Putting People First

A WORLD BANK PUBLICATION

Putting People First

Sociological Variables
in Rural Development

edited by

Michael M. Cernea

SECOND EDITION
Revised and Expanded

PUBLISHED FOR THE WORLD BANK
Oxford University Press

Oxford University Press

NEW YORK OXFORD CORBY LONDON TORONTO
NEW DELHI BOMBAY CALCUTTA MADRAS
SELANGOR SINGAPORE HONG KONG TAIPEI
TOKYO BANGKOK KARACHI LAHORE MELBOURNE
AUCKLAND CAPE TOWN JOHANNESBURG DURBAN
NAIROBI DAR ES SALAAM KAMPALA
JAKARTA IBADAN

Published October 1985
First printing of second edition, August 1991

Library of Congress Cataloging in Publication Data

The original edition of this title was cataloged as follows:

Main entry under title:

Putting people first.

Includes index.
  1. Agricultural development projects—Social
aspects.   2. Rural development—Sociological aspects.
3. Sociology, rural.   4. Rural poor.   I. Cernea,
Michael M.   II. International Bank for Reconstruction
and Development.   III. Title: Sociological variables
in rural development.
HD1433.P87 1985   303.4'4   85-11574
ISBN 0-19-520465-4

Contents

v

Preface
to the Second Edition

The second edition of *Putting People First* owes its publication to the spread and success of the first edition: both far surpassed the expectations of the authors and publishers. The volume found a wide audience in academia, in addition to the development community itself. It has been used in classes on development anthropology, development sociology, applied social research, social forestry, evaluation methodology, and other aspects of social change. *Putting People First* has been published in full translation into Bahasa-Indonesia, and partial translations have circulated in many other countries.

Soon after its publication in hard cover, demands for a paperback edition started to arrive. We have resisted, however, the temptation of a quick and simple reprinting of the initial volume, published in 1985. This second edition of *Putting People First* is a much richer book. In fact, to a considerable extent, it is a new volume.

In preparing it, the contributors attempted to weigh their earlier conclusions against development experiences accumulated during the second half of the 1980s. Their chapters seek to capture the newly emerging trends in development thinking and practice that are likely to characterize the 1990s. Some authors even went back to the field to update cases investigated earlier and report their new findings. As a result, most of the chapters have been rewritten and expanded, one chapter has been dropped, and two new chapters have been included. The volume's index has been made much more detailed to facilitate research, operational use, and classroom use of the volume.

Experience over the past five years has confirmed and reinforced the main themes of this volume. "Putting people first" in development programs is no less an imperative now than before: in fact, it is even more readily recognized as the crucial requirement for inducing accelerated development. The volume takes a firm stand against the technocratic and econocratic biases in development work. It criticizes explicitly or implicitly the neglect of social or cultural dimensions, the rigidity of blueprint thinking in project design, the focus on commodities rather than on the social actor, the disregard for farmers' knowledge, and the indifference toward people's grassroots institutions and organizations. Any intervention that does not recognize the centrality of the social actors in development programs is bound to clash, rather than to fit, with the natural dynamic of socioeconomic processes. And understanding the basic concept that unifies the volume—the concept of social organization—provides the main key for translating the prerequisites of people's centrality and participation into specific project strategies and approaches.

In preparing the second edition, it was gratifying to realize the great extent to which the "new" themes emerging on the development agenda and gradually modifying the development paradigm of the 1990s were already embedded in the volume's core. Emphasizing them further in the new edition was thus within the logic of our argument.

This edition highlights more explicitly the issues related (a) to natural resources management—particularly water, forests, and fisheries; (b) to the environmental implications of development programs; and (c) to the development of human capital through investments in forming grassroots organizations and promoting participation. After a decade of structural adjustment to financial crises, it is also appropriate to draw attention in this volume to certain adverse consequences of development, such as the risk of greater impoverishment for some marginal groups, the forced displacement and involuntary resettlement of populations, and the deterioration and dissipation of common property income-generating assets. All of the authors are concerned with understanding the conditions for long-term sustainability of development investments.

For those interested in how sociological and anthropological knowledge can be professionally applied in all stages of development work, this edition brings new experiences and methods. It analyzes specific cases in which the difficult transition from social science knowledge to the formulation of policy principles and institutional planning procedures was made successfully; it explores ways to overcome disciplinary limitations in social sciences; and it discusses new, recently invented or tested, rapid and participatory procedures for generating information. Altogether, the new edition strengthens the argument that sociological analysis brings an increment of professional precision to the thinking and practice of induced development.

The authors of this volume look forward to receiving as rich a feedback to this second edition as we did to the first. As editor, I full-heartedly encourage our readers—development practitioners and social scientists, teachers and students—to write and share their views, questions and comments about this volume with us.

Michael M. Cernea

Preface
to the First Edition

This volume is the joint product of a group of people much more numerous than the set of social scientists who wrote its chapters. Many managers, beneficiaries, and even victims of development programs, as well as technical experts, economists, and policymakers, have shared their experiences with the social scientists who carried out the research and operational work reported here. Benefiting from these various perspectives, the volume's contributors have undertaken to give sociological-anthropological analysis of issues that are central to induced, or planned, rural development. This volume thus critically discusses lessons of development experience, brings into the limelight both the obvious and the hidden (or the recognized and the denied) sociological variables of development activities, and presents new concepts, models, and methodologies for addressing these variables.

The basic tenet of the book is that people are—and should be—the starting point, the center, and the end goal of each development intervention. In sociological terms, "putting people first" is more than an ideological appeal. It means making social organization the explicit concern of development policies and programs and constructing development projects around the mode of production, cultural patterns, needs, and potential of the populations in the project area.

Several themes and concepts have consistently guided the authors of this volume toward unity of treatment in their chapters. Briefly, these refer to:

- *The social organization of production systems.* The authors started
  from the shared conviction that generalities about the processes of
  social change did not need to be rehashed, but that it was necessary
  to identify the type of social organization and the relevant sociocultural characteristics at work in the process of induced rural change.
  Although certain characteristics are common to the entire agricultural sector, others differ from one subsector to the other, depending
  on the technical production process and the type of population. For
  instance, the characteristics of pastoral populations differ profoundly from those of fishermen, which are different from those of
  farming communities, and so on. In the same vein, the use of
  irrigation systems requires a pattern of social organization that does
  not exist (and is not necessary) in rainfed agricultural areas. These
  sociocultural characteristics are intertwined in the social organization of the respective pastoral or farming communities and their
  mode of production. The authors of this volume believe that sociology and social anthropology can contribute more to planned
  development by supplying the understanding of these patterns of
  social organization, their dynamics and manner of change, rather
  than by offering Band-Aids, or piecemeal "solutions," to the problems.
- *Typology of development projects.* The generally accepted taxonomy of agricultural projects (based on subsectors such as irrigation,
  settlement, forestry, and livestock) is used here in addressing the
  various areas of development activities. The authors considered that
  development projects in any one subsector usually have more or
  less similar prerequisites for their preparation, and, apart from many
  local differences, they need the same kind of social information,
  general organizational arrangements, and basic implementation
  procedures and approaches. The challenge was to define, in connection with the overall social organization of production activities,
  the social and cultural issues most likely to emerge in each category
  of projects. Such an identification might help the practitioner and
  the reader understand the cultural issues underlying various types
  of agricultural development.
- *The stages of the project cycle.* To increase the operational relevance of the book, we have used the project cycle paradigm and
  discussed the sociologist's task and potential contributions within
  the broad framework of the main project stages: identification,

preparation, appraisal, implementation and supervision, and ex post evaluation. Just as the economist's or agronomist's project-related tasks differ at each stage, so should the contributions and methods of the social analyst be tailored to the specific needs of each phase of the cycle. The discussion of the sociologist's contributions can gain in specificity and relevance if critical cultural issues can be pinpointed for each phase. Of course, not every author in this volume has taken his or her recommendations through all stages of the project cycle: some address only one or a few stages. But since the project cycle is a structuring device for the work of many development practitioners, the authors have tried to sharpen the precision of their operational recommendations and improve the communication with practitioners by following this paradigm.

Lessons from many World Bank–assisted development projects are discussed in this volume, and the contributors reflect on these varied experiences, both positive and negative. Although this is the first book to discuss extensively World Bank experience with sociological work in rural development projects, the contributors also analyze development experiences of other international, bilateral, or national development agencies. This, we hope, will help give the authors' points relevance in various operational and national contexts.

One of the difficulties in writing this book was caused by the authors' desire to address two audiences simultaneously, both crucial. On the one hand, there is the large audience of development practitioners (project designers, managers, policymakers, technical experts, and others) for whom the authors wished to point out the sociological content that inevitably is present in the problems these developers handle daily. On the other hand, there is the audience of professional social scientists from developed and developing countries with whom the authors wanted to share their experiences in project work and information about the type of sociological "products" they found were needed and feasible for development work.

The authors hope that by suggesting practical approaches for addressing the social issues of several distinct categories of projects, pointing out typical pitfalls or fallacies, and recommending constructive and feasible alternatives, they will give the volume both practical and academic value. Although the book is not intended to be a simplified how-to-do-it manual, nonsociologist readers should be able to understand and use it to enhance the social quality of the design and strategies of their projects. Social scientists themselves, learning how to work in development interventions, will, we hope, find some guidance for making their efforts more relevant to the concrete needs of development-oriented research and operational work.

Michael M. Cernea

Acknowledgments
for the Second Edition

In preparing this second edition, considerably revised and enlarged, the editor and contributors to *Putting People First* have benefited from many public and personal reactions to the first edition, received through book reviews, discussion articles, letters, and face to face encounters.

Particular thanks are due to Theodor Bergmann, Subhash Chandra Sarker, Michael Schulman, Shiv Mehta, Mary Tiffen, Tim Allen, and others, who reviewed and discussed the volume in print and helped spread its message. David Brokensha, Ted Downing, Alan Hoben, Michael Horowitz, Gerald Murray, Michel Petit, V. Rajagopalan, G. Edward Schuh, H. Schwartzweller, Vijay Vyas, Thomas Weaver, and others generously shared their comments with us directly, and we are grateful for their valuable insights. A special word of thanks is due to Scott Guggenheim, research assistant for the first edition, who this time joined as a new chapter coauthor and gave a hand in some of the chores that are the editor's toil.

It was especially gratifying and encouraging to receive comments from numerous colleagues who used *Putting People First* in their classrooms and who conveyed their and their students' reactions. We hope that they will recognize their suggestions in the enriched substance of the new text.

The editor would like to acknowledge that a good part of his work on the new edition was carried out during the year he spent at Harvard University as Visiting Scholar, at the invitation of the Department of Anthropology and Harvard Institute for International Development

(1989–90). Thanks are expressed to David Maybury-Lewis, Nur Yalman, Dwight Perkins, Robert Hunt, Steve Gudeman, and to many other colleagues and graduate students, whose intellectual companionship during that year was of benefit for my work on this volume.

The word processing of the second edition demanded a substantial investment of skills and patience from Gracie Ochieng: authors and editor alike are thankful to her.

M. M. C.

Acknowledgments
for the First Edition

This volume has evolved over several years, and we are grateful to those who have assisted and helped in its preparation. The volume's chapters were reviewed by many readers—both social scientists and technicians with experience in the specific subsectors—and their comments greatly helped improve the manuscript; a general expression of thanks is offered to them. In particular, Leif E. Christoffersen, Donald C. Pickering, and Montague Yudelman were unwavering in their support and strong encouragement throughout the successive phases of generating and completing the manuscript. Clive Collins, Fred Hotes, and Francis Lethem were always ready to read yet another version and to share their advice. Michael Bamberger, Gloria Davis, Ted Davis, John Duloy, Hussein Fahim, Francine Frankel, Peter Hammond, and Maritta Koch-Weser contributed especially helpful comments and insight.

I owe a special debt of gratitude to my assistants—first Deborah S. Rubin, whose exceptional skills were not spared during the editorial preparation of the manuscripts, and then Scott Guggenheim, who took over from her in the final stretch and ran fast under the editor's prodding. Both were at the time graduate students in social anthropology at The Johns Hopkins University and both managed to complete and obtain their Ph.D. just before book went to print. Joy Vendryes, Mae Gahl, Sonia Moral, and Arda Kehyaian diligently typed their way through the many different handwritings that we inflicted on them.

Last but not least, to the volume's coauthors, too, I owe a special debt, for the forbearance with which they responded to my repeated rounds of demands and comments on their draft chapters.

To my children, Dana and Andrei, I owe gratitude for their warm overall support, and also an apology for the overtime that went into this volume that otherwise would have belonged largely to them. I hope they feel it was all worthwhile.

M. M. C.

Knowledge from Social Science for Development Policies and Projects

Michael M. Cernea

Several scientific disciplines, particularly economics, preside over the processes of planned development. But until rather recently, sociology and social anthropology have not been called on to serve extensively.[1] Though planning is a knowledge-based exercise, the storehouse of knowledge and knowledge-generating methods amassed within these social sciences has been largely overlooked. However, this imbalance is gradually (though too slowly) changing.

Why is this change occurring?

Increased Recognition of Social Science Knowledge

A key factor in this change is the increasingly widespread recognition that repeated failures have plagued many development programs, which were—and largely *because* they were—sociologically ill-informed and ill-conceived. Although uncomfortable for development agencies, this recognition heightens interest in identifying and addressing the socio-cultural variables of projects. The heavy influence of such variables upon the success or failure of projects is recognized more readily than before. Consequently, more efforts go into providing projects' "hardware" with indispensable "software."

A second process conducive to using more socioanthropological knowledge in project planning began in the mid-1970s. At that time, a reconceptualization of development policies—moving away from "trickle down" theories to poverty alleviation through development— was proposed, and it started to modify development interventions in third world countries. Perhaps for the first time the concept of "target group"—the poor, those with an income below the absolute or relative threshold of poverty—was brought to bear upon project strategies. With it came the need to define the target group, the social actor, the beneficiaries (and sometimes the victims, too) of development. The shift from a virtually exclusive emphasis on physical infrastructures to a recognition of social structures, and from free-swinging ethnocentricity in development interventions to recognizing indigenous cultures, was part of the shift in the direction of actor (people)-centered development projects.

The third factor is the work performed by development-oriented social scientists themselves who are demonstrating their usefulness and effectiveness for induced (planned) development programs. The prior absence of a critical mass of anthropologists and sociologists within the development community at large has long prevented them from asserting themselves systematically and has undercut the cumulative effect of their contributions. The 1980s have registered a change in this respect too. The former slow growth seems to have picked up speed, and although in my view such social science professionals are still too few, their steadily increasing number makes the intrinsic value of social analysis more visible to the rest of the development community. The 1980s saw a tremendous increase in the number of published (and gray) papers and reports on development anthropology and sociology. Furthermore, other factors are the rising public concern for environmental protection, *sustainable* development, and participation and institution building, as well as the sharpened public criticism of development allocations wasted on half-baked programs and backfiring inept interventions; these factors contribute powerfully to employing more behavioral scientists to improve the quality of development work.

Thus, at the beginning of the 1990s the noneconomic and social sciences are better positioned to influence development interventions. Their pleas, before dismissed as unproven claims, have become more "respectable." The practical uses of sociology and anthropology are regarded with a bit more confidence. Much of past beliefs about the exercise of noneconomic social sciences becomes now obsolete or obsolescent.

When the orientation to poverty alleviation started, there was little experience about *how* to do a socioanthropological analysis that would fit into the project process. In hindsight, it can be said that the social science community didn't then know how to use this opportunity and largely underused it. Today, almost two decades later, there is considerably more—but still not enough—experience.

Factors internal to the discipline also constrain the use of noneconomic social sciences in planning and policymaking. Most damaging is the fact that the accumulated experiences of applied social scientists have not yet been systematized, conceptualized, and codified either by these practitioners themselves or by academic social scientists; therefore, theory formation is sporadic and the epistemological and methodological concerns of applied science are insufficiently stated.[2] Hidden under an apparent but ambiguous truce, the split within these professional communities between those in academic teaching and basic research and those in development and applied work continues to exist and weakens both sides. There is limited mutual intellectual empowerment, and little deliberate building of the development-oriented enterprise, although this new enterprise is steadily laboring to expand the frontier of its parental disciplines. Such inner dysfunctions reduce the actual impact of the disciplines upon society.

If, nevertheless, development sociologists and anthropologists are entitled to rejoice in the growing demand for their expertise, then I believe that they are also under the obligation to define more clearly the types of contributions they propose to make. Will they simply supply baseline social information and background knowledge? Design social models? Formulate theories or strategies for social action? Or just offer methods for data gathering and evaluation? Furthermore, since some of these contributions must be context specific, how will they vary from one culture or location to another?

The contributors to the present volume attempt precisely to answer such questions in practice and to identify the entrance points to introduce knowledge emerging from noneconomic social sciences to planned development programs. They carried out these social analyses in the context of real development programs, and they have examined the social organizational and cultural variables, either to propose models, define methodologies for social action, or translate the lessons from past failures into improved approaches. Overall, this represents an effort to sharpen the tools of social science for inducing development.

Sociologists and anthropologists dealing with different production processes (farming, animal husbandry, fishing, forestry, and so on) not only have to address different patterns of social organization; they are also faced with several common issues that result from the nature of their operational involvement and are distinct from those encountered in academic research.

This opening chapter deals with some of these common issues that I regard as essential, yet are little addressed in the current literature: the nature of financially induced development; the development project as a framework for socioanthropological endeavor; the entrance points for sociological knowledge in development planning; policy-permeated social inquiry; the methodologies for social action; the role of social engineering; and the institutionalization of social science in development work.

In discussing planning, this chapter is concerned primarily with rural and agricultural change in developing (rather than developed) countries. Today, more than ever, this vast area is open to and in demand of sociological and anthropological inquiry. The role played by the state (as well as the state-sponsored international and bilateral aid agencies), in inducing and directing accelerated development in developing countries, has generated a demand for empirical knowledge and theoretical models about the structures and processes that such interventions aim to affect. The social scientists from developing countries are best positioned to respond to this demand.

The noneconomic social sciences have a long tradition of commitment to the betterment of society. Some of the founders of sociology and anthropology, from Comte to Lester Ward and from Lewis Morgan to Margaret Mead, have pioneered this respectable tradition, striving also to tackle the new ethical and methodological issues involved in such work. Their interests have been continued and refined by subsequent generations of scientists focusing on specific social problems that demand research-grounded solutions. Therefore, the call for social science contributions to development is hardly a new appeal. The challenge now, however, is to get involved in the extraordinary expansion of *planning* and of *state interventions* for inducing directed development.

There is a further intradisciplinary challenge as well. Social scientists must overcome the "disaffection for public service and governmental involvement," as Goldschmidt described it,[3] and the "disenchantment with . . . the validity of their involvement in official activities,"[4] in Hall's words, which was pervasive in the social science community until quite recently. If *systematic* interest in these issues increases among scientists from both developed and developing countries, these disciplines and development planning, will benefit substantially.

As a social scientist working for seventeen years within a large international development organization, I am involved in many World Bank–assisted development projects in various countries. I have observed the work of many sociologists and anthropologists in these projects and in programs assisted by other agencies, as well as the position that socioanthropological knowledge holds relative to technical or economic expertise. This chapter is rooted in some of my personal experiences that have shown what sociology and anthropology can or cannot do in such contexts.

Financially Induced Development and the Sociological Variables

How are projects instruments of intervention in development? And how propitious is the framework offered by a project for social inquiry and sociologically informed planning?

Projects are purposive interventions used for accelerating and targeting economic growth and social development. Notwithstanding the inherent limitations of their current format, I venture to say that development projects offer broad scope for intensive, applied socioanthropological work. In fact, they offer the context to employ a much wider array of social science "products" and approaches to inducing change than the professional social science community has invented to date. At the same time, the sociology of development offers the theoretical argument for an alternative model for projects, a model in which the social actors are the pivotal element, the central core around which all other resources should be marshalled for action, as will be explained further in more detail.

Social scientists make the distinction between spontaneous development, on the one hand, and induced or planned development, on the other. Yet it is worth remembering that an overall theory of *induced* social development has not yet been articulated. With measures (policies, programs, international aid, and state interventions of all types) for *inducing* development being multiplied and expanded enormously, practice has moved ahead of still absent comprehensive theory, and it suffers badly from this absence. An absence of concern with social dynamics has been inherent and endemic in the econocratic or technocratic models guiding planned interventions. Economists, as the professional body presiding most often over the rites of project making, have done little to incorporate cultural variables into project models.[5]

The neglect of social dimensions in intervention-caused development always takes revenge on the outcome. Contrary to myth, it is a grievous misunderstanding to imagine that project interventions are a simple linear unfolding of a well-reasoned, time-bound sequence of preprogrammed activities with all but predefined outcomes.[6] Beyond what *is* being planned, and often despite it, development interventions occur as processes subjected to political pressures, social bargaining, administrative inadequacy, and circumstantial distortions. A host of necessary or unwarranted reinterpretations modify the intended outcome.

It is true that development interventions do not take place through projects alone, but projects are the most widely used vehicle. Their underlying model contains a greater potential for case by case fine-tuning than planners typically use.

The debate over whether current projects are an adequate vehicle for development interventions has pointed out both strengths and weaknesses inherent in the project model of intervention. On the one hand, projects concentrate resources on selected priorities, focus on a circumscribed geographic area, and can address specific population groups. They zero in on identifiable constraints on development. Projects can also be social laboratories that use innovative approaches on a limited scale to gain experience for attempting large-scale interventions (for example, national plans). As a form of development investment, Hirschman noted, the very term project "connotes purposefulness, some minimum size, a specific location, the introduction of something qualitatively new, and the expectation that a sequence of further development moves will be set in motion."[7]

Nonetheless, development projects have been criticized because they are only segmented units of intervention; they often bypass overall structures, are subject to the hothouse overnurturing syndrome, and thus may develop atypically. Projects are also criticized because they tend to create enclaves and to siphon resources from nonproject activities, while sustained development at the same pace beyond their limited time frame may be doubtful. The flow of project allocations is also prone to diversionary pressures that often channel resources away from intended beneficiaries. These and other shortcomings of the project approach are further highlighted from a sociocultural perspective in several chapters of this volume.

Despite the recurrent debates on the merits and disadvantages of projects as instruments of development intervention, no effective alternatives have emerged, and projects are likely to remain a basic means for translating policies into action programs.[8] Therefore, as long as the project approach is routinely being used, it is both legitimate and necessary to identify and address the sociological requirements intrinsic to this model of development intervention. I contend that social scientists could gain from further exploring project potential and from overcoming its limitations, in order fully to use—and also broaden—the opportunities available for inquiry and action-oriented sociology. Since development anthropology and sociology are often defined as a "sociology of interventions"[9] or a "sociology of strategies," it is fitting to examine what in the nature of interventionist state policies and programs creates a demand for social knowledge.

The systematic use of social knowledge, as a complement to economic and technical knowledge, is indispensable for "putting people first" in planned development interventions. Putting people first in projects is not just a goodwill appeal to the humanitarian feelings of project planners, a mere ethical advocacy. It is a concept for constructing programs for inducing development and an imperative for their effectiveness. I submit that "putting people first" in development programs must be read as a scientifically grounded request to policymakers, planners, and technical experts to explicitly recognize the centrality of what *is* the primary factor in development processes. This interpretation implies a call for changing the approach to planning.

When the requirement to admit *the centrality of people in projects* is addressed to those who currently design projects—primarily, to the technical and economic planners of development programs—it becomes tantamount to asking for *reversal of the conventional approach to project making.* This is not to say that people are totally out of sight in conventional approaches. But many approaches are so overwhelmingly dominated by the priority given to technical factors or economic models stripped of the flesh and blood of real life that the characteristics of the given social organization and the very *actors* of development are dealt with as an afterthought.

The argument of this chapter, indeed of this volume in its entirety, is that *the model adopted in projects that do not put people first clashes with the model intrinsic to the real social process of development*, at the core of which are—simply—its actors. This clash seriously undercuts the effectiveness of projects that attempt to induce and accelerate development. Putting people first is a reversal because it proposes another starting point in the planning and design of projects than that taken by current technology-centered approaches. This specific "reversal" demands to identify—in every single technical, financial, or administrative intervention—the sociological angle and the variables pertinent to the social organization affected or targeted by intervention.[10] This is why putting people first is not a simple metaphor, but rather a tall demand to restructure the approach to planning.

Lately, support to "people-centered" projects is pledged even in the official planning rhetoric. But this is done in a manner that often reduces the concept's applicability to projects in the so-called "social sectors"— education, health, family planning, nutrition, and so on. The point is that "putting people first"—in other terms, the concern for social organization as the central issue—should be recognized as paramount for *all* projects, not only for projects in social service sectors such as those listed above. It should be recognized explicitly as a paramount objective for projects supporting productive activities, where the apparent primacy of technological or economic variables still serves as a fallacious justification for neglecting social organization variables.

Development projects are in essence vehicles for *financing induced growth and change*. Often financial resources are a project's single most massive input injected into an area to accelerate growth. The financial investments—resulting either from loans or from central budget allocations, in other words, from sources exogenous to the project area and its own capacity for capital formation—are used as the lever apt to eliminate constraints and set development in motion.

By their nature as financially driven interventions, such projects must—but often do not—provide explicitly for complementary social or institutional reorganization. This is so because the abrupt large infusion of external resources into a rural society modifies the internal and gradual processes by which resources for development are created, saved, and accumulated. When these resources are generated internally and gradually, they more or less commensurate with the capacity of the socioeconomic structure to absorb and use surplus. However, if the financial resources *alone* grow suddenly by external injection, while the patterns of social organization or the institutional structures remain the same and no matching change in the nonfinancial factors of development is sought, then serious discrepancies set in.

People's economic activities are embedded in a structure of social relations; therefore, for the theory and practice of *induced* development, defining accurately the levels of such embeddedness in different—market or nonmarket—societies becomes operationally relevant.[11] The degree of embeddedness and level of congruence between accelerated technoeconomic activities and the existing structure of social relations is not just an academic problem, but a practical one, inasmuch as the interventionist stand of the state should beware of causing desquilibria and discontinuities.

Indeed, when investments through state-sponsored programs are made only in the technological infrastructure, they are highly likely to be an implicit disinvestment in the *social* infrastructures of the given society. Often such disinvestment is only relative, but sometimes it is also an absolute disinvestment. Furthermore, the very know-how for investing financial resources in institutional structures is much less refined than the know-how for investing in technical and physical assets. Thus, when public investment in technical infrastructures proceeds alongside disinvestment in the social, cultural, and institutional structures within which the former are embedded, the sustainability of the technical advancement itself is undermined.

Massive financial resources may trigger a short-term development spurt, but without institutional and social scaffoldings built in at the same pace, the new edifice is not durably constructed. The long-term positive effects of financially induced changes will remain at risk. Such risks may initially stay hidden, but eventually they will surface into unanticipated and undesired outcomes.

It is important to emphasize that induced development depends ultimately on the overall quality of the program, rather than on the absolute amount of its financial inflows. In other words, the developmental impact of aid resources could be increased even if the financial flow levels are kept constant or at the limit reduced, provided the overall quality of project design and its effective implementation are enhanced. For instance, participatory project implementation and improved management are likely to extract *greater* "development mileage" from the financial investments of a project than what can be obtained by increasing the financial allocations while disregarding participatory implementation.

While the need for financial resources is indisputable, it should be understood that internationally assisted rural development programs have often languished not because of lack of finance, but because of either the inability of the given rural society to use external finance effectively or the planners' inability to formulate an *efficient social construction strategy* for absorbing those new financial resources. Money is not everything. In certain situations money may be the least important contribution to processes of change. The financial levers of development cannot soundly substitute for the nonfinancial ones.[12] The financial inflows of the project may temporarily create the appearance that anything can be done, but this appearance is misleading and transitional. Salient sociocultural factors continue to work under the surface. If the social variables remain unaddressed or mishandled, then the project will be unsustainable and fail, no matter which governmental or international agency promotes it.

Sociological knowledge—and the social analyst—can help identify, conceptualize, and deal with the social and cultural variables involved in financially induced programs. In doing so, the sociologist's contribution consists not just of uncovering social variables overlooked in the planner's approach; it often amounts, as Robert Merton pointed out, to a reformulation of the problem that requires solving. "Perhaps the most striking role of conceptualization in applied social research is its *transformation of practical problems* by introducing concepts which refer to variables overlooked in the common sense view of the policymakers. At times the concept leads to a statement of the problem that is diametrically opposed to that of the policymaker."[13] Or, we can add, is diametrically opposed to that of the project planner or manager.

Specifically, in situations like those discussed here, the social analyst participating in designing a project intervention will ask basic sociological questions: Can the existing social and institutional structures function effectively at the accelerated pace triggered by a large financial influx? What social adjustments are needed to keep step with the other elements of the intervention? The sociologist must help chart the operational steps for creating the institutional changes necessary for both the social and cultural sustainability of the financially launched development. As a result, the entire course of practical action can be changed.

The penalty for not carrying out the social analysis and not incorporating social knowledge into financially induced growth programs is costly and swift. An anthropological secondary study of fifty-seven World Bank–financed projects, which examined the association between the sociocultural fit (or misfit) of project design and the estimated economic rate of return at project completion (audit) time, found that attention to issues of sociocultural compatibility paid off tangibly in economic terms. Specifically, thirty out of the fifty-seven projects were judged to have a project design compatible with traditional cultural and local socioeconomic conditions, while in the other twenty-seven projects serious sociocultural incompatibilities were identified. The most significant finding was that the compatible set of projects had an average rate of return at audit of 18.3 percent, which was two times higher than the economic rate of return (only 8.6 percent) of the other twenty-seven projects in the second group (see chapter 12).

Another significant finding comes from analyzing twenty-five Bank-financed projects that were reevaluated several years *after* the financial flows channeled through the projects were terminated. The purpose of this analysis was to assess the long-term sustainability of those projects. Thirteen out of twenty-five projects were found to be nonsustainable; among the primary reasons for their nonsustainability was not insufficient financing, but factors of a sociocultural nature (mainly the lack of farmer organizations and participation) neglected during project formulation and implementation.[14]

Such examples only confirm with economic facts that financially induced growth interventions stand a high risk of being less effective than planned or of failing altogether, if they neglect to build up the sociocultural structures for development.

It is said sometimes that doing social analysis for each project would increase the cost of project design and waste scarce resources. In hindsight, one learns, however, that the cost of *not* doing social analysis is much higher. Projects should not bear the unaffordable expense of not addressing the sociocultural variables knowledgeably. In fact, as a culturally sensitive development economist argued, the "advances in social science knowledge *reduce the cost* of institutional change,"[15] the same way advances in the natural sciences reduce the cost of technical change.

Development-oriented sociologists and anthropologists have become not only more involved with projects in the past decades but also more able to insert their contributions effectively. Although sometimes still

uncomfortable with projects and straitjacketed by blueprints, technocratic biases, short time frames for fieldwork, and other restrictions,
many social scientists have gradually been learning, as the following
chapters in this volume demonstrate, how to make operational contributions within this planned approach to development. Applied social scientists have also developed new research procedures (see chapter 14) and
discovered that the project format opens up not one, but multiple points
of entrance for contributions of social knowledge.

Entrance Points for Sociological Knowledge

Where are the entrance points for effective incorporation of sociological knowledge into rural development planning?
Past errors and lingering misperceptions have clouded the answers to
this question. My argument is that the habitual entrance points used in
the past—"social impact assessment" or "ex post evaluation"—have
been few and not the most effective ones. They must be broadened.
Therefore, I argue (a) that entrance points should be multiplied and
opened up in every important juncture of the planning and execution of
projects and (b) that the single most important entrance area where
sociological knowledge can and must contribute is *the design for purposive social action.* A quick retrospective look reveals several fallacies
and lessons of experience in this respect.

Conventional Entrance Points

Historically, and until recently, the first and main entrance point for
social scientists was the ex post evaluation of development results.
Sociologists were sometimes called in to assess whether a certain project
had indeed accomplished its overall objectives and triggered the desired
consequences or some unanticipated ones. Unfortunately, this was the
wrong end of the cycle: it was then too late to affect the project process.
While the use of a sociologist or anthropologist for this task was positive,
it was not a substitute for multidisciplinary planning.
At issue here, of course, is the *role of the discipline as a body of
knowledge,* not the task given to an individual sociologist. Although an
individual expert can correctly perform a segmented role such as evaluation, the noneconomic social sciences as disciplines should not be

pigeonholed into only one segment of the project or planning process. If used only as evaluators, sociologists arrive late, long after other experts have made their contributions. They appear wise after the fact and are seen as those who only complain about what others have actually done. Their skills are not brought to bear on ongoing social action; since the social process has taken place before the evaluation study, it cannot be improved or redirected in retrospect.

It is often said (with a consoling undertone) that the lessons drawn from evaluation may, of course, be useful for the next program. However, many sociologists, the author included, have been generating evaluation findings that should have led to the modification of subsequent programs, only to find themselves in the unenviable position of having no part or influence in the actual formulation of the follow-up programs. Instead they watched new projects without sociological inputs being designed again by econocrats oblivious to earlier findings and repeating the same mistakes. Even when the sociological evaluation findings are correct and relevant, whether or not they will materially affect new programs or policies depends on the decision of others. Incorporation of past lessons is never automatic. Moreover, skills similar to those used for identifying the social lessons of past programs are best suited for incorporating such lessons into the new design. That is why it is necessary to involve professional sociologists in the preparation process for the new project. There is no legitimacy in relegating them to the function of ex post evaluators only.

Another role for the social sciences has emerged in what is called the social impact assessment (SIA). This is a kind of ex ante evaluation. In this role, the sociologist examines a development project prepared by a group of other experts and is asked to make a desk assessment about whether or not it will have positive or adverse social repercussions. Here again the social analyst is not called on to participate constructively in shaping the intimate structure and sequence of actions in development projects; rather, he or she is used simply to validate or partly modify a ready-made "package."

Sometimes the social impact assessment carried out by the social analyst is genuinely taken into account in modifying the project's plans, and this service is undoubtedly worthwhile. Some anthropologists have rendered important contributions this way. My point, however, is that the social analyst is not to be employed merely to anticipate the effects of plans conceived without him, for damage control and mitigation. The

point is to involve the social analyst in the advance planning of development. This is a much broader endeavor than just assessing impact.

A somewhat more promising "entrance" is offered to sociologists
when they are invited to generate the basic social information necessary
for a project. Such a contribution is often quite useful. But the role of the
supplier of descriptive information still allows the sociologist little
influence over what is done with the information; whether or not it is
used at all; or whether it is incorporated into the design for development,
into resource allocation decisions, and into the sequencing of planned
actions.

Thus, none of the entrance points noted above allow sociology to
participate fully in the interdisciplinary modeling of planned rural development. The narrowness of the assignment—evaluation or data gathering—blocks out the crucial contribution that sociology should make to
the actual *content* and *design for purposive action* in rural development
programs.

Going Outside the Cocoon of the Discipline

In a powerful analysis of "why sociology does not apply" in public
policy, Scott and Shore argue that sociologists have been largely ineffec-
tual in policy-relevant work because they have remained captive to their
disciplinary process and manner rather than interpolating themselves and
their work into the policymaking process itself. "A main source of the
present difficulty with applied sociology is that attempts to make sociology relevant to policy are conceived and executed with disciplinary and
not with policy concerns in mind."[16] This thesis is important and consequential. It entails that the work to be done by sociologists, the methods
used and their order of use should differ substantively in a policy
perspective from what is habitual in a disciplinary perspective.

When guided by an inward-looking disciplinary perspective, applied
sociological work begins and ends with sociology and may not fully serve
the specific purposes of policy (applied) work. Conversely, with a finality
oriented to the public domain, a sociological perspective would begin
and end with policy—not disciplinary—concerns. The "significant
other" for a social scientist writing up his field "product" in a policy or
project perspective is the policymaker or the development practitioner,
while the significant others for the one writing with a disciplinary
perspective are his academic peers. To carry out policy-permeated social

inquiry and analysis, one has to come out of the cocoon of the discipline in more than one way. When employing the policy perspective, Scott and Shore note, not only is the *order* of activities changed but their *nature* is different, too, since the purpose is "to adapt method to problems involving questions and variables outside the ken of the discipline."[17]

Scott and Shore focus their argument on applying sociology to policymaking, but their critical analysis is valid also with respect to applying sociology to the *planning* process. The two areas are not identical, since planning is essentially in the realm of policy execution rather than policy formulation. Applied sociological work in one is different from the other, despite similarities or overlap. If the goal is to use sociological knowledge in projects, then this work should start from the needs intrinsic to the project model itself.

The sociologist who decides to use his knowledge and skills in a project-related task needs to internalize the process of project making and to tailor his work so as to fit the structure of this process. He or she must then understand the project cycle, its specific stages (discussed in detail below), and how to relate to these stages as both starting points and intermediate ends of his or her activities.

More than any other development professionals, sociologists must labor to bring the social actors, the people themselves, into the processes of project formulation, planning, and creative execution, and attune the other specialists—technical and economic experts—as well to the demands of putting people first. The two tasks are not opposed, they are complementary. The vital need to promote public participation goes hand in hand with recognizing that preparing a complex development project is a job that requires the cooperation of a number of professional experts, including the social scientist. Adopting the project model as a common denominator for applied sociological work also has the advantage of enabling sociologists to interact better with the other project professionals (planners, technical experts, and economists, for example) and to overcome their intimate biases, often self-paralyzing, against such other professionals.[18] The better they grasp the "technical" criteria of the other professionals, the better able sociologists are to generate sociological answers (propose solutions) well-tailored to the project's circumstances. Furthermore, this engagement enables the sociologist in turn to raise his challenging questions, compelling the other professionals to reflect on them and generate project-related (and project-funded) solutions.

Rural development planning in many countries follows the format of the project cycle. Aside from some local variations, the essential stages of this cycle, to which sociological contributions can be matched, are:

- Project identification
- Project preparation (including design)
- Project appraisal (including design correction)
- Project implementation (including monitoring)
- Project evaluation.

Each stage of this cycle requires a different type of sociological contribution (either informational, analytical, or predictive) from sociologists and anthropologists, in much the same way that the specific contributions of economists vary from one stage to another.[19] Of course, the stage sequence of the project should not be fetishized or idealized as the ultimate embodiment of planning rationality or as an inflexible arrangement of time-bound activities. As shown before, the project model has its limits, and the project's *social* reality is much richer than its abstract model. It is the obligation of the social scientist to work so as both to adopt and adjust the model to the given social reality and to reject any procustian request to do the opposite.

Not only challenges, but sometimes barriers as well are built into this very format. Control over the project cycle is generally in the hands of government officials, local politicians, planners, administrators, and technical managers, who decide whether and when to call in sociologists and what to ask them to do. In real life, such calls may be half-hearted or may be narrowly restricted to only one stage rather than to all of them consecutively; they may even misspecify the tasks of the social analyst. In practice, project planners and other officials often do not know precisely what to ask the sociologist. Nor do they know particularly what they are entitled to receive from the project's social analyst.

To sum up, going "outside the ken of the discipline" means, in this case, adopting the stages of the project cycle listed above as the practical framework for organizing the activity of the social analyst. His or her contributions should be tailored to the specific purposes of each stage. To do so, most social scientists trained only in the ways of disciplinary academic research must go through a learning process. Numerous illustrations of how sociological work can fit into each of these stages are contained further in this volume, and I will provide here only a brief characterization.

Project Identification

Project identification is the stage when the potential of a particular development intervention is approximated. On the social side, this requires a definition of the likely social actors in that development, such as the project area population and the place of its various subcategories in the social structure. The social and economic goals of that development must be delineated, and their likely consequences, both positive and negative, must be subjected to an initial estimate—the first round in an iterative analytical process. During this stage, the social analyst has only little time for independent field investigation, but should be able to gather and assess all the available general social data (censuses, prior surveys, ethnographies, monographs, and so forth) relevant to the area and the type of intervention considered. For instance, if the potential of an irrigation dam is considered, at the identification stage the social analyst should broadly define not just the beneficiary groups in the command area but also the reservoir population certain to suffer the adverse impact—forced displacement. He or she should also consider the likely influx of construction manpower and the predictable boomtown effect at the construction site, and so on. At this preliminary stage, it is not possible, nor is it necessary to have definitive answers or the full set of social data. But it is necessary to identify the main risks and to set in motion the subsequent data gathering, social analysis, and social design processes to be carried out during the much longer, and more in-depth, preparation stage.

Project Preparation

This stage is the most important for the *social* construction of development interventions. At this point, the sociologist verifies the hypotheses about the development potential and translates them into planned sequences of actions. The social analyst, as a member of the preparation team, must use the full arsenal of relevant research tools, from surveys and case studies to piloting and other methods, together with his or her ability to anticipate changes in social arrangements and to design alternative organizations, institutions, or strategies for participation. Using the same example of an irrigation dam project, the social analyst must *plan* in detail the process of involuntary resettlement, involving both the displaced groups and the host population; plan for the displaced to be reestablished on a viable socioeconomic basis,[20] plan for the complex process of helping the future beneficiaries from irrigation organize themselves into a network of watercourse-based irrigators' associations (see chapters 2, 3, and 4).

Project Appraisal

The appraisal stage critically reexamines the preliminary version (feasibility study) of the project as produced during project preparation and, often, introduces significant corrections into the future project. Ideally, the specialist teams doing the preparation and the appraisal, including their social analysts, should not consist of the same individuals, so as to enable the second team to reassess freshly, independently, and critically the work of the first team.

The social analyst on the appraisal team should reexamine the project's assumptions regarding the social actors, their current needs and expected behavior; he or she should also reevaluate the social arrangements recommended to accompany the induced technical changes and reshape the relations between people and their environment.

In light of World Bank experiences with project appraisal, four main elements should be the focus of the sociological appraisal:[21]

- The sociocultural and demographic characteristics of local benefi-ciaries, including groups that may be adversely affected
- The social organization of productive activities of the population in the project area
- The cultural acceptability of the project and its compatibility with the needs of the intended beneficiaries
- The social strategy for project implementation and operation needed to elicit and sustain beneficiaries' participation.

A few details on each one follow.

The social appraisal of projects should first verify that project design has taken into account sociocultural and demographic characteristics— the size and social structure of the population in the project area and its density and stratification patterns (including ethnic, tribal, and class composition). This is particularly important for project components affecting specific target groups (such as ethnic minorities, resettled populations, and women). It requires an understanding of the receptivity of the existing patterns of population settlement and community organization to the proposed arrangements for supplying inputs, collecting outputs, facilitating access to education, health, or other social services, and for ensuring the desired distribution of project benefits.

Appraisal should further ascertain that the project design is based on an accurate understanding of the social organization of productive activities: (a) how the intended beneficiaries have access to, make use of, and exercise control over natural and other productive resources available in the area and what changes need to be promoted in the existing social arrangements; (b) how the characteristics of the household models and family systems prevalent in the area affect the development potential and constraints, labor availability, and ownership patterns; (c) whether small producers have reasonable access to and information on wider markets and regional economies; and (d) how land tenure systems and usage rights, as well as alternative employment opportunities, may affect intended beneficiaries' interest in the proposed project activities. In weighing the assumptions on which the project intervention is built, the social appraisal needs to ensure that the technological changes to be introduced will be complemented by supporting changes in local social organization patterns.

Projects must be culturally acceptable, that is, understandable, agreed to, and capable of being operated and maintained by the local social actors and their institutions and organizations. For instance, projects for joining herders and cultivators in combined rangeland and farmland management schemes may not be workable if they ignore the history of relationships prevailing between the two given groups. Similarly, the health benefits of improved water supply or waste disposal systems may not materialize unless the intended beneficiaries appreciate the linkages. A judgment on the project's cultural acceptability and on the beneficiaries' willingness to contribute to its success must therefore take into account their values, customs, beliefs, and felt needs.

The appraisal stage is not too late to carry out one more round of consultation and communication with the project area populations, thus facilitating various forms of *public* appraisal of the project as opposed to only *expert* appraisal. Moreover, the appraisal process must ascertain that the people likely to be affected—both positively or negatively—by the project were involved or consulted during the identification and preparation stages and that they will continue and expand their participation during project implementation, maintenance, operation, and monitoring. Whenever necessary, the project should contain explicit strategy provisions to help beneficiaries *organize* themselves to carry out these functions.

If the social appraisal determines that the project is likely to be highly risky in social terms, but inadequate information is available to support a firm conclusion, consideration should be given to either a pilot project or postponement of the project until sufficient information is available. If certain technical, administrative, or other aspects of a project make it socially unfeasible, they will have to be modified or eliminated. Often it may be desirable to include in the project an information, motivation, and education component to help accelerate the necessary changes in social attitudes, behavior, and organization. The appraisal should ensure that the implementation process contains a realistic time frame and mechanisms for the expected behavioral responses to occur, and that there is enough built-in flexibility for making design changes in response to sociocultural information obtained during implementation.

Project Implementation and Monitoring

The actual implementation of the project opens up a new territory for applied social science activities—in fact the broadest area in which sociologists and anthropologists can and should work. They can bring their knowledge to bear on the organization, communication, and managerial realms of projects, on the shaping of project approaches to specific tasks, on mobilizing participation, and on daily problem solving. Implementation is precisely the stage when it becomes most obvious that projects never unfold linearly, exactly as planned, but involve changes, struggles between interested parties, and reinterpretations. How social scientists can work within this vast domain is illustrated in detail with actual project experiences throughout this volume.

To summarize, the overview of the project cycle stages provides the development social scientist with an insider's key to open the entrance doors into the process of inducing social change through projects.

I must emphasize, in light of my own and other researchers' experiences, that by adopting the project cycle model as a framework for conducting applied sociological project work, the social researcher does not have to and should not abdicate his critical thinking. He must not surrender any of his tools of trade—conceptual or methodological—or his ability to critique or reject one course of project action or another. To the contrary, anthropologists and sociologists can assert their views more influentially by reorganizing the conduct of their work according to the project cycle model and by becoming *insiders* to the project-making process—both intellectually and organizationally. Sociological knowledge can thus aspire to statutorily *inhabit* the project process, rather than be temporarily called in from the cold for an in-and-out, yo-yo–type contribution.

Policy Formation Grounded in Social Knowledge

The *formulation of development policies* is a substantively different terrain for the use of social science concepts and research tools, distinct from the project planning process and its key stages. The important principle to be stressed, as Solon Kimball reminded us, is that basic conceptualizations guide the gathering, organization, and analysis of data. Therefore, these conceptualizations must differ in the case of applied work in a project context, from, say, an ethnographic exercise, or from the conceptualization required for policy formulation. "The simple conceptualizations of traditional ethnographic descriptions provide inventories of cultural items, but are inadequate for policy purposes."[22] The demands and methodological options for using policy formulation as an "entrance point" have been discussed in detail, and arguments in its favor continue to be added from within both anthropology (see Weaver, 1985; Grillo and Rew, 1985)[23] and sociology (see Hall and Midgley, 1988),[24] obviating the need to repeat them here. In fact, the theoretical argument for putting people first in development, for designing strategies around the social actor rather than starting with technical factors, concerns primarily the shaping of development *policy* and secondarily the shaping of *project* design.

The incorporation of socioanthropological knowledge into development policies is the most effective way of employing this body of knowledge, by far more effective than influencing one or another project piecemeal. It has a multiplier effect produced by the institutionalized recognition of sociocultural variables in the programs that follow policy formulation. Implicitly and explicitly, it causes multiple subsequent uses of social science knowledge in specific programs and projects. Two instances from the experience of sociological work in the World Bank prove this convincingly.

The first is the case of the elaboration of a social science–informed policy for projects that cause involuntary population displacement and resettlement. Forced displacements imposed by the construction of dams, highways, or ports dismantle people's settlements and their prior mode of production, shatter community networks and patterns of social organization, and cause homelessness, landlessness, and impoverishment. The seriousness of such negative consequences is compounded by the magnitude of forced displacement in certain projects: for instance, the Narmada Sardar Sarovar and Almatti dams in India will displace over 70,000 and 160,000 people respectively. The recently built Cirata and Saguling dams in Indonesia have displaced some 70,000 and 65,000 people, respectively; the Kayraktepe and Ataturk dams in Turkey, some 20,000 and 55,000 people, respectively; and the Sobradinho and Itaparica dams in Brazil, some 65,000 and 40,000 people, and so on.

Over many years, anthropologists and sociologists have carried out research and generated knowledge on people's responses to, and consequences of, exogenously imposed displacement. Nevertheless, the availability of knowledge-on-the-shelf about involuntary resettlement exercised hardly any influence on the governments and agencies engaged in the practice of forced displacement. Studies and books produced by social scientists kept accumulating, but they had little effect: they were by and large ignored by officials responsible for programs causing compulsory displacement. Development policies of most governments and major agencies, including the World Bank, did not formulate explicit demands that involuntary resettlement operations be carried out under more stringent criteria based on social science knowledge; displacement of people was usually dealt with last, as an afterthought. This lack of sociologically informed planning backfired during project implementation stages, causing underfinanced and unplanned relocation to be executed disastrously as a last moment crash operation. What was primarily missing was not "more research for better knowledge." Already accumulated sociological knowledge was not incorporated into an institutionalized policy for involuntary resettlement, which could guide the agencies dealing with forced relocation.

The significant turning point occurred when, for the first time, this body of knowledge was operationalized and translated into action guidelines adopted by the World Bank as an explicit policy statement addressing the "*social issues* associated with involuntary resettlement."[25] This happened initially in 1979–80 (when the first statement was issued) and was followed in 1986, 1988, and 1990 with new, strengthened policy papers.[26] The formulation of this policy was grounded in social science knowledge. The policy mandates that planning for projects that cause resettlement should start effectively with "putting people first," making the reestablishment of the living standards and productive capacity of those displaced a priority concern, favoring resettlement in groups, and protecting the interests of the host populations as well (these moves are treated in detail in chapter 6).[27]

Once a formal resettlement policy was instituted and enforced, the kind of social science knowledge that informs the policy *became manifestly in demand.* The policy itself explicitly prescribes the use of this specialized knowledge and, in fact, was the lever that increasingly moved the "knowledge-on-the-shelf" into actual application in operational work. Knowledge publicly available for some three decades but largely ignored or underestimated was now suddenly put to use (thus confirming Zuckermann's observation that social science knowledge informs policy making in a "more diffused fashion" than do physical and biological sciences, "involving longer intervals and more complex chains of influence"[28]). For instance, during 1985–90 more than 200 field missions that included one or more anthropologists or sociologists were sent by the World Bank to projects causing forced displacement, to assist in the preparation, appraisal, or implementation and supervision of the relocation operations at standards defined by the policy. This involvement of sociologists or anthropologists in resettlement work in Bank- financed projects the world over represents to date the highest density of sociological presence in a single sector of World Bank lending.

Even though formidable problems are always faced in resettlement, the practical results of the sociological contributions are visible and measurable in many projects. This does not mean that the social analysts were always free of mistakes in their work and certainly does not mean that it is sufficient to mobilize social knowledge to resolve all the major problems in such projects.

Another comparable example of social science–informed policy is the adoption by the World Bank of its policy guidelines concerning tribal or indigenous populations in Bank-financed projects.[29] Based directly on anthropological knowledge, these policy guidelines have directly contributed to a better protection of the cultural identity and socioeconomic rights—especially the demarcation of land rights—of vulnerable tribal groups and ethnic minorities inhabiting areas covered by projects. This policy led to substantive corrections in Bank projects and in the treatment of such population segments by many borrowing agencies.

Methodologies for Social Action

The need to go beyond explanation to action and beyond assessments to recommendations, raises requirements that make the *practice* of applied sociology and anthropology a *distinct* enterprise. This enterprise is not science in the classic sense and often may not be linked to policy formulation either. It is "simply" applied sociological or anthropological work, bound to generate new and valuable "products" that are different from the typical research products of science.

The concept of an "applied social scientist" who does not do "science" may at first seem paradoxical, but the contradiction is only apparent. The applied social science work often takes its practitioners far beyond what they have studied as trained social science professionals and beyond what has been conventionally regarded as the discipline's boundaries. Some practitioners of social and environmental impact assessment studies, for instance, have realized that important as such assessments are, "the assessment process is . . . *neither science nor policy*, despite the conventional wisdom which views it as a scientific procedure that lays the groundwork for well-informed policy."[30] And indeed, this is true not just for assessment studies, but for a much larger part of applied sociological and anthropological work. Moreover, much of the applied anthropological work cannot be called applied *research* either, as it often is labeled, simply because not every application of anthropological knowledge involves new research. This opinion, however, is not shared by all those who do applied sociology or anthropology, and a bit more consensus about the *nature* of this endeavor would much help this subfield. But if this view is accepted, it clearly ensues that new types of "products" of applied social science must be invented and defined.

One such product is the *methodologies for social action*. Such methodologies may be seen as a kind of applied social science product that is intermediate between general policy work and individual project (or case) social analysis. While it is essential to contribute to defining broad or sectoral development policies that indicate directions and goals, the formulation of policy does not usually include the elaboration of detailed methodologies for action to reach those goals: articulating them requires a distinct professional effort. Project-focused analyses must be specific-ally tailored to the given set of circumstances. Yet many social processes, under many different programs, share similar basic characteristics, and consequently the types of social actions required are in essence similar as well. For situations that are more or less recurrent (save different particular conditions), the elaboration of social action methodologies can supply what is missing in both general policy analysis and piecemeal project-focused social analysis. Such methodologies then can (must) be adjusted to individual situations, thus making tested approaches opera-tional and avoiding repetitive work in each single instance.

A case in point, which demonstrates the acute demand for social action methodologies, is the impasse with participatory planning for rural development. Among obstacles is also the absence of tested methodolo-gies for organizing people's participation. Now we often hear sudden declarations of fashionable support for participatory approaches from politicians, planners, economists, and technocrats. Social scientists should not confuse these statements with actual participatory planning because, under the cloud of cosmetic rhetoric, technocratic planning continues to rule.[31] The rhetoric of intent is still far ahead of the design for action to promote participation.

However, government officials or planners are not the only ones to blame for this gap. Anthropologists and sociologists have been busier advocating participation than working out social techniques for organiz-ing it. But without the know-how to organize it, participation will remain a hot ideology lacking a social technology. Many developing countries have authoritarian regimes that place structural and political restraints on grassroots participation, but often more participation is feasible even within existing political limits. We must ask and resolve pragmatic questions. Are the social sciences able to offer a methodology for organizing actual participation in different cultural contexts? Do social scientists have sets of procedures and methods transferable to planners and managers? What should be done during project preparation to shape the project so that it elicits and depends on participation? What should be done for organizing participation during implementation?

An interesting initiative to design such a social methodology was taken by a group of anthropologists, sociologists, and planners under the PIDER development project in Mexico. Against many odds, the team developed a model for participatory investment planning at the community and municipality levels. The team wanted to replace the top-down, paternalistic decisions imposed from on high with a methodology for eliciting farmers' own proposals and choices and for mobilizing their initiatives and material resources. The innovation was to develop this model itself not by a desk-bound effort but *through action-research*—actual tests in the field and community planning experiments—followed by iterative returns to the drawing boards.[32] The "product," the new methodology, consisted of a conceptual framework and a set of procedures, rules, and approaches that instituted field assessments, information exchange, and structured interaction between local and outside experts. Application guidelines and field manuals for planners were prepared. This methodology was then applied not only to many PIDER areas, but to planning for the entire Zacatecas state (over 1,000 municipalities). Such an approach can be replicated in other contexts where action research for this or other issues is needed, using similar social science–craftsmanship.

The interest in generating such methodologies usable in development interventions, still incipient, is nevertheless growing. Based on field-work, the Institute for Development Anthropology (IDA) has designed a methodology for identifying optimal locations for the siting of deep wells to provide potable water to dispersed rural homesteads and small settlements in Central Tunisia. Represented as a series of thematic maps overlaid on satellite imagery, the methodology employs sociological, demographic, and landuse criteria, as well as the more customary hydrologic and financial criteria, and takes into account projected population growth, political or administrative divisions, and environmental capacities. The institute also advised the government on the creation of organized, self-managed groups of potable water users, *Unités d'Autogestion*, to assume responsibility for the operation and maintenance of the new water points, fee collection, and the allocation of water surpluses. This social methodology appeared so effective that the government of Tunisia has invited IDA to participate in elaborating a national strategy for water user groups based on the Central Tunisia model.[33]

Another example comes from Sri Lanka's Gal Oya project area. Based on prior findings from the sociology of irrigation, and on action-research in the area, a team led by Uphoff developed, jointly with local water user associations, a social methodology for determining small group capacity to undertake development tasks and for building up this capacity.[34] A comparable methodology is described in chapter 3.

A domain that urgently calls for such methodology creation is organization building at the grassroots. All over the world, the degree of formal organization in rural communities lags far behind that of urban populations. This is a fundamental characteristic of rural underdevelopment that accounts largely for the vulnerability of rural societies. Many rural programs collapse for want of grassroots organizations able to foster collective actions (yet the same programs seldom attempt to establish organizations that aggregate and enhance individuals' capacities). Farmers' organizations, pastoral associations, credit groups, and water users' organizations, for example, are all critical for development, but the methods and knowledge to help construct them on a large scale have not been codified and made widely available. Informal organizations existing in traditional societies can sometimes be used as a matrix for building stronger formal organizations.[35] High-yielding social organizations are no less important for development than high-yielding crop varieties, and intensified agriculture cannot occur without intensified human organization. Sociological methodologies for building farmers' organizations or revitalizing existing ones are scarce. Sociologists and anthropologists should recognize this as a broad opportunity for institutional innovation.

There are, of course, complex epistemological and ethical questions about such methodologies as those mentioned in the examples from Mexico, Tunisia, and Sri Lanka. Would they be operationally valid across cultures? Any extrapolation would require testing adjustments and critical learning processes before they are actually offered for application.

The ethical legitimacy of preparing such methodologies is questioned by some, as on a more general plan the validity and legitimacy of action-research has also been both contested and defended in recurrent debates within the professional social science–community. Denying on ethical grounds the legitimacy of engagement in policy formulation and program work has undercut rather than empowered the transforming influence of social science. As has been correctly emphasized by many social scientists, given "the enormity of social illfare in modern times, . . . it is morally indefensible to adopt a noninterventionist stance when human suffering is all pervasive and when sociological technology has meliorative relevance."[36] Although these issues are not argued here in detail, my stand in brief is that action-oriented sociological work is ethically legitimate and that such sociologically informed methodologies for action are epistemologically feasible. The extent of crosscultural regularities in agrarian production patterns and social structures sets both the ground for, and the limits of, this feasibility.

Overall, these new applied science products, including methodological instruments, are insufficient and are being elaborated more by happenstance than by design. This mirrors the underdevelopment of development sociology and anthropology. The situation also largely reflects the fact that the academic mainstream of these disciplines gives little consideration to explicitly working out the theoretical and epistemological tenets of their applied domains.

At the beginning of the 1980s, a broad review of advances in development anthropology concluded that "anthropologists working in development have not yet created an academic subdiscipline, 'development anthropology', for their work is not characterized by a coherent or distinctive body of theory, concepts, and methods. Development anthropology has, however, become an incipient profession and field of study . . . (and) has produced a body of technically informed, substantive findings. . . ."[37] More or less the same can be said about development sociology, although the theoretical work is here more advanced. Furthermore, there is unacceptably little intellectual exchange and synergy between sociologists and anthropologists working on development. Although some significant advances have been made during the 1980s toward accumulating building blocks for a subdiscipline, the beginning of the 1990s finds the valid demand for a distinctive body of theory, concepts, and methods still wanting.

The idiosyncratic contribution of an individual anthropologist or sociologist to a certain project may be very valuable, but if it is mainly the product of this individual alone rather than the translation of a systematic methodology, it remains a piecemeal and particularistic contribution. Development agencies often have to rely excessively on a sociologist's personal aptitudes and on the accident of his or her flair and inspiration in the field, rather than on the discipline's methodological and conceptual tools. This reflects the infancy of the discipline itself. Although the creativity, intuition, and ad hoc judgment of the social analyst are critical for the project (and help develop the discipline itself), in the long term it is essential to have a *systematic body of sociological know-how* that is transferable and usable in operational work by sociologists and non-sociologists alike. Unless such methodologies are developed, behavioral sciences connected with development will only advance slowly.

Two Models: "Enlightenment" and "Social Engineering"

In discussing how social science knowledge can influence society more effectively, a distinction is often made between two models: *the enlightenment model* and *the engineering model.*[38] Generally, the differences between the two get stressed, while their complementarity is overlooked. Enlightenment counts on dissemination of sociological knowledge through education, which is a useful but obviously insufficient strategy. Enlightenment alone implies a tortuous, uncertain, and slow way to return the benefits of social knowledge to society and influence its progress. Moreover, the enlightenment model postulates the dissemination of findings and conclusions as available in academic social science, but it does not respond to the need of operationalizing social knowledge for action purposes. For this and other reasons, complementarity between the two models is necessary. The social engineering action model is rooted in knowledge of the social fabric and dynamics. It postulates the translation of social science knowledge into new know-how and change tools, and it uses this knowledge purposively to organize new social action and relationships.

For a while, social scientists have shied away from using the very concept of social engineering to avoid the unwarranted twin misinterpretations of applied social science as manipulation or as condescending paternalism. Lately, however, as the action-orientation in social research matures, the term is returning with renewed intellectual strength and validated usefulness. In fact, as Hirschman noted, it was on the crest of radical thinking and revolutionary action that the very idea of social engineering and of the perfectibility of the social order first arose—namely, at a time when "it was . . . novel to think that human happiness can be *engineered* by changing the social order."[39] Since that time, social knowledge has grown more precise, expanded, and deepened to levels at which it is increasingly usable as a guide to plan and as a means to democratize the planning process itself by facilitating broader participation in it of the development actors themselves. This meaning of social engineering is ethically and professionally acceptable. What should be avoided and opposed is not social engineering itself, but its abuse for reprehensible goals. As Rossi and Whyte wrote in a balanced definition,

> social engineering consists of attempts to use the body of sociological knowledge in the design of policies or institutions to accomplish some purpose. Social engineering can be accomplished for a mission-oriented agency or for some group opposed to the existing organizational structure, or it may be undertaken separately from either. . . . When conducted close to the policy-making centers, it is often termed social policy analysis. . . . When practiced by groups in opposition to current regimes, social engineering becomes social criticism.[40]

It is worth noting that nowadays social engineering is by far not a monopoly of social scientists. In fact, social scientists do a very limited amount of the "social engineering" that inevitably occurs in every plan and social policy decision in contemporary society. When technical specialists, economists, or managers decide on a development program without so much as consulting a social scientist, they do ad hoc social engineering of their own. When subsequently they implement that plan, they again do social engineering. Unfortunately, however, most often they aren't even aware that at least part of what they do is *social* engineering, the same way Molière's Monsieur Jourdain wasn't aware that he was making prose everyday, by simply speaking. However, just as Monsieur Jourdain made rather bad, ungrammatical, and halting prose, present day planners and technicians quite often do poor social engineering, unassisted by the professional competence derived from sociological and anthropological knowledge.

Planning agencies or policy bodies should be wary of relying on mechanical engineers to do social engineering. They should ensure the same level of professional competence for the social components of projects as they provide for the technical components. The applied social scientist who responsibly takes on the challenge of social engineering, for instance by planning for social development, provides an important service: he or she replaces the amateurish, do-it-yourself brand of social engineering of the nonsocial scientist with the state-of-the-art tools of understanding offered by a field of professional expertise. Certainly, social engineering does not decide upon or establish the *goals* of development. But with a clear understanding of what "putting people first" signifies, it can be employed to chart the relationship between means and goals in programs. For instance, in poverty-oriented rural development programs, it can bring about better strategies to support poverty alleviation. Another area concerns local institutions, where informal leadership identified through ethnographic analysis can provide efficient structures for reaching villages.

Although social engineering is only one way in which behavioral sciences can influence social action, it is the one that compels social scientists to descend from the realm of generalities to produce operationally usable know-how. It also requires sociologists to think through carefully the consequences of their recommendations rather than assume condescendingly that they know what is best for the people. In this vein, the sociologist should conceive of his or her role as not just a producer of expert solutions, but rather as a facilitator whose task is to free and bring to bear the huge innovation potential of the "plannees" themselves. The social scientist is the only kind of expert who is professionally trained to "listen to the people." Social knowledge thus developed becomes a "hearing system" able to amplify the listening for managers and policy-makers, too.

Hard dilemmas and controversial tradeoffs confront the development researchers doing social engineering. Sometimes they are required to compromise in their quest for data, to leap over unknown parameters and, yet, to provide their best judgment and advice with only imperfect information. But it is simply not possible to always know everything before doing anything. Dilemmas caused by imperfect knowledge are best addressed when recognized squarely and realistically, without ex-aggerated claims about the "scientism" of all that is done under the auspices of development anthropology or sociology. There must be concern for building in learning mechanisms and flexible adjustment procedures. The strictures of the planning process itself will never easily allow the ideal setting for generating and using social knowledge.

Experienced sociologists and anthropologists have struggled against such strictures; they have emphasized the need for applied work to both live with and overcome imperfect knowledge. Reflecting on his own work as sociologist-planner and simultaneously "certified" scholar, Herbert J. Gans described well the practitioner's dilemmas and the need for creative answers:

Most of the questions which must be answered before planning can take place on a rational basis have not yet been sufficiently studied; yet the planners cannot wait for further research. Sociologists who participate in guided mobility programs must be able to come to conclusions on the basis of past research, a modicum of impressionistic observations, and a large amount of freewheeling hypothesizing—that is, guessing. They must gamble further by being willing to build the products of this highly unscientific approach into experimental programs. There is no doubt that this type of sociological endeavor will lay the practitioner open to criticism from colleagues in the discipline as being unscientific or controversial, but it will be countered by appreciation and the surrender of an ancient stereotype about the unwillingness of sociologists to come to conclusions on the part of the planner. More-over, the sociologist must revamp the concepts that he uses so that they can answer questions posed by the plan and in such a way that they will lead to ideas and techniques for action programs.[41]

Breaking new ground by working on the cultural variables of major development programs, applied social researchers have the rare chance of making "social inventions," to use Whyte's felicitous concept; this is what they do, for instance, when they chart "new sets of procedures for shaping human interactions and activities and the relations of humans to the natural and social environment"[42] or when they develop new "incentive structures"[43] apt to help improve the involvement of social actors in purposive development activities.

Without discounting the caution dictated by limited knowledge, sociologists should become more operationally prescriptive. Sociologists and anthropologists often have many hundred "don'ts" to only five "do's." By focusing on program design and execution as entrance points, social scientists will force themselves to be more pragmatic, more operationally useful, and more versatile in development work. They will also become aware of variables and relationships that otherwise would have escaped their attention.

In sum, my overall argument is that applied social scientists have to learn to generate new products that are usable by development practitioners. These new products should not be regarded as replacements for the traditional products of research (such as taxonomies, explanatory hypotheses, concepts, and theories), but as supplementing them with methodologies for social action. Such new social science products and approaches—whether they are called social technologies, social engineering, sociotechniques or, in Firth's term, human engineering[44]— would respond to the needs of induced development, enrich the traditional spectrum of social science products, and make social knowledge more effective. The scope for such creative contributions is virtually limitless and they are needed urgently.

Institutionalizing Development Social Science

To generate new intellectual products, the noneconomic social disciplines have to work hard in their own gardens. Expansion of their research agenda and more concern with their own institutionalization are essential.

Promising new research areas and issues are emerging, both within sociology and anthropology and at their frontiers with other sciences: agricultural sociology; common property resource management; collective action; farming systems research; crop sociology; social forestry; the development role of the state and of the nongovernmental organizations; and others. Every one of these research areas is relevant for induced development and holds substantial potential for expanding applied social research.

The metaphor of entrance points in the process of planning development has obvious implications for the *institutionalization of development social science* and the actual settings within which development sociology and anthropology are practiced and taught. The process of institutionalization of development sociology and anthropology can be conceived, paraphrasing Robert Merton's analysis of the sociology of science, as a process of intensified "interplay between the *cognitive* and the *professional* identities"[45] of the development social sciences.

Solidifying our "cognitive identity" requires not just applied work; to a decisive extent, this cognitive identity will depend upon the general progress of basic theory and research in sociology and anthropology. Indeed, it is on the shoulders of basic research only that applied researchers can have the secure pedestal of a distinct body of knowledge, supplying them the lenses to see the wider horizons.

In turn, solidifying our "professional identity" requires other processes; in this respect, Merton has called attention to the definition of institutionalization suggested by Edward Shils that meticulously captures a set of organizational and intellectual dimensions:

> By institutionalization of an intellectual activity I mean the relatively dense interaction of persons who perform that activity. The interaction has a structure: the more intense the interaction, the more its structure makes place for authority which makes decisions regarding assessment, admission, promotion, allocation. The high degree of institutionalization of an intellectual activity entails its teaching and administered organization. The organization regulates access through a scrutiny of qualification, provides for organized assessment of performance, and allocates facilities, opportunities, and rewards for performance—for example, study, teaching, investigation, publications, appointment, and so forth. It also entails the organized support of the activity from outside the particular institution and the reception or use of the results of the activity beyond the boundaries of the institution.[46]

In the case of development sociology-anthropology, at least three processes appear critical: first, the position of the social analyst should be formally institutionalized within the organizational settings of technical, administrative, and development agencies; second, substantive changes must be made in the training of sociologists and anthropologists oriented to development work; and third, the equivalent of a sociological renaissance is needed in university curricula for training technical specialists and economists for development work.

As long as professional social researchers remain outside technical and administrative agencies, knocking on physical doors to gain intellectual entry, the actual use of sociological knowledge in planned development will be hampered by more obstacles than if sociologists were among the insiders. Their inclusion is necessary to reduce organizational ethnocentrism on both sides. Some agencies have begun to institutionalize sociological skills, yet these cases are still few and far between. National (governmental) and international organizations are lagging behind despite their professed creed or given mandate. There are, for instance, many livestock departments in agricultural ministries all over the world, which are properly staffed with veterinarians to deal with cattle but lack any sociological staff trained to understand the social organization of pastoral populations. Staff sociologists could certainly enhance the capacity of these agencies to work with cattle owners and thus improve animal husbandry.

It is of exceptional importance that indigenous sociologists and anthropologists from developing countries participate intensively in applied development activities. Unfortunately, however, this is still far from happening. In India, for instance, and this is true for virtually all developing countries, "most organizations, including those that recognize the value of anthropological contributions, are functioning without qualified anthropologists on a regular basis. . . . Obviously this situation must change if government-directed development is to benefit from anthropological knowledge."[47]

I have no naive illusions that the inclusion of sociologists or anthropologists in technical settings will solve all social problems, but in their absence many programs remain socially underdesigned and register a high rate of economic, technical, and sociopolitical failure. Cooperation across disciplinary fences is difficult enough; across additional bureaucratic walls it becomes virtually impossible. The issue is not just one of philosophical recognition but also one of resource allocation. The social scientist may have to play second violin to the technical experts, which is perfectly acceptable; in other circumstances he may fulfill the role of project manager;[48] but only the well-orchestrated joint efforts of technical and social experts can produce harmonized development work. The institutionalization of the social professions will generate various *patterned* models of interaction with other disciplines and enhance the quality of development planning.

The academic training of sociologists and anthropologists should be profoundly restructured if producing professionals with an action-oriented outlook is to be addressed responsibly. Enough has been written on this issue to make repetition unnecessary, yet it is unfortunate that the social science academic establishment reacts so slowly to this imperative.[49] True enough, all the textbooks for training such action-oriented sociologists and anthropologists are not yet on the shelves.[50] But there is little time to wait. Moreover, if the opportunities opened up by the pressure of practical demands are used, then both empirical and analytical materials for textbook synthesis would accumulate faster.

Last but not least, in my own experience at the World Bank and in different countries, an enduring obstacle to the influx of sociological knowledge into development work has been that many technical experts lack understanding of what social science and social engineering could bring to their own efforts. The magnitude of this intellectual obstacle on a global scale is underestimated. The gap persists. In fact, it is being recreated with every class graduating from technical and economic institutes, because of the manner in which technical experts are "grown" in the groves of academe. Biologists and economists, agronomists and veterinarians, urban planners or foresters, and industrial or irrigation engineers who tomorrow will have a strong say in the design and execution of development programs, are often being trained today as though people did not matter for the solution of technical issues. Thus, they remain ignorant of the sociostructural and cultural dimensions of technical/production processes because of outdated training philosophies and practices.

The experts produced by this training are being deprived of a crucial lens—the social one—for looking at and understanding their own technical field. They are not being prepared to cooperate later with the social experts, don't know what to ask from them, and remain unaware of what they are entitled, as technical specialists, to receive from the social specialist. Correcting this situation is not a task for only a year or two, but rather will require a generation at least.

If any renaissance is in store for social sciences in their development role, it will not take place unless social science knowledge (not just introductory principles, but the sociology of the specific subarea of technical activity) is diffused among technical specialists as well. Teaching social sciences to students in fields other than sociology and anthropology is at least as important and consequential as teaching future sociologists.

To sum up, putting people first is not simply a fashionable slogan but is a formidable work program for social sciences. It is also a heuristic device demanding always that we identify, in every seemingly "technical," "financial," or "administrative" intervention, the sociological angle and the variables pertinent to the social organization affected or targeted by the intervention. Sociologists have to face the nuts and bolts of development activities, to roll up their sleeves and deal with the mundane, pragmatic questions of translating plans into realities in a sociologically sound manner. They need to link data generation, action-oriented research, social analysis, design for social action, and evaluation into a continuum, and thus stretch sociology's contributions far beyond simple pronouncements.

The planning models for rural development are far from perfect, and although sociologists should learn to work within existing frameworks they must at the same time change them with their input. Financially induced change programs need sociological knowledge and must incorporate the sociocultural variables. Financial resources are not necessarily the key ingredient in all development programs. Sometimes they are the least important. The range of entrance points for sociological knowledge and skills should be expanded to all segments of development planning, from policymaking to execution and evaluation, and from theorizing to social engineering. It is essential to design purposively for social action.

The conventional range of operationally usable products generated by social scientists is still narrow and insufficient; forward-looking action methodologies should enrich the domain. The support for participation will be more effective if passionate advocacy is accompanied by social methodology. The newly emerging research orientations are more interdisciplinary than the old ones; they deserve the support and commitment of development-oriented social scientists. Training philosophies must change as a crucial step to avoid producing new cohorts of socially incompetent technical experts or technically illiterate sociologists.

Such changes and the new orientation toward increasing the action relevance of the social sciences will result in a better response to the fundamental calling of social sciences: not only to analyze and explain, but also to assist in transforming society and improving people's lives.

Notes

1. For the present argument, I use the terms sociology and social anthropology interchangeably. I believe that the broad substantive overlap between what sociologists and social anthropologists actually do within the framework of development programs justifies this use; the differences between the overall perspectives of the two disciplines, although real, are not treated here. References to social sciences in this paper should be generally read as references to noneconomic social sciences—particularly anthropology and sociology—but do not imply that there are no differences in approach between disciplines.

2. Other such internal factors, which cannot be elaborated here, but deserve wider discussion, include the state of the discipline's theory and body of knowledge, the quality of its practitioners' applied craftsmanship, the patterns of their professional formal organization, and obviously their views and value judgments on whether or how applied social research should be conducted. For the status of applied anthropology in the United States, see a broad and very instructive historical overview on disciplinary growth and internal problems in: William L. Partridge and Elizabeth M. Eddy, "The Development of Applied Anthropology in America," in E. M. Eddy and W. L. Partridge, eds., *Applied Anthropology in America*, 2d ed. (New York: Columbia University Press, 1987).

3. Walter Goldschmidt, "Anthropology as a Policy Science," in W. Goldschmidt, ed., *Public Policy: A Dialogue* (a special publication of the American Anthropological Association, no. 21, 1986).

4. Anthony Hall, "Sociology and Foreign Aid: Rhetoric and Reality," in A. Hall and J. Midgley, eds., *Development Policies. Sociological Perspectives* (Manchester and New York: Manchester University Press, 1988).

5. Vernon W. Ruttan, one of the few notable American economists who set out explicitly to explore what development economics "can learn from anthropology," noted that "almost no attention has been devoted by economists to the role of cultural endowments." He went on to observe that "professional opinion in economics has not dealt kindly with the reputations of those development economists who have made serious efforts to incorporate cultural variables into development theory or into the analysis of the development process. Their work has typically been favorably reviewed and then ignored. . . . But in spite of the failure of research on the economic implications of cultural endowments to find a secure place in economic development literature or thought, the conviction that "culture matters" remains pervasive in the underworld of development thought and practice. The fact that the scholars and practitioners of development are forced to deal with cultural endowments at an intuitive level rather than in analytical terms should be regarded as a deficiency in professional capacity rather than as evidence that culture does not matter." (See "Cultural Endowments and

Economic Development: What Can We Learn from Anthropology?" in *Economic Development and Cultural Change*, vol. 36, no. 3, 1988, pp. 250, 255–56).

6. For an analytical effort at "deconstructing" the concept of *planned intervention* and at reformulating its theoretical underpinnings, see Norman Long and J. D. van der Ploeg, "Demythologizing Planned Intervention: An Actor's Perspective," in *Sociologia Ruralis*, vol. 29, no. 3/4, 1989 (Van Gorcum, Assen, the Netherlands).

7. Albert O. Hirschman, *Development Projects Observed* (Washington, D.C.: Brookings Institution, 1967).

8. Dennis A. Rondinelli, *Development Projects as Policy Experiments. An Adaptive Approach to Development Administration* (London and New York: Methuen, 1983); see, in particular, Rondinelli's analysis of projects as public policy vehicles in social experimentation.

9. Yves Goussault suggests the following as a possible definition: "The sociology of development is a *sociology of intervention*. It is basically linked to the social changes provoked by the interventions of states and capital in various social sectors as well as in the overall structures of societies. In this capacity, it is a sociology of strategies. . . ." (Yves Goussault, "Où en est la sociologie du développement?" *Revue Tiers Monde*, vol. 23, no. 90, 1982, p. 242).

10. See Robert Chambers for a provocative discussion of the concept of professional "reversal" needed in development work. "Bureaucratic Reversals and Local Diversity," *IDS Bulletin*, vol. 19, no. 6 (1988).

11. Mark Granovetter, "Economic Action and Social Structure: The Problem of Embeddedness," *American Journal of Sociology*, vol. 91, no. 3, 1985.

12. The following comment was made by an anthropologist who reviewed an earlier version of this chapter: "Indeed, money is far from being everything. In the large institutional development project I did for the Treasury in Saudi Arabia, I discovered that even given unlimited funds, certain social and organizational changes were often impossible through money alone. In fact, the funds themselves became a problem. . . ." (Theodore E. Downing, letter to the author).

13. Robert K. Merton, "The Role of Applied Social Science in the Formation of Policy: A Research Memorandum," *Philosophy of Science* vol. 16, no. 3, 1949, p. 178 (emphasis added).

14. Michael M. Cernea, "Farmer Organizations and Institution Building for Sustainable Agricultural Development," in *Regional Development Dialogue*, no. 2, 1988.

15. Vernon W. Ruttan, "Social Science Knowledge and Institutional Change," *American Journal of Agricultural Economics*, December 1984.

16. Robert A. Scott and A. R. Shore, *Why Sociology Does Not Apply: Sociology in Public Policy* (New York and Oxford: Elsevier, 1979), p. 35.

17. Scott and Shore 1979, p. 2.

18. Edward C. Green insightfully captured such self-defeating disciplinary biases, when he wrote: "for their part, anthropologists may view economists, agronomists, engineers, and the like as narrowly focused technicians whose rigid professional mindsets and cultural distance from local populations prevent them from coping with human factors or seeing the larger picture, especially when dealing with cultures quite different from their own." (Themes in the Practice of Development Anthropology, in Edward C. Green, ed., *Practicing Development Anthropology*, Boulder and London: Westview Press, 1986, pp. 7–8).

19. Warren C. Baum, *The Project Cycle* (Washington, D.C.: World Bank, 1982).

20. For a detailed description of the preparation stage for an involuntary resettlement project, see Michael M. Cernea, *Involuntary Resettlement in Development Projects*, Annex 1, World Bank Technical Paper No. 80 (Washington, D.C., 1988).

21. In 1984, explicit guidelines to analyze these four sets of factors during the appraisal of projects were formally introduced in the World Bank's internal policy and procedural

directives. These guidelines are mandatory for Bank staff; they also strongly influence the work of planning staff of borrowing agencies in developing countries. These formal appraisal guidelines mandate a more in-depth analysis of the basic social variables than what was described as the "social aspects analysis" in the well-known manual published by the Bank: *Economic Analysis of Agricultural Projects*, edited by J. Price Gittinger (Baltimore and London: Johns Hopkins University Press, 1982), see pp. 15–16.

22. Solon T. Kimball, "Anthropology as a Policy Science," in E. M. Eddy and W. L. Partridge, eds., *Applied Anthropology in America*, 2d ed. (New York: Columbia University Press, 1987, emphasis added).

23. See Thomas Weaver, "Anthropology as a Policy Science, Part I and II," *Human Organization*, vol. 44, nos. 2, 3 (1985). See also Ralph Grillo and Allan Rew, eds., *Social Anthropology and Development Policy* (London and New York: Tavistock, 1985).

24. Anthony Hall and James Midgley, eds., *Development Policies: Sociological Perspectives* (Manchester and New York: Manchester University Press, 1988).

25. The statement, "Social Issues Associated with Involuntary Resettlement in Bank-Financed Projects," became part of the World Bank's internal operational manual in February 1980.

26. Michael M. Cernea, "Anthropology, Policy and Involuntary Resettlement," British Association for Social Anthropology in Policy and Practice Newsletter 4(1989).

27. The basic tenets of this policy are presented in detail in the paper "Involuntary Resettlement in Development Projects: Policy Guidelines in Bank-Financed Projects" by Michael M. Cernea, World Bank, Agriculture Department, Washington, D.C., 1988. See also chapters 5 and 6 of this volume.

28. Harriet Zuckermann, "Uses and Control of Knowledge: Implications for the Social Fabric," in James F. Short, Jr., ed., *The Social Fabric: Discussions and Issues* (Beverly Hills: Sage Publications, 1986).

29. These guidelines, "Tribal People in Bank-Financed Development Projects," became part of the World Bank's internal operational manual in 1982.

30. Steven McNabb, "Logical Inconsistencies . . .," in *Human Organization*, vol. 48, no. 2 (1988).

31. The question skeptically asked by Gelia Castillo—"how participatory is participatory development?"—is warranted and should be asked about every development program. (See *How Participatory Is Participatory Development? A Review of the Philippine Experience* (Manila: Institute for Development Studies, 1983).

32. See more details in Michael M. Cernea, "The 'Production' of a Social Methodology," in E. M. Eddy and W. L. Partridge, eds., *Applied Anthropology in America* (New York: Columbia University Press, 1987).

33. Michael M. Horowitz, personal communication, January 1990. Several reports dealing with this activity are available from the IDA: among these are Gordon Appleby, "Criteria and Methodology for the Delimitation of Water-Short Areas in Central Tunisia," 1987; Mohamed Fakhfakh and others, "Projet Eau Potable en Tunisie Centrale," Cartographie des Ressources en Eau et Population," 1987; Nicholas S. Hopkins, "Les Associations d'Usagers de l'Eau Potable dans la Tunisie Centrale, et la nouvelle Unité d'Autogestion au sein de l'ODTC," 1986. A final report by Muneera Salem-Murdock and Michael M. Horowitz describing how this methodology was produced is forthcoming.

34. Norman Uphoff, "Participatory Evaluation of Farmer Organizations' Capacity for Development Tasks," *Agricultural Administration and Extension*, vol. 30 (1988). Uphoff suggests that the methodology should be adaptable and generalizable for group credit programs, range or forest management, agricultural extension, and so forth. "All that is needed is

some modification in the questions that are formulated, though not even in the way the questions are derived and pretested" (p. 44).

35. Milton J. Esman and Norman T. Uphoff have extensively treated the topic of local organizations and their potential in *Local Organizations—Intermediaries in Rural Development* (Ithaca, New York: Cornell University Press, 1984).

36. James Midgley, "Sociology and Development Policy," in Anthony Hall and James Midgley, eds., *Development Policies: Sociological Perspectives* (Manchester and New York: Manchester University Press, 1988).

37. Allan Hoben, "Anthropologists and Development," *Annual Review of Anthropology* (1982), pp. 349–50.

38. Morris Janowitz, *Political Conflict: Essays in Political Sociology* (Chicago: Quadrangle Books, 1970), p. 247.

39. Albert O. Hirschman, "Rival Interpretations of Market Society: Civilization, Destructive or Feeble?" *Journal of Economic Literature*, vol. 20 (December 1982), p. 1463.

40. Peter H. Rossi and W. F. Whyte, "The Applied Side of Sociology," in H. E. Freeman, R. R. Dynes, P. H. Rossi, and W. F. Whyte, eds., *Applied Sociology: Roles and Activities of Sociologists in Diverse Settings* (San Francisco and London: Jossey-Bass Publishers, 1983), p. 10.

41. Herbert J. Gans, "Urban Poverty and Social Planning," in P. F. Lazarsfeld, W. S. Sewell, and H. L. Wilenski, eds., *The Uses of Sociology* (New York: Basic Books, 1967), p. 448.

42. William Foote Whyte, "Social Inventions for Solving Human Problems," *American Sociological Review*, vol. 47 (February 1982).

43. Edward H. Greeley, "Project Development in Kenya," in Edward Green, ed., *Practicing Development Anthropology* (Boulder: Westview Press, 1986). Greeley underscores that the first lesson he learned from his experience as an anthropologist working on USAID projects in Kenya was the importance of focusing "on the incentives of individuals, groups, and institutions."

44. Raymond Firth, "Engagement and Detachment: Reflections on Applying Social Anthropology to Social Affairs," *Human Organization*, vol. 40, no. 3 (1981).

45. Robert K. Merton, *The Sociology of Science: An Episodic Memoir* (Carbondale and Edwardsville: Southern Illinois University Press, 1979), p. 7 (emphasis added).

46. Edward Shils, cf. Merton (1979).

47. H. Mohan Mathur, *Anthropology and Development in Traditional Societies* (New Delhi: Vikas Publishing House, 1989).

48. Gerald Murray discussed the role of the anthropologist as manager in a social forestry project in Haiti that was managed over several years by several anthropologists in sequence (see G. Murray, "The Domestication of Wood in Haiti: A Case Study in Applied Evolution," in R. M. Wulff and S. J. Fiske, eds., *Anthropological Praxis* (Boulder, Colo.: Westview Press, 1987).

49. W. Goldschmidt has been among the few to raise his voice in criticism regarding the responsibility of the "more senior anthropologists" who have cultivated remoteness from applied tasks among their students: "Anthropologists . . . have not prepared themselves for the serious and difficult task of translating their deep understanding (of national cultures) into the workday realities of decision making and the crossfire that goes with such a role. Or perhaps, I should say, we more senior anthropologists have failed them, we have failed to prepare them for such tasks, and thus it is we who are to blame for not making them ready when they are wanted. Rarely in our curricula are there programs that translate theories into actionable

policies. . . . It is necessary for the anthropologists to prepare their students for public service" (Goldschmidt, 1986, p. 4).

50. For a notable exception, see William L. Partridge, ed., *Training Manual in Development Anthropology*, Publication No. 17 (Washington, D.C.: American Anthropological Association and Society for Applied Anthropology, 1984).

PART I

Irrigation Projects

Editor's Note

About one-third of the world's food supply is being produced from only one-sixth of its cultivated area—the lands that have been provided with irrigation. Globally, irrigated areas more than tripled between 1950–90. Satisfying the increasing demands generated by both population growth and higher per capita consumption will heavily depend upon improving the productivity of both irrigated and rainfed lands.

The water flowing in irrigation systems is as much a social product of human organization as it is a natural commodity. As the authors of the following three chapters jointly argue, sociological issues are embedded in the operation of all irrigation systems, small or large: people must organize socially in order to secure water, transport it, divide it into usable shares, enforce rules for its distribution, pay for it, and dispose of unused portions. Therefore, the in-depth understanding of technical and agronomic problems of irrigated agriculture is impossible without understanding the social organization in which it is embedded.

However, financially induced irrigation development programs have often focused only on technical and physical components: dams and canals, control systems, water levels, and drainage. Institutional concerns, when present, were limited mostly to strengthening central water agencies. It is being increasingly recognized now that major institutional weaknesses undermine the operation and maintenance of the physical infrastructure, that irrigation schemes perform below expectation, and that some even cause serious adverse environmental effects. These unintended effects often result not from technical causes, but from inattention to the social organization of the water users.

In the following chapters, social scientists with broad field experience in irrigation discuss several new models for identifying the social-organizational components intrinsic to irrigation development. Although their views do not coincide in all respects, the authors jointly stress the centrality of social organizational structures and propose sociological models to explain the operation of these structures. These models are directly usable, in turn, in designing either new irrigation systems or programs to rehabilitate the physical, organizational, and institutional arrangements of existing irrigation schemes.

Water Coward is concerned with the correlation between technical and social changes, especially when projects aim to rehabilitate or improve already existing irrigation systems. All too often, planners ride roughshod overall locally developed irrigation systems and self-management techniques in the rush to provide improved alternatives. Particularly interesting are Coward's recently discovered examples of indigenous social mechanisms for water allocation that cover the area of several villages. Coward argues convincingly that a more careful incorporation of existing social, technical, and managerial arrangements into irrigation project designs would make for higher success rates, avoid undermining existing grassroots institutions, and lower the maintenance costs of irrigation systems.

David Freeman and Max Lowdermilk also concentrate on the human networks which must organize and manage irrigation systems. Their structural-functional model looks at the different organizational levels needed to coordinate the different tasks involved in making irrigation infrastructure meet farm requirements. Freeman and Lowdermilk argue that their task-focused model can be usefully applied at three different levels: the farm, the command (irrigation) area, and the state bureaucracy. Freeman and Lowdermilk emphasize that the mid-level organizational structures, located between local and national management, are the most neglected in the irrigation design.

The contribution of these two frameworks lies in using a sociological perspective to understand irrigation organizations—formal and informal ones. Both chapters underscore the need to rely on fieldwork-based descriptions of the customary rules in order to understand how irrigation systems work. By clarifying the possible ways to involve better the users in system operation, and by clarifying the social principles that explain why the system is operated in a particular way, the social analyst can determine how to make system improvements more effective. The chapters draw upon ethnographic fieldwork: Coward in India and the Philippines; Freeman and Lowdermilk in Pakistan.

Benjamin Bagadion and Frances Korten, in their chapter, start from similar premises about the utility of discovering the social structure of local irrigation activities. They argue that the organizational fit between local institutions and state agencies should be based on complementarity rather than competition. Their particular concern is the empowerment of water users through establishing their own grassroots associations, and the coordination of local users' organizations with the state agency in charge of administering irrigation. Such coordination is not built overnight. Bagadion and Korten look penetratingly at what steps must be taken at the agency level to allow it first to recognize and then to deal with local capabilities.

The chapter documents the experiences of the Philippine National Irrigation Administration. Using a learning process approach, the agency gradually understood how to address social needs at the village level and how to interact with the water users, and then developed the necessary support systems for those field activities. The training of community organizers was reoriented to include social science skills, and social analysts learned to cooperate with engineers and other technical experts, with beneficial results.

The case study on the water users associations in the Philippines, begun a decade ago, is brought up to date with recent field data, which show that the measurable benefits of using community organizers in promoting grassroot organizations exceed the costs.

The type of analysis advocated in these three chapters is useful for the preparation and implementation stages of irrigation projects. Detailing the contours of the social organization of irrigation systems would permit field staff and project planners to develop the structures into which new technologies could be imbedded. This, of course, implies a planning strategy considerably different from most current models.

Harnessing local organizational innovations, talent, and experience in project design has the additional advantage of avoiding the costs and bureaucracy associated with unnecessary paternalistic control by governments. Social analysis, if properly inserted in the process for generating and implementing a project, is able to design and help construct socio-organizational structures. The local groupings identified during this process should be recognized, assisted, and strengthened in their own efforts for self development.

2

Planning Technical and Social Change in Irrigated Areas

E. Walter Coward, Jr.

Much of the state-financed contemporary irrigation development is directed toward improving systems that already exist. This includes the rehabilitation or improvement of (usually) large state-operated irrigation works, as well as technological change in smaller irrigation works operated by local groups. In either of these situations, the effective design and implementation of appropriate development interventions must begin with a thorough understanding of the sociotechnical context.

Projects to rehabilitate or improve systems should ideally proceed from a comprehensive understanding of the physical apparatus and the associated social organization of existing irrigation activities. From this understanding ought to emerge a refined analysis of the irrigation problems that need attention, and a strategy for implementation which recognizes both the local resources at hand (including knowledge, experience, and institutional capacity) and the preferred alterations in the existing state of affairs.

In all cases where irrigation systems have been in operation, there are institutional and social arrangements which organize fundamental tasks such as distributing water among users or maintaining the canals. These tasks may be performed by water users themselves or in conjunction with others such as local government officials or irrigation agency staff; the social arrangements may be formal or informal, highly individualistic or collective, chaotic or controlled—and, of course, judged (by outsiders or insiders) as effective or not. Nonetheless, we begin with the assumption that where canals (or wells, springs, or whatever) serve more than a single person, patterns of social interaction govern the use of those facilities.

Two other initial assumptions are equally important. One is that project implementation itself is also a social process that follows various rules and is conducted by individuals occupying specific roles in various organizations—namely, engineers of the irrigation agency, experts from donor organizations, and so on. The second assumption supposes that the final, post-rehabilitation situation requires a set of social arrangements to complement the new or rebuilt physical apparatus provided by the project. These future social arrangements may be implicit or explicit in the design and the project documents and, of course, may be formal or informal, dominated by the agency staff or not, may require individual or collective action, and so on. Most important, the future arrangements may or may not correspond with the preproject social patterns.

Agency planning for irrigation projects is already a lengthy and complex process covering (sometimes superficially) an array of social, technical, environmental, and economic factors. Given this complexity, one should hesitate to recommend including more in the feasibility study. Nonetheless, particularly in the case of rehabilitation, project preparation papers and appraisal reports often provide only the most meager information on the existing social arrangements for irrigation, or on the intended social organizational patterns to be associated with the improved facilities.

Because the *physical* apparatus of an irrigation system and the *social* structure for its use are necessarily intertwined, rehabilitation projects run a high risk of failure if they deliberately plan technical change but either ignore, or merely assume, the necessary social changes. Sometimes, failure is expressed in unimproved production levels; frequently, in the lack of farmer commitment to using and maintaining the new works. To correct this fundamental weakness in project design, preparation procedures should require more attention to existing irrigation institutions and organizations—the cultural ideas and social arrangements that organize activities such as system maintenance and water distribution.

Conceptualizing the Sociology of Irrigation

A sociological perspective on irrigation commences with two fundamental concepts (which are also part of project preparation terminology):
institutions and social organization.

"Institution" is a concept varyingly used in both sociology and in
everyday language, but here I employ it to refer to ideal behavior and
role expectations and as a generic concept for the variety of rules that
help pattern social behavior: norms, folkways, customs, conventions,
etiquette, and law. Economists sometimes use a similar notion when they
define an institution as a behavioral rule. In this sense, the rule of
continuous irrigation, the custom of performing a ritual ceremony at the
headwork of a local irrigation system, and the law requiring payment of
a water fee are all examples of irrigation institutions.

In addition to these institutions, there are, in any human group, actual
patterns of social interaction which are referred to as the social organization. These patterns of behavior are sometimes formal, purposive, and
enduring enough to warrant the use of a group name: the Royal Irrigation
Department, Subak Tamblang, the San Lorenzo Farmers' Irrigation
Cooperative Association, Inc., or the Muda Area Development Authority. Of course, social organization is also composed of patterns and
groups less formal, purposive, or enduring: an evening meeting between
irrigation authorities and an assembly of water users, a partnership
between two farmers which allows one to move water across the fields
of another, or a temporary band of farmers who share a common lateral
working to clean a canal.

An understanding of the basic relationship between institutions and
social organization requires recognition of the frequent inconsistency
between what people believe should occur (the institutional element) and
what actually occurs (the organizational element). The basic "lack of
close correspondence between the 'ideal' and the 'actual' in many and
pervasive contexts of social behavior" is one important force for change
in either the institutional or social organization arrangements.[1] A major
reason for this inconsistency is that changes in the social or physical
environment make it difficult or impossible to act in certain established
ways or make it easy or possible to act in certain new ways. Change in
either the institutional or the social organizational element creates demand for change in the other.

Institutions and social organization are fused through the basic concept of role which in turn is composed of two elements: *role expectations* (the institutional dimension) and *role performance* (the social organizational dimension). In part, a role can be thought of as the cluster of expectations associated with a given function. In addition, a role is associated with actual patterns of action. Roles help one to predict the actions and reactions of others and thus they enable social patterns and social organization to emerge. For example, in an irrigation system, a cluster of institutions associated with the function of water distribution may be found in the role of the ditchtender and another cluster found in the role of the water user. The presence of these two roles allows social organization to take shape in an irrigation system in the form of patterned relationships between the ditchtenders and water users. This perspective of institutions and organizations allows us to consider patterns of social organization in a particular irrigation system or between systems even though no formal irrigation associations may exist.

The general concepts of rules, roles, and groups are useful in understanding human behavior in many contexts and for a variety of purposes. To be useful in understanding irrigation, however, these concepts need to be matched with critical tasks or actions that occur in irrigation systems. Although many tasks must be organized to operate an irrigation system, five are of fundamental importance.[2]

Three of these tasks are somewhat specific: (1) *water acquisition*—the task of obtaining water for the irrigation system through regular or extraordinary means; (2) *water allocation*—the task of dividing and distributing the system's supply to its users; and (3) *system maintenance*—the task of repairing, cleaning, and otherwise reconditioning the physical apparatus of the system.

The remaining two tasks are more general and may, in fact, be directly related to one or more of the above tasks: (4) *resource mobilization*—the task of activating and accumulating labor, materials, funds, and other resources needed to implement such tasks as system maintenance; and (5) *conflict management*—the task of containing and adjudicating (though not necessarily resolving) disputes and disagreements arising from operations such as water allocation.

The above list of tasks can be used to create an analytical scheme for understanding the institutional and organizational aspects of one or more existing irrigation schemes before rehabilitation, and to examine the institutional and organizational assumptions embodied in the post-rehabilitation physical works. The matching of the basic concepts of rules, roles, and groups with the five fundamental tasks is illustrated in table 2-1.

Social analysts participating in the preparation phase of a rehabilitation project could use this analytical scheme to detail the existing social organization of irrigation systems and to clarify the organizational and institutional changes likely to be implied in various technological alterations introduced by the project.

Studying Irrigation Institutions and Organizations

Two main factors explain, in my view, why the planning for rehabilitation projects usually includes little analysis of social organization. The irrigation agency itself—the typical source of rehabilitation project proposals—frequently makes assumptions that blunt the demand for organizational analysis. If the works to be rehabilitated are publicly managed, the problems to be solved are typically identified by the agency as poor or absent infrastructure and inadequate social organization. If the rehabilitation is directed toward small, locally managed systems, the organizations currently operating the systems are often judged by the agency to be no longer successful or to be unsuitable for operating "modern" irrigation works. In either case, there is little or no demand to explore the current organizational arrangements.

However, even when applied social scientists have been engaged in project preparation work, their research may be difficult for planners to use. This can occur even when the project designers have called for sociological input—which usually is a request for a general analysis of "socioeconomic" factors.

When this is the request, what is it that sociologists supply?

Socioeconomic analysis, nearly always, is done by conducting a socioeconomic survey. Surveys are efficient ways of collecting and aggregating information about the characteristics of individual farmers or of individual farm units—information that is necessary to project planning as well as to some later project evaluation. But surveys are ineffective in revealing important dimensions of the structure of collective action related to irrigation, such as arrangements for water distribution or processes for mobilizing resources for maintenance. Thus, as with

Table 2-1. *Irrigation System Tasks, by Institutional and Organizational Element*

Institutional and organizational element	Task				
	Water acquisition	*Water allocation*	*System maintenance*	*Resource mobilization*	*Conflict management*
Key rules	Rules for acquiring extra water supplies for the systems	Rules for allocating water between subunits of system, farms, and so on	Rules for what repairs need to be done, where, and by whom	Rules for mobilizing labor, materials, money, or other resources needed to perform system tasks and for responding to shortfalls in resources	Rules for avoiding or resolving disputes between systems, zones of a system, or individuals
Important roles	Roles for planning and implementing water acquisition activities	Roles for establishing and implementing water allocation policies	Roles for identifying maintenance jobs and supervising repairs	Roles for implementing and monitoring the resource mobilization process	Roles for mediating disputes, making judgments, and enforcing sanctions
Significant social groups	Groups that seek additional water supplies	Groups that influence water allocation policies and implement water distribution	Groups that provide routine or emergency repairs to system	Groups that collect specific resources	Groups that participate in settling disputes and in enforcing sanctions

many other endeavors in sociology, a full sociological description of any particular irrigation situation requires multiple and complementary methods of acquiring the data. In this case, socioeconomic surveys must be supplemented with the in-depth regional field studies discussed below.

For a number of reasons, the socioeconomic survey remains the dominant tool for data collection in project design efforts, despite some inadequacies. First, the researchers implementing such studies are often economists by training and are interested in collecting data on some social characteristics (such as age, family size, or farm size), but not in doing sociological or organizational analysis of the irrigation relationships.

Second, the survey is usually perceived to fit better within the time frame for the feasibility phase of project design. It is viewed as a quick research style—even though, in actuality, the length of time required for such tedious tasks as sampling or preparation and analysis of large data sets can often extend the period significantly. In contrast, field studies are often viewed as being too long, requiring perhaps twelve or more months of actual field observations. While many comprehensive ethnographic field studies do require extended periods, it is also possible for field studies focused on more specific themes, such as irrigation activities, to accumulate important data in periods comparable to those of other data collection efforts typically included in feasibility studies.

A third important reason relates directly to the participation of sociologists themselves. Because of the dominant theoretical and methodological approaches in the discipline of sociology, many sociologists approach project design with a heavy emphasis on the perceptions and characteristics of individual farmers which, when combined with familiar reliance on sample survey methods, reinforces the likelihood that the socioeconomic survey will be used exclusively. Analogously, anthropologists tend to lean toward the use of field case study techniques (though they might also incline toward some "comprehensive" village study in the area).

Thus, substantial forces continue to press for the classic socioeconomic survey as an integral part of the feasibility study. The point, however, is not to substitute some other single method, but to complement the socioeconomic survey[3] with other research approaches such as the regional field study to which we now turn our attention.

Some recent irrigation studies have begun using a methodology—herein called the regional field study—that overcomes certain limitations found in both the socioeconomic survey and in field studies that focus only on a limited number of irrigation systems. There are two dimensions to this methodology, though a given regional study may not pursue both. The first dimension involves studying a large number of individual systems in a defined region (which may be cultural, ecological, administrative, or some combination of all three) to understand the distribution of common social and technical features as well as to identify any important subcategories of system types. The second dimension identifies and understands any regional mechanisms that articulate or mediate the activities of otherwise separate systems.

Regional field studies are designed to give in-depth attention to collective patterns, group actions, and institutional arrangements for irrigation that may already operate in the proposed project area. This information focuses on the social organization of irrigation and is gathered through discussions with key informants, observation of group activities (such as meetings and work parties), and the review of existing records and documents.

A later section of this chapter focuses on two recent examples of regional field study in settings with a high density of local irrigation systems—of which many, but not all, have small commands of 100 hectares or less. But beforehand, it is useful to illustrate briefly the practical problems that can arise when the state acts without sufficient institutional and organizational analysis in regions that possess rich local irrigation experience.

Ignoring Local Irrigation Institutions and Organization

To illustrate the propensity to ignore what might exist at the local level, I will examine two irrigation projects. The first example is the Palsiguan River Multi-Purpose Project in the Ilocos Region of the northern Philippines. In its initial phase, this project involved foreign assistance in the rehabilitation of 172 local irrigation systems, known in the region as *zanjeras*, covering approximately 10,000 hectares. Technical and economic feasibility studies were conducted.[4] However, no sociological studies addressed the organization and operation of local systems, nor did the feasibility report incorporate any findings on those associations from the studies published by several social scientists. Instead, the report contained only a very brief comment indicating that some traditional irrigation existed in the project area but that the systems were ineffective (and, by inference, unimportant).

In the absence of detailed organizational information and due to the misrepresentation of the elaborate network of local irrigation institutions, the project designers assumed they were creating irrigation *de novo*, rather than providing assistance to ongoing local systems. The de novo orientation led to the design of a 1,000 hectare pilot area in which major canals were radically realigned. This rearranged the internal segments and boundaries of the local systems and, though it was poorly recognized, the social organization required significant modification to fit these new canal layouts. As Visaya reported, "The design of the pilot project was based on maximum engineering efficiency, without considering the existing communal irrigation systems and the irrigation organizations in the area. [A] majority, if not all [of the] designed canals are new ones, crisscrossing the canals of the existing *zanjera* systems. The proposed rotational areas, consequently, disregarded existing area boundaries of the irrigation associations."[5]

The unavoidable question is, How could this have happened? How could such a large misunderstanding occur? I assume that projects are designed in this manner for several related reasons—all having to do with the nature of the planning agencies. First, there is bureaucratic arrogance—the assumption of superior engineering skills and technology that can certainly produce a better system of irrigation (how different the process might be if the designers approached the task with more humility—"perhaps we will not be able to improve things very much"). Second, there is the problem of the planners' definitions—irrigation is viewed primarily, if not exclusively, as a technical apparatus and the design of an irrigation system is seen as a technical-engineering process. If farmer organization is considered, it is viewed as secondary to, and needing to adjust to, the infrastructure. Third, there is agency centralization—the designers are either part of, or closely associated with, a centralized government bureaucracy which intends to design and operate its irrigation system.

Any concern with local and regional irrigation experiences and arrangements is clearly subordinated to this combination of factors. Given the scarce resources, limited time, and large agenda associated with most feasibility studies, it is not surprising that the sociology of irrigation in the rehabilitation project area is overlooked or addressed superficially.

One finds a similar approach in the Village Irrigation Rehabilitation Project in Sri Lanka, financed by the World Bank. This project attempted to improve the physical facilities and management arrangements in approximately 1,200 village irrigation systems, most of which, but not all, are tank systems.[6]

As with the Philippine case, it appears that the planning for this project was not based on an assessment of the existing local institutional and organizational arrangements for irrigation tasks. At least such an assessment is not presented in the Bank's appraisal report. In fact, the appraisal report, in its brief discussion of village irrigation and its context in Sri Lanka, uses rather vague information about village tanks and their operation.[7] It states that many schemes have deteriorated or have been abandoned; that head sluices are seldom operated systematically; and that the decline of traditional management partly explains the deterioration and underutilization of village irrigation systems.

If the above statements are accurate, they are significant symptoms of something gone wrong. One might expect that rehabilitation of the tanks would be directed at the causes of these symptoms. But, the "causal factor" on which the project seems to rest is that the tank community has lost the power to act effectively in irrigation matters. This, of course, may be an accurate assumption—though the basis for it is left unclear, as are the reasons for the community impotence. In particular, it is not clear to what extent inaction or erratic action by the government has contributed to this decline in local capacity.

This last point is the more important when one considers the fundamental assumption on which the project rests and the major objective that derives from it. The basic assumption is: "Since it is difficult for individual farmers to change this system, increased guidance by government will probably be necessary to make the best use of available resources."[8] On this powerful assumption, the project logically adopts as its main objective "strengthening the major government institutions involved in village irrigation."

The significance of this assumption is best illustrated by recasting the proposition (obviously paraphrasing the original): "Since it is difficult for individual farmers to change this system, and since outside government assistance alone is unlikely to be effective, it will be necessary to strengthen both government capacities and the capacity of the local group to make these changes." It seems likely that this altered assumption would lead to an additional project objective explicitly concerned with strengthening capacity at the village level to handle irrigation affairs.

As with the Philippine case, there was available for Sri Lanka some sociological field research on village tanks that might have been consulted for the feasibility study. These range from the classic study of Pul Eliya by Sir Edmund Leach to a more contemporary study of a single tank by two Sri Lankan researchers.[9] The latter conclude:

> Although the Kelegama tank and its operation were solely for the benefit of the users of the tank, these beneficiaries were made to feel that the ultimate control and custodianship of the tank lay with a somewhat nebulous body outside, namely, that is the State, whose powers and responsibilities were exercised by the Agrarian Services Department through its officials at the regional and village level.

They report that the community has failed to evolve new institutional arrangements that are consonant with the contemporary state presence, and there is thus a certain degree of community malaise with regard to tank maintenance and operation. Somewhat at variance with the assumptions of the village irrigation project, these authors suggest that state involvement, at least of a particular kind, may increase, rather than reduce community disengagement.

These examples illustrate an obvious but fundamental point—the factors investigated in the preproject studies represent the designer's judgments and understandings of what is important for the irrigation systems. Conventional thinking about irrigation subordinates social organization to other factors, such as the technical-engineering, which are perceived to be more critical. The result is that local irrigation organization, even when it exists, may be ignored, as in the Philippine case, or may be assumed defunct, as in the Sri Lankan case.

In sum, often there is simply no demand for sociological analysis of local irrigation institutions and organizations because designers are oriented toward other matters: the engineering works, the financial arrangements, the irrigation agency's resources, and so on. This narrow approach is consistent with the technocratic image that most planners hold of irrigation development.

In both of the cases discussed above, the events of early project implementation heightened awareness of, and concern for, local institutions and social organization. In the Philippine case, the local irrigation groups offered dramatic resistance when the irrigation agency began implementing its program in the pilot area. When these troubles arose, several outsiders, including some social scientists familiar with the remarkable capacities of the zanjeras, began sharing with the agency the results of past field studies. These standard academic studies were not done for the purpose of project planning but, nonetheless, contained highly relevant information. These data, as well as the monitoring studies subsequently conducted as part of the project, were then incorporated into project implementation. The best example of this reorientation is seen in the project manager's statement of the reformulated project goal: "To rehabilitate existing zanjera communal irrigation systems and construct facilities for new areas, through the maximum participation of the farmers in planning and implementation of the project, and improve the farmer's capability to effectively operate and maintain their irrigation systems."[10]

In the case of Sri Lanka, since the initiation of the project, the Department of Agrarian Services and the Agrarian Research and Training Institute have conducted detailed field studies in a few selected tanks, both to increase their knowledge of existing local organizational capacities and to understand more fully the government-community interactions produced by the village tank program.

Regional Field Studies of Local Irrigation: Two Examples

Many regions in Asia and elsewhere (for example, Ilocos in the Philippines, Tamil Nadu in South India, or the Peruvian Andes) are characterized by a high density or frequency of local irrigation systems. Their organizational shapes, while displaying variations, possess a degree of commonality resembling one another to the extent that we can recognize a Balinese *subak*, an Omani *aflaj*, or a Himachali *kuhl*. In part, of course, these resemblances may derive from similarities in the physical habitat, the cultural elements of the place, the historical processes that have occurred, or the political economy of the region. In short, the local systems are to be seen in light of the regional circumstances, past and present, in which they operate.

Thus far, regional analyses of local irrigation systems have been infrequent, though several scholars now have such work under way[11] and a few studies have recently been completed (two of these are discussed in the following sections). In this section, I propose to explore this new line of research on local irrigation, illustrating its application in two cases, and considering its policy relevance for designing effective state assistance to such systems.

Baskets of Stones: Local Irrigation in a District in Northern Sumatra

Research was recently completed examining government assistance to local irrigation systems in a region in northern Sumatra; Pidie District in the Province of Aceh.[12] Pidie was selected for this work because of the importance of irrigated agriculture, the prevalence of local irrigation networks and the variety of government irrigation assistance programs available in this region. The research which was conducted in three sequential phases—an inventory, followed by several case studies, and then by a survey of forty-nine local systems—provides a full description of regional commonalities and significant variations in local irrigation.

Most irrigation works in Pidie use surface water as their supply and nearly all of the systems utilize simple diversion structures to acquire this water. The structures that divert water are called *seuneulop*, or more familiarly, *neulop*, regardless of their size or location—the headwork on the river course or along the main canal at the point where a branch canal begins. The term seuneulop (or neulop) also is used to refer to the entire irrigation system. For constructing diversions, the most commonly used materials are bamboo, stones from the riverbed, wide timbers, or some combination of these. On some of the larger rivers in the narrow coastal plain area of Pidie, the neulop is of a particular type called *beuriyeueng*— a structure made by first weaving large cone-shaped baskets of bamboo which are then filled with stones from the riverbed. These baskets of stones are a kind of indigenous crate structure.

The canals (called *leung*) of these local systems are of unlined, earthen construction. Typically, in addition to the main canal, there are various branch or secondary canals. At each of the numerous branches of this canal network, one generally finds a proportioning weir (a neulop, as discussed above). The combination of neulops and canal network provides the physical apparatus that permits relatively complex management and distribution of water within a system when such management is required. Rotational water distribution during times of shortage is common.

Most local systems in Pidie have small commands—the forty-nine systems we surveyed had from 17 to 426 hectares and 70 percent of them irrigated less than 150 hectares in the wet season. However, in Pidie, there is also a special set of local systems whose overall command is very large, covering thousands of hectares and tens of villages. Leung Treung Campli is one such large network. It conveys water through a main canal approximately 15 to 20 kilometers in length. The canal passes through four subdistricts and irrigates about 2,000 hectares in over 100 hamlets.

Many of these large systems have an origin myth that features the prominent role of some special religious leader (*ulama*) of an earlier century who is regarded as having been central in inspiring and mobilizing people to construct the large system.

An important institutional component in the management of local irrigation systems in Pidie is the *keujreun* arrangement. The people of Pidie conceptualize the keujreun as operating simultaneously at several levels of civil administration and at several levels in the irrigation network. At the hamlet (*gampong*) level, the institution is represented by a man referred to as the *keujreun blang* who works closely with the hamlet head and the water users of that area. At the next higher level of civil administration, the village cluster (*mukim*), the institution is represented by someone called *keujreun muda* (there is some variation in the terminology), with responsibilities for irrigation activities throughout the mukim. At the next level, the *keujreun syik* (again there is some variation in the terminology) operates at the subdistrict level with its administrative head (the *camat*). In this way, the keujreun, while having responsibilities specific to irrigation, operate as an element of the civil administration. Also, the keujreun arrangement is sufficiently flexible to cover both administrative and hydraulic boundaries. For example, at the village level, several situations may exist. There may be facilities of an irrigation network that serve multiple villages. If so, typically, there will be a keujreun blang for each village served. If that network covers a group of villages, all of which fall within a single mukim, then the activities of the several keujreun blang will be coordinated by a mukim-level keujreun. At the hamlet level, the keujreun blang usually is selected by the farmers of that area with the approval of the village head. At the higher levels, the keujreun are appointed by the administrative heads of the units from among the existing keujreun at the lower levels.

While working closely with the various heads of the civil administrative units, the keujreun are also accountable to the water users, since they receive payments for their activities from them and not from the government. These payments are called *beuheuek bruek umong*. The literal meaning of this phrase is the "half of a coconut shell (bruek) share (beuheuek) of unmilled rice to be paid by each ricefield plot (umong)." In Neulop Amud, one of our case study locations, farmers made an annual payment to the keujreun blang of twelve kilograms of unmilled rice for each quarter hectare of rice fields that they irrigated.

In Seuneulop Beuracan, a network that has received little state assistance, we found the duties of the keujreun blang to include a wide range of activities—coordinating canal cleaning and system repair, distributing water within the village lands when rotation was in use, involvement in the various irrigation and rice production ceremonies (*khanduri*), and settling minor disputes among the irrigators. This range of reported duties is consistent with those detailed in an ordinance issued in 1973 by the head (*bupati*) of Pidie district. This ordinance, which deals with the organization of rice production activities in the district, includes an extended discussion of the keujreun institution. In it, the stated responsibilities of the keujreun blang are (1) supervising repair of the facilities, including the management of the farmers' collective work groups, (2) managing the distribution of water, (3) settling disagreements among farmers regarding water distribution, and (4) supervising and controlling timing of the planting of the rice nurseries and the subsequent transplanting to the fields.

Not all irrigation systems in Pidie have the keujreun arrangement. Our survey indicated that 65 percent of the systems utilized the keujreun; the rest did not. There are two situations in which the keujreun is absent. One is in very small systems involving only a few farmers who informally coordinate their irrigation operation and upkeep activities. The other situation involves numerous water users, but the local government authorities coordinate operations and maintenance without the aid of a keujreun.

The traditional view of neulop networks in Pidie is that they are public infrastructure, public utilities as it were, whose maintenance and operation lies jointly with the civil administrators, irrigation caretakers (the keujreun), religious leaders, and the related users, rather than as facilities owned by some private group of coproprietors. Initial decisions regarding the annual refurbishing and use of these facilities are made in a forum organized at the subdistrict administrative level by the camat. In this meeting, discussions of the coming agricultural season are held and dates are set for key activities, such as repairing and cleaning the neulop networks, initiating land preparation activities, and the various ritual activities to accompany these actions.

Thus, the neulop network is highly intertwined with matters of civic and spiritual order as well as agronomic practice. Its state of readiness and smooth operation are both necessary for, and a reflection of, order in the realm of governance and culture. The effectiveness of the neulop network is dependent on the synchronized individual behavior of multiple users as well as their timely collective behavior—a pulsating rhythm of aggregating and disaggregating in which people sometimes come together to act jointly, while at other times act singly but in a coordinated fashion.

One sees then that the order needed for effective wet rice production and neulop network operation is socially constructed by the Acehnese of Pidie. The Acehnese use an aphorism that irrigated agriculture requires men to act like brothers. However, unlike other regions of Southeast Asia in which the required social solidarity is supported through the formation of a specialized irrigation group (for example the subak of Bali or the zanjera of Ilocos Norte), in Aceh order is shaped through the actions of the civil administrative heads and the specialized irrigation institution called keujreun—accountable to both the civil administration and the water users.

While the keujreun do receive contributions from the water users, they are not the staff of some membership-based organization formed by the villagers. Rather, they are intermediate between government and farmers. The keujreun are arms of the local government officials and they derive part of their authority to direct farmers from their association with these local authorities but, however, local government has no budget to pay the keujreun. Thus, they depend on the farmers to provide support for their services. In this way, the keujreun also are accountable to the farmers. In short, irrigation order can be seen as one element of general public order.

State assistance to local irrigation in Pidie has been widespread. Nearly six out of every ten local systems in our survey had received some form of state aid. With a few important exceptions, this state assistance has served to complement rather than demobilize local resources.

Our case studies revealed the frequency with which resources supplied by the state are combined with local resources for the purpose of improving existing structures and canal networks. For example, in Neulop Taka Adan, where water from a swampy area is used for irrigation, in the budget year 1980–81, the camat combined the village subsidy funds from ten villages to purchase materials for improving the dike used to divert water from the swamp. Labor that farmers provided for the construction work supplemented the state assistance.

Overall, our research findings produce a positive picture of local irrigation in the Pidie region. These local systems function in the diverse ecological settings of the district—the hill areas, the fertile coastal zone, and even the low-lying swampy areas. In all of these locations, facilities are not only maintained, but also improved with locally mobilized resources. Local government officials, frequently assisted by local irrigation caretakers (keujreun), exercise leadership in mobilizing these resources and in the operation of the systems. These irrigation activities are punctuated with a special rhythm and given cultural meaning and order through the myriad ritual ceremonies that occur at the subdistrict, neulop network, and, sometimes, individual field levels. While farmer involvement in the operation and maintenance of these irrigation works is considerable, it is not accurate to label them farmer-managed systems. More to the mark would be to identify them as "locally managed," since it is the local authorities, often with assistance from the keujreun, who perform these functions.

This regional picture of irrigation in Pidie suggests important considerations for formulating policies in support of local irrigation development. For example, the widespread, but not universal, presence of a customary institution for local irrigation management suggests little need for the introduction by the irrigation agency or foreign donors of a standard water user organization model from another region. The earlier effort of the district government to strengthen the keujreun arrangements is more appropriate.

There are also opportunities for regional policies to build on the widespread customary practices of system management through water rotation. No doubt, improvements could be made in selected systems, but programs for improvement should recognize the local experience that exists and the principles in which these practices are rooted. Programs built on this approach have a much greater possibility of being sustained than those that assume little relevant local experience.

Plans for assisting these local systems also should recognize the history of, and continuing capacity for, local resource mobilization that exists—

local labor, funds, materials, and so on are regularly organized and applied to system development. Future state assistance should be designed to complement and not to replace or erode these valuable customary activities.

The Book of Irrigation Customs: Irrigation Rights in Palampur

The Kangra valley of Himachal Pradesh (India) is one of the most intensely irrigated regions of this mountainous state. Most of the existing irrigation facilities are so-called private kuhls, small gravity flow networks that are locally operated and maintained by the water users themselves. Recently, research was conducted in this region to explore the importance of water rights which were recorded during the British colonial period to the functioning of the contemporary systems.[13] As with the Pidie case discussed above, the results of the Kangra research also confirm that the understanding of kuhl irrigation stands to gain from taking a regional perspective.

The Historical Record

The functioning of these local irrigation networks was noted by the British as early as the middle of the nineteenth century, when they initiated procedures for assessing taxes in their newly acquired territory. As part of these procedures, they also recorded, and hence established within their legal framework, irrigation rights. The instructions provided to the staff implementing the tax assessment included directions to record rights to wells and other sources of irrigation. Thus, detailed records of customary rights and rules for operating these hydraulic works were produced.

Our research in one subdistrict of the Kangra region, Palampur, focused on the analysis of these historical records combined with fieldwork in a number of operating kuhls. In the revenue office of Palampur, one can find an important historical register called the *Riwaj-i-Abpashi* (the Book of Irrigation Customs). The title page includes the following statement: General Rules of Irrigation, Tehsil Palampur, Kangra District, 1918. It is written in Urdu and based on the findings of the 1915–16 Settlement Report. The register contains the following sections:

- A table of contents
- An introductory section discussing general rules for kuhl irrigation in Tehsil Palampur
- A glossary of irrigation terms
- A map of the Tehsil showing the location of rivers and streams
- An index of 298 kuhls existing in the Tehsil and arranged by river course
- A section containing details regarding each of the indexed kuhls
- A listing of smaller kuhls (with no additional details)
- A concluding section.

The General Irrigation Rules

Six general rules are discussed in this opening section of the register. The first rule deals with the construction of diversion structures on the rivers or streams. The farmer-built structures of today probably appear very similar to those constructed at the time these rules were recorded. They are temporary structures, built with the use of stones found in the river bed. In some cases, the stones are supplemented with the use of mud, grass, and other natural materials used to reduce leakage. Usually they are damaged one or more times during the wet season, when river flows increase significantly, and thus they need repair either within the season or before the start of the next cropping season.

The first rule simply states that if the diversion needs to be repaired, the work is to be done by the "members" of the kuhl. If the diversion needs to be rebuilt, it can be constructed anywhere between the nearest upstream diversion and the next diversion below. This latter point clearly deals with the rights of the various kuhls along the stream and limits the rights of any particular kuhl to diverting at some point between the diversions located immediately above and below the one being rebuilt. In short, the order of placement along the river course cannot be altered.

The second general rule deals with the matter of constructing a new diversion. It states that this is not to be done without obtaining permission from the (British) government as well as the local raja. In general, permission will not be given to construct a new diversion upstream from an existing one. However, if it is determined that there is surplus water in a river, permission could be granted to build a new diversion upstream with the provision that, in times of future scarcity, the earlier diversion would have priority to meet its needs. Likewise, if a new kuhl is built between two existing diversions, in times of scarcity the two original diversions would have priority in meeting their irrigation needs.

This second rule also discusses the characteristics of materials that can be used in constructing the new diversion. First, the materials must be approved by the members of the existing kuhls. Second, the materials for the new diversion cannot be different from those used in the diversion immediately above (thus protecting the rights of the lower kuhl). Finally, this rule notes that the landowner has three compensation alternatives if the channel for the new system passes through his land. He can receive a payment from the builders of the new kuhl, or he can make use of water from the kuhl to irrigate his land, or he can opt to become part of the group constructing the kuhl, which will later receive payment for providing the irrigation.

The third rule deals more specifically with the issue of distributing water among the several kuhls that may be drawing water from a common stream. To illustrate the sharing principle that applies in this case, the example of Baner Khad (river) is given in the record. In 1914, due to insufficient rain, water flow was low in this river. After the first sixteen kuhls along this river had diverted their water, there was none remaining for the lower kuhls. The Deputy Commissioner instituted the rule that the first sixteen kuhls had to allow at least one *nallah* of water for each of the lower kuhls. It also was noted that this principle had been used in earlier times. In 1868, farmers on Baner Khad had agreed to the same water-sharing arrangement.

The fourth rule concerns the use of seasonal creeks (also called nullahs) for irrigation purposes. The general rule allows villages where the creek originates to use as much of the seasonal flow as they require. The unused water can be claimed by the next lower village on the creek. However, water from the creek can only be used on the riparian lands of that stream. The water from the seasonal creek cannot be diverted to some nearby stream to augment the supply in it.

A fifth general rule relates to the organization of repair and maintenance activities for a kuhl. The general principle is that the "last" village is responsible for maintenance. But last is defined so that, in a set of four villages spread from the head to the tail of the canal, the last village will work alone from the tail upstream to the boundary of village three. At that point, village three will join village four to perform maintenance activities upstream to the boundary of village two, at which point it joins the maintenance work, and so on. Thus, "last" is redefined and expanded as the maintenance work progresses from the tail to the head. Each water user must supply labor in the form of a male at least twelve years of age. Those who do not supply labor will be charged the cost of hiring a replacement. If investments are to be made in systems improvements, funds will be collected proportional to the size of the irrigated holding.

The last general rule concerns water distribution procedures within a kuhl and states generally that these irrigation rules vary from system to system and are described in the section of the register containing details on the customary rules of the individual systems (section 6 in the Book of Irrigation Customs).

The irrigation register also contains a glossary of irrigation terms. A total of twenty-four terms are presented and defined. These terms deal with essential matters such as measurements of water, irrigation structures or technologies, agronomic terms, and the names of different irrigation cycles and their purposes. This set of irrigation vocabulary suggests the existence of a districtwide "irrigation culture," recognizable by its common terminology and the common material items, techniques, and concepts. The shared vocabulary contributes to the discourse among the users of a single kuhl as well as between kuhl groups.

The main canal of the Bharul Kuhl system irrigates about 145 hectares belonging to five hamlet clusters. Irrigation water is particularly scarce during the summer planting season. To cope with the water constraint, the people of Bharul Kuhl use customary rules of system operations, simple irrigation technology, and suitable agronomic practices. An intrahamlet distributional system assigns water to the five hamlets based on their location along the main canal. Each hamlet must, therefore, select agronomic technologies according to the available supply of water and labor. After the summer rice crop sowing is finished, each cluster receives an assured water supply appropriate for the crops that it planted.

Also consistent with the historical record, Bharul kuhl is served by a local irrigation foreman, the *kohli*. His responsibilities include two major activities: (a) mobilizing labor and materials and supervising routine and emergency repairs to the diversion structure, the main canal, and the water control structures along it, and (b) supervising the distribution of water along the main canal, including supervision of the guarding activities frequently required when cultivators in the lower reaches of the network receive their water supply.

Repairing and maintaining the physical facilities of Bharul kuhl is not an onerous task. The diversion structure is made of stones found in the bed of the Awah River. The main canal is unlined and courses through undulating countryside. When the canal reaches a gully, or seasonal creek, the canal water is channeled into the natural stream and then rediverted somewhere downstream back into the continuation of the canal, thus avoiding the need for complicated structures at troublesome, creek-crossing locations. The river water is relatively free of silt and thus little siltation occurs in the canal. Most bothersome is weed growth along the canal, which at times can be heavy. In addition to providing labor for repairing and maintaining these main system facilities, farmers must also provide labor and other resources for repair of the branch facilities within each of their hamlet clusters. In addition, farmers in the lower clusters have to provide labor for the guarding activities.

Over the last several decades, the state has been providing assistance to kuhls such as Bharul in the Kangra region—in the last decade at an increasing pace. While this assistance has sometimes been useful, discussion here of an unsuccessful case illustrates the shortcoming of a policy that is uninformed by regional realities.

Birari is an old kuhl that diverts water from the one of the largest rivers in the Kangra region, the Neugal. At the hamlet boundary where the main canal enters the village, stands a small Hindu temple dedicated to the goddess Birari for whom the kuhl also is named. Historically, the water supply in this kuhl has been good since the Neugal is a perennial river receiving snowmelt from the nearby Dhala Dhar range and Birari kuhl is in an upstream location. Some years ago the state irrigation agency approached the people of Birari kuhl with a plan to extend the main canal for approximately thirteen kilometers, to serve a set of hamlets which now irrigate from several seasonal creeks in their area. The Birari people report being told by the agency at the time of these discussions that, as part of this project, the water flow into Birari kuhl would be augmented to meet the additional needs of the new area.

Extending the canal for this purpose was not an entirely new idea. The Birari inhabitants indicate that a number of years previously, some people from the proposed extension area had approached Birari about extending the canal. Birari proposed that the extension people assume full responsibility for maintaining the entire main canal, including the portion then maintained by the Birari users. In exchange for this arrangement, the Birari inhabitants would have rights to two, or two and one-half, nallahs of water (a local measure of water volume described in the Book of Irrigation Customs glossary). No agreement was reached between the two groups at that time.

The original canal now has been extended by the irrigation agency to reach the new area. But, only infrequently does water actually reach this tail area. While the kuhl now is nominally under the control of the irrigation agency, the Birari people, located at the head portion, effectively operate it and water is supplied to the tail area only when there is surplus relative to the needs of the original rights-holders.

The disagreement between the agency and the Birari people is now in court. The dispute turns on the matter of "ownership" of the kuhl. The Birari people argue that their ancestors built the kuhl and they traditionally operated and maintained it—thus it is a private kuhl belonging to them. The agency argues that, based on earlier state assistance to the kuhl, it became a government kuhl and, consequently, they are in a position to modify and improve it as necessary.

There is a clear lesson for local irrigation development policies in the Palampur region when this case is placed in regional perspective. As a result of the colonial and subsequent settlement procedures and the continuing activities of the Revenue Department, the people of Palampur *are aware* of their legal rights to water and their ownership of the means of irrigation in the form of the diversion structures and the canals of their kuhl systems. Under certain conditions, they are prepared to take strong actions to prevent the invalidation of these rights. Thus, state actions in existing irrigation networks are not likely to be successful if they attempt to erode rather than enhance existing water rights.

Regional Field Studies and Project Planning

The two field studies just summarized, carried out on a regional basis rather than on only one or two irrigation systems, illustrate the range of data on patterns of social organization that can be assembled in areas thick with local irrigation systems. In this section, I want to step back from the location-specific data presented in those cases and ask the question: What of this information is relevant for project planning?

First, in both cases we see there are regional institutional arrangements in place that deserve attention by the project planners. In Pidie, the existence of the district ordinance which legitimates the traditional irrigation supervisor role (the keujreun) is an essential institutional resource for local irrigation in this region. It should neither be ignored nor unnecessarily modified, though it is certainly plausible that some changes might be required, in the name of rehabilitation or irrigation modernization. In Palampur, the water rights defined in the records of customary irrigation (the Book of Irrigation Customs) are equally fundamental underpinnings for everyday irrigation matters in the systems of this region and should be respected as far as possible in any state interventions. At a minimum, ignoring these rights greatly complicates the outcome of state assistance. Second, a point that derives from the regional approach is the ability to see both common patterns and important differences across systems. For example, in Pidie, we see a common element in that, for all cases, the various heads of the civil administrative units are involved in key activities related to irrigation management. But, while the keujreun institution is widespread, it is not ubiquitous—our regional survey indicated that 35 percent of the systems were without this irrigation supervisor. Good planning in Pidie will build on both the common elements and the differences found in local systems in the region.

Third, the regional sociological study, if targeted on a region that coincides with the territory of a meaningful unit of the bureaucracy, can give planners and program implementors confidence that they understand the situation of local irrigation in the region where they are working—rather than be left uncertain about the extent to which conditions found in one or a few systems studied apply throughout the area.

The virtue of such sociological studies is that they document for the planner and designer not just the existing physical works of the systems but the associated patterns of behavior and social relations. Through in-depth field studies, the research can display the rich texture of the sociology of irrigation systems, revealing the deep-seated rules for carrying out basic irrigation tasks, the expectations that various irrigation actors have of one another, and the functional fit between the engineer's canals and turnouts and the sociologist's institutions and organizations. Regional field studies can concentrate specifically on these institutional and organizational arrangements, and the qualitative picture they provide can alert the planner to the existing social organization of irrigation, which is a resource just as the existing physical works are seen as an important component of the given situation.

This may sound to some as though field studies are meant to paralyze the planner—to inhibit any, perhaps all, changes for fear that they will adversely affect the status quo. This is not the intent! With or without state-assisted rehabilitation work, many changes are constantly occurring in irrigation systems and adjustments are continually being made by and to the institutional and organizational arrangements. The point is that changes need to be made with sensitivity and awareness of their potential implications—with an understanding that irrigation systems are usually composed of a close congruence between the physical works and the institutional and organizational arrangements. Understanding the nature of that correspondence in the particular project provides a realistic base for planning new changes.

Even with this amount of knowledge it is difficult to anticipate the various implications and outcomes of proposed changes. This is why it is imperative to involve the people of the project area in the very process of planning and design (also see chapters 3, 12, and 13).

Some Suggestions for Action

When planning and designing rehabilitation projects for regions with existing local irrigation works, it is critical to understand the established social arrangements for implementing fundamental irrigation tasks. It has been suggested that information on these existing institutional and social patterns will be difficult to obtain through the usual method of the socioeconomic survey, but can be obtained by trained analysts using a focused regional field study approach. Such field studies should collect information required to complete the cells identified in table 2-1, both by studying a large number of individual systems in the region and by identifying any regional mechanisms that relate to these cells. The result would complement the statistical portrait produced by a socioeconomic survey with the structural principles and social organizational arrangements illuminated by the sociological analysis of the regional field study.

To implement regional field studies of this kind, the following recommendations are put forward. First, the terms of reference for the socioeconomic portion of a rehabilitation project preparation study should specifically identify the need to examine the existing social organization related to fundamental irrigation tasks.

Second, project feasibility studies and appraisal reports should include a subsection on the existing local irrigation organization in the project area. This subsection should report on the preproject organization of irrigation tasks, contrasting them with the social arrangements the planners intend to have upon completion of the project. There should also be a clear statement of the steps necessary to achieve identified changes of institution and social organization.

Third, national and international agencies concerned with the design of irrigation rehabilitation projects should consider holding periodic workshops for socioeconomic analysts and others working on studies for irrigation project proposals. The proposal specialists could then discuss their experiences with applying an organizational approach and identify better procedures for data collection and report presentation.

A detailed analysis of local activities by region will inform local project proposals and will shape thinking about irrigation organization. The accumulation of information on how much local groups are doing and, in some cases, how they are doing it, could influence policies regarding the appropriate mix of state and local responsibilities and rights in irrigation development. Knowing more about what local irrigation groups are doing could influence our thinking about what they *ought* to do.

Notes

1. Wilbert E. Moore, *Social Change* (Englewood Cliffs, N.J.: Prentice-Hall, 1965).

2. In previous writing I have emphasized only three fundamental tasks. Subsequent fieldwork has demonstrated the need to expand this list. The task of *resource mobilization* was first suggested to me by Romana de los Reyes ("Sociocultural Patterns and Irrigation Organization: The Management of a Philippine Community Irrigation System," Ph.D. dissertation, University of California at Berkeley, 1982). A detailed exploration of this system function has been presented by Uraivan Tan-Kim-Yong ("Resource Mobilization in Traditional Irrigation Systems of Northern Thailand: A Comparison between the Lowland and the Upland Irrigation Communities," Ph.D. dissertation, Cornell University, 1983). The task of *water acquisition* is discussed by Mark Svendsen ("Water Management Strategies and Practices at the Tertiary Level: Three Philippine Irrigation Systems," Ph.D. dissertation, Cornell University, 1983); John Duewel ("Promoting Participatory Approaches to Cultivating Water User Associations: Two Case Studies from Central Java," paper presented at the Workshop on Investment Decisions to Further Develop and Make Use of Southeast Asia's Irrigation Resources, Bangkok, 1981); and Ruth Meinzen-Dick ("Local Management of Tank Irrigation in South India: Organizations and Operations," M.S. thesis, Cornell University, 1983).

3. The critique of the survey approach, and particularly of its use as the single tool for gathering social information needed for project feasibility studies, is developed by Robert Chambers in chapter 14 of this volume.

4. See Visaya, "The PRMP and the *Zanjeras*," paper read at the Workshop on Organization as a Strategic Resource in Irrigation Development, Asian Institute of Management, Manila, November 1982. A full report on the organization and operations of a particular *zanjera* is

contained in E. Walter Coward, Jr.'s "Principles of Social Organization in an Indigenous Irrigation System," *Human Organization*, vol. 38 (1979), pp. 28–36.

5. "The PRMP and the *Zanjeras*," p. 6. The details of these changes have been monitored by a team of researchers from Central Luzon State University. See Honorato L. Angeles and others, *Process Documentation on the Development of the Palsiguan River Multi-Purpose Project* (Munoz, Nueva Ecija: Central Luzon State University, 1983).

6. For a description of the project see Jaliya Medagama, "Some Observations on Farmer Involvement in the Village Irrigation Rehabilitation Project in Sri Lanka," paper read at the Workshop on Organization as a Strategic Resource in Irrigation Development, Asian Institute of Management, Manila, November 1982. Recent field studies of village irrigation rehabilitation projects include Shyamala Abeyratne and Jayantha Perera, "Changes in Irrigation Management in Small Communities: A Tank and Anicut System in Moneregala District, Sri Lanka," *Sri Lanka Journal of Agrarian Studies*, vol. 5 (1986), pp. 20–27; and, for a more comprehensive examination within a historical context, Shyamala Abeyratne, "Rice, Rehabilitation and Rural Change: Social Organization and State Intervention in Small-Scale Irrigation Systems in Sri Lanka," Ph.D. dissertation, Cornell University, 1990.

7. World Bank appraisal materials for the Village Irrigation Rehabilitation Project in Sri Lanka, 1981.

8. World Bank appraisal materials. Note that there is a bit of a straw man in this statement. Few would expect that "individual farmers" could change things. But, as noted below, this does not necessarily imply a heavy government role. There is another alternative—strong local organization.

9. E. R. Leach, *Pul Eliya: A Village in Ceylon* (Cambridge: Cambridge University Press, 1971); and Wickrema Gunasekera and Sunimar Fernando, "Water Management in the Village of Kelegama in Sri Lanka" (Colombo: Marga Institute Final Report, 1981), p. 36.

10. Visaya, "The PRMP and the *Zanjeras*," pp. 13–14.

11. Those with interest in this topic should be aware of work in process by Nirmal Sengupta of the Madras Institute of Development Studies and John Ambler of the Cornell Irrigation Studies Group.

12. This research was carried out in 1986–87, and was funded by the Water Management Synthesis Project under USAID Contract DAN–4127–C–00–2086–00 to the Consortium for International Development and subcontracted to Cornell University. Fieldwork in Indonesia was supervised by Dr. Amin Aziz of the Center for Agribusiness Development in collaboration with Syaih Kuala University in Aceh Province. For a more detailed discussion of findings, see E. Walter Coward, Jr., "Basket of Stones: Government Assistance and Development of Local Irrigation in a District of Northern Sumatra," Water Management Synthesis Project, *WMS Report*, no. 80, March 1988.

13. This research was supported by Cornell University and assisted through an award from the Indo-U.S. Subcommission on Education and Culture. In India I was affiliated with the Himachal Pradesh Agricultural University and provided professional assistance and warm hospitality by Professor T. V. Moorti, chairman of the Department of Agricultural Economics. My reliable field assistant was Mr. Rattanchand Bhardwaj.

3

Developing Irrigators' Organizations: A Learning Process Approach

Benjamin U. Bagadion and Frances F. Korten

Examination of development projects worldwide indicates that social and institutional issues are often not adequately addressed. Although technical and economic considerations receive a great deal of attention, the people-related issues are frequently subordinated or ignored, with detrimental consequences for sustained development.[1]

In recognition of these failings, many implementing agencies, as well as donor large and small agencies, are giving greater attention to social issues and adding individuals trained in sociology, cultural anthropology, and other noneconomic social sciences to the project design and implementation teams. In many situations, these individuals have spotlighted key needs and helped shape project concepts that better fit the realities of the lives of the intended beneficiaries.[2]

Quite often, however, a wide gap remains between the needs that are spotlighted and the actual implementation of programs that address those needs. Sometimes this is because adequately addressing the social issues would raise political questions too large for the project to tackle.[3] In other cases, the implementing agency is not oriented to deal with those needs.

Addressing social issues often involves building new capabilities among the people at the community level. But many government agencies assigned to implement large projects have norms, procedures, policies, and attitudes which provide little support for building such capabilities. Thus, socially sensitive individuals who are trying to address social needs find they must work through implementing agencies that are oriented to very different issues.

As discussed in the final section of this chapter, the project development process commonly used by the large donors is likely to be of little help in solving this problem. While project design can be improved by considering social and institutional issues, implementation remains a problem unless the implementing agency can also address these issues. Furthermore, the organizational subsystems that the implementing agency needs for supporting such methods are rarely in place. The agency first has to learn how to address the social needs effectively at the village level, then develop support systems appropriate to the required field-level actions.

When new capacities need to be developed, the need is not for a comprehensive plan, but rather for a process. The process must allow for trial and error on a small scale; continuous examination of the village-level work to identify problems, issues, and successful approaches; and adjustments in agency policy, procedures, and organizational structures to accommodate responses to the field-level needs. The process itself must be shaped to develop both the individuals and the organizational systems needed for eventually implementing the new approaches on a broader scale. In short, what is needed is a learning process.[4] The conceptualization of a learning process for use in operational programs is an important contribution which the social sciences and professionals with a strong "people orientation" can bring to development policy and practice.

In irrigation development these concepts are clearly displayed. There is a growing consensus that farmer participation in irrigation development and operations is important to the effective operation and maintenance of irrigation systems.[5] Irrigation bureaucracies, overburdened by the rapid expansion of irrigated area, cannot serve every individual farmer throughout a populous nation or state. *Groups* of farmers who use the irrigation water are needed to maintain channels and allocate water locally. Further, the farmers' knowledge of local conditions is needed in the development of the physical system. Although there is increasingly wide agreement on these concepts, very few irrigation projects follow them consistently.

One reason is that the irrigation agencies executing the projects seldom have the capacity for working with the local people. Staffed mostly with civil engineers, these agencies are geared to constructing the physical system. To combine these construction objectives with the *social* objectives of developing strong irrigators' groups requires a variety of adjustments in the field-level approach, the management systems, and the policies of the implementing agency.

The exact nature of the changes needed in any specific agency would depend on various factors, including its current norms and structures, the culture of the farmers, the nature of the irrigation use, and the policy frameworks within which the agency operates. But in nearly all instances the changes needed are likely to be substantial. While the social scientists on a project development team can suggest that irrigators' associations should be created and involved in the development and management of the irrigation facilities, the suggestion can be implemented only in a most superficial manner if the agency has not systematically developed the capacity that supports such involvement.

To develop the agency capacity, a learning process is needed in which the agency first develops strong irrigators' associations on a small scale, examines the problems and issues in so doing, and adjusts its policies, procedures, and personnel to fit the field-level requirements. Such a learning process must begin long before the implementation of a major project.

The development of a participatory approach by the National Irrigation Administration (NIA) in the Philippines illustrates such a learning process. After searching for a number of years for better ways of working with farmers, in 1976 the NIA initiated a process which gradually and systematically created the capacity to develop strong irrigators' associations.[6]

In September 1981 when the World Bank appraised a $70 million loan for the NIA communal irrigation program, it was able to state that the loan would "support a national program under which farmers would effectively participate in planning and construction of communal irrigation systems and after completion would assume full control of the operation and maintenance of the system."[7] These were not just empty words in a project document. Rather, they referred to the results of a learning process which had been under way for five years: many field-level procedures had been developed, hundreds of agency personnel were involved in implementing them, the new approaches were being institutionalized on a nationwide basis, and the creative capacity existed for further improvement of the program.

The Bank's appraisal team included engineers and economists sensitive to social issues and a social anthropologist who lived for several days in a village where the NIA was using the participatory approach. The team members' careful examination of the existing program allowed them to shape the Bank's loan in a variety of ways supportive of the ongoing participatory program. But the team had only to understand and adapt to an existing process, not create it. The learning process which led to developing the national capacity was not part of a limited process of preparing for a Bank loan and was very different from routine procedures for the preparation of similar projects. Below, the discussion presents the path of the learning process in the NIA, the benefits and costs of the participatory approach developed, and the differences between the learning process and the usual project development process.

The Learning Process in the Participatory Irrigation Program

The National Irrigation Administration is the agency primarily responsible for assisting Philippine irrigation development. With more than 30,000 employees dispersed throughout the nation's twelve regions and seventy-two provinces, the agency has a leading role in the country's agricultural development program. Its work involves national systems, which are owned, operated, and maintained by the government and usually serve more than 1,000 hectares, and communal systems, which are owned, operated, and maintained by the farmers and usually serve less than 1,000 hectares. As of 1988, the service area of communals totaled about 600,000 hectares, and those of nationals about 500,000 hectares. While communal systems are often initiated by the farmers, the NIA assists them by constructing improvements such as concrete diversions, canals, and canal structures.

In its basic policies, the NIA has long recognized the importance of organized irrigators' groups. On its national systems the NIA has had a long-standing policy that irrigators' associations are responsible for operation and maintenance of facilities within the areas served by tertiary-level canals. Once NIA completes its construction assistance, communal systems are completely turned over to the local irrigators' associations. Although its policies assume the existence of strong irrigators' associations, before 1975 the agency did not have a systematic process for assisting the establishment and development of such associations. Like many large irrigation agencies throughout the world, the NIA viewed its work primarily as the construction of physical facilities and paid minimal attention to forming irrigators' organizations. Many of these associations were hastily created by calling a meeting and electing officers. Unless a strong association already existed in the area, this approach generally resulted in paper organizations that lacked the viability for good water management and maintenance.

Unease with this approach was widespread in the agency, and in 1975 a new government policy on communals highlighted its inadequacy.[8] The policy stated that farmers were to pay for construction or improvement costs incurred by the government on communal irrigation systems. The irrigators' associations were to provide 10 percent of the value of the construction assistance in the form of labor, materials, cash, and rights of way and to repay the remaining costs over a number of years without interest. To implement such a policy required an irrigators' association strong enough to comply with these conditions.

However, the gap between policy and implementation was wide. The NIA had limited institutional and staff capacity for developing strong irrigators' associations. As an interim measure it contracted a different governmental agency, the Farm Systems Development Corporation, to organize the farmers on communal systems, while the NIA concentrated on physical construction. This arrangement was based on the assumptions that organizing the farmers and constructing the physical facilities were separate tasks, appropriately carried out by different agencies; that problems in coordination at the field level would be minimal; and that most of the organizing could be done during or after construction.

Subsequent experience showed that these assumptions were wrong. The issues that most concerned the farmers during preconstruction and construction were technical ones, such as the location of the diversion and the canals, the timing of the construction activities, and the choice of laborers for the construction work. Because the socio-organizational tasks were not carried out by the agency doing the planning, design, and construction of the physical irrigation system, the social organizers could not deal with the issues of concern to the farmers—they approached the farmers empty-handed. To generate commitment and organizational strength, the irrigators' association needed to be organized long before construction, with the organizing and engineering tasks closely integrated. Seeing this, in 1976 the NIA attempted to learn how to work in this new mode.

Development of the Learning Process

Although the NIA had an ongoing program of some 250 communal irrigation projects a year, it began experimenting with the new approach on a small scale. With partial assistance from the Ford Foundation, the NIA began a pilot project in one municipality in central Luzon. Dubbed the "participatory approach," the basic concept was to field full-time community organizers to the project area well before construction began. The community organizers would live in the project area and help the farmers build or strengthen their association, using the intensive activities of planning, design, and construction to develop the skills of the association and to gain the farmers' full commitment and involvement in the development of their own irrigation system.

Although the initial pilot project was beset with numerous problems, the results appeared promising. The farmers were eager to participate in the development of their own system; they had considerable knowledge of the local area to contribute to planning and design; and through their involvement in the planning and construction activities, they developed the decisionmaking skill and organizational structures of their association.[9] The project also revealed that fully integrating the institutional and engineering aspects of the work was difficult and required a variety of adjustments on the part of the NIA.

At the time of this pilot project, the NIA contracted social scientists from the Institute of Philippine Culture to undertake a sociological study of fifty-one existing communal irrigation systems throughout the country. The field study was intended to provide knowledge of farmers' approaches to managing irrigation systems, and the results were later used in numerous training programs for NIA personnel.[10]

In addition to examining the existing communal systems, the social scientists examined NIA's pilot project to see if their findings could contribute to NIA's organizing work. Others from outside the NIA also became interested in the pilot project. Faculty from the Asian Institute of Management were intrigued with the management implications of the use of a participatory approach, and agricultural engineers from the International Rice Research Institute were interested in the potential for improved water management that strong irrigators' associations presented.

In 1979, when the NIA decided to expand the use of the participatory approach, it convened these individuals and its own key officials into a

Communal Irrigation Committee, chaired by an NIA assistant administrator. This committee, supported in part with funds and staff from the Ford Foundation, was charged with guiding the further development of NIA's participatory program. Two new pilot projects were started, which were explicitly conceived as laboratories in which the agency would learn how it would need to change in order to implement the approach more widely.[11]

The field-level activities of the new projects were intensively documented by a full-time social scientist residing in each of the project areas and supervised by the social scientists who had conducted the study of the communals.[12] Monthly process documentation reports were examined by the Communal Irrigation Committee for indications of problems, issues, and successful approaches. These were examined not to solve the problems of the specific pilot projects, but rather to develop agency capacities to deal with the problems on a program-wide basis.[13] Figure 3-1 depicts the process followed. New procedures and policies supported by field guidelines, manuals, and training were then developed, tested, refined, and gradually introduced throughout the country.

Figure 3-1. *Process Utilized for Program Improvement*

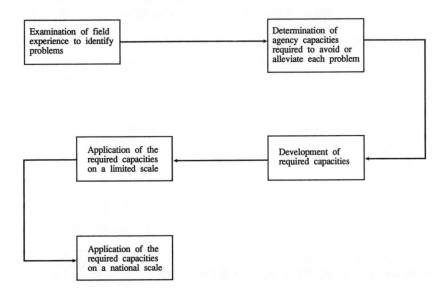

To build the decentralized capacity needed to implement the new approach nationwide, in 1980 twelve new participatory communal projects were started—one in each region of the country. In 1981, 24 new participatory projects were added—two in each region—and the following year a total of 108. In 1983 the participatory approach became the standard operating procedure on nearly all the NIA-assisted communal irrigation projects, including projects fully funded by the Philippine government and those funded through a World Bank six-year loan which took effect in June 1982. Later, loans covering communal irrigation systems by the Asian Development Bank and a grant from the U.S. Agency for International Development also supported the projects using the participatory approach. By 1987 participatory methods had been used in 1,335 communal irrigation projects covering 180,000 hectares.

The participatory concepts were introduced to national systems in 1981. By involving farmers in the rehabilitation of the irrigation system, irrigators' associations were developed, and subsequently they assumed responsibility for major sections of the irrigation system. Use of participatory methods on national systems expanded thereafter and by 1987 such methods had been introduced on 37 national irrigation systems covering 34,000 hectares.[14]

As the new methods were introduced to the agency, in-country training programs and workshops were held to develop attitudes and skills appropriate for the NIA employees dispersed throughout the regions and

Table 3-1. *Phased Expansion of the Participatory Projects*

Year	Participatory projects		Workshops and training courses	
	Number added	Hectares covered[a]	Number	NIA participants[a]
1976–78	1	400	1	25
1979	2	550	2	75
1980	12	1,800	6	150
1981	24	3,600	36	600
1982	108	16,200	50	1,700
1983	200[b]	30,000[b]	60[b]	2,000[b]
Total	347	52,550	155	4,550

a. Approximate number.
b. Estimated as of 1983.

provinces of the nation. Table 3-1 reveals the growth of both the projects and the training for the communals program from 1976 to 1983. This gradual approach to capacity building meant that when the program was applied on a nationwide basis, the personnel, policies, and procedures were in place, appropriate to the needs of the new approach. At the same time, NIA had developed a creative capacity for addressing new needs and problems as they arose.

Agency Change

The participatory approach required numerous changes in the NIA's approach at the field level. Some of the key changes in personnel, policies and procedures, and norms, attitudes, and expectations are discussed in this section.[15]

Personnel

Before the participatory approach was introduced, nearly all of NIA's professional field-level staff in charge of communal projects were trained exclusively in technical subjects such as construction, design, and survey. The participatory approach, however, required the addition of staff oriented toward people and trained in building the problem-solving capacities of local people. Consequently, NIA hired community organizers who could work with the farmers to develop irrigators' associations. The organizers came from a variety of educational backgrounds, but most commonly from applied social sciences such as community development and social work.

In 1976 when NIA initiated its first participatory project, it hired six community organizers. Over the ensuing years, the number gradually expanded, by 1987 reaching 395 organizers deployed to communal systems and 167 deployed to national systems. This was not simply a matter of hiring a new category of personnel. The approach the organizers used had to be developed and refined in ways suited to the needs of the farmers and the NIA's irrigation development program. The organizers had to learn by doing.

The gradual approach to expanding the program and the intensive observations of the early pilot projects allowed this new class of personnel to accumulate learning. Organizers who had worked out the initial strategies and solved innumerable field-level problems in the initial pilot projects became the supervisors and trainers of the new roster of organizers hired in 1980. When the program expanded again in 1981, the best of the 1980 recruits were added to the pool of supervisors and trainers of the new group. Training programs initially based on theory and anecdotal material gradually became more structured and program-specific until by 1983 detailed manuals based on extensive field experience had been written to assist organizers throughout the agency.[16]

The gradual expansion also allowed the progressive integration of the organizers into the NIA agency structure. At first they were simply part of the NIA–Ford Foundation pilot program. It was not clear where they should be placed organizationally or how a government budget for them should be provided. But as the program grew, the field-level organizers became part of the Provincial Irrigation Office staff, directly under the supervision of the provincial irrigation engineer who served as overall technical and institutional manager of the communal irrigation projects in each province. The organizers were budgeted as part of the regular communal irrigation program. At the regional level, one experienced community organizer was placed in each regional office to help recruit and train new organizers and work with provincial irrigation engineers and field-level organizers on site-specific issues. For the participatory projects involving national irrigation systems, the organizers were considered part of the project staff of the particular system on which they worked.

This expansion and integration into the NIA structure was not without problems. Living in the barrio and working closely with the farmers, this new class of personnel often saw projects from a different perspective than that of the regular NIA personnel. Their work habits were also different. Because farmer meetings were often held at night or on weekends, they could not keep the normal working hours of government employees. These differences became sources of tension between engineers and organizers at various times. As the program became better understood throughout the country, however, provincial irrigation engineers began to view the organizers as part of their staff and as helpful to the goals they wanted to accomplish.

Policies and Procedures

The NIA made six types of change in its field-level procedures, which are reviewed next.

SOCIOTECHNICAL PROFILES. Before the development of the participatory approach, NIA's feasibility studies for communal projects consisted of basic technical data on the water, land, and crops, and rough estimates of the construction costs and the extent of the area to be irrigated. Little or no information was available on the existing social arrangements for irrigation among the people, their organizations, leadership, conflicts, interest in NIA assistance, or landholding patterns. The technical data were often hastily gathered with only a few water availability measurements and minimal topographic investigation. One consequence was that many planned projects were discovered to be unfeasible shortly before construction was to begin. To make use of the available construction budget, other projects were then substituted at the last minute.

The participatory approach required better analysis of project feasibility. Once a community organizer had worked with the irrigators' association, it was important to be reasonably sure the project would be carried through to construction. It was also important that the NIA have basic social data so that the initial scheme of development could take into account social as well as technical issues.

To meet these needs, a sociotechnical profiling approach was developed. Anthropologists and NIA engineers from the Communal Irrigation Committee worked together with NIA organizers to develop comprehensive guidelines for collecting field-level data on each communal candidate for construction assistance. By following the guidelines, a regionally based NIA person could produce a profile in one month. It provided a good initial picture of the area to be assisted and the key social and technical problems likely to arise if assistance were made available. Formats were developed for the write-ups and analyses to help ensure that the data were used for decisionmaking.[17]

The NIA's use of these sociotechnical profiles accompanied the expansion in the participatory projects. By 1981 each regional office began to hold workshops on profile analysis to assist each province in assigning priorities to the communals seeking program support and in determining the key problems to be addressed in each. The sociotechnical profiles varied substantially in quality. In some cases shortcuts were taken to reduce costs, and data were sometimes inadequate for a full analysis. But in general the profiles provided a much improved data base for site selection and reduced the number of last-minute substitutions of projects. By 1983 the workshops on profile analysis had become a standard part of the NIA communal program.

Figure 3-2.   *Flow Chart of Preconstruction Activities*

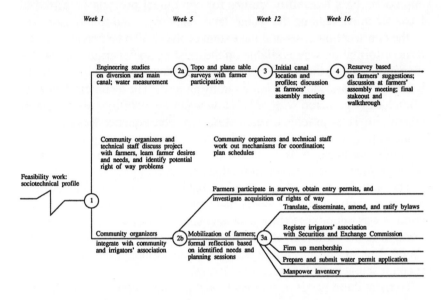

LEAD TIME. The initial pilot projects showed that involving the farmers in the layout and design of their irrigation system required a community organizer to be fielded eight to nine months before construction. During this time the organizer integrated with the community, helped develop or strengthen the irrigators' association, and encouraged the association to discuss the plans for the system with the NIA technical staff. Farmers accompanied the survey team and discussed alternative canal routes in meetings and walk-throughs of proposed routes with the NIA technical staff. Shortly before construction the irrigators' association and the NIA Provincial and Regional Irrigation Offices jointly agreed on the final design.

Figure 3-2 shows the flow of the technical and institutional (socio-organizational) activities during the preconstruction period. In some cases, problems interfered with the full implementation of this approach. For some projects the organizers were not fielded to the site for the full nine months of lead time; in others, there were difficulties in scheduling survey teams when the irrigators' association was ready to receive them; and in some there were misunderstandings on the respective roles of the

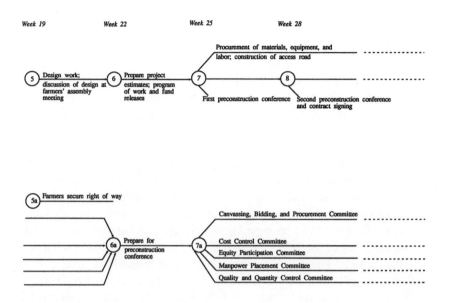

association, technical staff, and organizers. But as experience was gained in the participatory approach and NIA management systems were adjusted to fit the new needs, these problems lessened substantially.

The new procedures meant a major shift in the planning schedules of the provincial irrigation staff. Feasibility work had to be done more than a year earlier than previously and required adjustments in budgeting, scheduling, and the time horizons of provincial staff. Many provinces slipped behind schedule, but throughout the country there was steady progress in developing more orderly and better documented feasibility work and institutional and technical preparation for construction.

INSTITUTIONAL AND TECHNICAL COORDINATION. Before the introduction of the participatory approach, NIA field staff did not systematically consult the irrigators' association regarding the development of the physical system. Discussions were sometimes held with individual farmers or with the officers of the association, but full and regular interaction with the association on project planning and construction issues was rare. Achieving such regular interaction required a variety of coordination mechanisms. The community organizers encouraged the irrigators' association to develop task-specific committees to work with the NIA personnel on survey, design, and construction of the project.[18] Organizers needed to consult daily with the project-level engineer and biweekly with the provincial irrigation engineer to help link the technical decision making with the issues the irrigators' association was facing.[19]

To explain this coordinated approach, a flow chart based on the experience of the early pilot project showed the parallel activities of the technical and institutional staff in the preconstruction period (figure 3-2). Used in all organizer and engineer training, this helped everyone conceptualize their respective roles. In subsequent years the chart underwent substantial elaboration, though the essential elements remained the same.

The success with which this coordination was carried out varied from project to project. Many engineers were pleased to interact more fully with the farmers, to be welcomed in the villages, and to understand what was happening in the project area. Others found the approach a burden and the farmers' suggestions a threat to their technical expertise.

The early pilot projects had revealed the need for structured workshops with NIA engineers and community organizers in which the institutional and technical problems were aired and a common project perspective developed. Consequently, when the program expanded to all the regions, the Communal Irrigation Committee sponsored regional review and planning sessions for participatory communal projects. These workshops, in addition to the discussions in the field, helped build the technical staff's understanding of the institutional issues and the organizers' understanding of the technical issues.[20] The workshops were so helpful that by 1982 the NIA regional offices throughout the country had instituted them on a regular quarterly basis.

HIRING AND CONTRACTING FOR CONSTRUCTION WORK. NIA personnel were accustomed to hiring and contracting with little or no consultation with the irrigators' associations. But the early participatory projects revealed that these decisions were of great concern to the farmers. Association members were often eager to work as laborers or contractors in the project (though interest varied from one area to another depending on alternative employment opportunities). The association also needed full involvement in the construction work to generate the local equity contribution stipulated by agency policy.

One approach to meeting the concerns of the farmers was to negotiate contracts with the irrigators' associations for much of the work. Under this arrangement, the association contributed equity by having a percentage of the contract payment withheld and allocated to their equity account, which meant lower than normal daily wages for those who worked. One problem, however, was that workers did not receive their money on time. Although commercial contractors received payment only when the contract was completed, they would normally have "front money" to pay laborers their daily wages. The irrigators' associations, however, had no such funds. Experience showed that farmers could work for about two weeks without pay, but then became so desperate for money to feed their families that they left in search of other work. In some cases efforts were made to develop small contracts that could be completed and paid for within two-week cycles. In other cases NIA directly administered the construction and paid the farmer-laborers on a volumetric basis (that is, per cubic meter of canal earthwork).

Sometimes, when outside contractors were used, conditions were imposed to make this acceptable to the association. In some cases, prior to bidding, potential contractors were informed that the association wanted its members to have priority in getting jobs as laborers, and that a percentage of their pay would be deducted as their equity contribution. The association officials also observed the opening of the bids. With these kinds of arrangements the association was usually much more satisfied with the construction work and made higher equity contributions.

FINANCIAL RECORDING AND RECONCILIATION. Upon completing a communal irrigation project, NIA presented the irrigators' association with a statement showing the project costs that were chargeable to the association and the equity contributions. This was used as a basis for calculating the annual amortization payments due. The association was expected to verify this statement and sign it before the new or reconstructed irrigation system was officially turned over to the association.

Experience in the early participatory projects, however, revealed that it was difficult for farmers to verify what was often two or more years of project expenses. In nonparticipatory projects this problem caused widespread unwillingness among the associations to sign the final statement, with the result that the projects could not be officially turned over.

The Communal Irrigation Committee discussed this problem and in response NIA developed a system of periodic financial reconciliations.[21] Not only engineers and organizers, but also NIA accountants and billing clerks were trained in the new way of recording expenses. It was suggested that these reconciliations be done monthly but they were often done about every three months. Throughout the country, NIA personnel indicated that on the project expenses, this new approach led to much greater agreement with the irrigators' association than previously.

POSTCONSTRUCTION ASSISTANCE. Before the development of the participatory program, NIA terminated its assistance to an irrigators' association as soon as construction was completed. But, as a general result of the participatory process, irrigators' associations were sufficiently well-developed that it seemed appropriate to cap the NIA construction assistance with help on planning the operation and maintenance of the irrigation system and the financial management of the association.

During 1979–81 the attention of the Communal Irrigation Committee had concentrated primarily on the preconstruction and construction stages. But by early 1982 attention turned to these postconstruction issues. Since some research had already been done on these issues,[22] working groups were constituted to use that research to develop approaches that NIA could implement throughout the country. By mid-1983, approaches specifically tailored to communal systems had been developed to assist both system operations and financial management. NIA personnel throughout the country were trained to use these materials, offering system management training to irrigators' associations once construction was completed.

The financial management materials provided simple forms and instructions with which the irrigators' association could assess and collect irrigation fees, record receipts and expenses, and report financial information to its general membership.[23] These financial systems were viewed by many observers as important to the success of the associations. Many rural community organizations in the Philippines had collapsed because members suspected their officers of mishandling funds. It was hoped that these simple but precise recording systems would help the irrigators' associations avoid this fate.

With regard to irrigation system management, NIA's previous training for farmers had been done mainly on national systems and was designed to explain the water requirements for crops and NIA's rules for water allocation. Under the participatory program NIA's role switched from lecturer to facilitator. NIA personnel encouraged the farmers to hold a workshop during which the association officers and members would work out their own management plans. NIA would suggest types of problems the association might discuss; provide formats and data with which the association could assess its current operations; give examples of how other communal associations had addressed such problems; and encourage a structured planning process in which the association determined the steps it would take on these issues. The goal was not to give the associations a ready-made plan, but rather to give them a process by which they could make their own system management plans—a process they could use for many years to meet the system's evolving needs.[24]

Norms, Attitudes, and Expectations

Proper implementation of the participatory approach required some fundamental shifts in the norms and attitudes of NIA personnel. One such shift was in the perspective on basic goals. For many NIA personnel the goal of their work was to construct certain physical facilities. In contrast, the goal of the participatory approach was to build simultaneously both a physical system and a local social capability for using and sustaining that system on a long-term basis.

A second fundamental shift was in the relation of the NIA personnel to the farmers. Previously, the farmers had played a passive role in system construction, with NIA personnel making all the key decisions. The participatory approach, however, required a partner relationship between the NIA and the irrigators' association. Technical personnel needed to respect the knowledge and traditions of the farmers, while also recognizing the limitations of that knowledge. They needed skill in communicating their technical knowledge to the farmers so that technical decisions could be made jointly. And they needed to use an interactive style, working through farmer committees to accomplish the goals of the project.

Technical staff varied widely in the degree to which they developed the needed attitudes, and consequently in the degree to which their projects followed the true spirit of the participatory approach. Many had come from farm families and quickly came to appreciate the value of the new approach. Others, however, continued to work within the NIA's previous perspectives and found the new procedures frustrating.

Changes in NIA management systems helped create new expectations which supported the needed shifts in norms and attitudes.[25] One change highlighted the data on the equity contributed by the irrigators' association. Previously the 10 percent local equity requirement was viewed as so difficult to fulfill that it was not used as an indicator of project progress. Physical accomplishment and financial disbursement of construction funds were the primary indicators. However, when the fuller involvement of the farmers made higher equity contributions possible (as indicated below in table 3-2), equity data were brought "out of the closet" and the generation of equity contributions became a basic responsibility of every provincial irrigation engineer.

Another item relevant to the needed shifts in norms and attitudes was the area actually irrigated once construction was completed. NIA had tended to emphasize "area generated" as the key indicator of performance. This was an estimate of the area that theoretically could be irrigated by the canals that were constructed—whether the water actually ran in those canals or the farmers made use of them was not an intrinsic part of the indicator.[26] The introduction of post construction assessment helped focus more attention on actually irrigated area rather than simply on the construction of physical facilities.[27] Postconstruction assistance also helped support these shifts in norms and attitudes since it kept NIA personnel in contact with the farmers during the first two cropping seasons, when the farmers were wrestling with the problems of operating and maintaining the system.

Another element supporting the shifts was a stronger emphasis on the collection of amortization payments. The NIA devised cost account sys-

Table 3-2. *Farmers' Equity Contribution to Construction Costs*

Basis for measuring contribution	Participatory systems $(n = 21)$[a]	Nonparticipatory systems $(n = 22)$
Farmers' mean equity contribution per hectare of land irrigated in the 1984–85 wet season[b]	₱ 357	₱ 54
Farmers' mean equity contribution per 1984–85 wet season system user	₱ 348	₱ 44

a.   Data on the farmers' contribution to system construction costs were not available for three systems in which construction had not been completed.

b. $t = 5.31; p < 0.01$.

tems under which provincial irrigation offices were expected to support their operational costs from their equity and amortization collections—and which therefore gave provincial personnel a strong interest in the longer-term viability of the irrigation groups they assisted.

Such fundamental shifts do not take place easily or quickly. It was possible in the NIA because of a variety of factors: a general policy framework supportive of local self-reliance; strong and committed leadership from NIA's top management; the gradual expansion of the program; the addition of a new type of personnel oriented to social issues; appropriate changes in policies and procedures; extensive training and workshops; and the assistance of an able group of individuals from outside the agency, including social anthropologists, management specialists, and agricultural engineers with the time and creativity to assist in the change process.

By 1988 the participatory approach was well established within the communal irrigation program and its use had also been applied to substantial areas of the larger, national systems. Over the twelve year development of the participatory approaches, the agency had developed a new organizational culture more compatible with the need to build local social capacity for irrigation.

Benefits of the Participatory Approach: Key Findings

In 1985 a sufficient number of communal irrigation systems had been assisted using participatory methods that it was possible to quantitatively evaluate the impact of the new approach. A study was conducted by Romana de los Reyes and Sylvia Jopillo, social scientists from the Institute of Philippine Culture of the Ateneo de Manila University, who headed a team of thirteen researchers which examined forty-six communal irrigation systems. They studied the functionality and productivity of the systems, the structure and activities of the irrigators' associations, and the farmers' contributions to the costs of the system. They also examined both the construction and the institutional costs of assisting the systems. Twenty-four of the systems sampled had been assisted using participatory methods while twenty-two had been assisted using nonparticipatory methods. The systems were randomly sampled from five regions of the country from among systems irrigating over 50 hectares of land which had been constructed between 1981 and 1983 and which were fully or partially operational by June 1984.

Before examining the variables reflecting the impact of NIA participatory vs. nonparticipatory methods, it is useful to compare the basic characteristics of the sample systems *prior* to the NIA's intervention. With the exception of two variables, there were no significant differences in the basic characteristics of the two types of systems or the farmers using them. All sites were gravity fed, run-of-the-river irrigation systems, and forty-one of the forty-six had originally been developed by the farmers themselves. Farmers on all of the systems planted primarily rice and tilled about 1 hectare per family. The land tenure status of the farmers was similar, with 25 percent of the farmers being owner-tillers and the remaining 75 percent tenants.

One variable showing a significant difference between participatory and nonparticipatory systems prior to the NIA intervention was the size of the system. Nonparticipatory systems averaged 127 hectares while participatory systems averaged only 88 hectares. The other background variable showing a difference was the accessibility of the system. Participatory systems were somewhat more remote, averaging 5.5 kilometers from the nearest town, while nonparticipatory systems averaged 4.35 kilometers.

The nature of the construction done with NIA assistance was basically the same for both types of systems. Forty-three out of the forty-six systems existed before the NIA intervention, and the assistance involved upgrading the physical facilities to expand the irrigated area and increase the reliability of water delivery. The remaining three were new irrigation systems. Costs per irrigated hectare for the labor, materials, and supervision of the participatory and nonparticipatory projects were nearly identical, averaging $769 per hectare.[28]

In 1981 the NIA was still implementing most of its projects in a nonparticipatory way, however, by 1983 participatory methods had become widely used in the agency. Thus, more nonparticipatory systems were assisted in 1981 (86 percent) while more participatory systems were assisted in 1982 (33 percent) and 1983 (58 percent).

Key Findings

The following summarizes the key findings from the recent de los Reyes and Jopillo study.[29]

FUNCTIONALITY AND PRODUCTIVITY. One of the purposes of the participatory approach was to encourage farmers' involvement in the layout and design of the new canals and structures so that their knowledge of the local area and their desires could be incorporated into construction plans. Thus, an important issue in evaluating the impact of such participation was the farmers' degree of satisfaction with the resulting canals and structures. The research data revealed that farmers on participatory systems viewed their new facilities as more functional. On the nonparticipatory systems farmers abandoned or erased 18 percent of the canals constructed under NIA assistance and assessed an additional 20 percent of the new structures as defective. In contrast, on the participatory systems 9 percent of the canals were abandoned or erased and 13 percent of the structures were viewed as defective.

In terms of the expansion of irrigated area, as indicated in table 3-3, the NIA assistance produced a positive effect for both participatory and nonparticipatory systems. In the wet season, the proportion of expansion was similar for the two types of system—18 percent for participatory systems and 17 percent for nonparticipatory. But in the dry season there was a substantial difference between the two types of systems, with the participatory systems expanding their irrigated area by 35 percent, while the nonparticipatory systems expanded by 18 percent.

Regarding productivity, as measured by rice yields in the irrigated areas, the participatory systems showed substantially greater increases than the nonparticipatory systems. Table 3-4, contrasts the mean rice yields of these two systems. Prior to the NIA assistance, rice yields in irrigated areas on both participatory and nonparticipatory systems were just over 2.5 tons per hectare per season in both the wet and dry seasons. However, after the assistance, only the participatory systems showed significant gains in yields per hectare, a result that appeared to be a function of greater reliability of water delivery in the participatory systems.

ORGANIZATION. Data on the associations that managed the irrigation systems revealed that associations developed through the use of participatory methods were much more "rooted" in their communities than those of systems where such methods had not been used (see table 3-5). Associations using participatory systems were more likely to have a second organizational tier—the sector-level unit—based in the various geographical parts of the irrigation system. The sectors spread out the

Table 3-3. *Mean Areas Irrigated Before and After NIA's Construction Assistance*

Time period	Participatory systems (n = 24)	Nonparticipatory systems (n = 22)
Wet season		
Before the project	88 ha.	127 ha.
Crop year 1984–85	104 ha.	149 ha.
Expansion	16 ha.	22 ha.
Expansion as a percentage of area irrigated before the project[a]	18	17
Dry season		
Before the project	56 ha.	105 ha.
Crop year 1984–85	76 ha.	123 ha.
Expansion	20 ha.	18 ha.
Expansion as a percentage of area irrigated before the project[b]	35	18

a. $z = 0.08; p < 0.21$.
b. $z = 1.38; p < 0.08$.

Table 3-4. *Mean Rice Yields on Irrigated Land Before and After NIA's Construction Assistance*
(tons per hectare)

Time period	Yield on sample farms in participatory systems[a]	Yields on sample farms in nonparticipatory systems[b]
Wet season		
Year prior to the project	2.84	2.59
Crop year 1984–85	3.05	2.65
Difference in yields after the assistance	+ 0.21	+ 0.06
Dry season		
Year prior to the project	2.56	2.57
After the project	3.11	2.54
Difference in yields after the assistance	+ 0.55	– 0.03

a. $n = 350$ farms for the wet season and 230 for the dry season.
b. $n = 295$ farms for the wet season and 178 for the dry season.

responsibility for irrigation activities and enabled a more decentralized form of management, critical to the geographically dispersed membership for carrying out routine tasks. The greater use of sectors on participatory systems resulted in a higher ratio of leaders to members, which helped provide stronger links between the full membership and the management of the irrigation system (see table 3-6).

The land tenure status of association leaders also reflects the greater "rootedness" of the leaders of the associations on participatory systems. For both participatory and nonparticipatory systems, about three-fourths of the association members were tenants who owned no land of their own. For participatory systems 47 percent of the central-level leaders also owned no land, while on nonparticipatory systems 35 percent of such leaders owned no land. And for those who did own land, the leaders of nonparticipatory systems tended to have larger parcels than those of participatory systems. These differences indicated that in the associations of participatory systems, the socioeconomic status of the leadership was closer to that of the ordinary members than was the case for nonparticipatory systems.

The study also examined the activities of the associations in managing the irrigation systems. An important variable was water management, particularly the degree to which efforts were made to distribute water equitably among the members. A commonly used means of assuring such equity in water distribution is to rotate water according to a schedule, allowing each group in turn to make use of all available water for a specified amount of time. The associations on participatory systems were more likely to use this rotation when water became scarce, and were more likely to employ personnel to supervise the water distribution, than were associations on nonparticipatory systems (see table 3-7).

Table 3-5. *Organizational Structure*

Organizational unit	Participatory systems (n = 24)		Nonparticipatory systems (n = 22)	
	Number	Percent	Number	Percent
With central board of directors	24	100	18	82
With sector-level units	24	100	13	59
With central boards composed of sector-level representatives	12	50	3	14

Table 3-6. *Mean Number of Leaders per Association*

Type of leader	Participatory systems (n = 24)	Nonparticipatory systems (n = 22)
Central-level officials[a]	10.9	8.8
Sector-level officials[b]	6.8	3.5
Personnel[c]	2.7	1.8
Total[d]	15.6	12.0
Ratio of leaders to system users in crop year 1984–85[e]	1:9	1:14

a. $t = 1.59$; $p < 0.06$.
b. $t = 2.7$; $p < 0.02$.
c. $t = 1.09$; $p < 0.14$.
d. $t = 1.87$; $p < 0.03$. The total number of leaders is not a simple summation of the three subtypes of leaders because some individuals held positions at both the central and sector levels.
e. $t = 1.64$; $p < 0.05$.

Regarding maintenance, the study found that the associations on the participatory and nonparticipatory systems mobilized their members for about the same number of days of voluntary group work during the 1984–85 wet season—all averaging about twelve person hours per hectare of irrigated land. However, the associations on participatory systems had more hired personnel (2.7 persons per participatory system versus 1.8 per nonparticipatory system) and consequently had more total person power mobilized for maintenance activities.

Data on the financial practices of the associations revealed significant differences between the participatory and nonparticipatory systems. Less than one-fifth of the associations on nonparticipatory systems used vouchers for expenditures, conducted an annual audit of their accounts, prepared financial statements, or monitored payments and collectibles on each member's card. For participatory systems the rate of use of such practices ranged from 21 percent to 50 percent which, while significantly greater for nonparticipatory systems, still indicated considerable room for improvement.

FARMERS' CONTRIBUTIONS TO CONSTRUCTION COSTS. Philippine government policy required farmers to contribute to the costs of construction in two ways. Farmers contributed "equity"—labor, materials, and land—at the time of the construction—and they also made annual repayments of

Table 3-7. *Water Distribution Methods*

Method	Participatory systems (n = 24)		Nonparticipatory systems (n = 22)	
	Number	Percent	Number	Percent
Rotational distribution in the wet season	6	25	4	18
Rotational distribution in the dry season	14	58	8	36
Special personnel to distribute water	16	67	9	41

the construction costs, which were amortized over a period of years. For their equity payments farmers were asked to contribute 10 percent of the construction costs or P300 per hectare, whichever was less. Farmers on systems using NIA's participatory methods exceeded the minimum, raising an average of P357 per hectare of irrigated land. In contrast, nonparticipatory systems raised only P54 per hectare (see table 3-2).

Regarding the payment of amortizations as of 1985, associations on participatory systems had paid 82 percent of the amount due, while those on nonparticipatory systems had paid 50 percent. However, most of the nonparticipatory systems had been built a year or two earlier than the participatory systems and, consequently, had more payments due, as indicated in table 3-8. It was not yet known how well the payments on each type of system hold up over time.

Costs of the Participatory Approach

Under its participatory approach, the NIA conducted a number of activities not done in the nonparticipatory projects. These included writing sociotechnical profiles, fielding community organizers, providing financial management and system management training to the irrigators' associations, as well as recruiting, training, and supervising the organizers and profile writers. The costs of these additional activities, shown in table 3-9, averaged a total of P498 ($25) per hectare, or 3 percent of the construction costs of the participatory projects. Interestingly, when the total development costs (institutional and construction expenses) of the two types of systems were compared, the participatory systems cost a mere P48 ($2.40) per hectare more than the nonparticipatory systems because of the slightly higher costs per hectare for construction of the nonparticipatory systems (see tables 3-9 and 3-10).

Comparison of Costs and Benefits

As indicated above, substantial benefits were reaped from the small investment in institutional activities, including more functional physical structures, greater increases in rice yields, larger increases in dry season irrigated area, and stronger irrigators' associations.

But how do these benefits compare to the costs? The benefits, in terms of recovery of the construction costs, were substantial. The farmers' equity contributions at the time of construction were ₱303 ($15.15) per hectare greater for participatory than for nonparticipatory systems, which represented an immediate recovery of 60 percent of the cost of institutional development activities. Moreover, based on the experience of the initial few years, loan repayment rates were ₱87 ($4.35) per hectare per year higher for participatory than for nonparticipatory systems. If that differential rate of repayment is maintained for three years, the remaining cost of the participatory methods would be completely recovered (assuming a 10 percent discount rate), and if the higher repayment rate were

Table 3-8.   *Construction Loan Repayment*

Payment	Participatory systems (n = 17)[a]	Nonparticipatory systems (n = 19)[b]
Mean amortization payment due[c]	₱ 15,088	₱ 41,667
Mean amortization payment remitted to NIA	₱ 12,429	₱ 21,005
Mean percentage of amortization due actually paid[d]	82	50

   a.   Of the twenty-four sample participatory systems, four were still under construction during the research fieldwork, one had no loan because the association raised a 30 percent equity, and two were not yet due to begin paying their amortization.

   b.   Of the twenty-two sample nonparticipatory systems, two associations had not accepted the final turnover of the system, while one association had no loan because it raised a 30 percent equity.

   c.   Nonparticipatory systems had larger amortization payments because most had been completed in 1981. Participatory systems were more often completed in 1982 and 1983.

   d. $z = 2.17; p < 0.05$.

Table 3-9. *Institutional Design, and Construction Costs per Hectare of Wet Season Irrigated Land*

Costs	Participatory systems (n = 24)		Nonparticipatory systems (n = 22)	
	Pesos	U.S. dollars	Pesos	U.S. dollars
Institutional costs				
Profile preparations	36	1.80	—	
Community organizer salaries and field supplies	293	14.65	—	
Community organizer training and supervision	82	4.10	—	
Financial and system management training for irrigation associations	87	4.35	—	
Total institutional costs	498	24.90	—	
Design & construction costs[a]				
Chargeable to farmers	12,666	633.30	12,000	600.00
Not chargeable to farmers	2,484	124.20	3,599	179.95
Total design and construction costs	15,150	757.50	15,600	780.00
Total development costs	15,648	782.40	15,600	780.00

Note: Costs have been standardized in 1984 pesos: ₱20 = $1.00.
a. Includes costs of materials, labor, equipment rental, and technical supervision.

Table 3-10. *System Construction Costs per Hectare*

Category	Participatory (n = 21)[a]	Nonparticipatory (n = 22)
Mean per hectare project cost[b]	₱15,150	₱15,599
Mean per hectare chargeable cost[c]	₱12,666	₱12,000

Note: Adjusted to 1984 prices using the implicit price index for government construction. Based on area actually irrigated 1984–85 wet season.
a. Data on system construction costs were not available for three systems in which a turnover of the system had not been made.
b. $t = 0.08$; n.s.
c. $t = 0.14$; n.s. Excludes equity contribution of association. This is payable in fifty years without interest.

maintained longer, the investment in the participatory methods would provide a direct positive financial benefit to the NIA. In investment terms, if the differential repayment between participatory and nonparticipatory systems remained at ₽87 for a total of seven years, the rate of return over a ten-year period would be 25 percent.[30]

For the individual NIA staff member, that financial benefit provided an important reason to make use of the new participatory methods. Provincial irrigation offices needed to support their routine operating costs (but not project costs) based on income generated through the equity and amortization payments from communal irrigation associations. Thus, the differences in financial results between the participatory and nonparticipatory methods were important to NIA staff and were one of the reasons for their strong support of the participatory program.

Determining the economic returns from using participatory methods is difficult because of the problems of assigning monetary values to the benefits revealed by the field-level impact data. Even to estimate the benefits simply in terms of increased rice production cannot be done based on the results of the de los Reyes and Jopillo study. Their study revealed that participatory systems produced greater increases in rice yields than nonparticipatory systems due to higher yields for previously irrigated areas, and also due to greater expansion of dry season irrigated area. However, because the study did not examine the related increases in costs associated with the production increases, an economic rate of return cannot be determined for the sample communal irrigation systems.

Another type of benefit of the new methods was the goodwill generated between the farmers and the NIA personnel. At the completion of construction, systems were officially turned over to the irrigators' associations. On participatory systems, the opening ceremonies were much more likely to be festive village events, reflecting the warm relationships that had developed between the NIA and the farmers through the new approach. For the thousands of NIA personnel and the farmers, that benefit may have been one of the most important of all.

Developing Local Capacity

The participatory approach described above was developed specifically to fit the Philippine context. It cannot be extrapolated directly. But the critical characteristics of the program may be relevant to irrigation programs in other settings. In fact, many Asian irrigation leaders have already found many of the concepts and methods used by the NIA highly relevant to the needs of their countries. Based on their observations in the Philippines, leaders from Sri Lanka, Indonesia, Thailand, Nepal, and India have initiated policy changes and pilot projects directed toward making greater use of some or all of the basic concepts outlined below.

AUTHORITY OF THE ASSOCIATION. The authority given to an irrigators' association can range from cleaning the ditches to having full responsibility for operating and maintaining the entire system. While irrigation agency officials in many countries are eager to have irrigators' associations responsible for cleaning the ditches, some are more skeptical of empowering local associations with control over water allocation.

It is sometimes thought that water control should be left to an impartial government authority to avoid inequities in water allocation. Particularly on small-scale systems, government contact is likely to be so limited that the concept of government control is only a myth. The myth, however, officially removes the local authority to run the system, leaving a vacuum where individualism could reign.

The appropriate degree of authority to be given to the local irrigators' association needs to vary according to each local program. It should be recognized, however, that the less authority the local association has, the weaker it is likely to be. Farmers are not likely to be eager participants in an association that is simply expected to clean the ditches. Chambers suggested a useful guideline for determining the appropriate degree of authority: "In general, government should unambiguously avoid doing that which communities can do for themselves in their own interest, but should intervene when exceptional problems are beyond a community's power to overcome."[31]

One of the strengths of the Philippine communal irrigation program is its clear policy regarding the authority of the local associations. Each system of less than 1,000 hectares has one association which owns the irrigation system and has responsibility for operating and maintaining the entire system. The association is a legal entity with water rights registered in its name. This provides the farmers with a clear rationale for committing their time and energy to developing their association.[32]

USE OF EXISTING IRRIGATION GROUPS. In developing an irrigators' association, the organizers can either ignore existing groups or explicitly build on them. In some places this is not an issue as irrigation groups do not exist. But elsewhere, particularly in the humid tropics, there are likely to be many—even though irrigation bureaucracies tend to be blind to them. A number of factors encourage this blindness. Many irrigation agencies prefer to assume they are generating new irrigated hectarage rather than improving existing systems, and therefore they ignore existing irrigation groups. Another factor is the lack of data about these local groups. Even when local socioeconomic data are collected, they usually focus on characteristics of individual farmers such as farm size, crops grown, and yields, but do not reveal the local social organizational arrangements for irrigation.[33] Consequently, existing irrigation groups may be ignored and are wasted as an organizational resource. Although these groups do not always operate as effectively as the government would like, they often have withstood the test of time and evolved useful traditions and leadership roles which are not easily replaced.[34]

The participatory projects of the Philippine communal irrigation program explicitly tried to build on existing irrigators' groups. It was normally the local irrigation group that made the request for assistance from the government in the first place. The sociotechnical profile then highlighted current irrigation arrangements in the area, providing the NIA technical and organizational team with the basis for making maximum beneficial use of those arrangements.

CONTRIBUTION OF ASSOCIATIONS TO CONSTRUCTION COSTS. The Philippine experience reveals the beneficial effects of requiring some immediate contribution to construction costs from the irrigators' association.[35] Since the irrigators' association was expected to contribute an immediate 10 percent of construction costs and subsequently repay the remainder, agency personnel needed to concern themselves with developing irrigators' associations. On the farmers' side, the requirement that their association make a 10 percent contribution was an immediate and tangible organizational task that mobilized membership participation. The arrangement also bestowed greater equality on relations between the agency and the local association. The association's power to withhold its contribution provided some leverage with agency personnel not available in the case of a handout.

ASSOCIATION INVOLVEMENT IN PLANNING, LAYOUT, AND CONSTRUCTION. A common assumption is that there is no reason to develop an irrigators' association until there is water running in the canals. If this assumption is followed, social organizers are not fielded until after the system is built, and the local people have no involvement in developing the system. The detrimental effects of this approach are discussed in chapters 2 and 4.

The Philippine experience reviewed here corresponds to that of numerous indigenous irrigation systems around the world and reveals the importance of *early* involvement in developing the capacities of irrigators' associations to manage and maintain their system.[36]

Development of Implementing Agency Capacity

The dimensions of program design listed above are likely to contribute to developing strong irrigators' associations. But a program design is meaningless unless the implementing agency can carry it out. The Philippine experience reveals some key questions regarding implementational capacity. (These questions do not deal with the purely technical issues, though of course engineering capacities are crucial.)

Does the agency have the technology for a rapid assessment of the current irrigation arrangements and other operationally relevant social characteristics of the people to be affected by the system? Does it have a way of using that knowledge in developing the irrigation system? Does it have a way of estimating with reasonable accuracy the area to be irrigated?

Does the agency have socially oriented personnel who can develop the irrigators' association, working closely with the technical personnel? Is there a training program that develops field workers' capabilities for the specific tasks of developing associations?

Is there a clear framework for relating the socio-organizational and the technical work at each step of a project so that the field-level technical and organizational staff and the farmers understand their respective roles? Are there mechanisms (such as workshops) to help these two types of personnel develop common plans and perspectives?

Has the agency closely examined the procedures for its field staff to make sure they fit the operational requirements of the strategy for developing strong irrigators' associations?

Are there training programs for technical staff to develop the attitudes, skills, and knowledge suited to the strategy?

For many national irrigation agencies the answers to most of the above questions would be no, although recent developments in a number of

Asian countries are beginning to change the situation. When there are no such capacities, those concerned with "putting people first," must confront the need to develop such capacities within national agencies. The issue poses a dilemma for members of project development or appraisal teams because the project cycle followed by many international or bilateral aid agencies is not well-suited to developing such capacities.[37]

Project Cycle Issues

The learning process described here differs from the project cycle commonly used by major international aid institutions.[38] The main elements of the learning process are initial small-scale pilot action, use of the pilot projects to build program-wide agency capacity, and gradual expansion of the pilot projects.

Small-scale Pilot Action

A number of people at the NIA felt that involving farmers in the preconstruction and construction stages of an irrigation system would help build farmer organizations better able to handle the operation and maintenance activities once construction was completed. But the NIA did not know exactly how to implement such involvement. Three small-scale pilot projects were carried out to learn how.

Such learning through action sharply contrasts with the preparation for a large loan, which consists of data collection, not action. Feasibility work uses data to determine whether some set of activities will produce sufficient benefit to justify the investment. Then a set of plans and budgets for a five- to six-year implementation period are drawn up on the assumption that experts can figure out in advance what has to be done.

But usually in rural development projects—particularly those intended to involve the beneficiaries in some significant way—the steps to be taken have not been tried before, and no one knows exactly what the steps should be or what management procedures the agency needs to support them. This must be learned. While data collection may be helpful to this process, appropriate methods must be developed through action. Just as a person cannot learn to swim by doing a socioeconomic survey of swimmers, an agency cannot learn to implement a new approach through feasibility studies alone.

Mechanisms for Building Agency Capacity

The NIA developed a variety of mechanisms to use the pilot project experience in building program-wide capacity. A Communal Irrigation Committee composed of key NIA officials and individuals from Philippine academic institutions and the Ford Foundation continually examined the pilot project experiences. The committee helped identify agency procedures that interfered with successful work, and it encouraged written documentation of successful methods for later use in training. The committee members also helped develop new agency capacities when field-level experience indicated new approaches were needed and sponsored workshops to spread awareness of the new approaches within the agency. In addition, to bolster NIA training for irrigation associations, the committee examined approaches already in use by some of the most successful indigenous communal irrigation systems.[39]

To ensure that the pilot project experience was fully captured, a researcher documented the daily interactions among the farmers, and between the farmers and NIA personnel. Thus, the issues and problems occurring in the field could be fully understood by a range of people who could contribute to solutions—not just for a specific project, but for eventual broader implementation in many projects.

Large loans by foreign donors occasionally have pilot activities associated with them. In some cases the pilot is done simultaneously with the main project activity, while in others it is attached to a loan for a different purpose, as a means of testing a new idea for a larger, later loan.

Usually the pilot does *not* contain mechanisms that enable the agency to use the pilot activities to improve its own capacity. The staff that oversees the pilot activity is burdened with meeting disbursement schedules on the broader loan, which sometimes forces a pace too fast to allow a thoughtful examination of the small-scale pilot project. There is usually no careful documentation of the field-level activities in the pilot area, nor is there a specially formed group of agency and nonagency individuals committed to extracting from the pilot the knowledge for developing broader implementation capacities. When the pilot and the larger project are carried out simultaneously, it becomes particularly difficult to use the pilot project for developing methods and training with a broader application. Even if methods and training are developed from the pilot experience, by the time they are available, the personnel on the other parts of the project have usually already pursued their own approaches.[40]

Gradual Expansion of the Pilot

A third element in NIA's learning process was the expansion of the pilot projects at a rate gradual enough to build broad program capacity and to ensure that staff had the understanding and capability to implement the new approaches. The first step in the expansion process was to implement one pilot project in each administrative region of the country. This gave key personnel throughout the country some acquaintance with the new approaches so that later, when more projects were added, they would be prepared to oversee their implementation. This gradual expansion allowed personnel experienced in the new methods to become the direct supervisors and trainers of others who were implementing the new methods for the first time. It also allowed the gradual shift in NIA policies and procedures to fit the needs of the new program.

Planning and funding for the expansion were also done gradually. When examination of the field-level activities indicated the program was ready for some degree of expansion, plans were formulated in workshops by the people who would implement that expansion. Ford Foundation grants totaling $1.4 million over twelve years, matched by NIA funds, were provided at one- to two-year intervals, with each grant fitted to the needs apparent at that stage of the program.[41] Flexible budget categories allowed deployment of funds to meet the needs as they emerged from the action.

In the case of large loans from international agencies, a gradual expansion is also sometimes built into the plans. But to fit the usual project cycle, this expansion and the associated budget items are programmed in advance over a five- to six-year period. However, when the methods to be used are not yet developed, it is difficult to predict how quickly appropriate methods will be created and what budget items will be needed to support them. Furthermore, what is learned from the initial activities may call for significant changes in the plans. But plans that have already undergone a variety of bureaucratic approvals may be difficult to change.

Another problem is that often a large loan concentrates on a particular geographical area within the country, militating against a focus on nationwide capacity building. Exceptions do exist, however, where a

enous irrigation associations which the NIA incorporated into its participatory program can be found in Robert Y. Siy, "A Tradition of Collective Action: Farmers and Irrigation in the Philippines," in Frances F. Korten and Robert Y. Siy, eds., *Transforming a Bureaucracy: The Experience of the Philippine National Irrigation Administration* (West Hartford, Conn.: Kumarian Press, 1988, and Quezon City, Philippines: Ateneo de Manila University Press, 1989).

11. For a description of process documentation and the action-related learnings that emerged from it, see Romana de los Reyes, "Process Documentation: Social Science Research in a Learning Process Approach to Program Development," *Philippine Sociological Review,* vol. 32, pp. 105–20.

12. For a brief summary of the events in one of these two projects, see Jeanne Frances I. Illo, "Farmers, Engineers and Organizers: The Taisan Project," in Frances F. Korten and Robert Y. Siy, eds., *Transforming a Bureaucracy: The Experience of the Philippine National Irrigation Administration,* (West Hartford, Conn.: Kumarian Press, 1988, and Quezon City, Philippines: Ateneo de Manila University Press, 1989).

13. Benjamin U. Bagadion, "Developing Farmers' Participation in Managing Irrigation Systems under the National Irrigation Administration," paper read at Second Social Forestry Forum of the Bureau of Forest Development Upland Development Program, November 1981, Asian Institute of Tourism, Manila.

14. Reports on participatory work on national irrigation systems include: Jeanne Frances I. Illo and Ma. Elena Chiong-Javier, *Organizing Farmers for Irrigation Management: The Buhi-Lalo Experience* (Naga City, Philippines: Ateneo de Naga, 1983); and Sylvia G. Jopillo and Romana de los Reyes, Proceedings from the IPC/NIA Profile Analysis Workshop on National Systems (Quezon City, Institute of Philippine Culture, 1988).

15. For a more-detailed description of changes made during the feasibility, preconstruction, construction, and operations and maintenance stages of the projects, see Frances F. Korten, *Building National Capacity to Develop Water Users' Associations: Experience from the Philippines,* World Bank Staff Working Paper no. 528 (Washington, D.C., 1982).

16. In 1988 the NIA was producing revised manuals on every aspect of the communals' program. These manuals included: 1) *Manual on the Participatory Approach in Communal Irrigation Projects (Preconstruction Phase)*; 2) *Manual on the Participatory Approach in Communal Irrigation Projects (Construction Phase)*; 3) *Communal Irrigation System Management, A Manual for Trainers (Operation and Maintenance Phase)*; 4) *Communal Irrigation System Management, A Manual for Facilitators*; 5) *Simplified Financial Management System Manual for Irrigators' Associations*; 6) *A Manual of Procedures for Participatory Irrigation Projects.* Revisions of earlier work carried out by Sylvia Jopillo, the Communal Irrigation Committee, and Arturo Margallo, were led by a team composed of Susan Leones, Grace Ignacio, Vicky Pineda, Karen Jacob, and Carmelo Cablayan.

17. For a fuller description of the development, content, and impact of the sociotechnical profiles, see Romana de los Reyes, *The Socio-Technical Profiles: A Tool for Rapid Rural Appraisal* (Quezon City, Philippines: Institute of Philippine Culture, 1984).

18. Different committees were created at different times depending on the needs of the project. Examples included committees for survey and design, bylaws, water permits, Securities and Exchange Commission registration, right-of-way, manpower survey, quality and quantity control, canvassing, bidding and procurement, and cost control.

19. An example of an issue requiring tight coordination between technical and institutional work was the acquisition of rights-of-way. The communal irrigators' association was expected to obtain right-of-way waivers for all canals from the individual owners of the land. Once

tentative locations of canals were determined the association would begin work on this. But if a particular right-of-way appeared to be unobtainable, the technical staff needed to be informed and alternative routes discussed. If the association was eventually able to obtain the right-of-way the alternatives could be abandoned. But if not, new efforts were needed on the alternative routes. Other activities such as the deployment of labor for construction and the receipt of construction materials required similarly close coordination.

20. Asian Institute of Management faculty played an important role in these initial workshops. Representing neither the institutional nor the technical viewpoint, and well-practiced in leading discussions, they were able to draw out both viewpoints and orient the discussions toward problem solving. For a fuller description of some of these differing viewpoints, see Edilberto de Jesus, "Managing Bureaucratic Reorientation," in John C. Ickis, Edilberto de Jesus, and Rushikesh Maru, eds., *Beyond Bureaucracy: Strategic Management of Social Development* (West Hartford, Conn.: Kumarian Press, 1986).

21. Arturo N. Margallo, *Cost Reconciliation Manual (Construction Phase)* (Quezon City: NIA, 1981).

22. Two studies were funded to develop ideas on how to help irrigators' associations with water management. In 1979 the APTECH Research Foundation was contracted by NIA to conduct water management studies on some of NIA's initial pilot participatory projects. In 1980 the Central Luzon State University received a grant from the Ford Foundation to study the water management of an indigenous communal irrigation system. The directors of these studies (Alan Early and Honorato Angeles) then became members of the System Management Working Group, along with key NIA personnel and other outside contributors. This group developed an approach to be used nationwide by NIA personnel.

Two studies were also undertaken to develop ideas on how to help irrigators' associations with financial management. In 1980 the BIOS Corporation was contracted by NIA to develop a financial management system and test it in three participatory communal projects. In 1982 the Development Academy of the Philippines was contracted by NIA to study financial management systems of some existing communal irrigation associations which had well-developed record keeping systems. The lessons from these efforts were applied in the financial management system in which NIA personnel were trained nationwide in 1983.

23. The details of the system are contained in Margallo, *Simplified Financial Management System Manual*.

24. This approach is fully described in two NIA manuals: *Communal Irrigation System Management Manual for Trainers* and *Communal Irrigation System Management Manual for Facilitators*. These manuals cover the development of plans for a cropping calendar, water distribution, maintenance management, conflict management, duties and responsibilities, and farm-level facilities.

25. David Korten provides an analysis of key internal management changes within the NIA which supported the participatory methods in "From Bureaucratic to Strategic Organization" in Frances F. Korten and Robert Y. Siy, eds., *Transforming a Bureaucracy: The Experience of the Philippine National Irrigation Administration* (West Hartford, Conn.: Kumarian Press, 1988, and Quezon City, Philippines: Ateneo de Manila University Press, 1989).

26. Felipe B. Alfonso, "Assisting Farmer Controlled Development of Communal Irrigation Systems," in David C. Korten and Felipe B. Alfonso, eds., *Bureaucracy and the Poor: Closing the Gap* (West Hartford, Conn.: Kumarian Press, 1983).

27. Paddy mapping was helpful in assessing this area—for both the NIA and the irrigators' association. For a description of this technique, see Alan C. Early and Benjamin U. Bagadion, "Custom Fit Design of Farm Ditches: A Participatory Approach to Making Irrigation Systems

Responsive to the Needs of the Farmers" (Los Banos: International Rice Research Institute, 1982; processed).

28. Costs are reported in standardized 1984 dollars, with a conversion rate of 20 pesos per U.S. dollar.

29. For a comprehensive report of this study, see Romana de los Reyes and Sylvia G. Jopillo, *An Evaluation of the Philippine Participatory Communal Irrigation Program* (Quezon City, Philippines: Institute of Philippine Culture, 1986). A shorter version of that report is also available in Romana de los Reyes and Sylvia Jopillo, "The Impact of Participation: An Evaluation of NIA's Communal Irrigation Program," in Frances F. Korten and Robert Y. Siy, eds., *Transforming a Bureaucracy: The Experience of the Philippine National Irrigation Administration* (West Hartford, Conn.: Kumarian Press, 1988, and Quezon City, Philippines: Ateneo de Manila University Press, 1989).

30. The financial rate of return is calculated assuming that the costs of the NIA's institutional activities were incurred as follows: 33 percent in year one; 55 percent in year two; and 12 percent in year three. The farmers' higher equity contribution on participatory systems of ₱303 is assumed to occur in year two. Repayment on the loan is assumed to begin in year four, with participatory systems paying on the average ₱87 per hectare per year more than nonparticipatory systems and maintaining that incremental rate of repayment through year ten.

31. Robert Chambers, "Men and Water: The Organization and Operation of Irrigation," in B. H. Farmer, ed., *Green Revolution? Technology and Change in Rice-Growing Areas of Tamil Nadu and Sri Lanka* (Boulder, Colo.: Westview Press, 1977), pp. 250–63.

32. In recognition of the importance of meaningful rights and authorities for water user organizations, in 1988 the Indonesian government began a program, with assistance from the World Bank, the Asian Development Bank, and the Ford Foundation, to transfer to water-user organizations the full management responsibility of the more than 2,000 government-run irrigation systems of under 500 hectares each. For a more comprehensive discussion of the importance of the rights and authorities of water user organizations see Frances F. Korten, "The Policy Framework for Community Management," in David C. Korten, ed., *Community Management: Asian Experience and Perspectives* (West Hartford, Conn.: Kumarian Press, 1986).

33. This point is elaborated in chapter 2.

34. This point was emphasized at a conference of Asian irrigation agency personnel, social scientists, and donors; see Walter Coward, Bruce Koppel, and Robert Siy, "Organization as a Strategic Resource in Irrigation Development: A Conference Report" (Honolulu: East-West Center Resource Systems Institute; and Manila: Asian Institute of Management, 1983).

35. A study of thirty-six small-farmer development projects worldwide found that the two components "most important in promoting overall success (were): small farmer involvement in decision making in the implementation phase of a development project; and small farmer resource commitment (labor and cash) to a development project." See Morss and others, *Strategies for Small Farmer Development*, p. 203.

36. Data on the spontaneous development of indigenous irrigation systems in the Philippines indicate that they follow a pattern. Local farmers band together to put logs and stones in a river and dig channels to bring water to their fields; the same individuals who initiate the system serve as the leaders for operation and maintenance; during the construction of the system, the farmers informally agree on rules and obligations for operating and maintaining it; later, farmers farther from the water source join in, committing themselves to the same rules and obligations for planning and constructing their own part of the system. Thus the social and physical systems develop simultaneously—often over a period of many years. See Romana

de los Reyes and others, *Communal Gravity Systems: Four Case Studies* (Quezon City: Institute of Philippine Culture, 1980); de los Reyes, *Forty-seven Communal Gravity Systems: Organization Profiles* (Quezon City: Institute of Philippine Culture, 1980).

37. In responding to this dilemma some programs have commissioned a different agency, with presumably greater capacities for dealing with people, to do the social organizing. However, such a solution divorces the organizational and technical activities and makes it difficult to involve the farmers in the key questions of planning, design, construction, and operation.

38. In the description of the NIA work, the term "project" was used to refer to a specific irrigation project. In the following section the term is used in the sense commonly used by the large international aid agencies to refer to a financial package to support a set of activities which may involve many different villages, provinces, or regions.

39. A more complete description of the structure, functions, and internal dynamics of the Communal Irrigation Committee can be found in Frances F. Korten, "The Working Group as a Catalyst for Organizational Change," in Frances F. Korten and Robert Y. Siy, eds., *Transforming a Bureaucracy: The Experience of the Philippine National Irrigation Administration* (West Hartford, Conn.: Kumarian Press, 1988, and Quezon City, Philippines: Ateneo de Manila University Press, 1989).

40. An interesting example of the use of a pilot activity within a large-scale loan is the Gal Oya irrigation project in Sri Lanka. Built into a large loan from the U.S. Agency for International Development (USAID) for system rehabilitation was experimental work in a pilot area where farmer involvement in rehabilitation, operation, and maintenance was encouraged. Although the pilot was originally to be concurrent with the larger project, delays in the larger project gave the pilot a significant head start. In this example, personnel from the Agrarian Research and Training Institute and Cornell University provided the special attention needed for learning from the pilot project, though it also meant that the Irrigation Department was not the central implementor of the pilot activity. For more details on this project, see Norman Uphoff, "Experience with People's Participation in Water Management: Gal Oya, Sri Lanka," in Jean-Claude Garcia-Zamor, *Participation in Development Planning and Management: Cases from Africa and Asia* (Boulder, Colo.: Westview Press, 1985).

41. The costs of implementing the projects were covered by other sources. Ford Foundation funds, in combination with NIA's own funds, were used for research, training, and workshops to support the learning process elements of the program.

42. For a useful discussion of social experiments and learning that took place during implementation of the large World Bank–funded PIDER project in Mexico, see Michael M. Cernea, *A Social Methodology for Community Participation in Local Investments: The Experience of Mexico,* World Bank Staff Working Paper no. 598 (Washington, D.C., August 1983), in particular section 2 on "The Production of a Methodology for Participation."

43. For example, the World Bank's Communal Irrigation Development Project in the Philippines included components for developing all of NIA's provincial irrigation offices and for training NIA personnel and farmers for communals regardless of whether they would be implementing the communal subprojects covered by the loan. The project thus has some generalized capacity-building orientation.

4

Middle-level Farmer Organizations as Links between Farms and Central Irrigation Systems

David M. Freeman and Max K. Lowdermilk

Engineering is not the fundamental problem underlying irrigation development in the LDCs. Engineering principles are known and can be adapted, but the major problem . . . is to discover ways to utilize farmer clients more effectively in operations and maintenance and in development programs which will create rural transformation. Rural transformation essentially requires changes in farmers' behavior, motivations, and expectations which is hardly possible until institutions exist to provide them with increased production possibilities and incentives.

—Aaron Wiener, *ICIDD Bulletin*

The communal task of creating and operating organizations has always been at the center of societal development. People in all cultures have recognized that they must make permanent arrangements to secure and manage collectively what they could not obtain individually. Irrigated agriculture has always meant the organized, collective attempt to control water efficiently to fulfill crop consumptive needs; and the progress of irrigation systems has always depended upon the design and quality of their respective irrigation organizations.

Irrigated agriculture has been disproportionately productive. At present, only about 18 percent of the world's cultivated land is irrigated, but it produces roughly 33 percent of this planet's human food supply.[1] But the fact that many landscapes of the world are now dominated by dams, reservoirs, and canals cannot hide a disquieting fact. Many irrigation projects have not served the needs of farmers and agricultural production.

Too many accounts of irrigation projects are notable for their reports of failure to meet projected agricultural production targets, of poor maintenance, of disappointing economic returns to investment, and of farmers who not only make little attempt to exploit their expensive water supplies to the degree which had been planned, but who undermine the functioning of the systems developed ostensibly to serve them. Montague Yudelman, reflecting on World Bank experience, has suggested that Bank irrigation projects have seldom met expectations.[2] The story of poor irrigation water management unfolds around inefficient water use, distributional inequities, disappointing cropping intensities and yields, and irrigation bureaucracies apparently unaware of farmers' needs to control water.

The thesis is that many recurrent problems in large-scale gravity flow irrigation systems stem from a failure to couple social rules with physical tools in local farmer irrigation organizations. To improve matters, farmer water demands must be linked to main system water supply management by an intermediate organization. This discussion thus focuses on designing irrigation organizations in the middle ground between central bureaucracies and farmers. It will formulate strategic propositions which can contribute to improved design of local irrigation organizations.

The model of sociological analysis suggested here has emerged from several years of fieldwork by the authors, primarily in irrigation systems in Pakistan and other Asian countries. Its central argument is that the design of the middle-level interface between farmers and the bureaucracy is a strategic determinant of farmers' water control and, therefore, of their productivity. With regard to the practical aspects of designing and implementing irrigation projects, the claim is a strong one: by ferreting out key variables affecting irrigation water control, social obstacles constraining the social and agricultural potential of irrigation can be avoided or removed.

The Dry and the Wet: Sociology and Irrigation

Development planners increasingly recognize that social organization is as fundamental to adequate project design as are accurate economic forecasting and precise technical design. This recognition is creating a constituency for increasing sociological participation in project preparation and implementation.

The irrigation systems referred to in this paper are primarily large, public, gravity systems. They have at least three organizational tiers: a centralized public bureaucracy, a local command area organization, and a farm level organization. Irrigation water management in South Asian organizations can be defined as a process by which large, technical bureaucracies capture and control water through central irrigation works, deliver it to local command areas which divide and control it further, and in turn pass it on to the farmer. The essential purpose, therefore, of construction or rehabilitation, allocation, maintenance, and conflict management at all levels of any irrigation system is to provide ultimate control over water to its users—the farmers. The extent to which this purpose is fulfilled indicates the effectiveness of the organization.

Only one individual—the farmer—combines the factors of production in a particular field and he or she either succeeds or fails to bring in a crop. Whatever the attributes of upstream organizations, the farmers must possess adequate control over water to place it in the crop root zones when it is most productive. Their requirements for water control too frequently go unnoted, and their attempts to gain effective control are too typically viewed as subverting the interests of more powerful interests at higher levels in the irrigation hierarchy.

Irrigation system components have been visualized in various ways.[3] There are, however, certain functions basic to all models. Figure 4-1 expresses two strategic aspects of canal systems. First, main system water supply managers approach water control with a fundamentally different set of interests than do farmers. The difference in interest, knowledge, and perspective necessitates an intermediate organizational level which can reconcile the farmer's water demand with central management's supply. Second, figure 4-1 asserts that, at each level of irrigation organization, physical works must be constructed and periodically rehabilitated in a nonroutine manner, water must be allocated, facilities must be routinely maintained, and conflicts arising over each activity must be managed so that the collective effort will be sustained. Irrigation organizations must be designed at several levels in order to perform the essential functions noted on figure 4-1.

Because the water supply provided by main system managements must mesh (top figure 4-1) with farmer crop water demand (bottom figure 4-1) in some organized fashion (middle figure 4-1), even if middle-level

irrigation organizations are not officially recognized by the state, patterned interaction must occur in an organized manner among farmers,
and between farmers and main system management.

Two examples of organizational levels drawn from recent case studies
illustrate this point. In the large, highly centralized irrigation system of
the Pakistani Punjab, main system management takes responsibility for
administering water supply from rivers through primary, secondary, and
tertiary canals to a fixed outlet (*mogha*) for each local watercourse. As
the water flows through each mogha, water responsibility shifts from the
main system to the local community of irrigators. Middle-level watercourses are collectively administered by farmers on a rotational scheme

Figure 4-1. *The Organization of Irrigation Systems*

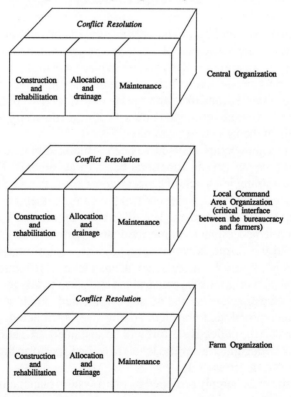

(*warrabundi*). Whatever water is available in a watercourse during a given time period flows through the watercourse outlet (*nacca*) to a farmer's field or field ditch, where the water flows into the domain of the individual farmer. Varying crop consumptive demands must be melded with main system supply via the middle-level watercourse organization. Farmers individually and in groups unofficially go upstream beyond the mogha on the main system distributary to make arrangements for water. The de facto middle-level organizational interface, therefore, is not confined to the local watercourse. In the case of two adjacent tank systems in Sri Lanka, main system management assumes official responsibility for construction, water allocation, maintenance, and conflict management all the way from rivers and reservoirs through primary, secondary, tertiary, and quaternary channels, ostensibly to the farm gate. However, the de facto arrangement is that a traditional local water manager, known as a *Vel Vidane*, who lives in the local command and has no officially sanctioned status, works with farmers to allocate water. This system enjoys variable success during periods of low to moderate water demand. On sample distributaries, however, none of the Vel Vidanes could stand up to allocation pressures during periods of peak demand. Local farmers, knowing well that the role of Vel Vidanes was not supported by an adequate middle-level organization, referred to him as ". . . a cup without a saucer." The research question is not whether middle-level arrangements exist between farmers and main system managements; it is whether the middle-level organizational arrangements provide farmers with viable water control arrangements.

The extent to which the water supply is in tune with biological requirements of crops depends on the operations of all three organizational levels. Water control at the levels of the command area and the farm is the most basic yardstick against which to measure the effectiveness of irrigation. Water control is never absolute at any level of an irrigation system; it relates to the particular needs of the crop at a particular moment. The term as used here means the relative control over quantity and timing of supplies.[4] Actual control over water at the farm is a direct outcome of the organizational networks established to operate the physical structures at higher levels. The effectiveness with which irrigation water gets to root zones is a function of the organizations created to allocate water, maintain and rehabilitate works, and manage conflict within and among all levels.

The systemic meanings and requirements of water control typically shift as one moves from level to level within the irrigation system (depicted in figure 4-1). The critical differences are:

- At the highest organizational level, water control means keeping the flow of large volumes of water within key parameters so that the main system functions smoothly. The many requirements of diverse local commands are aggregated and dealt with on the basis of average requirements and behaviors. Managers of the central system are not rewarded or punished according to the farm productivity of the water. They can depend on the knowledge of engineers, public administrators, sociologists, economists, and the like, without knowing specific details of the operations of local command areas and farms. They think of water control in terms of operational smoothness.
- At the farm level, water control means primarily the capacity to place relatively small volumes of water in particular crop root zones at the proper time and in the required amounts. The farmer cannot focus on average behavior in the main system or command area, but must distribute water according to the unique conditions of particular fields and crops. Farmers are rewarded and punished according to the controllability and productivity of water. Farmers think of water control primarily as the capacity to adapt rapidly to changing field conditions. These may vary widely within fields, among fields, and among farms.
- At the level of the local command area, where the main system and farm systems meet, water control primarily means dividing the water of the main system into volumes appropriate for farm application.

The Problem: Farmer Water Control

In irrigated agriculture, farmers must get moisture to crop roots in the technically dynamic and socially tumultuous environment of an irrigation system which has all too often been designed by distant administrators, engineers, and politicians.

The problems of water control at the local level cannot be solved exclusively by social scientists, technical professionals, or farmers operating independently of each other. The sociologist who finds reasons in the local system to advocate a particular combination of share types but does not consider the cost and technical feasibility of the necessary physical structures, is guaranteeing great organizational difficulty, just as is the engineer who designs control and measurement structures without knowing much about local organizations. Representatives of technical disciplines must not be viewed as irrelevant to the problem of the social organization design; nowhere is the contribution of the engineer, agronomist, or economist more required than in selecting the type of share system.

The problems of water control are fundamentally conditioned by technical constraints. One such constraint is often inadequate capacity for water storage surface reservoirs. Clearly, if no storage is available, water use flexibility is substantially reduced, but share arrangements which maximize the possibilities for local water exchange can enhance even the limited control available on run-of-the-river systems. Interdisciplinary analysis, with farmer participation, is needed to determine which share arrangements will best allow groundwater or reservoir water to compensate for deficiencies in water flow.[5]

It has been estimated that more than 50 million farmers in Asia with 1 hectare of land or less have access to undeveloped fresh water within 2 meters of the surface.[6] Groundwater is a public good—a common resource available to any farmer with sufficient capital to exploit it. But, as a collective good, it requires social-organizational rules to guide and discipline its use. Since aquifer recharge is a dynamic process in which pumping rates interact in complex ways with river and canal depletions and recharges, the social scientist and the farmer cannot blithely make organizational rules for its use without careful collaboration with technical specialists. Engineers and hydrologists, in turn, cannot specify pumping regimes without regard to impact on organizational charters and social dynamics.

In most large-scale systems, especially in Asia, upstream control systems are designed without regard to the problems faced by farmers in securing local control over irrigation water.[7] Engineers have provided a transport system for water via rivers, canals, reservoirs, and diversion structures. Planners have assumed that if water flowed in the general direction of command areas, good water management at the local level would evolve automatically simply because it was needed.

The lack of adequate local control embodied in effective organizations that can provide for effective water management brings with it economic, agronomic, social, and ecological costs. Many so-called management problems in irrigation projects are in fact rooted in poor organizational design.[8] Because high-yielding plant varieties demand precise applications of water, farmers with inadequate control are rational to refrain from investing in those varieties and in the associated inputs such as fertilizers and pesticides. As control over water diminishes, farmers find it necessary to use increasing quantities of water whenever it is available to meet minimum crop needs. Thus, overirrigation and associated problems of waterlogging and salinity are exacerbated by poor water control.

Irrigated agriculture creates new forms of uncertainty while overcoming the uncertainties associated with rainfed agriculture. In bureaucratically rigid, large-scale surface irrigation systems, these may be greater than the original uncertainty of the rainfed situation.[9] Because political pressures have historically spread available supplies thinly over wide command areas, they face rigid systems of distribution.[10] In much of South Asia, farmers face the worst of both worlds: they receive inadequate quantities of water and they confront rigid distribution systems. Analysts have reported the variability of crop yields actually increasing in Indian-irrigated agriculture. This disturbing phenomenon has been associated with the failure to provide minimally adequate water control in many surface irrigation systems.[11]

Given their double bind, farmers in India and Pakistan appropriate all ways possible that will allow them a minimum of water control. Such control comes at high costs, and sometimes through "deviant" behavior—illegal purchases and trade, water theft, and bribery of officials to secure concessions—or by investing in private tubewells.[12] Of all these options, investment in private tubewells has been the most examined.

The evidence for the desirability of tubewells which permit local control is overwhelming. Because tubewell water is available on demand, it is of higher value than the canal water provided by rigid large-scale surface irrigation systems.[13] Table 4-1 displays evidence from a sample of forty Pakistan command areas which shows that access to private tubewell water is significantly associated with increased yields and farm incomes. Yields and gross income per hectare jump substantially when farmers are able to secure greater water control via tubewells.

Given the value of controllable tubewell water, farmers in certain areas in India have revealed a willingness to pay from six to ten times the water charges levied for canal supplies.[14] Fixed weekly rotation schedules, associated with so much South Asian surface irrigation, may provide a constant quantity of water per week regardless of local conditions. Variations in weather and crop requirements, however, require unequal water applications within farms, within command areas, and within larger sets of command areas. In this context it is no surprise that farmers should be willing to go to great lengths to obtain a modicum of water control.

Organization Building for Irrigation

Despite impassioned calls for farmer participation in irrigation water management, in much of South Asia command area organizations do not exist to provide means through which farmers can hope to secure control over their irrigation water.[15] This harsh fact lies at the basis of the severe problems of local farmer water control.

The practical question is: what sociological variables must be considered in an analysis of the requirements for creating such middle-level organizations or for rectifying deficiencies in existing ones? We detail a set of strategic sociological variables relevant to this problem. In this section, the suggestions are based on our field experience in various Asian countries and require modification and adaptation to the situations prevalent elsewhere.

Table 4-1. *Average Yields for Sample Wheat and Cotton Farms, with and without Tubewells, Pakistan, 1975–76*
(kilograms per hectare)

Crop	Private tubewell	No tubewell
Wheat	2,199.5	1,649.5
Cotton	1,191.5	641.5

Note: During 1975–76 intermittent rains in the Kharif (summer) season created soil crustation that inhibited the emergence of the plants. Yields were especially low because some farmers had two plantings. Private tubewell farmers were able to provide a thin, timely irrigation to soften the soil crust and thus achieved better plant populations. This explains the low yields of nontubewell farmers.

Source: These data result from a field study carried out in Pakistan as part of a larger Colorado State University research Project, sponsored by the U.S. Agency for International Development (USAID). For more details, see Max K. Lowdermilk, Alan C. Early, and David M. Freeman, *Farm Irrigation Constraints and Farmers' Responses: Comprehensive Field Survey in Pakistan*, Water Management Technical Report no. 48 A-F (Fort Collins, Colo.: Colorado State University, 1978), vol. 4.

To rehabilitate an existing system or build a new one, a technological package must be developed to control the water. The technologies, which must be project and site specific, might include: main system control structures, measuring devices, management information systems, rational water codes, and other software or hardware (social or physical infrastructure) to supply water on a reliable basis to the middle-level reaches. Again, at the middle level, the proper mix of hardware and software will be needed for water allocation and conveyance from the main system outlet to each farm. Both the organizational mode and the infrastructure must be designed and implemented together. This obvious coupling of the water technology with the management organizations rarely extends past project appraisal. In India, for example, the conventional approach is to design the physical infrastructure of the main system and to deliver water to the heads of command areas with no organization or infrastructure beyond the main system outlet. Ten to fifteen years later, as the command area is developed, there is a panic-stricken search for some organizational mode to handle water management. Clearly the cart has been placed before the horse![16]

Once the technology has been established, central and local command area organizations must be designed to operate the new technological package. The design must provide specific means to fulfill the four functions of any irrigation organization: nonroutine construction and rehabilitation, water allocation and proper disposal of unused water, routine maintenance, and management of conflicts between members.

Each local organization must be soundly linked to individual farmers and to middle-level servicing and monitoring organizations. Development of the new organization breaks down into two fundamental tasks: the design of the organizational charter and the management of ongoing organizational activities after acceptance of the charter. The fundamental problem is to structure these linkages so that irrigation water control at the farm level is increased to the maximum level possible given social, physical, and economic constraints.

Design for Precarious Partnerships: The Charter

Water control is a function of collective actions and can be enhanced only through disciplined organizations.[17] The power of any organization lies in the agreement among members that rewards and punishments will be employed in certain specific ways to get members to do what they would not do if detached from the network. Organizations without predictable rewards and punishments have no capacity to deliver joint action in predetermined, predictable ways. These joint agreements about the use of rewards and punishments in the collective interest are critical for at least two reasons. First, such agreements on joint action constrain brute coercive force. Second, they constrain the use of money to its proper sphere in the marketplace and prevent it from unjustly distorting the distribution of nonmarket resources through corruption, connections, and political exchange.

In any viable irrigation association, each irrigator has certain specified organizational rights and duties by virtue of joint collective agreement rather than by personal physical prowess or wealth. Any leadership which cannot enforce joint agreements on particular members with the consent of the general membership is not a viable entity. Formalized joint agreements, or charters, are codifications of precarious partnerships which are always subject to test and renegotiation among farmers themselves, the local command area personnel, and the central bureaucracy.

Charters specify rules for behavior within and among organizations. An effective organizational charter is not simply handed down by the irrigation agency authorities, but evolves from experimentation with farmers. Maximum feasible control over water should be given to the smallest organized group of farmers possible, but such small organizational units are constrained by the operating requirements of the larger system.

There are, then, at least three basic research and design problems recurrent in middle-level organizational planning. First, ascertaining the appropriate social group—the "smallest possible unit" that can manage water delivery is a matter of empirical investigation. Cooperating groups are not given automatically by kinship or neighborhood. As one anthropologist commented, social relationships in extended families and corporate villages are as likely to be back-to-back as face-to-face. Second, the social structural architecture, norms, and principles of behavioral interaction must be understood clearly before they can be expected to work in the context of the systemic stresses that will be placed on them once incorporated into the irrigation bureaucracy. And third, project planners must understand and overcome the constraints currently limiting existing local organizations' interaction with regional and national groups.

These precarious, delicately balanced partnerships must be incorporated in the design for charters of local command area organizations. Two great faults in the construction of charters, which often occur under the pressure of time during the implementation of irrigation projects, are the failure to include staff with sociological skills to help prepare the charter, and the failure to coordinate properly the simultaneous development of hardware and software.

The general organizational charter must be defined and accepted by the users of the new technology before ditches are built or rehabilitated, before tubewells are installed or overhauled, before new or rehabilitated canals deliver water, and before reservoir gates are opened. It is always disastrous to proceed with the physical technology to get the water flowing with only vague notions about what joint agreements should be devised for rehabilitation, allocation, maintenance, and conflict resolution. The reason is simple: when water flows, some farmers are in better initial positions than others to take advantage of the resource. They quickly employ their good fortune to consolidate disproportionate advantages, and then oppose later attempts to reform the situation—usually with success because of their hold on critical resources.[18] Forms of joint action can hardly be optimum if they must operate in a context of distorted resource distribution.

What must be done to build viable organizations? Since each local command area is physically and socially distinct, general principles of organization must combine with local realities. Any organization must begin with a general description of its goals and structure. This is the charter.

Farmers require and respect solid, enforceable agreements which provide the basis for trust and genuine cooperation, but agreements can emerge only when the collective organizational units can constrain the brute power of force and money. This requires that members perceive their organization as politically neutral, neither acting against their collective interests in relation to outsiders, nor favoring any particular group within the membership. Thus, in India farmers at times ask government authorities to intervene to settle volatile local disputes. As one Indian farmer remarked, "We need an outside source to intervene at times because we who must live and work here want to avoid the repercussions which often take place between groups with age-old enmities."[19]

The key sociological variable is organizational credibility: Do farmer participants believe it will do any good to appeal to organizational joint agreements when they are threatened by money or force? Do they genuinely believe that, if an important agreement is violated and a member is wronged, the organization will come to the defense in a predictable manner according to prearranged procedures? If not, the organization exists in name only.

The problem of organization neutrality raises deep sociological questions about the meaning of local control, questions that require carefully analyzed empirical data about any given field situation. Rural communities are characterized by socioeconomic differentiation and political schisms. These differences can be overcome, as they often are by NGOs and indigenous organizations, but the problems are particularly pronounced when large, external bureaucracies are involved.

Without close attention to sociological design, local control will quickly degenerate into local domination. Fortunately, even among the best-intentioned technological populists, the pattern of neglecting local culture because it was archaic and irrelevant has too often been replaced by one where the same neglect can be justified because the "people can do it all." The "people," however, do not live in a sociological vacuum; without a full understanding of local social structure and systemic linkages, there is little reason to expect increased local accountability, or improved performance.

In certain projects—in Nepal, Indonesia, Philippines, and the Republic of Korea—the World Bank has specified the formation of viable water users' associations as a precondition for disbursing funds for construction.[20] When project designers have been aware of and have cooperated with local irrigation groups, such associations have proven to be important sources of information and project support. Generally, however, such associations are established during the start-up phase of the project or in midstream—if at all—although some experiences suggest that they can be organized effectively *before* the project begins.

The Bangladesh deep tubewells project provides an example of what frequently occurs when water is allowed to flow through new irrigation technology before the organizational charter has been drawn up with local command area farmers. A study of deep public tubewells has revealed that, at five sites, the groups or individuals who had made the initial efforts to locate the tubewell subsequently controlled its management for years.[21] Four or five systems were operated by small, informal groups of farmers who had organized on their own to procure and operate a deep tubewell from the Bangladesh Agricultural Development Corporation. In each case, the system was a product of the effort of one farmer—a large landlord who owned about 20 hectares of land in the command area. One system has evolved a relatively broad-based, participatory farmer management structure, while three systems operate under the guidance of a few influential local farmers. In the fifth instance, one farmer became a virtual water lord. In at least one case, influential people pressured to have the tubewells placed in less than optimal locations. Their own needs were met, but water could not be run up the gradient to many farmers who would otherwise have been well served; in one case, a tubewell with the capacity to irrigate approximately 70 hectares was effectively irrigating about fifteen.

Throughout the study area, rules for allocating water and maintaining infrastructure were never formulated. Pump and channel maintenance is poor. In short, while individual farmers did apply the water that arrived with considerable efficiency, in no case were there organizational arrangements for exploiting the potential of available tubewell technology. The lack of necessary agreements for joint action translated into technical deficiencies.

All of the systems we studied in Pakistan, Thailand, Sri Lanka, Bangladesh, Egypt, and India needed to evolve and define mutually reinforcing, functional roles for irrigation and agricultural authorities and farmers, and provide training commensurate with the roles. The perceived roles are often in direct conflict with each other and, while studies are needed to ascertain the magnitude of this problem, delineating role boundaries within organizations is clearly a general problem.

The discussion turns now to choices that must be made in the initial design of organizational joint agreements, as summarized in figure 4-2.

Staffing

The organizational charter must establish rules for staffing. Small differences in these rules can have large consequences for organizational behavior.[22] Students of irrigation have come to some common conclusions about a staffing strategy.

On the one hand, the charter can specify that the local command area organization be staffed by "cosmopolitans," who may be recruited from outside the local command area on the basis of educational qualifications. These counterbalance technical expertise against a substantial social distance between staff and farmers. The nature of their employment and

Figure 4-2. *Key Variables in the Construction of an Organizational Charter*

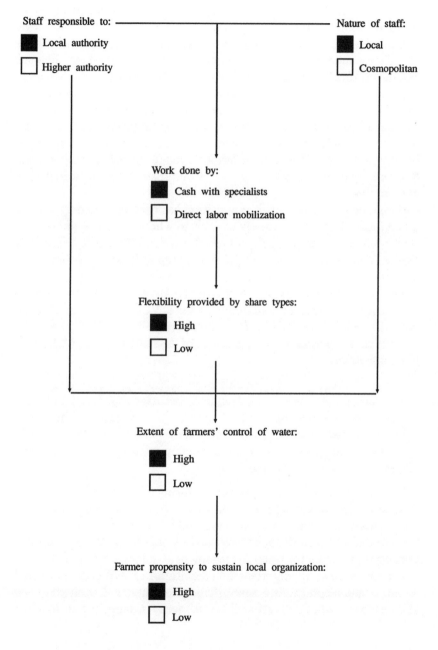

the criteria used to define success are given by their superiors. The cosmopolitan staff aspire to upward, or at least diagonal mobility, which often means short-term involvement with the local command area.

On the other hand, the charter may specify that the middle-level organization be staffed by locals who are recruited on the basis of local experience and social ties. The nature of the tasks performed by this staff and the criteria for success will derive from farmers within the irrigation command. Locals tend to be more accountable to farmers, more subject to local pressures, and more inserted into local communication networks. Local staffs accountable to farmers have greater incentives to increase their competence because incompetence is punished. They are seen as being more responsive to local farmers' requirement for water control than are cosmopolitans who are more marginal to the local irrigation community.

Evidence in support of this proposition has been provided by, among others, A. F. Bottrall, in a study of Taiwan where farmers employ local staff to manage the command area. Bottrall has seen this as a key explanation for the relatively high level of organizational responsiveness to the farmers' need for water control.[23] Clifford Geertz, in an anthropological study of the Balinese *subak* (irrigation society) drew the same conclusion: command area staffs consisting of locals produce greater and more dependable water control than do cosmopolitan staffs.[24] In another context, and looking at the opposite side of the same variable, M. E. Abel has commented:

> The appropriate government unit hires and (rarely) fires management. The farmers who use, or wish to use, the irrigation water have little direct control over the performance of the managers. This weak linkage between management and farmers can—and does—lead to inefficient distribution of water and makes it difficult to adjust water distribution to changes in technology.[25]

Evidence to support the importance of hiring locals in the middle-level water organizations also comes from cross-national case studies recently completed in Pakistan, India, Thailand, and Sri Lanka.[26] In each instance, the substantial social distance between cosmopolitan staff and farmers presented problems for water management at the middle level.

Perhaps even more important than the origins of staff is the system of authority and responsibility established by the charter. The charter must also establish whether staff will be primarily responsible to local or higher authority. Typically, staff responsible to a higher authority are paid by the higher organization, are affiliated with the civil service, and have ambitions for promotion in the central hierarchy which will take them from the command area. It is hypothesized that the more the command area staff are responsible to local farmers and are compensated from command area resources, the greater the local control over water produced by the organization.

The work of Robert Wade in the Republic of Korea is relevant to both of the above propositions. Parastatal organizations currently irrigate approximately 36 percent of Korean irrigated farmland. The majority of the command area organization staff are born and raised in the locale in which they work and are from the same social class as local farmers. So attached to the local area are staff members that transfer out of the command area is a major threat for breach of duty. Yet, interestingly enough, these locals are not formally responsible to local farmers, who play a relatively small role in decisionmaking. The staff look to higher bureaucratic authority for definitions of success, are not directly accountable to local command area farmers, and look upon their positions as lifetime employment in the bureaucracy. Salary scales are based on length of service and promotion is based on a merit system beyond the reach of farmers. Although, in theory, water allocation is centralized, command area irrigation staff possess such poor operational information that farmers have evolved a local demand system, which works largely because water is abundant and little pressure is placed on the command area organization.[27] Because water control structures are poorly maintained, the potential for water control is far from fully realized. This pattern suggests that the structure of authority is at least as relevant to water control as the pattern of staff recruitment (local or cosmopolitan).

An important subset of the general staffing problem is staffing for routine maintenance. Middle-level organizations should undertake routine maintenance with local resources, in our view, for at least two reasons: the central bureaucracy is unlikely to be in a position to bear recurrent local maintenance costs; and central irrigation authorities are typically unable to secure adequate information about local maintenance requirements. Local command area organizational charters must, therefore, provide for agreement among farmer members for maintenance.

There are, again, two strategic options. Routine maintenance can be performed by staff hired full- or part-time for the purpose and paid in cash or kind, or by farmer members who must perform maintenance work in specified periods or be subject to penalty.[28] It is hypothesized that the more maintenance is performed by full- or part-time employees of the local farmers' organization, the greater the control of local farmer members over water. Individuals who work full- or part-time on maintenance acquire specialized skills and knowledge not available to the general farm membership. There is greater response flexibility to a problem from full- or part-time maintenance staff, because the work can be performed when required, not just during slack labor periods of the general farm membership.

Relying only on farmer labor allows much opportunity for "free riding." It may appear rational for certain individual farmers to schedule other activities during the time that labor is to be mobilized so as to avoid contributing their labor share, but the irrigators' organization is then on the defensive; it must proceed against free riders in ways which may erode support for the organization or at the very least cost dearly in resources expended. Our experience with difficulties of mobilizing labor contributions suggests that it is less disruptive to the farmer organization to collect revenue in advance of water delivery according to some concept of water share (see allocation section in this chapter) and hire staff to perform routine maintenance.

Improved maintenance is not just a matter of local control. A study of forty watercourse commands in Pakistan in which we participated, found a generally low level of maintenance, and estimated that 5 million acre-feet of scarce water could be saved in the Punjab and Sind for field application simply by proper maintenance of the local community watercourses.[29] All watercourses in the sample were cleaned and maintained by mobilizing farmers, who worked together at certain periods to clean the main channel or were assigned to kinship groups to clean certain sections. Everywhere, large landlords and other village influentials could escape maintenance duties, and the quality of maintenance was low. Sanctions against a free rider who wished to use irrigation water without providing a fair proportion of labor were divisive and difficult to enforce.

Effective labor mobilization for maintenance requires great social cohesion because all farmers must collectively harness themselves to the communal duty. In the many cases where the cohesion to do this is lacking, organizational forms that permit local-level cooperation must be adapted from other arenas or, at times, invented, to override schisms within and between levels.

Developing these organizational forms demands in-depth knowledge of local sociocultural systems and it is impossible to overstress the value of this understanding if participation is to mean more than a slogan. The assumption that local social organization can be ignored because the technical planners know better too often has been replaced by the equally blithe assumption that social organization can be ignored because irrigators will perceive their own best interest and transcend the social and cultural barriers to cooperative action.

The difficulties posed by trying to form local organizations without incorporating general principles of social interaction, which often include hierarchy and conflict, is illustrated by Merrey's description of efforts to form local-level water management associations in Pakistan's Indus valley region. After several attempts to form local water users' associations to improve water delivery efficiencies, he found that ". . . these organizational and cultural impediments, together with the ineffectiveness of the overly centralized bureaucratic management structure of the system, are at the root of the low productivity of the system . . ."[30]

In our view, the Pakistan case illustrates the desirability of hiring full- or part-time maintenance staff who will develop the necessary skills and information and be available at all times for duty. In India's Maharashtra State, for example, there is a community system known as *Phad*. In this system, farmers hire "community irrigators" to irrigate all the fields in the command area. They thus ensure that all fields are irrigated with roughly equivalent amounts of water.[31]

Water Allocation

Organizational charters must address the problem of resource allocation. What rules will determine who shall get what water and how the costs of providing it shall be paid? Gilbert Levine has noted that irrigation planners have rarely given these considerations meaningful attention.[32] In India, for example, adherence to bureaucratic tradition leads to the absurd situation in which each state applies the same water-sharing formulas throughout its irrigated area irrespective of agroclimatic and other significant differences.[33] Again in India, there are those who advocate extending the northern India *warabundi* system to all states, overlooking the special conditions and the infrastructure that make the system work fairly well in Punjab and Haryana.[34]

The concept of "share" is central; members of the local organization possess shares of water resources. To exert demand on the organization for water service, one asserts a right to that service based on shareholding rules. A share is always two-sided: it confers a resource within certain prearranged rules, and it imposes a cost or assessment on the user to pay costs of local water control, not the water per se. The concept of share, therefore, unites two essential aspects of organizational life: the gathering of revenues through assessments and the delivery of water to the members. The question is, then, what joint actions will be organized by the charter for the management of shares?

Organizational charters can specify water shares in some combination of the following: (1) fixed percentage allotments by volume or by time period rotation, (2) a priority system based on location (near the head or the tail of the channel), farm characteristics (time of settlement), or economic value of the crop, and (3) user demand placed on a surface reservoir or on groundwater. Depending on local circumstances many combinations are possible.[35]

Share systems may be combined by constraining one type of share by another—for example, shares by volume subject to crop priorities. Two types of shares can be used simultaneously, as when shares by time rotation are supplemented by higher-priced demand water. Share systems may shift in response to changes in the environment; for example, from shares by volume to shares by time of settlement. The many different irrigation allocation arrangements are various combinations of these basic share types. For example, the warabundi systems of the Pakistan and Indian Punjab are simple combinations of shares by time period rotation and priority-based on location.

Martin and Yoder have presented a case study of two Nepali systems—Chherlung and Argali—which makes clear how farmers have successfully created distinctly different organizations around purchased water share arrangements, each of which closely tie water delivery to farmer payment of assessments.[36] In Argali, farmers devised a system of sharing water by allocating channel flow in proportion to the area irrigated whereas, at Chherlung, water was shared out by fixed proportions of flow volumes which could be detached from any given piece of land. The latter provided an incentive to increase water use efficiency by obtaining the greatest possible productive value from each unit of water, so that the water saved could be transferred to other irrigators who were willing to pay that fraction of the costs of managing it.

Water control problems assume different forms depending upon which combination of share distributional types manage the resource from the main system to the middle level and, in turn, from the middle-level organization to the farm gate. There are three facets of the organizational problem: (1) defining membership in the irrigation organization, (2) connecting water supply and control with member fulfillment of maintenance obligations to the organization, and (3) addressing the differential impact of head and tail location in the system on water access.

First, to be a member of the irrigation community, one must be defined as such. Designers of middle-level irrigation organizations must address the issue of membership in the irrigation community and the nature of the share system devised will have everything to do with how the issue is resolved. One does not become a member of an irrigation community simply by living in an area proximate to canal flows. Each observed water distributional system specifies a means by which people are defined as legitimate irrigators. For example, in a typical Indian or Pakistani warabundi system built on the principle of allocating a share of the 168-hour week in direct proportion to the amount of cultivatable land both owned or operated by the irrigator in the approved command area, one becomes a member of the irrigation community by owning or using land within the main system-approved command area. However, if one operates a local organization on the principle that proportions of channel flow shall be allocated on the basis of proportions of investment in the organization without regard to acreage, then ownership of organizational shares or "stock" defines organizational membership, as is the case at Chherlung in Nepal, and in some systems in Spain and the United States.[37] In these cases, joint agreements about distributional shares become agreements about who is, or is not, a member of the irrigation organization.

Secondly, those who work with farmers to create effective water-share systems must confront another strategic choice—how closely will water service be connected to the fulfillment of organizational obligations for maintenance? Virtually everywhere, water ownership is retained by the state for public direction and purpose and farmers cannot pay assessments to "own" water. Yet, water supply and control exacts costs throughout the system, including the lower, more decentralized levels, just as it does in the upstream reaches under the jurisdiction of main system management. Controlling water on tertiary or quaternary channels closer to specific farmer demand schedules may present problems substantially different from managing water in a given set of primary and secondary canals, but water control costs must still be paid—costs of staff, measurement and division devices, channel maintenance, and conflict management. If one designs a program for recruiting local people who will be responsible to the farmer irrigation community, then the local organization must pay, if not all, at least a significant fraction of the wages and salaries or it will lose control over the ability to hire and dismiss such personnel and to define the degree of their success, and the nature of their job priorities. Middle-level organizations do not raise resources to "own" water, but to pay operation and maintenance costs for managing water under the organization's jurisdiction. Two questions arise:

- Are organizational joint agreements about water distributional share systems established such that water service depends directly upon member payment for one's share of the cost? Alternatively, is water delivery divorced from fulfillment of members' cost obligations?
- Are farmer shares of organizational costs at least roughly proportionate to water service received?

Patterns of water management observed at four case study sites—in Pakistan, central India, Northeast Thailand, and Sri Lanka—establish that in no case was there a close connection between water delivery and farmer contribution of payment in cash or kind for local maintenance. In the Pakistan case, farmers pay an assessment based upon crop type and estimated yield and they make such payments in a manner unrelated to water supply or control received at the farm gate. Therefore, a farmer receiving relatively good canal water service pays according to the same assessment schedule as one who receives relatively poor service. In the Indian, Thai, and Sri Lankan cases, water service and fee collection were also found to be unrelated. In each of the case study systems, those who fail to pay their assessments are not meaningfully penalized; farmer free-riding is the norm, and in the Indian case at least, uncollected revenues had mounted to considerable sums. Farmers are quick to see that, from an individually rational standpoint, one is foolish to pay water assessments—especially those whose water supply and control are decidedly inferior—when water service is not substantially affected by making payment. To disconnect farmer payment of assessments for maintenance, whether in cash or kind, from water delivery is virtually to invite organizational decay.

With regard to the second question, farmers in each of the case studies referred to above were intensely interested in having their water assessments reflect something of the absolute volume or proportion of water flow obtained. A share system which connects variation in volume or proportion of water flow to variation in assessment is likely to earn greater enthusiasm from farmers than one which does not. For example, in the Pakistan case study site located on the Niazbeg distributary, there is a strong inverse relationship between water cost and control. Given a canal system operated under a fixed rotational system, and given irrigation revenue assessments disconnected from actual water deliveries, the more disadvantaged farmers pay much more per unit of water delivered than those advantaged by head locations where canal water supplies are greater. A perverse relationship emerges—the worse the water supply and control situation, the higher the cost per unit of water delivered. This situation did not earn warm support from farmers to whom such matters are most important even if it is not a central consideration on the main system management agenda. The cost of tubewell water in the Niazbeg distributary sample watercourse command area was roughly 340 percent more than the cost of canal water, but not only was it worth more due to its high controllability but the relationship between amount of payment and amount of water received is direct. Data presented in the Pakistan case study shows strong farmer preference for the tubewell water arrangement as compared to the canal water system even though their tubewell water costs were substantially higher.

A third aspect of the share distributional problem can be stated as a question: does the share system reinforce or resolve the problem of "head" and "tail" location given by geography? Water must flow in channels from point A to B. Farmers toward point B are, by definition, nearer to the tail and—all else being equal—will be disadvantaged in terms of receiving water allocations relative to those increasingly near point A. The more one proceeds towards the tail of an irrigation channel, the more one is vulnerable to: (1) losses due to leaks, seepage, and evaporation, (2) self-interested manipulations of others toward the head as the number of irrigators intervening between farmer X and the head increases, and (3) nonroutine breakdowns in the system—there is simply more to go wrong when one is dependent upon longer channels.

Engineers must construct canals with head and tail positions, but it is up to designers of social organizations to decide whether the potentials for head-tail distinctions are to be realized by organizational share systems.

Case studies of Pakistani, Indian, Sri Lankan, and Thai rotational water delivery systems show that they reinforce and solidify the head-tail discriminations. Allotting water by time and location reinforces what engineers and geography have already done; it creates a fundamental difference in interest between irrigators at head and tail positions which inevitably threatens the solidarity of any local farmer organization. Irrigators located near the head do not experience the same water supply and control problems faced by their neighbors toward the tail and they typically find their relatively advantageous situation to be threatened by the desires for reform on the part of tail-enders. Satisfying tail demands for more timely water thus appears to come at the expense of relatively advantaged head-enders who, not unexpectedly, show less enthusiasm for solving problems of tail-enders.

Water supplies at tail positions are, however, a problem only to the extent that the organizational design of the share system fails to overcome them. If the middle-level organization should employ a combination of share types that impose the costs of "water loss" or "shrink" on all members without respect to location, then all members have an equal incentive to pay maintenance and operation costs for the system as a whole. If channel losses anywhere are distributed by the share system to all, irrigators at all locations have an equal concern to reduce losses at any one point. If, for example, the organization should charge for shares defined by volume, or by volume combined with some form of demand, and if volumes are measured so that losses anywhere on the common channel reduce volumes to all irrigators, then all farmers absorb the "shrink" and all have an incentive to reduce losses through better channel maintenance. In short, views of "head" and "tail" as inevitable natural phenomena must be set aside. Uncritical willingness to accept "heads" and "tails" in irrigation commands is the result of poor organizational analysis of share types, and is not a reflection of universal physical necessity.

Conflict Management

Organizational charters must address the problems of conflict management. Conflict over matters of allocation, maintenance, and construction and rehabilitation is inevitable, and there should be procedures for its effective resolution which strengthen commitments to the joint enterprise. For disputes to be resolved impartially, they should not be investigated and heard by regular managers: no person should be in the position of judging his or her own case.

The social organization of an irrigation system must provide for a local council or water court capable of adjudicating the interests of members and managers. This judicial council must interpret and apply organizational rules in specific cases of conflict and then pass on its interpretations to organizational executives for implementation. Members of the council should be from the local community; access to the council must be cheap, quick, and easy.[38] In some form, the charter must provide a routine for resolving conflict so that commitment to the organization will not be eroded, and the norm of due process will earn the allegiance of the members.

Organizational Behavior and Deviance

The result of a set of negotiated agreements on joint actions, the command area organization is inherently the dynamic outcome of continuous bargaining and struggle among its members and between the local organization, the central irrigation bureaucracy, and other non-irrigation groups in the area. Canal maintenance, construction, and water allocation always occur within a nested set of other social relationships—kinship, political, religious, educational, work, and recreational. Compliance with the rules of the local irrigation command organization will be judged not only according to the expectations of local irrigators, but also according to rules formulated for behavior in these other networks. To judge one party as not complying with the irrigation rules may be to reject or compromise other important social rules, a fact that can make life complicated for promoters of irrigation organization.

Anthropologists who studied the organization of the subak in Balinese villages in Indonesia concluded that the more inclusive and precise the set of irrigation rules or customs, the more dependable the distribution system.[39] To provide the common understanding essential to dependability, the process of organization building must go beyond specification of the charter and address questions of actual organizational behavior.

These conditions are widely unfulfilled in large-scale South Asian surface irrigation systems. The rules are not generally known or agreed on, and farmers often see them as biased toward the privileged. Compliance is often viewed as imposing costs on the conscientious irrigator which are not borne by the less responsible. A classic misunderstanding has to do with responsibility for the maintenance of local watercourses. For example, in the Mahi-Kadani system in Gujarat, India, farmers overwhelmingly indicated that, since the government had built the irrigation system and had constructed local watercourses, the Irrigation Ministry should maintain them. Yet irrigation personnel strongly believed that regular maintenance of local watercourses was the farmers' responsibility. The situation remains unresolved and regular maintenance is virtually nonexistent.[40]

Project analysis carried out by the World Bank in India suggests that if relevant information about expected seasonal water supplies and the timing of those supplies is provided to the farmer before crop decisions are made, farmers are more likely to cooperate with an improvement plan.[41] Insofar as this information is not given, irrigation behavior in the command areas will become most problematic and organization viability will decline. The sociologist must do the field assessment and research necessary to measure whether charter rules fulfill the specified conditions and make sense given sociopolitical conditions. When problems are found, it is necessary for the sociologist to work with local people and technicians to discover the source of the difficulty and to design alternatives.

Conclusion

Irrigation organizations at all levels—central, command area, and farm—must allocate water, routinely maintain facilities, periodically construct or rehabilitate facilities, and manage conflicts occasioned by these activities. Physical technologies deliver the water but their effectiveness depends on how central irrigation bureaucracies interface with farmers through middle-level command area organizations. This analysis has therefore focused on the command area organizations which occupy the critical interface between central irrigation bureaucracies and farmers.

Proper water management at the farm level is difficult. It involves supplying variable amounts of water to crops in an environment that is often tumultuous and bureaucratically rigid. Whether farmers attain their targets is a direct function of how well higher-level organizations operate. Farmers' deficiencies in irrigation management are the outcome of ineffective, inappropriate, or nonexistent social and technical arrangements—especially at the levels of the central bureaucracy and the command area. Irrigation planners have too often failed to analyze the requirements of the interface between central irrigation authorities and local farmers—an interface which is very sensitive at the command area level. The middle level of organization should provide a place where farmers and irrigation personnel can adapt to local realities and farmers can participate meaningfully in decisionmaking processes which affect their lives.

This chapter has hypothesized that maximum possible local control over water is best secured by a sociotechnical middle-level organization that:

- Makes staff responsible to local authorities
- Recruits local staff from command area labor markets
- Provides for routine maintenance by local specialized staff
- Provides a combination of share types which deliver forms of water control appropriate for farmer crop demand within physical and technical constraints, which connect fee assessments to water service, and which eliminate head-tail distinctions.

Between farmers and central bureaucracies, the command area organizations that possess the above attributes will secure greater farmer involvement and commitment. The failure to secure farmer commitment can be investigated by examining a set of variables having to do with organizational behavior.

The nonadaptation of irrigation subsystems seems to have been a foremost preoccupation of many officials in central irrigation authorities. Central officials are typically quite eager to decentralize the unglamorous and costly tasks of routine ditch maintenance, but fear to empower local command area organizations with real authority over water allocation, conflict management, and rehabilitation work. The argument is usually that control should be left to the impartial central authority to ensure equitable water management. It is, of course, a self-serving myth that the central bureaucracy can meaningfully control local irrigation affairs. Real central power would be quickly dissipated if it was expended in countless local interventions; information is too scarce, and the energy of central personnel too limited. Precise behavioral control escapes the center. Attempts to exert such control only succeed in cutting off the flow of information on which control is predicated. The effect of this myth is that central officials remain remote from the problems of local control, and farmers are too often left in a debilitating organizational vacuum or, equally bad, in capricious organizational settings where the only norm is unpredictability.

Bureaucrats blame farmers for not behaving in ways mandated by regulations and seek to expand their own incomes by extracting value from every exchange with farmers. Farmers, in turn, learn to distrust entanglements with powerful and remote officials. Given separate interests, farmers eke out as much room as possible through bribery, deception, and maintaining their distance. If all this undercuts farmer productivity, it is too bad for the farmers; central irrigation bureaucrats almost everywhere in South Asia, at least, obtain their budgets in ways unconnected to the productivity of the resource they control and deliver.

Widespread failures of irrigation bureaucracies have reinforced calls for farmer participation in irrigation management. Authentic farmer participation, however, requires more than the authorization of the central authority, a willingness to decentralize aspects of management, and the goodwill of the agents of change. It requires an understanding that the loose coupling of local irrigation command area organizations is necessary to provide local control. In addition, it requires an understanding that such loose coupling cannot go so far as to undercut the viability of the larger central efforts to control water upstream. Irrigation interdependencies require balancing the control needs at the center, the command area, and the local farm.

Farmers must be placed first in the planning priorities of those who design new and rehabilitated irrigation systems. It is only farmers who combine the factors of production to produce the wealth which justifies investment in irrigation. By providing the farmer with the maximum control over irrigation water, organizations endowed with the attributes discussed here will indeed help put the farmer first.

Notes

1. W. Robert Rangely, "Irrigation and Drainage in the World," in Wayne R. Jordan, ed., *Water and Water Policy in World Food Supplies* (College Station, Texas: Texas A & M University Press, 1987), p. 29.

2. Montague Yudelman, "The World Bank and Irrigation," in Wayne R. Jordan, ed., *Water and Water Policy in World Food Supplies* (College Station, Texas: Texas A & M University Press, 1987), p. 420. There have been many other similarly pessimistic retrospectives; see, for

example, Anthony F. Bottrall, *Comparative Study of the Management and Organization of Irrigation Projects*, World Bank Staff Working Paper no. 458 (Washington, D.C., 1981). Daniel W. Bromley, "Irrigation Institutions: The Myth of Management," in Wayne R. Jordan, ed., *Water and Water Policy in World Food Supplies* (College Station, Texas: Texas A & M University Press, 1987) pp. 173–76. Robert Chambers, "In Search of a Water Revolution: Questions for Managing Canal Irrigation in the 1980s," *Irrigation Water Management* (Los Banos: International Rice Research Institute, 1980), pp. 23–37. Naranjan Pant and R. K. Verma, *Farmers' Organization and Irrigation Management* (New Delhi: Ashish Publishing House, 1983). David I. Steinberg, *Irrigation and AID's Experience: A Consideration Based on Evaluations*, USAID Program Evaluation Report no. 8 (Washington, D.C.: Agency for International Development, 1984). Robert Wade, "The World Bank and India's Irrigation Reform," *Journal of Development Studies*, vol. 18, no. 2 (1982), pp. 169–80.

3. Norman Uphoff, *Improving International Irrigation Management with Farmer Participation: Getting the Process Right* (Boulder: Westview Press, 1986), p. 42. David M. Freeman, "Water, Water Everywhere in Irrigated Agriculture and Not a Drop with Constant Meaning," in John W. Bennett and John R. Bowen, eds., *Production and Autonomy: Anthropological Perspectives on Development* (Washington, D.C.: University Press of America, 1988).

4. Uphoff 1986. Raymond Z. H. Renfro and Edward W. Sparling, "Private Tubewell and Canal Water Trade on Pakistan Punjab Watercourses," in K. William Easter, ed., *Irrigation Investment, Technology, and Management Strategies for Development* (Boulder: Westview Press, 1986), pp. 193–210.

5. Ian Carruthers and Ray Stoner, *Economic Aspects and Policy Issues in Groundwater Development*, World Bank Staff Working Paper no. 496 (Washington, D.C., October 1981) p. S-1.

6. Carruthers and Stoner 1981, p. 29.

7. Gilbert Levine, Harold Capener, and Peter Gore, "The Management of Irrigation Systems for the Farm," ADC/RTN Irrigation Seminar Summary Report, Agricultural Development Council, Cornell University, October 16–18, 1972; Max K. Lowdermilk, Alan C. Early, and David M. Freeman, *Farm Irrigation Constraints and Farmers' Responses: Comprehensive Field Survey in Pakistan*, Water Management Technical Report no. 48 A-F (Fort Collins, Colo.: Colorado State University, 1978); Anthony F. Bottrall, "The Management and Operation of Irrigation Schemes in Less Developed Countries," *Water Supply and Management*, vol. 2 (1978); Bottrall, *Comparative Study of the Management and Organization of Irrigation Projects*, World Bank Staff Working Paper no. 458 (Washington, D.C., May 1981), p. 122; Gary Posz, Bodh Raj, and Dean F. Peterson, "Water Resource Development in India," appendix A, in Keller and others, *India/USAID: Irrigation Development Options and Strategies for the 1980s*, Utah State University Water Management Synthesis Project, Report no. 6 (Logan, Utah, July 1981); Richard B. Reidinger, "Institutional Rationing of Canal Water in Northern India: Conflict between Traditional Patterns and Modern Needs," *Economic Development and Cultural Change*, vol. 23 (1974); and Robert Wade, "Managing Water Managers: Deterring Expropriation, or Equity as a Control Mechanism," in Wayne R. Jordan, ed., *Water and Water Policy in World Food Supplies* (College Station, Texas: Texas A & M University Press, 1987), pp. 177–83.

8. William E. Smith, Francis J. Lethem, and Ben A. Thoolen, *The Design of Organizations for Rural Development Projects: A Progress Report*, World Bank Staff Working Paper no. 375 (Washington, D.C., March 1980).

9. Daniel W. Bromley, *Improving Irrigated Agriculture: Institutional Reform and the Small Farmer*, World Bank Staff Working Paper no. 531 (Washington, D.C., 1982), p. 30.

10. Lowdermilk, Early, and Freeman, *Farm Irrigation Constraints*; Reidinger, "Institutional Rationing of Canal Water in India," in Keller and others, *India/USAID: Irrigation Development Options*.

11. Shakuntla Mehra, *Instability in Indian Agriculture in the Context of the New Technology*, Research Report no. 25 (Washington, D.C.: International Food Policy Research Institute, July 1981).

12. For a discussion of the several ways farmers in a sample of watercourse command areas in Pakistan secure a degree of control, see Lowdermilk, Early, and Freeman, *Farm Irrigation Constraints*, vol. 5.

13. Carruthers and Stoner, *Economic Aspects and Policy Issues in Groundwater Development*, p. 34; Lowdermilk, Early, and Freeman, *Farm Irrigation Constraints*, vols. 2 and 4.

14. T. K. Jayaraman, Max K. Lowdermilk, Larry J. Nelson, and Wayne Clyma, "Diagnostic Analysis of Farmer Irrigation In the Mahi-Kadana Irrigation Project, Gujarat, India" (Fort Collins, Colo.: Colorado State University Water Management Synthesis Project, December 1981), p. 28: Keller and others, *India/USAID: Irrigation Development Options*, p. viii.

15. Many analysts have recognized that the lack of appropriate local organizations to link local people with state bureaucracies is a significant constraint upon development. Two noteworthy efforts are: William Foote and Damon Boynton, eds., *Higher Yielding Human Systems for Agriculture* (Ithaca: Cornell University Press, 1983); and Milton J. Esman and Norman Uphoff, *Local Organizations: Intermediaries in Rural Development* (Ithaca: Cornell University Press, 1984).

16. David M. Freeman, *Technology and Society: Issues in Assessment, Conflict, and Choice* (Chicago: Rand McNally, 1974); Duncan MacRae and James A. Wilde, *Policy Analysis for Public Decisions* (N. Scituate, Mass.: Duxbury Press, 1979). For a discussion of the problems of engaging in viable policy assessment and the opportunities to do so, see David M. Freeman, "Choice against Choice: A Sociological Science of Fact and Logic of Value for Public Policy Assessment" (unpublished manuscript).

17. Arthur Maass and Raymond L. Anderson, *And the Desert Shall Rejoice: Conflict, Growth, and Justice in Arid Environments* (Cambridge: MIT Press, 1978), p. 1; and Bottrall, *Comparative Study*, p. 203.

18. This point is reinforced by Bromley, *Improving Irrigated Agriculture*, p. 36; Robert Wade and Robert Chambers, "Managing the Main System: Canal Irrigation's Blind Spot," *Economic and Political Weekly*, vol. 15, no. 39 (September 27, 1980), pp. A-109–10; Frances F. Korten, *Building National Capacity to Develop Water Users' Associations: Experience from the Philippines*, World Bank Staff Working Paper no. 528 (Washington, D.C., July 1982), pp. 3–7; and Felipe B. Alfonso, "Assisting Farmer Controlled Development of Communal Irrigation Systems," in David C. Korten and Felipe B. Alfonso, eds., *Bureaucracy and the Poor: Closing the Gap* (West Hartford, Conn.: Kumarian Press, 1983).

19. Keller and others, *India/USAID: Irrigation Development Options*, p. 32.

20. Michael Cernea, "The Social Organization of Irrigation Users: Experience with Water Users' Associations in Bank-Assisted Projects" (Washington, D.C.: World Bank, Agriculture and Rural Development Department, 1982; processed), pp. 6–8.

21. Z. Karim and others, "Diagnostic Analysis of Five Deep Tubewell Irrigation Systems in Joydebpur, Bangladesh" (Fort Collins, Colo.: Colorado State University Water Management Synthesis Project, October 1983).

22. Robert Hunt, "Water Work: Community and Centralization in Canal Irrigation," unpublished manuscript, Department of Anthropology, Brandeis University, Waltham, Mass.

23. Bottrall, "Evolution of Irrigation Associations in Taiwan," *Agricultural Administration*, vol. 4 (1977), p. 247.

24. Geertz, "Organization of the Balinese Subak," in Coward, *Irrigation and Agricultural Development in Asia* (Ithaca: Cornell University Press, 1980), p. 81.

25. Abel, "Irrigation Systems in Taiwan: Management of a Decentralized Public Enterprise," Staff Paper, Department of Agricultural and Applied Economics, University of Minnesota, July 1975, pp. 22–25.

26. David M. Freeman, "Water Management Synthesis Project Report," no. 69.

27. Robert Wade, *Irrigation and Agricultural Politics in South Korea* (Boulder, Colo.: Westview Press, 1982), pp. 7, 21, 109–13, and 58.

28. This kind of labor mobilization system is employed in Pakistan; Lowdermilk, Early, and Freeman, *Farm Irrigation Constraints*.

29. Lowdermilk, Early, and Freeman, vol. 3, pp. 67–68, 77–87.

30. D. Merrey, "Reorganizing Irrigation: Local Level Management in the Punjab, Pakistan," in Douglas Merrey and James M. Wolf, *Irrigation Management in Pakistan: Four Papers*, IIMI Research Paper no. 4, 1986, p. 42.

31. Niranjan Pant and R. K. Verma, *Farmer's Organizations in India* (New Delhi: Ashish Publishing House, 1983), p. 25.

32. Levine, "Management Components in Irrigation Systems Design and Operation," *Agricultural Administration*, vol. 4 (1977), p. 43.

33. Bottrall, *Comparative Study*, p. 124.

34. S. P. Malhotra, *The Warabundi and Its Infrastructure*, Central Board of Irrigation and Power Publication no. 157 (New Delhi, April 1982). For a description of the warabundi, see Reidinger, "Institutional Rationing of Canal Water in Northern India."

35. This discussion of shares is influenced by, but not identical to, the work of Raymond Anderson and Arthur Maass, *A Simulation of Irrigation Systems*, U.S. Department of Agriculture, Economics, Statistics, and Cooperative Service, Technical Bulletin no. 1431 (Washington, D.C., January 1971; rev. ed., August 1978).

36. Edward Martin and Robert Yoder, "Water Allocation and Resource Mobilization for Irrigation: A Comparison of Two Systems in Nepal," Nepal Studies Association, Annual Meeting, Madison, University of Wisconsin, 1983.

37. Martin and Yoder 1983. Maass and Anderson, *And the Desert Shall Rejoice*.

38. The Water Court (Tribunal de las Aguas) which meets every Thursday morning outside the Apostles Door at the Cathedral of Valencia, Spain, to hear all disputes which have arisen during the preceding seven days is a local adjudication system that is much admired (Maass and Anderson, *And the Desert Shall Rejoice*, p. 24).

39. Geertz, "Organization of the Balinese Subak."

40. Jayaraman and others, "Diagnostic Analysis," pp. 52–53, 56.

41. Personal communication from Gilbert Corry and Christopher Perry of the World Bank in New Delhi, India, December 10, 1983.

PART II

Settlement and Involuntary Resettlement Projects

Editor's Note

The first edition of *Putting People First* noted that agricultural land settlement is one of the most difficult of all development interventions. But as difficult as voluntary settlement on new lands may be, *involuntary* population resettlement has turned out to be a process even more complex and painful, and of course at least equally in need of sociologically informed strategies.

Agricultural settlement (also called agricultural colonization) and involuntary resettlement programs share many characteristics. Both involve developing entirely new production systems, as well as viable patterns of community organization, often in unfamiliar environments. Both are high risk enterprises for the affected families: few settlers have reserves to sustain them if the crops fail. Finally, both voluntary and involuntary settlement programs raise issues of cultural integration and of environmental sustainability as population densities increase in the newly settled areas.

However, there are also important differences between voluntary and involuntary resettlement. Most new settlement programs involve a pre-selection of settlers; some programs develop formal screening criteria so that only the strong families, those likely to readjust and succeed, are selected for the program. By contrast, when people are involuntarily displaced, everybody must be resettled, including the old, the weak, the infirm, and the incomplete family households. Voluntary settlers see an attraction in the new sites that makes them willing to tackle the risks and uncertainties of a new environment. By contrast, involuntary resettlers have no say in whether they move; the forcible expropriation of their land impels their relocation. Finally, whereas in agricultural colonization programs developing new and viable socioeconomic systems is the primary aim of the project, involuntary resettlement situations are the side effect of another, more central investment such as a dam, a mine, or a thermal plant.

Both Scudder and Cernea note that settlement and resettlement programs have been among the least satisfactory type of development interventions. Many of the problems have been traced to a failure to appreciate the socioeconomic and cultural complexities involved in re-creating human communities and building a viable productive basis for them.

More recently, however, some agencies have started to use social scientists to formulate policies and assist in settlement project design on a large scale. How social science knowledge can be applied in settlement and involuntary resettlement projects is the theme of the two chapters in this section.

Thayer Scudder's contribution develops a settlement model drawn from a worldwide experience with colonization projects. Its core consists of the proposition that settler families everywhere pass through regular developmental sequences as they voluntarily move away from the old and adapt to their new environments. Although the length of each stage can vary, their sequence is both similar and predictable. Each stage is marked by distinct attitudes toward risk, innovation, and receptiveness to development opportunities. Scudder's model can both explain settler responses to new opportunities and guide the design of better-phased settlement projects. The long process of adaptation described by Scudder typically extends well beyond the planning horizons of most development projects. Scudder suggests that one implication of this discrepancy is that settlement projects often suffer from evaluations carried out too soon, when in fact the model he describes suggests that their full benefits are not realized until the late phases of settler development. Similarly, the model predicts that most settlers will develop mixed production systems as a way to reduce risk, rather than relying exclusively on the agricultural endeavors facilitated by projects. This reliance on off-farm income sources should, in theory, be an asset to project planners seeking to stimulate regional development; in practice, however, multiple-income source development is left out of settlement planning models.

Cernea's chapter about involuntary resettlement raises the issue of adverse, counter-developmental consequences from induced development processes. It describes at length how displacement tears apart the social fabric of existing communities and creates risks of impoverishment. A risk model is outlined to guide the planning of preventive measures. From this starting point, Cernea argues why population displacement caused by development projects requires a policy informed by social science research and how such an explicit policy has been formulated and institutionalized in the World Bank. Analyzing this case of policy formulation, Cernea argues that transforming social knowledge into building blocks for policy is a three-stage process, and documents each one of these stages. An effective social science approach is one that can use the "culture" of the development project cycle to establish a planning framework and processing criteria for projects that cause human displacement.

The content of the new resettlement policy establishes a normative framework for the planned reconstruction of the socioeconomic and cultural organization of the people displaced by development. Cernea's chapter synthesizes this normative content and shows how social scientists have helped formulate institutional procedures for implementing the policy. As a direct result, the adverse effects of many projects have been mitigated and the chapter provides examples of important improvements achieved in resettlement practice due to the sociologically informed new policy.

Cernea's and Scudder's chapters mirror an advance over the traditional use of social science research as a tool just to document development's impacts. Incorporating social science knowledge into development policies and planning frameworks is a key step for improving the outcomes of financially induced development programs.

5

A Sociological Framework for the Analysis of New Land Settlements

Thayer Scudder

Throughout human history enterprising individuals, families, and communities have sought new land for agricultural settlement. Though the majority of such settlers continue to move spontaneously even today, in recent decades national governments, often with international assistance, have sponsored their own settlement projects. While these cover a wide range of interventions, including sponsoring large-scale voluntary settlement, facilitating spontaneous new settlement, rehabilitating older settlement schemes, or relocating people who are in the way of large national development projects such as dams, this chapter is primarily concerned with government-sponsored voluntary settlement schemes.

The World Bank has become the major international donor in land settlement, assisting projects around the world financially and technically. Some of the most important projects have been in Malaysia (the FELDA projects), Sri Lanka (the Accelerated Mahaweli Project), Indonesia (transmigration projects), Sudan (Rahad, New Halfa, and Gezira), Kenya (Bura), Brazil (Polonoreste), and Colombia (Caqueta).[1] A recent World Bank evaluation of thirty-four Bank-assisted projects reported that over one-fourth had major multiplier effects and nearly two-thirds were considered adequate or better in terms of a wide range of development criteria. However, some recent Bank-financed projects have been legitimately criticized for their failure to benefit from lessons learned from prior projects, and for their adverse effect on tribal populations and the environment. The Bura project in Kenya illustrates one such major failing, while the transmigration projects and Polonoreste have been singled out for strong criticism by environmentalists. Such a spotty record does not come as a surprise to social scientists who have studied land settlement. They have long pointed out, and the Bank and many other development agencies have discovered in practice, that creating an economically viable, socially satisfying, and environmentally sustainable settlement "from scratch" is a complex endeavor and one of the more difficult of all development interventions. The task is often made still more difficult by unfavorable government policies which force low-income people into problem-prone frontier lands where many continue to live in poverty.

While my involvement in the research of resettlement processes extends over a thirty-year period,[2] the findings and conclusions that follow draw particularly on three major studies that I carried out over the last decade. First was a 1979–81 study of the development potential of voluntary land settlement in the tropics and subtropics, sponsored by the Institute for Development Anthropology and funded by USAID. Involving over 100 projects, this research included an extensive review of the literature as well as supervision of field work by colleagues in spontaneous and sponsored settlements in Egypt, the Sudan, Nepal, and Sri Lanka, and site visits to five other countries. Second was an extended desk review, carried out in 1984 and 1985 with the assistance of Gottfried Ablasser and Andrew Waite, of the World Bank's experience with thirty-four completed settlement projects. Third is a longitudinal study, started in 1979 and still continuing in 1990, by Kapila P. Vimaladharma and myself, on the Accelerated Mahaweli Project in Sri Lanka. Thus, in preparing the present chapter, I have drawn on three main sources which are not available to most readers.[3]

Sponsored Settlements and Social Science

The purpose of this chapter is to show why a wider social science perspective is essential if the development potential of new land settlements is to be realized. By wider social science perspective, I mean utilization of the results of relevant research in anthropology and sociology as well as the work of economists, political scientists, human geographers, and the like. The contribution of sociology and anthropology to settlement theory and practice is especially relevant since no other social sciences have had the same long and intimate association with community studies. These disciplines have built up a useful body of knowledge on community structures and social change that is especially applicable to projects involving compulsory relocation and voluntary land settlement. Both sponsored and spontaneous settlement provide the social scientist with an exceptional opportunity to study the processes whereby new production systems, communities, and belief systems come into existence and evolve in problem-prone habitats.

Though the accumulated knowledge of sociology and anthropology is basic to theories on the nature and evolution of human societies—especially peasant societies, which provide most settlers in the tropics and subtropics—time and again it is ignored by development planners and agency officials. Why this is so is unclear. One example among many is the accelerated Mahaweli project in Sri Lanka. Though this is one of the world's largest settlement schemes, little social science expertise was used by the community of donors, including the World Bank, in connection with Mahaweli I, II, and III.

The problem relates not just to lessons learned through social science analysis, but often also to the use of biological or soil sciences. For instance, in addition to weaknesses relating to inadequate application of social knowledge, a major weakness in many settlement projects continues to be inadequate soil surveys, with serious negative environmental consequences.

Regardless of the reasons, blame for failure in settlement planning can be placed on both social scientists and project planners. For their part, social analysts have not codified their insights into theoretical and operational constructs. The lack of a systematized, operationally usable conceptual framework about settlement processes has in part accounted for the tendency of project planners to bypass the contributions of social analysts. The planners, in turn, in designing settlement programs, have too often conceptualized their projects only in technological terms—building housing, creating technical packages for agricultural development, and providing water systems—and have ignored or undertreated the socioeconomic aspects of the settlement process. In effect, most land settlement schemes are planned and implemented as agricultural production schemes rather than as schemes designed to stimulate regional development through increased production, rising living standards and disposable income among the settler population, and nonfarm employment generation. Though they are the social actors who will make the scheme work or fail, the settlers themselves receive little attention, and so knowledge on how to realize their potential is ignored.

The main contribution of this chapter is to present a four-stage framework for the analysis of land settlement as a process and to discuss a range of critical issues which must be addressed if current and future settlement, and especially government-sponsored settlement, is to benefit larger numbers of low income settlers without environmental degradation. The analytical framework is derived from the study of that minority of settlements which can be considered successful. The critical issues are those identified by researchers looking at both successful and unsuccessful settlements.

Many developing countries have attempted to plan and implement sponsored settlements as one of a variety of mechanisms to realize economic, social, and political goals. Sponsored settlers are recruited from established communities according to a relatively narrow set of criteria and are required to follow a closely supervised agricultural development program. Though many settler families in these cases see themselves as better-off once the most difficult pioneering years have passed, opinions among experts vary concerning the effectiveness of new land settlement as a development intervention.

The capital development costs of sponsored settlement are high and rising. During fiscal years 1962–75, they averaged $8,650 per settler family for World Bank–assisted projects. By 1985 costs per settler household usually exceeded $10,000 in irrigated settlement schemes (even running over $20,000 in the case of Kenya's ill-fated Bura Project) while costs for rainfed settlement schemes ranged above $5,000 per household. At those levels of investment host country governments, international donors, and various evaluators are often disappointed by the low economic rates of return from investment in new land settlement, especially in relation to initial appraisals. According to the Bank's *Agricultural Land Settlement* issues paper, "typically, evaluation of settlement projects three to five years after the start of implementation shows economic rates of return at least 50 percent below those in project appraisal documents." A major argument of this chapter is that this discrepancy is due more to a misunderstanding of the settlement process than to unsatisfactory progress on the part of settler households. And this misunderstanding is directly related to a failure on the part of development planners to familiarize themselves with, and utilize, social science expertise on new land settlements.

Although planners tend to overemphasize the short-term benefits of new land settlement, they can also seriously underestimate the potential long-term benefits. Indeed, several evaluators view the long-term prospects favorably, with Hans van Raay and Jos Hilhorst even suggesting that "land settlement may be an attractive alternative to the further intensification of agricultural production in already settled areas, especially if low-cost solutions of land settlement can be developed."[4] Perhaps the most important conclusion of these studies is that sponsored settlement can catalyze regional development with greater long-term spread effects (including the generation of both farm and nonfarm employment), *provided* that national policies are not unfavorable and certain basic features are built into the project design with sufficient time allowed for them to take effect.

These features include scale (settling thousands of families); rural-urban linkages through a hierarchy of service centers (including regional towns); economic diversification at household, community, and project levels; and sufficiently high settler incomes to stimulate the purchase of a wide range of locally produced goods and services. In particular, it is the rising disposable income of large numbers of settlers which is the "engine" that "drives" development forward within the encompassing region, with case studies throughout the world indicating that settlers purchase remarkably similar goods and services, the demand for which stimulates nonfarm employment and enterprise. The point is an important one which warrants documentation. Referring to tropical rural economies in general, Johnson and Kilby note "that as per capita output in the economy rises a growing share of household expenditures is devoted to manufactured and processed commodities." Furthermore, "where income is more or less evenly distributed over broad segments of the population, the result is large markets for comparatively simple goods."[5]

As for settlement projects, Bell, Hazell, and Slade note that there were 83 cents of indirect benefits for every dollar of direct benefits from Malaysia's Muda Irrigation Scheme. Breaking down the 83 cents, the authors reported that 50 cents were from increased farmer demand for goods and services, significantly exceeding value added from production linkages.[6] Though not many land settlements have actually catalyzed a process of regional development, there are examples from Latin America, the Middle East, Africa, and Asia including San Lorenzo (Peru), Northern Parana (Brazil), Abis (Egypt), Gezira (Sudan), Minneriya (Sri Lanka), and Metro (Indonesia) of such major multiplier effects as nonfarm enterprise development, employment generation, and the growth of market and regional towns.

In summary, not only can new land settlement stimulate integrated area development, but it can also spread the development effects over large numbers of low-income families, since the rural poor are disproportionally selected as settlers. For this reason, and because of the high costs per settler household and per hectare developed, the creation of such multipliers should become a major goal of land settlement.

New Land Settlement and Settlement Success Defined

New land settlement is generally defined as the spontaneous and sponsored settlement of areas which are largely uncultivated at the time of their occupation. It includes what is referred to in the literature as "colonization" (especially in Latin America and in pre-independence Indonesia), "resettlement," and "transmigration." All these terms emphasize the settlement of land by people rather than the reclamation or initial preparation of land.

The distinction between spontaneous and sponsored settlers refers to whether the settlers are self-recruited or respond to the recruitment initiative of a sponsoring agency. It has nothing to do with the reasons or motivation for leaving the original residence for a new settlement area.

Though government administrators with settlement experience often remain skeptical, evidence from different parts of the world suggests that spontaneous settlers usually make better farmers in less time and at a lower financial cost than do government-sponsored settlers.[7] The comparison here is with pioneer settlers, that is, those who arrive during the first phase of the settlement process.

A range of explanatory factors appears to account for this. There is considerable evidence, for example, that spontaneous settlers have access to more resources than do the majority of government-sponsored settlers, most of whom are poor and likely to be landless laborers or sharecroppers. Spontaneous settlers, however, often have resources that place them above the lowest 20 percent of the sending population in terms of income. The evidence also suggests, however, that without government or other external assistance spontaneous settlement alone can hardly generate a process of integrated development. Under such circumstances, it makes sense to combine both types of settlers in the settlement process rather than to favor one type to the exclusion of the other.

In the definition of new land settlement, the wording "largely unculti-vated" is important since most new lands are in fact occupied by others (hereafter called the hosts) at the time of settlement or, if currently unused, are almost always subject to rights of customary use and tenure by the hosts. Because population densities tend to be relatively low and the hosts tend to have relatively low social status and little regional (let alone national) power, their lands are frequently taken away without the provision of compensatory land, or adequate cash compensation. Even if they do not lose land, rarely is a systematic attempt made to incorporate the hosts within the settlement design (Mahaweli and New Halfa being major exceptions), and this omission increases the chances of conflict between hosts and settlers.

While the World Bank defines settlement success in terms of economic rates of return, "which in turn emphasize increases in agricultural pro-duction, the nature of land settlement schemes suggests that in the future the Bank should pay more attention to benefits accruing to a majority of the settler households and to the potential of projects to catalyze a process of integrated area development."[8] Two factors support this statement. The first is the rising costs of land settlement projects. The second is the rising disposable income of thousands of settler households which gen-erates the main multipliers. In this chapter success is defined in terms of the ability of a land settlement project to facilitate regional development.

Types of Settlement

In classifying settlements it is necessary to distinguish both the type of settler and the nature of the involvement of the sponsoring agency or agencies. Four types are distinguished for the purpose of analysis, although several may in fact be represented in a single settlement:

- Spontaneous settlement with very little government or other assistance
- Spontaneous settlement facilitated by government and other agencies
- Voluntary settlement sponsored by government and other agencies
- Compulsory resettlement sponsored primarily by government agencies.

One tends to forget that the inhabited portions of the world have been largely populated by spontaneous settlement with very little or no gov-ernment support. Even today the majority of settlers moving into the last frontiers of the humid tropics are primarily spontaneous, whether to locales in South America, the equatorial belt of Africa, Nepal, Indonesia, or the Philippines. Government and other agencies have rarely facilitated spontaneous settlement, however, despite impressive evidence that spontaneous settlers time and again make better farmers. As with poorly planned and implemented government-sponsored settlement, the major disadvantages of spontaneous settlement are the lack of legal access to land and secure land tenure, environmental degradation resulting from movement into marginal lands, a tendency for spontaneous settlers to displace the host population, and relatively low levels of productivity with few multiplier effects.

Settlement sponsored by governments or other agencies takes two main forms: voluntary and involuntary. The importance of government-sponsored voluntary settlement has been proportionately increasing in recent decades and has opened up the opportunity for substantial use of social science knowledge in designing and implementing settlement policies.

Involuntary resettlement, on the contrary, is generally a by-product of events such as the construction of highways and major hydroelectric and irrigation systems (see a detailed analysis in chapter 6 of this volume). Because it represents such an extreme example, settlements resulting from involuntary relocation spotlight a number of problems which, to a lesser extent, characterize all types of new land settlements. These have been studied sociologically in considerable detail, particularly in connection with relocation in the tropics and subtropics. The results of such studies have improved our understanding of settler responses to settlement, of settlement stages, and of a wide range of issues associated with each stage. Such sociological knowledge has been effectively incorporated into the World Bank's policy guidelines dealing with the social issues associated with involuntary resettlement in Bank-financed projects.[9] These guidelines have definitely improved the content of involuntary resettlement planning. Their implementation, however, is confronted with major problems, and the guidelines themselves will need continuous strengthening to protect better the interests of the landless and to ensure that projects provide real opportunities to improve living standards following removal.

The Magnitude of Potential Settlement

Both spontaneous and government-sponsored settlement have increased since the end of World War II. Assessing the potential for future settlements on the basis of FAO data, Goering stated that "cultivated land in 1970 was about 57 percent of the world's total potentially arable land," with over 40 percent of the estimated reserves in Latin America (459 million hectares), and between 15 and 20 percent in tropical Africa. Though Asia contains only about 5 percent of the global reserves, approximately 50 million hectares are involved.[10]

Although there is still scope for new settlement projects, some governments have exaggerated the capacity of frontiers to absorb population surpluses. For example, massive government-sponsored settlement in Kenya has absorbed only about 10 percent of the population increase over a ten-year period. In Latin America, new settlement has absorbed only 2 percent of rural population increases. This is the general situation.

The largest areas of underutilized potentially arable lands are in the humid tropics, where approximately 75 percent of settlement is spontaneous. At present rates of settlement much of the remaining land in the humid tropics will be occupied before the end of the century. The same applies to the savanna in Africa, the most extensive area of this type in the world. More systematic use of social science knowledge now is critically important in order to multiply the socioeconomic and cultural benefits of new settlement and to mitigate its negative aspects and consequences.

The Relevance of Social Scientists and Social Science Research

Existing economic techniques for project appraisal are not adequate and sufficient for assessing the advantages and disadvantages of land settlement compared with other alternatives. Cost benefit analysis does not emphasize multiplier effects, the assumption being that the multipliers for any given investment will be roughly similar. While that assumption may be justified for projects in old lands, it is less applicable in new lands where market and regional towns, highways, and other essential communication links may be virtually nonexistent. Under such circumstances, multipliers associated with land settlement may be very low unless the necessary communication and rural-urban linkages are designed and implemented; it should be kept in mind that the high costs per hectare and per household are hardly justified unless land settlement does lead to major downstream benefits.

There are significant differences between settling people in old and new lands. In old lands, developers start with existing societies; in new lands viable societies have to be formed from individually recruited families moved to unfamiliar problem-prone pioneer zones. To build productive communities in which people wish to live and raise their children, not only must production goals be met and living standards raised at the household level but also new societies must be formed where none existed before. Throughout, the main risk-takers are not government officials but settler families. They are the ones who must pioneer difficult areas and overcome a wide range of trials, including sickness, if production goals are to be met. Although there are many reasons that most new land settlements do not live up to planning expectations, inadequate attention to settler families and the communities in which they live is certainly a major cause.

The conventional wisdom, still strong among settlement planners and administrators, is that settlers are drawn primarily from traditional societies that are conservative and therefore must be carefully supervised and led. To the contrary, families of voluntary settlers tend to be open to innovation, as shown by their willingness to leave a familiar home environment for a frontier. Usually arriving as strangers, these families initially tend to be risk-averse, perpetuating the myth of their basic conservatism. Their risk-averse stance, however, is a logical response to a new habitat, as is their attempt to meet their subsistence needs from their own lands as soon as possible. My own research shows that having once replicated a subsistence mode of production, settler households easily shift into a risk-taking stance that allows them to follow a range of investment strategies which are not only remarkably similar throughout the tropics and subtropics but also tend to be more dynamic than the production strategies of planners for the settlement project as a whole.[11]

Other social science research is clarifying the processes whereby settler families adapt to a new habitat and shift from a risk-averse to a risk-taking stance. Current research in the Amazon basin is isolating such characteristics as "previous management experience, residential stability, previous credit experience, and initial capital or liquid assets" which enable certain individuals to play key roles in forming new communities out of an aggregate of pioneer families from different areas and backgrounds.[12] This research has important implications for the criteria used to select settlers for government-sponsored settlements. Research in the Philippines emphasizes the importance of kinship in speeding the adjustment of settler families in the years immediately after arrival. This point has been broadened to include neighbors and co-ethnics of spontaneous settlers in Indonesia and in Nepal and spontaneous and sponsored settlers in Latin America.[13]

Social science expertise is needed for a variety of issues addressing the very nature of the settlement process: the recruitment of settler families; promoting cooperation among those families in productive activities; community formation, whereby an aggregate of families becomes a viable community which can take increasing responsibility for self-management; and the spatial arrangement of communities in a regional hierarchy which ascends from the village to the regional town. Since these issues relate to all stages of settlement, planners and managers need the assistance of social scientists throughout in the same way they need the assistance of agricultural economists and agronomists.

Although the dynamics of the settlement process and their policy implications will be dealt with in the next section, it is important to emphasize here that this process includes the complex interrelationship between the community of settlers and the settlement agency—a relationship which has been best analyzed by Chambers.[14] With regard to the issue of recruitment, sociological expertise can provide information on the type of people who are most likely to adapt to new settlements and to work together in building productive societies. A common mistake is to focus attention on the male farmer as an individual rather than as a household head and family member. The basic building block of any frontier society is the family. Both spouses ideally should be interviewed by settlement authorities prior to recruitment, since the reluctance or unsuitability of one spouse can have an adverse effect on productivity and family stability. Yet in spite of the high stakes involved, with the major exception of FELDA projects, joint interviewing is rarely done.

Another issue requiring social science inputs is the promotion of cooperation among settlers for productive activities. During the initial months of settlement, settler families often must clear new lots, build temporary houses, prepare and sow fields, learn new production techniques, and adjust to new neighbors and to the management style of the settlement agency. The majority of early settlers are either individual household heads (followed subsequently by other family members) or small family units. The serious labor constraints that usually occur at this time can be eliminated best if planners adopt policies which facilitate (or at least do not hinder) labor recruitment and the establishment of work networks and associations, especially for house construction and land preparation. Here it is crucial to have sociological knowledge of how settlers (usually strangers to each other) establish and broaden work and residential networks and social groups.

Studies have shown that the formation of local participatory action groups among settlers is associated with higher productivity. By frequently settling people who are alien to each other side by side in the same community or assigning them contiguous fields, administrators run the risk of increasing stress among settler families and of delaying the cooperative activities which raise production and help community formation. Unaware of the importance of participation, they also impede group formation for fear of its political consequences (an ongoing problem within the areas covered by the Bank-financed Accelerated Mahaweli Project). There may also be an unwillingness, especially in the later stages of settlement (as in the Sudan Gezira Board), to share management responsibilities with local settler organizations such as water user associations or rural and urban councils.

Because of a one-sided preoccupation with agricultural production, settlement officials tend to recruit individuals with similar skills and of similar age, creating a highly artificial society of peers. The formation of viable communities, however, requires diversification—a wider range of backgrounds, best obtained by also recruiting some young and middle-aged couples with nonfarm skills and older couples with social, political, and religious leadership skills. By definition, societies are specialized and stratified by sex, age, occupation, and status. Careful use of sociological expertise can facilitate the building of more productive societies not merely by establishing selection criteria but also by monitoring and evaluating the settlement process so that potential problems can be identified and dealt with as they arise. Finally, there is a well-informed, case-oriented literature concerning the spatial integration of communities into a regional hierarchy, written primarily by geographers and anthropologists, which contains unutilized but useful operational advice that should be consulted.

A Dynamic Model of Settlement Process: Four Stages

A major goal of our 1979–81 global evaluation of new land settlements was to develop a conceptual framework which could be used for the systematic analysis of settlements and, more specifically, for their planning, implementation, management, and evaluation. In attempting to explain settlement processes as well as the relative success or failure of projects which have been in existence for a number of years, I developed a four-stage framework which builds on the three-stage framework of Robert Chambers. Before outlining this, a cautionary warning is warranted about the use of stages. These are merely tools for coming to grips with a complicated and dynamic process. They involve some simplifying assumptions that attempt to break the settlement process into a series of critical periods, during each of which a range of basic issues needs to be addressed. These stages necessarily overlap somewhat in reality, which must be recognized, although for taxonomic purposes I emphasize the distinctions and dissimilarities between them.

The four stages cover at least a generation and are:

1. Planning, initial infrastructural development, and settler recruitment
2. Transition
3. Economic and social development
4. Handing over and incorporation.

To be successful, a new land settlement *must* pass through all four stages, though the order of the third and fourth may be reversed.[15] These last two stages are crucial if disposable income is to rise and multiplier effects are to continue. Though ideally a settlement area should pass rapidly through the entire sequence so as to realize its development potential at the earliest possible date, in fact a wide range of internal and exogenous factors are apt to interfere, so that a steady movement through the four development stages tends to be the exception rather than the rule. Furthermore, many spontaneous and sponsored settlements never reach the third stage of economic and social development but evolve directly from stage two to stage four. Though individual settler households may be better off than in their previous homes, few spread effects occur, and the project merely replicates a subsistence mode of production (as is frequently the case in Latin America and tropical Africa).

It is relatively easy to place different settlements within a particular stage or between two stages. Furthermore, the very concept of stages draws attention to the fact that new land settlements have histories and that these histories are remarkably similar. It follows from this that people and the sociocultural systems in which they are imbedded and interrelated (including settlement agencies) respond to new land settlement in predictable ways. These responses have major policy implications.

Stage One: Planning, Initial Infrastructural Development, and Settler Recruitment

The first stage covers the initial activities related to feasibility studies, planning, and design—and the subsequent ones related to settler recruitment and the construction of such infrastructure as roads and irrigation facilities.

FEASIBILITY STUDIES, PLANNING, AND DESIGN. Feasibility studies should consider a range of alternatives before proceeding with a particular type of settlement. The planning and design activities that follow need to consider a range of issues including the scope and scale of the intended farming systems and the relation of the settlement to regional development. Some researchers (including myself) believe, for example, that multiplier effects are correlated primarily with diversification of the farming system, farm family income, and the scale and scope of settlement.[16]

Often not enough emphasis is given to the type of land tenure for the settlers and to negotiations with the host population to reduce the potential disruption of land disputes and uncertainty over tenure. Even where host-settler land rights are negotiated and legalized, subsequent conflicts can be expected. Adjudication procedures are therefore needed from the start. During the planning phase, consideration should also be given to the extent to which the hosts will be included in the settlement project on social equity, economic, and political grounds.

INITIAL INFRASTRUCTURE AND SETTLER RECRUITMENT. The term "initial infrastructure" suggests that infrastructural development should be phased, with planners establishing priorities for implementing different types of infrastructure for settler families, administrators, and other nonfarm families. During the design stage, it should be decided whether an elementary "sites and services" approach or a more ambitious approach will be taken. In either case, implementation of infrastructure should be sequenced, with only the essential items—such as access roads and irrigation structures—constructed during stage one.

Settler recruitment is a crucial operation that can benefit enormously from intelligent social analysis. As previously noted, far too much emphasis in the past has been paid to recruitment criteria related to individual men rather than to settler families. Recruitment should be linked to considerations such as the type of production system, the type of community, and the type of society desired, so as to acquire both farm and nonfarm families with the necessary aptitude and orientation, experience and skills.

When designing and establishing new production and social systems, planners need to rely more on the initiative, experience, institutions, and symbols of the settlement population (including hosts and settlers, and farm and nonfarm families). Especially in this first stage, more attention to the needs of the main risk-takers (that is, the settler families, not the planners and managers) would help deemphasize agricultural production as an end in itself and focus instead on the income-generating activities and the net income levels needed to encourage both greater settler initiative in agricultural production and employment generation through nonfarm enterprise development. Settlement project design should build in ways for the settlers to modify the plan: for example, carrying out their own negotiations with the hosts, selecting from a variety of housing options, and so forth.

Stage Two: Transition

This stage is poorly understood by project planners in both the World Bank and borrower agencies, as illustrated by the expectation of rapid gains in production in the years immediately following settlement. The use of the word "transition" emphasizes two points. First, in this stage settlers are still moving from one habitat to another and, second, this transitional period must come to an end before settler families can be expected to significantly increase their productivity. Although the transition stage may last less than a year for a minority of families in settlements which subsequently reach stage three, for the majority it would appear to last for at least two years and more often for five or more years.

During the transition stage many settlers are risk-averse, which explains why few technical, organizational, and sociopolitical innovations are adopted at this time. Risk aversion is a coping response to the stress and uncertainty associated with not only a new physical and biotic environment but also new neighbors, an increased government presence (in the case of government-sponsored settlement), and frequently a new host population. While learning the ropes, most settlers adopt a conservative stance, their first priority being to meet their subsistence needs. They favor continuity over change; where change is necessary, they favor incremental change over rapid and radical change. Where possible, they cling to the familiar by moving into new settlements with relatives, former neighbors, and co-ethnics. They also try to transfer house types, farming practices, and other skills from their original area even though they may not be suited to the new habitat.

The transition stage comes to an end when enough settler families shift from a conservative stance to a dynamic open-ended one, initiating the third stage of economic and social development. This shift is most likely to occur after the settlers begin to feel at home in their new habitat and are able to produce sufficient food to meet family needs. In light of the security-oriented and conservative stance of the settlers at this time, it is unreasonable for governments and donors to expect rapid increases in productivity through agricultural intensification during the first five years. Yet such unrealistic expectations all too often characterize both national and international planners. Project appraisal estimates frequently ignore the production implications of the transition stage and tend to overestimate initial benefits.

The logical way to improve project performance during these early years of implementation is to shorten the length of the transition stage. This can be done in a number of ways; one way relates to settler recruitment. There are two overwhelming advantages when settlers are recruited for specific communities from villages of the same locale and ethnic area instead of from different ethnic areas. First, neighbors and co-ethnics are much more likely than strangers to form self-help groups for land clearing and house building during the early years of settlement in which serious labor shortages are common. Second, the potential stress and uncertainty of adapting to new neighbors is lessened when those neighbors come from a similar background.

Another way to shorten the length of the transition stage is to adopt policies that distinguish between the settlement or transition stage and the development stage. During the settlement stage, the emphasis should be on helping the settlers feel secure in their new habitat at the earliest possible moment. Such an approach does not mean that developmental activities should be ignored at that time; quite the contrary. Just as land negotiation and tenurial arrangements should be completed during stage one, and agricultural research and pilot projects undertaken, to expedite subsequent development, so too can developmental activities be implemented during the transition stage. These include, for example, continual provision of crucial physical infrastructure, and continuation and evaluation of agricultural research and pilot projects; the development of credit, extension, and other agricultural services; and the construction, equipping, and staffing of schools and health facilities.

Because settler families are especially susceptible during the transition stage to a wide range of illnesses owing to contact with new diseases, stress, inadequate water supplies (and often inadequate nutrition, as reported for the Accelerated Mahaweli Project), health services are especially important. Schools are equally important because settlers usually invest first in their children's education. If schools are inadequate in number and quality, government-sponsored settlers are less apt to bring their families to settlement areas, and this will contribute to instability and labor bottlenecks.

Other developmental activities which sponsoring agencies can undertake include fielding an appropriate, unified extension service; encouraging appropriate private and public sector credit and marketing services; and building up, through extension and training, settler-dominated participatory action organizations.[17] These activities must be carefully formulated and implemented to facilitate settler initiative and independence. A too paternalistic approach risks promoting a sense of dependency which can bog down a settlement leaving it in the transition stage for years.

To sum up, the early years of pioneering a new settlement area are difficult and stressful. They require a period of adaptation which is rarely less than two years and usually longer. Though timely governmental interventions can shorten the length of this difficult period of coping and transition, it cannot be eliminated. Expectations that settlers will intensify their production from the very start are therefore unrealistic.

Stage Three: Economic and Social Development

The contrast between stage two and stage three is dramatic: the second stage is characterized by a population of risk-averse settlers and the third by a settled population ready to take risks. Since the same people are involved, an important change has occurred.

Instead of producing primarily for subsistence, as in stage two, settlers act on a wide range of investment strategies in stage three to achieve higher levels of productivity through diversification of the family estate.[18] They appear to follow the same sequencing of investment activities in different parts of the tropics and subtropics. Initially they invest in education for their children and expand their farming system to include both cash crops (including labor-intensive, higher-value, and higher-risk crops) and livestock. Subsequently, additional farmland is reclaimed, sharecropped, leased, or purchased; and the settlers branch out into nonfarm activities.

Nonfarm activities tend to start on the farm homestead in the form of small business enterprises such as crafts (carpentry, masonry, and so forth), baking, and tailoring. Investment then expands to nonfarm activities off the homestead but within the settlement area, including small general stores and transport for hire (two- and four-wheel tractors, trucks, taxis, and mini- and other buses). Still later, as observed in Egypt and the Sudan, investments may be made in urban real estate and business.

While this sequence of investments has rarely been studied in any detail, it has been documented among a minority of settlers in both rainfed and irrigated settlement areas. Examples include Abis (an irrigated area) in Egypt where urban investments have been made in Alexandria; Gezira (irrigated) in the Sudan where settler households have invested in trucks that travel between the northern and southern Sudan and in Khartoum real estate and businesses; and Kariba (rainfed agriculture) in Zambia where settler households have built rental housing and small businesses in the capital city of Lusaka.

Stage three is crucial for economic development. As net incomes rise, settler families begin to purchase production and consumption goods and services. The indirect benefits coming from the increased purchasing power of thousands of smallholders have been underestimated in the past. Not only can it have a significant impact, but it generates more value added than does agroindustry.

Throughout the tropics and subtropics settlers tend to spend rising net incomes on similar items. These include education of children; expansion and improvement of housing (with temporary materials replaced by kiln-fired brick and cinder block walls, and tile and metal roofs); and purchase of household furnishings such as tables and chairs, glassed-in cupboards for displaying tea and coffee sets, better beds and mattresses, sewing machines, wall clocks, battery-operated radios and radio–cassette players, and—where electricity is available—electrical appliances. Bicycles, plows, and other production equipment are also acquired. Such purchases can generate new demand for nonfarm employment in a range of commercial and service enterprises within the settlement region.

Increased productivity and rising net incomes also tend to increase onfarm employment, since even smallholders intensively cultivating two acres or less of irrigated land need outside labor for certain operations. Furthermore, as incomes rise, many settlers prefer to hire labor for the more arduous agricultural tasks and to use family labor for social or more lucrative economic activities. Especially in irrigated settlements, the number of seasonal and permanent laborers may become significant. Partly influenced by the image of a simple family farm (whereby settlers utilize only family labor), most governments ignore or underestimate the onfarm employment potential of successful new settlement projects. A major exception is the Rahad Project in the Sudan where an equal number of village allotments were set aside for farm labor and nonfarm families. A partial exception is the Accelerated Mahaweli Project, where one out of every six household allotments in System B is being set aside for nonsettler families. Though a step in the right direction, this ratio still underestimates the employment potential of the Mahaweli program as shown by Kapila Vimaladharma's research at the older Sri Lankan settlement scheme of Minneriya.[19]

In stage three, settlers begin to pay more attention to organizing themselves, and aggregates of households change into communities in the process. Initial emphasis tends to be placed on welfare organizations and on associations for building such religious structures as churches, mosques, shrines, and temples. Production organizations such as water user associations and marketing cooperatives come next. All too often the tendency of governments is to try to control such organizations rather than to encourage their independence and ability to take over increased responsibilities for self-management. This is most unfortunate since their appearance and growth are associated with more viable communities and increased productivity, as emphasized by World Bank–reports on such projects as Peru's San Lorenzo.

During stage three, careful government monitoring and intervention can help identify and offset difficulties which, if allowed to continue, might cause the project to regress into a subsistence mode of production. This happened at Kariba in the mid-1970s because rural-urban terms of trade continued to be unfavorable after Zambia was adversely affected by a series of international events. Potential problems include providing land and employment for the second generation of settlers; the upkeep of physical and social infrastructure; changing rural-urban terms of trade, especially pricing policies for agricultural products and agricultural inputs as they affect farm income; and provision of farm services including extension, credit, and marketing. Government agencies can also anticipate increasing labor demands by developing appropriate measures to assist farm laborers. Settlement agencies should actively encourage training and institution-building programs so that managerial responsibilities can gradually be delegated to rural and municipal councils, settler organizations, and line ministries (especially decentralized departments dealing at the local level with health, education, agriculture, and the like).

Stage Four: Handing Over and Incorporation

Settlement cannot be considered a success until control of project activities has been handed over to the settlers and their local organizations; a second generation of settlers has started to take over; and the project is incorporated within the encompassing region. Handing over activities to departmental, local government, and settler organizations is a tricky business which can proceed both too rapidly and too slowly. Certain health services at Mwea (Kenya), for example, tended to break down because they were handed over too soon, but usually settlement agencies tend to retain authority which would be better handed over. This tendency is explained in part by the inefficiency of long-established agencies, in part by the authoritarian attitude of officials, and in part by the fact that jobs and prestige are at stake. Regardless of the reason, restructuring the settlement agency may, in time, be as necessary as rehabilitating the physical infrastructure of a settlement project. The Sudan Gezira Board and the Agricultural Production Corporation (New Halfa) are two Sudanese examples of settlement agencies whose inefficiencies have become major developmental constraints. The problem may become especially acute with highly centralized, hierarchically organized agencies.

While highly centralized agencies may effectively plan, secure funding, and implement the early stages of settlement, during the later stages they can become major constraints to further progress. The Sudan Gezira Board has been resisting for several decades the devolution of certain management functions to the strong tenants' union. Notwithstanding the undeniable advantages of centralized agencies during the initial stages, governments need to evaluate the comparative advantages of centralized versus decentralized management of settlements at later stages.

Another serious problem may arise when it is time for the second generation of settlers to take over from the first. The Gezira scheme is again illustrative (but not unique: the older FELDA projects could also be used as examples). Pioneering families there made a special effort to educate their children and have sent a disproportionate number of students to the major universities. Since many children do not wish to take over from their parents, the settlement is inhabited by an aging population. In such cases, innovative policies may be needed whereby sharecroppers or those leasing the land are given an opportunity to procure title to it.

Development Issues Associated with Stage One

In many settlement projects worker-settlers clear and prepare their own lands for cultivation and construct the infrastructure serving those lands. These workers often arrive without their families simply because living conditions tend to be extremely difficult. Every effort should be made to ready the land for cultivation and family occupancy during the first year or else the hardship and suffering of the settlers may be reflected in low morale, increased illness, suspicion of government intentions, and high dropout rates.

Roads and government-built permanent housing are usually the two costliest items associated with settlements based on rainfed agriculture. While the former are necessary, the latter are not. Also, government-provided housing is likely to be culturally inappropriate and poorly constructed. The Bura project is a case in point. Housing made there by European contractors was not only very expensive but its design ignored significant Kenyan experience with the construction of low-cost housing. Similar cultural inadequacy occurred at Kom Ombo, where Egypt relocated the majority of people from the Aswan High Dam project. Regulations about how the housing and the house plots are to be used may constrain family activities and the normal developmental cycle of the family. Permanent housing tends to be associated with plots too small to permit the settler's heir to build his or her own housing near aging parents. In effect, government-provided housing restricts the social organization of the settler family, while the size of the plot more often than not is inadequate for keeping animals and planting household gardens. For all these reasons, it makes sense for settlers to build their own housing on larger household plots wherever possible.

Settler Recruitment and Policy

Pioneer families tend to be relatively young, often with only one or two small children. But over the years, the number of children can be expected to increase significantly, usually exceeding the national average. In their old age the first generation of settlers will probably wish their heir to build on the same plot. The size of household sites should therefore be planned with the future needs of the family unit in mind, at least for the next generation.

The Institute for Development Anthropology (IDA) research and other sociological field studies conclude that spontaneous settlement should be facilitated and combined with sponsored settlement much more than at present. This would tap the initiative of spontaneous settlers, diversify settlement areas in terms of occupational specialization, and cut the financial costs of the settlement process. The desired nature of the mix should vary between countries and from one agro-ecological zone to another. The World Bank has in recent years financed several projects to encourage people in the overpopulated areas of Indonesia to move to the outer islands. Spontaneous migration has occurred in tandem with the more formal government-sponsored programs. In addition to the advantages mentioned above, spontaneous migration has the capability to affect large numbers of people and, because it is self-motivated, is less likely to result in settler dependency. A community study in Indonesia revealed that almost without exception migrants to the new community had some kinship connection with settlers who had arrived at an earlier date. These relationships formed a network through which information was conveyed and social support provided to the new migrants.[20]

Opportunities for paid employment in the receiving area have been shown to be an important incentive to spontaneous migration. Communities should therefore be planned in such a way that new migrants can be absorbed and settled in the area. In countries with both large areas of underutilized humid rain forests and heavily populated old lands with a significant proportion of landless farmers, spontaneous settlers tend to outnumber sponsored settlers by three or four to one. The proportion of spontaneous settlers tends to be significantly smaller in areas with insufficient rainfall during the main cultivating season. Better cooperation between planners and sociologists might reveal the possible responses of spontaneous settlers to the opening up of new areas, and such estimates could be used to calculate the optimal settler mix. What the mix should be will also depend on other factors. Since financial costs per family tend to be lower for spontaneous settlers, this factor alone (as at Caqueta in Colombia) may be significant—although a "sites and services" approach to sponsored settlement can also reduce settlement costs.

Recruitment Criteria

Where land settlements are a major development intervention, serious thought should be given to formulating a national set of recruitment criteria. Although desirable criteria will vary, some generalizations appear valid. Perhaps the most important is to recruit settlers as families rather than as individuals. Another is to use a formal point system to evaluate both spouses and to recruit the families attaining the highest number of points. Sponsoring agencies make little effort to learn if spouses wish to move—and, if they do, whether they have appropriate skills. It makes sense to recruit only families in which both spouses wish to become settlers.

Establishing a point system requires careful thought about the relative merits of different criteria, but it reduces the possibility of favoritism within the selection process. Specific selection criteria most frequently utilized are health, education, skills, previous experiences, and number of children. Throughout the tropics and subtropics, sponsored settlers are overwhelmingly recruited from among low-income farmers or landless laborers. But if a new settlement is to initiate a process of regional development, obviously people with both farm and nonfarm skills must be recruited. This applies at all community levels, since even small communities need carpenters, masons, blacksmiths, curers, barbers, midwives, religious leaders, and other skilled personnel.

The last criterion, family size—more specifically, number of children—is a criterion with which most settlement planners are very concerned. They are faced with a relatively difficult choice. Although younger couples can be expected to be in better health and hence more capable of dealing with the early rigors of settlement, older couples with more and older children will have a larger labor force of family members during those same critical years. Usually ignored is the sociological implication of a settlement population which contains very few three generation families and a very small proportion of older people. If a broader age mix of people is desirable, older couples could be actively recruited to provide the necessary nonfarm occupational skills. Older women, for example, could be recruited as midwives and older men as carpenters, masons, and blacksmiths. Of course, where older couples are recruited the employment needs of their children must be met if subdivision of holdings is to be kept within desirable (economic) limits.

Involving the Host Population

Involving the host population has two meanings. One is utilizing the "indigenous knowledge" of the hosts during project planning and implementation. The other is physically incorporating the hosts within the settlement project if they so wish, or protecting their land rights if they wish to remain outside the project. Time and again settlements are planned and implemented without adequate information on the social, physical, and biotic environment, which is a major reason for their subsequent nonsustainability or inability to realize their development potential. Socioeconomic surveys of the hosts should provide population data, information on their system of land tenure and land use, their water rights, and, to an extent, their socioeconomic systems. Surveys of the host population are needed to establish the total number affected by a possible settlement project and to assess their attitudes toward being incorporated, should settlement proceed. It is fair neither to the hosts nor to the settlers to ignore customary tenure, since future land disputes can jeopardize the entire settlement process. A study of host systems of land and water use can yield invaluable information on the resources of the area and how best to utilize them.[21]

Land settlement projects, including Bank-assisted projects, have a poor record with regard to incorporating the host population. Just how poor that record is, is hard to evaluate since host populations are frequently not even mentioned in project evaluations. Such was the case, for example, in regard to nearly 50 percent of the thirty-four Bank-assisted projects which we reviewed. Though hosts may have been satisfactorily incorporated within some of those projects, in others—including Alto Turi in Brazil and Caqueta in Colombia—the project had an adverse impact on the host population.

While the Bank has become more aware of the problem, encouraging host incorporation, for example, in transmigration projects and in recent FELDA projects, this complex process is still not handled satisfactorily during project implementation. In the transmigration case in Indonesia, usually less than 20 percent of the settlers are hosts and, in some instances (parts of South Sumatra, for example), they have lost parts of their better land. Though the Bank's guidelines regarding tribal groups were applied to the host population in connection with the Polonoreste project in Brazil, both the Bank and the government have been severely criticized because of adverse impacts on hosts during project implementation. Various foreign donors have also been lax in insisting that Sri Lankan agencies implement their government policies on host incorporation in the Tamil-speaking areas of the Mahaweli project, and that the agencies do not mix Tamil-speaking hosts with Singala-speaking settlers in the same community.

Middle-class Settlers

Periodically, governments and settlement agencies have experimented with the recruitment of middle-class settlers—usually as a minority within a settlement dominated by lower-class settlers, but occasionally within their own settlement. Two reasons often cited to justify including middle-class settlers are that they will make more successful farmers and provide leadership within the settlement. There is no evidence, however, that middle-class settlers make better farmers. On the contrary, available evidence suggests that yields per hectare are usually lower on middle-class allotments than on peasant holdings within the same settlement.[22]

The leadership issue is more complex. Middle-class settlers in Sri Lanka "have on the whole done little or nothing to provide any form of leadership for nearby peasant colonists,"[23] but smallholders at Tahaddi (Egypt) told researchers that graduates were useful in pressuring the settlement authorities to live up to their responsibilities for operating the irrigation system and providing inputs. At Way Abung, a World Bank Indonesian transmigration settlement in Sumatra, middle-class settlers were instrumental in establishing a senior secondary school and other social services which were made available to all settlers. On the negative side, however, middle-class settlers tend to dominate positions of leadership within cooperatives and other production and marketing organizations. In the process, they become a new rural elite which impedes the subsequent development of more broadly based settler organizations.

Against this background, there appears to be little justification for combining middle- and lower-class settlers in the same settlement. Settlements of smallholders should instead produce their own leaders.

Settler Homogeneity

Though governments continue to see land settlement as a nation-building mechanism for integrating heterogeneous population groups, the evidence is overwhelming that settlers prefer to live and work with co-ethnics and that ethnically homogeneous settler populations facilitate cooperation and community formation, reduce potentially disruptive conflict, and make for a shorter transition stage.

Even where settlement policies stress homogeneity, those policies are often ignored for a variety of reasons during implementation. In some cases the reasons are technical; in others they are political. In either case there is the risk of factionalism or even communal strife arising in mixed communities. The Accelerated Mahaweli Project is a case in point. Government policy aimed to resettle hosts in their own communities, to settle sponsored settlers according to their electorate of origin, and to keep irrigation turnouts as homogeneous as possible. In fact, Singala-speaking settlers were mixed in System B in the same community with Tamil-speaking hosts, while elsewhere both hosts and sponsored settlers were mixed in turnout units of twenty farm families and less. In the former case, the recommendations generated by social research in the area warned ahead of time about the risk of ethnic strife, should recruitment policies mix different ethnic groups and alter the balance in numbers between those groups. Unfortunately, ethnic strife erupted sometime later with a loss of life that would probably not have occurred if the Mahaweli Authority of Sri Lanka had followed its own policies. The researchers recommended that the settlement agency make "a stronger effort to aggregate people of common origin in the same communities and place neighbors within the same turnout group wherever possible" since field findings indicated that "poor functioning of turnout groups and community factionalism is often attributed to too much heterogeneity."[24]

Although it is recommended that co-ethnics from the same locale be settled within the same community, one advantage of large-scale settlement is that there is room for a range of ethnic groups within the settlement as a whole. It makes sense for co-ethnics to be clustered around their own rural service centers. Adult members of different ethnic groups would then come together at the next level in the settlement hierarchy—that of the rural town where their children, for example, would mix in junior and senior secondary schools.

Layout of Settler Communities

Planning and laying out new communities and settlement patterns for people also require sociological expertise. Although a homestead pattern in which the family house is surrounded by its fields may have obvious benefits for the settler, many sociological and economic assessments have concluded that a clustered settlement pattern in most cases has comparative advantages in generating employment, providing services, and facilitating area development. Thus, "the interests of both settlers and their children are best served in most instances by larger, nucleated settlement. . . . The benefits are of several types—greater employment opportunities, higher service standards, reduced infrastructure costs, reduced migration to large urban centers, and more balanced regional growth."[25] The nucleated settlement pattern at San Julian, a rainfed project in Bolivia, is an imaginative attempt to combine access to fields with access to the local service center.

Social scientists have also arrived at a consensus that the new settler communities should be sited with a spatial distribution that would maximize their functional interaction and rural-urban linkages. Settlement projects "must be based on a hierarchy of communities,"[26] with smaller communities linked to rural service centers and rural and regional towns. Settlement planning throughout the tropics and subtropics tends to overlook the importance of rural towns as opposed to smaller rural service facilities with virtually no industrial capacity. In a sample of more than a hundred cases that I have examined, rural towns were planned in only eleven cases. Regional towns—which retain multiplier effects in the area—received the least attention.

The importance of regional towns is illustrated by the fact that "most of the more successful settlement schemes are either adjacent to thriving regional centers or cities or are associated with the development of such centers on their periphery or within their boundaries."[27] In spite of this, World Bank funds and expertise are seldom involved in the puposive development of rural-urban linkages, even in projects like Bura, FELDA, Rahad, and Mahaweli which involve urban development.

A frequent preference of settlement planners, where they do attempt urban development, is to ignore adjacent regional towns in favor of new town construction within the settlement area. Not only do such new towns usually fail to develop as regional centers but they also are apt to slow down the development of existing towns. One reason why the otherwise successful FELDA-administrated Jengka Triangle Projects in Malaysia produced "fewer multiplier effects than might have been expected in terms of either the emergence of secondary economic activities or urban development"[28] is probably because the Jengka Triangle area was developed as if it existed in a vacuum. In attempting to develop three new towns within the Jengka Triangle, not only did settlement planners ignore already existing adjacent towns but they also tried to restrict the development of secondary economic activities to settler households.

Planning for Farming Systems

Planned agricultural diversification, combining farming, fisheries, and silviculture in an integrated framework, is a rare feature of settlement projects. Instead, throughout the tropics and subtropics, new settlements have been planned and implemented as agricultural schemes to produce a relatively small number of crops for export and, to a lesser extent, for domestic consumption. Yet diversifying farming systems increases the development potential of new lands.[29]

There are four important socioeconomic reasons for diversifying the farming systems of settler families by encouraging multiple crops and combining farming and livestock components. First, such systems tend to be more resilient and ecologically more stable. Second, they are more productive, providing settler families with higher net incomes. Third, diversified farming systems distribute family labor more evenly throughout the annual cycle, providing each family member with a variety of activities: "only through the introduction of properly planned additional enterprises into the crop pattern is it possible to fill the gaps of underemployment in the slack season of the agricultural year."[30] Finally, diversification provides foodstuffs for nonfarm families and raw materials for agroindustries, building a base for more rapid area development.

In semiarid rainfed areas, especially in savanna habitats with irregular rainfall and a lengthy dry season, planning the farming system is a particularly difficult task. Knowledge of viable farming systems is still inadequate and further research is needed on crop rotations, cropping techniques, and the integration of livestock into the farming system. In addition, the balance between industrial crops such as cotton (varieties of which have considerable drought resistance) and food crops is difficult to decide. If too much emphasis is placed on cash crops (such as cotton) as in certain Kariba resettlement areas in Zambia, nutrition may suffer and settler families may lose their resiliency. If no hardy cash crops are grown at all, however, settlers may have insufficient income to meet other needs or to purchase food when consumption crops fail.

In irrigated settlement schemes, the design of irrigation systems should be based on an informed understanding of possible and desirable farming systems. Otherwise there is the danger that the irrigation system will favor a single crop (rice in the case of the Accelerated Mahaweli Project) at the expense of other possibilities. In the humid tropics, whenever tree crops are emphasized, a range of annual crops can be underplanted in maturing orchards, which reduces the dependency of settlers before the first commercial harvest.

Net Income of Settler Families and Employment Generation

If new settlements are to initiate the development of an area, much more attention should be paid to the net income of settler families. In the thirty-four Bank-assisted projects, for example, farm models projected at the time of appraisal were more apt to be calculated on the basis of family labor rather than being designed to take advantage of possible multiplier effects. "Ignoring the probability that successful settler households tend to employ labor regardless of plot size (with family labor reallocated to more lucrative or socially approved activities), too much emphasis is placed on limiting plot size to the minimum that can be worked efficiently with family labor."[31] As a result all too often plot size and cropping patterns are insufficient to move settler households beyond subsistence, or, for that matter, beyond poverty.

Furthermore, it is not in the interests of either employment generation or the welfare of farm laborers to pretend that hired labor does not exist or to de-emphasize its existence. In settlements based on large-scale irrigation, seasonal workers may outnumber adult settlers at certain times in the cropping cycle. In farming systems based on rainfed cultivation, the use of hired labor is less significant.

It is worth repeating that the settler family—not the land or the water—is the main resource of the area, and the new settlement can catalyze a process of development only if the settler family has the incentive and the opportunity to produce. As long as settlers remain close to the subsistence level, it is reasonable to expect them to be risk-averse, as most of them are. As net incomes go up, however, investment strategies change, consumption goes up, and the increasing demand for goods and services in turn increases nonfarm employment opportunities and enterprise development.

Almost by definition, a successful settlement process will create a new rural elite among both settlers and nonfarm families. As they move from the transition stage to the stage of economic development and their incomes go up, successful settlers can be expected to pursue more dynamic investment strategies. The challenge for planners is to set the stage in such a way that settler initiative is encouraged without its being exploitative of others. This can be done in a number of ways. The ready availability of appropriate credit for annual production, mid-term and emergency needs, and strong settler-dominated producer and marketing organizations, can help to spread the benefits of settlement to a larger proportion of the settler population (one of the more attractive features of successful land settlements is their potential to benefit a broadly based settler population as opposed to a small rural elite).

Analysis of existing linkages between agriculture and industry suggests, first, that the potential multiplier effects of agricultural development on general employment are considerably greater than normally realized and, second, that national development policies must share much of the blame for the failure of new settlements to realize their potential for generating nonfarm employment. Nonfarm activities in rural areas provide a primary source of employment and earnings to approximately one-third of the rural labor force (including workers in rural towns). This proportion rises to 40 percent where the town population in rural settings increases to 20,000–30,000 residents. In general, government-sponsored settlement schemes fail to replicate, let alone improve on, such percentages.

Status of Women and Extension Services

Though impacts vary according to the status of settler households, there is a tendency for government-sponsored land settlement to adversely affect the status of women. Examples are worldwide. J. Schrijvers discusses how the Accelerated Mahaweli Project in Sri Lanka has marginalized women (as well as causing undernutrition in children). Even though both spouses are interviewed during recruitment, the 1987 World Bank evaluation of the Jengka Triangle Projects notes not only that "women's rights under the FELDA system have been downplayed," but also that "the inconsistent application of Islamic principles in Jengka has probably served to erode women's rights overall when compared with those prevailing in the traditional *kampung*." Similar impacts have been reported from settlement schemes in Africa, including Kariba (Zambia), Mwea (Kenya), New Halfa (Sudan), and various rice-growing schemes in West Africa.[32]

Women's status is adversely affected for a number of reasons. Settlement projects are planned by men for men rather than for families. Rarely are holdings registered in the name of both spouses and women most frequently gain access to land only after the death of the husband (and even then they may lose out to male relatives of their husband). This is true even where crops grown were formerly women's crops as with rice and groundnuts in West Africa. While women may provide much of the labor, payout is to men, and extension services, with few exceptions, are staffed by men who provide advice only to men. Solutions to these problems must not only protect women's legal rights in settlement plots but also emphasize payout to women for women's crops.

Granted the importance of extension in new land areas, recruiting women as extension agents and providing extension to both men and women are of special importance. Throughout the tropics and subtropics the majority of settlers are unfamiliar with their new habitat at the time of their arrival. To avoid costly mistakes and a lengthy period of adaptation, both orientation and extension are crucial. Although there are exceptions, such as San Julian in Bolivia and Mahaweli in Sri Lanka, orientation programs are virtually nonexistent in new settlements. As for extension, of the thirty-six government-sponsored settlements on which we have sufficient information from the Institute for Development Anthropology's global evaluation, extension services were either nonexistent or minimal in nineteen cases (53 percent), moderate in thirteen projects (36 percent), and good to excellent in only four cases (11 percent). Of the ten spontaneous settlements on which we have adequate data, extension services were either nonexistent or minimal in nine (90 percent).

Development Issues Associated with Stage Two

Generally speaking, planners are least aware of the development implications of stage two. It is a pioneering stage during which settler households must regain self-sufficiency before they can take risks with new forms of production and new types of organization.

Dropout

During the early years of settlement, it is not unusual for relatively large numbers of both spontaneous and government-sponsored settlers to drop out. Although there is little quantified data as to why settlers leave their new homes, case studies indicate a variety of reasons. The two most often mentioned are illness and indebtedness, with the first not infrequently leading to the second.

Indebtedness can occur for a variety of reasons, including illness and death; crop failure owing to pest damage, drought in the case of rainfed agriculture, or poor design or construction of irrigation systems; social events such as weddings; and fiscal mismanagement. Because of the general absence of other forms of credit, settlers are usually indebted to local moneylenders whose credit, although better than none, is usually provided at such high interest rates that debtors may find it virtually impossible to meet their debt servicing responsibilities, with the result that they either sell out or have their land taken over by their creditors. The solution to this problem, which may affect 10 percent or more of settler households during the initial years, is to provide midterm credit for hardship—the legitimacy of which is certified by project staff.

Dependency

Although spontaneous settlers frequently suffer because of inadequate government assistance, the amount of assistance and the way it is delivered may make sponsored settlers dependent on the settlement agency. Dependency is undesirable: it delays the arrival of stage three and reduces the development potential of new lands by curtailing settler initiative. Where settler organizations do form, there is the danger that their activities will be disproportionately concerned with relations with the settlement agency. Finally, dependency increases the financial cost of settlement since the agency must retain a large staff and continue carrying out a range of activities which could otherwise have been handed over to local management. The best way to avoid this is to attempt to involve the settlers in decisionmaking and management from the very start.

Subsidization of settlers should be kept to the absolute minimum at all times, even though during the initial years special assistance may be necessary. Especially in the case of worker-settler programs, the settlers may need shelter, water, and food while preparing the settlement area or before the first food crops are harvested.

Social planners should carefully assess ways to help the settlers become self-sufficient at the earliest possible moment with the least danger of a dependency relationship developing. That said, more often than not governmental aid will be necessary until the first adequate harvest occurs. Various options are available here, including food aid, wage labor on the project, and subsistence allowances until settlers are self-supporting. Where there is a choice, in my experience government-provided food for work produces the best results if the food is distributed in a timely fashion. Wages can be an alternative, but there is the possibility that settlers may come to see themselves as laborers on a government farm rather than as owners and operators preparing their future holdings.

Although some form of food aid, wages, or allowances is usually necessary for a while on sponsored settlements, other types of subsidization should be avoided wherever possible. As a general proposition, settlers should be taxed so that, at the very minimum, they pay for recurrent project costs. Whether they can be expected eventually to repay the government for a portion of the capital investment will depend on the nature of that investment, and the earning capacity of settler households. Recurrent costs are best covered when taxes (on land development or water) have been carefully explained to the settlers from the start.

Settler Organizations

Project success is positively associated with active local participation. Given the lack of social integration which initially characterizes new settlements, agencies should be prepared to facilitate the development of settler participatory organizations. Indeed, the establishment of such organizations is so important for stimulating development and avoiding dependency that they should be mandated by the legislation-establishing settlement authorities. At best, such authorities are apt to be ambivalent about nurturing strong settler organizations, which is another reason for including them in the enabling legislation. Even where settler organizations are encouraged by national leaders, the opposition of local politicians and the authoritarian attitudes of settlement agency officials (plus fear for their jobs) may delay or even inhibit their formation. In the Sudan Gezira scheme, the settlement agency has resisted the devolution of authority to the Gezira Tenants Union. This strong organization represents a federation of tenants at the project level and could play a much more important role in settlement management.

Water user associations of settlers at the turnout, distribution, branch, and main canal levels can be especially effective in improving water management.[33] Although there is no equivalent organization for settlements based on rainfed cultivation, production-oriented organizations could be formed more easily if settlers who lived together also had adjacent fields, as is the case with the San Julian settlement in Bolivia. In Burkina Faso, promising results have come from participatory land management committees that have the support of the government and private voluntary organizations and that emphasize activity zones (cropping systems, pastoralism, classified forests, and so on) for sustainable development.[34]

In general, it is best not to combine multiple functions in the same organization during the initial years of settlement because of the danger of overloading a new organization. Hence water user associations should stick to the operation and maintenance of the water conveyance system rather than expand into a wider range of activities, although subsequently strong organizations should have the option of becoming multifunctional.

Most settlement projects start with no local organizations and with virtually no community structure. In time, settlers can be expected to form their own funeral aid and religious organizations (indeed, their formation is one indicator that the transition stage is drawing to an end), but in most settlement areas they need assistance in forming production-oriented associations. For this, a variety of training programs is needed. The training should involve as many settlers as possible since there is always the danger that elitist programs may separate the trainee from his or her peers, who subsequently view the trainee and the local organization as representing government interests rather than their own. This risk becomes even greater if the settlement agency, as with the Accelerated Mahaweli Project during the early 1980s, places its own staff in leadership positions within what are supposed to be settler-dominated organizations.

Development Issues Associated with Stages Three and Four

As mentioned earlier, stages three and four represent the successful transformation of the new settlement into an economically and socially viable entity. The shift to these stages occurs as an increasing proportion of settlers begin to experiment with new economic opportunities and to participate in settler and other organizations. In this section, however, I will not discuss both stages in the same detail, but will focus on one issue of stage four, the problem of handing over.

From the start, very careful attention should be given to how government inputs can best be provided. Government initiative should therefore be combined with local participation and with the cooperation of the private sector and private voluntary organizations. A special or national settlement agency should have built into its enabling legislation or terms of reference not only mechanisms which encourage it to hand over at appropriate times certain managerial and other functions to the decentralized departments of relevant ministries, rural and municipal councils, and local and participatory agencies but also fiscal and other mechanisms to ensure that such handing over occurs. In this way, successful handing over is the culmination of a planning process which has been directed toward this goal since the inception of the project.

When building settler organizations is emphasized during stage two, useful returns can be obtained at the time of handing over. Strong settler groups can take over certain functions of government or agency officials without confusion when this has been part of the program from the outset. In the same way, building up the infrastructure for an educational system in stage one pays off in literacy and in management skills among the staff of the settler organizations at the handing-over point.

Handing over enables settler organizations not only to play a leading role in managing their own affairs but also to compete in the future for resources at the regional and national levels. Ability to compete is especially important if the settlement area is to catalyze a broader process of integrated area development. When the functions of the settlement agency itself are handed over to other government departments, of course those inheriting this responsibility must have the resources and the will to maintain essential services. Once again, the stronger the settler organizations, the better able they are to act as political pressure groups to obtain the necessary services.

Conclusions and Policy Implications

Creating an economically viable, socially satisfying new land settlement in a problem-prone pioneer zone is one of the more complex tasks attempted by planners and development administrators. Certain production goals must be met, living standards must be raised at the household level, and households must be integrated into viable communities and societies. The conventional wisdom, still strong among settlement planners and administrators, is that settlers are drawn primarily from traditional societies that are both static and conservative and that they must therefore be carefully supervised and led. This view is simply wrong. A recent review of long-term community studies in anthropology concludes that contemporary societies are dynamic, open-ended coping systems, while recent studies of farming communities emphasize time after time the rationality of agricultural decisionmaking at the household level.[35] Voluntary settler families tend to be even more open to innovation than rural communities in old lands areas, as shown by their willingness to leave a familiar home environment for a less familiar frontier and their ability to follow new development strategies once they have established themselves.

On arrival, however, settler households tend initially to be risk-averse, perpetuating the myth among observers that they are basically conservative. Their temporary risk-averse stance, however, as well as their efforts to meet their subsistence needs from their own land as soon as possible, is a logical response to a new habitat. Having once established their own self-sufficiency as food producers, the majority can easily shift into a risk-taking, innovative stance provided opportunities for development are available.

The dynamics of the settlement process can be best understood by breaking it down into a series of stages. During the initial stage settler households are recruited and initial infrastructure is provided in the settlement area. The second stage is a period of adaptation during which the settlers try to come to terms with their new habitat including the communities of strangers among which they find themselves, the settlement agency and the host population. This period of transition is stressful and while it lasts it is unrealistic for planners to expect rapid increases in production.

With good planning and adequate implementation the transition stage can be reduced to two to five years. In the more successful settlement schemes settlers follow a range of investment strategies during the third stage which is remarkably similar throughout the tropics and subtropics. The fourth and final stage involves handing over and incorporation. Handing over has two components: handing over from the settlement agency to line ministries and local organizations and handing over from the first to the second generation of settlers. Incorporation involves integration of the settlement area in the surrounding political economy in such a way that the settler households are able to compete effectively for scarce resources.

Because of poor planning and implementation, a majority of new land settlements never pass through the third stage of economic development and community formation. While settlers tend to be better off than in their previous homes, they are still poor and the settlement process has merely transferred poverty from one area to another. Since sponsored settlement is expensive, with costs frequently exceeding $10,000 to $15,000 per household, and economic rates of return are often low, the economic justification of land settlement projects has been questioned.

While donor evaluations and research show that project appraisals significantly overestimate returns to be expected during the first five years, recent studies also show that longer term benefits are underestimated. Also noting that new land settlement can be an effective mechanism for raising the living standards of the very poor, those studies conclude that settlement can catalyze sufficient regional development to justify, in economic terms, the high costs per household and per hectare. The engine that drives that development through enterprise establishment and employment generation is the increased demand for goods and services of tens of thousands of settlers as their disposable incomes rise.

In conclusion, much has been learned in recent years about the settlement process and the potential of land settlement projects. Much of this knowledge has been incorporated within World Bank policy statements and publications. Increasingly it is being incorporated within the planning process at the time of appraisal, although some offices within the Bank have been slower than others to incorporate lessons learned. For both government agencies and multilateral or bilateral donors, the challenge for the future is to work out mechanisms to ensure that improved plans are actually implemented. Awareness of the sociological issues of new land settlement discussed here, and of their implications for the practice of development interventions, will increase the effectiveness and sustainability of settlement programs.

Notes

1. During fiscal years 1962–75, the World Bank committed $429 million for twenty-eight settlement projects, with almost equal emphasis on irrigated and rainfed settlement (Theodore J. Goering and others, *Agricultural Land Settlement Issues Paper* [Washington, D.C.: World Bank, 1978], p. 16). After 1975, lending for settlement projects increased considerably.

2. This work led to a series of publications; see, in particular, the study by Thayer Scudder and Elizabeth Colson, "From Welfare to Development: A Conceptual Framework for the Analysis of Dislocated People," in Art Hansen and Anthony Oliver-Smith, eds., *Involuntary Migration and Resettlement* (Boulder, Colo.: Westview Press, 1982).

3. These three sources are the following: first, my unpublished report, "The Development Potential of New Lands Settlement in the Tropics and Subtropics: A Global State of the Art Evaluation with Specific Emphasis on Policy Implications," resulting from the 1979–81 research project sponsored by the Institute for Development Anthropology and funded by the U.S. Agency for International Development (USAID) under grant no. AID/DSAN-G-0140. Second, the 1985 report of the Operations Evaluations Department of the World Bank, of which I was the main author, on *The Experience of the World Bank with Government-Sponsored Land Settlement*. This study covered thirty-four projects and built upon an assessment carried out at an earlier date (1978) by T. Goering on twenty-eight of these thirty-four projects. The third source is a series of seven Institute for Development Anthropology reports on the Accelerated Mahaweli Project by Kapila P. Vimaladharma and myself. Grateful thanks are expressed to USAID, the World Bank, the Institute for Development Anthropology, and all individuals—settlement managers, settlement inhabitants, and colleagues—who in one way or another assisted me in my field investigations and in writing this paper.

4. Hans G. T. van Raay and Jos G. M. Hilhorst, "Land Settlement and Regional Development in the Tropics: Results, Prospects, and Options" (The Hague: Institute for Social Studies Advisory Service, 1981; draft), p. 5. See also Raanan Weitz, David Pelley, and Levia Applebaum, *Employment and Income Generation in New Settlement Projects*, World Employment Paper no. 10, Working Paper no. 3 (Geneva: International Labour Office, 1978); and Thayer Scudder, "Increasing Employment Potential of New Land Settlement in the Tropics and Subtropics," in *Transforming Rural Livelihoods: A Search for Asian Alternatives* (New Delhi: Tata McGraw-Hill Publishing Company, Limited, for Marga Institute, Colombo, Sri Lanka, 1986), pp. 64–98.

5. Bruce F. Johnston and Peter Kilby, *Agriculture and Structural Transformation: Economic Development Strategies in Late Developing Countries* (New York: Oxford University Press, 1975), pp. 301 and 304.

6. Clive Bell, Peter Hazell, and Roger Slade, *Project Evaluation in Regional Perspective: A Study of an Irrigation Project in Northwest Malaysia* (Baltimore, Md.: Johns Hopkins University Press, 1982).

7. See, for example, Michael Nelson, *The Development of Tropical Lands: Policy Issues in Latin America* (Baltimore, Md.: Johns Hopkins University Press, 1973).

8. Report on *The Experience of the World Bank with Government-sponsored Land Settlement*, Operations Evaluation Department, World Bank, 1985.

9. See Michael M. Cernea, *From Social Science Knowledge to Policy Formation: The Case of Involuntary Resettlement*, Development Discussion Paper no. 342 (Cambridge, Mass.: Harvard University, 1990); see also Michael M. Cernea, *Involuntary Resettlement in Development Projects: Policy Guidelines in World Bank–financed Projects*, World Bank Technical Paper no. 80 (Washington, D.C., 1988).

10. Goering and others, *Agricultural Land Settlement*, pp. 19–20.

11. Scudder, "Increasing Employment Potential."

12. Emilio Moran, "Government-directed Settlement in the 1970s: An Assessment of TransAmazon Highway Colonization," pp. 12–23, in Debra A. Schumann and William Partridge, eds., *The Human Ecology of Tropical Land Settlement in Latin America* (Boulder, Colo.: Westview Press, 1989).

13. Miriam Chaiken, *Social, Economic, and Health Consequences of Spontaneous Frontier Resettlement in the Philippines*, Ph.D. dissertation, University of California, Santa Barbara, 1983; Gloria Davis, "Beyond Subsistence: A Report on the Agricultural Economies of Way Abung and Baturaja" (Washington, D.C.: World Bank, East Asia and Pacific Projects Department, June 1978); and Tulsi Uprety, *Rural Settlement Policy Processes: A Comparative Study of Government Planned and Spontaneous Settlement Schemes in Nepal*, Ph.D. dissertation, University of California, Berkeley, 1981.

14. Robert Chambers, *Settlement Schemes in Tropical Africa* (New York: Praeger, 1969); and Robert Chambers and Jon Moris, eds., *Mwea: An Irrigated Rice Settlement in Kenya* (Munich: Weltforum Verlag, 1973).

15. In another study of settlement projects, I have divided the first stage into two separate stages dealing (a) with planning and (b) with the initial development of infrastructure and recruitment of settlers. Although this division is useful for managing the detailed practical aspects of the settlement process, I believe the four-stage framework presented here is better for focusing attention on the major phases through which the population itself should go.

16. Weitz, Pelley, and Applebaum, *Employment and Income Generation*; see also Shawki Barghouti, *Diversification in Rural Asia*, World Bank Working Paper no. 98 (Washington, D.C., 1989).

17. See Michael M. Cernea, "Farmer Organizations and Institution Building for Sustainable Development," *Regional Development Dialogue*, vol. 8, no. 2 (1987).

18. While the emphasis here is on the type of diversification that occurs when disposable income and living standards rise, diversification as a survival strategy also occurs when living standards from agriculture fall below subsistence, forcing settlers to add other components (like petty trade and wage labor) to their production systems.

19. Kapila P. Vimaladharma, "Non-farm Employment in the Major Settlements of Sri Lanka," in Kapila P. Vimaladharma, ed., *Land Settlement Experiences in Sri Lanka* (Colombo: Karunaratne & Sons for Kapila P. Vimaladharma, 1982).

20. World Bank appraisal materials for Indonesian transmigration projects.

21. While such studies should be part of feasibility studies, sponsored settlers should also be encouraged to learn from hosts. In the Altamira Zone along the TransAmazon Highway in Brazil, Moran (1989) noted that the more successful settlers sought out hosts "and followed their advice in managing their farms from the start" ("Government-directed Settlement in the 1970s: An Assessment of TransAmazon Highway Colonization," p.13).

22. See, for example, Pacific Consultants, "New Lands Productivity in Egypt," report prepared for USAID (Washington, D.C., 1980); and B. F. Farmer, *Pioneer Peasant Colonization in Ceylon: A Study of Asian Agrarian Problems* (London: Oxford University Press, 1957).

23. Farmer, *Pioneer Peasant Colonization in Ceylon*.

24. Thayer Scudder and Kapila P. Vimaladharma, "The Accelerated Mahaweli Programme (AMP) and Dry Zone Development: Report Number Six" (Binghamton: Institute for Development Anthropology, 1985), p. 31.

25. Goering, *Agricultural Land Settlement*, p. 40.

26. Weitz, Pelley, and Applebaum, *Employment and Income Generation*, p. 70.

27. Report on *The Experience of the World Bank with Government-sponsored Land Settlement*, Operations Evaluation Department, World Bank, 1985.

28. The World Bank, *The Jengka Triangle Projects in Malaysia: Impact Evaluation Report* (Washington, D.C., 1987), p. 63.

29. A detailed and broadly informed technical, economic, and social argument in favor of diversification together with a critique of single-commodity projects is given in: Barghouti, *Diversification in Rural Asia*.

30. Weitz, Pelley, and Applebaum, *Employment and Income Generation*, p. 4.

31. Report on *The Experience of the World Bank with Government-sponsored Land Settlement*, Operations Evaluation Department, World Bank, 1985.

32. Joke Schrijvers, *Mothers for Life: Motherhood and Marginalization in the North Central Province of Sri Lanka* (Delft: Eburon, 1985); World Bank, *The Jengka Triangle Projects in Malaysia*, pp. 29, 30. See also Muneera Salem-Murdock, "Hunger and River Basin Development in Africa: Some Socioeconomic Issues," *GeoJournal*, vol. 14, no. 1 (1987), pp. 37–47.

33. See chapters 2, 3, and 4 in this volume for a more detailed treatment of the establishment and functions of water users' associations.

34. Della McMillan, Thomas Painter, and Thayer Scudder, *Settlement Experiences and Development Strategies in the Onchocerciasis Controlled Area of West Africa* (Binghamton: Institute for Development Anthropology, 1990).

35. George M. Foster, Thayer Scudder, Elizabeth Colson, and Robert V. Kemper, *Long-Term Field Research in Social Anthropology* (New York: Academic Press, 1979); Peggy F. Barlett, ed., *Agricultural Decision Making: Anthropological Contributions to Rural Development* (New York: Academic Press, 1980).

6

Involuntary Resettlement:
Social Research, Policy, and Planning

Michael M. Cernea

Development, either spontaneous or induced, brings not only benefits;
but often causes social disruption. Many planners and policymakers find
it difficult to recognize this double impact, precisely when it matters:
when a development plan is being designed and approved. But it must
be recognized for acknowledging rather than denying it is the beginning
of dealing responsibly with the inevitable disruption.

Social scientists, by contrast, are all too aware of how development
projects can make certain people worse off. But social scientists all too
often speak to themselves: historically they have been much better at
recording development's tragedies than preventing them.

One type of profound social disruption that occurs under certain
development programs is the forced displacement of populations. As I
will discuss below, involuntary displacement and resettlement raises
critical questions for applied social scientists. But beyond the specifics
of the resettlement case, the experiences discussed in the present chapter
suggest, in my view, a valid pattern for treating other kinds of adverse
disruptive consequences of development programs.

Despite a vast literature on the sociology of voluntary settlement,
development research has given comparatively less analytic attention to
involuntary displacement and resettlement. This situation has considerably changed in the latter part of the 1980s. Involuntary population
displacement and resettlement are widespread enough, big enough, fre-

quent enough, complex and consequential enough, to merit the full mobilization of the conceptual, analytical, and operational tools available to address it. For social scientists, this specifically means to assist in: (a) identifying potential disruptions caused by displacement, (b) minimizing them, and (c) formulating countervailing policies and strategies to turn constraints into development opportunities.

The social science analysis of involuntary population displacement is also a test for the contention underlying all the chapters of the present volume: that sociological knowledge can improve the formulation of development policies and operational approaches, so as to substantially enhance the benefits of induced development. In this vein, the present chapter will discuss a case in point: the history and content of the World Bank's policy for dealing with involuntary displacement and resettlement. This policy drew upon social science contributions both to understand the causes of resettlement's adverse outcomes and to develop a pragmatic planning framework that would redress them.

This chapter argues that social scientists working in large development institutions must expand their horizons to focus on policy work, not only on discreet project interventions. Policy development is the active process of introducing constitutive rules about how to approach development in terms of basic goals and compatible means. Policies provide guidelines for allocating development resources in general, as well as for structuring individual projects. Turning social science knowledge about resettlement into organized "do's" and "don't's" for projects financed by governments and international agencies—policies—is as important as understanding resettlement's causes and outcomes.

To develop the argument, the chapter examines two processes occurring during displacement and resettlement: first, the unraveling of the existing social organization because of involuntary displacement; second, resettlement as planned reconstruction of the socioeconomic organization of the affected people.

The chapter also argues that transforming social science knowledge into building blocks for development policymaking is actually a three-stage process. The case at hand will illustrate well this three-step process.

The first step is for social analysis to delve beneath the ethnographic surface to identify the processes happening "on the ground" that must be addressed by development planners. This is social analysis in both its academic and applied forms.

The second step is to formulate and recommend, based on accumulated and systematized knowledge, the basic principles that should become the normative content of the policy.

The third step consists of translating sociological knowledge into a vocabulary of procedures (for planning, reviewing, supervising, and other internal processing activities) that can be used by large bureaucratic organizations such as the World Bank. Doing this successfully requires understanding the organization's complex of rules, values, internal knowledge flows and incentives, structural relationships—in other words, its culture—every bit as much as grasping the field-level realities of the displaced people.

Social anthropology and sociology have provided path-breaking analyses of what happens to uprooted and resettled populations. Their increased use by development planners reflects recognition of this expertise. Examples from several large scale displacements, discussed in the last section of this chapter, will document the difference that the conscious use of social science analysis can make in dealing with the adverse effects of development.

The Unraveling of Social Organization during Displacement

Forced population displacement always creates a crisis. The disruptions and changes it triggers are unequaled in the normal processes of development. Deliberately displacing people exacerbates the difficulties usually confronting planning and implementation. This section discusses why displacement occurs in development projects and what are its common outcomes.

Types of Programs Requiring Displacement

What kind of development programs typically cause forced displacement of people?

Forced relocation is widely but mistakenly seen as a consequence of constructing irrigation or hydropower dams only. In fact, it also occurs in many other sectors. Several categories of development interventions—primarily those predicated on major changes in land and water use—are likely to require mandatory population dislocation. Typically, such projects are those that construct:

- dams for irrigation, hydroenergy, and drinking water that create lakes on previously inhabited areas
- transportation corridors—railways, highways, airports, transmission lines, irrigation canals, and others that require right of way
- new ports and towns
- urban infrastructure, such as sewerage systems, intracity roads, and subways
- new mines, particularly open pit mines
- major industrial estates or zones that require considerable land
- protection for forest reserves or national parks.

The political and economic conflicts embedded in such projects (and in the processes of induced development generally) result from the fact that certain national or regional interests cut across the interests of smaller groups and some individuals. The former interests usually prevail, especially when confronting poor and politically weak population segments. Conflicts emerge also when gains expected in the long term impose losses and hardship in the short term.

Although the argument of the preeminence of national needs can be abused, induced development is in fact predicated on raising production, increasing energy use, and improving transportation; that is, building the irrigation, dam, and road projects that cause displacement. Development can never be completely free of such contradictions and conflicts, and population displacement imposed by more broadly based interests is only one case in point. Recognizing that some degree of displacement cannot be avoided during development does *not* mean, however, that induced development should accept it as a God-given tragedy worthy of little more than a compassionate shrug of the shoulders.

Inasmuch as development projects make a prevailingly positive contribution to national well-being but also have unavoidable negative impacts on certain groups, some means of reconciling the conflicting interests must be found. Firm measures must be taken to protect the lives, productive systems, culture, and human rights of those displaced by such projects,[1] as well as to redress the loss of economic potential incurred by the local or regional economy.

Quantified Measures of Displacement

Is population displacement caused by development a rare and small-scale phenomenon, or is its magnitude sufficient to justify concern?

To quantify the losses caused by displacement several indicators may be used: the number of displaced people; the number of people who lose part of their productive assets, though their houses or houseplots are not necessarily lost; employment losses; environmental losses; costs of moving, and so forth. Aggregate statistics for all these indicators are rarely compiled. But the most important indicator—the overall number of people adversely affected—is significant not only in itself, but also as a proxy for the other indicators. Table 6-1 shows the magnitude of adversely affected populations in irrigation and hydropower dam building projects in twenty-eight cases. This group includes projects financed by a variety of national, bilateral, and international development agencies, not only by the World Bank.

During 1980–90 the World Bank approved financing for 101 projects that entail population displacement. Although they represent a small part of the total number of projects approved by the Bank during this period (below 5 percent), an adjusted estimate of displacement indicates that some 1.6 million to 1.8 million people are affected adversely by these projects.

On a global scale, no hard statistics about development-induced displacement are available. This absence contributes to insufficient public awareness of this issue. A rough assessment of dam-caused relocation worldwide can be made, however. In a 1986 study, I found that only the major and medium dams constructed under World Bank–financed projects approved during 1979–85 would eventually displace approximately 750,000 people. Using this 1986 study in combination with information from the World Inventory of Dams, I arrived at the rough estimate that each year between 1.2 million and 2.1 million people are displaced worldwide as a consequence of new dam construction alone. Caveats notwithstanding, such magnitudes are staggering. Aggregate hard statistics for China, for example, document that the water conservancy projects of the last thirty years have alone caused the evacuation of over 10 million people.[2]

However, reservoir populations are not the only people involuntarily displaced by development programs. Massive additional population dislocation is caused by other types of constructions, such as urban

Table 6-1. *Number of People Displaced by Major Dam Projects*

Dam	Country	Number of People
Already built		
Akosombo	Ghana	84,000
Aswan High dam	Egypt	100,000
Danjiangkou	China	383,000
Kainji	Nigeria	50,000
Kossou	Côte d'Ivoire	85,000
Mangla	Pakistan	90,000
Nangbeto	Togo and Benin	12,000
Portile de Fier	Romania and Yugoslavia	23,000
Saguling	Indonesia	65,000
Sobradinho	Brazil	65,000
Srisailam	India	100,000
Tarbela	Pakistan	86,000
Currently under construction		
Almatti	India	160,000
Itaparica	Brazil	40,000
Kayraktepe	Turkey	20,000
Narayanpur	India	80,000
Narmada Sardar Sarovar	India	70,000
Shuikou	China	68,000
Yacyreta	Argentina and Paraguay	45,000
Under design		
Casecnan	Philippines	4,000
Gandhi Sagar	India	100,000
Kalabagh	Pakistan	80,000
Karnali (Chisapani)	Nepal	55,000
San Juan Tetelecingo	Mexico	22,000
Soubre	Côte d'Ivoire	40,000
Subarnarekha[a]	India	80,000
Three Gorges	China	750,000[b]
Xiaolangdi	China	170,000

a. Includes five dams.

b. Minimum estimate; maximum estimate is 1.2 million.

Source: This table is based on data from project documents and public sources. Some of these projects were cofinanced by the World Bank, while others were financed from other sources, both domestic and international.

renewal, mining, tourist resort development, and new industrial estates. Sometimes even seemingly innocuous programs (for example, establishing an agricultural research and experimentation center, building a hospital complex within an urban settlement, or constructing a drinking water storage basin) also involve land expropriation, depriving many families of their livelihood and habitat and forcing them to relocate. Some estimates put the numbers of people affected in India during the last four decades by such projects to between 2 million and 20 million.[3] It is likely that the need for involuntary displacement will even increase as part of future urban and agricultural development.

Anthropological field studies have also described populations displaced because governments attempt to protect forests and other wildland resources or reserve them for production. Turnbull's controversial study of a starving East African people displaced by a game reserve is perhaps the most well-known example. Lane and Pretty have documented the displacement of pastoralists in Tanzania to convert grassland areas into large-scale wheat farms.[4] Displacement of forest-dwellers creates particularly severe problems for the culture and livelihood of these people.

Another kind of massive displacement consists of state-sponsored resettlement programs that claim to be undertaken to benefit primarily the displaced. Such relocation programs include, for instance, the forced transfer of the Bulusu of East Kalimantan, Indonesia, and of other interior Dayak groups to government-established resettlement centers, with the stated purpose of providing them with services; or the imposed population transfer away from Ethiopia's drought prone areas. Appell, Clay, and other social researchers have concluded, in light of their field investigations, that these programs are politically motivated government operations that are disguised under a "development" rhetoric, but have little to do with real development.[5]

In summary, even if magnitude were the only factor considered, population displacement caused by development programs fully calls for more attention from policymakers and social scientists.

Tearing Apart the Social Fabric

To some planners or administrators it is not obvious why development-induced displacement is so disruptive. They argue that long-distance movement is a constant of human history, at times to environments more hostile than those facing resettlers from development projects. But it is not the movement itself that is so traumatic: rather, it is its impact on the structures of economic and cultural life. The fundamental feature of *forced* displacement is that it causes a profound and sudden unraveling of existing patterns of social organization.

This unraveling occurs at many levels. When people are forcibly moved, production systems are dismantled. Long-established residential communities and settlements are disorganized, while kinship groups and family systems are often scattered. Life-sustaining informal social networks that provide mutual help are rendered nonfunctional. Trade linkages between producers and their customer base are interrupted, and local labor markets are disrupted. Formal and informal associations or self-organized services are wiped out by the sudden departure of their membership, often in different directions. Traditional authority and management systems tend to lose their leaders. Abandonment of symbolic markers, such as ancestral shrines and graves, or spatial context, such as sacred mountains, water courses or trails, severs physical and psychological linkages with the past and saps at the roots of the peoples' cultural identity.[6] Not always visible or easily quantifiable, these processes are nonetheless real. The cumulative effect of all these processes is that the social fabric is torn apart.

Many anthropological and sociological field studies have documented in vivid detail the qualitative consequences of forced displacement.[7] These consequences vary enormously with local circumstances, with the extent of loss of income-generating assets and with the degree of resilience or vulnerability of the affected population, among other factors. But there are also basic features these cases share. Those at the economic level are most obvious. Comparing the empirical findings of many field monographs, I found that the ultimate common factor underlying the broad spectrum of reported displacement consequences is the *onset of impoverishment*.[8] Extending far beyond its immediate (visible) effects, forced displacement can trigger a spiral of impoverishments that amplifies and worsens the initial damage. Sometimes, under favorable subsequent circumstances, this process may slowly subside or even be reversed at the relocation sites. But the evidence strongly demonstrates that impoverishment often tends to deepen with time.

The impoverishment process caused by forced displacement typically occurs along the following seven main dimensions:

- landlessness
- homelessness
- joblessness
- marginalization
- food insecurity
- increased morbidity and mortality
- social disarticulation.

A few examples illustrate the above points. The development of the São Francisco river basin in Brazil, for instance, included the construction of several major dams and polders: Sobradinho, Paolo Alfonso, Itaparica, and other dams. The new irrigation, flood control, and power generation capacities are of national importance, but the reservoirs have also entailed massive human dislocation. Lake Sobradinho displaced 65,000 people and caused a major socioeconomic disorganization. Although 24,000 people were "planned" to relocate to Serra de Ramalho, an area about 800 kilometers upstream of Sobradinho, only about 28 percent actually relocated there. Many settlers got off to a disastrous start: during the five-day boat and bus journey upstream, they lost their possessions and many farm animals; they received no compensation for these losses and at the new site were left to fend for themselves as best they could. Moreover, about half of the land allocated to them was unsuitable for agriculture. Even fourteen years after the move, the precarious economic situation at this location site has not significantly improved.[9]

Under Brazilian regulations, compensation for expropriated land can be paid in cash. However, field investigations have proved that the actual payments offered in the Sobradinho resettlement, as well as in other cases like Itaipu dam resettlement[10] and Tucurui dam resettlement,[11] were woefully insufficient for the purchase of comparable land by those displaced. This made many farmers from the Itaipu and Tucurui areas slide toward complete landlessness, or left them with smaller, marginal holdings. Moreover, many farmers were not compensated because they had only customary but not formal legal title to land. For example, in the Tucurui reservoir, only 20.8 percent of the 4,334 properties surveyed had property title, while in the Sobradinho area as much as two-thirds of the farmers lacked titled ownership.

The denial of compensation entitlements instantly decapitalized many independent smallholders and made it harder or impossible for them to reestablish themselves. Furthermore, the loss of consumers from the reservoir area reverberated throughout the regional economy, well beyond the immediately affected area.

In Kenya's Kiambere reservoir area, the sociological impact study carried out by Mburugu found that resettlers' average land-holding size dropped from 13 hectares to 6 hectares. Their livestock was reduced by more than a third; yields per hectare decreased by 68 percent for maize and 75 percent for beans, while the drop in income (from Ksh. 10,968 to Ksh. 1,976) amounts to a loss of 82 percent. More than one-third of the resettlers were still without new houses by the end of the project's initial period.[12]

In Indonesia, the Institute of Ecology of Padjadjaran University carried out in 1985 a social survey among reservoir families who were given cash compensation and resettled in the Saguling dam shoreline area. The survey found that after relocation the income of these families was 49 percent lower and their land ownership 47 percent lower than before development.[13] Impact studies for the Cirata dam, also located in Indonesia, found that, while 59 percent of the poor households improved their incomes after relocation, about 21 percent were worse off, with a 25 percent loss from their previous income levels.[14]

Research has shown that compulsory dislocation causes special cultural, economic, and technical problems that are not only largely different from, but usually more severe than, those entailed by voluntary migration and relocation. A feeling of alienation, helplessness, and powerlessness is instilled in those uprooted. Social cohesion is weakened, and increased psychological and sociocultural stress diminish the initiative and capacity for collective action of those affected.

The negative consequences of involuntary displacement have been aggravated, in countless cases, by (a) the absence of a strategy for redressing the problems resettlement creates and (b) the inadequacy of planning and execution for projects that cause dislocation. Many of the findings about social disorganization have been known for a long time. In addition, many of the studies commissioned by planning agencies reported the same unfortunate outcomes as professional social research did, albeit without the same in-depth analysis. Thus, population displacement is not an unanticipated and unpredictable adverse consequence of development: in most cases it is fully predictable. What comes as a surprise is not that adverse effects result from drastic change processes, but that they continue to be overlooked and low on the planners' agenda, and that measures to avoid them are not thought through in advance. The effect of neglecting to plan for resettlement adequately is, for the affected people, tantamount to induced impoverishment rather than development. In plain terms, this means that tens of thousands of people are undergoing amplified losses, hardships, and suffering that could have been avoided or mitigated if the attempt had been made.

Consistent with the thrust of this volume, describing how social organization is torn apart by displacement is important not as an exercise in sociological prowess or in signaling development's shortcomings. Such analysis is necessary for identifying *what needs to be done* to help resettlers reconstruct their social fabric. Unveiling the fallacies of conventional resettlement planning is needed to signal what needs to be changed about how institutions intervene in processes that are only partially understood and never fully controlled.

How can sociology and anthropology help improve resettlement?

The knowledge developed in this domain through sociological and anthropological research can make, and in fact has already made, a substantial difference in the way involuntary displacement and resettlement are being carried out, at least in some projects. Next, I will examine how social science knowledge contributes to:

- the formulation of an explicit policy for resettlement
- the content of the policy
- the translation of policy into operational strategies and plans for reestablishing those displaced
- the actual execution and monitoring of resettlement.

Formulating a Sociologically Informed Policy

Over the years, anthropologists and sociologists of various countries have generated a corpus of professional knowledge about the effects of socioeconomic uprooting and the patterns of people's responses to exogenously imposed displacement. Nevertheless, until recently the availability of sociological "knowledge-on-the-shelf" about involuntary resettlement exercised very little influence on governments and relevant agencies.

Believers in the "enlightenment model" of social science influence over social affairs assume that simply exposing social ills will lead to measures for their correction (for a broader discussion of enlightenment versus social engineering, see chapter 1). This assumption was soundly disproved in the case of involuntary resettlement. Although studies and books produced by social scientists kept accumulating, their effect was very limited. By and large, they were ignored by the officials responsible for programs entailing compulsory displacement. Development policies of most governments and major agencies, including the World Bank, did not explicitly demand that involuntary resettlement be carried out under more stringent criteria, based on an adequate social understanding of the nature of this process. Worse, major engineering consulting firms that designed projects usually left out population relocation from their feasibility studies and cost- estimates. This practice backfired during the implementation stage, when underfinanced and unplanned relocation had to be executed as last- moment emergency operations. Critical conclusions about such adverse consequences have been reached both by the Bank and by many socioecological and environmental studies.[15]

A significant change in this situation occurred when, for the first time, a major development agency—the World Bank—adopted an explicit policy statement addressing the social issues inherent in involuntary resettlement operations. The World Bank's initial resettlement policy was issued in February 1980.[16] An unusual feature of this policymaking process, in comparison with the formulation of Bank policy on other issues, was that the resettlement policy statement was grounded in *social science* knowledge and was prepared primarily by sociologists inside the World Bank.[17]

In the preparation of the policy and of the procedures for translating it into project work, we have used research findings, concepts, and conclusions that have emerged from pioneering anthropological and sociological studies on forced resettlement. These include the many essential contributions by Scudder in this field,[18] the studies on the Volta reservoir in Ghana by Chambers and associates,[19] on the Gwembe Tonga from the Kariba reservoir by Colson,[20] the study of urban displacement carried out in the United States by Gans,[21] and others. Blended into the new policy and procedures were also the evaluation lessons fed back from the Bank's own projects in the 1970s.

Further, in 1985–86, a new sociological analysis of the Bank's experience with resettlement and with the application of its own policy was carried out in-house. The findings of this comprehensive analysis led to a reexamination of the Bank's policy, and an additional "operational policy" paper on resettlement was written and formalized inside the Bank in October 1986.

In 1988, both policy documents (1980 and 1986) were integrated into one paper that, for the first time, was publicly issued by the Bank and made widely available.[22] This paper specified in more depth and detail the Bank's policy, and further translated it into practical measures and steps for project work. The Bank's resettlement policy guidelines were again examined, strengthened and revised in 1990.[23]

The description above demonstrates that the formulation of the resettlement policy was not a one-shot affair, in which principles are stated and then gradually forgotten or allowed to become irrelevant, as circumstances change. On the contrary, it was—and is—a continual, steady process which proceeded in an iterative manner through several rounds of substantive improvements.

In actual project practice, the tangible results of the resettlement policy and of its improvement rounds consisted in major changes in many Bank-assisted resettlement project components. Previously, certain statutory limitations of the Bank's role were interpreted in a way that led to a less-active-than-possible position for the Bank in displacement operations. This referred, for instance, to the treatment of land acquisition for project purposes, the application of eminent domain law, the levels of compensation payments, and other aspects. Moreover, the Bank's financial resources were generally not used for assisting the resettlement and related activities. In turn, this was broadly (even though inadequately) interpreted to mean that the Bank could not or would not demand conditions and standards on how to conduct operations that it was not financing.

The adoption of a policy gradually changed the Bank's public discourse about population displacement and cast it into a new conceptual framework. First, it rejected the argument that impoverishing resettlers was an unavoidable, if lamentable, facet of development. Second, it was predicated on the argument that there were development strategies that could produce better outcomes. Third, while declaring that the borrowing governments, as executing agents, retain ultimate responsibility for carrying out resettlement, it expanded the scope of the Bank's internal obligations to ensure the quality of resettlement planning and execution, as it was already required to ensure the soundness of the other economic and technical components.

The Content of Resettlement Policy

As noted in the prior section, the Bank's resettlement policy, and its definition of the issues at hand, were illuminated by a set of concepts borrowed from social science that changed the previously strictly technical or economic discussions of relocation. For instance, the new policy referred explicitly to "community structure," "moving in groups," "kin-groups," and "cultural identity"; talked about "settler-host integration," "social networks," and "social cohesion"; about "dependency syndrome" or the cultural meaning of "leaving behind lands, deities, and ancestors," and so on. The use of such a vocabulary is not customary within agencies seeking econocratic or technocratic "precision." Yet the new public discourse arose precisely because a new *content*, new *variables*, and new *dimensions* of project processes were recognized and defined in order to guide operational activities. This modified in-house conceptualization compelled staff members to think in new ways about what they were doing, to see dimensions of their own work which previously passed unobserved, and to act according to new, modified criteria.

The normative content of the resettlement policy guidelines can hardly be compressed here in a manner that will do them justice, and a more detailed presentation is available in print elsewhere.[24] In a summary manner, however, the main substantive elements of the policy are the following:

- Involuntary displacement should be avoided or minimized wherever feasible, because of its disruptive and impoverishing effects. To avoid displacement, all viable alternative project designs should be explored. Where displacement is unavoidable resettlement plans should be formulated with due care given to peoples' needs and to environmental protection.
- All involuntary resettlement should be conceived and executed as a *development program*, providing sufficient investment resources and opportunities to assist resettlers in their efforts to improve their former living standards and earning capacity, or at least to restore them. Displaced persons should be (a) compensated for their losses at replacement cost, (b) given opportunities to share in project created benefits, and (c) assisted with the move and during the transition period at the relocation site.

- Displaced people should be moved in groups, as social units of different kinds, to preserve (inasmuch as possible and desired by the affected people) the preexistent social networks and local forms of organizations. Group or individual self-resettlement should be facilitated whenever it represents the preferred option.
- Minimizing the distance between the new and old sites can facilitate the readaptation and integration of resettlers into the surrounding social and natural environment, provided the economic and natural resource potential at the new site is adequate. The possibilities of tradeoffs between distance and economic opportunities must be taken into account and balanced carefully.
- The existing social and cultural institutions of resettlers and their hosts should be relied upon in conducting the displacement, transfer, and reestablishment process. Community participation in planning and implementing resettlement should be encouraged.
- The new communities of the resettlers, often created by regrouping several prior smaller villages, should be designed as settlement systems equipped with infrastructure and services, with due consideration to their integration in the encompassing regional economic contexts.
- Host communities that accept resettlers should be considered in the overall planning process and assisted to overcome possible adverse socioenvironmental consequences from the resettlement.
- Indigenous peoples, ethnic minorities, pastoralists, and other groups that may have informal customary rights to the land or other resources taken for the project must be provided with adequate land, infrastructure, and other compensation. The absence of formal legal title to land by such groups should not be grounds for denying compensation and rehabilitation.

These basic policy guidelines created a totally new framework for planning displacement and resettlement operations. This framework cannot be compared to any previous one, since a formal policy simply did not exist previously. But if the "practical policy" is considered, in other words if the pattern of routine practice in resettlement is taken as reference, the difference is enormous. In fact, what I call the previous "pattern of routine practice" continues to be today the *current* pattern in forced resettlement in many projects that are not related to World Bank activities. Hence, the importance of disseminating and instituting formal national policies with a normative content similar to the one previously described.

Formulating Institutional Procedures

Formulating policy guidelines in the context of a large development agency like the World Bank implies not only defining general resettlement principles, however important these are. As mentioned at the beginning of this chapter, a distinct step of the "knowledge-translation" process by the social scientist is proposing *institutional procedures* for implementing the general principles derived from a theory of action. This exercise is far from pedestrian, as academic purists tend to regard it from afar. Without sanctioned procedures, policy cannot be applied, especially those policies that require new ways of doing business. Without congruence between policy and procedures, there also is no way to measure policy implementation and effects.

Formulating institutional procedures in the specific case analyzed here meant designing the sequence of practical steps for addressing involuntary resettlement issues during each stage of the project cycle: project identification, preparation, appraisal, and supervision (see a discussion of these stages in chapter 1). The procedures had to prescribe both what the staff of the Bank must do and what must be done by borrowing agencies in their own countries.[25]

Developing an institutional awareness of the policy and of how it can be practically incorporated into daily operations was a gradual process. Overviews of policy implementation beginning in 1984 identified bottlenecks in various operational divisions and ambiguities in interpretation. Thus, for example, while the policy required developing a full resettlement plan (describing where and how displaced people would be reestablished) *before* appraising a project, for some highway projects the actual layout (and hence the displacement) was decided year by year during the project. More commonly, however, the chief difficulty was that national governments lacked the legal framework and the appropriately skilled institutions to carry out resettlement; assisting in their build-up became a major long-term activity in which both policy and operational staff have collaborated.

Thus, during a full decade—1980 to 1990—an iterative "dialogue" took place between the body of social science knowledge on resettlement, on the one hand, and the Bank's institutional policy and procedures, on the other. In substance, this meant that the body of knowledge on resettlement went through a thorough test of "translatability" into the World Bank's development dialects. The results proved that the conscious application of this knowledge led to a better development policy and to ameliorated planning procedures. In turn, the application of the new policy to projects, the many sociological research projects initiated in this period, and the vast operational activities for improving resettlement practice, have enriched the social science empirical and conceptual understanding of resettlement.

From Policy to Practice: Reestablishing the Displaced

To translate the normative content of the resettlement policy into an operational approach, the concept of *resettlement plan* was introduced. Such a resettlement plan is expected to be part of every project that causes involuntary displacement. A generic structure was developed and prescribed for such plans, to ensure coverage of the key variables in each individual case. The resettlement plan must be funded through the project and be implemented on a timetable coordinated with the progress of the project, to prevent crash relocation or delays in project advance. The provisions of the relocation plan must be consistent with the requirements, norms, and objectives set by the resettlement policy.

The demand that project designers prepare from the outset a distinct plan for resettlement has redefined many of the practical problems at hand in project processing. Forced displacement has been treated in the past as an administrative problem of mere physical removal of people out of the path of the flooding reservoir waters or the coming highway.[26] With such an approach, the "planning" was usually reduced to the legal procedures for expropriating land and paying compensation: project planners and appraisers have little to do regarding resettlement.

In contrast with this treatment, when resettlement is treated as an opportunity and mandate for reconstructing production systems and human settlements, the whole project planning must be broadened so as to include a strategy to reestablish people: goals, resettlement sites, new productive basis, organizational responsibilities, timetables, budgets, and so on. The former approach aggravates the disruptive effects of displacement and is a proven recipe for failure. The latter approach is clearly preferable, but is costlier. The difference between them is major. What we call the "resettlement plan" is the planning and financial instrument that must embody and carry out the new approach.

Defining and prescribing a generic structure for resettlement plans is intended to make sure that all real-life plans to be prepared under various projects will (a) cover the main issues that arise in all resettlement processes; (b) pursue development rather than merely relief; and (c) remain flexible enough to allow for adaptation to local circumstances.

The generic components of the resettlement plan refer to: (a) the development "package" and strategy; (b) the social organization of resettlers; (c) valuation and compensation; (d) habitat and social services; and (e) environmental protection and management. The plan is expected to start from an explicit policy statement and legal framework defining the overall objectives, the entitlements of those affected, and the allocation of organizational responsibilities to carry out each resettlement activity by an agreed upon timetable. Of course, this generic structure leaves room for considerable flexibility in selecting specific solutions and modes of implementation suitable in any particular situation.

Most essential among these elements are the development strategy and the reconstruction of the social organization of resettlers. These are closely related in that the reestablishment of a productive basis for the resettlers is seen as the backbone of their social organization patterns.

A brief discussion of these generic components of the resettlement plan follows.

The Development Package

Extraordinary difficulties await both the people displaced and the relocation agencies because the starting point of resettlement is the setback caused by the loss of key productive assets and social networks. Therefore, the development package is the set of provisions intended to reconstruct the production base of those relocated. It must offer sufficient opportunities and resources for their economic and social reestablishment as self-sustaining producers or wage earners.

Two basic strategies may be pursued for reestablishing those dislocated from rural settings: land-based strategies and employment strategies.

In *land-based strategies*, the policy affirms that adequately compensating for lost property is important, but that the crux of any viable resettlement is providing economic opportunities to reestablish the displaced populations as agricultural producers, rural artisans, and so forth. Components based on technically feasible agricultural activities are likely to be the main avenue to restoring the production systems. Such components may be: land reclamation, irrigation schemes, agricultural intensification, tree crops development, fisheries, commercial or social forestry, vocational training, off-farm employment, and other kinds of lasting income-generating activities. Reforestation schemes are of particular importance not only for their income-generating potential, but also for mitigating some of the environmental losses usually caused by reservoir submergence. In planning agriculturally based relocation strategies, there is much to be learned from the approaches developed for the voluntary settlement of new lands (see chapter 5).

Land is a crucial factor in reestablishment strategies. Since the vast majority of those displaced tend to be farmers or agricultural laborers, the reconstruction of their productive potential essentially depends on the availability of land. The experience in a number of projects, however, is not very encouraging, since implementing agencies are often reluctant (or not competent enough) to take all the steps necessary for making land available to those dispossessed of their land. Most often, however, the unavailability of land is the result of (a) lack of adequate project planning, (b) lack of effort to identify existing land reserves, (c) lack of political will to use government authority for providing land that legally can be made available, or (d) lack of imagination to design proper solutions. Therefore, rural resettlement plans should start by establishing the basic indicator: the *amount of land necessary* to reestablish those displaced on a productive base. This requires, in sequence, identifying economically and technically viable sites acceptable to relocatees and timetables for obtaining and preparing the new farming land.

Alternative strategies *based on employment* (rather than land) become imperative in situations of extreme land scarcity. For some of those displaced, such employment alternatives are required even when land is available. Opportunities then need to be opened up for those displaced to reestablish themselves in the industrial or service sectors of the local or regional economy. Jobs may need to be created through new investments. Vocational training alone does not restore income, unless those displaced can actually get jobs with their newly acquired skills. This is why restoration of productive systems and substitution for lost income-generating assets should go beyond simple cash payments to providing an alternative income basis to the affected people.

Those displaced from urban or peri-urban settings usually derive their livelihood from jobs in the industrial or service sectors or from self-employment, but sometimes they may own some farm land as well. The approach to their situation should therefore pursue their access to employment opportunities and, when warranted, to some land for farming or gardening (in addition to new housing plots). Depending on local circumstances (rural, urban, or peri-urban), a combination of land-based and employment strategies may be adequate. Whichever strategy is followed, however, it must be flexibly translated into specific steps to be taken and funded by the project.

When urban settlements are affected, the resettlement plan must give special attention to the complexities of site ownership, the legality of site occupation, and the site-related economic (productive or service) activities. The policy directs that squatter communities slated for removal receive alternative locations for housing *although they may lack the legal title or rights* to their land (or other property) that would ensure their compensation. Given the likelihood of increased involuntary *urban* resettlement in developing countries in the 1990s and beyond year 2000, finding alternative options for urban relocation will become even more necessary.[27]

The Social Organization of Resettlers

Another policy prescription drawn from social science research is that strong support for self-organization within the new human settlements is indispensable for relocation with development. The policy explicitly directs that resettlement plans should support the settlers' social and cultural institutions and rely on them as much as possible, while the initiative of resettlers should be encouraged through self-help and incentive programs. This can be seen particularly in the several recent Bank-assisted projects which have, for the first time, recognized traditional land tenure systems as a valid basis for full resettlement entitlements.

Because the dismantling of previous authority systems weakens the self-mobilizing capacity of the community and tends to induce helplessness and social apathy, careful work with the resettlers, the hosts, and their leaders prior to and after the move is crucial. At the same time, to be ultimately successful, resettlement operations require a gradual transfer of responsibility from settlement agencies to the settlers themselves.

The policy guidelines explicitly ask that resettlement agencies beware of the bureaucratic tendency to retain decisionmaking and managerial functions among agency personnel and instead should encourage the emergence of recognized community leaders.

When relocation takes place downstream or around the reservoir, or in both areas, the resettlement plan must pursue the involvement of local authority systems of *both* resettlers and hosts to avert "second-generation" environmental effects, including encroaching on forests, soil-erosion, and overgrazing. Local leaders must eventually take over from the settlement agency the responsibility for environmental protection and management and for the maintenance of infrastructural assets.

The majority preference of those displaced to move in groups as cultural or social units (for example, as entire kin groups, extended families, ethnic groups, neighborhoods, whole hamlets, or village units) also bears on their potential to become socially organized and economically productive quickly at the new location. This preference must be supported as long as it does not adversely affect the choice of feasible redevelopment options or the genuine preference of some for individual self-relocation. Planned support for relocation of integral cultural units would protect an important social resource—the viable patterns of group organization—which once revived at the new location can cushion disruption caused by resettlement.

Shelter and Social Services

Turning displacement into development also calls for reconstructing settlements with enhanced standards of physical planning and services, rather than just replicas of those existing previously. The reconstruction of the habitat must be done along two social dimensions: (a) building new community settlements as livable systems and (b) building houses for each individual family.

The new settlements will be expanding sociocultural systems whose collective needs will increase over time. Planning of social services gains a high profile. The social infrastructure, school and health services, road access to employment opportunities, and the size of the housing plots and dwellings should be carefully designed to meet the needs of resettlers' growing families, taking into account at least the first and second generation in the settlement.

Social Skills in Resettlement Projects

The basic prescriptions for preparing and implementing involuntary resettlement were structured along the World Bank's project cycle model and its key stages: project identification, preparation, preappraisal, appraisal, implementation, and supervision. Underlying the operational procedures is the idea that professional social skills are necessary throughout the process, not only on the Bank's side but on the borrower's side as well. Minimizing the hardships of dismantling a human settlement, planning the transfer of population, and establishing a new rural settlement involves social engineering.[28] This is why the Bank's policy explicitly mandated that preparation of the resettlement component, which requires expertise from many disciplines, should normally involve the on-site services of at least one sociologist or anthropologist, preferably a national from the country and specialist in resettlement. In hindsight, this recommendation can be credited with the substantial increases in the number and duration of employment of professional anthropologists and sociologists in such projects. It also requires a stronger involvement of the academic social science community in this field.[29]

The above discussion of the resettlement plan reflects how the recognition of sociocultural variables has led to different operational guidelines, including also different allocation of project financial resources, compared with earlier situations in which the absence of such considerations caused underfinancing and misallocation of human skills and capital resources.

To support the claim that the resettlement policy and planning approach described here have made a substantive difference in practice, I will briefly describe the types of actual improvements achieved in Bank-assisted projects in many countries. These, in essence, are: a vast improvement in the planning of involuntary resettlement; the promotion of development-oriented, production-based relocation strategies, instead of relief-oriented, cash-compensation approaches; increased allocation of financial and institutional resources to assist resettlers; stronger protection of the livelihood and rights of the adversely affected people. In certain projects, tradeoffs have been found to minimize displacement; in others, such as the Colombia Power Sector Project, some intended dams (for example, Urru II) with otherwise high technical payoffs were excluded from the proposed projects because of their unacceptably high displacement effects. Under the impetus of the Bank's resettlement policy, governments and concerned agencies in India, Mexico, Brazil, Colombia, and other countries have started to elaborate explicit legislation, domestic policies, or formal rules regarding development-caused displacement or have updated, and strengthened existing regulations.[30] Some bilateral donor agencies are also preparing their own guidelines for such projects (for example, the Overseas Development Administration in the United Kingdom), which largely draw on the Bank's policy as described above.

In turn, this policy and the large body of applied sociological work it has triggered have also generated clear-cut disciplinary gains for the social sciences. Newly commissioned sociological research has expanded the body of empirically based knowledge about resettlement; applied work has gained a sharper professionalism and increased competence; and anthropologists and sociologists have gained more recognition and credibility as experts with skills and knowledge that make a difference in development work. It is particularly encouraging to see that much of the increase in applied social work for resettlement is due to social science researchers from developing countries.

A significant example of how this policy has changed the project-making *processes* and in turn many projects themselves, is the Upper Krishna Irrigation II Project in Karnataka state, India. The two dams being built under this project, Almatti and Narayanpur, cause massive displacement: 160,000 and 80,000 people, respectively. The first phase of this project started in 1978, before the Bank's policy on resettlement was enacted: as usual then, it bore the typical and unfortunate imprints of inadequate resettlement planning. At completion of phase I of the project, the overall evaluation report had to direct its sharpest criticism to the project's unsatisfactory resettlement component.

In 1986–87, when the borrowing agency prepared the project's phase II for subsequent Bank financing, the continuation of resettlement was initially "planned" by the borrowing agency in much the same vein as in phase I. However, this time a policy was already in place in the Bank. It led to the rejection of the proposed but inadequate plan for phase II. The field appraisal of the project was delayed by the Bank several times specifically because the resettlement component was found each time to be incomplete, misdesigned, and underfinanced.

To improve it, Karnataka's government involved a local nongovernmental organization named MYRADA in the planning process and carried out social surveys, tested out a land-pool approach through a special pilot project, and prepared new state legislation, which was informed by the lessons learned from past experience and from the new pilot project.[31] This incremental sixteen to eighteen months of *policy-driven project preparation work* produced a much improved resettlement plan. Only then was the full project appraised by the Bank, with its own anthropologists on the appraisal team.[32]

The resettlement component of the new Upper Krishna II Project is designed to help reconstruct a production basis for the relocated people and new settlements well equipped with infrastructure services. Some categories of affected people will be assisted in acquiring 1.5 hectares of irrigated land in the downstream benefiting zone or equivalent non-irrigated land, with an ex-gratia grant of Rs. 30,000 per family. Other groups will be offered a choice among several income-generating schemes: these may include pumplift irrigation, dairying, transport using bullock carts, sheep rearing, fishing, and others. It is estimated that the plots of irrigated land in the command area, or of equivalent nonirrigated land, could provide for the average relocated family an income of Rs. 7,260 to Rs. 13,500 per hectare each year, which is equivalent to 1.8 to 2.5 times the annual poverty-level income of Rs. 4,500 per family. This would be higher than the income of the majority of project-affected families who lived below the poverty line before displacement.[33] Implementation of this development package had started by the end of 1989.

Comparable examples of substantial resettlement components—planned better, embodying innovative policy and operational approaches, and benefiting from financial and institutional allocations much higher than the average allocations in the past—can be found in other Bank-assisted projects of the late 1980s: for example, the Shuikou Hydropower Project in China, the Punjab Irrigation and Drainage Project in India, and the Zimapan Hydropower Dam and Resettlement Project in Mexico.[34] Practically every case requires a special effort to break away from the old and unsatisfactory ways of handling involuntary displacement, entrenched in the bureaucratic practices of various executing agencies; but the existence of an explicit, standing policy is the powerful force that, time and again, leads to a substantive turnaround.

Sociological Monitoring

It is of paramount importance to ensure sociologically informed monitoring of the economic, cultural, and psychological processes that unfold within the population subjected to displacement and relocation. Often, unjustified departures from the policy or from the agreed project provisions undermine the development objectives and render the policy less effective. Such departures happen for various reasons, not least because borrowing agencies do not comply with the explicit legal covenants regarding resettlement.

Of course, as has been observed, "simply having a good resettlement policy on the books is not enough. Turning a good resettlement policy into good resettlement action is not easy: governments resist, managers equivocate, and line agencies are not always willing to back up brave words with hard cash."[35] When such departures occur, not only is the policy compromised, but the quality and soundness of people's resettlement is lowered.

The Bank's policy requirements regarding the standards for adequate resettlement are, in general, considerably higher than the current practices in many borrowing countries and usually are more demanding than the norms contained in the regulatory frameworks (if any) of the borrowers. This gap resists closure and is difficult to overcome in one step. Old mentalities and bureaucratic routines often actively oppose the resettlement standards and provisions agreed upon and designed into Bank-assisted projects; discrepancies therefore occur between plans and practice. Sometimes, levels achieved in actual resettlement represent significant improvements over prior local practices, yet they may still fall short of project goals.

To carefully review the unfolding of the relocation processes, clear operational procedures for monitoring have been instituted, as have legal instruments for enforcing compliance. Bank supervision teams are directed to pay careful attention to the sociocultural, economic, and technical aspects of resettlement as a whole. Increasingly, however, project monitoring is carried out by independent organizations within the country. Monitoring these dimensions during the different phases of displacement and relocation—before transfer, during transfer, immediately after transfer, and after reestablishment—provides feedback for managing this process and for reducing its adverse consequences.

Institutionalizing sociocultural monitoring, as opposed to watching only the physical indicators, provides both a warning system for project managers and a channel for the resettlers to make known their needs and their reactions to resettlement. Since recovery from displacement can be protracted, it is often necessary to continue such sociological monitoring well after populations have been relocated, frequently even after a project has been closed.

Even under a carefully applied policy, involuntary resettlement is, and will always remain, a traumatic process in the life of the affected groups, as well as a formidable task to solve for any development project that causes it. Since such social disruptions will continue to accompany future technical and economic change, further improvements in relocation policies, in legal frameworks, in implementation, and in the social science research on resettlement remain imperative.

Notes

Thanks are expressed to Ruth Cernea, Scott Guggenheim, Michel Petit, V. Rajagopalan, G. E. Schuh, and T. Scudder for their perceptive comments and suggestions on earlier versions of this chapter.

1. Displacement caused by development projects has certain features in common with the displacements that occur as a consequence of wars, political turmoil, and natural disasters—such as droughts, floods, and others. There are, however, important social differences between them. A detailed analysis of commonalities and differences between these populations can be found in Michael M. Cernea, "Internal Refugee Flows and Development-Induced Population Displacement," *Journal of Refugee Studies*, no. 4 (1990).

2. Liang Chao, "State Plans New Rules for Dam Resettlement," *China Daily*, no. 2632 (January 4, 1990).

3. Kashyap Mankodi, "Displacement and Relocation: Problems and Prospects," in W. Fernandes and E. G. Thukral, eds., *Development, Displacement, and Rehabilitation* (New Delhi: Indian Social Institute, 1989), p. 150.

4. Charles Lane and Jules N. Pretty, *Displaced Pastoralists and Transferred Wheat Technology in Tanzania*, no. SA20 (Dar-es-Salaam: IIED, Sustainable Agriculture Programme, Gate Keeper Series, 1990); Colin M. Turnbull, *The Mountain People* (New York: Touchstone Books, 1987).

5. George N. Appell, "The Bulusu of East Kalimantan: The Consequences of Resettlement," in George N. Appell, ed., *Modernization and the Emergence of a Landless Peasantry*, Studies in Third World Societies, vol. 33 (Williamsburg, Va.: College of William and Mary, 1985); see also Jason W. Clay, Sandra Steingraber, and Peter Niggli, "The Spoils of Famine: Ethiopian Policy and Peasant Agriculture," *Cultural Survival* (1988).

6. See Martin Silverman, *Disconcerting Issue* (Chicago: University of Chicago Press, 1971) for an ethnography of how Pacific Islanders moved off their home island attempted to reassign symbolic values to their new geographic environment.

7. Thayer Scudder, "Man Made Lakes and Population Resettlement in Africa," in R. H. Lowe-McConnell, ed., *Man Made Lakes* (New York: Academic Press, 1966); W. Ackerman, G. F. White, and E. B. Worthington, eds., *Man Made Lakes: Their Problems and Environmental Effects*, Monograph no. 17 (Washington, D.C.: American Geophysical Union, 1973); Kurt Finsterbush, *Understanding Social Impacts: Assessing the Effects of Public Projects* (Beverley Hills, Calif.: Sage Publications, 1980); William L. Partridge, A. B. Brown, and J. B. Nugent, "The Papaloapan Dam and Resettlement Project: Human Ecology and Health Impacts," in A. Hansen and A. Oliver-Smith, eds., *Involuntary Migration and Resettlement* (Boulder, Colo.: Westview Press, 1982), in this volume, see other studies as well; Walter Fernandes and E. G. Thukral, eds., *Development, Displacement, and Rehabilitation* (New Delhi: Indian Social Institute, 1989); and Muneera Salem-Murdock, *Arabs and Nubians in New Halfa* (Salt Lake City: University of Utah Press, 1989).

8. Michael M. Cernea, *Poverty Risks from Population Displacement in Water Resource Projects*, Development Discussion Paper no. 355 (Cambridge, Mass.: Harvard University, Harvard Institute for International Development, 1990).

9. Anthony Hall, "São Francisco Valley: Report on Human and Environmental Impacts," processed, December 1989.

10. Gerd Kohlhepp, *Itaipu—Socioeconomic and Ecological Consequences of the Itaipu Dam* (Vieweg: GATE-GTZ, 1987).

11. Luc J. A. Mougeot, *Hydroelectric Development and Involuntary Resettlement in Brazilian Amazonia: Planning and Evaluation* (Edinburgh: Cobhan Resource Consultants, 1988).

12. Edward K. Mburugu, "A Resettlement Survey in the Kiambere Hydroelectric Power Project—Preliminary Report," processed, March 1988.

13. Similar results are reported in an internal report of the World Bank, Operations Evaluation Department, on project performance audit reports for three Indonesian power projects in 1989.

14. Padjadjaran University, Institute of Ecology, "Environmental Analysis of the Cirata Dam," processed, March 1989.

15. Among the many environmental studies on these issues, see Edward Goldsmith and N. Hildyard, *The Social and Environmental Effects of Large Dams*, 2 vols. (Cornwall: Camelford, 1984); also Pat Aufderheide and Bruce Rich, "Environmental Reform and the Multilateral Banks," *World Policy Journal* (Spring 1988).

16. World Bank Operational Manual Statement no. 2.33, "Social Issues Associated with Involuntary Resettlement in Bank-Financed Projects," February 1980.

17. In addition to the author of this chapter, a small group of consultant sociologists and anthropologists consisting of David Butcher, Lois Gram, and Deborah Rubin took part in this preparation work.

18. Thayer Scudder, "The Human Ecology of Big Projects: River Basin Development and Resettlement," in B. Siegal, ed., *Annual Review of Anthropology* (Palo Alto, 1973); see also D. Brokensha and Thayer Scudder, "Resettlement," in N. Rubin and W. M. Warren, eds., *Dams in Africa: An Interdisciplinary Study of Man Made Lakes in Africa* (London: Frank Cass, 1968); see also some studies listed in note 7.

19. Robert Chambers, ed., *The Volta Resettlement Experience* (London: Pall Mall Press, 1970).

20. Elizabeth Colson, *The Social Consequences of Resettlement* (Manchester: Manchester University Press, 1971).

21. Herbert J. Gans, *People and Plans: Essays on Urban Problems and Solutions* (New York: Basic Books, 1968).

22. Michael M. Cernea, *Involuntary Resettlement in Development Projects: Policy Guidelines in World Bank–Assisted Projects*, World Bank Technical Paper no. 80 (Washington, D.C., 1988); for more details about the history of this policy, see also Michael M. Cernea, *From Unused Social Science to Policy Formulation: The Case of Population Resettlement*, Development Discussion Paper no. 342 (Cambridge, Mass.: Harvard University, Harvard Institute for International Development, 1990).

23. World Bank Operational Directive no. 4.30, "Involuntary Resettlement," June 1990.

24. See the documents and papers referenced in notes 16, 22, and 23.

25. A detailed description of these procedures by stages of the project cycle is contained in Michael M. Cernea, *Involuntary Resettlement in Development Projects*, World Bank Technical Paper no. 80 (Washington, D.C., 1988); see in particular pp. 33–42 and annexes 1, 2, and 3.

26. This, in fact, is how displacement caused by development projects has been treated historically by virtually all national agencies in developing countries, as well as by multilateral and bilateral donors. Many such agencies continue even today to handle relocation with low standards, as a rescue or welfare operation. For instance, analyzing current approaches in Brazil, L. J. A. Mougeot observed that "when put in charge of resettlement, hydropower developers have tended to view it as a self-contained social assistance, not as a highly interactive component of integrated area development" (see note 8). The redefinition of resettlement by the World Bank's policy is still far from being generally accepted outside Bank-assisted projects, but the influence of the Bank's policy is slowly expanding.

27. Michael M. Cernea, "Metropolitan Development and Compulsory Population Relocation: Policy Issues and Project Experiences," *Regional Development Dialogue*, vol. 10, nol 4 (1989).

28. Barbara E. Harrell-Bond, *Imposing Aid: Emergency Assistance to Refugees* (New York: Oxford University Press, 1989).

29. Scott Guggenheim, "Development and the Dynamics of Displacement," paper presented at the Workshop on Rehabilitation of Displaced Persons, Bangalore, India, December 1989.

30. Ibrahim Shihata, "Some Legal Aspects of Involuntary Population Displacement," in Michael M. Cernea and Scott E. Guggenheim, eds., *Anthropological Approaches to Involuntary Resettlement: Policy, Practice, and Theory* (Boulder, Colo.: Westview Press, 1991).

31. Jayendra P. Nayak, "Resettlement Anthropology and the Upper Krishna Irrigation Projects," *Current Science*, vol. 59, no. 2 (January 25, 1990).

32. A substantial sociological contribution to resettlement planning and design in this new projects was provided by William Partridge and Abdul Salam.

33. According to World Bank appraisal materials on the India Upper Krishna II Irrigation Project, prepared in April 1989.

34. Interesting details and reactions about the changes introduced by this Bank-assisted project, as compared with the practices of disastrous resettlement under Mexico's domestically financed dam and resettlement projects, are provided by David Clark Scott in his two-part series of articles: "Mexico Resettles Uprooted People," *Christian Science Monitor*, October 11 and 15, 1990.

35. V. N. Rajagopalan, "Policy and Planning in Involuntary Resettlement," *Bank's World*, no. 9 (September 1989).

PART III

Livestock Projects

Editor's Note

Extraordinary environmental and socioeconomic pressures have beset pastoral societies over the past three decades. Throughout Africa they have struggled against the ravages of increased drought and famine. There, as in other parts of the world, natural disasters have often been exacerbated by war, political repression, and economic deterioration. Growing populations and diminishing resources bring competing pressures from agriculturalists even on the marginal lands occupied by pastoral groups. Traditionally famed for their economic and political independence, pastoralists are increasingly pulled into broader systems of production and administration—a process of change and integration that has often created new problems for pastoral peoples.

By improving the technology of animal husbandry and thus modifying traditional pastoralism, livestock development projects are an attempt to address these hardly tractable problems. However, they have probably been the least successful subgroup among agricultural projects. Neville Dyson-Hudson's lucid assessment attempts to answer why. He bases his interpretation on a careful sociological analysis of the social organization the pastoralists have developed to adapt to an inhospitable environment. He forcefully argues that the pressures acting on pastoralists clash with their complex and delicately balanced system, which often cannot rapidly absorb the changes promoted through financially induced development programs. By misunderstanding the intricacy of the pastoral socio-ecosystem and failing to develop projects compatible with its structural characteristics, development planners themselves may often add to the conditions for failure.

Defining the social and cultural features of East African pastoralist societies, the chapter highlights the social organizational variables that must always be considered if the planned interventions are to be effective in gradually modifying the existing social systems.

A frank and most significant case analysis is the rather unsuccessful Kenya First Livestock Development Project, for which Dyson-Hudson himself served as anthropologist-consultant, first as a member of the project appraisal team and years later as an evaluation analyst. As he readily recognizes, the presence of social anthropologists on the project design team is by no means the definitive guarantee of project success. Sociocultural input in project design is indeed indispensable but, as the case proves, other factors are also required to ensure the project's effective implementation.

Reflecting on the faulty efforts of the past, in light of the experiences of the late-1980s, Dyson-Hudson proposes five additional guidelines for the new generation of livestock development projects in the 1990s: these refer to the need for longer-term financial commitments, a deconstruction of the "integrated" approach, attention to the new family units within pastoralist populations, the promotion of smaller-scale experimental interventions, and the need to decentralize and localize development programs.

7

Pastoral Production Systems and Livestock Development Projects: An East African Perspective

Neville Dyson-Hudson

By the early 1960s, the World Bank had already been successful in lending for general agricultural development in Africa and for livestock production in Latin America. With some courage, but no doubt with some confidence also, it then attempted to merge these two streams of experience and venture into livestock development projects in Africa.

Both the needs and the opportunities must have seemed clear. Enormous areas of Africa provide a variably harsh environment, which is sparsely settled and seems usable only for livestock management. Existing techniques of exploitation seemed to be minimal, controversial, or both: range burning, cutting trees for browse, supplementary use of small stock (especially goats), digging shallow pans for rain catchment. Livestock conditions did not impress visitors familiar with genetically manipulated breeds; disease and seasonally inadequate forage were evident and poor breeding knowledge was assumed. It was also widely supposed that the condition of African livestock was less important to its owners than the number, and that animal productivity mattered less than the sociocultural status and complex social manipulations which evidently accompanied livestock ownership. The human populations of the pastoral areas seemed to live with a minimum of material comfort, at hazard to disease, starvation, and sometimes to warfare. In many places they seemed to be ruining their environment.

To outsiders acquainted with the effective use of equally harsh environments in America and Australia by a modern, market-oriented animal husbandry system, it seemed feasible to increase livestock production, transform the human standard of living, and improve the environment itself by introducing relatively simple technology, limited inputs of capital, and expertise available from the Amero-Australian ranching experience. To quote one commentator, it was necessary to direct an effort "towards transforming subsistence pastoralism into the beginnings of commercial livestock production."[1] The social magnitude and the enormous complexity of the changes implied in this simple, brief sentence seem to have escaped many who were ready then to endorse such prescriptions.

As is often the case, where the World Bank led, other donors followed and invested aid resources in African livestock development. The results of the experiments with these various social and technological innovations have generally been very different from what was anticipated by planners, and more often than not the effect has been disappointing.

It must be understood at the outset what this chapter tries—and what it does not try—to do. First, it does not attempt an overall comparative review of the World Bank's operations in livestock development. Livestock development projects assisted with international funding have utilized social institutions: parastatal ranches, private producers, and cooperatives. They have had very varied emphases: market structures, slaughterhouses, range water installations, railway transport for livestock, trekking routes, dipping facilities, and feed lots. Some have focused on beef cattle, some on dairy cattle, some on sheep. Some have been concerned with improving the local food supply, some with national meat marketing, some with developing an export meat trade. Some have addressed bull breeding, others have emphasized range improvement by rotational grazing plans. Some have been exclusively livestock-oriented, others have attempted to integrate livestock production with crop production or with forest resources. It would be nonsensical to assume that any one person could claim the depth of knowledge necessary for identifying and assessing all sociocultural variables in such a broad spectrum of projects in so many diverse places across the African continent. Consequently, I do not attempt to keep a score card of projects' successes and failures.

Second, it is not a simple exercise in fault-finding with the developer cast as an idiot-villain. Most people intimately involved with African livestock development feel disappointed and frustrated by what everyone's best efforts have been able to achieve. But to conclude that all the development agencies and national governments have therefore been merely inept is, I think, quite mistaken. It has taken fifteen years to realize the full operational implications of the basic sociological contention, which the World Bank did in fact partially perceive at the outset: that traditional range systems for livestock production in tropical Africa are not as modest as their frequently simple tools would imply. Technologies comprise social organization, technical skills, and knowledge, as well as tools: the skills of African herders are ingenious and their knowledge is extensive. They are not as inefficient as their herd structures first suggested to Westerners raised on a livestock taxonomy of beef ranches and dairy farms. Rather, they employ a highly complex (and previously highly successful) strategy for survival in a severely fluctuating environment. Indeed, the age-sex-species structure of their livestock herds is a key element in the resource-use strategy of African pastoral peoples. Even the basic architecture of African pastoral societies (their group organization and decision procedures) is related to the efficiency with which they must meet the daily requirements of animal production.

A characteristic of first-generation African livestock development plans is that they were rooted in what now seem oversimplified models of traditional livestock production and savanna ecosystem dynamics. More effective livestock development planning may well have to wait upon advances in basic research in both ecological and human sciences, research which most projects have been, so far, unable or unwilling to fund.

Third, the chapter is concerned mainly with systemic problems. That is to say, although some project problems arise from single elements of a livestock production system,[2] other, more complex problems arise from the manner in which an *entire* production system operates. In implementing African livestock development programs, one in fact faces the problems of *two* production systems. On the one hand, there is the indigenous pastoral production system, which can be seen as an evolutionary response to environmental pressure; it is a pattern for survival which has proved successful insofar as the pastoral populations continue to exist. On the other hand, there is the new pattern for survival, based on the technical rationale brought in from the outside but not yet adjusted to social factors and subjected to the test of time; its technical innovations are promoted by the livestock projects. It is in dealing with problems which relate to the entire social system, including the interaction of new and old strategies for pastoral production, that social scientists can be most useful to those who plan and operate development projects.

Fourth, the chapter is not about all forms of livestock production, even in East Africa. Development interventions focused on dairying (for milk production to urban populations) have had quite a successful record. Again, peasant livestock development (whereby a beast or two is provided to the agricultural smallholder to increase his self-sufficiency) is a policy with obvious potential. The concern here is with total livestock production systems, which have in the past focused to a considerable (though variable) degree on feeding their owners rather than on market supply. For unsurprising ecological reasons such systems are found on rangelands. The issue of development is therefore immediately complicated since one is speaking of developing two things which are not identical, though they often coincide: a natural resource with its own potential and limitations (the dry rangelands) and an animal resource with its own potential and limitations. Both these forms of intervention have the appeal (for livestock developers) that they do increase livestock productivity. Neither addresses the major African livestock problem, however, which is that extensive areas seem suited only for livestock production and the considerable populations they support.

Fifth, this chapter takes an approach common in social anthropology: the detailed consideration of a single situation to see whether it can provide insights and prompt reflection on more general issues. The hope is that limitations of breadth may be compensated by the revelation of linkages, and eventually causal connections, which may then help interpret other situations.

The case chosen is the World Bank's first confrontation with African pastoral production in the form of the Kenya Range Livestock Project, which I followed from the beginning, as a consultant on the appraisal team, to the end, as a social evaluator several years after completion of project disbursements. Without implying that this project is a paradigm for all other livestock projects in East Africa, I think it is adequate, as case material, for identifying some recurrent social issues of livestock development: the problem of focus in project design, the cultural assumptions on which livestock development appears to be predicated, the social structure of existing production systems, the relevance of project characteristics, the present character of social anthropology, and the state of knowledge of rangeland ecology. By examining it I hope to suggest that, despite early disappointments, we are now coming to the end of the first generation of attempts to grapple with an enormously difficult problem. With a careful look at past experience we may chart another, better attempt.

One basic problem of African range development is technical and so far intractable: how to provide increased nitrogen in the form of fodder to a production system with a severe seasonal deficit of animal foodstuffs. Other problems suggested technological solutions which now appear dubious. Attempts to deal with the problem of water scarcity, for example, have shown that water installation is problematic or negative without an appropriate organization for its control. Improved breeds may not be physiologically adapted to withstand the stress of the dry seasons. The crucial problem, however, in African range livestock development now seems to be organizational and behavioral, rather than technical. That is to say, what social forms of production are likely to be viable in the changed situation that faces most African pastoral populations?

Pastoral Production Systems

In the perspective of behavioral ecology, a wide range of human behavior can be viewed as directed toward survival through the development of efficient strategies of production and reproduction. So viewed, the production system itself is the aggregate behavioral response of a human population to the resources and risks of the environment as they are perceived.

Because it is population-specific, a production system will show many idiosyncratic features. For instance, all pastoral production systems need water and must develop procedures for water use. For the Borana populations of Ethiopia and Kenya, this seems predicated on restraint, queuing discipline, and careful treatment of watering facilities (perhaps related to the limited number of deep wells in their homeland, which they know how to repair but not how to build). For the nearby Somali, water use seems defined much more as a scramble for self-interest and a disregard of the condition of water facilities for communal use.

Obviously, such specificities are of relevance to the design of development projects: one set of behavior will ruin the range much more quickly than the other. It is, however, possible and useful to go beyond such extreme empiricism to establish general features of human behavior and social organization which seem entailed (or, for reasons of efficiency, preferred) in particular modes of production.

Range livestock production by the pastoral populations of eastern Africa is one such generalizable production system. Some of its features are common to African pastoralism as a whole or to arid land pastoralism anywhere. But there are conditions that distinguish the East African model both from the Sahelian model (in which the much greater latitudinal movements of the population have led to regional integration into multi-economy markets and negotiated relationships with agricultural populations) and from the southern model (in which the absence of predators and the presence of crops alter settlement patterns and disrupt the demographic linkage between human and livestock populations which marks purely pastoral production).

East African pastoral systems in their traditional form combine range and dairy operations, which Western livestock technologies keep separate, and involve various features which Western livestock technologies do not encompass at all. A reasonable model may be constructed with about thirty features, though how well it corresponds to any given pastoral situation in East Africa will of course vary.

The environmental setting for East African livestock production is dry range—plains or undulant topography, mainly sandy soils, and an evaporation rate greater than rainfall. The dry season lasts for three to seven months of the year, and the grasslands are wooded, bushed, or shrubbed according to the severity of the moisture deficit. When the mean annual rainfall is over 250 millimeters, perennial grasses of numerous species generally occur; otherwise, there is a variety of annual grasses. In Kenya the pastoral areas average roughly less than twenty inches of annual rainfall, and over 80 percent of the rangelands are dry bushland savanna, grassland, or semi-desert.

Since East African savannas do not constitute a single uniform environment, primary productivity (which is a function of both grazing intensity and rainfall) ranges from about 100 grams per square meter per year where annual rainfall is under 400 millimeters and grazing is relatively light, to about 1,500 grams per square meter per year where rainfall is over 1,000 millimeters and grazing is intense. These savanna regions provide a problematic resource base for human populations. Plant cover is often thin, scattered, and mainly not directly usable by humans; rainfall usually comes as convective rainstorms which can leave a thousand square kilometers without moisture and produce widely spaced water supplies; surface water is subject to rapid loss by evaporation, and subsurface water must be dug for; vegetation and accessible water may be separately distributed, and the periodicity and locations of either are often highly unpredictable.

To exploit this environment the pastoralists have a low energy, labor-intensive production system which utilizes both sexes and all ages between infancy and senility in support of a technology which is high in skills and low in tools. Labor demands show sharp seasonality, negatively correlated with food supply. Labor is grouped into a large number of small, autonomous production units, each of which has a herd of livestock which supposedly matches both the labor capacities and the food needs of the production unit. Production units are autonomous and (given scarce natural resources) competitive. They are also mobile, with groups separating and recombining in response to perceived environmental change, socioeconomic advantage, or the often divergent demands of multiple species of livestock. Decisionmaking is nominally in the hands of a single owner-manager for each production unit, but spatial separation effectively creates a hierarchy of decisionmakers for management purposes.

The competitive interaction of production units is ameliorated and controlled both by small-scale, transitory alliances and by permanent affiliation to a large social grouping for the gross allocation of grazing and water resources. Continual dispersal and reaggregation (mainly in response to environmental dynamics) inhibit the development of political leadership. Leadership is in principle associated with some social feature such as age or descent, but in practice it depends on the size and composition of any gathering and the nature and urgency of the problem. Politically centralized leadership was a colonial creation, now in the hands of the national civil service, and is usually regarded with suspicion. Pastoral populations in East Africa are not integrated into national politics—except where the political elite and their policies are identifiably pastoral, which is rare.

Social Organization and Pastoral Production

Since their lives depend on their domesticated animals, the production problem facing the people of the dry rangelands of Africa is twofold. The population must be dispersed in consonance with the overall low density of natural resources, with livestock demands matched to plant biomass and water as closely as possible. The population must also be ready to move among resource patches as their distribution changes over time, and in groups of a size that will achieve an efficient ratio between time spent exploiting resource patches and time spent moving among them. If the resource patches are fairly small (as is usually the case) the moving groups must be small. If the populations are quite large (as is usually the case) the number of moving groups will also be large. This creates a problem of traffic control, of ensuring that numerous groups seeking limited and separated resource patches do so as amiably as possible, because violent competition cuts down the time each group has for foraging and disrupts movement (resource seeking) over a wide area.

The organization of social groups in pastoral populations, the ground plan for society itself, seems to be a direct response to these major production constraints.

Allocation of Natural Resources

Typically, a pastoral society in East Africa will be divided into a fairly small number (say, twenty or less) of large territorial units (of several thousand square miles) and correspondingly large populations (of approximately 10,000–20,000 persons). These units provide the largest permanent groups in the society and give individuals their principal social identity and principal claim on natural resources, for each territory is perceived as the home range of the group concerned. Outsiders may use the area only with the permission of the group and in accordance with certain restrictions.

This social organizational device creates subpopulations, which in the event of anything less than a general disaster facilitates the recolonization of areas whose local population becomes reduced or extinct. It also greatly reduces and regulates traffic flow among foraging groups. Instead of being scattered over, say, the full 20,000 square miles of a pastoral territory, they are scattered over only 2,000 or 3,000. This increases the frequency with which small groups are likely to encounter each other over the years and presumably makes for more peaceful interactions. Previous acquaintance may either moderate competitive behavior or allow groups to avoid those who precipitate hostility; and those with grievances must take into account the repercussions their present disputes will have in future years.

In a highly changeable environment, it is possible that the stochastic model of natural resource distribution is learned more efficiently for a limited area than for a larger one. The territories concerned are large, however, and it seems possible (though the data are not available to prove it) that their size accommodates the short- and medium-term fluctuations of the environment quite well. For short runs of years the associated population can find resources by redeploying themselves within their allotted area. In the years when they cannot do so, there are established procedures by which groups disperse into smaller aggregates to seek temporary refuge in the territories of other groups.

Allocation of Animal Resources

Although large territorial units with large populations seem to reduce some problems of production in African rangelands, they clearly leave others unresolved. As noted, foraging groups must adjust to the available resources if they are not to spend a disproportionate amount of time searching for forage and thereby expend energy which otherwise would go into animal products for human consumption. This requires small aggregates of animals and people. Such small groups are also effective for animal management: keeping away predators, watering animals, and rationing and physically drawing water from below ground surface.

Typically, the other permanent group in a pastoral society is modeled on kinship ties—a large family. It can be either a three-generation family of perhaps fewer than fifty people or a group of small families (whose family heads may be relatives or friends) characterized by cooperation, amiability, and mutual assistance as in a single family.

While the large social unit is territorially based and associated with the ownership of *natural* resource, this smaller unit is based on blood ties and associated with the ownership of *livestock*. A production unit is therefore a composite of a human family and an animal herd, each dependent on the other for survival, with the humans seeking some balanced adjustment between the labor capacities of the family (to tend and to exploit the animals) and the food capacities of the herd (to sustain both the family and newborn livestock for the herd of the future). The dynamics of herd increase and of family expansion (typically, in a polygynous setting) are thus intimately related.

Patterns of behavior link marriage and inheritance to this family/herd relationship, as if to perpetuate it. Men are encouraged to match the acquisition of livestock with the acquisition of wives, to generate the labor needed by a growing herd. Older successful men usually have priority in marrying young women, thereby matching human fertility with the food resources needed to sustain children after weaning. The serial secession of grown sons from an established family/herd operation is controlled so that livestock resources are transferred from aging to growing owner-managers without putting either at risk.

Integration of Natural and Animal Resources

The territorial and the family units, the two organizational building blocks of African pastoral production systems, interface with a third unit, intermediate in size, and unlike the others, temporary. Although autonomous production units modeled on the family-herd move across the landscape in a highly efficient search for grazing, browse, and water, they cluster into small, temporary communities. These can consist of two or three or even twenty or thirty family-herd groups, depending on the production system in question, the time of year, or other local circumstance, such as threat of warfare or disease. Not to be in such a small community is an aberration—and in a sense impossible, because they break up and reform every so often. The frequency with which communities regroup is, as might be expected, population specific: a community may last for days among the Turkana, for years among the Maasai, but usually for weeks or months.

Apart from the enormously important task of meeting human requirements for sociability (by providing an audience, entertainment, and psychological support), neighborhood groups offer more security from animal or human threats to herds or people; they provide assistance for herding emergencies if family labor is inadequate; they allow people to share their knowledge of environmental conditions as they move their herds in different directions each day. For the period they are together, neighborhood groups acknowledge some common interest, but they break up because the common interest is subordinate to the individual opinions of herd owners about animal management and environment use, and to their freedom to act on those opinions.

Systems vary in the extent to which membership changes from one neighborhood shift to another. The costs to individuals may be quite high if they have to spend time and energy to renegotiate mutual acceptance of neighbors every few weeks. But the overall gain to the production system is probably high in terms of increasing traffic control and encouraging peaceful foraging behavior, without imposing rigidities which would interfere with the group's adjustment to environmental fluctuation.

Organizational Flexibility

African rangelands are frequently struck by environmental distur-
bances that are highly unpredictable in part because they seem to be
multicyclical at best. The organizational flexibility of pastoral systems
has probably evolved as a deliberate response to this unpredictability of
ecological and technical variables. The flexibility occurs at all significant
levels in the social organization and is outlined in table 7-1.

Groups of different size and social complexity have different functions
related to the control of the herd and its human owners. At the upper level
of organization, as noted, members of territorial groups operate mainly
in their own territories (after all, if people can claim rights of exploitation,
they will exercise them if possible). But pastoral societies in East Africa
have procedures for sharing their territories with nonmembers when
necessary, and they usually justify these procedures explicitly by saying
that in other years the situation could well be reversed. The degree of
control maintained over incursions seems to vary from one system to
another and from one degree of drought or disease to another within the
same system. Most pastoral societies have somewhere within their
territories one or more centers of markedly better resources (in East
Africa, commonly in the highland, where greater rainfall provides higher
densities of water). In years of hardship these are treated as refuge areas,

Table 7-1.   *The Social Organization of African Pastoral Production Systems*

Group size	Social organization	Type of activity
10,000s	Political society	Permanent, ideological (rarely operates as concrete unit)
1,000s	Territorial unit	Permanent (natural resource allocation)
100s	Local group (neighborhoods, based on information exchange, visiting, and some cooperation)	Transient, low predictability (constantly shifting units)
10s	Production unit (autonomous, self-reliant feeding and foraging)	Permanent, with predictable development cycle

or resource reservoirs, in which people will pack themselves as closely as necessary without too much argument over priorities of use. This flexible but orderly interpretation of large group membership is matched by the explicitly transient nature of neighborhood communities and people's freedom to join or leave them according to their individual perceptions.

At the lowest level of organization, the family and its herd, flexibility takes the form of people with few or no livestock being accepted as dependents by people whose livestock resources strain their limited supply of labor. Dependents have little or no opportunity to share in the livestock capital, but they are fed in return for labor, as are other family members. Like all organizational flexibilities, it is a short-term solution.

The ultimate flexibility in pastoral production systems, and one that has most caught the attention of outsiders over the years, is the autonomy of the individual producer. Herd owners are commonly considered as owning both their animals and their families: it is a straightforward position of power and responsibility. This independence of herders is of course a mixed blessing and is grounded in rangeland realities. Given the stochastic nature of African range environments, no citizen can be guaranteed the right to survive. Some will survive, but African pastoralism is a population strategy, an evolutionary success, not an individual guarantee. Since the only guarantee that can realistically be extended is the guarantee of a chance to survive, the producer is "free" to do the best he can. Within broad social guidelines about what constitutes acceptable behavior between members of the same family, neighborhood, or territorial group he is "free" to take his competitive chances with others.

The pastoral production system everywhere recognizes that competition will sometimes lead to violence, and that is accepted—minimized, deplored, but accepted because unavoidable. Despite this drawback, competition offers certain advantages in the long run. Many thousands of autonomous herd owners mean many versions of a herding strategy, with the opportunity to copy success and eschew failure by observation. The learning opportunities are probably not measurable, but seem obvious and immense.

Table 7-1 attempts to go beyond the culturally idiosyncratic features of pastoral populations in East Africa and identify a common organizational form which seems responsive to the requirements of survival through pastoral production in a harsh, fluctuating environment. There are quantum jumps in the size of the groups at each of the four levels of organization suggested. The smallest unit, based on a large extended family or several cooperating smaller families, will commonly vary from ten to a hundred depending on its point in a development cycle (see below) and its livestock resources. These small production units combine temporarily into a local group, or neighborhood, of a hundred or a few hundreds, depending on the density allowed by natural resources and the threat of competitors. This unit is based on the temporary exploitation of a single patch of resources and the general sociability which stems from it. Above this level is a permanently named, demarcated territorial group comprising some thousands of people. These in turn are aggregated into a single ethnic group, or tribe, which numbers in the tens of thousands and provides the largest permanent unit of organization for pastoral populations. As the actual numbers for pastoral populations in Kenya will demonstrate, these sizes merely indicate the general range, but they are realistic. Anomalies may occasionally occur for local historical reasons: for example, the Samburu were at one time a component territorial section of the Maasai but later split off and now exist as an independent entity. In their case both upper levels of this organizational chart are fused together. Nonetheless, I believe this general organizational form to be a real phenomenon and regard it as a behavioral solution to several problems facing any pastoral population in East Africa.

Each level of the social organization seems to address different problems, which are indicated parenthetically in the table. Each has different dynamics and a different operational mode. Along with the territorial delimitation of an owned universe, the largest unit provides political identity and the security of person and property that goes with it, as well as established procedures for resource sharing in emergencies. Outside this affiliating unit, no such ties are officially and regularly recognized, though of course the modern nation-state is attempting to override that exclusive level of affiliation. Although important, the total polity (tribe, ethnic group, or whatever term is preferred) is invoked only symbolically because it is too large to assemble as a group for concerted action. This is an ecological matter since there are seldom if ever enough natural resources to support large, dense populations of humans and livestock gathered in one place. The same is largely true for the next descending level of organization, the territorial section, or subtribe.

By contrast, the two lower levels of organization are the context of everyday interactions among the people, largely to decide how far they will act as a unit and how far separate action is preferable. For this reason, the local organizational unit is a transient collection of people who agree to act together, and it breaks up and reforms as opinions change. The smallest level of organization, however, is permanent and geared to the efficient management of livestock and to the secure reproduction and growth of the human population in families. Unlike the large units of organization, which are thought of as continuing indefinitely, families more visibly come and go as people are born, age, and die. There is therefore a visible cycle of development for production units, which is also more predictable than the ebb and flow of people into and out of local groups. Spatially even the smallest unit in the organization may be dispersed into several fragments at different times of the year if the demands of the livestock, the needs of the people, and the scattered pattern of grass and water require it.

Leadership and Decisionmaking

Individual modes of activity fit into this overall organization in different ways. The careers of individual herd owners can be linked to the different stages of the development cycle of the production unit. In local groups temporary leaders emerge on the basis of their experience, insight, and rhetorical powers. Individuals are connected with the upper levels of this organization usually by virtue of occupying socially recognized positions of rank (individually or collectively held offices). Truly outstanding idiosyncratic features, such as an assumed ability to be a prophet, may lead to preeminence at these upper levels of organization, but it is uncommon and does not necessarily create a permanent overall leadership role.

Herd-owner autonomy, and the reasons for it, have consequences for leadership patterns and decisionmaking in pastoral production systems. Flexible organizations require contingent leadership: East African pastoral societies seem to have settled for low-investment politics, in which the problem situation is allowed to throw up its own leader, who speaks for a consensus of essentially independent producers. Without a problem to be addressed, there is no need for a leader; without a consensus on what to do there is no leader; and the difficulty of assembling audiences and the tendency of groups to turn into quite different sets of people within a short time means that would-be leaders raising artificial problems have little sustained attention. Limited leadership in public affairs would, then, seem another form of organizational flexibility in pastoral societies—and one appropriate to highly dynamic, poorly predictable external situations.

Pastoral Strategies

East African livestock production systems are probably best understood as human population strategies which attempt to optimize resource use in a competitive situation. For the competing population, a foraging strategy of high mobility is the most opportune response to savanna rangeland conditions.

Environmental Tracking and Manipulation

Environmental tracking and manipulation are basic elements of the pastoral strategy, but they are achieved indirectly rather than directly. Direct tracking of a highly perturbed environment in any predictive sense seems to be as difficult for pastoral peoples as it is for ecologists. Both may be said to sense multiple periodicities (for example, a short-term stress, such as an unusually extended dry period perhaps every ten or eleven years, which may be compounded by coincident effects such as disease in livestock or humans). Both seem better at describing it than predicting it or preparing for it. East African pastoral groups were badly hit by drought in the 1920s, 1960s, and 1970s, and almost obliterated at the turn of the century by epidemic disease. Apparently, however, all they could do as a society was recognize it when it happened, rather than mobilize for it ahead of time.

Direct control of the environment is only incidentally achieved by pastoral populations, since skill rather than tools is the major component of their technology. Their intervention comes at significant points, however: burning of old grass to promote the growth of more nutritive shoots; exploitation of natural (subsurface) water and occasional cooperative creation of surface water storage; occasional enclosure of a grazing area to reserve feed for calves. This is balanced intervention aimed at both plant and water resources. Unbalanced improvement (of water without regard for plants) seems to be a later discovery.

Indirect environmental tracking and manipulation, however, seems to be achieved with a high degree of skill. This is shown by the structure of their herds, the species composition, the way the total livestock enterprises are handled, and the social processes governing the search for, use of, and distribution of natural resources by the human population.

Species Mix and Herd Structure

Livestock herds in pastoral production systems in East Africa show some general structural characteristics which indicate that herd design is not haphazard but, on the contrary, an adaptive response by pastoral populations to their environment: its level of primary productivity, its plant structure, its water resources, and its frequent perturbations. At the time the World Bank and other bilateral agencies started lending for livestock development in Africa, this was barely acknowledged even by social anthropologists, let alone by technical experts. Most development practitioners simply assumed that cultural idiosyncrasy of a nonrational sort was governing the herd structure of traditional pastoral groups, as it did other features of pastoral behavior.

Briefly, all pastoral systems raise multiple species of livestock. Commonly, they include one large-animal species (cattle in more favored conditions, camels where water is less available and the woody component of vegetation is higher), small livestock (sheep and goats being usually run together), and donkeys. Occasionally, all domestic stock may be exploited for food purposes, as with the Turkana in northwestern Kenya, who use the milk and meat of cattle, camels, goats, sheep, and donkeys according to circumstance, as well as the blood of all but the donkey.

The general mix of species can be illustrated by the 1978 figures for Kenya rangelands livestock populations from the Kenya Rangelands and Environmental Monitoring Unit (KREMU) 1979 Annual Report:

	Millions	*Percent*
Cattle	4.2	31.15
Sheep and goats	8.5	62.75
Camels	0.64	4.72
Donkeys	0.19	1.38

The proportions of one species to another within the total production system vary regionally, principally according to environmental factors. It may also vary widely within a single production system according to the relative skills, preferences, and labor capacities of the human groups.[3]

The salient point of species mixing is that different food and water requirements and reproductive cycles are manipulated to damp down fluctuations in the food supply under the wide range of expectable savanna conditions. Small ruminants hold a key position in any pastoral production system. In particular, goats' milk is crucial for the survival of weaned human infants, especially in the dry season, and small stock are the main source of meat for the human population as a whole. That this is a conscious strategy is clear from Wilson's work on African goats: three-quarters of the herd is likely to be female, with breeding females consistently at about 50 percent and only enough males for reproductive purposes.[4] In an analogous way, camels may be valued for their milk supply (roughly two to four times that of cattle in the same environment), especially at times of environmental stress, and also for the greater carcass size of males. But these advantages have to be set against slower reproductive rates and (probably for management reasons in fully mixed systems) apparently higher calf mortality.

Cattle, however, rather than small stock or camels, have been the focus of attention in African livestock development programs. The structure of cattle herds therefore warrants particular attention. There is a consistently high proportion of adult animals, in particular females, because pastoral production systems operate to deliver milk products as continuously as possible from animals which are often at a low level of nutrition. Herds with a high proportion of breeding females also track environmental fluctuations quite closely. Deteriorating range conditions depress fertility, drought produces anestrus, yet animals get in calf quickly with returning rains and the subsequent return of grass. It was noted that 60 percent of Maasai cows calved in the first year after the 1960–61 drought, and almost all calved by the second year.[5] Others calculate that the Maasai herds doubled within three years of the drought and reached predrought levels within seven years.[6] Adult males are kept after an initial discrimination which creates a two-to-one ratio of female to male calves. Males are retained because they appear to increase their efficiency as energy converters with maturity, which they reach rather slowly (five to seven years). Moreover, in a number of East African pastoral production systems, adult males are regularly tapped for blood, especially at those times when female cattle fail to give milk.

Calving rates seem generally low. The data contain anomalies, but suggest a range around 40 percent. A survey of Isiolo in 1970 by the Food and Agriculture Organization found 57 percent calving rates; Meadows and White use a range from 15 percent to 80 percent in their herd model for Kenya to cover conditions from drought to plenty, which is realistically dynamic although the upper figure may perhaps be appropriate only to the Maasai ranges with their bimodal rainfall and increased plant productivity.

Less in dispute is the general two-to-one ratio of female calves. This reflects both the major objective and the major constraint in pastoral production systems. Continuous milk production adequate to sustain high labor inputs is the objective, but the needs of young humans compete with those of calves. The resolution seems to be a compromise on calf/child needs by favoring the female calves, which are the long-term guarantee of the viability of this production strategy, by eliminating a high percentage of male calves. Meadows estimates that 40 percent of male calves disappear before the age of twelve months throughout northeastern Kenya and Maasai rangeland, compared with only a 5 percent mortality for female calves.[7] This difference is puzzling because the Maasai claim they look after both sexes of calves equally well.

Of all the features of pastoral herd structure, it is perhaps the high percentage of breeding females that marks the herd design as an adaptive response to savanna fluctuation. But the twin features of removing male animals before one year or retaining them for five or more years emphasize how far this particular design is from a Western beef herd designed for the world market.

The Twentieth-century Context of Pastoral Strategy

Pastoral production systems are a highly efficient response to an environment which began to disappear in the early twentieth century and has been disappearing at an accelerating rate ever since. Around the turn of the century, a succession of epidemics among livestock and humans led to widespread starvation and almost emptied the East African ranges of both. Medical intervention, though not always efficient, has frequently prevented similar epidemics in subsequent years, and insofar as the data are reliable, human populations have grown steadily in the range areas. Veterinary medical intervention has not eliminated stock loss to the same degree, because drought more often than disease causes the livestock population to decline, but frequent campaigns against major livestock diseases have presumably helped build up analogous pressure on range areas.

Two political factors also contribute to pressure on the ranges. In the past, pastoral populations could always fall back on large-scale movement out of their defined (tribal) grazing areas, and they used physical confrontations to gain dominance where necessary. To an increasing degree, national governments prevent this. Instead, pastoral areas are being invaded by cultivators who are driven from their own lands by population pressure. Pastoralists are poorly placed to resist this because they are less likely to be represented in the governing political elite than are the agriculturalists. In the past, nonpastoral groups have been kept out of seasonally vacated range areas only by the threat of pastoral force.

The clarity and conviction of the pastoralists' own views of their lifestyle are also being interfered with. The coherence of the nonliterate pastoral value system is under pressure from competing literate and urban values. It is likely that this will gradually drain the number of people able and committed enough to continue a pastoral way of life. Pastoral strategy is also subject to outside technical interference—water installations, rotational grazing plans, and pressure to market beef. The people who propose these changes may be expert in specialized ways but are often less knowledgeable about local range capacities or the organizational constraints of present production capacities. Even where such interference is an improvement (which is not always the case) the pastoralist has not yet internalized it and the result, again, is a loss of coherence.

In sum, the pastoral strategy so successful in the past is no longer possible because three of its essential features—spatial movement, periodic devastation of human and livestock population, and aggressive confrontation—are no longer tenable. The problem for national governments is how to achieve the political and economic integration of pastoral populations without destroying their special skills and cultural variety and without causing human misery.

Livestock Development Projects

Livestock projects have proposed alternatives to traditional pastoral strategies. They have appealed to different groups for different reasons: to national politicians eager to develop national markets and provide for growing urban populations, to animal breeders convinced of pastoral inefficiency, to range managers alarmed at environmental deterioration, and to administrators trying to govern pastoralists and to integrate them into the national framework. Beginning as small-scale, simple plans for a water supply, improved breeds, or fixed rotational grazing, some livestock projects evolved into complex attempts to transform localized subsistence pastoralism into market-oriented commercial ranching on a national scale.

The more ambitious commercial ranching projects were often initiated by East African governments and agencies hoping to expand on successes based on European models before independence. Their requests for financing were answered by several donors, bilateral or international, but none of the projects were entirely successful.

Of course, not all development interventions were based on the Amero-Australian ranching model. Some tried for a less comprehensive overhaul of the production process and concentrated on improving specific components: support for dairying or for veterinary services, research on breeding and disease control, and facilities for marketing and slaughtering. Some projects included training and extension components, especially for agropastoral populations which depend on agriculture and raise livestock as a secondary occupation.

These projects have varied enormously in their design and objectives, as well as in the extent of their success. To comment comparatively on the whole range of projects would be beyond the scope of both this paper and my experience. Even within East Africa, some projects have encountered problems too idiosyncratic for profitable generalization: for example, the peculiar development context created by parastatal livestock agencies and compulsory village resettlement in Tanzania, or the development of rangeland in Ethiopia in the middle of Somali-Ethiopian conflict in the Ogaden and a violent national revolution. There are, however, certain characteristics shared by livestock development projects of all sorts. They are fixed-length interventions (usually with a short-term disbursement period) which are planned by outside technical experts for implementation by national government officers. The projects often depend on high levels of capital and technical inputs and most commonly, though not exclusively, attempt in one way or another to increase the supply of beef for the national market. Although progress is being made, the pastoral populations most often affected by the projects have relatively limited participation in the project planning. The reasons stem from the characteristics of the pastoral groups themselves (their geographic dispersal and weak political voice) as well as the institutional framework in which projects are designed and carried out.

In summary, it would seem that the first generation of internationally financed attempts at livestock development in East Africa shares five major defects, all of which are facets of being unrealistic. Since most projects have failed, to call them unrealistic would seem trite. However, I mean unrealistic not merely in their expectations (which failure shows) but in their assumptions, which involved a distortion of reality.

First, as already noted, they embodied an unreal environmental assessment. A lack of data contributed to this; but simulation can often temporarily stand in for data, as for herd projections, which donors commonly accept. A realistic simulation, with worst-case scenarios for dry years, however, would not leave a bankable project.

Second, and surprisingly, the failed assumptions rested on an unreal technological assessment. The critical constraint in African dryland grazing is not water but nitrogen—that is, fodder—which is deteriorating or absent far more than half the lifetime of the system. There is no technology for economic, large-scale nitrogen inputs; there is for water. Once again possibilities, not difficulties, have molded the strategy.

Third, failure stemmed from an unreal power assessment of herder relationships. Such assessment sees production as a neutral process related primarily to efficiency and to rationality as the preferred view of efficiency. In real world terms, livestock development targets pastoral populations who are commonly powerless in relation to national governments. Within pastoral populations, the poor are powerless in relation to the rich, women in relation to men, and young in relation to old. All these power relationships are capable of distorting project aims and operations.

Fourth, an unreal efficiency assessment of the agencies delivering change built false expectations. More often than not the agencies involved are short of personnel, skills, equipment, and finance and need to develop themselves before they can realistically transmit development to others. The agencies are also an arena for power dynamics of their own.

Fifth was an unreal assumption that traditional pastoralism could be updated as a holistic design, on the same territory with the same population but now with greater production for export and improved well-being. But the territory shrinks and rigidifies, the population grows, and the production is already so efficient that not much growth margin exists.

This last assumption is still the central unreality, and is perhaps worth restating in terms noted recently by Homewood and others.[8] Pastoralism is an efficient exploitation strategy—indeed a great human invention—for many arid regions of Africa. But it is not a feasible strategy for the present populations of those regions, which are allowed neither to fight to cross their boundaries nor to starve and die within them. Some pastoralists can doubtless pursue some version of pastoral production for some time to come without damaging the dry regions. But they cannot all do so and indeed they never have. Probably all pastoral production systems "shed" people (and livestock) at intervals as a condition of their continuance.

These general issues can be addressed more explicitly with reference to the project with which I am most familiar, the Kenya Livestock Development Project. Although its design and implementation are not necessarily typical of other East African livestock projects, it is a significant and early example of what has been or can be done to address such issues. Other ongoing projects in East Africa, despite their differences, face some similar issues, and the Kenyan experience has, in certain respects, a cross-cultural validity for other areas.

Project Design

In the mid-1960s six types of development measures were proposed by the Kenyan government for incorporation in the World Bank–assisted livestock project to increase livestock production and productivity.

Ranked according to the degree of social and technical sophistication involved, these measures ran from water development schemes (involving minimal changes and the simplest inputs) to community ranching schemes, group ranching, company ranching, and individual ranching, and culminated in commercial ranching (with complex inputs, essentially similar to ranching operations in more developed areas of the world). The first five of these assumed economic and cultural changes for traditional tribal societies, while the sixth implied continuing support for established commercial ranching activities in Kenya.

For water development, Kenya proposed the installation of additional supplies in its arid northeastern region, on the assumption that provision of water alone would increase productivity by allowing the more systematic use of available grazing. There were no associated proposals for stock control, for changes in the ownership of land and animals, or for efforts to increase the market orientation of producers, although stock-route development was proposed.

Community grazing schemes involved the demarcation of land areas for controlled grazing on an agreed rotation and the limitation of live-stock numbers in accordance with the assessed carrying capacity of the land. There were no changes in ownership of land or animals and no measures to initiate or increase a market orientation of the stock owners. Livestock above the assessed carrying capacity of the land was only to be moved out of the area, not disposed of entirely. The schemes were proposed by the government for areas not thought suitable for the fuller development implied by group ranching.

Group ranches are production enterprises in which a group of people jointly have title to land, collectively maintain agreed stocking levels, market the surplus in rotation, collectively herd sex-age aggregates of livestock, yet continue to own the livestock as individuals. They were proposed by the government as appropriate for areas which offered environmental and livestock potential, yet in which a subsistence econ-omy, decentralized tribal organization, and conservative values all pre-vented any immediate and general transition to more advanced forms of ranching. Four pastoral groups (Maasai, Samburu, Pokot, and Turkana) and several agricultural groups (Embu, Kamba, and coastal peoples) were proposed for this purpose.

Company ranches were proposed on land leased from the government by a number of shareholders who put up cattle or a cash equivalent to stock it. Animals were to be collectively owned and disposed of, and the profit shared according to prior agreement. Day-to-day direction of ranch affairs would be under the control of paid management hired by or on behalf of the shareholders. The government proposed the Kamba, Meru, and Taita peoples as suitable for this form of livestock development. These groups were engaged in predominantly subsistence agriculture with ancillary livestock raising and cash cropping on small plots in densely populated areas (mainly 100–500 persons per square mile); many of the people were educated and progressive and showed a high demand for consumer goods and services.

The scale as well as the complexity of this alternative pastoral strategy was considerable: 29 cooperative ranches on 1.3 million acres, 203 group and individual ranches on 5.4 million acres, and 96 community grazing schemes on 7.6 million acres. The land development was to be comple-mented by extensive water development (which amounted to further ranch development, although this was not realized), the improvement of commercial ranches on existing range, the development of untouched coastal areas for range on 2 million acres, and the development of stock routes with holding grounds and quarantine facilities. The cost was estimated to be more than $26 million, over half of which was to be lent by the World Bank. The time allowed for this transformation was five years.

The new pastoral strategy also entailed significant social change. Communally held rangeland (tribal areas) were to be permanently divided among small groups and individual pastoralists, who would receive ownership deeds to small areas but, of necessity, be permanently excluded from rights of any sort in any other area.

The Kenya case reveals three difficulties which have continued to affect other attempts at creating alternative African pastoral strategies for the twenty-first century. The first is the tendency to see technical intervention as the key, whereas behavioral change is more likely to be the key to production changes. The second is the great difficulty of using the impressive social forms evolved by traditional pastoralists for any purpose other than range subsistence—in particular, the difficulty of using those social forms as a vehicle for "development" interventions. The third related difficulty arises from the attempt (usually unsuccessful) to create an appropriate new social organization of production.

Out of this third difficulty has come an insight, however: a new style of development intervention (vector development, so to speak) in which pastoralists and planners interact more experimentally over longer periods of time with a much lower level of input but in a conscious search for organizational alternatives. This approach may yet succeed in finding a viable new production strategy for range livestock in the African savannas.

These problems affect all livestock projects to a greater or lesser degree. The greater the extent to which the structure of a project is tailored to match the structure of the beneficiary population, the greater the likelihood that the project will be successful.

In the case of the Uganda Beef Ranching Development Project, for instance, a close fit existed between the objectives of the project and those of the participants, and despite enormously difficult economic and political conditions in the country the project was able to achieve a good measure of success. The Ugandan project, like the Kenyan one, was meant to initiate a long-term expansion of beef production for the domestic market. The greater part of the investment went for improved breeds and disease control, however, rather than for ranch infrastructure. The population of the project area was familiar with private livestock production and their land tenure patterns permitted fencing and individual use of pasture. Previously prevented from expanding into the project area because of the tsetse fly, the ranchers were now able to take advantage of the new breeds and raise them successfully. Because the indigenous patterns of livestock ownership and land tenure were very compatible with the requirements of the project, the experience was relatively successful. In contrast, the Kenyan project attempted to impose a foreign system of livestock control on a population which traditionally used far different methods, and consequently it ran into serious difficulty.

Alternative Pastoral Strategies

Although livestock development projects are deliberately created as alternatives (indeed, improvements) to what African pastoralists are doing, those who design and implement them are not always aware of all the contradictions between the old and the new livestock production strategies. To understand the difficulties which livestock development projects have encountered and to illuminate the points at which solutions must be found, it will be useful to compare the livestock project and the pastoral system as alternative strategies for range livestock populations.

First, a pastoral strategy of the traditional sort is a *population* strategy. It is more intelligible in ecological than in economic terms, because its beneficiary is a breeding population, not an individual. This is why pastoral populations are still so much in evidence in Africa, despite the numerous flaws in their way of life which have brought criticism successively from colonial administrators and national politicians. As noted earlier, the traditional division of pastoral populations into large groups of equivalent status allows small production units to fend for themselves in essentially orderly but ultimately zero-sum competition. This practice maximizes the chance of securing some survivors from even the worst conditions, who can then recolonize the habitat as conditions gradually improve. The objective is population persistence through time, at whatever numerical level, rather than a maximized number of animals or people at any given point in time. Whether pastoral populations are aware of, or recognize, this objective is another point altogether.

In a pastoral system, the individual producer is, however, always at risk. The hazards of the environment, disease, animal predators, and human competitors mean that African range pastoralism is a high-risk activity. The limited figures I have for a single pastoral population suggest that there may be a failure rate of more than 50 percent of attempts to start new herds, as fathers hand over to sons.

A double shift takes place in this strategy when one moves to a livestock development project. A project will have both ostensible and actual beneficiaries, but neither encompasses the whole pastoral population. The ostensible beneficiary is the pastoral producer, whether an individual or a small group. I believe the controlling factor in the project design is the planners' model of the business firm as a unit in Western economies, but I know of no explicit argument along these lines in development documents. It comes close to surfacing in proposals such as those for cooperative or company ranches in Kenya. If the target producer units are thought to be completely generalizable across the entire population, the population does benefit in the aggregate. If the target producers are seen as a subset (often already wealthy) who will prosper from the project, then the rest of the population is left to provide labor or to depart from the system as a result of malnutrition and sickness or poverty and urban migration.

Apart from the ostensible beneficiaries there are the actual beneficiaries. It has become commonplace for project plans to list the objective of improving the standard of living and thereby the quality of life of the target population. This obscures the fact that range livestock development projects have multiple beneficiaries, some of whom gain at a faster rate or on a larger scale than the pastoral producers. Some of the more obvious unstated beneficiaries are urban populations being provided with meat, livestock buyers and sellers, butchers, and the political elite who may benefit because they are part of the politico-economic pipeline of development funding and legislation.

This shift in beneficiaries is not accidental or merely the result of abused plans. It is inherent in the difference between livestock projects and pastoral strategies. Both are successful solutions to the problem of rangeland utilization. But one solves for maximizing the persistence of a regional population; the other solves for maximizing disposable livestock. The two solutions cannot sustain comparable densities of population. From a human point of view the project strategy is therefore incomplete unless it is supplemented by proposals to take care of excess humans. Any human group may choose either a ranching (project) strategy or a pastoral (population subsistence) strategy, but it may not choose both at the same time or assume that both sets of benefits may be had for only one set of costs.

Design Problems

Every project has a fixed spatial scale of operations that limits responsibility to selected problems and goals and allows an unambiguous assessment of performance. But it also creates problems. First, national officials charged with implementation often regard the scale of the project as more rigid than the World Bank appraisal team intended, and the final plan is locally given the status of scripture rather than of guidelines. Second, both the designers and the appraisers (technicians and anthropologists) of range livestock development projects may be flying blind on the matter of scale. Many planning issues are as yet unanswered questions.

For example, what are the upper and lower limits of size if a grazing control unit is to be effectively managed or a group ranch is to achieve stable market entry? What is the safe ratio of member equity to collective debt in a company livestock operation? Are there socially useful, or inimical, ratios of individual to collective ranching in a single region? How many livestock development units of any given form need to be started simultaneously for that new form to have a chance of success? Or is the danger only of starting too many, not too few? I see many adaptations of project design in recent implementation experiences, but social scientists are still far from being able to identify adequately the sociological solutions to these problems.

The fixed spatial scale of a project is matched by a fixed time scale, the period within which specified objectives are to be achieved by activities and expenditures which are carefully budgeted. Time horizons are essential for planning and psychologically useful for securing performance. The Bank has been constrained, however, by one of its own useful inventions, the so-called project cycle, which is geared to a five-year period for disbursement. That periodicity was not devised for agricultural investment, though it has been adapted to it with varying degrees of strain—usually by extending the time.

Range livestock development is poorly served by this short time horizon, and quite unrealistic dynamics are assumed in project design to accommodate it. As is evident from other sections of this chapter, the social engineering and changes in values entailed by livestock development are far beyond what can be achieved in five years—perhaps even in twenty-five. Stringing a succession of project applications together as an expected set of phases, more or less guaranteed some degree of support, has been tried as an ameliorative measure, but this hardly answers either. Typically, preparations and applications for the second phase of development have to be completed well before the lessons of the first phase have been crystalized and absorbed; thus it is impossible to take advantage of any improvements of knowledge or adjustments of direction that might be gained by segmented investment.

An open-ended time horizon would be better for livestock development but runs into the unavoidable restrictions created by the time horizons in which donors must themselves raise funds. Perhaps the flexibility already shown by the Bank in extending disbursement schedules could be used even more effectively in prolonging the preparation and identification phase to plan for implementation difficulties.

An intermediate level of organization (described earlier as a "neighborhood") does exist in a pastoral production system, but it is a changeable and temporary unit. The conditions of development intervention (security for a capital investment and control of a technological input for the sake of both efficiency and security) at present presuppose permanent organizations, not occasional ones. A set of permanent debtors whose personal identities change from month to month is not a concept that banks can deal with, and they can hardly be blamed for that.

Attempts to create a permanent group at the intermediate level of organization—some sort of association of pastoralists—can lead to a unit which falls between two stools, being too small to cope with environmental fluctuation and too large to cope with social coordination. Two proposals from the Kenya Livestock Development Project illustrate this sort of difficulty: grazing blocks for northeastern Kenya and group ranches for southern Kenya.

The root difficulty in achieving flexibility and feedback is the lack of information. There is probably seldom enough information to plan, justify, and predict the performance of a livestock development project at the time the project is identified or appraised, and it may still not be adequate when the project is being evaluated. This is not the fault of the donors. Of the mountain of data accumulated for East Africa by numerous scientists in the past fifty years, surprisingly little can be used in a dynamic, stimulating, predictive mode to manipulate efficiently the conditions of human existence. For example, we know quite a lot about the taxonomy of East African vegetation, but very little about the phenology of grass and browse in rangelands. Our data on population processes in livestock are miserable, and scarcely better for humans. Socially, we know, for museum purposes, more about cultural subdivisions of humans into tribes than we know how social processes operate to keep these groups both viable and identifiable. Development programs should certainly do more to build a capacity for improving their own information base.

Complexity is another feature of livestock development projects, though it may vary in degree and may not be necessary at all. Sometimes the complexity is built into a project, as when one part is dependent on another (for example, when one component group supplies immature animals to another, or when the success of marketing depends on disease control). At other times the complexity is created by the coexistence of other, uncoordinated development enterprises in the same area, which will affect the project (for example, when seasonally important pastoral areas of high productivity are exploited for agriculture, or mechanized farming intrudes across migration routes).

This combination of organizational complexity and low flexibility in livestock development projects is the reverse of pastoral production systems, whose response to savanna fluctuation seems based on organizational simplicity and flexibility. Recent projects for the improvement of smaller components are one way to achieve a less complicated, more successful design.

Projects are the outcome of an explicitly positive approach. An appraisal mission can fairly be described as charged to assess or, where necessary, to redesign a feasible project, if at all possible, even though the identification effort was less than satisfactory. This positive approach generates a phenomenon which might be described as "treading the edges of possibility." When an appraisal reveals that a project was built on an inadequate data base, team skills of a professional and forensic sort are mobilized, and a more convincing case is created by extrapolation and inference than might have been created by fact alone. At various points there is an assumption of optimality: optimal commitment, energy, and ability in government institutions, for example; optimal official response on key factors such as beef pricing; optimal weather; optimal calving rates; optimal market capacity to create producer response; optimal producer participation; and so on. These assumptions are drawn forth in the attempt to make a feasible proposition from fragmentary data: they are legitimized by the ideology that it is the task of development to discover potential, to push the system. The outcome is that plans (for rangeland livestock development in particular) tread the edges of possibility. This peculiar mixture of fragmentary information and optimal assumption may, from the very beginning, build unrealistic expectations into the project and to that extent set the stage in advance for some degree of failure.

Leadership and Participation

Pastoral organization is so flexible that the relative roles of leading and following, argument and arbitration, and information seeking and information management can change according to context. As a result, there are insufficient permanent and stable patterns for a development project to incorporate.

Ultimately, the herd owners are the autonomous figures; the transient state of their ability or willingness to reach mutually acceptable courses of action is reflected in the making and breaking of neighborhood groups and individual contracts. Given the lack of clear-cut means of coordinating animal management strategies over long periods, a peaceful existence is fostered more by decision-avoidance than by confrontation. Crisis management is more characteristic of larger groups than of a single production unit, for if a problem is large and immediate, then some choice must be made—however acrimoniously. Since development projects are plans for deliberately induced and phased change, they are not well served by this traditional pattern whereby decisions are deferred as long as possible and disagreement is expressed by simply parting company, with spatial separation reflecting the divergence of opinion. On the whole, projects do not anticipate, and find it hard to remedy, this distinctive mode of pastoral decisionmaking. Under these circumstances, the operation and outcome of livestock development projects is obviously affected by the participants: designers, implementers, and producers—groups with little overlap and less interaction than might be expected.

Project implementers are for the most part nationals, agency officials in an established hierarchy, who are concerned with the project for its duration. The hierarchy constrains what the implementers may achieve.

For an individual, the project may represent a personal power base and career opportunity as well as a job responsibility. His own political affiliations may include specific attitudes toward pastoralists, and he is more aware than the project designers that he works in a political arena. For example, he is subject to review by donor agency staff, who are likely to attribute project difficulties more to the incompetence of implementing officials than to flaws in the project design or to political obstacles. This constellation of factors severely limits the performance of implementation officials, especially the project manager when, in the nominal interests of efficiency, a separate project unit has been established with little regard for the actual distribution of power in government.

The other participants, the pastoral producers, are more often merely informed rather than consulted, and during implementation rather than at the time of identification. Formerly they were thought to be the one nonrational group of participants. Although this view is fading, there is still a tendency to regard pastoralists' lack of response as due to perversity rather than to flaws in the project design or unreasonable demands to take risks for unknown and undemonstrated benefits. As an autonomous manager totally responsible for his own animals and people, and free and obligated to exercise his independent judgment to secure their welfare, the pastoral producer is poorly prepared for the narrow role left for him within such projects. He is expected to respond readily to the plans of little-known outsiders, whose reputation of superiority may be difficult to reconcile with the value of their explicit suggestions and their level of knowledge of local conditions. Much in his prior way of life, social organization patterns, views, and needs prevents him from giving the expected response.

Issues for the Second-generation of Livestock Development Projects

Is it possible to infer from the admittedly faulty efforts of the past a set of guidelines for a new generation of livestock development? I believe it is: five items are clear to me, but there may well be more.

First, flexible financing is effectively the foundation of project improvements. We may still be uncertain whether livestock development is finally possible, but surely we are certain that quick livestock development is not. This would seem to entail longer-term financial commitments from donors to a program (for example, an expectation of twenty-five years, with some phasing sequence), which would be a line of policy or a set of project options, rather than a single project package (with more rigid structure-budget schedule). An array of smaller development initiatives could be tried. It would be expected that some would be small, some exploratory, and some divergent (even competitive) in their assumptions, aims, and strategies.

Second, a deconstruction of livestock development project designs should reemphasize their disparate components. This is counterintuitive: it would seem a reversion to older, discredited practices of trying to achieve disease control, marketing, pasture improvement, and the like without regard to the implications of each. But it is really an attempt to flush out the contradictions that may be concealed in a project's intentions. There would be clear focus on livestock or pastoral population or range environment as the primary objective or frame of reference. The relevance of each for the other is not denied, and a form of impact statement can be required to elucidate what is relevant in a given instance. Integration has entered our rhetoric as an easy assumption (about existing production systems) or a premature objective (for development projects) and we might benefit by deferring integration until we better understand the elements.

Third, for similar effect, we should cease trying to analyze or manipulate whole systems and alter our scale—whether of investigation or intervention—to deal with specific linkages. The system (which is anyway only a model) remains a useful frame of reference: the complex interrelationships will of course persist, undeniably, in the form of the real world. But since our attempts to understand or affect whole systems have been disappointing (except, ironically, in accidental adverse form as with boreholes creating desertification), we should operate for a while on a smaller scale. I offer two examples of linkage, one natural, one natural and social. (a) Sheep and goats are a significant element in many range livestock systems. In many situations, and paradoxically, they die in large numbers, not during the severity of the dry season but from the cold just after the rains recommence. To affect, by investigation and then therapeutic intervention, this particular linkage would significantly improve pastoral livelihood. (b) In many pastoral situations, the basic production unit is provided by an extended (three generation) family and its attendant herds and flocks. Such units begin when a grown son splits from his natal family to create his own independent household. This is a time of great strain and high risk, involving loss of labor and animals for the parent unit and (often) barely sufficient herd and labor resources for the new unit. Unexpectedly high failure rates occur among the new units: the stock loss and human trauma are considerable. This phase of production is one link in the system where intervention to reduce the failure rate would be of benefit to overall production.

Fourth, we should generate a new form of development initiative—a hybrid between project and experiment. The failure of experimental stations to deliver results that affect producers is notorious. The failure to create livestock experiments which are transferable even in principle is also well-known. A combination of the first three guidelines, however, would eliminate this difficulty. Adaptation is the real-life process whereby intentions (projects) are continually tested (as experiments) with observable results which are then incorporated or avoided. A pastoral society is typically composed of thousands of small production units who react variably to ambient conditions, observe each other, and adopt or avoid the strategies of others. With small-scale design and flexible financing, we would follow real world behavior (instead of denying or defying it) and try small innovations. These could be dropped if they fail (not all experiments yield anticipated results), or reinforced, or modified and tried elsewhere. Examples of such small-scale interventions would be: can a family with only young children produce more efficiently by herding only small ruminants; can a local trading role be combined with herding in an area where all traders are at present ethnically alien and resented; can production alternatives be found within the society for women who flee or are abandoned by their husbands. If attention is focused on development opportunities at this level, it will be discovered that many "experiment-projects" are already in place, because individuals are already trying these options.

Fifth, the distorting effects of political power on project intentions and execution (in the case of internationally financed projects) should be faced as openly as issues of national sovereignty allow. Accordingly we should try to decentralize and localize development. The channels that function to carry out development projects deserve, but do not get, as much attention as the target populations at the project site. The political dynamics of the process are seldom factored into project design, but are likely to be responsible for shaping the outcome and design itself. It is accepted that even if better information were available for project design, it is unclear whether the national organization would grasp and employ it. Centralized bureaucracy is the antithesis of most forms of pastoral social organization, and this distance creates mutual suspicion, inaccessibility, and above all inefficiency. Central-bureaucratic project development is subject to those political pressures (including abuses) that are extrinsic to project design but unfortunately not to project experience. Flexible financing, focus on small-scale interventions, the use of local example, and a continuing search for suggestions from the local population, could all reduce the role of a central bureaucracy to the minimum necessary for supply and accounting.

The cumulative effect of these five propositions—at least in intent—is to bring "livestock development" more closely in conjunction with real world conditions. If, as I believe, the common characteristic of African livestock development projects in the past twenty years is that they lacked realism (and thus were unrealizable), then whatever moves project design and procedure towards real world conditions will improve project realization. If the points offered are unconvincing, then this central guideline may be used by the reader to construct his or her own.

Incorporating Anthropology in the Project Process

It is more than twenty years since the World Bank first used consultant anthropologists to help appraise a livestock project; and if anthropological participation guaranteed success then livestock development projects would be in better shape than they are. If anthropologists have, nonetheless, a useful role to play in livestock development (and I think they have) then the question arises of what alteration in their present role might improve both their own performance and that of livestock projects.

The issue seems linked to the place of the anthropologist in the project cycle. Anthropologists have usually been used at the time of project appraisal. This is ironic. Although at this phase (depending on the team leader) genuine weight can be given to the anthropologist's views, it is the phase which puts the greatest strain on an anthropologist's capacity to respond. Typically, the anthropologist is set the task of unraveling complex social issues in less than a month of on-site observation. (If they are not complex, an anthropologist is not even looked for.) Another few weeks are allowed later for reflection, analysis, and conclusions which should be operational and should interact constructively with the findings of other specialists on the team. Unless the anthropologist has prior detailed knowledge of the area or extensive experience with the operational problem-set likely to be encountered, his or her input may even

become negative, suppressing the commonsense, relevant social observations that appraisal team members might otherwise make for themselves.

A more efficient use of social analysis would be to give it a place,
though of varying style and degree, at each stage of the project cycle (see
the discussion of this point in chapter 1). An anthropologist could be
usefully employed at the preparation stage to assemble relevant data and
identify those needed but missing. Whether to acquire such data could
be a project-specific decision. The anthropologist could be of better use
at the preparation stage, however, if allowed to begin with project
identification.

Anthropologists and other social analysts are essentially translators
(they differ in how they acquire what information to translate), and the
discipline's utility lies in the conviction that it is both necessary and
possible to explain human groups to each other. An anthropologist might
therefore be used (for example, by an international development
agency's country mission) on a roving commission, collecting potential
cases for project identification by surveying the aspirations and discon-
tents and difficulties of people in a specific area or of a particular sort
(women factory workers, irrigation farmers, and so on). From this
beginning could come a three-way conversation between government,
agency, and people, with the social analyst acting as broker. It would be
a particular use of professional skills in two respects: conveying to
outsiders a sense of prevailing values and present social forms, from
which action of any sort would have to start; and helping the people to
participate in identifying new groupings and new roles which the new
activities or technologies might call for. This would be a long overdue
attempt at participatory planning.

The use of social analysis and of anthropologists in project identification would certainly not eliminate all project problems. But it would
eliminate some of the needless uncertainty about whether the people will
respond to the project. It would accord to project populations the dignity
to which they are entitled in speaking to their own future. It would coach
them in the difficult process of learning how to influence their own
development. It would, for example, bring the knowledge of the pastoral
social system to bear on the design of livestock projects. It would put the
skills of a valuable perspective to work where they would be most
efficient. A logical extension of this process would be to have the social
analysts take their turn with other types of experts in the follow-up

activity of supervision missions. Finally, they should be able to make a useful contribution to the evaluation phase of projects.

There are, however, two difficulties in using social anthropology in development as part of the attempt to put people first. First is the difficulty of finding anthropologists or sociologists at the right level of ability (given other institutional competition for the best scientists): there is no point in using others just for a dubious anthropological imprimatur. Second is the nature of social anthropology itself. For much of its history, the thrust of anthropological theory has been toward retrodictive and aggregate statements. "Tradition," "culture," "society," after all, refer to what people *in general* do, what they do *most of the time*, what they have done *up to now*. These are valuable notions; but for development purposes there is also need to know the idiosyncratic, the predictive: what is the *full* range of behavior, what are behavioral frequencies, what alternative forms of procedure and organization might people take up as necessary? A shift from determinism to a probabilistic frame of reference in social anthropology began in the mid-1950s (with the work of Raymond Firth), but its takeover is slow and its implications have yet to be fully worked out. Encouraging new steps, however, have been made in several subfields during the second half of the 80s.

The effort to bring social anthropology into the practice of development planners is surely worth continuing. Development is of, for, and by humans. And it is no less logical to have the human sciences involved at all stages of a human enterprise than to have economists involved at all stages of projects because they have been overwhelmingly yet onesidedly perceived as economic activities.

Addenda

In the natural sciences, the opportunity to revise an essay after five years would necessarily involve a new set of references and, as often as not, different conclusions. Sadly this is not true where livestock development is concerned. We still lack data on rangelands, livestock dynamics, and pastoral production sufficient to create an adequate foundation for planning. Homewood and others (1987) demonstrate for one part of the Maasai pastoral production system over a two-year period, what such a data base might look like. But their conclusions are not new: "contrary to popular opinion pastoralist land use is an ecologically appropriate and efficient form of livestock management." Ellis and Swift (1988), p. 450, with a good deal less data but more speculation, reach comparable conclusions for the Turkana—that development should "build on and facilitate pastoral strategies rather than constrain them."[9]

Part of the difficulty (to confine myself to the Maasai case) is that some of the most interesting work that has been done in terms of animal holdings—such as wealth polarization—remains unpublished or exiguously presented (Graham 1988).[10] This presentation also makes it impractical to deal with a variety of interesting social phenomena such as whether new social forms actually work in Niger (Hiernaux and Diara 1984[11]; Sollod and others 1986[12]), whether the restocking of failed pastoralists is a useful development strategy (Morris 1988), or the spontaneous emergence of range enclosure in Somalia (Behnke 1988).[13]

I have therefore tried to use the opportunity of a second edition at the beginning of the 1990s. for further reflection: to see if it is possible to diagnose the essential character of first-generation livestock development projects—the classic livestock development project, so to speak—as a way of moving to some guidelines for second-generation livestock development possibilities.

Notes

I gratefully acknowledge the assistance of Deborah Rubin, who patiently helped construct this paper out of several unpublished reports and improved it in the process; despite my long work and various writings on East African pastoralists, this particular paper would not have existed without her help.

1. D. J. Pratt, "Rangeland Development in Kenya," *Animals and the Arid Zone*, vol. 7 (1968), pp. 177–208.

2. Examples would be stock routes for marketing, repayment schedules for loans to ranches, throughput rates in slaughterhouses, or market prices for beef. Such problems are readily recognized and are susceptible to technical solution or political negotiation.

3. See also Rada Dyson-Hudson and Neville Dyson-Hudson, "The Structure of East African Herds and the Future of East African Herders," *Development and Change*, vol. 13 (1982), pp. 213–38.

4. R. T. Wilson, C. P. Peacock, and A. R. Sayers, *A Study of Goat and Sheep Production on the Maasai Group Ranch at Elangata Wuas, Kajiado*, Working Document no. 24 (Nairobi: International Livestock Center for Africa, 1981).

5. J. H. B. Prole, "Pastoral Land Use," in W. T. W. Morgan, ed., *Nairobi: City and Region* (Nairobi: Oxford University Press, 1967).

6. S. J. Meadows and Judy White, *Structure of the Herd and Determinants of Offtake Rates in Kajiado District, Kenya, 1962–1967*, ODI Pastoral Network Paper 7d (London: Overseas Development Institute, 1979).

7. S. J. Meadows, personal communication.

8. K. Homewood and others, "Ecology of Pastoralism in Ngorongoro Conservation Area, Tanzania." *Journal of Agricultural Sciences, Cambridge*, vol. 104 (1987), pp. 47–72.

9. J. E. Ellis and D. M. Swift, "Stability of African Pastoral Ecosystems." *Journal of Range Management*, vol. 41 (1988), pp. 450–59.

10. O. Graham, *Enclosure of the East African Rangelands*. ODI Pastoral Network Paper 25a (London: Overseas Development Institute, 1988).

11. P. Hiernaux and L. Diarra, "Is it possible to improve traditional grazing management in flood plain of Niger River in central Mali?" In P. J. Joss and others, eds., *Rangeland: Resource under Siege*, pp. 214–15 (Cambridge: Cambridge University Press, 1984).

12. A. Sollod and others, "Development of a Successful Range Program in Niger." In J. T. O'Rourke, ed., *Proceedings 1986 International Rangeland Development Symposium*, pp. 83–88 (Morrilton: Winrock, 1986).

13. R. Behnke, *Range Enclosure in Central Somalia*. ODI Pastoral Network Paper 25b. (London: Overseas Development Institute, 1988).

PART IV

Fishery Projects

Editor's Note

Descriptions of picturesque fishing communities have occupied a central place in the ethnographic literature since fieldwork was first carried out among the Trobriand Islanders. Yet systematic sociological consideration of the productive activities and development needs of fishermen has not followed accordingly. In development interventions, sociological knowledge has been more frequently applied to farming activities. Planners tend to mechanically extrapolate the model of farming communities to fishing communities, without consideration of the social, organizational, and cultural differences between the two.

Richard Pollnac offers a concise, yet comprehensive overview of the characteristics of fishing communities and of their relevance for development design. The social and cultural characteristics that distinguish fishing communities from other types of productive communities are used to explain why the changes induced by fishery development projects tend to unfold differently than changes in other subsectors.

The first section of Pollnac's chapter identifies those unique social and cultural characteristics which are rooted in fishermen's mode of production and ecological constraints and thus require special attention when planning for induced development. Harvest (capture) fisheries are distinguished from aquaculture, and both types are further defined by scale and aquatic niche. The amount of cooperation among producers, their shifting residence and irregular work hours, the unpredictability of resources, and the high perishability of the product—all entail some unusual consequences for development interventions.

Pollnac also addresses the issue of incremental income distribution in small-scale fishing communities. Frequently only wealthy fishermen, or others who are already well-off, can afford the costly new technology to increase productivity. This new technology gives them a further advantage over the poorer fishermen, increasing social and economic stratification, polarization, and other disruptive consequences.

The second section of chapter 8 outlines the structure of the small-scale fishery development process and suggests how sociocultural information can contribute to the correct design or to the failure of a fishery project. Tradeoffs between increased technological efficiency and adverse social effects such as unemployment and greater social stratification are examined. It is argued that, in some instances, existing labor-intensive fishing systems are preferable to technologically more efficient systems, which may displace local labor and thus create social problems outweighing the anticipated gains in economic efficiency. Sometimes, perceiving the costs of reduced employment, the fishermen maintain the traditional work force, even though it decreases the efficiency of the new technology. They may, as a result, become worse-off economically, because they bear both capital investment costs as well as high labor costs.

How, then, can new fishing technology be introduced without increasing community stratification and polarization? The author's response points toward specific organizational arrangements which could help keep the ownership of the new means of production in the hands of the fishermen. Along this line, the third section of the chapter addresses the role of cooperatives in fishery development projects. Changes in social organization are perhaps the most difficult to initiate, and the fishermen's cooperative is a problem-prone organization—yet the governments of many developing countries consider cooperatives to be the most adequate institutional vehicle for fishery development projects. Therefore, Pollnac proceeds to examine, in the fourth section, the relationships between occupational characteristics, sociocultural context, and factors which influence the success or failure of fishermen's organizations under fishery development projects.

The final section is directed toward the fishery project planners or managers and discusses how to use sociological information needed for project design and implementation. Examples of how the data can be obtained and converted into operational recommendations are provided. The costs of such sociocultural information programs are low in relation to the expected incremental benefits.

8

Social and Cultural Characteristics in Small-scale Fishery Development

Richard B. Pollnac

Many of the problems associated with development and change among fishermen are shared with other productive sectors. These general problems will not be reviewed here for they are adequately covered elsewhere.[1] It is clear, however, that fishery development programs face some specific cultural and institutional impediments to successful implementation. One recent study notes that the constraints on small-scale fishermen are usually socioeconomic and rarely due to the absence of a specific technology. Another study suggests that fishery development programs need at least ten to twenty years of commitment on the part of involved governments and agencies due to the complexities involved in project design and implementation.[2] Difficulties faced by fishery projects are perhaps best indicated by the fact that fully one-half of the World Bank–assisted completed fishery projects either failed in achieving major objectives or had uncertain or marginal outcomes.[3] The purpose of this chapter is to identify the sociocultural characteristics of fishing communities which are significant for development interventions and to trace their origins back to features of the occupation and of the aquatic environment.

Adaptation for humans has been defined as the process by which humans make effective, productive use of the energy potential in their environment. It is an interactive process between the physical environment, technology, social organization, social environment, ideology, and individual biopsychological needs and characteristics. These components form part of an interlocking system; thus, changes in one part can affect others. The various components of fishing communities have adapted to the aquatic environment and associated occupations through years of trial and error so that these systems are usually balanced to some degree. Introducing new elements through development programs can upset this balance. The new characteristics may either be rejected or may result in social stress. It is, therefore, important to understand human adaptations to aquatic environments to enhance the likelihood that proposed changes will fit the needs of fishing communities. This does not mean, however, that either technological or social changes are to be avoided. As will be seen below, social engineering—the development or enhancement of organizations or institutions (as in the case of cooperatives)—can be used effectively to reduce or eliminate potential conflicts. Social engineering, however, cannot be appropriately accomplished without an understanding of the sociocultural matrix within which it is carried out.

Sociocultural Characteristics of Fishing Communities

Two primary categories of fishery must be distinguished at the outset: aquaculture as opposed to capture fishing. Most international development agencies classify them together in the fishery sector, thereby compounding the erroneous belief that the two types have a great deal in common. In fact, one of the few things they have in common is the product—fish.

In its work patterns, aquaculture is more like agriculture or animal husbandry than capture fishing. Usually an aquaculturalist improves a specific area to promote fish growth and gain rights to the fish. Property rights in aquaculture are thus like those in agriculture. Harvest fisheries, however, depend on open access—the fishermen have common rights to the resource. Because the prey is wild—moving from place to place—there is an element of risk involved, and fishermen must be mobile. In contrast, the harvesting of aquaculture products is more controlled. In most cases the aquaculturalist knows where the fish are and when they are ready to be harvested. The product has more predictability. Finally, the manpower and capital requirements differ between the two types.

Capture fishermen need only to harvest what grows naturally, and in small-scale fisheries this is done with a relatively low capital investment. In contrast, aquaculture systems can require both cultivation and harvesting, which depend on more complex labor arrangements and training. Many aquaculture systems also require pond excavation, stocking, maintenance of water quality, and feeding—operations which have a relatively high capital investment.[4] To limit the scope of this paper, subsequent discussions are concerned only with the capture fishery.

Capture Fishery

The category of capture fishery also includes several distinct types. The most frequently recognized factor is scale, leading to a distinction between large- and small-scale fisheries.

Large-scale fisheries are organized in a manner similar to agroindustrial firms in the developed countries; are relatively more capital intensive; provide higher incomes than artisanal fisheries, for both boat owners and crew; provide most of the canned and frozen fish; and produce most of the fish earmarked for reduction and export markets.

Small-scale fisheries are generally located in rural and coastal areas, near lagoons and estuaries; they typically overlap with such rural activities as agriculture, animal husbandry, and aquaculture; they are highly labor intensive and use a minimum of mechanical power; while they may include some motorized boats, they generally exclude mechanized gear; they retain primitive technology for handling and processing (few of them use ice or cold storage facilities) with the result that harvesting losses are significant; they harvest stocks with a small biomass, compared to deep-sea pelagic fish stocks, which contain a large variety of species suitable for domestic consumption; and they supply most of the cured fish and fish intended for direct human consumption.[5]

This categorization is related to the sociocultural characteristics of the communities in which small- or large-scale fishing is found. Some of the processes discussed later deal with changes along the continuum from small- to large-scale. In the real world these categories are somewhat mixed, scale is only one factor, and "small" need not be equated with artisanal or unmechanized. Some changes in small-scale fisheries, for example, involve introducing mechanized gear such as winches to haul nets. A distinction by scale is useful, however, in analyzing fishery development.

Another important distinction is between capture fisheries in large as opposed to small bodies of water. The technologies, the risks involved (both to person and equipment), and the distances from residence to workplace differ greatly between these two types. These differences are reflected in the work patterns and the structure of different fishing communities.

Sociocultural Aspects of Resource Variability

Capture fishery resources are usually characterized by a high degree of variability. This variability is of three types: (1) long-term, predictable (seasonal); (2) long-term, usually not predictable (because of population changes associated with overfishing, climate, or other external factors); and (3) short-term, unpredictable (variation in the day-to-day catch). As a result, most fishing communities have developed specific sociocultural attributes.

Predictable long-term variations have local differences with respect to both the periodicity and relative availability of the various fish species exploited. These variations have elicited behavioral responses manifested in the social environment. For example, in both arctic and tropical regions periodicity in the availability of desired species leads to annual movements between seashore and interior settlements. Some fishermen respond to this variability by living on their boats and following the fish, as among the boat-dwelling Bajau of the Sulu Archipelago; others, such as those on the Azuero Peninsula of Panama, shift residence to different parts of the coast. Since coastal strips are often agriculturally unproductive, maritime people who also practice agriculture must decide whether to live inland and travel to the sea to fish, or live along the shore and farm inland. Fishermen who shift residence are not always accompanied by their families. Women and children may remain behind in the home community, which creates imbalances in the sex ratios in both the home and temporary fishing communities. When the adaptation to aquatic environments leads to shifting residences, annual movements between the coast and inland, and temporary imbalances in sex ratios, the fishermen are more like pastoralists than settled agriculturalists.

Short-term, unpredictable variability influences the hours that fishermen work. When the weather is good and fish are available, good fishermen are out fishing. Thus, their day-to-day work schedule frequently differs from those in other occupations. Even more variance in schedules can be introduced by other factors unique to fisheries, such as currents and the relative visibility of gear at night versus day.

Short-term, unpredictable variability is basically due to three important characteristics of fisheries: the prey is mobile; it is usually not visible under water; and bad weather may make it dangerous or impossible to fish. A great deal of day-to-day variation in catch and income is the result. Primary fish buyers in most fishing communities have long-standing relationships with fishermen and are familiar with their problems. Because they understand these environmental constraints they can provide loans and permit a great deal of flexibility with respect to repayment.

Sociocultural Implications of Relative Isolation

In many instances fishermen, like other occupational subcultures, form societies unto themselves. Capture fishermen are frequently also isolated because they must live along the narrow margins of lakes, rivers, or the sea. This relative isolation is increased among large lake and marine fishermen by their separation from land-based society while fishing. In addition, because many fishing people work at night or extremely early in the morning, times when most others are asleep, fishermen are often treated as social outcasts. Fishermen in India, for example, are classified among the lowest castes;[6] in both China and Korea they are the object of considerable prejudice and oppression, and they are ranked very low on the social scale in Japan.[7] In Africa, the Somali leave the fishing to "the Midgan and other despised groups,"[8] and in Mauritania, the Imraugen, a low-status coastal group, conduct the fishing.

This residential and social isolation affects other sociocultural variables, which in turn affect development. It may contribute to the low level of education of many small-scale fishermen in the developing world. I have visited many fishing villages in Africa which are so isolated that children must live with relatives in other villages in order to have access to schools. Even where the residential isolation is not so great, the social isolation may cause fishermen and their families to form negative attitudes toward the formal education of the nonfishing society. For example, ridicule of fishermen's children for their poor dress and relatively impoverished family contributes to their dropping out of school early.

Organization of Work

A great deal of attention has been given to the interdependent and cooperative nature of fishing activities. It has been suggested that the need for coordination within fishing crews, combined with the physical risks associated with the marine environment, increases both the need for interdependence and the importance of each worker.[9] In conjunction with the rapid depreciation of equipment and the possibility of equipment loss, this cooperation decreases the social and economic distance between owners and laborers. Work relationships in fishing crews, it is argued, are therefore more egalitarian than among farmers. The ethnographic literature supports this proposition.[10]

In Micronesia the exploitation of terrestrial resources is an individual act, while marine resources are exploited by cooperative groups. Similarly, in Nicaragua among Miskito turtle fishermen, while land hunting partnerships are loose, close cooperation is demanded between turtle fishermen. Turtle men must have partners they can rely on; thus, partnerships form around each individual's skill, reliability, and temperament. On Saint Kitts in the Caribbean, fishing crews, in contrast to cane cutter groups, are integrated and cooperative with little stratification. Fishermen are likely to view their captain as helpful and nurturant, unlike cane cutters who view the head cutter negatively because they think he takes advantage of the men. Finally, the need for cooperation is so important to the fishermen of Caleta San Pablo, Peru, that all arguments must stop short of the beach.[11]

Paradoxically, numerous researchers have also noted that fishermen can be characterized as "independent" types.[12] This stems from the environmental and technological conditions of the occupation of fishing. It has been argued that independence helps fishermen adapt psychologically to their occupation. They are forced to make decisions quickly and in the face of uncertainty—decisions that have immediate effects on the safety of the vessel and its crew as well as on the success of the hunt. Furthermore, fishermen are often physically removed from the help and support of land-based society. At sea, fishermen carry out complicated tasks independently, with little verbal communication. Each crewman works and makes independent decisions.

The apparent paradox of the egalitarian, cooperative, independent fisherman is reconciled by emphasizing that "egalitarianism is the only non-coercive way that individuals with high need for independence can be organized into a crew."[13] It is important to note that the egalitarianism and interdependence between fishermen discussed here refers to *within* a crew, *not between* crews.

Safe and profitable operations on a fishing vessel depend on an interdependent and cooperative crew. The use of kinsmen in a crew enhances cooperation within the work group and is a common practice in many parts of the world.[14]

Division of Labor by Sex

Although in some economies women can combine subsistence and child care functions, in fishing, especially deep-sea or lake fishing from boats, it is difficult to include less than fully active members in the crew. The size of most small-scale fishing vessels and the degree of coordinated activity required in relatively cramped work areas simply will not allow it. Women are therefore usually confined to shoreline activities (including fishing and shell fishing in the shallows) where the work will not conflict with child care.

A gender division of labor is often evident in the distribution and marketing system. Fish is a highly perishable product not easily stored without complex techniques for drying or freezing and a relatively large outlay in equipment and labor. The distribution of the surplus catch is thus usually performed by a middleman or fish dealer who has the time and resources to process and distribute this highly perishable product. In many fishing communities, females take over the function of buying and selling fish. This division of labor sometimes serves to keep at least some of the profits within the family: the males fish and their female relatives sell the product. The role of fish trader makes women the primary element of economic stability in some fishing societies, since males may fish only intermittently but the females can work year-round.[15]

Rights to Aquatic Resources

One extremely important element of social organization is the control or ownership of natural resources. The importance of land tenure systems is widely recognized with respect to agricultural societies, but until recently sea tenure was rarely considered when discussing fishing communities. Perhaps the Western legal definition of the sea as an open-access resource has influenced the way we view sea tenure in other societies. Furthermore, the flat, relatively featureless nature of the sea and large lakes presents boundary-marking problems not associated with land. In some regions waves and currents shift lagoonal, estuary, and coastal boundaries so that it is practically impossible to maintain boundaries on a micro level, as is done in agriculture. Finally, since the prey is mobile, rights over a specific, small fishing spot would become worthless as fish move around. In most fishing societies, therefore, individuals rarely "own" specific fishing areas as they do plots of land. Communal rights are found somewhat more frequently, but they often run counter to national laws which designate the sea as an open-access resource.

Several types of sea tenure operate in fishing communities.[16] Least frequent is individual ownership. In some cases, shellfish beds and fishing areas have been formally owned by important men in the community, with rights to this property claimed through inheritance.[17] Communal ownership is perhaps the most frequent form of sea tenure. In Polynesia, areas of ocean are the corporate estates of groups of people, with title associated with the group leader. Although all group members have use rights, the leader has the prerogative of administering use.[18] In South India, villages as a whole have rights to specific fishing grounds.[19] Japanese fishing waters are defined by prefectural law, which usually conforms with the traditional assignment of fishing waters.[20] Even in present-day U.S. society where the sea is legally defined as an open-access resource, Maine lobstermen claim fishing rights to particular areas. The lobstering territories are associated with harbor gangs, who have destroyed equipment in retaliation for territorial violations.[21]

Where there is no formal recognition of sea tenure rights, fishing spots are often secret. At Arembepe, Brazil, fishermen view the sea as an open-access resource, but good fishing spots are kept secret. A complex system of named fishing grounds and landmarks exists among the raft fishermen of Brazil.[22] Location of the fishing grounds is made by visual triangulation, and knowledge of fish within them is transmitted from father to son over the generations. The difficulty of maintaining boundaries, however, means that most fishermen exploit the resources on a first-come, first-serve basis.

Although some of the characteristics mentioned above, such as seasonal residence changes and irregular work schedules, are not unique to fishing communities, their particular *combination* does require specialized consideration and planning in the design and implementation of development programs for fisheries. In summary, the following aspects of the society and culture of fishing peoples are significant for development. First, seasonal resource variability and the generally infertile nature of the coastal strip frequently causes a pattern of shifting residence among fishermen. Short-term, unpredictable resource variability causes irregular work hours and variable incomes which require special financial services.

Second, residence along the narrow margins of waterways, lakes, or the sea and the unusual characteristics of their occupation (irregular work hours, out-of-sight of land-based society) often cause fishermen to be socially isolated. This social isolation inhibits their access to formal education and also influences their attitudes toward members of other social groups.

Third, the physical risks associated with some forms of fishing, the need for coordination within crews, and the rapid depreciation of productive equipment all require an egalitarian, interdependent, cooperative crew, frequently based on kin relationships. Furthermore, to minimize discord the turnover within crews is rapid. Nevertheless, the same physical risks associated with the need for rapid decisionmaking produce fishermen who are relatively independent. This independent nature is further enhanced by the fact that in most fisheries harvesting rights are based on arrival time as opposed to some type of tenure. This general lack of sea tenure systems is associated with the unpredictable, short-term periodicity of the resource and the relative featurelessness of the aquatic environment.

Fourth, the special handling, processing, and marketing needs of fish lead to the need for specialists. In most cases, this division of labor is based on sex since the limited and frequently dangerous work space on a fishing vessel discourages the presence of children. Women consequently often take over the processing and marketing of fish, which can be combined with child care.

Sociocultural Information Needed
for Developing Fishery Programs

Starting from the development process of the small-scale fishery this section attempts to indicate how sociocultural information can facilitate planned interventions in this process and what kind of sociocultural data are needed by development planners in connection with specific projects.

It is assumed that adequate preliminary analyses by resource economists and biologists have already determined that certain changes in the fishery are important in the development strategy of the specific target population being considered. Sometimes these changes involve a management plan, such as a reduction in overall fishing effort, to improve the potential of the fishery resources. In regions where acceptable alternative employment opportunities for displaced fishermen exist, the decisionmaking process is simplified: it is necessary only to perform biosocioeconomic cost-benefit analyses of effort-reducing alternatives.

Where acceptable alternative employment opportunities do not exist, but the price of fish can be increased so that fishermen can maintain existing levels of profit with reduced effort, or where projected decreases in income are within limits that are ascertained to be acceptable to fishermen, effort-reducing alternatives can be evaluated. If the level of financial strain is not acceptable, it will be necessary to retrain fishermen for other employment.

If the fish stocks can support greater effort, then a decision can be made concerning techniques for increasing effort. Certainly the degree of unemployment in the target region should be considered. If many people are unemployed, the rational decision is to increase the number of fishermen, both to augment the supply of fish and to provide productive employment. If unemployment is low, the introduction of more efficient technologies should be considered. If analysis shows a more effective technology to be warranted, alternative technologies should be subjected to a sociobioeconomic cost-benefit analysis. Biologists, for example, should consider the relations of the technologies to maximum sustainable yield; economists should conduct standard cost-benefit analyses and consider the cost of the technology in relation to the fishermen's purchasing power. In all cases, attempts should be made to select a technology that is within the means of working fishermen. This is sometimes impossible.

The attitudes of the participants toward the proposed change must be considered. New technologies or new people cannot be introduced into the fishing industry unless the participants are willing to change. It is obvious—but the point is often overlooked—that if the participants refuse to cooperate, the project will not succeed. Often this reluctance to cooperate is based on rational considerations that can be worked into the project design if they are known beforehand. It is therefore necessary to consider the likely attitudes of the participants toward the proposed changes and how their beliefs and values will be affected. Involving the target population in early stages of planning is an important ingredient in the success of a project.

If attitudes are negative, it is essential to determine the reason and attempt to adjust the changes to the perceived needs of the people. If attitudes are positive, success in introducing a new technology or more fishermen depends on the availability of skilled personnel—another decision point where detailed information is needed. If there is a lack of skilled personnel, a program should be developed to train fishermen in the new technology or to teach unemployed people how to fish.

Once sufficient skilled personnel are available, the remaining obstacle between the fishermen and the capture technology is the ability to finance the changes. If financial resources are inadequate, decisions must be made concerning the extension of credit. If capital is distributed unequally in the target region, the project could increase social stratification and create other social problems. In many instances, only people who are already well-off can take advantage of new opportunities so that the new technology improves their situation relative to others. This problem—though not unique—is common in fishery projects, since the technology for development (such as nets, motors, vessels, and processing equipment) is relatively expensive and producer financing is frequently a component of the project.

Introductions of new or improved technology can also affect the distribution of wealth in a situation where the same fishing ground is used by groups employing different fishing gears for the same or different resources. Improvements restricted to only one of the user groups can provide them with an advantage to the detriment of other users of a common property resource.[23]

Changes in the scale of technology can alter the distribution of wealth and quality of life on a macroscale in a fishery. For example, the introduction of larger scale, more-industrialized fishery technology in many West African countries would result in a concentration of fisheries in the few areas with sufficient infrastructure to support the larger vessels and increased production. This could result in increased urbanization as small-scale fishermen move to areas (usually urban) with adequate infrastructure, thus causing a decrease in the number of rural fishermen who provide high-quality fresh fish to local markets. Additionally, there is a potential loss of agricultural products from part-time fishermen-farmers who move to urban fishing centers as well as the possibility of increased unemployment resulting from a less labor intensive technology.[24]

The costs and benefits of such changes obviously need to be carefully evaluated by resource economists, but the socioeconomic value of small-scale fisheries at the local, rural level is difficult to determine; hence, frequently it is examined superficially in macro analyses. As McGoodwin points out with respect to small-scale shrimp fishermen on the Pacific coast of Mexico, it is difficult to calculate the economic value of fish supplied to kinsmen or neighbors for food or bartered for other foodstuffs or supplies along the isolated, rural coastal zone. This is especially true when community members both depend on the fish and lack viable alternatives. Nevertheless, these calculations concern a major social impact—the distribution of well-being among a dispersed, coastal population.[25]

Finally, some changes in fisheries involve a shift to export-oriented species such as shrimp. These shifts are often promoted by governments interested in foreign exchange earnings. Such changes can have a negative impact on local nutrition as well as on the relative independence of small-scale fishermen who must adjust to considerably more unpredictable and more fluctuating external market forces and technological inputs. Initially high prices paid for the product, in addition to government promotion, sometimes result in overexploitation of the resource base and subsequent declines in catches and incomes.[26] Cost-benefit analyses of this type of development run into many of the same social questions posed above concerning the industrialization of a fishery. It is clear that changes in a fishery are not without social impacts that pose value-laden questions concerning social organization, the division of labor, and distribution of wealth.[27]

Some concrete examples from fishery development projects are in order. In Grenada, ownership patterns of fishing boats were altered when the price of equipment increased. Before mechanization, 90 percent of the fishermen owned their own boats; afterward this figure dropped to 25 percent.[28] In another case, as Peruvian small-scale fishermen began to depend on expensive, highly specialized equipment, their formerly egalitarian community began to manifest signs of social stratification.[29] Among Malay fishermen, too, rises in the costs of productive equipment associated with modernization have created a class of equipment owners. Although modern equipment has produced greater overall returns, increasing capital costs have led to a marked drop in the earnings going to the labor force. The fisherman has become an employed laborer, but he is treated as a participant in a common enterprise and thus is not paid regular wages. His income is still based on a share of the catch, but costs are subtracted from the proceeds before shares are calculated. Because the size of the catch varies widely, fishermen often receive next to nothing. Fishermen were in a less advantageous position after these changes than when they were first studied in 1939–40; the entrepreneurs are much more powerful than their predecessors were a generation earlier.[30]

Even when governments are aware that the high cost of new technology is likely to bring greater social stratification, problems arise and disparity in wealth widens. In Sri Lanka, because the government was aware of the problems of financing costly new fishing technology, it introduced a hire-purchase scheme. Participants were selected by ballot from among qualified applicants. Each fisherman made a deposit and received a government loan, repayable in the course of five years, to purchase a hull and engine. Unforeseen problems arose, however. First, the deposit and the loan together covered only the vessel and engine, but not the gear, so that the fisherman had to go to private moneylenders for additional funds. Second, the new equipment deteriorated faster than the old, and there were no maintenance funds. Third, the loan repayment terms were not related to the value and the periodicity of the catch, but required fixed monthly payments. Thus, during an off period the payment might exceed income. Since production increased, however, the government saw the project as a success and invested more funds in it. The total income to the fishing village also rose, but other, less visible problems developed. The number of fishermen remained nearly stable, but the population continued to increase and unemployment grew. New boats were allotted only to experienced deep-sea fishermen. Since inexperienced recruits were drawn only from relatives of experienced fishermen, those not related to the boat-owning elite had few opportunities to acquire the prerequisite experience. The elite in the community is larger and more substantial than in the past, but the large group of free middle-class peasants is finding life much more difficult, and the majority of the population has been reduced to the poverty level. Since the elite use their political power to control recruitment to the most favorable occupations, the degree of social stratification will become even more marked in the future.[31]

The introduction of new, relatively costly technologies can clearly exacerbate disparities in income and increase social stratification. If decisionmakers deem such a situation undesirable, other ways of extending credit to the needy should be investigated. Local structures for extending credit, such as development banks and fishermen's cooperatives, should be used if they are adequate to handle the financing needs of the project. In many cases, however, they will require a great deal of assistance to develop their management skills to the point where donor agencies can have confidence in their ability to handle the task at hand. One cannot assume that merely because the target region has development banks or fishermen's organizations these institutions will be capable of managing the necessary credit systems.[32] The possibility that existing organizations can be used must not be overlooked—but they must be carefully evaluated.[33]

Care must be taken in determining the processes for extending credit. The distribution of wealth is closely related to the distribution of power and reciprocal obligations in a community. Unless these aspects of the social structure of target communities are investigated in advance, the credit system designed may prove inadequate or potential problems may fail to be anticipated. In some cases, attempts to bypass traditional owners of equipment and moneylenders when introducing new technology have failed because fishermen accepted the traditional relationship with the middlemen as legitimate and saw the government's efforts to circumvent it as illegitimate.

Other problems in extending credit concern fishermen's perception of the immediate source of the loan. In one fishery development project in Malaysia, for example, the source of credit for the fishermen was a government-sponsored cooperative. Many of the fishermen in the region reasoned that since the function of the government is to help them, the loans were like charity and did not have to be repaid. As a result of the fishermen's perception of the government, neither the loans nor the equipment provided were treated as a scarce resource, and the project encountered serious difficulties.[34]

It should be clear that this final decision point, determining locally appropriate structures for extension of credit to fishermen, is as important to the success of a project as any other decision in the project planning process. Decisions other than to extend credit to fishermen could be made at this point. For example, the equipment could simply be donated to the fishermen—an unlikely and unrealistic decision. A more likely alternative would be to establish a producers' organization, such as a cooperative, which would own the equipment, and member fishermen would pay a share of their catch to the organization for the use and upkeep of the equipment. In this case credit would be extended only to the organization; the organization would not extend credit to individual fishermen. As will be seen below, several structures have been proposed, but many developing countries have selected the cooperative as the ideal form of organization.

Cooperatives for Small-scale Fishermen

This section illustrates how an understanding of social and cultural aspects of fishing communities can facilitate the design and implementation of fishery projects. Since institutional change is perhaps the most difficult to implement, the example given focuses on one of the most problematic of institutions—the fishermen's cooperative—to demonstrate the utility of this approach.

The purpose of this section is neither to advocate nor condemn fishermen's cooperative organizations, but rather to give an objective examination of their use within the special context of small-scale fishery development programs. Experience around the world has shown that while no predetermined cooperative model can ensure success in different fishing societies, a sociologically sensitive approach can be used to adjust the cooperative framework to the specific needs of fishing communities.

Cooperatives in Development Projects

Many governments, international organizations, and individuals see the fishermen's cooperative as the ideal means to improve small-scale fisheries. In some instances marked success has been reported; in others, failure.[35]

In the late 1950s and early 1960s the Food and Agriculture Organization (FAO) of the United Nations identified cooperative organizations as a means of reducing inequities in development that had been caused by an emphasis on wealthier and more efficient producers who had been properly identified as having the greatest potential for making good use of new inputs and techniques.[36] The cooperative, as well as other farmers' organizations, was seen as a means of overcoming the logistical problems of reaching large numbers of often illiterate farmers with both technical and financial assistance. Consequently, the governing body of the FAO began to encourage the development of cooperatives in various sectors, including fisheries. Many FAO fishery projects prepared in the 1960s and 1970s made the cooperative the key institution in the development of the small-scale fishery.[37]

Nevertheless, things were not going well with the use of fishermen's cooperatives. In 1974 an expert who held the post of FAO regional fisheries officer in Latin America for ten years wrote that cooperatives had failed so often and with such notoriety that there was widespread skepticism among fishermen concerning their usefulness.[38]

It is not being suggested here that the FAO was ignorant of the very real problems associated with the establishment of successful fishermen's cooperatives. In some early reports, difficulties were noted and in 1975 many of the shortcomings of cooperatives were detailed along with suggested causes. Nevertheless, the report concluded that "cooperatives appeared to offer the best means for assisting fishermen."[39]

By 1977 the accumulating weight of evidence against traditional approaches to the establishment of fishermen's cooperatives began to have some effect. In 1977 an FAO report concluded that classical European cooperative systems will fail in small-scale fisheries in developing countries unless they are adapted to local realities, and that a minimum of five to ten years' preparation is needed.[40] Around 1977 a new concept was developed, that of community fishery centers that included an optional cooperative element. This concept did not insist on ready-made solutions such as the cooperative, but stressed that solutions must be appropriate to the environment.[41] As long as all sectors of the fishery—such as harvesting, processing, marketing, and supplies—and their infrastructure were given adequate consideration, the various sectors could manifest any combination of appropriate patterns of ownership—private enterprise, cooperative, government enterprise, or community enterprise. Gone was the stress on the cooperative. Related to the concept of the community fishing center is that of grass-roots groups and associations of both small farmers and fishermen. Proponents of this concept make little mention of cooperatives but emphasize the formation of small groups with many of the same functions as cooperatives such as group planning, mutual aid, group action for credit and marketing, group self-study, and group bargaining for social justice.[42] It appears to be a means of avoiding both the stigma of the term "cooperative" and the rigid rules and regulations that often surround cooperatives in the developing world.

Cooperatives in World Bank Projects

In many countries, aid programs for fisheries, funded nationally or internationally, use and support cooperatives to one degree or another. The First Open World Conference on Cooperative Fisheries, for example, concluded that cooperatives were the agencies best suited for fishery development and that "aid to fishermen should be channelled through cooperative organizations."[43] The World Bank has stated:

> Local institutions, such as farmers' associations and cooperatives, have obvious potential advantages for coping with administrative difficulties in reaching the rural poor. On the one side, they provide some measure of participation through the involvement of their members. On the other, they perform intermediary functions which make it possible to provide credit to larger numbers than can be done through official agencies. Group members can be held jointly responsible for repayment of credit and for acceptance of input supplies or other produce.[44]

The Bank goes on to note that almost 20 percent of its farm credit is disbursed through this kind of organization. A recent review of the use of organizations in Bank-assisted agricultural and rural development projects indicated that, in fiscal 1981, 51 percent of the projects involved some form of farmers' organizations, 84 percent of which were cooperatives.[45] The important role played by these organizations emerged from a recent analysis of twenty-five World Bank–financed projects which indicates a strong association between long-term economic sustainability and the development of support organizations such as cooperatives.[46] A review of a sample of Bank-assisted fishery projects over the past decade showed (see table 8-1) that cooperatives figure in 48 percent of them.

The extent of the use of fishermen's cooperatives in World Bank fishery projects has varied considerably through the years. The paucity and limited geographical distribution of projects that strictly concern fisheries make it impossible to discern trends, but a project-by-project examination of the planned use of fishermen's cooperatives as described in staff appraisal reports of the past few years clarifies their relative importance.

Of the two projects appraised for 1986, neither made explicit use of cooperative organizations, but the freshwater fisheries project for China will use fish farmer collectives composed of approximately seventy-five households. Although technically not cooperatives, collectives share some features of cooperatives such as economies of scale. The 1985 Bangladesh Shrimp Culture Project assumes that loans will be made to groups of farmers because individuals are not creditworthy. Although it is not explicitly stated in the appraisal report, these farmer groups, which

Table 8-1. *Cooperatives in World Bank Fishery Projects, 1976–86*

Country	Year	Project	Use or possible use of cooperatives
Indonesia	1986	Fisheries support services	No
China	1986	Freshwater fisheries	No (collectives)
Zambia	1984	Fisheries development	Yes
Yemen	1982	Third fisheries development	Yes
Maldives	1983	Second fisheries	No
Bangladesh	1985	Third flood and drainage	Yes (potential)
Somalia	1984	Fisheries exploration pilot	No
Philippines	1982	National fisheries development	No
Egypt	1981	Fish farm development	No
Yemen Arab Republic	1980	Fisheries development	No
Kenya	1980	Fisheries	Yes
India	1979	Inland fisheries	Yes
Yemen PDR	1979	Second fisheries development	Yes
Tunisia	1979	Second fisheries	Yes
Philippines	1979	Fishery training	No
Bangladesh	1979	Oxbow Lake fishery	Yes (potential)
Maldives	1979	Fishery	No
India	1978	Andhra Pradesh fisheries	Yes
India	1977	Gujarat fisheries	Yes
Panama	1977	Second fisheries	No
Burundi	1976	Fisheries development	No
Philippines	1976	Fisheries	No
Tanzania	1976	Fisheries development	Yes

Note: Data for this table were extracted from World Bank internal documents related to the appraisal of these projects.

are to be formed by a subcontracted NGO, could be considered as cooperatives.

Two projects were appraised for 1984, one making explicit use of cooperatives, while the other seemed to avoid the issue in a country where a large number of fishermen have been organized into cooperative organizations. The Zambia Fisheries Development Project (1984) explicitly states that the most effective means of group lending would be through small primary cooperatives. The loans would be primarily for boats, engines, and nets. Despite the fact that the 1984 Somalia Fisheries Exploration-pilot Project appraisal notes that some 7,000 fishermen are organized into cooperatives, the report makes no mention of them in the artisanal fishery development component.

Of the four projects appraised during 1981–83 only the third Fisheries Development Project for the People's Democratic Republic of Yemen explicitly plans to use fishermen's cooperatives. The fisheries village development component of this project will transform four fisheries cooperatives from their present function as production units into independent commercial enterprises which will undertake all activities from catch to final retail marketing. The appraisal makes it clear that realizing project goals depends on a considerable amount of cooperation from fishermen as well as competent cooperative management.

A fishery project in Kenya, appraised in 1980, indicates extensive reliance on fishermen's cooperatives. Eleven fishermen's cooperatives will participate in the project and will be the ultimate borrowers of more than 90 percent of project credit funds. The appraisal report notes that while some of the marine cooperatives have been relatively successful, many of the inland cooperatives manifest signs of financial weakness such as losses on loans and lack of services. The possibility that cooperatives will fail to manage the fishing centers effectively is seen as the primary risk; substantial support and guidance of management was therefore written into the project. But as the authors of the report note, risk of failure is likely to be mitigated if the cooperatives receive the support and confidence of most fishermen in the areas they are serving. As will be seen, such confidence and support are related to a host of sociocultural variables that were not addressed in the report.

Of the six 1979 appraisal reports examined, four mention the use or possible use of fishermen's cooperatives. Development of fisheries with the use of fishermen's cooperative organizations is government policy in the People's Democratic Republic of Yemen. These cooperatives are assisted by a Cooperative Department within the Ministry of Fish Wealth. It is reported that approximately 50 percent of the fishermen belong to cooperatives. The Yemeni Second Fishery Project will provide credit to cooperatives for the purchase of vessels, engines, and gear.

The second Tunisian Fisheries Project notes the potential for cooperatives. The Fisheries Authority, a semi-autonomous public agency, will take a significant part in promoting the formation of fishermen's cooperatives or similar professional organizations and supervising their activities. Fishermen's cooperatives may eventually guarantee mortgages on new boats, provided at the early stages of the project by the Banque Nationale de Tunise. Construction of new ports is seen as an opportunity to reorganize fishermen into cooperatives or other organizations that could eventually take over the leases of shore facilities.

The potential for cooperatives in the Bangladesh Oxbow Lake Fishery Project is substantial. First, the project will create a source of fish fry and fingerlings that will eventually be used throughout the country. Whether this new resource is used effectively depends largely on the success of the fishery cooperatives that are organized by the Integrated Rural Development Program and given the exclusive right to manage and harvest village ponds. Second, project monitoring and evaluation studies are to explore the feasibility of using cooperatives and other institutions for the management of future projects.

Finally, the 1979 staff report on the Indian Inland Fisheries Project noted that Fish Farmer Development Agencies funded by the government of India will help arrange fish pond leases between government bodies and private individuals or cooperatives. Project credit for fish ponds will go through participating banks refinanced by the Agricultural Refinance and Development Corporation to individual fish farmers, groups, or cooperatives. Thus, cooperatives have a potential place in the project, but their nature is unspecified.

The project in Andhra Pradesh, India, was the only fishery project appraised for 1978. The principal objectives were to improve three harbors, access roads, and seafood plants and provide credit for fishing vessels to be owned and operated by individuals, companies, and cooperatives. Approximately half of the vessels were to be financed.

Of the two fishery projects appraised for 1977 only the Gujarat, India, project mentioned the use of fishermen's cooperatives. In this project the Fishermen's Primary Cooperative Society (FPCS) is expected to operate the hire-purchase scheme through which canoes and outboard motors will be provided to fishermen. The Gujarat Fisheries Central Cooperative Association Ltd., which includes some sixty FPCSS, seven of which are defunct, will be responsible under the project for constructing fishing vessels and importing outboard motors. It will receive trucks to serve the fishing villages and two net-making machines. The fishermen's cooperative thus has important functions to perform in this project.

Table 8-1 and the brief summaries just presented should convince the reader that fishermen's cooperatives are of at least some significance and can be utilized, promoted, and supported in fishery projects, including those assisted by international or bilateral development agencies. Often development agencies have little choice but to use a cooperative. Nearly all the governments in the developing world support cooperative development in one form or another for rural areas and have cooperative departments or ministries and training facilities which encourage their use. In a recent survey of West Africa, for example, it was found that of the six countries covered, five have an established policy to encourage the formation of fishermen's cooperatives. The sixth is proceeding cautiously because of past failures.[47] This emphasis on fishermen's cooperatives clearly indicates that, despite failures in the past, national and international development agencies have to decide on the use of fishermen's cooperatives for every new project. Such decisions must be made on the basis of adequate information. The remainder of this chapter will demonstrate how knowledge concerning the social and cultural characteristics of fishing communities can be used effectively to design and implement fishery development projects.

Sociocultural Aspects of Developing Fishermen's Cooperatives

This section focuses on relations between characteristics of the occupation of fishing, its sociocultural context, and factors which influence the success or failure of fishermen's organizations. There is nothing to be gained from rehashing generalities about social change processes and cooperative organization in general. The focus here is on aspects of fishermen's society and culture which have a positive or negative effect on the formation of cooperatives.

Shifting Residence Patterns

The pattern of shifting residence among fishermen affects the establishment of fishermen's cooperatives. For example, although farmers' organizations can have residency requirements for membership, such rules would not work for the organization of migratory fishermen. In one fishery development program in West Bengal, fishermen were required to live in the region of the cooperative in order to become a member. Since many fishermen were migratory they could not join.[48] These mobility patterns make it extremely difficult to get in touch with fishermen to obtain essential data (such as the number of active fishermen) or to organize an appropriate cooperative; they also make it difficult for fishermen to attend the meetings essential to the proper operation of a cooperative.[49]

The cooperatives would have a better chance of success if cooperative organizers could adapt their rules to reflect this common residence pattern. This requires prior sociocultural information on residence patterns. Such information could also be used to define effective methods for contacting fishermen and establishing realistic meeting schedules and attendance requirements. Once the cooperatives were established, they would facilitate communication between personnel responsible for fishery development and the fishermen; this essential interaction would help tailor the cooperative to the needs of the fishermen and provide the information needed to establish appropriate development programs.

Financing Needs

Primary fish buyers (who often act as moneylenders) and traditional moneylenders in most fishing communities have had a long relationship with fishermen and know their problems: they understand the environmental constraints and usually adapt to the short-term, unpredictable variability of the catch by permitting flexibility in repayment of loans. The variability of fishery resources often places the middleman in a role of benefactor to fishermen when catches are light, and his ability and willingness to provide loans when rough water or corrosion destroys or damages productive equipment reinforce this role.

If fishermen's organizations are to succeed, they must manifest the same flexibility. Loans made by the government to Sri Lankan fishermen through cooperatives did not take this fact into account. Because fixed payments were required monthly, irrespective of catch size, there were many defaults and the cooperative effort was weakened.[50] A different type of inflexibility plagued cooperatives in India. Madras fishermen were reluctant to use cooperative marketing schemes because the cooperatives, unlike the traditional middlemen, did not make loans for weddings, funerals, holidays, and expenses incurred during unproductive periods.[51] Meeting loan repayment schedules was one of the problems contributing to the decline of Mexico's inshore Pacific fishing cooperatives. The cooperatives, based on the nation's agrarian collectives (*ejidos*), did not take into account the periodic nature of marine production.[52] Similar failures among cooperatives in Ghana occurred because herring fishermen found it difficult to meet loan payments during the months herring were scarce. To be successful, fishermen's organizations will have to adapt to this periodicity with flexible loan repayment schedules similar to those used by existing middlemen.

Another factor with implications for the design of the financing component of fishermen's cooperatives is the destructive effect of the sea on equipment. Not only is salt water corrosive, but also bad weather causes the relatively rapid depreciation of gear. This high rate of depreciation is not always taken into account by planners, who may introduce costly new fishing gear, which deteriorates more rapidly than traditional gear, without making provisions for financing its replacement. The form of fishermen's cooperative organizations is sometimes transferred directly from farming where, in contrast to fishing equipment, the major resource, land, appreciates through time. This failure to take basic differences between farming and fishing into account can also cause difficulties.

Irregular Work Hours

Irregular work hours also have an impact on the development of fishermen's cooperatives. When the weather is good and fish are available, fishermen are out fishing and will miss scheduled meetings, such as cooperative planning or training sessions. In my experience, the better fishermen take advantage of good fishing conditions; less successful fishermen attend meetings. These less successful fishermen then become most active in agency-sponsored meetings to form fishermen's organizations. This is perhaps one of the reasons that good fishermen in some regions view cooperatives as havens for the incompetent. Planners should consequently be flexible in scheduling meetings with fishermen. For maximum participation, meetings should be scheduled during traditional days off (if such exist), slack fishing periods, or bad weather. If meetings have to be held during peak fishing periods, they should not be scheduled during traditional hours for fishing or resting. These times must be determined for each region and season—fishermen's hours differ significantly from those of other occupations.

Social Isolation and Level of Education

The social isolation of fishermen is frequently associated with low social status. This low social standing may make fishermen unreceptive to the cooperative movement as a consequence of their suspicious attitude toward outsiders and their advice.[53] Their long history of being an oppressed lower class may also condition them to accepting exploitation as a way of life; thus, they do not view organizations such as cooperatives as a mechanism tor achieving their aspirations.[54]

The relatively low level of formal education characteristic of many fishing communities in the developing world also has a negative effect, particularly on the management of cooperatives. Since fishermen are often illiterate, it is difficult either to train them or to find qualified managers and accountants among them.[55] Illiteracy also exacerbates problems of corruption—which plague the development of fishermen's organizations—since corrupt cooperative clerks can easily cheat illiterate fishermen. Thus, by way of contrast, the fairly high standard of education in Belize fishing communities is cited as contributing to the success of their fishermen's cooperatives.

The residential and social isolation of small-scale fishermen, combined with their tendency to work offshore where they cannot be readily observed, make it possible for them to sell part, and sometimes all, of the harvest outside cooperative marketing organizations. This practice has been reported in areas as diverse as Ireland, the Philippines, and Malaysia, and I have observed it in Central America and Panama. Selling outside the organization diminishes its ability to make a profit, but it is especially harmful when gear has been sold to fishermen through the organization on a hire-purchase scheme, and the fishermen avoid repayment by outside selling. The fact that fishermen work out of sight of land has also given rise to nonverifiable claims concerning lost cooperative gear.

Crew Structure

The need for egalitarian, independent, cooperative crews among small-scale fishermen frequently results in crews based on kin relationships. If part of the cooperative program includes the introduction of labor-saving equipment, it may fail unless adequate alternative employment is available for crew members. Such a failure could reduce the potential for overall success of the cooperative. For example, when labor-saving winches were introduced to a group of small-scale fishermen in Malaysia, traditional crew sizes were maintained to provide employment for members of the extended family.[56] The expected labor savings were not realized, and the change was an economic failure. In another area of Malaysia, C. L. Yap reports that improved technology brought about a reduction in the crew size and significant unemployment among fishermen who had no alternative occupations.[57] The creation of this impoverished class of unemployed fishermen increased the degree of social stratification within the fishing community—a result inconsistent with the goals of both the cooperative movement and small-scale fishery development.

In addition, to minimize discord within crews, the crew membership changes when irreconcilable arguments develop. This practice is inimical to a hire-purchase scheme based on joint ownership by an entire crew. For example, the Kuala Linggi Fishermen's Cooperative Credit and Marketing Society in Malaysia established a system whereby crew members would jointly sign a hire-purchase contract. Subsequent crew changes made it difficult to settle loans and thus contributed to the decline of the association.

Decisionmaking and Sea Tenure

The independent nature of fishermen, which is fostered by the need for rapid decisionmaking, is further enhanced in most capture fisheries by a system of harvesting rights based on arrival time rather than a sea tenure system. The independence of fishermen and the absence of sea tenure systems are interrelated in their impact on cooperative development programs.

When harvesting rights are based on arrival time at the fishing spot, the first vessel there deploys its gear and continues to fish until enough has been captured. There is a great deal of competition between vessels and a need for independence in decisions concerning where and when to fish. These two factors are important considerations with respect to developing fishermen's organizations. Unless the cooperative is able to develop a consensus among its members and mutual help and trust, joint ownership and use of tow vessels would probably run a high risk of failure.

It would be a mistake to try to assign fishing spots to fishermen's organizations in the same manner that land is assigned to agricultural cooperatives. It was tried on the Pacific coast of Mexico, where production sites for fishermen's cooperatives were fixed in the same manner as they were for the agricultural ejidos. Lagoonal boundaries in this region, however, are subject to erosion and shifting, while the location of agricultural land remains constant. Thus, within a period of only several years, a fishermen's cooperative could lose nearly all of its productive harvesting areas. In the Gulf of California farther to the north, however, a fishermen's cooperative succeeded in part because the cooperative members were all Yaqui Indians, and the tribe was given exclusive rights to fish resources in the tribal reserve. In this case the sea tenure covered a relatively large area which was not susceptible to changes in the distribution of target species that characterized the fishery in the south.[58]

On a more positive note, however, in areas (such as Japan and Korea) where sea tenure systems have existed for some time, the guilds holding fishing rights have been effectively used as the basis for cooperative organizations. As an outgrowth of this system, Japanese law grants property rights in the coastal fishery to fishermen's cooperative associations; one must be a cooperative member in order to fish. This has been regarded as a key factor in the success of the Japanese fishermen's cooperative development program.

Division of Labor

The special handling, processing, and marketing needs associated with fishery products require specialists. In most small-scale fisheries the division of labor is based on sex, with females processing and marketing fish. Organizing fishermen in cooperatives is often viewed as a way to eliminate exploitation by middlemen. In areas such as West Africa, female fish processors and vendors would therefore be displaced. Where fishermen are related to the middlemen, the cooperative movement would probably be resisted; in other areas, the effects on a relatively large, economically productive sector of the population would be disastrous. It is suggested that when women perform an economic role in fishing communities, they need to be included either in fishing cooperatives or other organizations. This would not be difficult. In areas where women process the fish, the organization could provide facilities, and they could continue their work within the cooperative. If women are traditionally the "middlemen," it would be easier to have them fulfill the same role within the cooperative than to retrain men and then cope with the problems of the women who are displaced.[59] The addition of functions in a fishermen's cooperative must be approached with caution. It has been noted that the various demands posed by different sectors (for example, processing, harvesting, and marketing) within a fishermen's organization can create internal conflicts which can lead to failure.[60]

Unlike a farmer's product, fish is highly perishable and cannot be stored without complex technologies for cold storage, freezing, or drying. This creates an initially high demand for capital for the development of multipurpose fishermen's organizations. It is often difficult to meet this demand because fishermen are commonly among the poorest of the poor, living from day to day with little or no slack capital for investment. Thus, in regions where fishermen's organizations are most needed, they often run into difficulties because of a lack of funds. This need for capital is further intensified by the relatively high price of boats, motors, and other supplies and by their higher rate of depreciation in contrast with the major investment of an agricultural cooperative—land. This greater need for capital in combination with the relative poverty of fishermen must be met by careful planning.

Although it is tempting to claim that there are some intrinsic aspects of the occupation of fishing which make fishermen less likely than agriculturalists to cooperate in organizations, it must be remembered that there are successful fishermen's cooperatives. Most of the projects discussed thus far have been failures, in part because of the stress on failures in the literature. It results in a false impression that all, or nearly all, fishermen's cooperatives are doomed.

It should be clear from the presentation so far that there are several factors known to contribute to the success of fishermen's cooperatives. In both industrial and developing countries, fishermen's cooperatives that have succeeded have been socioculturally compatible with the structure and outline of the fishing society, that is to say, where social perturbances are kept to a minimum. The significance of this point cannot be overstated: obvious in principle, few projects possess either the data or the mechanisms to make it a practice. Fishermen's cooperatives are quite successful in areas with a long history of cooperative religious and secular societies, as in Italy, or where cultural patterns encourage deeply rooted group consciousness and loyalty, as in Japan.[61]

Fishermen's cooperatives which are generated by the fishermen themselves, rather than by the government or some external agency, have also been successful in many parts of the world.[62] When development proceeds from below it is more likely that the cooperative structure was selected because it was seen as compatible with the society, culture, and needs of the fishermen. With involvement of the target group from the beginning of development, the structures which evolve are more likely to be compatible and thus more likely to be accepted by the participants. This is related to the concept of popular participation in development. A recent study has indicated that the degree of fishermen's participation in decision making is positively correlated with relative success of fishermen's organizations.[63] Some fishermen's organizations have encountered problems because an agricultural cooperative model was used, and aspects of the occupation of fishing conflicted with some of its structural features.

Cooperatives can succeed if they take into account the sociocultural characteristics of fishing communities as well as provide necessary technical and economic inputs and competent leadership. The features unique to fishing must be stressed in the appraisal of fishery projects, however, especially when they involve agencies such as government cooperative departments which are not accustomed to working with fishermen.

Designing and Implementing Projects

This section suggests to the fishery project planner and manager how to obtain and use social and cultural information for the design and implementation of fishermen's organizations. Other aspects of fishery development programs such as technological change also require a base of sociocultural information to carry out social engineering, as discussed above. Since institutional change is more complex than technological change, however, it will more fully illustrate the use of social and cultural information in project design and implementation. The logic of the approach can then be applied to any type of change proposed.

Background Information

The essential types of background information necessary for decision making in the design of projects using fishermen's organizations are: source of the idea for organization, degree of participation by fishermen in development and management of the organization, local laws regarding organizations, existing social groups in the target community, attitudes of members of existing groups toward the proposed organization, size of existing groups in the target community, and source of the structure of the proposed organization.

The collection and analysis of these types of sociological data complement the technical evaluations routinely done in project preparation and appraisal work. For example, many studies have noted a relatively high success rate for organizations which were initiated by the fishermen involved. Though this does not guarantee success, it eliminates the hurdle of outsiders trying to convince the fishermen that they need an organization. If the idea has a source external to the target group, education programs need to be developed to influence fishermen's attitudes toward the organization. No such organization should be imposed administratively.

Local social groups can sometimes provide the basis for the proposed organization. These organizations must, however, be carefully evaluated to determine whether they will fit or can be made to fit project needs. The type of social group that is desirable for such ends is one that is successful and is composed of members who cooperate to achieve a common goal. In addition, one must determine whether members of the old group are favorably disposed toward the new. If not, the new group should be formed separately, and it should be made clear that the new group is not a threat to the old. The size of existing groups is also important. The proposed organization must be compatible with traditional group size—if not, traditional forms of group interaction may not be able to cope with the size difference, and the organization may not be able to function effectively.

SOCIAL ORGANIZATION OF FISHING. Various aspects of the social organization of fishing activities are consequential for the design of fishermen's organizations: the traditional division of labor, the crew or work group structure and stability, traditional sea tenure systems, and the settlement pattern.

If the proposed organization conflicts with the traditional distribution of labor there are bound to be problems unless the conflicts are settled in advance. Those who will be displaced by the functions performed by the proposed organization will work against it unless acceptable, alternative positions are found for them. It was argued above that acceptable, appropriate roles may be found in the organization for those who would be displaced. For example, it may be possible for female middlemen to use their entrepreneurial skills *within* the organization both to help it succeed and at the same time to sustain their livelihood.

Existing crew structure and stability can also be important elements. For example, if there is rapid turnover in crew membership, joint hire-purchase contracts should not form part of the proposed organization's operational strategy. Further, if new technologies will affect crew size or structure, they may be resisted unless social engineering can produce alternative and acceptable forms of work organization compatible with the proposed technologies.

If traditional systems of sea tenure exist and organizational charters can be made compatible with the existing system, exploitation rights can be tied to group membership—a system that facilitated the success of Japanese cooperatives. If no tenure systems exist, care must be exercised in associating organization membership with exploitation rights. The absence of traditional tenure systems may reflect aspects of the resource (such as unpredictable location or shifting lagoons and sand bars) which would make tenure systems unrealistic.

ORGANIZATION MANAGEMENT. Inadequate administration of fishermen's organizations has frequently been cited as a reason for failure. Several important bits of information can help project administrators design organizations which will be more likely to avoid managerial and administrative pitfalls. This information includes the identification of managerial and leadership ability in the target community, fishermen's work schedules, availability of accountants to carry out (or monitor) financial activities, government agencies involved in organizational and fishery development, and the availability of a suitable location for meetings.

It is most desirable to draw on the fishing community itself for the organization's leadership and management in the early stages. If this is not possible, the fishermen's distrust of outsiders may cause problems. A recent comparative analysis of twenty-six fishermen's organizations in eleven countries indicated that the majority of the successful organizations have a board of directors elected by the membership, while over one-half of the failures had boards selected largely by outside organizers.[64] Three stages in the early development of leadership in successful fishermen's cooperatives are: founding by a fisherman who is recognized as a leader; appointing a director who has some connection with fishing (through his family or past experience) or who holds a respected position in the fishing community but is somewhat detached, often by being better educated; and finally the complexities of management force the fishermen to admit that they need outside expertise.

Fishermen's work schedules must be known so that meetings can be scheduled. The fishermen must be available to attend preliminary planning meetings or they will be unable to provide the necessary input. The location of meetings must also be compatible with fishermen's residences and their perceptions of appropriate meeting places, or it will be difficult to get them to attend.

Provision must be made for adequate monitoring of the organization's activities. Experience has shown that the generally low educational level of fishermen leaves them vulnerable to exploitation by unscrupulous administrative staff, which frequently causes organizations to fail. Advance identification of monitoring personnel such as accountants, and the establishment of adequate monitoring procedures may eliminate this problem; this is also a fruitful area for NGO involvement.

Fishery development programs that involve organizations such as cooperatives frequently involve more than one government agency, such as, for example, the fishery department, a department responsible for cooperatives, and a social service agency. Often interdepartmental rivalry or bureaucratic inefficiency causes these agencies to work against one another to the detriment of the project. If more than one agency is involved, the project must develop adequate means to coordinate the various agencies' activities, especially if preliminary investigations suggest a historical rivalry or lack of cooperation between them.

SOCIOECONOMIC ASPECTS. Socioeconomic factors also influence the success of fishery development projects involving organizations: the willingness of potential participants to make a substantial investment in the organization; the adequacy of projected working capital to pay for fish on delivery; the compatibility of loan repayment procedures with traditional techniques; and the adequacy of planned credit available for the maintenance, repair, and replacement of equipment.

One factor that influences the success or failure of fishermen's organizations is the degree of personal investment on the part of members. Since fishermen are frequently among the poorest of the poor, it would be unrealistic to expect a substantial monetary contribution on their part. But the planners must determine if potential members are willing to make at least a substantial labor commitment: for example, by building facilities or cutting and donating logs for dock construction.

Analysis must show that projected working capital will be sufficient to pay for fish on delivery. If not, more working capital must be arranged. Marketing cooperatives have been known to fail when they could not compete with existing middlemen in this respect.

If one of the functions of the organization is to provide credit to the fishermen, it is essential that loan payment procedures fit the structure (though not the rates) of traditional moneylending practices, which are well adapted to an unpredictable, highly variable harvest. If the procedures do not account for these differences, many defaults will occur and the organization will fail. Finally, these credit functions must be adequate to meet the unique needs of fishermen for the maintenance, repair, and replacement of their equipment.

MEMBERSHIP. The organization must fulfill functions viewed as essential by its potential members. It is a relatively simple matter to survey potential members concerning what they expect the organization to do for them. Characteristics of the members influence the success of fishermen's organizations. It is important to determine potential members' level of formal education and their perceptions of important functions of the proposed organization. Members should have sufficient education to understand the routine operations proposed for the organization, or they may be suspicious of some procedures. The organization can develop educational programs which will allow it to grow along with its members. Educational programs can be developed to explain the relationships between the perceived functions and the new functions built into the project design.

The foregoing has identified twenty-one important elements of information that are needed to design and implement fishery development projects involving fishermen's organizations effectively. These elements are summarized in table 8-2.

How can such relevant information be generated? How can a development agency take these factors into account? The following examples suggest techniques to generate knowledge of sociocultural variables that can influence the success or failure of fishery development projects.

Table 8-2. *Relation of Information Needs to Specific Characteristics of Fishing Communities*

	Information need	Relation to characteristics
1.	Source of idea	Not related
2.	Laws regarding organizations	Fit with characteristics
3.	Existing social groups	Fit with group requirements of fishing
4.	Attitudes of existing group members	No clear relationship
5.	Existing group size	No clear relationship
6.	Organizational structure	Fit with all characteristics
7.	Traditional distribution of labor	Fit with proposed organization[a]
8.	Work group structure and stability	Fit with proposed organization[a]
9.	Sea tenure system	Fit with proposed organization[a]
10.	Settlement pattern	Fit with proposed organization[a]
11.	Managerial and leadership ability	Attitudes toward outsiders
12.	Fishermen's work schedules	Fit with organization[a]
13.	Availability of accountants	Formal education level
14.	Government agencies involved	No relationship but must be coordinated
15.	Suitable meeting location	Settlement pattern
16.	Participants' willingness to invest	Distrust of outsiders, level of formal education, degree of poverty, alternative
17.	Adequacy of working capital	Degree of poverty
18.	Compatibility of credit procedures	Income unpredictability
19.	Adequacy of credit	Unique needs for maintenance, repair, and replacement of fishing equipment
20.	Level of formal education	Fit with proposed organization[a]
21.	Perceived functions of organization	Can be used to determine fit with needs and characteristics[a]

a. In these cases the information needed refers to one of the sociocultural characteristics of fishing communities noted in earlier sections.

Fishermen's Perceptions of Existing Socioeconomic Arrangements

STUDY 1. One of the most frequent goals of fishermen's cooperative organizations is to replace the middleman, who is widely regarded as an exploiter of the fishermen. Nevertheless, as noted earlier, cooperatives often cannot compete with established middlemen who provide efficient marketing and other services to the fishermen. Unfortunately, this is too often discovered only after a cooperative has failed or when it is in the process of failing. If a cooperative is to replace the middleman, it is essential to have the fishermen's evaluation of his or her services before the cooperative is established. Once these services have been identified and evaluated they can be worked into the project design.

A study I conducted in Costa Rica illustrates the methods for determining perceived functions of existing middlemen.[65] In the Gulf of Nicoya, Costa Rica, some thirty-four primary buyers were operating in the port of Puntarenas and various outlying sites around the gulf. Eighty small-scale fishermen were interviewed from two communities served by twelve middlemen who were active during the research period. Fishermen were simply asked why they sell to one middleman rather than another. The responses are shown in table 8-3.

Middlemen clearly perform more functions than simply buying fish. In addition, fishermen select middlemen for more reasons than price paid. A further analysis of the data indicated that urban fishermen are more likely than rural to select primary buyers on the basis of price, and that rural fishermen are more interested in the other types of (nonmarketing) assistance that the middlemen can provide through loans, storage, supply of spare parts, and so forth.

Table 8-3. *Distribution of Rationales for the Selection of a Middleman*

Rationale	Percentage[a]
Gives better prices	48
Provides help, such as loans	45
Gives fair treatment	31
Is owed money by fishermen	9
Is a friend of fishermen	8
Always buys fish	6
Is close to fisherman's residence	4
Other	10

Note: $N = 80$.

a. Total exceeds 100 percent because entries reflect categorization of the first three responses to an open-ended question.

Although more sophisticated techniques of collection and analysis of data could have been used, this relatively simple study was sufficient to produce information on which to base two operationally significant recommendations concerning the design of marketing cooperatives among these fishermen. First, an analysis of the services included in the category "provides help" would indicate the functions a cooperative would have to fulfill to compete with middlemen. Second, the rural-urban differences indicate that cooperative structures cannot be uniform for an entire country.

STUDY 2. When changes are proposed at the productive level of any sector of the economy it is important to understand existing social relations among individual workers at that level. Work groups with which individuals are personally identified provide a degree of psychological security and satisfaction, and innovations perceived as threatening the structure of these groups often meet resistance. Among small-scale fishermen, changes in the nature or size of technology can drastically change the composition of work groups. In addition, changes that restrict access to resources can exclude some group members who would normally enter the occupation. These individuals would be dispossessed of what they consider a right, and they would probably resist the new regulations. The introduction of labor-saving devices such as winches, for example, could reduce the number of necessary crew members. In societies where kinship plays a role in the selection of crew members, technological changes which eliminate the need for large crews are either rejected or used inefficiently.

The sample for this study was drawn from the town of Rabo de Peixe, one of the largest concentrations of fishermen on San Miguel in the Azores. The men of Rabo de Peixe fish from open boats ranging from three to twelve meters in length. The larger vessels are powered primarily by inboard diesel engines. The smaller are powered by gasoline outboard engines ranging from five to seven and a half horsepower. Only one fisherman in the sample fished from a vessel powered only by oars. Since the larger vessels tend to use hand-hauled nets, the crew is relatively large, ranging from six to sixteen. The smaller vessels get along with only two to five crew members.

Among other questions, fishermen were asked how many fishermen in addition to themselves live in their household, how many of their kinsmen fish with them in the same vessel, and what their kinship is with other members of their fishing crew. The results showed that 39 percent of the fishermen interviewed had other fishermen in their households; only 15 percent reported that they fish with no kinsmen.

The significant amount of kinship links within the fishing crews suggested several operationally significant recommendations for project design. Modifications of the fishery which affect, especially reduce, the size of work groups will be resisted or inefficiently employed if the proposed reduction means laying off a kinsman. Furthermore, strains will probably develop between families if the reductions differentially affect the various kin groups making up the crew. When the alternatives are either continued positive relationships with and employment of a kinsman or unemployment of the kinsman, accompanied by hard feelings and the possibility of having to provide support for this kinsman anyway, fishermen will frequently reject or inefficiently use new labor-saving technology. Projected changes or developments among the fishermen of Rabo de Peixe which will affect crew size or structure must be evaluated in terms of the substantial amount of kinship links within existing crews. Changes must be introduced with acceptable alternatives for the displaced kinsmen or they will probably not succeed.

These brief examples illustrate techniques that can be used to generate and analyze sociocultural data to develop operationally significant recommendations. While they may be simple, they are far from obvious. Given factors such as highly culture specific long- and short-term economic interests among fishermen, predicting development impacts and interpreting sociocultural requirements are not always amenable to rapid diagnostic techniques. Experience amply demonstrates the need for technical expertise in obtaining and interpreting the data needed for cooperative development. Of course, the techniques described here do not exhaust the wide range of sociocultural information required for effective decisionmaking.

Conclusions

Although social analyses alone cannot guarantee a successful project, attention to important sociological variables, when combined with good technical design, can help match the goals of a project with the needs of the population. In the case of fishery development projects, an understanding of the special social characteristics of fishing communities can greatly enhance the compatibility of project design with the constraints of fishing.

The chapter has identified a set of sociocultural characteristics of fishing communities which can be said to influence the design of development projects. Although certain elements of the set are not unique to fishing communities, in combination they both qualitatively and quantitatively set fishing societies apart from those engaged in other productive activities. The role of sociocultural factors in development projects was examined, and it was emphasized that these factors should not be regarded as a constraint on development efforts; rather, a correct understanding of their importance as a resource for development can inspire the social engineering of the proposed changes so that they fit the social and cultural systems of the fishermen. Attention to these kinds of social variables is important for successful project design.

Notes

I would like to acknowledge the valuable insights provided by the thousands of fishermen I have interviewed in various parts of the world over the past fifteen years. I would also like to thank the numerous government fishery officers who provided me with another perspective on fishermen's cooperatives. Special acknowledgment must be given to my colleagues Jan Peter Johnson (Food and Agriculture Organization fishery officer), J. R. McGoodwin, and J. J. Poggie, who have acted as willing sounding boards for many of my ideas. Finally, I am grateful to the World Bank, especially Leslie Brownrigg, Michael Cernea, Fujio Kada, Eduardo Loayza, Deborah Rubin, Alfredo Sfeir-Younis, Lucian Sprague, and Lars Vidaeus, who made many helpful comments concerning the structure and content of this essay.

1. David Stevenson, Richard Pollnac, and Philip Logan, *A Guide for the Small-Scale Fishery Administrator: Information from the Harvest Sector* (Kingston, R.I.: International Center for Marine Resource Development, 1982); Ian R. Smith, "A Research Framework for Traditional Fisheries," ICLARM Studies and Reviews no. 2 (Manila, Philippines: International Center for Living Aquatic Resources Management, 1979).

2. National Research Council, *Fisheries Technology for Developing Countries* (Washington, D.C.: National Academy Press, 1988); and W. H. L. Allsopp, *Fishery Development Experiences* (Farnham, England: Fishing News Books, Ltd., 1985).

3. World Bank, "Harvesting the Waters: A Review of Bank Experience with Fishery Development Facts and Figures" (revised version prepared for the Fishery Development Donor Consultation, 13–15 October 1986, Paris, France).

4. For a more detailed comparison of aquaculture and capture fisheries, see Richard Pollnac, "Sociocultural Aspects of Implementing Aquaculture Systems in Marine Fishing Communities," in Susan Peterson and Leah Smith, eds., *Aquaculture Development in Less Developed Countries* (Boulder, Colo.: Westview, 1982).

5. Alfredo Sfeir-Younis and Graham Donaldson, *Fishery Sector Policy Paper* (Washington, D.C.: World Bank, 1982), pp. 27–29.

6. Kathleen Norr, "The Organization of Coastal Fishing in Tamilnadu," *Ethnology*, vol. 14 (1975), pp. 357–71.

7. Edward Norbec, *Changing Japan* (New York: Holt, Rinehart, and Winston, 1968).

8. George P. Murdock, *Africa: Its People and Their Cultural History* (New York: Mc-Graw-Hill, 1959), p. 321.

9. Kathleen Norr and James L. Norr, "Environmental and Technical Factors Influencing Power in Work Organizations: Ocean Fishing in Peasant Societies," *Sociology of Work and Occupations*, vol. 1 (1974), pp. 219–51.

10. For a summary of this literature, see Richard Pollnac, "Sociocultural Aspects of Technological and Institutional Change among Small-scale Fishermen," in John Maiolo and Michael Orbach, eds., *Modernization and Marine Fisheries Policy* (Ann Arbor, Mich.: Ann Arbor Science Publishers, 1982).

11. K. E. Knudson, "Resource Fluctuation, Productivity, and Social Organization on Micronesian Coral Islands," Ph.D. dissertation, University of Oregon, 1970; Bernard Nietschmann, *Between Land and Water* (New York: Seminar Press, 1973); and Joel Aronoff, *Psychological Needs and Cultural Systems* (Princeton, N.J.: Van Nostrand, 1967). These are but a few of the many sources which comment on the high degree of cooperative behavior within fishing crews.

12. Conrad P. Kottak, "The Structure of Equality in a Brazilian Fishing Community," Ph.D. dissertation, Columbia University, 1966; and Thomas H. Harrisson, *The Malays of South-West Sarawak before Malaysia* (East Lansing: Michigan State University Press, 1970).

13. John J. Poggie, "Small-scale Fishermen's Psychocultural Characteristics and Cooperative Formation," *Anthropological Quarterly*, vol. 53 (1980), pp. 20–28.

14. Richard Pollnac, *Panamanian Small-scale Fishermen: Society, Culture, and Change* (Kingston, R.I.: International Center for Marine Resource Development, 1977).

15. Richard Pollnac, "The Sociocultural Correlates of Fishing as a Subsistence Activity," Anthropology Working Paper no. 4 (Kingston, R.I.: Department of Sociology-Anthropology, University of Rhode Island, 1974).

16. Robert E. Johannes, "Traditional Marine Conservation Methods in Oceania and their Demise," *Annual Review of Ecology Systems*, vol. 9 (1978), pp. 349–64; Kenneth Ruddle and Robert E. Johannes, *The Traditional Knowledge and Management of Coastal Systems in Asia and the Pacific* (Jakarta: UNESCO, 1985); and Bonnie McCay and James Acheson, *The Question of the Commons* (Tucson: University of Arizona Press, 1987).

17. Wayne P. Suttles, *The Economic Life of the Coast Salish of Haro and Rosario Straits* (New York: Garland, 1974).

18. Marshall Sahlins, *Social Stratification in Polynesia* (Seattle: University of Washington Press, 1958).

19. Kathleen Norr, "A South Indian Fishing Village in Comparative Perspective," Ph.D. dissertation, University of Michigan, 1972.

20. Edward Norbeck, *Takashima: A Japanese Fishing Village* (Salt Lake City: University of Utah Press, 1954).

21. James Acheson, "The Lobster Fiefs: Economic and Ecological Effects of Territoriality in the Maine Lobster Industry," *Human Ecology*, vol. 3 (1983), p. 207.

22. Shepard Forman, *The Raft Fishermen* (Bloomington: Indiana University Press, 1970).

23. Francis T. Christy, Jr., "A Reevaluation of Approaches to Fisheries Development: The Special Characteristics of Fisheries and the Need for Management," paper prepared for the Agriculture Sector Symposium, The World Bank, 8–9 January 1987; Richard B. Pollnac, "Sociocultural Issues in West African Fisheries Development," Anthropology Working Paper no. 45 (Kingston, R.I.: International Center for Marine Resource Development, University of Rhode Island, 1985).

24. Pollnac, "Sociocultural Issues in West African Fisheries Development."

25. James R. McGoodwin, "Mexico's Conflictual Inshore Pacific Fisheries: Problem Analysis and Policy Recommendations," *Human Organization*, vol. 46 (1987), pp. 221–32.

26. John R. Bort, "The Impact of Development on Panama's Small-Scale Fishermen," *Human Organization*, vol. 46 (1987), pp. 233–42.

27. Conner Bailey, Dean Cycon, and Michael Morris, "Fisheries Development in the Third World: The Role of International Agencies," *World Development*, vol. 14 (1986), pp. 1269–75.

28. George M. Epple, "Technological Change in a Grenada, West Indies, Fishery, 1950–1970," in M. E. Smith, ed., *Those Who Live from the Sea* (San Francisco: West, 1977).

29. James Sabella, "The Fishermen of Caleta San Pablo," Ph.D. dissertation, Cornell University, 1974.

30. Raymond Firth, *Malay Fishermen*, 2d ed. (Hamden, Conn.: Archon Books, 1966).

31. Paul Alexander, "Innovation in a Cultural Vacuum: The Mechanization of Sri Lanka Fisheries," *Human Organization*, vol. 34 (1975), pp. 333–44.

32. Managerial inadequacy in project countries was identified as one of the key factors influencing failure of World Bank fishery projects. See World Bank, "Harvesting the Waters."

33. H. D. Seibel and A. Massing, *Traditional Organizations and Economic Development* (New York: Praeger, 1974).

34. Udhis Narkswasdi, "An Evaluation of the Kuala Linggi Fishermen's Cooperative Credit and Marketing Society, Ltd." (Kuala Lumpur: Ministry of Agriculture and Cooperatives, 1967).

35. For examples of success, see Food and Agriculture Organization, *Manual on Fishermen's Cooperatives* (Rome: FAO, 1971); examples of both successes and failures can be found in United Nations Research Institute for Social Development, *Rural Cooperatives as Agents of Change: A Research Report and a Debate* (Geneva: UNRISD, 1975).

36. A. F. Laidlaw, "Training and Extension in the Cooperative Movement" (Rome: FAO, 1962); Eberhard Dulfer, "Training Facilities for Cooperative Personnel in African Countries" (Rome: FAO, 1971).

37. FAO and Banco Interamericano de Desarollo, "Informe sobre un proyecto de pesca artesanal en Panama" (Panama City: FAO and BID, 1973); FAO and BID, "Programa de desarrollo pesquero en Costa Rica" (Washington, D.C.: FAO and BID, 1972).

38. Acisclo Miyares del Valle, "Fishermen's Cooperatives" (1974, unpublished).

39. FAO, "Report of the Expert Consultation in Small-scale Fisheries Development," FAO Fisheries Report no. 169 (Rome, 1975), p. 7.

40. FAO, "FAO Expert Consultation on Experiences and Models of Cooperatives and Other Rural Organizations Engaged in Agricultural Production: Conclusions and Recommendations" (Rome, 1977).

41. Menachem Ben-Yami, "Community Fishery Centers and the Transfer of Technology to Small-scale Fisheries," IPFC/80/SP/2 (Rome: FAO, 1980).

42. FAO, "Small Farmers Development Manual" (Bangkok: FAO Regional Office for Asia and the Far East, 1978).

43. R. P. B. Davies and K. Sakamoto, "Conference Summary: Prospects for the Future of Co-operative Fisheries in Developing Countries," in *Report of the First Open World Conference on Co-operative Fisheries* (London: International Cooperative Alliance, 1975), pp. 82–84.

44. World Bank, *The Assault on World Poverty* (Baltimore, Md.: Johns Hopkins University Press, 1975), p. 37.

45. Michael Cernea, "Rural Cooperatives in Bank-Assisted Agricultural and Rural Development Projects" (1982, unpublished study for the World Bank).

46. Michael Cernea, "Farmer Organizations and Institution Building for Sustainable Development," *Regional Development Dialogue*, vol. 8, no. 2 (1987), pp. 1–24.

47. G. N. Lamming and M. Hotta, "Fishermen's Cooperatives in West Africa," CECAF/TECH:79/17/(En) (Dakar: FAO, 1980).

48. FAO, "Project for Development of Small-scale Fisheries in the Bay of Bengal—Preparatory Phase," Working Papers, vol. 2 (Rome: FAO and UNDP, 1978).

49. J. Ho Toh, "A Study in the Camarines Norte Area Fishing Cooperative in the Philippines," paper delivered at the Symposium on Development and Management of Small-scale Fisheries, May 1980, Kyoto, Japan.

50. Alexander, "Innovation in a Cultural Vacuum."

51. B. A. Blake, "Cultural Adaptation and Technological Change among Madras Fishing Populations," in M. E. Smith, ed., *Those Who Live from the Sea* (San Francisco: West, 1977).

52. James R. McGoodwin, "Mexico's Marginal Inshore Pacific Fishing Cooperatives," *Anthropological Quarterly*, vol. 53 (1980), pp. 39–47.

53. Margaret Digby, *The Organization of Fishermen's Cooperatives* (Oxford: Plunkett Foundation for Cooperative Studies, 1973).

54. FAO, *Small-scale Fisheries in the Bay of Bengal* (Rome, 1978).

55. G. M. Gerhardsen, "Strategies for Development Projects in Small-scale Fisheries," W/L0595 (Rome: FAO, 1977).

56. Jahara Sabri, "Small-scale Fisheries Development in Peninsular Malaysia: Problems and Prospects," in Brian Lockwood and Kenneth Ruddle, eds., *Small-scale Fisheries Development: Social Science Contribution* (Honolulu: East-West Center Press, 1977).

57. C. L. Yap, "Trawling: Its Impact on Employment and Resource Use on the West Coast of Peninsular Malaysia," in Lockwood and Ruddle, eds., *Small-scale Fisheries Development*.

58. McGoodwin, "Mexico's Marginal Inshore Pacific Fishing Cooperatives," pp. 39–47; and Thomas M. McGuire, "The Political Economy of Shrimping in the Gulf of California, *Human Organization*, vol. 42 (1983), pp. 132–45.

59. C. L. Yap, "Women in Fisheries," in *Indo-Pacific Fishery Commission Proceedings*, 19th sess. (Bangkok: FAO Regional Office for Asia and the Pacific, 1980).

60. Svein Jentoft, "Fisheries Cooperatives: Lessons Drawn from International Experiences," *Canadian Journal of Development Studies*, vol. 7 (1986), pp. 197–209.

61. Bernardo Cattarinussi, "A Sociological Study of an Italian Community of Fishermen," in Peter Fricke, ed., *Seafarer and Community: Towards a Social Understanding of Seafaring* (London: Croom Helm, 1973); and R. Hamlisch and M. Hotta, "What Happened on Hokkaido," *Ceres*, vol. 7, no. 1 (1978), pp. 29–32.

62. See also, for Belize, Janet Gibson, "The Successes and Failures of Fishing Cooperatives of Belize," in J. B. Higman, Francis Williams, and Phil Roedel, eds., *Proceedings of the 30th Annual Gulf and Caribbean Fisheries Institute and the Conference on the Development of Small-scale Fisheries in the Caribbean* (Miami, Fla.: University of Miami, 1978); for India, see John Kurien, *Fishermen's Cooperative in Kerala: A Critique* (Madras: Bay of Bengal Programme, 1980); for the Philippines, see Rolando Castillo-Obispo, "Madridejos Fishermen's Cooperative Marketing Association, Inc.," paper read at the Symposium on Development and Management of Small-scale Fisheries, May 1980, Kyoto, Japan; and for Malaysia, see Udhis Narkswasdi, "An Evaluation of the Henghwa (Chinese) Cooperative Credit and Marketing Society Ltd., Malacca" (Kuala Lumpur: Ministry of Agriculture and Cooperatives, 1967).

63. Richard B. Pollnac, "People's Participation in the Small-scale Fisheries Development Cycle," Anthropology Working Paper no. 47 (Kingston, R.I.: International Center for Marine Resource Development, University of Rhode Island, 1987). Further evidence supporting this finding in non-fishermen's organizations can be found in Milton J. Esman and Norman T. Uphoff, *Local Organizations: Intermediaries in Rural Development* (Ithaca, N.Y.: Cornell University Press, 1984).

64. Pollnac, "People's Participation in the Small-scale Fisheries Development Cycle."

65. Pollnac, "Sociocultural Aspects of Technological and Institutional Change," in Maiolo and Orbach, *Modernization and Marine Fisheries Policy*.

PART V

Forestry Projects

Editor's Note

Adverse environmental consequences of development programs are present in many domains, but one in which they are particularly noticeable is the forestry subsector. For a long time development policies and projects have paid rather scant attention to the environment and to deforestation. But over the last decade or so, accelerated deforestation has been recognized as one of the most serious problems confronting the world as we near the crossroad between the twentieth and twenty-first centuries.

The deforestation crisis has hurt primarily the developing countries, but it entails global consequences. Its causes are many. In the 1980s, the tropical rainforests in Asia, Latin America, and Africa have been subjected to unprecedented commercial exploitation, planned clearings, and uncontrolled burning. The agricultural frontier is encroaching further and further into forest lands. Nearly 70 percent of the population of the developing world (excluding China) depends on fuelwood as its main source for cooking and heating, while out-of-forest tree resources, like forests themselves, are shrinking. Continuous population growth is increasing the twin pressures on forests—for more farming land and more fuelwood.

Forest-dependent groups are directly hard-hit by the drastic reduction in the world's forest areas, but environmental effects such as increased erosion, flooding, accelerated reservoir siltation, loss of biological diversity, and the threat of global climate change are affecting hundreds of millions of people more. Acute fuelwood shortages also vastly increase workloads for women, who must find the wood needed for cooking and heating. Figuring out how to halt such deterioration and increasing deforestation are among the highest priorities for development workers.

Forestry policies and programs thus face two major tasks: slowing down deforestation and intensifying tree planting both inside and outside forests. Rural populations must become more involved in tree planting activities, for without their massive participation afforestation activities cannot possibly make headway against the current rates of tree consumption and destruction. Therefore, the social and cultural issues involved in forestry projects, particularly in social forestry, are every bit as important as (a) the economic issues, (b) the technical issues, and (c) the environmental issues. To address them, the two chapters in this part of the volume propose a sociological framework for designing social forestry strategies and programs.

The chapter by Guggenheim and Spears discusses the key sociological dimensions of social forestry projects and some of their policy and design issues. Concerned with how to provide effective incentives for smallholders to grow trees, the authors' argument proceeds on three levels. First, at a general policy level, policymakers must recognize the pivotal role of small farmers in both environmental preservation and in tree production. National policies span a range of legal, financial, and institutional topics that set a macroscopic context that can encourage, as well as constrain, smallholder tree production. At present, few countries have policy frameworks designed to stimulate small farm tree production. Second, development projects must adapt their means—allocations, institutional arrangements, and incentives—to local situations. Guggenheim and Spears use a large body of field evidence to show how some projects still compete with and undermine local approaches to natural resource management. Third, on the positive side, local level institutions governing land tenure, labor availability, production orientation, technical innovation, and access to capital must be brought into project planning through good social research and participatory project approaches.

Cernea's chapter on participatory strategies for forestry projects revolves around the social actors of afforestation or regreening, as these social actors work within specific land tenure and tree tenure systems. Cernea argues that the profound behavioral changes to be elicited on a gigantic scale among farmers through social forestry are a shift from wood gathering behavior to tree cultivating behavior. The chapter proposes strategies able to engage the rural consumers of fuelwood into organized activities for producing trees and managing forests, and suggests a variety of organizational models for creating production-oriented user groups. The author's case study of a reforestration intervention in Azad Kashmir reverses the usual story told by development social scientists: while in that case project planners sought to promote reforestation on traditional corporate (common) property land called *shamilat* lands, it was the social scientist who pointed out that *shamilat* no longer worked on genuine corporate management principles.

Broadening the analysis to a number of recent projects that promoted "community woodlots" but largely failed, Cernea argues that these projects were socially ill-conceived and predicated on inadequately selected or defined units of social organization (or social actors). "Community woodlots" represented a program launched through many projects. However, in absence of good understandings of the kind of social process and social system required for such programs, the investments in the technical process outpaced by far the investment in the human and institutional process.

Cernea recommends specific options for replacing the diffuse "community" approaches with two basic strategies for social forestry, relying on clearly identified social actors: (a) family-centered strategies and (b) group-centered strategies (farmers' groups, associations of landless tree growers, age groups, women's groups, and other groups), both supported by sound organizational and distributional arrangements.

Asserting the centrality of people in forestry, and proposing ways for enabling fuelwood users to become producers, the chapters by Cernea and by Guggenheim-Spears break with the stereotype that tree growth is the business of professional foresters alone, or of mother nature alone. The practice of social forestry is wide open to—in fact, demands—the formation of patterns of social organization propitious for afforestation activities.

9

Sociological and Environmental Dimensions of Social Forestry Projects

Scott Guggenheim and John Spears

The 1990s may well be remembered as the decade when the dire predictions of environmental disaster came true. In recent years, environmentally aware researchers have pointed repeatedly to the dangers posed by mankind's assault on the natural world. But it was perhaps only in 1988, when satellite eyes in outer space could no longer even see the burning Amazon forests, that the public at large came to realize the immediacy of the global environmental threat.

The smoke signals from the Amazon carried an urgent message about deforestation. The quintessential renewable resource, forests are increasingly unable to recover from human depredation. Worldwide deforestation is accelerating just when more sustainable development strategies in developing countries are needed.

Solving the deforestation problem in large part depends on finding ways to promote forest protection, improve forest management practices, and carry out the macro level policy reforms that will provide people now clearing the forests with more attractive alternative uses for their labor and money. Properly planned development assistance will be a basic part of introducing these environmental reforms.

Small farmer-oriented forestry projects have come to play a pivotal role in the investment programs of international aid agencies as they have become aware of the causal connections between deforestation, rural poverty, and agricultural development. Starting from the late 1970s, aid agencies' traditional interest in commercial forestry and government-owned forest reserves expanded to include the role played by trees in farmers' production systems. The 1978 World Forestry Congress held in Jakarta, for example, had as its theme "Forestry for People," and recommended that forestry projects should address farmers' basic subsistence needs. Social forestry projects would supply fodder, fuelwood, poles, and other forest products to rural people whose dependence on forests and tree crops was in crisis.

Many lessons have been learned over the last decade about how and why small farmers grow trees. The World Bank has financed sociological studies of farmers' attitudes toward tree planting in India, Kenya, Malawi, Yemen, Zimbabwe, and elsewhere, but the overall understanding of smallholder tree farming still lags behind knowledge about other aspects of agriculture. Many of the most useful insights about small farm agroforestry have come from innovative research and projects carried out by nongovernmental organizations and self-help associations. Several critical insights on how to design forestry projects can be gleaned from the Bank's already extensive experience.

Four lessons stand out. First, tropical deforestation, rural poverty, and agricultural development are inextricably linked. Second, projects intended to support smallholder tree growing have been hampered by basic ignorance about when and why farmers decide to grow trees. Third, forestry projects have all too often been poorly designed and organized; in particular, their social strategies have been skimpily formulated. Finally, the institutions operating between those who make forest policy and those who plant trees are not working well. This critical lacunae in our knowledge of how to develop the institutional transmission gears between macro policy and micro farming has brought many promising projects to grief.

Sociologically intelligent strategies to implement forestry projects have been in short supply. Project experience and socioeconomic analysis show that project management requires substantially more local participation for social forestry projects to make a significant impact on rural well-being and natural resource management. Nonparticipatory social forestry projects are flawed by definition, yet few social forestry projects have been based on good anthropological analysis of the key social actors, indigenous land tenure systems, patterns of rural differentiation, local forms of labor organization, and other factors needed to design good participatory approaches.

If these are some of the main lessons to emerge from a decade of Bank experience with social forestry, then it is easy to see why the traditional barrier between forestry and sociology—a separation that was born as much out of disinterest as from antagonism—is gradually crumbling. This chapter examines some of the sociological dimensions of social forestry projects undertaken in the decade after the World Bank's forestry sector policy paper was released in 1978. The first section provides background policy information about the Bank's involvement in forestry, particularly the overall increase in forestry lending and a concomitant shift into social forestry. The second section summarizes various ways that trees fit into farming systems. It focuses particularly on how traditional farming systems deal with the challenges to tree management posed by environmental stress since this is, unfortunately, typically the time when forestry projects are most likely to be considered. The third section considers potential sociological contributions to forestry projects, such as ways to use local knowledge, social organization, and cultural preferences to help shape project designs. The paper winds down with a discussion of forestry planning issues relevant to the World Bank's project cycle.[1]

Policy: Forestry Lending and the Environment

Deforestation

International interest in forests has risen tremendously over the past decade, primarily because of two major developments of the 1970s. First, the rise of politically influential environmentalist movements in the developed world helped turn attention to the appalling rates of deforestation occurring in developing and, in particular, tropical nations. The approximately 900 million hectares of remaining tropical rainforests are disappearing at a rate of 7 million hectares per year (11 million hectares per year counting nonrainforest areas), and there is reason to believe that this rate will increase.

Most analysts attribute the primary cause of deforestation to small farmer, shifting (swidden) agriculture. Deforestation stems from several causes, but the breakdown of any previous equilibrium between small farmers and forests clearly suggests that farmers' current resource base is inadequate for their needs. For most rural people, and certainly for the people traditionally most dependent on forest products, this resource base has declined precipitously in recent decades. In the closed tropical forest zone, shifting cultivation accounts for about 70 percent of total deforestation in Africa, 50 percent in Asia, and 35 percent in tropical America.

Pressure on swidden systems comes from market incentives to increase farm sizes, overlogging, population increase, forest colonization, and forest titling; all causing formerly balanced swidden cycles to deteriorate.[2] Forest conservation must be backed up by a range of agricultural incentives and policy reforms. There is, in short, little chance to slow tropical deforestation without resolving basic issues of rural poverty: some of the most severe deforestation could be remedied by agricultural improvement and income redistribution in areas far removed from the tropical forest. For many areas, forest conservation programs will work only if they are backed up by more general policy reforms that will slow down migration into forest lands, encourage agricultural intensification, and limit the incentives to clear forests.

Successful forestry projects help sustain agricultural productivity by: protecting soil and water resources and replenishing soil fertility; ensuring adequate supplies of fuelwood so that rural people no longer need to burn animal dung or crop residues which can instead be ploughed back into the farming system; protecting watersheds that release water gradually throughout the year; slowing desertification by reducing wind erosion in arid zones; and helping to preserve the flora and fauna of rainforests, the planet's most biologically diverse ecosystem.

In addition to the international community's increased awareness of environmental degradation, the second push toward social forestry has come from the growing concern of international donor and lending agencies about poverty in developing nations. Detailed studies of rural populations revealed the extent to which tree and forest products are basic elements of peasant economies. Few rural populations live from agriculture alone; in many areas forest extractive activities are as important for the household economy as wage labor and agriculture itself (Hecht, Anderson, and May 1988). Dependence on forest products is inversely correlated with income: the poorest income groups are precisely those most dependent on the diminishing forests.

The linked issues of deforestation and poverty must be addressed at national levels. First, national policies should encourage farmers to plant trees on degraded lands or manage existing tree stands (see also chapter 10). Government regulations and programs have often accelerated forest loss. Elaborate licensing procedures to obtain wood or other forest products encourage both illegal harvesting and mutual distrust between local populations and forest management agencies. In some parts of Latin America, anachronistic and environmentally blind regulations grant a property title to those who clear the land, with the predictable outcome of extensive tree removal. Forest land nationalized for protective reasons has had the unintended consequence of discouraging tree conservation and management. Fortmann correctly observed (1984) that legislation vesting land ownership in the government can discourage tree planting because of farmers' fear that wooded lands will be expropriated. Throughout India, for example, many species growing on private land can be harvested only with written permits issued by the government.

Second, forest policy options in the humid tropics should address the development of settlement frontiers. Choices include whether to promote specialized agriculture on the development of a range of resources; integrated development on incremental approaches; wide geographical coverage versus concentration on model or pilot projects, and so on. Faced with choices of such formidable complexity, only *selected* policy reforms that address real constraints and incentives will discourage continued migration into forest lands.

Project experience, however, amply confirms that simply increasing forest productivity does not automatically relieve rural poverty. Very often, productivity gains both come from and are captured by relatively well-off farmers. Case studies show how the very success of a project that develops markets for wood can deprive poor people of necessary tree products. Increasing tree production without aggravating social inequality is a major challenge to which strategic answers should be formulated jointly by sociologists and forest project managers.

Forest Policy History and the Growth of Social Forestry

The World Bank's 1978 forestry sector policy paper advocated significantly increased lending for the 1980s compared with the 1970s. It also proposed a shift away from industrial forestry and toward social forestry and fuelwood programs. Bank forestry lending, which averaged less than $20 million a year throughout the 1970s (mainly for industrial plantations, sawmills, and pulpmills), increased to an average of $130 million a year during the first half of the 1980s. How that money was spent can be seen in the breakdown of forest lending by project type shown in table 9-1.

The table shows that Bank forestry lending strongly supports tree growing by smallholders. In fact, the change in lending priorities toward small farmer-oriented tree projects is striking. Between 1967 and 1976, 95 percent of the $115 million loaned by the Bank in the forestry sector was for industrial forestry. Nearly 80 percent of the $8.8 billion loaned since then has supported communal and smallholder forestry, spread over 62 specialized forestry projects and the forestry components of another 72 projects.

Policy Reforms

Containing deforestation requires new approaches to land settlement, tenure, and pricing policies, (particularly for fuelwood, charcoal, and industrial timber concessions), as well as ways to involve smallholders in forest management. Reforms will mean little to rural people unless they are accompanied by new approaches to project design. In this sense, the basic conceptual changes being proposed here parallel changes proposed in other chapters of this volume, and for similar reasons of growth, alleviation of poverty, and effectiveness.

Bank support for social forestry must be understood as a policy initiative in this direction. Social forestry (also called community forestry or agroforestry) is a broad term covering roadside strip planting, community woodlots, farm forestry, and tree planting on marginal lands by the landless. The novelty of social forestry lies in beneficiaries' direct involvement in tree planting and management.

This effort, however, has not yet been very successful. Despite the obvious centrality of small farmers in social forestry programs, during the 1980s more than 75 percent of the Bank's lending went to *government* forestry institutions and programs, rather than to small farmer projects. Even the rare plans to gradually turn forest management over to area residents have rarely worked out in practice.

The World Bank has only recently been able to define a substantive research agenda for making social forestry projects more effective. Research in the coming decade must concentrate on (a) small farmer incentives; (b) comparative study of the official and nongovernmental institutions that have the capabilities to manage social forestry projects;

Table 9-1. *World Bank Forestry Lending, 1977–89*

Type of project	Number of projects	Total loan/credit allocation (millions of dollars)	Percentage of total lending
Social forestry (including agroforestry fuelwood/ community forestry)	62	2,643.0	29.9
Watershed rehabilitation	15	929.5	10.5
Forestry components of agriculture and rural development projects	72	4,488.1	50.8
Forest management, and industrial plantations	30	606.8	6.9
Sawmills/plywood mills	8	172.8	2.0
Total	187	8,840.2	100.0

and (c) methodologies that can integrate local social structure and tree planting practices into effective project designs. Such research is worthwhile because, despite the mixed results from the social forestry projects carried out thus far, social forestry still offers the greatest promise for helping rural populations increase their access to tree resources.

Economic Viability of Bank Forestry Investments

In many cases the economic rates of return of the social/agroforestry/ fuelwood projects financed by the Bank over the last decade have been as high or higher than those yielded by the industrial plantation forestry projects that were predominant in earlier Bank lending programs. Table 9-2 shows that agroforestry projects require no special economic dispensation on humanitarian or environmental justifications, but can survive as economically attractive investments in their own right. Agroforestry projects can increase farm productivity and income for rural people as well as protect the environment (particularly soil and water resources).

Evolution of Forest Projects

The Bank has focused on changing the farmer's relative costs, benefits, and risks in growing trees. Farmers have been encouraged to grow trees

Table 9-2. *Economic Rates of Return for Forestry Products Financed by the World Bank between 1978 and 1986*

Category of project	Number of projects financed	Range of economic rate of return (percent)
Social forestry	62	10–50
Watershed rehabilitation	15	13–38
Forestry components of agriculture and rural development projects	72	12–100
Forest management and industrial plantation	30	10–200
Sawmills/plywood mills	8	12–100
Total	197	

through technical advice, free seedlings, planting grants, concessional loans, and so on. Many additional incentives for tree cultivation and management have had no project relationship whatsoever. These have included robust cash markets for construction poles and charcoal; subsistence demands for fodder, fruit, fiber; and occasional national efforts to encourage environmental protection.

The Bank and other development assistance agencies have historically pursued four strategies for encouraging rural people to plant trees:

- Improve the farmer's technical knowledge through *extension and education* about the costs and benefits of tree growing and by disseminating tested and proven tree technologies and growing techniques.
- Provide *inputs such as seedlings and tools* to decrease costs and increase production.
- Where cash crop tree farming is a viable option, provide *access to credit* to ease capital constraints during peak harvesting periods.
- Promote *secure land tenure or guaranteed usufruct rights* to alleviate equity and distributional problems and reduce risks, especially for the landless.

Distribution, Equity, and Risk

Unequal distribution has been the root of the failure for many forestry projects. Social structures are for the most part inherently unequal. How they respond to development interventions is an open question: in some cases they redistribute benefits to worse-off members, while in other cases the minor cracks separating one social stratum from another split into major class distinctions.

Socioeconomic status may place stringent limits on the extent to which certain groups are able to participate in a project. The landless, agropastoralists, and other politically and economically marginalized user groups may not be able to take advantage of incentives for tree growing. Landless farmers will be able to benefit from a project only if they are given access to land; otherwise they simply lose access to grazing areas, or organic residues for fuel are reduced when trees are planted on degraded lands (Chowdhry 1983). Evidence from South Asia suggests that the rapid growth in tree farming for poles and other commercial products has decreased food production and increased rural unemployment (Shiva and others 1982).

Few projects consider the effects of tree planting on competing demands for capital, land, and labor from the farmer's point of view. For instance, farmers seldom agree with development planners that fuelwood is the best forest product to grow, even during a fuel shortage: other tree-based products such as fodder or building materials, are often considered much more valuable. Understanding such tradeoffs from the farmers' viewpoint is essential for designing culturally and economically intelligent projects.

Forestry projects in general have also overlooked women's particular interests as the principal users (and gatherers) of fuelwood and other tree products. The species planted in collectively managed or state forests rarely reflect the uses to which women put tree products. While some of the deficiencies in this area can be overcome by including women staff members in forestry projects, and making sociologically guided efforts to build in women's access and involvement, local gender-based differentiation often causes conflicts, few of which have been resolved in favor of women.

Village woodlots in South Asia illustrate the sharp equity problems present elsewhere. These woodlots were supposed to help the poorest of the village population, lighten women's workloads, and relieve family budgets. The products of many such village woodlots, however, have been sold and the income invested in schools, roads, and village water supply systems. Apart from some employment and the right to collect minor forest produce (grass, leaves, twigs and fallen branches, and fruit), the landless and poor have hardly benefited. One solution being tried in a West Bengal project is to lease land to the landless for tree growing and to reserve the benefits of plantations on government land for the poor and landless. The potential for such landless-oriented special programs is vast in India and other countries with large reserves of degraded forest, but the work needed to organize landless families into groups with acceptable managerial patterns and enforceable production and distribution rules has not been carried out.

While equity problems are inherent in nearly all development projects, they have been particularly pronounced for projects affecting tribal and indigenous peoples. Most tribal people live in forested areas and practice shifting cultivation. They are often blamed for forest destruction; the conclusion is that their agriculture must be "improved"—in their own best interests.

These charges should be weighed in light of the fact that the remedy seems to kill more often than cure the patient. Official agencies' understanding of how tribal production systems work remains remarkably superficial. Swidden cultivation is usually only one aspect of more complicated production systems that include sophisticated fallow management and multiple resource extraction (Alcorn 1983, Padoch and others 1985, Hecht, Anderson, and May 1988). Many tribes are careful conservators of their environment and have made impressive, sustainable adaptations to agriculturally difficult environments. By the same token, however, these adaptations are fragile and not amenable to sweeping outside interventions. The disappearance of traditional tribal agriculture results not only in the irreparable loss of valuable information about tree species and their uses, but also about their efficient ecological adaptations. In other areas, tribal populations have increased thanks to public health improvements even as their traditional lands have been reduced, mainly as a result of inroads by nontribal agriculturalists. All of the problems with distinguishing between state claims to land and customary usage are magnified in the case of tribal peoples.

The policy implications of this situation should be analyzed. When a project is likely to have a direct or indirect impact on tribal populations, special efforts above and beyond normal social impact assessments are required. The key lies in building into project structures mechanisms that allow tribal people increased control over their resource base. Clear proprietary regimes for tribal residents on forested lands would provide some power to keep out encroachers. Very often, it is necessary to demarcate and legalize title on tribal land. Indigenous institutions should take on decisionmaking powers about project design and execution, rather than be substituted wholesale by outside project planners. The common attitude that, at best, tribal populations should be mollified so they do not interfere with a project must be replaced by development efforts that place the improvement of tribal living standards at the forefront of project objectives.

At least as important as simply protecting tribal populations from misconceived development projects, however, is the need to assist them with project activities that are consonant with their sociocultural practices. Species selection should reflect the diverse needs of the local population rather than seek a single economic maximization. Only recently have some forestry projects sought to benefit tribal people directly without imposing on them unfamiliar sociocultural values and unmanageable economic pressures. Efforts to build upon indigenous systems of tree management that focus on community organization have considerable potential for helping tribal populations.

The Social Organization of Agroforestry

A common mistake of routine forestry planning lies in thinking that forest management is an activity unfamiliar to rural populations, requiring major changes in how people think about their natural environment. Farm communities virtually everywhere require trees for timber, fuel, and fruit to meet household needs for fodder, soil nutrients, and other inputs into the farm or for cash income. Many (though not all) farm communities have long established tree cultivation systems or ways to manage natural forests. Several protective mechanisms have emerged to ensure that locally valued tree species remain available (Okigbo and Greenland 1977). However, pressures on tree and land resources have often outrun these conservation traditions and have exposed populations that had previously enjoyed an abundance of tree resources to scarcity.

Natural Tree Management

Where population densities are low and relatively stable, tree management is usually passive, relying on natural regeneration to offset harvesting, waste, or natural damage. In many areas increasing population pressure has led to more intense conservation and management of existing trees. In Malawi, for example, 34 percent of the farmers surveyed had planted trees without assistance from the forest department or the project. In the Nepal Terai, a limited survey showed that half the farmers had planted an average of fifteen trees (mainly multipurpose fruit and fuelwood trees) on their homesteads. Yet within a general pattern of tree planting, the extent to which people cultivate and manage trees varies widely. Some societies strongly emphasize tree cultivation and management; in others, it is peripheral or even negligible.

Some forest and tree management strategies reflect the land's carrying capacity. Individuals, households, or kinship groups may restrict access to trees. User groups in the hill areas of Nepal have long limited the harvest of wood, grass, and other products to a sustainable level (Campbell 1978; Molnar 1986). The use of the baobab in southern Niger is defined by very old traditions which specify strict proprietary rights. In Sudan, palm trees may be subject to a complex system of fractional ownership defined by traditional laws of inheritance. In Western Sumatra, the decision to cut a valuable tree is made by the extended family (Fortmann 1984).

More intensive tree management practices include pollarding, coppicing, and pruning techniques. For instance, reports from Bangladesh (Douglas 1981), the Philippines (Wiersum and Veer 1983), and Burkina Faso (Ben Salem and Tran Van Nao 1981) show that such techniques permit harvesting a sustained yield of wood or fodder over long periods. The total lifetime contribution of a tree used in this way can be considerably greater than the volume it will produce if it is simply felled. Coppicing and pollarding by farmers have often been overlooked, although indigenous silvicultural technologies are increasingly being recognized and validated by "scientific" foresters.

Other peoples actually protect and cultivate naturally germinating seedlings. Cultivators may leave certain desirable tree seedlings when weeding and might even build barriers to protect them from grazing livestock. In parts of southern Mexico, for example, farmers protect indigenous leguminous trees, such as *Prosopis*, which provide shade and edible pods and enhance soil fertility (Wilken 1978). Certain acacias and other leguminous tree species are widely protected for similar reasons in cropland across the drier zone of Africa.

Trees as Components of Agroforestry Systems

In some countries, rural people plant trees (especially fruit trees) in addition to managing existing stands. In one of the most densely populated areas of Bangladesh, each household on average had planted or naturally regenerated 68 trees, of which 16 had been established in the previous year (Byron 1985). In Panama, fruit trees are planted on almost every small farm (Jones 1982). Nearly half of the farmers interviewed in the Valle Occidental region of Costa Rica said that they had planted trees as windbreaks (Gewald and Ugalde 1981). A survey in the hill areas of Nepal showed that on average each household owned 28 trees, around a third of which had been planted and cultivated (Campbell and Bhattarai 1983). Of rural households in the Kakamega District of Kenya, nearly 40 percent maintain small nurseries and nearly 80 percent have planted trees on their land (van Gelder and Kerkhof 1984).

In most farming and rural land use systems, trees have multiple functions and produce several outputs. Recent research on shifting cultivation has shown that fallow lands are far from unused lands. While the primary cereal or starch crop is grown on cleared agricultural lands, recovering fallow lands provide farm populations with fuel, medicines, building material, raw materials for artisanal production, food sources, fiber, and fodder. The socioeconomic importance of secondary forests for rural economies is for the first time receiving attention from development specialists. Extractive reserve systems, where ethnoagronomic knowledge is used to harvest multiple products from natural forest, are only just being seriously analyzed by resource scientists, yet already there is considerable evidence that forestry projects can effectively reach the rural poor by fortifying extractive reserves (Hecht, Anderson, and May 1988).

It is seldom reported that rural people have spontaneously planted trees specifically for fuelwood, except where they intend to sell it. In Malawi, a large number of farmers plant trees, mainly for poles to be used by the family; only 15 percent of the people interviewed in a study of tree planting practices planted trees for fuelwood (Energy Studies Unit 1982) although a higher percentage may subsequently use the trees for this purpose. Reports from Nepal show that people plant fruit and fodder trees but obtain their fuelwood from the remaining natural forest (Campbell and Bhattarai 1983).

Rural people in many areas combine tree growing with a variety of agricultural and pastoral activities. These activities benefit from the presence of trees that provide shade, protection against wind, or nutrient enhancement. Shade trees are commonly planted around coffee, tea, and cardamom crops. Windbreaks are prominent in the drier, cultivated parts of Africa and Asia, and contour plantings that incorporate trees are commonly found in hill areas through the tropics. Contour or boundary-grown trees frequently provide green mulch, and nitrogen-fixing tree species in some places are grown in alleys specifically for this purpose (Raintree 1985). Fodder trees are also widely planted to provide an important source of livestock feed, as in Nepal (Campbell and Bhattarai 1983).

Among the most complex and intensive systems which incorporate planted trees are the home gardens and compound farms of the humid tropics in Asia (Wiersum 1984), Africa (Okigbo and Greenland 1977), and America (Wilken 1978; Gliessman et al. 1981). These multilayered mixtures of a large number of species produce a variety of foods and other products. Plants and trees are grown in different strata according to their light and humidity requirements. The ways in which most of these plant combinations respond to specific local edaphic, agronomic, and soil conditions is still poorly understood.

Trees as Cash Crops

Figure 9-1 provides a schematic model of incentives and constraints on smallholder tree growing.

Tree cultivation is usually less intensive than other types of crop cultivation within the farming system. Trees generally complement other crops and are grown on land not otherwise occupied. Trees can also be grown as cash crops. Many tree-farming systems include at least one income-generating coproduct such as gum arabic from *Acacia Senegal*, a tree planted as a fallow species in Sudan which provides farmers with important cash income. In a number of situations, markets for wood products encourage tree farming.

For some time, fuelwood has been produced to supply large, concentrated demands such as for tobacco curing. In Malawi, tobacco curing accounts for more than half of all fuelwood consumption. Some urban

Figure 9-1. *Costs, Benefits, and Risks of Smallholder Tree Growing*

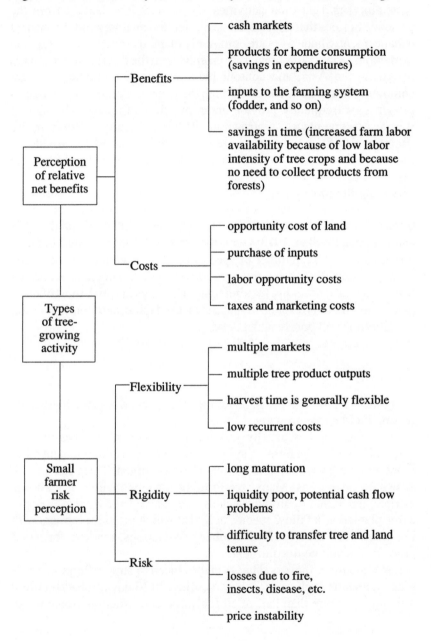

fuelwood markets which are remote from forests, such as the Addis Ababa and Madras markets, have long depended on farmer-planted trees. Most commercial tree farming, however, has been to supply more highly valued wood products. The rapid growth of this kind of tree farming in many parts of India has been primarily to produce building poles. In south India, match stock is also produced, and farmers in north India and the Philippines produce pulpwood (Hyman 1983). In Bangladesh, a study of private tree farming revealed that 70–90 percent of all wood produced and sold throughout the country came from private farmer's fields (Byron 1985).

Tree farming as an agricultural monocrop often relies on fertilizer and irrigation water. Tree farming of this type is quite different from the widespread selective type of tree growing which characterizes traditional systems. The failure to distinguish clearly between the different kinds of tree planting has sabotaged many forestry project designs since, in one system, the tree crop *mix* is fundamental to the farm system, whereas in the other, the goal is single species maximization.

Project planners must understand that, for the vast majority of the world's farmers, the operative question is how farmers already manage trees. Once it can be shown that tree management is already known, then the analytic focus must shift to the real constraints on traditional management systems. Project design must begin with an understanding of the constraints on traditional management, and the organizational requirements for establishing new (group, communal, or individual) management systems before tree planting can be either induced or improved.

Sociology and Social Forestry Projects

There is a role for project intervention where rural people have been unable to develop strategies of tree cultivation and management, especially in areas of growing scarcity, or where traditional management systems have been overwhelmed by external interventions. Experience with these projects has been variable. In some cases, farmers' access to forest-based products has been accomplished by creating large stocks of on-farm trees. In other cases, farmers have had little interest in tree cultivation and management. In others still, farmers have taken up tree growing, but their responses and the social outcomes have often proved to be quite different from those anticipated during project preparation

and allowed for in project design. Below we discuss some of the main
planning weaknesses that have plagued forestry projects.

Data Sources

Forestry projects frequently suffer from a lack of reliable baseline and
diagnostic data concerning the population to which the project is directed.
Figures used for project planning are usually extrapolated from national
aggregates or generalized from local estimates supplemented by limited
cross-checking during short field missions.

The lack of data reflects both the composition of project design teams
and cultural conditions. Foresters are skilled in sylvicultural issues but
are not well versed in sociological analysis. Although in theory multidisciplinary in practice design teams rarely include ethnographic skills for
blending information about the physical and economic dimensions of
tree production with a knowledge of the people. In addition, design teams
usually include only men. This is particularly problematic in the many
countries where men do not communicate well with the women who are
the main collectors of fuelwood and fodder.

The consequences of overreliance on aggregate statistics in many
developing nations are well known. Problems are multiplied when dealing with particular geographic areas, where firsthand, field-based knowledge is imperative. There is a sophisticated methodological toolkit
available to social scientists involved in developing social forestry projects. Participant observation, and basic research methodologies—
ethnotaxonomies, community energy-product flow diagrams, social network analysis—have already proven to be useful for formulating appropriate project strategies. Cost-effective tools for designing and
monitoring specific projects, so-called "rapid rural appraisal" methods,
are increasingly accepted in development project work. These are examined in this volume and Molnar 1987. On-farm research programs such
as "farmer-back-to-farmer" or Ashby's participatory research models
(1986), could also be used to incorporate sociological expertise into
forestry project approaches.

Sociological field studies can document the quantities and types of
fuelwood and fodder used. They can also provide essential information
about the number of people and the amount of time typically involved in
collection, competing uses for wood products, seasonal variation in

demand, and the effect of proximity to urban markets and forest reserves on wood use. The studies can also deal with access to environmental resources and their use by different socioeconomic, occupational, and ethnic groups. Questions, for example, about the time involved in fuelwood collection can usefully lead researchers to ask what people would rather do if collection times were reduced and resources were available in their own compound.

Sociology of Risk Management

How can forestry projects be made attractive to farmers? At the very least, tree planting incentives can only be effective if they reduce the farmer's risks. Farmers often refuse to adopt a system of production that might improve their situation because of the chance that failure might leave them even worse off. To a certain extent, the farmer's perception of risk is defined by an implicit, and often very high, discount rate: a tree planted this year is much more valuable to a farmer in three to five years than in ten to fifteen years. Risk aversion affects tree growing in several ways:

- Farmers often minimize their risks and maximize their benefits by growing trees which provide multiple outputs. Trees that provide fruit, fodder, and fuelwood, and enrich the soil are likely to be preferred to those used only for fuelwood, despite the higher net economic return obtained by concentrating on a single product.
- Trees can diversify the farmer's sources of income, flexibly providing income when other crops have failed during the dry season, or when household needs for income are greatest (for dowry, school fees, and so on).
- Farmers are sometimes more interested in growing trees that require only small changes to existing systems, rather than the introduction of new and unfamiliar species and management practices.
- Fast-growing tree species are the most acceptable to farmers who need to recover initial investment costs rapidly because of a high implicit discount rate.
- Farmers will grow trees more readily if markets are assured, either through direct marketing agreements between large wood consumers (such as a pulpmill) or by obviously robust, lucrative, and expanding markets.

Incentives

Depending on farmers' land, labor, and capital constraints, patterns of resource allocation can be altered to favor planting trees or to encourage more intensive management of existing tree resources. However, changes in broader land use practices can also threaten tree management, such as when tree cover is removed to eradicate the tsetse fly. Monocropping and mechanization militate against tree growing, since trees get in the way of tractor operation (Wilken 1978). Serial tenure patterns, where usufruct for a given plot is periodically redistributed, make the protection of privately planted trees extremely difficult, since the farmer who plants the tree does not receive benefits from it. Similar difficulties also appear when farmed lands revert to community grazing land following the harvest (Raintree 1985). Burning old growth grass to encourage pasture regrowth also makes tree growing difficult (Openshaw and Moris 1979). Incentives which may encourage smallholders to support tree cultivation and management strategies are summarized in table 9-3.

The most challenging issue confronting a project designer is to determine how different incentive and constraint structures operate in specific sociocultural areas. This issue is not simply a question of finding the right price to attract individual farmers. Just as traditional agricultural practices are channeled through a social structure that assigns incentives, resources, and the organizational forms needed to link them, social engineering is needed to provide a mechanism to recombine production factors in new ways.

Four main areas for sociological inquiry are necessary in the design of forestry projects: population, land, labor, and social organization. The last allocates human resources and is thus implicitly present throughout this discussion.

Population

At a minimum, two aspects of population need to be examined: settlement patterns and social heterogeneity. Settlement location affects the design of extension, the location of nurseries, and estimates of personnel required to implement the project. For instance, where settlements are clustered together, one nursery can provide seedlings for the population. Where they are dispersed, allowance must be made for the time and energy of travel to collect seedlings, seedling loss during travel, and the effects of technology on the demand for seedlings. For example,

Table 9-3. *Incentives for Smallholder Tree Cultivation and Management*

Type of incentive	Advantage
Prevailing economic and social incentives	
A. Land Availability	
Abundance	• Trees can be grown in a way that does not compete with other agricultural land usage
Scarcity	• Trees must be grown to meet household demands for tree products because existing tree resources are inadequate
Features of the agroclimate	• Good soils and rainfall favor tree cultivation and management
Land tenure	
Corporate	• Corporate property resource management strategies incorporate trees into corporate land-use approaches
Individual	• May bring privately owned trees under more intensive management
Fragmentation of holdings	• Increases tree planting as an outcome of tree scarcity and encourages tree planting for land demarcation
B. Capital Availability	
Market access	• Trees can provide a lucrative source of on-farm income
Substitute markets	• Trees can meet multiple market demands, diversifying the farmer's sources of income
Low recurrent costs	• Have an advantage over other cash crops, particularly among the poor who may have no access to capital for investment and maintenance
Other values of trees	
Subsistence products	• Tree browse; livestock production; fuelwood
Sustained production	• Support agricultural production through soil conservation
C. Labor Availability	
Employment creation	• Can create jobs in areas of rural unemployment
Increased access to forest products	• Incentive to plant trees where there are shortages of on-farm agricultural labor
Low labor intensity for tree growing	• Optimizes household's use of capital and labor resources; provides the opportunity for the household to maximize income by freeing up farm labor for wage employment
D. Risk Reduction	
Diversify smallholder	• Reduces exposure to environmental risk; risks of crop failure; dry season fodder
Flexibility of harvesting schedule	• Can wait until markets are right; market demands change for different age-classes

(table continues on next page)

Table 9-3 *(continued)*

Type of incentive	Advantage
Policy and project-related incentives	
A. Land Availability	
Legalizing corporate land tenure	• Strengthens corporate land-use management strategies
Land distribution or privatization	• Can encourage farmers to invest in land improvement
Tenure reform	• Reduce conflicts between formal and local tenure systems
B. Capital Availability	
Subsidized inputs	
Free seedlings	• Can provide access to fast growing species
Other inputs	• Reduce farmer's costs and can increase productivity
Tree-planting subsidies	
Cash	• Can give trees an advantage over other crops
Food-for-work	• Important in famine areas
Credit market	• Increases access to capital for cash crop tree farming
Concessional	• Subsidized production
Tax concessions	• Reduce costs
Market support	• Increases prices of undervalued tree products to reflect their economic value
C. Labor Availability	
User organizations	• Can provide credit guarantee
	• Cushions risk
	• Facilitates marketing
	• Improves extension
D. Risk Reduction	
Fast-growing trees	• Guarantee faster returns
Market guarantees	• Link farm production with market demands
Price supports	• Reduces market volatility and increases viability of trees in relation to other crops
Market information	• Increases farmer's access to markets
Extension/education	• Increases knowledge, can increase productivity
Research and analysis	• Identify new options, reinforce good existing management practices
Infrastructure development	• Promotes appropriate tree technologies
	• Increases farmer's access to inputs/markets

in Haiti and Nepal the use of polyurethene bags makes seedlings too heavy to carry in great numbers. As a result, far fewer seedlings have been taken from the nurseries than project planners anticipated.

Heterogeneity of project area population is the rule in most countries. Although class, ethnic, or caste divisions affect the ability of the intended beneficiary communities to work in common, such variables have generally been ignored in forestry projects. Different groups in the same area may need alternative models of social organization; access to a common resource may be based on ethnic affiliation; priorities may differ between subgroups; and extension media may need to be adapted to reach various subgroups effectively.

Land

Probably the most crucial element in any social forestry project is the way in which land is used, held, transferred, or inherited. Differences between formal and informal legal systems concerning land tenure are a recurring stumbling block in project design. One of the most common objections to forestry projects is that they prejudice nonlandowning groups that are nevertheless dependent on land access: village livestock owners, landless people dependent on gleaning rights, and so on.

Village-level landholding and land use patterns largely determine the land actually available for a forestry project. Without an investigation of traditional practices, and with undue reliance on official statements, the assessment of the distribution of project benefits is often erroneous. A distinction must be drawn between title to the land—particularly in the Western sense of the term—and actual use of the land. The state may claim as "unused" or "vacant," land that is subject to well-defined use rights allocated under traditional systems. In numerous instances, this failure to distinguish between statutory and traditional title has resulted in a shortfall in the lands said to be available for a project.

Although an individual may have no title to the land, he or she may be entitled (*inter vivos* or through inheritance) to use the land permanently and dispose of it to other members of the community. This right is often found where group title prevails, as in parts of Africa, Andean and tropical Latin America, Oceania, and Melanesia.

Land ownership can also be separate from the ownership of its products. Land, its crops, and its trees may belong to three different people. The relationship of tree planting to land title and access must be considered. Planting a tree may mean claiming title to the land. One study in Nigeria in the 1930s found that trees could not be fertilized with green manure—an herbaceous crop plowed under to enrich the soil—because women grow crops between them, which they did not want to lose.

The second question concerns the nature and duration of land use. Where a piece of land is held for life, the potential for growing trees is normally greater than where shifting cultivation is practiced, although, as the evidence from several lowland South American swidden groups shows, there are several major exceptions. In many instances where only one crop is cultivated, land is used successively: it produces a crop in one season, and in the off-season it is used for grazing. Social arrangements may permit and support concurrent use of land: one person can have the right to farm the land, and another can have the right to the trees on the land. In rotating field systems, although a member of the group may be entitled to a plot of land, it is not the same plot every year. Systems of rotating ownership and usufruct can undo the best-intentioned project that is based on unchecked assumptions of individual ownership. This is not to say that there are no strategies other than privatizing land (see chapter 10), but few forestry projects have done the background research needed to match tenure systems with project goals.

Labor

Sociological research on how a project conforms to the local division of labor—that is, who will provide labor, and whether labor should be voluntary or paid—should influence decisions about the use of labor or mechanization, the timing of work, and project costs. General unemployment or underemployment statistics cannot replace field surveys for determining whether sufficient labor is available. Labor may be scarce for a variety of reasons: the payment offered for work may be lower than the potential worker's valuation of leisure; a certain caste may not permit manual labor; able-bodied men may leave the project area during the agricultural off-seasons, and so forth.

Paralleling the importance of the traditional gender-based division of labor for project design are traditional labor-sharing arrangements.

Where such arrangements exist, are they limited to traditional crops (for example, subsistence paddy) and not cash crops? In traditional labor-sharing arrangements, how much time has to be spent on common operations? If tree crops are considered cash crops, would the traditional labor-sharing arrangement apply? Assessment of the social imbalance from technological interventions—a subject well studied by anthropologists—rarely figures in technical evaluations.

Many forestry projects have come to grief through overoptimistic or simplistic assumptions about abundant labor supplies. Where other tasks are more important than growing tree crops, it may be necessary to schedule forestry operations during the off-season. The scheduling of work is partly a technical decision for forestry specialists. However, a sociologist may be able to point out in advance that scheduling work at a time other than the ideal one for the forests themselves may be the only way to get any work done at all.

Social Organization

Models of social structure and social organization implicitly undergird all development projects. Forestry projects often come to grief because they fail to grasp basic social organizational issues, both those that govern resource management and those that depend on behavioral changes in local practice. Without an acceptable vehicle for introducing new technologies and management techniques to a large population, projects doom themselves to rejection.

There are four basic social organizational issues that should be studied for forestry projects. First, it is important to understand which are the appropriate *social units of analysis*. The "family farm" is obviously a basic decisionmaking unit in virtually all rural economies. Too often, however, the family farm is simplistically equated with the individual, decisionmaking family farmer.

The family farm is rarely the only analytically relevant group functioning at a local level. Corporate kinship groups and village structures, for example, are often key actors that decide which crops are planted by members and how they are managed. Similarly, for many decisions, the local group might not be relevant at all. For example, a lack of regional markets for wood products, rather than any unwillingness to change a farming system, might be the primary reason why trees are not grown commercially.

Second, the *internal structure* of the domestic group must be understood as it reflects who does what. While an understanding of the local division of labor is obviously important for forestry projects, other topics—such as the developmental cycle of domestic groups, which focuses on how rights, opportunities, and ratios of family producers to consumers vary as families mature—are rarely studied and never included in project design.

Third, *internal social dynamics* play a tremendously important role in determining the acceptability of a project intervention. One of the authors has documented a case of "rotational inheritance" in southern Colombia, in which a plot of land owned by a father would pass from son to son approximately every three years; this obviously was not conducive to any long-term investment, although it did encourage cooperative management between brothers (Guggenheim 1984). In several parts of the mid- and high-altitude Andes, sharecropping is a practice which, when carried out within the local community, appears to promote rather than discourage technological innovation (Lehmann 1986). Many of the failures of community woodlots in rural India have been attributed to a poor understanding of village-level social heterogeneity. When local communities are seen as *systems* of social relationships, then project interventions can be studied in terms of their differential impacts, both positive and negative.

Fourth, *external linkages* between the local community and the regional or national society should be considered in project design. Throughout much of highland Mexico, for example, Indian producers have no marketing alternatives for forest products other than through a politically controlled, monopsonistic trucking industry. Conversely, a World Bank–assisted hydroelectric project in Colombia was recently able to establish a successfully forested reservoir buffer zone by transferring forest management from the central government to the municipal council.

Projects all too often accept a formal administrative structure at face value, rather than analyze the ground-level connections between communities and outside groups. As a result, they end up with decisionmakers who cannot make binding decisions, trainers whose messages are instantly discounted, and community motivators whose main accomplishment is often to motivate the community to reject the project. Field-based social analysis is urgently needed for early project design.

Social Forestry Projects and Project Cycle Issues

Development projects assisted by donors rarely introduce a totally new type of activity. Usually they provide technical know-how, design, and finance to expand or strengthen an ongoing program in the country. The reasons for the success or failure of previous programs in the country (including those supported by other donors) are crucial background for any new project.

Defining the Beneficiary Population

Definition of the target population influences the choice of species, location of nurseries, means of communication selected, and the organizational design—to mention only a few aspects. A few examples will suffice. Herders or people living in drought-prone regions mostly need fodder rather than fuel. If the topography includes both hills and plains, nurseries may need to be located in both areas. If the target population consists mainly of women, female extension workers are crucial. Whether forestry products are to be used for handicrafts, fuelwood, housing material, or cash must be assessed during project preparation.

Needs, Perceptions, Priorities

It would be a banality to say that project design must relate to the needs of the target population were it not so often overlooked, with the resulting design based on an armchair assessment of needs. Such an approach leads only to "surprises" when the project is implemented—for example, the demand for certain types of seedlings is less than estimated.

Local priorities may differ from those of the proposed forestry project. Villagers may see their greatest need as being water or roads, not forest products. Thus, in one Niger project, villagers pulled down trees that had been planted under a Bank-assisted project in order to let their cattle graze freely (Falconer 1987).

Differential needs should not form an insuperable barrier to a project. For example, if the greatest perceived need is for a village water supply, the designers should estimate whether the sale of produce from the proposed village woodlot could help attain that goal while also demonstrating other benefits of tree planting. In Nepal and in some projects in

India, a percentage of the proceeds from community forests are plowed back into reforestation.

Organization

Basic to project success is the design of the organization that is expected to carry it out. Of course, the design cannot be determined by the anthropologist alone, but he or she can make a significant contribution by working closely with foresters, economists, and public administration specialists, particularly by building links between the implementing organization and the beneficiary population. Relations between these two levels can be shaped by anthropologists who are predisposed to "listen to the people," and whose professional training in cultural interpretation, social organizations, and authority and leadership patterns helps them understand what "the people" say.

Although there is general agreement that it is necessary to deal with the priorities of the villagers while promoting forestry, there is much less consensus on how to find out what village priorities are. As discussed throughout this book, anthropologists and sociologists serve a vital role, not just as "bridges" between the people and the project, but as designers of participatory procedures that directly involve people with project planning. A number of successful, small forestry efforts have in effect "cut deals" with local populations, obtaining local labor for the forestry work in return for a capital contribution to a school being built by the community. Being able to set up local negotiating systems invested with power to allocate and manage resources is participation's bottom line.

Implementing Agencies

The organizational forms commonly used for forestry projects span the entire institutional spectrum. They range from the completely integrated approach followed in China and Korea, where professional foresters and other specialists guide and assist rural residents through all stages, to the decentralized approach of Tanzania, where the forest department distributes free seedlings to villagers through extension agents and then leaves the other tasks entirely to the villagers to complete themselves.

The World Bank has tended to use and strengthen official agencies such as forest departments. Although this approach is not universally accepted, there is widespread agreement that forestry projects need government support of some kind: finance, staff, policy declarations, and, where necessary, legislative amendments. Preparation and appraisal teams must satisfy themselves that such official commitment exists.

Unfortunately, however, villagers' relationships with the National Forest Service are often hostile. Forest department employees frequently double as forest guards, enforcing state rights and levying fines over a resource that most villagers regard as legitimately theirs. Lai and Khan's analysis of the policy and institutional background to villager-forester hostility in Mali could easily characterize other countries:

> The Forestry Code was essentially restrictive and punitive, and the accompanying system of permits and fines became the normative structure within which foresters worked. Antagonism rapidly developed between foresters and villagers due to the expropriation of wooded fallow land (considered vacant and without ownership) to create state forests, and due to the emergence of abusive and randomized fining practices. The traditional role of the forester and its negative consequences on forester-villager relationships are key constraints which must be overcome if the forester is to become an effective catalyst in social forestry development (1986, pp. 4–5).

Shepherd (1986) has also pointed out that there is an inherent conflict in most villager-forest department relationships if the forest department is expected to guard state access to standing timber, which can be leased to commercial enterprises, while villagers must plant trees under social forestry projects for their own timber needs. Social forestry projects that do not change this hostile relationship cannot expect to see many trees planted.

Alternatives and complements to official forest departments, which may be inexperienced or understaffed, include using nongovernmental organizations (NGOs). NGOs can often reach into the lowest levels of rural society. Thus, the anthropologist G. F. Murray, writing on a successful tree planting program in Haiti sponsored by the Agency for International Development (AID), says that: One of the central features of this project, and one of its major operational strengths, has been its decision to work outside of the formal governmental structures through which such projects are generally channeled. Our nongovernmental approach is motivating peasants to plant large numbers of trees on their own land with an enthusiasm that may be unique in the annals of tree planting projects around the world. (Murray 1983). NGO disadvantages can include poor organization, inadequate funding, and government hostility (Cernea 1988). Sociologists can help assess whether specific NGOs are viable.

Extension

The weakest aspect of ongoing forestry projects is commonly the extension mechanisms—the contacts with people—especially when the project is implemented by a government's forestry department. The basic conceptual problem is that extension is designed by "sector," whereas the farmer must manage an integrated set of economic activities. Until recently, foresters have not been trained in agricultural extension methods. Furthermore, countless case studies document the prevalence of top-down—and ineffective—extension systems (Falconer 1987, Aguilar (in Agarwal 1986), Sen and Das 1987). Very often, the most successful forestry projects are those that introduce neither new species nor new management systems but that restructure the relationship between the forestry project management and villagers.

Recent World Bank-assisted projects in India have used "motivators," selected villagers who are paid an honorarium to disseminate silvicultural information. One section of the Portuguese forestry department has been trained specifically in extension methods, but this remains the exception. Future forest policy discussions should seek to develop a comprehensive approach that coordinates silvicultural and agricultural activities and methods for the benefit of small farm forestry projects.

Sociological studies, both in India and Africa, have repeatedly pointed out that extension workers tend to concentrate on the more affluent farmers. Forestry projects have paid insufficient attention to social barriers impeding the flow of information. The frequent omission of concerted efforts to contact women directly is even more glaring although their role in forestry is well recognized. It is also well known that in many societies women can be contacted only by women. Few women extension workers are employed in forestry projects—a fact which must be considered at the stage of project preparation, when there is sufficient lead time to arrange for the selection and training of women, to examine whether they should be employed in pairs, and to decide who would convey the message of forestry most efficiently. One successful extension effort in Kenya hired local women on short-term contracts to manage the nurseries. After their contract was finished, they returned to the villages where they became the accepted authorities on forestry.

Local Participation

A major incentive affecting farmer response to social forestry projects is the extent of local involvement in the design and implementation of a project and the linkages between official and local groups. If local participation is to be encouraged, the planners must first accept the validity of local views and incorporate local participation as a regular feature of project formulation and decisionmaking. Planners who assume that people do not know what they want—an assumption that is palpably inaccurate—are guaranteed that the only question about the failure of their projects is how long it will take to happen.

Most important is convincing the people that only they, and not others, will reap the benefits if the trees grow. Land tenure issues play a central role here. External land claims provide strong disincentives to tree planting. Clarifying or modifying land tenure systems is an important activity which well-informed donor agencies can readily undertake as part of project preparation.

Social forestry encourages a readiness on the part of the community to place long-term goals ahead of current needs. Community participation and local leadership must be expressly recognized in the project's organizational arrangements. It is not necessarily the elected leader who is the most efficient, the most influential, or the most respected. Forestry projects often neglect traditional leaders. In one Malawi forestry project, for instance, although traditional organizations were identified, the project did not provide for links between the traditional rural institutions that regulate resource use and the formal forestry organization. In Rwanda, too, there are no formal links between farmer associations or the *umaganda* (traditional labor-sharing) system and the project organization. In one Moroccan forestry project, however, traditional associations are involved in one of the most difficult components of the project: controlling stocking rates and organizing pastoralists into grazing associations responsible for maintaining improved pastures. The tendency in India has been to use the *panchayat*, a locally elected body, as the main medium for community forestry. In some cases, however, these bodies are not very effective and tend to represent the more affluent villagers.

Despite the problems generated by local level stratification, there is a growing trend in forestry projects (especially those backed by NGOs) to transfer most responsibilities directly to participating farmers. The USAID/Energy Council-sponsored project in Sudan found that the most successful and innovative projects were those where foresters advised primarily the farm communities that were assigned the greatest responsibility for nursery and plantation design (Gamser 1987).

Forestry technology can play an important role where different social groups have different needs for forest products. Government forestry plantations and reserves can be designed specifically to meet the needs of the rural poor. Appropriate tree species and management techniques— short rotation shrubs, coppicing and pollarding, and multipurpose specie selection—will help meet the needs of the poor while limiting usurpation by the wealthy.

A more difficult social problem is getting agreement from individuals and groups. When entering into contractual agreements with individuals the most important questions are: Is the agreement simple enough to be understood? Are the rights and obligations of the parties clearly spelled out? Can the terms be enforced consistently? Is there a penalty clause and, if so, is it fair? Groups raise additional but similar questions: How will forest products be distributed? Who will be responsible for management and maintenance, and when? What are the costs? Which items can be collected free of charge, who is to be employed and when? Formal agreements are only as effective as the meaning they convey to the participants. Project agreements must be made in ways that convince the population that the project is theirs. Typically, the more people who can be contacted by project staff, the better. Project authorities must make concerted efforts to involve a broad representation of participants in decisionmaking. Since it is not always possible to involve the entire population directly, projects need a clear-headed community analysis of how to involve local decisionmaking groups—and groups excluded from the local power structure.

Monitoring and Evaluation

The need for a monitoring and evaluation component is more often honored in the breach than in the observance. Furthermore, social forestry projects differ significantly from other agricultural projects in that the benefits normally appear only after the project disbursement period has been completed, when the need for monitoring is no longer perceived. General monitoring should be punctuated by periodic in-depth reviews— a mid-term review at the minimum—to reevaluate the assumptions that fashioned the project's design. These reviews permit project managers to adapt to new conditions or to correct earlier errors, and they provide a balance between overgeneralization and excess precision.

The Road Ahead

The design of forestry projects is being transformed. Through the increasing involvement of sociologists, as well as through a greater willingness to use existing ethnographic sources to learn how environmental resources are managed, much has been learned about how to identify local needs and development opportunities. Successful projects in Haiti, India, and elsewhere have shown that the incentives needed to promote tree cultivation may be both created by carefully planned projects and discovered by prior agronomic, environmental, sociological, or economic research. Good sociological preparation can ensure that these incentives are understood before a project begins.

Social forestry research for the coming decade should concentrate on three main areas. First, the issue of small farm incentives is poorly understood and social forestry projects by and large assume the economic incentives and constraints of small farm production systems rather than empirically unravel them through project design.

Second, the argument presented throughout this volume—that local participation in development projects is a *technical* issue that will lead to better projects—is true for social forestry projects. Participation is not an absolute guarantor of project success, but its absence is a surefire prescription for project failure.

Third, policy dialogues with national governments must concentrate on using field-based research to create a macrolevel policy environment more favorable to small farm forestry. Researchers have repeatedly noted that the contemporary forest policies and institutions found in most developing nations were formed by historical chance with means and ends far removed from those needed today (Shepherd 1986). Neither the King's hunting reserve nor the industrial tree plantation provides useful models for countries whose most pressing need is to aid their small farmers.

Reorienting forest policy to favor rural users is a task that must proceed on many levels. Comparing national tradeoffs between urban-oriented development and development of tree resources; restructuring forest and agricultural extension agencies so that they are seen to aid rather than oppose village interests; redefining legal systems to incorporate the various forms of local land tenure; and redirecting project goals to benefit villagers; these are the processes that must be researched and pursued over the coming decade if social forestry projects are to live up to their potential.

A great deal is known about how and why social forestry projects succeed or fail, and the myriad gradations that separate the two outcomes. Throughout the field there is a grudging but tacit admission that natural resource management is as much a social issue—socially defined, socially created, and socially solved—as a matter of building better technology. Social forestry offers an exciting opportunity for social scientists to collaborate with foresters and policymakers to transform the ways that forestry projects are conceived and executed.

Notes

1. Thanks are due to Michael Cernea, Alice Ingerson, Augusta Molnar, and Raymond Rowe for their perceptive comments on an earlier draft of this paper. John Spears would also like to thank Raymond Noronha, with whom he collaborated in the first edition of *Putting People First.*

2. Overall statistics about the role of shifting cultivation in deforestation can be misleading. For example, whereas the long fallow cycles of swidden cultivators typically allow for forest regrowth (and in some instances swidden type clearing may even be necessary for forest growth), this is rarely true of logger's clearcutting techniques, or forest clearing for building roads. These produce permanently deforested areas.

References

Agarwal, B. 1986. *Cold Hearths and Barren Slopes: The Woodfuel Crisis in the Third World.* London: Zed Books.

Alcorn, J. 1983. *Huastec Mayan Ethnobotany.* Austin: University of Texas Press.

Anderson, Dennis, and Robert Fishwick. 1985. *Fuelwood Consumption in African Countries: A Review.* World Bank Staff Working Paper 704. Washington, D.C.

Ashby, J. 1986. "The Effects of Different Types of Farmer Participation on the Management of On-Farm Trials: A Comparative Evaluation." Muscle Shoals, Alabama: International Fertilized Development Center.

Ben-Salem, B., and Tran Van Nao. 1981. "Fuelwood Production in Traditional Farming Systems." *Unisylva* 33, 11–51.

Brokensha, D., and B. W. Riley. 1978. *Forest Forage, Fences, and Fuel in a Marginal Area of Kenya.* USAID Africa Firewood Workshop, Washington, D.C.: U.S. Agency for International Development.

Broksensha, D., et. al. 1983. *Fuelwood Use in Rural Kenya: Impacts of Deforestation.* Revised draft report. Binghamton, New York: Institute for Development Anthropology.

Byron, R. 1985. *Supply and Demand of Forest Products and Future Development Strategies.* FAO Terminal Report. Rome: Food and Agriculture Organization.

Campbell, J. G. 1978. *Community Involvement in Conservation.* Katmandu, Nepal: United States Agency for International Development.

Campbell, J. G., and T. N. Bhattarai. 1983. *People and Forests in Hill Nepal.* Project Paper 10. Katmandu, Nepal: HMG/UNDP/FAO Community Forestry Development Project.

Cernea, M. 1988. *Nongovernmental Organizations and Local Development.* Discussion Paper 40. Washington, D.C.: World Bank.

Chowdhry, K. 1983. *Social Forestry and the Rural Poor.* Discussion Paper 10. New Delhi: Ford Foundation.

Douglas, J. 1981. *Consumption and Supply of Wood and Bamboo in Bangladesh.* Dacca: FAO/UNDP/Bangladesh Planning Commission.

Dove, M. 1983. "Swidden Agriculture, or the Political Economy of Ignorance." *Agroforestry Systems,* 1:85–89.

———. 1987. "Prospects for Farm Forestry on Rainfed versus Irrigated Farms: Punjab, NWFP, Baluchistan." Report 5. Islamabad, Pakistan, Office of the Inspector General of Forests and Winrock International Technical Assistance Team.

Energy Studies Unit. 1982. *Malawi Smallholder Tree-planting Survey.* Lilongwe, Malawi: Ministry of Forestry and Natural Resources.

Falconer, J. 1987. "Forestry Extension: A Review of the Key Issues." ODI Social Forestry Network Paper. London: Overseas Development Institute.

Fortmann, L. 1984. "The Tree Tenure Factor in Agroforestry with Particular Reference to Africa." *Agroforestry Systems,* 2:231–48.

Fortmann, L., and D. Rocheleau. 1985. "Women and Agroforestry: Four Myths and Three Case Studies." *Agroforestry Systems,* 2(26):253–72.

Gamser, M. 1987. "Letting the Piper Call the Tune: Experimenting with Different Forestry Extension Methods in the Northern Sudan." ODI Social Forestry Network Paper. London: Overseas Development Institute.

Gewald, N. J., and L. A. Ugalde. 1981. *Proyecto Lena y Fuentes Alternas de Energia.* Informe del seminario movil del proyecto lena, realizado en Costa Rica y Nicaragua. Turrialba, Costa Rica: CATIE.

Gliessman, S. R., et al. 1981. "The Ecological Basis for the Application of Traditional Agricultural Technology in the Management of Tropical Agro-ecosystems." *Agroecosystems,* 7:173–85.

Guggenheim, S. 1984. "Farming Systems in Dagua, Colombia." Cali, Colombia: Centro Internacional de Agricultura Tropical.

Hecht, S. B., A. B. Anderon, and P. May. 1988. "The Subsidy from Nature: Shifting Cultivation, Successional Palm Forests, and Rural Development." *Human Organization,* 47(1):25–35.

Hoskins, M. W. 1983. "Rural Women, Forest Outcasts, and Forestry Products." Draft. Food and Agriculture Organization, Rome.

Hyman, E. L. 1983. "Pulpwood Tree-farming in the Philippines from the Viewpoint of Smallholders: An Ex-post Evaluation of the PICOP Project." *Agricultural Administration,* 14:23–49.

Inglis, A. 1988. "Rural Women and Urban Men: Fuelwood Conflicts and Forest Sustainability in Sussex Village, Sierra Leone." ODI Social Forestry Network Paper. London: Overseas Development Institute.

Jones, J. F. 1982. *Diagnostico Socioeconomico sobre el consumo y produccion de lena en fincas pequenas de la peninsula de Azuero, Panama.* Turrialba, Costa Rica: CATIE.

Lai, C. K., and A. Khan. 1986. "Mali as a Case Study of Forest Policy in the Sahel: Institutional Constraints on Social Forestry." ODI Social Forestry Network Paper. London: Overseas Development Institute.

Lehmann, D. 1986. "Two Paths of Agrarian Capitalism, or a Critique of Chayanovian Marxism." *Comparative Studies in Society and History,* 28(4):601–27.

Lundgren, B. 1982. "The Use of Agro-forestry to Improve the Productivity of Converted Tropical Land." Draft. Office of Technology Assessment, U.S. Congress, Washington, D.C.

Molnar, A. 1987. "Review of Rapid Appraisal Methods for Use in Community Forestry." Forest Department. Food and Agriculture Organization, Rome.

———. 1986. "Social Forestry Experience in India and Nepal: A Review of Community Woodlots, the Involvement of Women, and the Introduction of Wood-saving devices in Various Projects." World Bank, Asia-Technical Department, Washington, D.C.

———. 1988. "Women and Social Forestry Issues." World Bank, Asia-Technical Department, Washington, D.C.

Murray, G. F., 1983. "Haitian Peasant Tree Planters: An Anthropological Solution to an Environmental Problem." Gainesville, Florida: Anthropology Department, University of Florida.

Nair, P. K. R. 1984. *Soil Productivity: Aspects of Agroforestry.* Nairobi: International Center for Research on Agroforestry.

Okigbo, B.N., and D. Greenland. 1977. *Intercropping Systems in Traditional Africa.*

Openshaw, K., and J. Moris. 1979. *The Socio-economics of Agro-forestry.* Morogoro, Tanzania: University of Dar es Salaam.

Padoch, C., C. Inoma, J. Jong, and J. Unruh. 1985. "Amazonian Agro-forestry: A market oriented system in Peru." *Agroforestry Systems,* 3:47–59.

Posey, D. 1985. "Indigenous Management of Tropical Forest Systems." *Agroforestry Systems,* 3:139–59.

Raintree, J. B. 1985. *Agro-forestry, Tropical Land Use and Tenure.* Background paper prepared for the International Workshop on Tenure Issues, May 21–27. Nairobi: International Center for Research on Agroforestry.

Rocheleau, D. E. 1984. "Criteria for Re-appraisal and Re-design: Intra-household and Between-household Aspects of FSRE in Three Kenyan Agroforestry Projects." Paper presented at the Annual Farming Systems Research and Extension Symposium, Kansas State University, Manhattan, Kansas.

Sen, D., and P. K. Das. 1987. "The Management of People's Participation in Community Forestry: Some Issues." ODI Social Forestry Network Paper. London: Overseas Development Institute.

Shepherd, G. 1988. "The Reality of the Commons: Answering Hardin from Somalia." ODI Social Forestry Network Paper. London: Overseas Development Institute.

————. 1986. *Forest Policies, Forest Politics*. ODI Social Forestry Network Paper 3. London: Overseas Development Institute.

Shiva, V. et al. 1982. "Social Forestry: No Solution Within the Market." *Ecologist*, 12(14):158–68.

van Gelder and P. Kerkhof. 1984. *The Agroforestry Survey in Kakemega District*. Working Paper 3. Kenya Woodfuel Development Program, Nairobi.

Spears, J. 1988. *Containing Tropical Deforestation: A Review of Priority Areas for Technological and Policy Research*. Working Paper 10. World Bank, Environment Department, Washington, D.C.

Ugalde, A. L. and H. Gregerson. 1986. "Incentives for Tree Growing in Relation to Deforestation and the Fuelwood Crisis in Central America." United States Agency for International Development, San Jose, Costa Rica.

Weber, F., and M. Hoskins. 1983. "Agro-forestry in the Sahel. University of Virginia, Department of Sociology, Charlottesville.

Wiersum, K. F., and C. P. Veer. 1983. "Loan Financing of Smallholder Treefarming in Ilocos, a Comment." *Agroforestry Systems*, 1(4):361–65.

Wiersum, K. F., ed. 1984. *Viewpoints on Agroforestry*, Department of Forestry, Agriculture University, Wageningen, Netherlands.

Wilken, G.C. 1978. "Integrating Forest and Small Scale Farm Systems in Middle America." Draft.

World Bank. 1984. *Fuelwood Consumption and Deforestation in African Countries*. World Bank Staff Working Paper 704. Washington D.C.

10

The Social Actors of
Participatory Afforestation Strategies

Michael M. Cernea

When government agencies launch programs that attempt financially to induce development, the key difficulty soon becomes a social one: *how* to generate and sustain the *involvement of the social actors*, the people who give life to the project?

If such involvement is indeed to be stimulated and organized, then the grandstanding but fuzzy rhetorical pledges to "people's participation" must give way to the precise identification of *who* "the people" are and *how* they are *organized* for development action. In this light, the present chapter discusses policy and operational options for improving current social forestry strategies by enhancing the role of self-managed *groups* and grass roots organizations as vehicles for people's participation in forestry.

Participatory strategies in social forestry must aim at engaging the rural *users* of fuelwood in organized action for *producing* and *managing* forestry resources. Such strategies should elicit a mass shift from simple *gathering* to *cultivating*. In forestry development, as often in natural resource management, strategies are needed that would, first, organize the individual users of natural resources into *groups* and second, enable such groups to act *as producers* and *managers* in order to generate increased benefits for themselves.

Social forestry programs, if properly conceived, can become a mechanism for establishing producer *groups* as social actors, that is, creating enduring units of social organization. Such enduring groups or units are particularly important in the case of afforestation strategies, given the long production cycle that requires structured support over an extended time.

These social strategy issues are addressed in this chapter under seven sections. The first section discusses the social-cultural prerequisites of participatory forestry programs. The next two sections focus on land tenure variables in forestry development, particularly under conditions of common property ownership or joint usufruct rights on state lands. The case of Azad Kashmir is used to highlight the subtle and pervasive process of privatization of the commons; the three key stages of this process—(a) informal partitioning, (b) incremental appropriation, and (c) formal privatization—are identified. The fourth section concentrates on the definition of social actors and the role of self-managing groups in sociologically guided strategies for reforestation. The disappointing performance of "communities" as agents of community woodlot schemes in many World Bank–assisted programs is discussed in the fifth part. The last two sections explore and recommend options to replace the elusive and unfocused community woodlots either with family-centered strategies, or with group-centered reforestation strategies. The latter would rely on alternative units of social organization such as group farm forestry, tree growers' associations, age groups, women's groups, watershed forestry, and so forth. Sometimes such social structures already exist and need to be strengthened; at other times they need to be created anew as a social scaffolding able to sustain purposive collective action.

The Social Premises of Reforestation Programs

What is *social* in social forestry?

The term "social" almost never appears in the language used by development practitioners to describe agricultural programs. One conspicuous exception, however, is social forestry development. Who introduced the term "social?" And *why* this exception? In other words, what is social about afforestation programs?

Defining Social Forestry

The concept of *social forestry* as a strategy in forestry work was introduced at least as early as 1973 in India, where precise goals were set for the new approach.[1] Since then, a broad consensus has developed about the content of social forestry. The current concept of *social* forestry recognizes that such programs must be so designed as to (a) motivate large numbers of *people* to plant trees, (b) promote the kind of tree growing that will best supply fuelwood, small timber, grasses, and income to the small producers themselves, and (c) provide increased benefits to the poorer strata. Social forestry programs are primarily aimed at involving the farmers and the landless. They attempt to influence the key variable—a variable usually bypassed in the design of conventional afforestation programs: people's *behavior* toward trees.

Furthermore, the *social* in social forestry should be understood to signify a broader meaning than *individual* behavioral change alone: it includes collective action, institutional development, and the establishment of enduring social structures and value systems that activate and organize individual actors.

While commercial or industrial forestry programs are not a recent invention, social forestry projects are. Under the conventional type of industrial forestry program, business corporations or government agencies hire laborers to establish plantations on large tracts of land that the businesses or agencies control; the wood is harvested for use in industry or construction. The alternative approach, *social* forestry, is to induce a large number of small farmers to plant fuelwood trees systematically for their own needs and on their own (and other available) lands. Foresters gradually come to recognize that behavioral and cultural (not just technical) changes are needed to intensify reforestation. By definition, social forestry programs demand massive farmer participation and rise or fall depending on whether or not the farmers engage in the program.

From Gathering to Producing

The social innovation called for through social forestry programs appears formidable indeed if contrasted with the long history of the patterned behavior of *gathering* fuelwood.

Humankind long ago moved out of the hunting and gathering era in virtually all respects except the procurement of fuelwood (and, to some extent, fishing). Throughout history, rural populations in general have been foraging for their fuelwood in naturally grown forests.

This continues today. While many members of the global human society have substituted the use of fuelwood for heating and cooking needs with other energy sources, a large part of the world population continues to use wood as fuel. How do these users obtain their fuelwood? Now, as in earlier times, essentially by *gathering*, and not by *cultivating*. By and large, for the bulk of their fuelwood needs, people have cut naturally grown trees and relied on the *spontaneous* regeneration of trees, without *systematically* planting trees for fuelwood over large areas.

The current challenge, of global proportions, requires a shift from merely gathering trees to cultivating them. How this can be done is shown clearly by the major exception to the pattern of tree gathering: humans long ago learned to domesticate, cultivate, and propagate fruit trees. Fruit trees are now incorporated in various agricultural strategies, while wood for fuel continues to be acquired mostly by cutting natural forests and gathering. Given need, scarcity, and certain prerequisites and incentives, "gatherers" can shift to cultivating fuelwood for themselves and for the market. Such a historic shift may take generations, but large masses of fuelwood users must become *producers*-cum-users.

Several factors underscore the urgency of the problem. The world's looming energy crisis has turned the spotlight on three fundamental facts. First, over 3 billion people, the majority of humankind, still rely on fuelwood as the main source of cheap everyday energy. Second, in the tropics, the annual rate of deforestation currently exceeds the rate of reforestation through natural regeneration and plantation combined. Steady environmental degradation and fuelwood shortages of virtual crisis proportions have already struck many countries or extended regions of them, particularly in Asia and Africa. Developing countries account for 75 percent of the world's population, but only for about 50 percent of the forests. Africa and Latin America have nearly 2 hectares of forest per person, while Asia has less than 0.2 hectares per capita. Third, current and projected increases in population and food needs cause accelerated shrinkage of forested areas because of conversion to agriculture. There is a growing awareness that, without new and vast worldwide planting, the present use-rate of forest resources will accelerate deforestation and cause a worldwide fuelwood scarcity.

The advent of what are now called *social* forestry programs and policies on a worldwide scale could be regarded as part of the growing global response to that threat. Such programs were strongly recommended by the 1978 World Forestry Congress, by the forestry policy paper issued the same year by the World Bank, and by national agencies in some countries.[2]

The *social* innovations fostered through such policies are two-pronged. They attempt both to involve large groups of people in the *conservation* and better management of existing forests and, since this alone would not be enough, to stimulate the widespread adoption of a "new" productive activity: the systematic planting of trees for fuel.

Collective Action and Group Formation

Several social prerequisites must be met if these innovations are to succeed. Financial investments alone, however large, cannot make such programs a success. These prerequisites go beyond the dynamics of individual adoption of innovations to lay the ground for the more complex processes of *collective* adoption. In social science research, although the adoption of innovations by individuals has been subjected to much investigation (spearheaded by Rogers and others[3]), the *collective* adoption of innovation, as correctly pointed out by West,[4] has received far less attention and needs to be understood better for many development purposes.

By collective adoption I understand not a mere aggregate of many acts of innovation adoption by atomistic individuals, but a process of inter-linkage among individuals and their purposive action for achieving a new common objective. Processes such as reforestation, environmental protection, watershed rehabilitation, and in general the group protection and management of natural resources, depend largely on collective action and collective innovation. Therefore, a development program must often trigger collective action among its target group, rather than only discrete individual responses to the program.

But how can this be accomplished?

Collective actions have the highest chance to occur and be effective when people belong to organized groups, when they are informed and consciously perceive that it is in their best interests to act purposively in a coordinated manner, and when the group has developed leadership structures and internal norms and procedures suitable to organize and manage its members and to overcome conflicts and deviant behavior. The common position of many people as direct *users* of a certain resource is a propitious social condition that often turns itself spontaneously, and can certainly be turned deliberately, into a powerful motivating and organizing force for *producing* the needed resource. The deliberate construction of user groups is, therefore, particularly important for using and husbanding a common pool resource in programs such as afforestation or irrigation, which depend on sustained, long-term consensual action by many individual actors.

When an innovative program is deliberately pursued, a unit of social organization to sustain that program features centrally among the social prerequisites for success. Therefore, afforestation strategies or projects must start with the identification (or the establishment) of such a viable unit or group; aim to engage the rural users of fuelwood in patterns of collective action for producing the fuelwood they need; tend to ensure a match between the sylvicultural technologies they promote and the social groups they address; and deal with the issues of *social* engineering (group formation, leadership, participation in decisionmaking, intragroup structures, incentives, penalties, communication, benefit distribution, and so on) with the same scrupulous attention given to the technical or financial elements of the strategy.

Group formation is an acute need particularly in development programs that involve (even to a small extent) natural resources that are either (a) under a common property regime or (b) lend themselves to group management even if they are under a state property regime. To ensure both the immediate use and the long-term renewal and sustainability of a commonly owned natural resource, the owners must act in consensus as a group that subjects itself to the same norms. In order to act as a group, they need to *be* a social group, not a simple set of unlinked individuals. Intragroup connections are forms of mutual conditioning, mutual help, and mutual control. The absence of structures and strictures leaves open the way to unchecked, contradictory, and counterproductive individual behavior such as free riding. This is the opposite of common property as a social construct and leads to the destruction of the natural resource itself.

Unfortunately, the planners of financially induced social forestry programs often do not yet realize that consideration of these social factors has to be woven into the very fabric of such programs from the outset. There is often a contradiction between the theory and the practice of social forestry and "many projects that are called social forestry are a far cry from the theoretical vision of social forestry."[5] The penalty for ignoring the social factors is project failure.

Practical recipes for *how* to incorporate these social prerequisites into action plans are not readily available. Culturally informed forestation strategies have to be produced, tailored, and retailored anew for each socioecological context. For that, foresters, planners, and action-oriented sociologists and anthropologists have to cooperate, search, predict, design, test, monitor, learn, redesign, and retest to combine effectively the technical and social approaches into coherent reforestation programs (see chapter 9). In the quest for creative *new* solutions, much of the already existing sociological know-how can be mobilized and used as a stepping stone to action, testing, and new knowledge. There is no justification for sociologically illiterate social forestry programs.

Land Tenure and the Anatomy of Trial and Error

To illustrate some of these issues, this section analyzes a case in which good intentions to experiment and innovate were not backed up by the necessary social knowledge. The case exhibits the fallacies of planning without an in-depth sociological understanding of the socioeconomic forces spontaneously at work and without a social strategy for translating goals into collective action.

Salient sociological factors are always at work, and forcefully so, under the thin layer of the "new reality" temporarily constructed by the financial inflows of the program; if these salient factors are not deliberately considered, they trigger unanticipated consequences. Such factors in the case of afforestation are: the existing land ownership system and the usufruct rights system; the local power and authority system; farmers' traditional attitudes and behavior regarding tree planting; and the absence of social structures for collective action aimed at reforestation.

Our case consists of two successive World Bank–assisted projects in the same area over a period of ten years: the first was the pilot forestry program under the Azad Kashmir Hill Farming Technical Development Project (HFTDP) in Pakistan, which started in 1978.[6] The second was the follow-up project, called the Azad Kashmir Integrated Hill Farming Development Project (IHFDP), which started in 1984 to continue into 1990.[7]

The lack of a preproject sociological study in the HFTDP (as is known, field-based socioanthropological research in Azad Kashmir had been discouraged by state authorities during the preceding twenty to thirty years) paved the way for false design assumptions about land tenure. The project strategy predicated on these assumptions backfired.

A sociological analysis, undertaken at the mid-term of the first project revealed the array of unanticipated consequences that had built up during the implementation process. The following summary of that sociological analysis[8] shows why seeing the people beyond the trees should be the first commandment in social forestry.

The Hill Farming Technical Development Project (HFTDP) was started in 1978 in Azad Jammu and Kashmir as a test of new approaches to several agricultural subsectors, with the intention of replicating the successful ones in a subsequent larger project. The pilot forestry component was one of the first explicit *social forestry* interventions assisted by the World Bank. It financed fuelwood planting, testing of new tree species under local conditions, and the establishment of nurseries for supplying seedlings; this component was included as a result of the area's alarming deforestation and environmental deterioration, both demographically and culturally driven. It intended to involve the participation of local communities and to benefit primarily the small farmers.

Increasing demand for fuelwood and timber had caused large-scale deforestation in Azad Kashmir over the preceding thirty years. In 1972, about 1.5 million residents, or 300,000 families, relied entirely on gathering fuelwood for cooking and heating. At the local high rate of population growth (3 percent annually), the population will double by the year 2000. Pressure on government forests is increasing as people cut trees both for fuel and for clearing forest land for farming (through illegal encroachments).

Both the formal regulations (enacted under British colonial rule[9]) and the old customary rules in Azad Kashmir have allowed rural inhabitants to remove deadwood, branches, and noncommercial species from reserved forests without payment, primarily for personal consumption. Both the formal and customary systems allowed and regulated wood gathering, but did not demand cultivating. In practice, however, customary user rights have been very liberally interpreted and broadened, while the use-limits set through formal regulations have been transgressed. Within a radius of several miles from many human settlements, virtually all trees were debranched beyond the limits set by sylvicultural recommendations. In many locations only the top ten to twenty percent of the crown of trees remains. Outright topping has also occurred and prematurely killed the trees. In the Chir pine areas, long, thin vertical slices of the bole of the tree are removed at stump level for home lighting. Roadside trees are similarly molested. On community lands, open access and the absence of community management have fully consumed the tree cover.

Forest resources have also been devastated by local livestock allowed to graze without adequate controls. The situation is aggravated by the transhumant livestock of seminomadic populations coming from Punjab and the North-West Frontier Province to use the Azad Kashmir alpine rangeland during summer.

Under such circumstances, the Forest Department needed the cooperation and support of the area population to stop and reverse deforestation. Instead, however, it got into open conflict with many local inhabitants. When the project started, over 50,000 cases of forest offenses were pending in the Azad Kashmir courts. This amounted to about one family in six involved in an alleged forest offense.[10] Farmers were reluctant to participate in reforestation schemes and were suspicious of the Forest Department.

Far-reaching changes were therefore required, both to improve the management of existing forests and to reforest depleted areas, if the increasing fuelwood demand was to be met.

In preparing the HFTDP's forestry component, the technical experts estimated the average annual consumption of firewood per family at two to four tons, amounting to some 800,000 tons in total.[11] The scale of reforestation needed to produce this supply was estimated at 330,000 to 400,000 fully planted and well-managed acres. At the cost of establishing fuelwood plantations (then about 2,000 rupees an acre), such a program would have incurred expenditures far beyond the available government resources. The government therefore needed to examine the extent to which the private users of fuelwood could contribute to these costs.

When the pilot project was prepared, it was thought that social support for the program (contributions from private users) could be blended with public support (government financing). Accordingly, the strategy was designed to experiment with both the technical and the social variables of developing forestry, particularly to involve local users in planting and maintenance. Community acceptance was regarded as crucial for the project's success. The government was to finance the establishment of four nurseries (at Patika, Kotli, Hajira, and Bagh) to produce seedlings for sale at a low price to the area farmers. The government was also prepared to finance the costs of planting trees in several communities on common property lands in order to work out a model replicable by other communities and benefiting primarily the small farmers.

The project design was based on a set of assumptions made by technicians and planners about the tenure of the land to be reforested,

about community processes, and about farmers' willingness to participate. In hindsight, these assumptions appear rather naive and uninformed.

Lacking a sociological field analysis, the appraisal report relied on
explanations about land tenure offered by local officials to the members
of the appraisal team. The report vaguely identified *shamilat* land as
"land generally left uncultivated, owned jointly by a number of families."[12] It took the official description of shamilat land at face value, as
community land, over which alledgedly all villagers had decisionmaking
authority as well as rights to share in its use. The appraisal report
estimated the existing shamilat areas to be a major resource, totaling
some 325,000 acres. This was equivalent to more than half the total
farmed area in Azad Kashmir, then about 500,000 acres.

Based on these estimates, the project was set to finance the pilot
planting of 3,000 acres of fuelwood, mainly on shamilat land; only a small
proportion was expected to be planted on government or private lands.

The key assumption was that the village communities would act as the
social units supporting the pilot fuelwood plantations. Community consent was expected to make portions of shamilat land available for tree
planting. Another explicit assumption was that the community institutions would mobilize community members' investments in fuelwood
planting in the form of labor, payments for seedlings, tree protection, or
other contributions toward reforestation costs, in exchange for which the
project would generate tangible benefits for the people involved. The
beneficiaries of project-financed planting on common land were expected to be the small farmers who otherwise faced constraints in their
access to scarce firewood. The community structures were assumed to
be strong enough to enforce the temporary closing of reforested areas to
prevent indiscriminate grazing and protect the tree seedlings.

Thus, typical features of "social forestry" were conspicuous in the
project's design. The project was setting goals that required farmers to
modify their economic behavior. The question was: would the target
communities and individual farmers respond as expected?

During the first project year the physical reforestation target was met,
the nurseries were established, and the project identified 100 acres of
community and private land, in addition to government lands. The project
staff reported that the owners and users of the private and community
land agreed to allocate the lands for fuelwood plantation, although no
formal contract was signed.

For the second year, the project had an increased planting target of 1,250 acres. Other landowners came forward and volunteered their nonarable lands for tree plantations, and the project staff tentatively identified for planting about 750 acres of commons and private land and 500 acres of government land. This was a larger proportion of nongovernmental land than had even been optimistically assumed at appraisal. The farmers' response seemed to suggest that significant tracts of community (shamilat) and private lands could be incorporated into the fuelwood production circuit.

Given the pilot nature of this project, its sociocultural aspects received more attention during implementation than was usually given to comparable projects. I was asked to undertake a social analysis of the progress of the forestry component between 1978 and 1980, to ascertain the mechanisms of community contributions in land and labor for fuelwood plantation, and of distribution of the expected benefits. Significantly, this social analysis was not triggered by a crisis, nor by slow progress, but was initiated to examine what seemed to be a successful project advance.

The study assessed the socioeconomic status of the farmers reached by the reforestation component; determined the tenurial status of the lands involved in the project in the first two years and estimated the likely beneficiaries; and evaluated the procedures used in implementation, as well as the communication between the project staff and the farmers. Attention was also paid to the mechanisms of community decisionmaking and to the envisaged distribution of expected profits from the forestry investments. Part of this study's findings follow.

There was also considerable serendipity in this research: the study uncovered a historical process not known and conceptualized previously. It established how a considerable part of the common land was privatized and how surreptitious and gradual encroachments over time into state forest lands caused the shrinkage of forested areas.

The Privatization of the Commons

The analysis of the tenure system in Azad Kashmir showed that there were three basic legal categories of lands:

- *Khalsa* (*khalisa*) or crown land,[13] is land that is "reserved," land unassigned and unencumbered by title; the authority over this land is vested in the government. Khalsa land usually consists of "de-marcated" and "undemarcated" forests.[14]

- *Shamilat* land is land that is attached to the communities or their members and derives its name from the concept of "getting to-gether." These lands are used as grazing areas, forests, sites for village public buildings, village graveyards, and so on.
- *Malkiat* land is privately owned. Ownership rights are recorded in the revenue register and are validated by it.

The field assessment of the status of specific land plots discovered, in addition, significant differences between the legal or formal status of the lands as recorded in the land register and the de facto situation.

Contrary to expectations, what was called shamilat land appeared to be, for the most part, not true *community* land. Over time, cumulative changes in most of Azad Kashmir had resulted in a dual, divergent de jure and de facto status. Although shamilat continues in principle to be considered common property land, in real life much of it is operated and used as private land. Usufruct benefits from this land are now accessible to selected individuals, rather than to the whole community. There is no pattern and mechanism of community management, neither on the re-maining patches of joint shamilat, nor, obviously, on those patches appropriated by individuals.

Thus, the sociological inquiry invalidated a basic assumption made when tree planting on shamilat land was originally planned. The different tenure was likely to cause unanticipated consequences of the planting program, mainly by diverting the intended flow of benefits away from the target population.

How did this major change in tenure come about?

Historically, shamilat land was set apart for joint possession and use by a village as pasture, graveyard, woodlot, or a location for drinking water facilities for people and cattle. Sometimes, administrative "muta-tions" of khalsa wastelands into shamilat released the land either to village landholders as a group for common use, or directly to certain individuals. After a while, such conversions were recognized and enacted retroactively (thus legalizing de facto encroachments), or were pre-scribed through government decisions like the *Ailan* (Proclamation) of 1927, which sanctioned several subclasses of shamilat.[15] The village's shamilat was not necessarily one consolidated plot; rather, more fre-quently the village shamilat consisted of several plots of land located at various distances from the core settlement. The shamilat plots had often both different uses and users. Villagers located closer to one or another plot (or side) of the commons became its more frequent users and sometimes encroachers. Increasing needs and uneven family abilities in using shamilat resources asserted themselves over time. Patterns of differential use and access gradually crystallized, and subtle modifications in the actual status of various plots cumulated into major changes.

Three broad historical stages in the evolving condition of shamilat can be roughly distinguished over time:

- *Informal partitioning.* Village families whose farmed land directly adjoined the shamilat areas became gradually associated with the use of specific sections of shamilat, thus beginning in practice, though informally, an allocation of common land among themselves. Population increase from generation to generation and a nonexclusionary (at least for male offspring) inheritance system led toward gradual de facto partitionings of family lands and also caused increased pressures on commonly held parcels.

  Within the traditional institution of *brotherhood*, which allowed each one of a number of peasants linked together by common ancestry to have distinguishable, individual, separate possession of the land he cultivated, the plots of partitioned farming land were not necessarily equal. This entailed uneven uses of the land held jointly (shamilat) by the members of a whole brotherhood or by a subdivision of it. Strong group entitlements were gradually eroded by recurrent individual use, and recurrent use evolved into privileged use. In the process, the smaller and more remotely located farms were left out of this informal, gradual partitioning of shamilat lands.

- *Incremental appropriation.* Although the land laws formally forbid co-sharers of shamilat to encroach on it for private exclusive use, farms adjoining shamilat or powerful village families nevertheless began to illegally take over segments of community lands and even to cultivate them.[16] Increasing socioeconomic differentiation and stratification processes within the communities subverted the unity of community interests and institutional arrangements and increasingly weakened the communities' ability to defend the commons against private appropriation. Power played a role in the use, control, and appropriation of the jointly held land, as it did in reinforcing and expanding inequality in the ownership of disproportionate shares of farming land.[17] Some shamilat tracts were customarily transferred through inheritance or sale of fractions of the privately owned (malkiat) adjacent areas. Thus, these malkiat lands carried with them more or less recognized "rights" to proportionate fractions of the shamilat plots.

Even as this de facto appropriation was advancing, most shamilat lands maintained their status in formal terms as common lands and were not entered in the revenue records as belonging to private families. As a result, the benefiting families did not have to pay land taxes on "their" shamilat plots. At the same time, khalsa lands as well were gradually encroached and portions were appropriated for unauthorized private cultivation (this kind of encroachment was called *Nautor*[18]).

- *Formal privatization.* During the 1960s and 1970s, the pressure grew to have shamilat plots *formally* entered in revenue records in the names of the families who appropriated them; the goal of these families was, and is, to have such lands validated as privately owned lands. With community power weakened, the last line of defense of the formal status of shamilat as commons shifted to the state administrative power, as custodian of the land records in which shamilat was officially registered.

However, the government also yielded to pressure, both incrementally and locally as well as through two sudden and general formal decisions. One was the Shamilat-Deh Act of 1966, which formally allowed up to 75 percent of the shamilat area to be used by private landowners, while only 20 percent was "to be reserved for common purposes of villages."[19] The second was the government's 1974 Land Registration Ordinance which gave legal recognition to most of the unauthorized use of land (Nautor).[20]

In 1974, the tax on land was abolished in Pakistan. Subsequently, the pressure and the illegal encroachment on both shamilat and khalsa increased further. The interested families resorted to various means, many illegal, to change the formal registration of tracts of both shamilat and khalsa lands.

Through such processes, the nature of the commons as a property regime has been considerably changed in large areas of Azad Kashmir, with village communities progressively losing control, de jure or de facto, over land resources they previously owned and used. The physical extent of the commons has altogether shrunk, even though the historical process of partitioning, appropriating, and privatizing community land has advanced at uneven speeds in various areas of Azad Kashmir. For instance, significant differences in land registration and tenure remain between Mirpur and Poonch districts; some Azad Kashmir areas still maintain considerable pieces of shamilat as true community possessions.

Overall, the historical cycle described above is continuing. Its creeping advancement is facilitated both by certain regulations and by backdoor influence or corruption. In the colorful words of a former senior Azad Kashmir official, the 1974 Land Regulation Ordinance was

> a legislative disaster (that) . . . opened the floodgates of encroachments. . . . The result was that brazen-faced encroachments were made into the very heart of forest lands. Here was an opportunity for unscrupulous revenue officers to oblige friends and relatives or make hay while the sun shone at the cost of rich forests and vegetative covering of hills.[21]

Against the backdrop of such incremental but profound historical changes in the land tenure system, it becomes understandable why the staff of the first pilot project (HFTDP) was not able to identify larger areas of genuine community land for project financed reforestation. On close inspection, I found that the planting reported by project staff to be on shamilat land turned out in fact to be on land under individual private control. Social analysis revealed that the tracts of shamilat land that had been offered for planting—and assumed by the project staff to benefit the communities—had surreptitiously changed their tenurial status to become private land. The de facto owners hoped to get "their" shamilat lands planted at government expense, without making repayment commitments. No community decisionmaking was involved and no community woodlot was established. Wherever there were still some genuine communally used plots of land, the communities did not come forward to offer them in support of reforestation, but preferred to save them for other uses.

The community forestry component, based on inaccurate assumptions and lacking from the outset a social structure to sustain it, couldn't accomplish its "community" objectives, even though overall the first pilot project did stimulate reforestation work.

Further analysis of the set of farmers who offered their private (malkiat) land for project reforestation and of the farmers who were in control of the nominally shamilat plots revealed that *the larger* landholders tended to take advantage of the project. The wealthiest landowners, who have the resources to contribute to the costs of establishing and protecting tree stands, had not done so, nor did they intend to do so in the future. At one of the reforestation sites, I found that the main part of the 100 acres planted in the first year belonged to one influential family of six brothers, only one of whom was "almost" a full-time farmer, while the others were absentee landlords operating shops and small enterprises in Muzaffarabad. Another landowner, who offered about 125 acres of land for planting in the second project year, flatly refused to contribute any payment. He justified his position by arguing that "the government of an Islamic country should provide for its citizens." A third large farmer, who wanted his fifty-six acres planted, asked for government-paid guards to protect the plantation and to restrict the access and customary rights of smaller farmers to collect grass and tree branches.[22]

The smaller farmers hesitated to accept project planting on their private lands. They were fearful of losing possession or control over their land to the government once it was planted by the Forest Department, or of being deprived of rights to collect fodder and graze their cattle. Most of the smaller farmers interviewed indicated that they might offer small plots for project planting, provided they could be convinced that the Forest Department would not alienate their lands and that they would be able to cut grass for their cattle.

In significant contrast, the larger landowners did not perceive tree planting by the Forest Department as a threat to their ownership of land and trees because they were confident of their political power. They tended to manipulate available project opportunities and resources to their own benefit. Their attempt was facilitated by the absence of a legal definition of the obligations, not merely the rights, of the large farmers whose land was being reforested through government contribution. The absence of a *contract* with the project or the Forest Department left a huge loophole that enabled the large landowners to avoid making contributions.[23]

The findings of the sociological analysis were considered operationally right away. They led to midstream changes in the forestry component of the HFTDP and generated several lessons of broader validity. The project's management was asked to reexamine the plots identified for fuelwood planting and to stop planting on fictitious shamilat land. During the following year the project resurveyed the 800 acres of allegedly community and private lands that had been identified initially for planting, and retained only 400 acres, of which only 25 acres were shamilat land. The intent was to prevent the slide of the pilot project into a full "giveaway" program, before a cost-sharing system could be designed. The funds left available were redirected in the short run to planting on khalsa land. The project's selection of private (malkiat) plots for experimental planting with fast-growing species was more emphatically oriented toward the smaller farms. However, it proved impossible in midstream to maintain priority for reforestation on communal lands and, according to the ex-post evaluation report, the fuelwood plantations on shamilat land ended up being the smallest fraction (15 percent) in the total area, compared to planting on khalsa (30 percent) and on malkiat (55 percent).[24] Moreover, various delays cumulated and the pilot project initially planned for three years took some six and a half years to complete.

Nevertheless, in addition to making possible immediate corrections in the ongoing pilot project, the sociological analysis prevented the initial pilot approach, based on wrong assumptions, from being extrapolated on a much larger scale as originally intended. The practical failure proved (more convincingly than intellectual arguments) that social analysis should have been carried out earlier, namely at the time of project preparation and appraisal, when it could have steered the pilot project on a path consistent with the local social landscape.

Though done relatively late, the social analysis was nevertheless instrumental and consequential.

When the follow-up Integrated Hill Farming Development Project (IHFDP) in Azad Kashmir was appraised in 1983, an attempt was made to avoid the earlier errors with regard to forestry. The IHFDP appraisal report stated that in the new project "overcoming the *social* constraints to a systematic hill development program would constitute the real challenge."[25] It recognized that most hillsides were controlled under various tenure systems of private land, government forests, and community land (shamilat), and that the land plots under these systems were intermixed.

Since a hillside is a natural ecosystem that must be treated as such, the new project concluded that it was of little use to implement conservation measures on one part of the hill when runoff from another part remained unchecked at the same time. Consequently, the new project began to pursue agreements (contracts) between the individual owners in each catchment area (or relevant communities) and the government; the objections of their contracts were to the definition, acceptance, and implementation of "hill management plans," based on specified cost- and benefit-sharing arrangements.

Since strong sustaining structures within the farming communities were neither identified nor established in the available time, the IHFDP is currently being implemented mainly by government departments in a rather paternalistic, top-down manner; some 9,000 acres are to be planted with fuelwood species on hillsides and additional land is being planted to coniferous species within demarcated state forest areas. Additionally, IHFDP is promoting an alternative approach to reforestation—"farm forestry" (discussed below)—that encourages farmers to plant within, or near to, their homesteads; the project finances the distribution of 12 million seedlings free as an incentive for such planting.

In summary, the sociological analysis discussed above brought three sets of social variables into the limelight: the complex land tenure system and the processes affecting it; the community as a cluster of nonhomogeneous groups, with differential access to "common" goods and limitations on consensual action; and the behavioral patterns of individual farmers.

It bears repeating that no social forestry project can be conceived and prepared without the in-depth and timely recognition of at least these three sets of social variables.

Designing Strategies around Social Actors

The variables discussed in connection with the Azad Kashmir project have relevance far beyond this specific case. So do the findings about common property erosion and privatization processes. Sociologists and foresters together should translate such findings into learned guidance for future action.

The most critical factor in designing the social strategy of forestry programs is, in my view, the adequate identification of the *unit of social organization* able to carry out the program and the definition of the conditions under which this unit (the social actor) can act effectively. Many ongoing forestry projects have lumped together, under the broad umbrella of "social" or "community" forestry, different objectives with vague or unfocused appeals to heterogeneous or undefined populations. This is bound to result (as it did in the Azad Kashmir Project) in an ambiguous (or even mistaken) definition of the social unit which could perform the intended activities.

Contributing to this insufficient clarity are the loosely defined concepts of community forestry used by some national or international development agencies. For instance, FAO has defined social forestry as "including *any* situation which intimately *involves local people* in a forestry situation" (emphasis added).[26] This is an overly broad and imprecise definition, of little practical help when it comes to saying *which* people, under *what* structured arrangements, and so on.

Operationally it is not only a challenge but an absolute necessity to disaggregate the broad term "people" and to identify precisely *who* and *how*: what units of social organization can and will do afforestation, and which social units and definable groups can act as sustaining and durable social structures for long-term production activities.

In my view, such units of social organization can be:

a.   Natural (existing) social units, such as the individual family household or a tightly knit kinship group or subgroup

b.   Groups organized purposively to plant, protect, and cultivate trees

c.   Groups established for other purposes than forestry, but which are able to undertake forestry-related activities as well.

Examples of units of social organization for each one of these three categories are discussed in the following sections. Before that, however, a few general considerations will introduce the discussion.

A distinction obvious in the above typology is between the *single* farm family as an actor (category a), on the one side, and the *groups* of families combined in different manners as collective actors (categories b and c), on the other side. First, therefore, it must be stated unequivocally that *social* forestry strategies can be designed around the *single* family household as their pivot and executing agent. It is a misconception to equate social forestry just with the so-called community forestry, village forestry, or other forms and terms that imply groups. The family, seen as a production unit, is a microsystem with extraordinary capabilities, resilience, and flexibility and is historically and structurally well-equipped to perform multiple functions. Tree cultivation for fuelwood and construction needs can certainly be accommodated within family-managed farming systems.

But if the individual family can act effectively in such programs, why then do we need groups? Why is it necessary to identify or establish groups as social actors supporting afforestation programs?

Forming enduring units of social organization is particularly important in the case of afforestation strategies, given the long duration of a production cycle. Self-managing small groups cooperating in afforestation tasks enhance the individual productivity of their members: they increase the cumulated impact of individual contributions and enable members to perform work and achieve goals that might not be attained by each acting separately.

In forestry, self-managing groups acting as economic agents can achieve for their members significant economies of scale in several respects: (a) primarily (but not only) with respect to labor required for tree planting and cultivating; (b) in labor for harvesting and transporting; and (c) groups usually can bargain more effectively than individuals when selling the harvest or when negotiating with authorities. Furthermore, some specific technological needs or constraints may be more easily solved by groups. Particularly for watching and protecting tree plantations for a long time and over large areas against theft, fire, or destruction by animals, producers associated in groups are usually much more effective than individual families. Small, self-managing groups can also act as psychological motivators for the consensual action of their members.

Like any development activity, reforestation requires investments and other resources. Opening up social forestry strategies to many potential social actors—including discrete families and multiple group structures—is a way to amplify investments and resources for afforestation. Social forestry programs need both public and private investments. The establishment of groups as action units opens up opportunities to mobilize and use resources that would not be used otherwise. There are, for instance, significant land areas under state control for which the public sector may not have the investment resources required for tree planting. By leasing such lands to organized groups ready to invest their labor in planting and protecting trees (as will be shown further), those lands are put to use without the risk of fragmentation or alienation and with lower transaction costs. In sum, group-based strategies, combined with some public sector support, can make better use of available but dispersed resources.

In other situations, lands that in principle are under common property regimes (forest commons or grazing commons) are often not managed as a group-owned natural resource because of the dissolution of group cohesion, linkages, and authority systems. Their use slides toward a condition of open access abuse, lacking protection, yielding diminishing returns, and suffering increasing ecological destruction. Reestablishing or strengthening, when possible, the group's structures and functionality recovers the resources of that social actor for its own benefit.

Thus, the need to identify or establish social units capable of collective action introduces one more sociological dimension in forestry development projects and into the work of forestry departments. If properly conceived, social forestry projects can become a mechanism for encouraging and forming groups, thus building up the social capacity for development. Helping users to organize themselves into groups and to undertake production and management functions in forestry would, in fact, restore the "participation equation" to normalcy: the users of forests and forest products act as *the* primary producers and decisionmakers, and the forest departments "participate" in their activities, rather than the other way around.

Establishing a functional social group means, of course, much more than simply lumping individuals together into an artificial entity given the label "group" on paper. It implies a process of selection or self-selection of the members, the willingness to associate, the members' perception of both self-advantage and coresponsibility, and the establishment of an enduring intragroup structure with well-defined functions. This in turn helps mold patterned behavior among members and is the essence of grass roots, purposive institution building.

At the same time, however, social forestry modeled on groups has to address complexities resulting from the actor being a group of farmers, rather than an individual farm family or household—namely, issues of joint dependence over a piece of land and, sometimes, group tenure over trees; issues of group management, labor allocation, and monitoring; and, probably the most sensitive, the issue of benefit *distribution.* Therefore, organizing and promoting *groups* as units of social organization for social forestry programs (where groups are pivotal "actors" or "economic agents" of such programs) means more than just lumping together a number of individual farmers; it means designing clear social arrangements for tenure, management, and distribution, arrangements that are known, implemented, and adhered to consensually. Such arrangements between members are the very glue and fabric of the group.

The social arrangements required for group forestry may need to vary with the *technologies* envisaged for reforestation in different ecological areas. The appropriateness of various tree husbandry technologies to one or another local situation is not neutral with respect to social structures. The technical-cum-physical characteristics of a forestry program and the sociostructural characteristics of the unit that is its social actor should be compatible.

When forestry programs are designed, it is essential to realize that there are a number of different potential "social actors," but that they are not equally fit for carrying out each and all technical (sylvicultural) approaches to forestry. Such technologies refer to species selection, site selection, nursery development, planting technology and configurations, fertilizing, plantation managing, enclosure or other protection, marketing, and so on. For instance, to determine which of three types of tree arrangements—block planting, linear planting, or alley cropping—is most adequate in a particular case requires identification of the needs of the farmers themselves, and assessment of the local land tenure systems and land availability. Calibrating the proper fit between the technical or biological elements of afforestation and the social units around which an afforestation strategy can be built is the aim of the cooperation between foresters, planners, and sociologists.

Taken alone, however, group creation or strengthening is only one part, albeit central, of designing strategies around specific social actors. At least two more key elements are required: providing economic incentives and tangible benefits to the envisaged social actors, and increasing their awareness about the need for afforestation. Economic incentives can be introduced through public sector contributions (for example, free seedlings, technical extension advice, and others), by encouraging the development of markets for fuelwood, through tax mechanisms, and in other ways. Markets make fuelwood producers price-responsive and may encourage the production of fuelwood beyond the subsistence needs of the cultivators. The need for individual economic incentives is also strong in group approaches to reforestation.

In turn, increased awareness about afforestation needs may shorten the time-lag or tardiness with which diminishing wood resources and shortages are usually perceived, and may energize individuals into collective action to satisfy their shared needs. Better communication, extension, and education can also open farmers' eyes towards the more subtle, less immediately perceivable, benefits of tree growing, like retaining soil moisture, decreasing wind effects and soil erosion, improving agricultural productivity, or building up savings over time in the form of valuable trees that can be drawn upon in times of sudden need.

The range of social actors apt to get involved in forestry projects is broad: communities, village governing bodies, farm families, groups of farmers, cooperatives, schools, private companies, public agencies, non-government organizations, and so on. Some of these potential actors are analyzed below in light of their sociological advantages or disadvantages for social forestry. The next section examines the village "community"; subsequent sections focus on the individual family as an actor in social forestry and examine other units of social organization that provide alternatives to building social forestry programs either upon whole "communities" or upon discrete single families.

Community Woodlots: Programs without Participating Actors

Until recently, the community woodlot has been widely promoted as the desirable model in social forestry. Many planners and foresters assumed that massive planting of fuelwood could best be induced on *communal* lands by involving large numbers of people in planting, tree protection, and in sharing the benefits. Therefore, it seemed at first natural to introduce this innovation through the community as the support group. The term "community forestry" became a buzzword, even though very few bothered to define the community. The emphasis was put on establishing woodlots either on communally owned lands (or lands assumed to be owned communally, as we saw in Azad Kashmir), or on certain state-owned lands.

The *apparently* plausible social assumptions were that communities would influence their members to plant, mobilize labor and promote self-help, and collectively protect the young plantations on "their" land. Donors and governments also optimistically assumed that community forestry could ensure the wide distribution of benefits among the small farmers who make up the majority of the community. Successful village woodlots in countries such as Korea and China, which had been supported authoritatively by the government, lent credibility to this approach and were assumed to be valid models for other social contexts.

However, when replicated in other countries the community woodlots fared much worse than expected. Azad Kashmir is but one example. Results in Uttar Pradesh, Karnataka, Gujarat, and other Indian states, in Niger and other African countries, and elsewhere have been, and continue to be, similarly disappointing.

Evidence about community woodlots increasingly documents that, at close scrutiny, they *are not* what their name suggests them to be and, therefore, do not achieve their stated objectives. Over the last ten to twelve years, considerable financial resources have been channeled by both international donor agencies and national governments in many developing countries to induce forestry programs that pursued the community woodlot model. Between 1977 and 1986, about 50 percent of the World Bank's lending for forestry went to twenty-seven projects, which included, among others, some form of community forestry. Next, the Bank's lending for social forestry tripled during 1987–89, compared with the prior decade. Major resources came also from bilateral donors like USAID, CIDA, ODA, SIDA, and others. Yet in most cases, according to evaluation reports, the actual plantings accomplished under the "community" model fall below targets and don't justify the investments made.

The analysis of these projects reveals that their initial assumption— namely, that communities (villages) would be effective actors for implementing "community forestry"—were not confirmed. This assumption was sociologically naive, lacking understanding of the nature and structure of village communities. Furthermore, these uninformed assumptions evolved crude project approaches and led to inadequate implementation that ignored the social prerequisites for generating collective action.

Indeed, after the Azad Kashmir case, strong empirical evidence in the same sense came around the mid-1980s from three large social forestry projects assisted by the World Bank in India (in Uttar Pradesh,[27] Gujarat,[28] and West Bengal[29]). None of these three projects managed to achieve or to come close to their targets regarding the establishment of *community* woodlots, while they were effective in other approaches and—to some planners' surprise—even surpassed their targets in *farm* forestry. In Uttar Pradesh, for instance, against a project target of 3,080 hectares, village woodlots could be established only on a total of 136 hectares (two-hectare woodlots on average). In Gujarat the self-help village woodlots component achieved only two-thirds of the 9,200 hectares targeted, while in West Bengal, because of similar low performance, some of the project allocations for village woodlots had to be shifted at mid-term to farm forestry. Summarizing the causes of such failures, a Bank report on the Uttar Pradesh project noted: "poor villagers proved unwilling to contribute their labor as expected by the project in exchange for rather limited potential benefits from a small woodlot, after many years of protection and maintenance. . . . The social forestry organization lacked relevant know-how and resources to deal with the sociological and technical problems associated with densely cultivated areas and very small farms."[30]

At the time these unsatisfactory results became known, a new National Social Forestry Project for India (covering four Indian states: Himachal Pradesh, Rajasthan, Uttar Pradesh, and Gujarat) was already advanced in the appraisal process; it included again a significant component of "village woodlots" (85,000 hectares), although now this component represented only a relatively small fraction of the total projected planting (708,000 hectares). On account of the little interest shown by community members, the model was modified to give considerable management authority over village woodlots to the village panchayats. Of course, this was an administrative substitute for both user and producer responsibility, wholly missing the crux of the social forestry strategy.

The slippage of community woodlots into panchayat woodlots did not remedy anything. The subsequent mid-term assessments in 1988 and 1989 again confirmed the earlier conclusion about the absence of a pivotal social actor at the center of such schemes. Many of the newly established village woodlots are beset with social, management, and distributional problems that prevent the accomplishment of their *community* fuel supply and poverty alleviation objectives. A Bank staff sociologist concluded that no user-created management system for the protection and maintenance of "community" woodlots has emerged so far.[31] Communities as a whole are not getting involved and hardly can; instead, the village panchayat (or the state forestry department) takes over the administration of the woodlot, often commercializes the products outside the village, and invests the revenue in other assets.[32]

Among the subsistence farmers, disappointment with the distribution of benefits from these woodlots saps future interest in maintaining or expanding them. A 1987 evaluation of Orissa Social Forestry Project found that 82 percent of the villagers did not know how the produce from village woodlots would be distributed; most of the people did not expect any share from the final output and looked upon such woodlots as another category of reserved forests.[33] It is therefore not surprising that in such social forestry programs "on village commons and wastelands . . .

villages have proved most reluctant to manage trees planted as a corporate resource."[34]

Convergent conclusions result from observing community woodlots in other geographical contexts. In West Africa's "bois de village" (village forests), the community system was also found "ill-suited . . . to serve as a vehicle for reforestation,"[35] and in several other Asian countries its adequacy was questioned as well.[36] Often forestry departments were asked to fully set up the village woodlots and then to hand them over to the village committee. This deprives the community woodlot of all or most of its *social* forestry content and makes the social forestry label a mere untrue slogan. It also appeared in numerous cases that the village committees were uninformed and unaware of what they should do with the woodlots.

Synthesizing the findings of numerous evaluations of woodlot projects on communal lands in India during the 1980s, Arnold and Stewart provide a description replete with references to the missing social arrangements:

> The communal groups charged with the dialogue with forest departments over the planning of woodlots and with their eventual take over have nearly everywhere been panchayats . . . rather than a user group or a body selected by a village specifically for managing the woodlot . . . .
>
> Mechanisms for direct consultation by the forest department with villagers have generally not been put in practice . . . . (forest committees) have been formed in an ad hoc manner without much, if any, prior consultation among the various groups in the village about their composition and in many cases [they have not been] functioning at all actively. . . .
>
> The literature reports an almost universal failure to precede woodlot establishment with public discussion. Repeatedly reports record villagers being unaware that the woodlot had been established for the community; it was a "government woodlot". . . . Benefit-sharing agreements are frequently neither finalized nor formalized . . . . Most of the people did not expect any share from the final output.[37]

Altogether, the findings discussed above, and many others, support the same essential conclusion. The many community woodlot projects initiated during the last dozen years amount to an extraordinarily telling case of an international program intended to capture popular participation, which nevertheless was launched and generously financed without having an elementary understanding of the kind of social process and system it needed to put in motion. Financial resources were made readily available to induce the *technical act* of planting tree lots, but before the *cultural* construction of new norms and institutions to support such tree lots was formulated theoretically, tested experimentally, and attempted in actual practice.

Investment in the technical process outpaced by far the investment in the human resources and in the social institutional process. The latter was not recognized either as a basic cost, or as the unavoidable learning curve that it must be. There was undisputedly a lack of knowledge about even *how* to invest in the human resources and institutional components of social forestry. Although the institutional arrangements should have been the building bricks for the success of the technical process, the financial outlays were rushed into the latter without a prayer for the former. The final outcome could be no other than the dismal evaluation findings proved it to be.

The absence of the basic sociological knowledge to guide social forestry policies and actual work is much more consequential than the routine bureaucratic hindrances that always appear during the implementation of induced-development programs. Bureaucratic hindrances aside, the weaknesses or distortions during project execution are not the primary cause that renders community woodlots ineffective. I argue that community woodlots *cannot* be effective as such because woodlot schemes inspired by the romantic myth of homogeneous communities are misconceived from the outset and because appropriate social actors and social arrangements have not been put in motion.

Even though it seems that the common interests of individual village inhabitants converge in having and exploiting a common tree lot, this commonality turns out to be insufficient in itself for generating collective action toward this goal. Cultural dimensions—such as *awareness* of goals to be pursued, consensus about *what* work is to be done, suitable social organization, group size and coherence, and authority mechanisms and systems for benefit sharing—are critical parameters of collective action. In many of the project cases referred to in this chapter, *such variables are not knowledgeably woven into the strategy for building the desired models*.

To propose a generalized formulation, there are seven basic sociological reasons why "communities" as population clusters cannot and should not be treated as ready-to-use corporate actors (units of social organization or economic agents) for afforestation programs:

1. Communities and villages are geographical residential units, not necessarily corporate organizations. Physical vicinity alone is not sufficient to engender the type of long-term collective action required for a woodlot enterprise.

2. The interests of community subgroups often differ to such an extent that the kind of collective action required by a long-term afforestation program is generally not possible. Usually, communities are heterogeneous population clusters, stratified and split into factions and subgroups with fragmented socioeconomic interests. What is advantageous for one subgroup is not necessarily advantageous for another.

3. Community land is limited and often there is reluctance to make it available for tree planting. Tree block sites are small, costs are high. The poorest households have a vested interest in not allowing the commons, which to them are a continuous, even if meager, source of products, to become a closed and unaccessible woodlot. As Jodha's research in India has demonstrated, the poor households are dependent on products from the commons much more than those that are better off.[38]

4. The tenure status of the common lands is often uncertain and engenders uncertainty about the tenure of planted trees. It is similarly unclear what social body has jurisdiction over the allocation of common lands.[39]

5. Authority systems have uneven power over community subgroups. Local community leaders often appear reluctant, or not strong enough, to mobilize the individuals belonging to different subgroups to work for establishing woodlots, or to enforce restrictions to protect the trees.

6. Distributional arrangements for benefit sharing to ensure that the woodlot products reach the entitled recipients are usually not thought through at the outset and have not worked in practice. Specified intragroup rules and guarantees for distribution *commensurate* with labor contributions are lacking, and this alone is sufficient to doom the wholesale community approach. Exclusionary rules against noncontributors are absent as well. The long production cycle for trees weakens the confidence of those

planting today that they will get wood eight or more years later, and it favors the lingering suspicion that the authorities will appropriate the wood anyway.

7.   Last but not least, most often communities are not organized as joint producers in other respects and thus do not offer a matrix on which additional joint activities can be grafted. Externally designed programs, which do not bother to establish grass roots organizations, cannot foster by decree the kind of close interdependence of members required by community schemes.

Because such characteristics tend to be widespread, disappointing results have also been recurrent; I am arguing that results are likely to be poor in the future as well, whenever such corporate woodlots are expected to be sustained by noncorporate communities.

Implied in most community woodlot schemes is also a reversal in tenure. Such schemes often aim to revert the open access regimes that took hold of nominally communal lands (or even on lands under nominal state ownership) and return them to genuine common property management vested in a group that must be well-defined. This, in principle, is not unfeasible. Many development theorists argue that converting open access to common property is superior to etatization or conversion to individual property systems.[40] But rarely is such a reversal *designed with conceptual* clarity and carried out with adequate social means. Moving from open access to common property demands a conceptually clear and operationally refined sequence of steps. Such culturally attuned social engineering are simply not present in most of the hurriedly put together "community" woodlot projects.

On the other hand, it has to be stated also that positive results with community woodlots are sometimes achieved; but they tend rather to be exceptions linked to particular circumstances in one community or another.[41] When they occur (some are reported in Orissa and Haryana by Chambers, Saxena, and Shah, others in Thailand by Kasetsart University—RECOFTC[42]), it is important to identify the specific structural, cultural, or political conditions that make them possible or replicable.

Anthropologists and sociologists have long called attention to the processes that have changed the internal structure of village communities as social units. As settlements, villages are, of course, units of social organization. But that is not synonymous with saying that they are units capable of undertaking collective or coordinated action in any and all respects.

Although historically various forms of corporate villages have over-lapped with kinship units of a corporate kind, Eric Wolf noted already a quarter of a century ago that "corporate peasant villages are growing fewer in the modern world."[43] Moreland made a similar observation in 1929 for Muslim India (and, by extension, for Azad Kashmir as discussed earlier) when he rejected the concept of village community; he notes that the peasants forming the brotherhoods "are sometimes referred to in the aggregate as the 'village community' but this term frequently covers other elements of the population and, apart from this ambiguity, it has gathered so many vague connotations that I prefer to avoid it."[44] Louis Dumont similarly emphasizes that in India, given its caste system, the very expression "village community" is not adequate because it conceals the existence of factions and the omnipresence of hierarchies.[45] Dumont does not see the village as a significant unit for social action in India and stresses that what is generally called a "village panchayat" is actually a "caste panchayat."

More recently, in an excellent field study of Indian community-based irrigation systems, Robert Wade engages Dumont in discussion, defend-ing the opposite view—namely, that the community can act as a unit of social organization.[46] Wade's field findings indeed prove that the villages he studied were able to develop collective action for irrigation. This points to the need to qualify the *kind* of collective actions and the *kind* of natural resources that are to be developed by the community. While communities, as argued here, have not proven to be effective actors for "community woodlots," under certain conditions they may be effective actors for other types of activities such as irrigation schemes, fire- protection, or road building, and so on. No a priori blanket judgment will do.

The key characteristic of the *type* of action required must be pondered together with the social needs, pressures, and group or individual benefits related to such action. For instance, the pressure to manage water allocations under conditions of scarcity may overcome built-in contra-dictions and motivate the community to perform water-related actions collectively as *a unit*. The various "conceptual and operational fallacies" that circulate in connection with common property natural resources need to be clarified, in order to improve the management of such resources and the strategies for using them effectively.[47]

The Family as Actor in Social Forestry

Returning to afforestation strategies and to their potential actors, two questions to address are:

First, if the community as a whole can hardly be a homogeneous collective actor *in afforestation*, are there other units of social organization able to assume and to execute such a role?

Second, are any tenurial *innovations* possible (in either land or tree tenure or in granting usufruct rights), whose introduction could mobilize such alternative units of social action?

The answer is affirmative to both questions. There are such social groups *within* the stratified, nonhomogeneous communities—namely, specific subsections of such communities, which can act collectively. Moreover, and this is crucial, such groups can be purposively organized. Furthermore, understanding better the distinctions, as Fortmann proposes, between forms of land tenure and various systems of tree tenure would allow designing imaginative combinations between them that can be promoted through social forestry projects to meet the needs and the abilities of various groups.[48] The challenge is to *identify* the population subsections able to implement and viably sustain such innovative approaches, and carry out the work with them.

Family Agroforestry

The increasing evidence that the community-centered approach is less effective than assumed has led to a perceptible shift in thinking and strategies among foresters and planners. They have begun to focus on the *individual* family farm unit as an alternative to the community-based programs in social forestry. This approach goes by various names: farm forestry, family woodlots, agroforestry, and others. But the common denominator behind this nomenclature is that the family household increasingly becomes the social unit around which reforestation is planned and financed. The technical approach to family farm programs also differs from that proposed for community woodlots: it is designed to suit the land and labor resources available to the individual family farm.

Of course, this is not to say that either all interest in promoting village treelots has now disappeared, or that promoting tree planting on individual farms is a totally new orientation. What I want to underscore is a shift in emphasis, a reallocation of priorities, and a diversification of social forestry strategies. This also implies a change in the sociological under-pinnings of certain forestry programs. In turn, this shift implies a need for social researchers to formulate the social and cultural strategy for stimulating *family*-based forestry.

Various World Bank–assisted forestry projects—in Karnataka, Kerala, Haryana, and other Indian states, as well as in Mali, Tanzania, Nigeria, Nepal, Haiti, and elsewhere—now provide support and incentives for tree planting on small family farms. Family farm forestry is now a substantial part of the follow-up IHFDP in Azad Kashmir, for instance, as mentioned previously.[49] In the design of India's Jammu and Kashmir and Haryana social forestry project, village woodlots represent only 11.3 percent of the total planting program, while farm forestry represents about 43 percent, supported by a distribution of about 47 million seedlings free to individual farmers.[50] A similar approach was taken in an ongoing Kerala Project.[51] Some of the most spectacular results in family forestry are being obtained in Gujarat and Himachal Pradesh, demonstrating a receptive response by farmers to project-provided incentives (free seedlings, for example) and technical assistance. During the first three seasons of the National Social Forestry Project in India (1985–88), family farms planted approximately 500 million seedlings, the equivalent of more than 325,000 hectares on their private lands, exceeding the already high target by some 18 percent.[52]

The vast potential of the family farms to incorporate tree planting was dramatically proven in Haiti by the Agroforestry Outreach Project (AOP) funded during 1981–85 by USAID. Guided by prior ethnographic knowledge of Haitian tenure systems and cropping patterns, the AOP stands out as one of the few social forestry projects with a clearly thought-through *sociological* strategy, purposively designed around the family farm as its central social actor—and it promoted a technically appropriate reforestation package; in other words, the technical and social approaches were well intertwined. The project *started* from the farmer's needs, values, and actual behavior; it proposed that the family farm (the average peasant holding in Haiti is about a hectare and a half) plant 500 trees of fast growing fuelwood and pole-producing species by intercropping and border planting, to reduce the opportunity cost of land; it produced lightweight microseedlings and provided them free to the peasants, together with technical assistance; and, most importantly, the project guaranteed that "the peasants themselves, and not the government or the project, would be the sole owners of the trees and that the peasants would have unlimited rights to the harvest of the wood whenever they wished."[53] Social anthropologists directed the implementation of this social forestry project, in close cooperation with technicians, involving also nongovernmental organizations. The results were spectacular: while the four-year project target was to plant 3 million trees on the land of 6,000 peasants, it accomplished the planting of 20 million trees on 75,000 family farms. The success of this project's sociologically informed reforestation strategy holds a powerful lesson about the importance of providing good economic incentives and tree-tenure security to the farm family, and of fully recognizing its autonomy in decisionmaking.

Social and Technical Variables

Sociologically, the significance of a strategy centered on family forestry is manifold. Instead of joint (community) responsibility for planting and protecting, it deals with individual (family) responsibility. Instead of promoting joint tenure and ownership of trees, it promotes individual ownership. The family-centered strategy also vests the management authority over the planted trees in a real person—the man or woman of the household—rather than in a large, nonhomogeneous entity. Land tenure and tree tenure are much less ambiguous and thus agroforestry approaches can adjust more easily to the enormous variety of local customary norms of tree and land ownership or usufruct. Of great importance is that the divisive problems of intragroup benefit distribution are eliminated. Overall, the transaction costs entailed by establishing groups are much reduced or eliminated by the family-centered strategy.

The result is that the user's (family's) needs for fuelwood are satisfied more securely through stable production rather than through chancy gathering. Inasmuch as the correlation between the farmer's inputs (labor or cash) and the output becomes direct and clear *to the farmer* himself, in a manner that is understandable, proportionate, and less risky, his production-oriented behavior is reinforced.

Of course, the structure and size of family units vary considerably across cultures: the farm family unit as economic agent may be a nuclear family in one case, an extended family in another, or even a lineage group living in the same compound, as is often the case in Africa. Agroforestry projects centered on family units need sociological guidance to understand the social space created by the customary rights systems regulating access to land and trees.

Technically, trees can be grown on individually owned land not necessarily in small blocks (family woodlots) but also along linear landscape features such as farm boundaries, internal field borders, roads, and watercourses. Under conditions of wood scarcity, the economics of family agroforestry favors expanding tree planting. The resources required by agroforestry are limited, but smallholders tend to weigh the opportunity costs of labor and land more than planners usually realize. Tree planting technologies that maximize the use of interstitial locations and other marginal land patches are particularly suitable for individual small farmers because they do not compete with existing land uses and other crops. Even small farms that cannot afford to set aside an arable plot for a tree block can use their hedgerows for planting. Thus, technical options for expanding tree planting are indeed numerous.

Individual trees scattered on and around the family farm's cultivated areas generally grow faster than plantation trees, which compete with each other in dense tree lots (for example, the volume of free-growing eucalyptus at the age of ten years is at least five times that of trees grown at a stand density of 1,600 trees per hectare). Moreover, since farmers secure most of their fuelwood by lopping branches, trees along homestead boundaries can produce more volume per tree and more frequent supplies of small quantities of wood than those felled on far away plantations. This option can go a long way towards mitigating fuelwood shortages, since it is easier to persuade a farm family to plant on its own farm boundaries than to persuade communities to provide scarce land for block plantations.

The sylvicultural technology recommended for family forestry programs usually differs from the one recommended for block tree planting, because of the socioeconomic context of farm forestry. Under this approach, tree planting is incorporated into the farmer's own farming system, rather than remaining parallel to it on a remote communal lot. Technologically, this integration may promote multipurpose tree species, since these will respond to several user needs: not only the need for fuelwood but also needs for fodder, shade, small timber, and so on. Species suitable for animal fodder, with fuelwood as a secondary rather than primary benefit, often integrate more organically into the farming system than species such as eucalyptus widely promoted by many programs. If marketable species are selected, trees can become a cash crop, bring income, and not serve merely as a product for household consumption. Forestry can complement, rather than compete, with agriculture. In favorable ecological circumstances, with reasonable rainfall, an average rural family needs comparatively few mature trees to cover its cooking and heating needs. Therefore, small landholdings are not a prohibitive barrier to family forestry.

Since family farm forestry is introduced through individual decision-making, it can spread without having to confront the limiting social factors that impede collective adoption in the case of community forestry. Adopting family forestry represents a significant change in the farmer's behavior, in the sense discussed at the outset, inasmuch as he or she did not previously plant fuelwood systematically. In India, for instance, it was estimated that in 1984 only a small fraction (no more than 10 percent) of all farmers planted fuelwood trees. This low proportion suggests the gigantic dimension of the changes that are necessary. Recent studies in Haiti, India, Malawi, Yemen, Zimbabwe, and other countries indicate some increase in farmers' interest in planting multipurpose trees—for poles, fodder, fuelwood, and as a cash crop.

Eliciting and motivating such change in users' behavior is precisely a part of the *social* strategy for reforestation. Every technical approach must incorporate extension[54] for communicating sylvicultural *information* to farmers, influencing their perception of existing opportunities, and activating the little used thesaurus of farmer's indigenous knowledge about trees. Successful forestry programs (for example, in West Bengal, Jammu and Kashmir, and Haryana) employ special agents of change (extension agents called *motivators* or social forestry workers) to persuade farmers to plant trees and to assist them in doing so. Good progress has been made recently by social scientists in refining extension techniques tailored to the specifics of reforestation.[55]

However, economic factors may also reduce the incentives to the family farm in tree planting, namely in situations when naturally grown fuelwood is available abundantly. A study of agroforestry in Sub-Saharan Africa concluded that "as long as wood can be collected from common lands at a low cost by rural producers, there will be little economic incentive to plant trees on family farms to meet fuelwood demands."[56]

Supportive evidence for such conclusions comes from field investigations like those in Malawi, which found that the returns to labor invested in gathering fuelwood are fifteen times higher than the returns to labor invested in growing fuelwood and over five times higher than to labor invested in growing trees for poles.[57] In light of such and other findings, the study on Sub-Saharan agroforestry pessimistically predicted that "agroforestry for fuelwood will not be widely adopted in Africa until the 'free' wood resources of the commons have virtually disappeared."[58]

Such broad pessimistic conclusions may be disputable, but nonetheless they are a reminder that agroforestry has its own limits. This is why alternatives to family-centered forestry strategies, as well as conservation measures, must also be promoted in parallel.

Because of the *long-time lag* between planting and harvesting trees and because small farmers can rarely afford to wait several years for income, special incentives are often needed to induce behavioral change. Economic incentives, though necessary, are difficult to provide when government funds are scarce or when there are limited cash markets for forest products. Alternative incentives, perceivable to the farmer, should therefore be sought as well. Chambers and Leach, for instance, call attention to a long overlooked aspect of the value of trees to farmers— trees as saving banks—a perspective that gives additional options for imaginative motivation efforts.[59] The use of incentives is an important aspect of responsible social engineering and sociologists must contribute to incentive system design.

The sociological understanding of the local culture, value systems, and symbolic behavior can help develop noneconomic but powerful incentive systems and motivation tools. Farm forestry activities can be linked to events that stimulate the farmers' interest. For instance, under (nonforestry) projects that aim at regularizing land tenure (as in Brazil or Thailand), large numbers of farmers who have had only customary rights to land receive formal legal title to it. Since land titles are important to farmers, the very process of granting them can be turned into an incentive for farm forestry: farmers may be asked to plant trees along the boundaries of their demarcated plots as part of the title-receiving process or ceremony, and free seedlings can be supplied to facilitate it. Farm forestry can also be linked to irrigation, settlement, or infrastructure projects. The symbolism of tree planting can be linked to events in the farm family's life that are imbued with positive values, to help adopt the new behavior—*cultivation* of fuelwood trees.

As an enduring social unit able to sustain forestry development, the farm family is a powerful social resource. Tapping its potential requires integration of technical, sociological, and economic elements, as well as

cooperation between foresters and sociologists in designing and implementing this strategy.

Alternative Units of Social Organization

The current expansion of family-centered forestry may, but should not,
obscure the fact that *group*-centered approaches retain development
potential that must not be written off because of the ineffectiveness of
the wholesale "community approach." It would be throwing out the baby
with the bath water if the deemphasis of community woodlots were
interpreted as renouncing *all* group-centered approaches. Common property resource management is not wedded exclusively to the pattern of
whole-village involvement. Even the community-centered strategy
should not be dismissed altogether, however, because under certain
sociopolitical and institutional contexts it may produce some results.

Small Groups

Sociologists are well placed to point out to planners and foresters that
communities are just one *type* of group and that the community forestry
approach is only one particular case of many conceivable group-centered
strategies.

The foresters, in turn, can and must ask the sociologist: which groups
can act between the entire community and the individual farmer as
supporting structures for the development of forestry? Is it possible to
avoid the weaknesses of the community-based approach, yet elicit and
make use of the social synergy of group-powered efforts in forestry?

The sociologist's answer can only be affirmative. Sociologically,
alternative types of groups can definitely be identified or organized.
Some have already been formed as a result of local social invention under
favorable conditions. The key is to identify a group that is free from the
inner conflicts of large communities, yet able to generate the synergy that
makes groups more effective than the sum of their members.

The limitations intrinsic to communities as social actors result, as
discussed earlier, from their large size and internal splits. Homogeneous
groups of an easily manageable size could prove more functional. Their
small scale would not create difficult problems of system maintenance.

(Otherwise, maintenance problems can become more complex than the very tasks the group is called upon to solve.)

Through small groups, a common need can be pursued more effectively by joint action than by individual actions. Individuals' needs as users of fuelwood can aggregate powerfully not only for joint procurement but possibly for joint production as well. Further, a simple rule for members' contribution and benefit distribution (for example, equal shares for all) would eliminate actual disadvantages or misperceptions of advantages. A small group can also *enforce* rules through peer pressure and mutual control, so as to arrest free rider behavior. Members of such small groups enter in face to face contacts simultaneously as users, producers, and enforcers.

Small groups often manage other natural resources (as in the case of a water users' association formed around a small branch of the irrigation system) and could operate a woodlot largely without the conflicts that surround community plantations. Also, given their ability to speed up the dissemination process, groups may become "contact" partners (more effective than individuals) to extension agents that diffuse technological innovations.

Two West Bengal experiences relevant to group formation and group roles are the group farm forestry and the Arabari socioeconomic experiment. They demonstrate the vast potential for group formation and the advantages that grouping brings to both farmers and forest departments.

Group Farm Forestry

The first pattern, group farm forestry, consists of a group of landless families to whom the government leased marginal public land on a long-term basis (ninety-nine years), to enable and motivate them to grow trees. The lease was offered to the clusters of landless with the guarantee that it can be inherited but with the restriction that the land cannot be alienated (sold or used for nonforestry purposes). The plots of land are contiguous, thus facilitating collective action in planting and protecting (such as taking turns in watching the plantations), as these tasks are performed more rapidly and effectively than if carried out individually. However, tree ownership, maintenance obligations (application of fertilizer or replacement of dead trees), and the right to dispose of the products are vested in the individual leaseholders. Under this system there is not only legal, but also group control over the temptation to change land use or mortgage the land.

The target group of this West Bengal scheme, being landless, was highly dependent on the immediate income from their labor, for daily sustenance. Some incentive payments for labor have therefore been made to help meet consumption requirements of the families during the early stages of the plantation. Incentives are also given for each surviving tree to encourage maximum survival rates.

The area allotted and the number of trees to be planted guarantee enough wood from lops, tops, dead trees, and branches to meet a substantial part of a family's domestic requirements. The stem volume is then available for sale, and the total output ensures participant interest. The group strategy thus not only maximizes land use for forestry but also provides the users with fuel or construction materials, as well as with cash income. These plantations generated good revenues which some families invested in purchasing land, planting potatoes, and other such gains.[60] Overall, some 20,000 hectares have been successfully planted under group farm forestry arrangements in West Bengal during the last six to seven years.

The potential for multiplying such small groups is substantial, as the pattern of group farm forestry can be introduced not only for the landless, but for small farmers as well. However, a socio-organizational effort is required to form such user-cum-producer groups. The advantage is that they will then supply the social structure necessary to transform little-used natural resources (wastelands) into an income source for landless or marginal farmers who supply labor at low opportunity cost and reap the benefits. Both government agencies and NGOs envisage a considerable expansion of group farm forestry on public wastelands in India.[61]

This social innovation privatizes the use, but not the ownership, of public wastelands, providing an economic incentive to landless people to raise trees as a cash crop. Where surplus labor is available and employment is scarce, this option can significantly benefit the landless. However, it also requires prudent implementation to prevent the risk of depriving other vulnerable households dependent on wasteland products.

The Arabari Experiment

In the Arabari socioeconomic experiment, the innovative idea was to stop forest depletion (encroachment, theft, and such problems) by providing villagers with an amount of employment in forest protection-cum-replanting work, which in monetary terms, would be equivalent to what villagers earned by sale of stolen forest products. The Arabari is the name of a *mouza* (the smallest revenue subdivision in West Bengal, usually coextensive with the village boundary) in the Midnapore district. The small team of three researchers led by A. K. Banerjee who started the experiment in 1970 assessed, through a house-to-house survey in eleven villages (some 1,300 people), that the underemployed villagers earned a significant part of their income (some Rs 80,000) through illegal firewood cutting; the researchers understood that the villagers could not simply give up that income and survive, unless they could get access to equivalent income from paid employment.[62] With support from the Forest Department, the research team designed an action-research experiment consisting of several elements:

- employing villagers in planting trees (acacia and eucalyptus, for example) and grasses (such as *mesta*, a poor man's jute) on blank patches
- spreading and phasing employment creation over the year to match the seasons of most severe underemployment in the area
- entrusting protection responsibility to villagers with minimum official interference
- ensuring fuelwood supply to the villagers at a nominal, low price
- supplying smallwood, plough pieces, and the like, from outside at cost prices, to meet villagers' domestic and productive needs
- offering a revenue-sharing arrangement under which the Forest Department would pay the villagers 25 percent of the selling price of the mature trees in cash (this element was introduced later)
- carrying out an intensive communication effort to explain the incentives and the experiment's rationale to the villagers
- establishing institutional arrangements such as the election of rotating representatives to monitor work attendance and to collect or distribute payments.

The results confirmed the experiment's assumptions (with the exception of relocating grazing outside the forests), in that the villagers enforced total protection of the forest, primarily by desisting from making illegal cuttings, while their employment in replanting generated revenue for them and for the project as well. The self-imposed and self-enforced reduction of firewood cutting and the watching and patrolling by villagers acted as a social fencing around the state forest. The tensions between the villagers and the Forest Department eased.

The upshot of this successful experiment was that the once degraded forests were rehabilitated spectacularly within three to five years, and have continued to grow since. Moreover, other villages joined and the experiment soon expanded from eleven to sixteen villages, covering 1,506 hectares by 1978. Some of the newly included blank areas were planted with cashew nuts, which in a few years provided a cash crop sold on the open market, with part of the sale proceeds going to the villagers.

Recent (1989) assessments confirmed not only the sustainability of the initial Arabari model but also its rapid spread in the mid- and late-1980s to many more areas. While the experiment started without formal group formation in each of the small villages involved, the subsequent follow-up took on stronger characteristics of group creation, with the establishment of village protection committees. Banerjee reports that some 700–800 such groups were formed in the southwest zone of West Bengal, protecting over 70,000 hectares of degraded and replanted forests: "in this area, people have formed formal groups composed of one member from each family. These groups meet once in a while, take decision and keep minutes. Each family provides a forest watcher at regular intervals . . . . The will to do so developed as these groups believed in the assurance of sustained benefits . . . . Their collective action is productive as there is an action plan" for the group.[63]

Both the group farm forestry and the Arabari model are more feasible when the location of the groups' residence borders the forest lands to be planted and protected. Furthermore, tailoring these approaches to particular sites and social strata requires land-use surveys and population surveys as baselines for targeting. The basic sociological principle is *to create a clear link between a well-defined small group and a well-defined piece of forest land* that is to be protected or planted. In addition, the group members need to perceive a clear correlation between their contributions and the returns they get, and with this awareness be prepared to act consensually. Authority and benefits must be restricted to the members of the group, not left open to free riders.

Interesting developments regarding the creation and productive activities of small user groups have been reported also from Nepal,[64] Indonesia, and Niger. Analyzing the collective management of hill forests in Nepal, Arnold and Campbell emphasize user group motivation, organization, and establishment of legal agreements between the governments, the panchayat, and the people who comprise the user groups. The core content of the legal agreement is in fact the management plan which regulates the cutting regimes, product collection, and group harvesting.[65] From Niger, Floor reports experiments that encourage charcoal user groups to take over management responsibility for areas of savanna woodland in producing charcoal with more efficient practices.[66]

Overall, the quasi-ubiquity and diversity of such arrangements show the potential for varying the degree and forms of group cooperation as called for by the task at hand and by people's preparedness for cooperation.

Forest Cooperatives and Associations

Even when tree planting is done by farmers on private, individually owned land, the creation of some form of farmers' association may be beneficial for specific activities such as the management of tree lots or the marketing of tree products. In some countries, the forestry departments help establish tree growers' associations or similar organizations to assist farmers in marketing the wood produced under individual family forestry.

The forestry cooperative is one such structure. Although forestry cooperatives are less common than agricultural cooperatives, in some regions (such as Scandinavia) forestry cooperatives are numerous and their organizing principles work effectively.[67] When they have a well-defined and not-too-large membership, cooperatives might be a more coherent and goal-oriented organization than the village community as a whole. In the North-West Frontier province of Pakistan a pilot program to revive forestry cooperatives in the Guzara forest was started to establish fifteen cooperatives, each with a minimum of 500 acres of forest land. Each cooperative has responsibility for managing only the forests owned by its members, in accordance with a plan approved by the Forest Department. The cooperatives receive technical assistance in preparing the management plan and the services of field foresters, both paid for by the provincial government. No other subsidies are given, and all other forestry costs (replanting felled areas, maintenance, extraction, and so on) are borne by the cooperatives. For this purpose, cooperatives are authorized to retain at least 40 percent of the revenue from the sale of trees, and receive credit if needed. A sociological study found that Guzara farmers strongly value the contribution cooperatives can make toward protecting their ownership rights to the forests, but they see government interference and the intrusion of party politics as a mortal threat to these cooperatives.[68]

An expansion of cooperative forestry structures is happening currently in India, due to the initiative to form "tree growers' cooperatives" launched by the country's National Dairy Development Board. Its essence is the attempt to transfer and adjust the pattern used by the well-known Anand dairy cooperatives. Such tree growers cooperatives are envisaged on unencroached wastelands in Orissa, Andhra Pradesh, and other states, with each cooperative covering some 100 hectares of private marginal lands and 50 hectares of common wastelands.[69]

Age Groups

Many traditional societies, particularly in Africa, entrust to subgroups certain maintenance or service functions in the society. Some of these groups are defined by age or gender. They are accountable to appointed group leaders as well as to the overall authority structure. I think that these types of groups could also be used for certain forestry development activities.

One of the notable successes in recent years has been the involvement of school-aged youths in establishing tree nurseries for social forestry (in Kenya, Malawi, Gujarat, and Haiti). The characteristics of such groups are propitious for certain collective actions: school children form a homogeneous age group, concentrated and organized by virtue of their main activity—going to school—and with a built-in leadership system. Although the transitional nature of this age group hinders its participation in activities of long duration, it is perfectly suitable for short-term collective efforts such as the production of seedlings. To formalize and expand this group's support to social forestry, it is possible to promote institutional arrangements in the form of a "partnership between schools, communities, and government agencies."[70]

An example from Gujarat is impressive: at the outset of a social forestry program in 1980 there were less than twenty schools with tree nurseries. The Forest Department decided to encourage schools and private farmers to raise seedlings rather than to expand the state's nurseries. In three years about 600 schools opened nurseries in which schoolchildren, with guidance from foresters and teachers, produced several million seedlings a year.[71] The persuasion and motivation required to generate such action was combined with one economic incentive: a guaranteed price for seedlings; when ready for transplanting, the state forest service buys the seedlings for distribution to local farmers. This economic incentive was backed by technical advice from extension workers to help schools construct and operate small tree nurseries. The program has thus made wise use of available social units as a lever for amplifying tree planting and ownership. In addition, many schoolchildren took the seedlings home and planted them around their family homestead.

Women's Groups

Experience with women's groups in forestry is expanding every year. Since in many cultures women are the direct users and gatherers of fuelwood, they would appear to be the ones most directly interested in producing it; women also possess a good knowledge of the growing requirements of various tree species.[72] And indeed, recent evidence analyzed by Molnar from many social forestry programs points out the major contribution women are making.[73]

Although women's associations for various productive or household-related activities have been promoted in many countries, until recently little has been done to encourage women's organized group action for cultivating woodlots. Even in a country such as Kenya, where women's groups are widespread and effective, a sociological field study reported a few years ago that out of 100 women's groups active in one district (Mbere), none was directly involved with tree planting.[74] Things have changed in recent years, however, and various field reports for 1988 and 1989 describe hundreds of women's groups involved in forestry in Kenya.[75] There are indications that similar trends are getting stronger in other countries as well. In India's Himachal Pradesh, multipurpose women's groups called *Mahia Mandals*, which have been in existence for many years already, are now frequently including tree planting among their activities.[76]

Women's groups are the prototypical grouping of discrete "users" turned "producers" in forestry. In many places women and children are compelled to make enormous efforts to collect wood for cooking and heating. In certain areas of Nepal, for instance, the time a woman spends collecting fuel is estimated to total between twenty and forty days a year. Therefore, producing rather than gathering the fuelwood may save both time and labor. Adjustments may be needed in their other productive and household roles, given the inelasticity of rural women's time.[77] But promoting group patterns for tree growing activities may maximize output without necessarily creating new time constraints on the women. What is required is a policy that facilitates women's access to suitable land tracts and organizes the establishment of groups.

Establishing reasonable-size women's groups that induce mutual help and cooperation is likely to be a more effective social device than if each woman spends the same amount of time and labor on individual farm forestry. This is certainly an area for action-oriented research and sociological experimentation, in which creative social engineering could make a valuable contribution to foresters' efforts.

Watershed Forestry

Environmentalists, foresters, planners, and policymakers alike are increasingly concerned with the rehabilitation of watersheds. A legitimate question which development sociologists therefore have to answer is what social unit can effectively sustain watershed rehabilitation and management?

Watersheds are geophysical entities and the people who inhabit them are not organized as one social unit. But the topographic pattern of the watershed and its resources shape human activities, division of labor, settlement patterns, and so forth. It has been observed that human societies in different parts of the world have frequently adapted themselves to the watershed landscape in similar manners and there are often "parallels between the ways in which human groups are organized and spatially distributed and the physical characteristics of the watersheds."[78] It is the physical potential and resources of watersheds that are used—and often abused—in people's productive activities. This is why watershed-use planning, erosion control, or watershed reforestation cannot be effective and sustained unless they are designed to enlist watershed inhabitants in rehabilitation work.

The need for an explicit sociological dimension in watershed resource management programs is being increasingly realized. A forward-looking strategy proposal for rehabilitating about 150 million hectares of degraded watersheds in developing countries strongly urges the recognition of this sociological dimension:

Watershed projects deal with people. The key to securing people's participation in such programs will lie in designing broad strategies based on a better understanding of their perceived needs and priorities and in particular of local land tenure . . . . This implies that enough time will have to be spent at the outset of project development on sociological studies in order to define the type of incentives needed to elicit farmers' cooperation.[79]

The challenges for sociology contained in such strategies, and the call for specific answers and implementable social engineering, are pressing. There are important practical questions to be asked from a sociological angle. For instance, if a watershed is treated in physical planning as an ecological system, can the ecosystem users be regarded as a constituted *social* system? What is the need for, and the degree of actual cooperation among inhabitants in their productive activities? Can ecosystem inhabitants act collectively, in a more or less coordinated manner, to protect and develop the natural resources of the watershed? If not, how can such collective action be encouraged?

A single watershed may contain a broad diversity of tenurial arrangements, stratified social groups, and various farming systems and land use patterns, evolved as forms of adaptation to the various physical segments of that watershed. Moreover, rehabilitation of deforested watersheds demands much more than massive planting of trees. It involves flood control and soil conservation; often bench terraces need to be built, requiring excavation, leveling, and refill work; farming systems need to be adapted to the ecological characteristics; and changes may be needed in the land use rights, in the rules of land transmittal, and in settlement patterns and the number of inhabitants. The work that needs to be done is therefore usually beyond the scope of what individual farmers can do as discrete actors.

Again, *group* action is required, as well as support from technical agencies. But as pointed out earlier, coordinated and collective action does not ensue *automatically* just because individuals stand to gain from such consensual action. They must (a) understand subjectively the commonalities underpinning their objective interests, (b) be willing to act consensually, and (c) organize themselves into some kind of group structures, with goals and rules conducive to carrying out the requisite activities. Coordinated social action for the management of watershed resources is probably one of the most complex types of collective adoption of innovation, particularly when it has to start from the absence of structured groups.

Organizing structures for social action and engineering the formation of a group from discrete and not necessarily interactive farmers is a task no less difficult than any of those previously discussed. Watersheds and microwatersheds could be used as the physical subdivisions within which some coordination of farmers' activities can be attempted as a group effort. Farmer groups should be promoted and thus should be involved in the design of a land use plan for the watershed and gain the strength to sustain it through convergent practices based on perceived common objectives and jointly enforced rules.

In such an approach, the sociologist would be called upon not only to design the social mechanism for a watershed strategy through applied fieldwork but also to provide an indispensable contribution by actually implementing it along with the land use planner, the forestry agent, and others. In the case of the very successful agroforestry project in Haiti discussed earlier, which was designed and directly managed for several years by social anthropologists,[80] sociological knowledge, applied with commitment and creativity, contributed decisively to success and created a tested model for guiding future social forestry efforts.[81]

Conclusions

The alternative types of social units examined above do not exhaust the list of potential social actors for afforestation programs. The same line of thinking can be continued in order to spotlight other kinds of social units and thus multiply the array of social actors able to involve themselves in forestry development.

In a broad sociological sense, the forest departments themselves are also a form of social organization created to perform, by using state investments, the functions of conserving, managing, and developing forests. As administrative bodies, forest departments are of a different organizational nature than the types of social units—organized population groupings—that have been discussed in this study. But forest departments may play a critical role in fostering and encouraging the formation of such groups among users of fuelwood, and in providing them with sylvicultural, organizational, and economic assistance to produce trees.

Foresters, by and large, are still far from knowing how to accomplish the social side of their task, but they must learn to work with people as well as with trees.

In turn, the many nongovernmental organizations that make forestry and environmental conservation their own agenda, may become also the organizers of people's productive *organizations* and help users to act and structure themselves as producers. Identifying or creating social units is a task that requires both informed sociological understanding of what is to be done and methods for social organization. The point is that such social forms need not necessarily predate the development intervention, nor should they all be created from scratch. In order to grow trees on the gigantic scale necessary now, people's capabilities must be enhanced through organizational strengthening, adaptation, and innovation. Such enhancement itself is part and parcel of the development process.

In conclusion, it may be adequate to stress that social forestry carries with it the connotations of both a philosophy of development and a pragmatic operational strategy. The philosophy postulates the centrality of people in forestry, the centrality of the masses of users becoming producers. It breaks radically with the stereotype that forest growth is the business of professional foresters alone, or of mother nature alone. In turn, the operational strategy to service this philosophy pertains to the "how-to" questions and is being fashioned with every new project or bold social experiment that attempts to involve people in tree growing.

The practice of social forestry is wide open to multiple approaches, open to the creation of diverse patterns of social organization as matrices for action. It is open to imaginative and informed combinations of innovations in land tenure and tree tenure, of various forms of ownership or usufruct, of tested or unorthodox tree-growing techniques, and of age-old or novel social structures ranging from the farm family to all kinds of purposively created groups.

The analysis of many available options shows that there is no single "best" social approach that will prove optimal for all situations of forestry development: the possible strategies span a broad spectrum. Sociological knowledge is instrumental and indispensable for conceiving and implementing each new approach. Alternatives can be devised through testing and learning. To use William Foote Whyte's term, such alternatives should be encouraged as "social inventions" for performing more effectivly productive and distributional functions.[82]

Notes

The author wishes to express his appreciation to the foresters, social scientists, and colleagues who have helped him during the fieldwork and postfieldwork phases of the preparation of this chapter. Particular thanks go to V. Rajagopalan, J. Spears, R. Rowe, L. Christoffersen, S. Draper, O. Baikal, T. Masud, Q. Aftab, A. H. Suhrawardi, Akbar Ahmed, D. Pickering, S. Guggenheim, Augusta Molnar, and A. K. Banerjee for their valuable comments and suggestions. The chapter was completed during the author's work at Harvard University as visiting scholar in the Department of Anthropology and Institute for International Development (HIID) during 1989–90, and grateful thanks are due to David Maybury-Lewis, Pauline Peters, and Ricardo Godoy for their assistance.

1. I found a relatively early use of the concept "social forestry" (perhaps the earliest use in an important government program) in the *Interim Report of the National Commission on Agriculture and Social Forestry* prepared in 1973 for the Government of India (Ministry of Agriculture, New Delhi, August 1973). "Social forestry" was proposed and advocated in that report in contrast with, and as an alternative to, what was then called "extension forestry"; the latter was criticized as inadequately meeting the "social demands on forests" (p. 10).

The objectives specific to "social forestry" were defined in that 1973 report as follows: (i) fuelwood supply to the rural areas and replacement of cow dung; (ii) small timber supply; (iii) supply of grasses and fodder and provision of grazing; (iv) protection of agricultural fields against wind; and (v) recreational needs (see p. 12 of that report).

2. *Forestry Sector Policy Paper*, prepared by G. Donaldson (coordinating author), J. Spears, G. Temple, J. Goering, and D. Dapice. World Bank, Agriculture Department, Washington, D.C., February 1978.

3. See Everett Rogers and F. Shoemaker, *Communication of Innovations: A Cross-Cultural Approach* (New York: Free Press, 1971); see also E. Rogers, *Diffusion of Innovations*, 3rd ed. (New York: Free Press, 1983).

4. Patrick C. West, "Collective Adoptions of Natural Resource Practice in Developing Nations," *Rural Sociology,* vol. 48, no. 1 (1983); and Patrick C. West and S. Light, "Community Level Change Strategies for the Management of Fragile Environments," in K. Shapiro, ed., *Science and Technology for Managing Fragile Environments in Developing Nations* (Ann Arbor: University of Michigan Press, 1978).

5. Louise Fortmann, "Great Planting Disasters: Pitfalls in Technical Assistance in Forestry," *Agriculture and Human Values* (Winter–Spring 1988), p. 51.

6. World Bank, Staff Appraisal Report for the Azad Kashmir Hill Farming Technical Development Project (HFTDP), 1978.

7. World Bank, Staff Appraisal Report for the Integrated Hill Farming Development Project (IHFDP), 1984.

8. For a more detailed account of this field study, see Michael M. Cernea, *Land Tenure and the Social Implications of Forestry Development Programs*, World Bank Staff Working Paper no. 452 (Washington, D.C., 1981).

9. *The Jammu and Kashmir Forest Regulations No. 2 of 1930*; see also the "Act to Amend the Jammu and Kashmir Forest Regulations of 1930," published as Act V of 1976 in the *Gazette of Azad Jammu and Kashmir*, vol. 22, no. 36, Muzaffarabad (May 13, 1976).

10. The literature is replete with evidence about such conflicts, crying for radical reversals. Simon Commander, commenting upon a similar state of acute conflict in the Chatanogpur region of Bihar between the Forest Department and the adivasi population, called it a "deterioration to quasi-insurrectional proportions" (see S. Commander, "Managing Indian

Forests: A Case for the Reform of Property Rights," *Development Policy Review*, vol. 4 (1986) p. 332.

11. Sydney Draper, personal communication.

12. World Bank, Staff Appraisal Report for the Azad Kashmir Hill Farming Technical Development Project (HFTDP), 1978.

13. W. H. Moreland, in *"The Agrarian Systems of Moslem India,"* considers that the usual naming of Khalsa as "crown land" is somehow "misleading." He emphasizes the meaning of Khalsa as "free," reserved land, which is not assigned to individual owners, land over which the government, through the Revenue Department, exercises will and authority, or virtual ownership (see W. H. Moreland, *The Agrarian System of Moslem India. A Historical Essay with Appendices*, Central Book Depot, Allahabad, 1929, pp. 29 and 273).

14. The official definitions of these two categories of forest land, given in the 1930 Jammu and Kashmir Forest Regulation Act, No. 2, are:

Demarcated Forest means forest land or waste land under the control of the Forest Department, of which boundaries have already been demarcated by means of pillars of stone or masonry or by any other conspicuous mark, or which may hereafter be constituted as a demarcated forest;

Undemarcated Forest means and includes all forest land and waste land (other than demarcated forest and such waste land as is under the management and control of the Revenue Department), which is the property of the Government and is not appropriated for any specific purpose.

As a rule of thumb, the demarcated forests are of higher density and better quality than the undemarcated ones, which are often located between the demarcated forests and the cultivated lands.

15. Ailan (Proclamation) No. 17 of the Jammu and Kashmir Government issued on September 13, 1927, gave permission to record as Shamilat the Khalsa waste areas already in joint village possession and also sanctioned; some restrictions notwithstanding, the recording of certain tracts as Shamilat private holdings in the Jamabandi (the register of holdings of owners and tenants) under three subclasses: Shamilat Malikan, Shamilat Malguzaran, and Shamilat Maurusian, according to the nature of rights of the respective village landholder in the register.

16. Land Revenue Act, sec. 150 A. In principle, according to the law, when a cosharer of shamilat encroaches upon it and includes it in his cultivated area, he can be ejected at the request of another cosharer. However, such grievances, and particularly their enforcement, have been rather infrequent. A rigorous land census in the late 1920s, for instance, would have found nowhere in the area of today's Azad Kashmir as much as the 325,000 acres of shamilat lands assumed to exist at the appraisal of the Hill Farming Technical Development Project. Even less land in this category could be found now, in the late 1980s.

17. W. H. Moreland quotes the following description from the revenue records of 1822–33:

The strong and crafty too frequently in past and present times have got the better of the weak and simple; the absence of those entitled to share, or the incapacity (from old age or other causes) of some of the resident proprietors, has enabled others, on pretence of deposit or management, to obtain and keep possession of shares very disproportionate to their hereditary rights (1929, p. 163).

18. *Nautor* is a piece of state-owned Khalsa land that is encroached for cultivation; the encroacher is called *Nautor Kumanda*.

19. The Azad Jammu and Kashmir Grant of Khalsa Wasteland as Shamilat-Deh Act, 1966 (Act I of 1966) in the *Extraordinary Gazette*, vol. 18, no. 20, Muzaffarabad, August 4.

20. *Azad Jammu and Kashmir Regulation of Nautors and Grant of Khalsa Land Ordinance*, 1974.

21. Suhrawardi, A. H., *Land Tenure Patterns and Customary Usage Rights in Azad Jammu and Kashmir*, paper prepared for HFTDP, 1981, processed.

22. The wealthier farmers benefited most from the project's financing of all the costs of the fuelwood planting, which included seedlings and the establishment of nurseries, labor for planting and filling in, transport of plants, and protection (wages for guards) for several years. The cost for planting was estimated to be Rs. 1,300 per acre, which excludes the costs of annual maintenance and protection between planting and harvesting, estimated at an additional Rs. 600–700 per acre per tree-crop rotation.

23. In a neighboring province of Pakistan, the North-West Frontier Province, the Hazara Forestry Act (1936) provides an interesting example of a contractual relationship that ensures legal protection for the group-ownership rights of the farmers, while vesting the authority to manage their forests in the Forest Department. This act also institutionalizes a contractual mechanism whereby the government costs for management and commercial exploitation are covered by a fraction of the proceeds from sold timber, which go to the owners.

24. See Operations Evaluation Department, Project Performance Audit Report for the HFTDP, World Bank, Washington, D.C., December 1986.

25. World Bank, Staff Appraisal Report for the Integrated Hill Farming Development Project (IHFDP), 1984.

26. See Y. S. Rao, "Community Forestry: Requisites and Constraints," in *Community Forestry: Some Aspects* (Bangkok: United Nations Development Programme, East-West Center, and RAPA/Food and Agriculture Organization, 1984); see also *Forestry for Local Community Development*, FAO Forestry Paper No. 7, 1978, Rome.

27. World Bank, Uttar Pradesh Social Forestry Project, Staff Appraisal Report, May 1979.

28. World Bank, Gujarat Community Forestry Project, Staff Appraisal Report, 1980.

29. World Bank, West Bengal Social Forestry Project, Staff Appraisal Report, September 1981.

30. World Bank, India: National Social Forestry Project, Staff Appraisal Report, May 1985.

31. Abdul Salam, Field report on sociological aspects in the National Social Forestry Project, Gujarat Sub-project, January 1989, processed; also Dr. A. K. Banerjee, personal communication.

32. Mid-term review materials for the National Social Forestry Project in India, World Bank, June 1988.

33. J. E. M. Arnold and W. C. Stewart, *Common Property Resource Management in India*, Report to the India Agriculture Division, World Bank, June 1989, p. 25.

34. Shepherd, Gill, *Forest Policies, Forest Politics*, ODI Social Forestry Network, Network Paper 3, (London: Overseas Development Institute, 1986).

35. See J. T. Thomson, *Bois de Villages (Niger): Report of an Investigation Concerning Socio-Cultural and Political-Economic Aspects of the First Phase of the Project and Design Recommendations for a Possible Second Phase* (Montreal: Canadian International Development Agency, February 1980).

36. See Rao, 1984; Raymond Noronha, "Village Woodlots: Are They A Solution?" Paper prepared for the Panel on the Introduction and Diffusion of Renewable Energy Technologies (Washington, D.C. : National Aeronautics and Space Administration, November 1980).

37. Arnold and Stewart, 1989.

38. Jodha, N. C., "Rural Common Property Resources: Contributions and Crises," Foundation Day lecture, Society for the Promotion of Wasteland Development, New Delhi, May 16, 1990; see also "Common Property Resources and the Rural Poor in Dry Regions of India," *Economic and Political Weekly,* no. 27, July 1986.

39. Michael Horowitz, analyzing rural afforestation alternatives in Zimbabwe, pointed out that "the important issue where communal lands are involved is correctly identifying the locus of authority over land use allocation." See Michael M. Horowitz, *Zimbabwe Rural Afforestation Project, Social Analysis Working Paper* (Binghamton, N.Y.: Institute for Development Anthropology, 1982), p. 51.

40. Daniel W. Bromley, "Closing Comments," in *Proceedings of the Conference on Common Property Resource Management,* (Washington, D.C.: National Academy Press, 1986); Elinor Ostrom, "Issues of Definition and Theory: Some Conclusions and Hypothesis," in *Proceedings of the Conference on Common Property Resource Management* (Washington, D.C.: National Academy Press, 1986); Pauline E. Peters, "Some Observations on the NAS volume on Common Property Resource Management." Paper presented at the Sociological Roundtable on Common Property Resources, World Bank, February 1988.

41. Mathew S. Ghamser, for instance, reported on an interesting community forestry project in Sudan (Um Inderaba) where the village community (some 600 families) was effective in planting, hand-watering, and maintaining the trees against extremely adverse conditions: complete lack of rain and large transient animal herds; it appears that the village committee and the local sheikh were able to aggregate effectively the villagers' activities, while incentives and protection payments were provided, together with technical advice from foresters (see Mathew S. Ghamser, *Letting the Piper Call the Tune: Experimenting with Different Forestry Extension Methods in the Northern Sudan,* ODI Social Forestry Network, Network Paper 4a, London: Overseas Development Institute, 1987).

42. Robert Chambers, N. C. Saxena, and T. Shah, *To the Hands of the Poor. Water and Trees* (New Delhi: Oxford and IBH Publishing Co., 1989), pp. 155–7; see also the *Asia-Pacific Community Forestry Newsletter,* RECOFTC, vol. 2, no. 1 (1989).

43. Eric R. Wolf, "Kinship, Friendship, and Patron-Client Relations in Complex Societies," in Michael Banton, ed., *The Social Anthropology of Complex Societies* (London: Tavistock Publications, 1966), p. 4.

44. Moreland, 1929, p. 161.

45. Dumont wrote: "The overall point is that within the village and within the dominant caste itself there is division into units which spring from no traditional principle, and in which each man's adherence is mainly or to a large extent governed by his interests." (L. Dumont, *Hommo Hierarchicus. The Caste System and Its Implications,* Chicago: University of Chicago Press, 1980, p. 164.)

46. Robert Wade, *Village Republics: Economic Conditions for Collective Action in South India* (Cambridge: Cambridge University Press, 1988).

47. Daniel W. Bromley and Michael M. Cernea, "The Management of Common Property Natural Resources: Some Conceptual and Operational Fallacies." Paper presented at the World Bank Agricultural Symposium, January 1989.

48. Louise Fortmann, "The Tree Tenure Factor in Agroforestry with Particular Reference to Africa," in L. Fortmann and John W. Bruce, eds., *Whose Trees? Proprietary Dimensions of Forestry* (Boulder, Colo.: Westview Press, 1988).

49. World Bank, Staff Appraisal Report for Azad Kashmir Hill Farming Technical Development Project, 1978.

50. World Bank, Staff Appraisal Report for Jammu and Kashmir and Haryana Social Forestry Project, September 1982.

51. World Bank, Staff Appraisal Report for Kerala Social Forestry Project, December 1984.

52. Mid-term review materials for the National Social Forestry Project in India, World Bank, 1988.

53. Gerald F. Murray, "The Domestication of Wood in Haiti: A Case Study in Applied Evolution," in Robert M. Wulff and Shirley J. Fiske, eds., *Anthropological Praxis* (Boulder, Colo.: Westview Press, 1987); see also "Seeing the Forest while Planting the Trees: An Anthropological Approach to Agroforestry in Rural Haiti," in D. W. Brinkerhoff and J. C. Garcia-Zamor, eds., *Politics, Projects and People. Institutional Development in Haiti* (Denver: Praeger, 1989).

54. Julia Falconer, *Forestry Extension: A Review of the Key Issues*, ODI Social Forestry Network, Network Paper 4e (London: Overseas Development Institute, 1987).

55. FAO, "Planning Forestry Extension Programmes." Report of a Regional Expert Consultation, Bangkok, May 1988; see also Indian Institute of Management, "Planning Forestry Extension Programmes, India." Papers presented at an IIMA/FAO-RWEDP Workshop, Ahmedabad, January 1988.

56. Cynthia C. Cook and Mikael Grut, "Lessons from Agroforestry in Sub-Saharan Africa: Some Farmer Perspectives," World Bank, Technical Department, Africa Region, Washington, D.C., p. 55.

57. World Bank, *Malawi: Forestry Subsector Study* (Washington, D.C.: 1984).

58. Cook and Grut, *op. cit.*

59. Robert Chambers and Melissa Leach, "Trees as Savings and Security for the Rural Poor," in *World Development*, vol. 17 (1989).

60. The economic analysis of such a land lease scheme indicates that if some 2,500 seedlings can be given free to each participating family for staggered, year by year planting over ten to twelve years, the family would become self-sustaining on tree cropping alone when the first year's plantation will reach maturity. The family would satisfy its domestic fuelwood needs from lops, tops, and fallen wood and could sell the main stem volume for cash, replanting anew each year to replace the mature trees harvested.

61. A. U. Ramakrishna Rao and Daman Singh, "Wastelands Developments—A People's Movement." Paper presented at the Regional Seminar on Wasteland Developments for Fuelwood Energy and Other Rural Needs, Vadodra, India, November 1988.

62. A. K. Banerjee, personal communication; see also Banerjee, A. K., "Local Needs of Small Timber and Fuelwood in India," in K. Shepherd and H. V. Richter, eds., *Forestry in National Development*, The Australian National University, Development Studies Center no. 17.

63. A. K. Banerjee, "A Case of Group Formation in Forest Management," June 1989.

64. Donald A. Messerschmidt, "People and Resources in Nepal: Customary Resource Management Systems of the Upper Kali Gandaki," in *Proceedings of the Conference on Common Property Resource Management*, (Washington, D.C.: National Academy Press, 1986).

65. J. E. M. Arnold and J. Gabriel Campbell, "Collective Management of Hill Forests in Nepal: The Community Forestry Development Project," in *Proceedings of the Conference on Common Property Resource Management* (Washington, D.C.: National Academy Press, 1986).

66. Willem Floor, Report on Charcoal User Group Involvement in Forest Management in Niger, World Bank ESMAP Program, 1986.

67. Kjell Kilander, "Cooperatives for the Promotion of Forestry in Rural Development," *Unasylva*, vol. 39, nos. 3 and 4 (1987).

68. Mohammad A. Rauf, "Sociological Perspectives of Forestry Development in Pakistan," Report of Guzara Forest Owners Task Force (Islamabad, processed), pp. 101–4.

69. V. K. Misra, personal communication. See also report on "Meeting Rural Fuelwood and Forage Needs Through Tree Growers' Cooperative Societies—a Pilot Project Proposal," National Dairy Development Board, Anand, August 1985, processed.

70. Kamla Chowdhry, *Schools as Partners in Social Forestry*, Ford Foundation Discussion Paper Series (Delhi, August 1983).

71. John Spears, "Appropriate Technology in Social Forestry." Paper presented at the Interregional Workshop on Appropriate Technology, Kathmandu, Nepal, November 1983.

72. Marilyn W. Hoskins, "*Women in Forestry for Community Development*" (Washington, D.C.: U. S. Agency for International Development, 1979).

73. Augusta Molnar and Götz Schreiber, "Women in Forestry Operational Issues," PPR Working Paper Series, World Bank, Agriculture Department, Washington, D.C., 1989.

74. David W. Brokensha, B. W. Riley, and A. P. Castro, *Fuelwood Use in Rural Kenya: Impacts of Deforestation* (Binghamton, N.Y.: Institute for Development Anthropology, 1983), p. 9.

75. Dianne Rocheleau, "Women, Trees, and Tenure: Implications for Agroforestry Research and Development," in John Raintree, ed., *Land, Trees, and Tenure* (Nairobi: ICRAF, 1987); also, personal communication, 1990.

76. D. R. Dioman, "Involvement of Women in Social Forestry in Himachal Pradesh." Paper presented at the NWDR seminar, New Delhi, February 1989.

77. An interesting analysis of the issues of human energy and women's work, including the implications for women's gathering, using, and producing firewood, is contained in Irene Tinker, "The Real Rural Energy Crisis: Women's Time" (Washington, D.C.: EPOC, 1984, processed); see also Irene Tinker, *Women, Energy and Development* (Vienna: Centre for Social Development and Humanitarian Affairs, 1982).

78. G. W. Lovelace and A. Terry Rambo, "Behavioral and Social Dimensions," in Easter, Dixon, and Hofschmidt, eds., *Watershed Resource Management* (Boulder: Westview Press, 1986).

79. John Spears and Edward Ayensu, "Resource Development and the New Century: Sectoral Paper on Forestry," World Resources Institute, Washington, D.C., 1984.

80. Gerald F. Murray, "Anthropologists and the Tree Planting Transition in Haiti." Paper presented at the 88th annual meeting of the American Anthropological Association, Washington, D.C., November 1989.

81. Frederick J. Conwey, "Broadening Fields of Action: Anthropologists and Project Implementation in Haiti." Paper presented at the 88th annual meeting of the American Anthropological Association, Washington, D.C., November 1989.

82. William F. Whyte, "Social Inventions for Solving Human Problems," *American Sociological Review*, vol. 47 (1982).

PART VI

Rural Road Projects

Editor's Note

A road can dramatically alter an area's growth patterns by providing access to markets, services, and employment opportunities. The location of roads in relation to particular villages causes some communities to experience rapid change while others remain relatively stagnant. Roads that open up tropical frontiers can have positive or adverse social and environmental effects transforming land use, facilitating commercial activities, encouraging immigration, and at times leading to social conflicts. These and other socioenvironmental consequences can be anticipated—and mitigated when needed—if, as the following chapter by Cynthia Cook proposes, social analysis is made a regular part of the preparation of rural road projects.

The construction of rural roads, as of other kinds of major physical infrastructures, has often been treated as a purely engineering task. The social implications of constructing rural road networks have long been overlooked or considered in an improvised manner. Cook identifies the main sociocultural issues relevant for rural road building and formulates specific questions about community activities and structures that need to be answered when road projects are designed.

What role can sociologists play as part of a technical design team for rural road projects? Depending on overall project objectives and the sociocultural context, some design issues are best addressed by a trained social scientist, even though predicting subsequent impact is a very difficult task. However, if the technical planners and supervision staff who will be involved with the project over the long term are not themselves sensitive to the cultural issues, the chances for adverse social impacts of roads are far greater. Cook thus suggests that some sociological education is necessary for the technical experts as well. She also suggests that sociologists interested in this area must absorb complementary technical know-how to become effective project co-planners, better able to merge their contribution with the economic and engineering expertise.

Participatory approaches in managing rural transport systems are critical for development, yet the actual experiences with such approaches are very limited. Although roads are frequently the largest single investment made in the context of a rural development program, much of this investment is often lost in a relatively short time because of lack of road maintenance. Social engineering to mobilize human resources, catalyze local initiative, and organize social entities to manage the physical infrastructure may thus go hand in hand with the civil engineering required to develop road networks.

11

Social Analysis in Rural Road Projects

Cynthia C. Cook

This chapter presents a case for incorporating social analysis into the planning and implementation of rural road projects. There are few types of investments which have more direct impact on overall rural development than rural roads; and there are few areas of infrastructure development where project planners could gain more by putting people first. Infrastructure projects traditionally have been designed according to economic and engineering criteria. These do not always fully meet the needs of the intended beneficiaries nor do they fully take advantage of local social, cultural, and technical resources.

A growing body of empirical evidence demonstrates that project design which pays close attention to social variables as described in this paper not only enhances the immediate usefulness of a project but also promotes more systematic maintenance and often triggers local economic multiplier effects. There are, in short, powerful utilitarian and humanistic arguments in favor of adding a sociological perspective to road planning, not least of which is to help project designers save time and money.

Although social analysis is needed at all stages of the project cycle, the skills of the professional social scientist are particularly essential during identification, preparation, and evaluation. A social perspective in the design of rural road projects and programs can help develop long-term community capabilities for self-directed and self-sustained growth.

This chapter attempts to show that there are indeed many sociological issues inherent in the design and implementation of rural road projects. The order of presentation adopted here follows that of the project cycle (see chapter 1): identification, preparation, appraisal, supervision, and evaluation. This chapter identifies issues that need to be addressed at each stage of the road project cycle, appropriate methods for field investigation, data needs, social variables, and analytical frameworks derived from sociological theories of social change. Some of the tasks suggested here can be most efficiently carried out by professional social scientists (sociologists or anthropologists), while others can be done by any socially sensitive member of a project planning team.

Although infrastructure projects are frequently portrayed as "hardware" projects with precise, measurable inputs and outputs, this chapter contends that social and cultural considerations are as important to the success of such projects as they are to the success of projects in "softer" sectors, particularly when viewed in the broader context of the rural development process.

Why is social analysis useful for rural road projects? First, it provides a better understanding of the characteristics and concerns of the proposed beneficiaries. This improves the basis for estimating project inputs and outputs in relation to real needs, and should enhance the economic rate of return, which is in large measure determined by the use made of the facilities. Second, the sustainability of rural road projects frequently depends on local involvement in road maintenance. There is obvious value in understanding which social groups can and will do this, how they are formed, and ways of involving community leadership so as to stimulate local interest in maintaining the project. Third, in addition to contributing to the economic success of the project, social analysis may also improve the impact of infrastructure investment on development in a broader sense, both by avoiding or compensating for negative social consequences, and by helping attain national social objectives.

The Role of Infrastructure in Rural Development

Classical, growth-oriented economic development strategies have been criticized for their excessive dependence on infrastructure investments. In the early years of development planning, major infrastructure investments were designed primarily to support the modern sector in developing countries, particularly export industries. They provided access to world markets and made it possible for an expanding urban elite to enjoy a life-style approaching that of the developed world. But they did little to alleviate the growing gap between the rich and the poor in developing countries.

Rural development projects started in the 1960s as a way to address the equity concerns and the long-term growth objectives of developing countries. These projects initially viewed the provision of services as the most effective way to meet basic human needs in rural areas, with income gains trickling in from the dynamic urban economy. Project planners soon realized, however, that industrial growth would not generate sufficient resources to meet rural needs simply through income transfers. Improving rural living standards would require increasing rural people's productivity. Programs to stimulate rural development generally included infrastructure as a significant component of the proposed investment package.[1] Four principal categories of infrastructure investment in early rural development projects were irrigation, water supply, rural electrification, and roads.[2]

Road projects produce profound socioeconomic effects in rural areas. Transport improvements may create significant changes in rural production strategies. Cash crop cultivation often becomes more profitable than producing food crops, and the resulting decline in local food production may create a potentially dangerous dependency on external sources of supply. Access to credit, extension, and marketing services will strongly influence whether and which households switch to cash crops and the types of new cropping systems adopted. Change (or lack of change) in production strategies will also reflect household structural variables such as size, age, and income sources. Greater cash incomes may bring about a substantial shift in the distribution of power and dependency within rural households.

Roads help to structure population growth and settlement in rural areas. New households cluster in the vicinity of roads and crossroads and may place excessive pressure on local resources such as water and wood. If a road opens access to good agricultural land, there may be significant in-migration of new farm families, with all that this means for future social relations between newcomers and old-timers. Roads also provide local residents with access to opportunities outside the project area and may cause significant temporary or permanent out-migration. Both patterns will have major consequences for the social structure of the project area. In the Philippines, for example, a new road connecting a remote area to the national highway network brought in large numbers of farmers familiar with modern production and marketing systems. They revolutionized the social structure which had prevailed when the area was isolated from the modern economy.[3] In Kenya, road improvements in densely populated areas provide access to urban job opportunities for men leaving farm management largely in the hands of women.[4]

In addition to the short-term job opportunities in road work and the broad opportunities for increased employment in agriculture (including diversification into cash crops, livestock and dairy operations, fish, and fruit and vegetable production for urban markets), rural road improvements also encourage the growth of nonfarm employment opportunities in commerce, services, and rural industries. The market for unskilled labor in rural areas expands and becomes more responsive to external pressures.[5] Thus, some of the benefits of transport cost savings may even be passed on to landless laborers and their families.

Road improvements provide a powerful inducement for service providers to extend into rural areas. Rural communities may build schools and clinics for themselves, but they are unlikely to receive adequate service until the center is staffed by a professional with ready access to supplies, supervision, and support from a central agency. Service providers frequently make their plans for rural areas contingent on improved access. However, road improvements alone cannot ensure successful service delivery. Service providers must have the funds to support travel costs, and their clients must be able to get to the service center. In addition, the services provided must be appropriate to the needs of the community if they are to have a positive impact on rural development.

Project planners, service providers, and beneficiaries agree that rural road investments should have high priority. Inadequate road access often constrains the delivery of other development inputs, both the physical inputs needed to increase production (for example, fertilizer, cement, and fuel), and the people required for the successful delivery of services (teachers, health workers, and extension agents). Rural or feeder roads play an important role in the collection and distribution of goods, generating the traffic volumes needed to support major investments such as highways and ports. Local planners and politicians like roads because they provide ready access to people and facilitate information flows in rural areas. Agency staff, local officials, and project staff are keenly aware of road deficiencies which inhibit the success of their programs.

If prospective development beneficiaries are consulted, they usually place rural road improvements high on their list of priorities.

Rural people want road improvements, however, for reasons that are often different from those of planners. Planners tend to think primarily in terms of the movement of goods and the efficiencies to be achieved by motorized transport. Local people are interested in these too, but they are also motivated by opportunities for personal mobility and improvement in the quality of their lives. Roads provide access to a larger labor market or to better markets for their farm products; they make it possible to send a child to secondary school in a nearby town or to visit a health center or hospital in case of emergency; they allow people to maintain contact with relatives or friends who have moved away, or to move away themselves without losing touch with their roots in the village. Furthermore, in areas which have recently experienced food deficits, planners, politicians, donors, and beneficiaries all agree on the importance of reliable road access for the timely delivery of emergency food supplies.

During the 1970s, the World Bank undertook a number of "integrated" rural development projects, many of which had major rural road components. These projects were often overly complex and ambitious; many failed to achieve their targets. Lessons drawn from the first generation of such projects led project planners to conclude that resources might be better focused on those sectors, like roads, which had shown a relatively high degree of success in terms of project implementation.[6]

During the latter part of the decade, therefore, a number of rural road projects were initiated in Africa, Asia, and Latin America. These projects were designed to strengthen institutional capacity to meet rural road needs by establishing suitable selection criteria, determining appropriate design standards and the optimal use of labor and equipment, and developing local skills in construction planning and management.[7] A decade later, the results of these initiatives can be evaluated on the basis of empirical evidence. Some rural road projects have been quite successful, while others have been conspicuous failures.[8] The successful projects are those which have created a lasting institutional capacity and have been drawn into the political process at the local level. The failures are those which became bogged down in bureaucratic battles and failed to establish effective communication with their constituencies.

Improved road infrastructure does not necessarily guarantee improved access, however. Road improvements must be accompanied by a growth in transport services, either public or private. It is often important to analyze the policy context, which may be a significant determinant of the extent to which transport service improvements will take place.[9] Other factors may include the availability of vehicles, fuel, and spare parts; access to credit by entrepreneurs and community groups; the structure of local employment; and the relationship of road improvements to the possible use of adaptive or appropriate transport technology.[10] Road infrastructure may play a different role in rural development than the one implied by classic economic models. Without complementary agricultural investments and a favorable macroeconomic climate, road improvements do not necessarily result in an increase in agricultural production. They do, however, reduce distortions in rural markets due to poor communications, and thereby facilitate a more efficient and equitable use of human and physical resources.[11]

Sociological Perspectives on Rural Road Projects

The problems of designing infrastructure projects to improve the welfare and stimulate the productivity of small farmers are quite different from those of designing major civil works. The former call for understanding local resources, skills, and capabilities, as well as forms of social organization and decisionmaking processes in households and communities. Infrastructure projects essentially alter the physical environment in ways that change the structure of opportunities for growth in rural society. To understand and predict how people will react to these changes, the relationship between social organization and control over the physical environment must be analyzed within each specific rural setting.

Sociology provides a number of theoretical perspectives useful for addressing these issues. Systems theories of modernization and social change stress the complex interactions between physical environment, behavioral reactions, and sociological response. Human ecology focuses on the mechanisms by which human societies adapt to changes in their environments. These can include social arrangements, technology, and certain aspects of culture. By emphasizing the complex linkages found within and between systems, human ecology can make predictions about responses to perturbations such as road projects. Organizational theory, particularly as it emphasizes the importance of interorganizational relationships and boundary transactions between organizations and their environments, provides useful insights into the institutional requirements for rural development projects.[12]

There is by now a substantial literature on the socioeconomic impact of rural road improvements.[13] In addition to the immediate consequences of rural roads, which are apparent to both planners and beneficiaries, there are many long-range social impacts that are likely to be less recognized in advance by either group. These consequences, some of which will be seen as positive and others as negative by different social groups or in different cultural settings, need careful consideration during the project design process and should form part of the basis for subsequent monitoring and evaluation activities.

The social aspects of rural roads projects should be considered at project identification, examined during project preparation, critically reviewed at appraisal, carefully monitored during implementation, and assessed at the end of the project. Of course, the aspects that should be reviewed will vary by project and location. At the level of the individual, key descriptive indicators normally include: age, sex, ascriptive characteristics such as ethnic identity, and achieved characteristics such as education and employment. Relevant variables at the household level are farm size, land tenure, cropping patterns, other forms of production or other sources of income, vehicle ownership, travel patterns, and service utilization. At the community level, descriptive variables may include settlement patterns, migration, social organization, self-help traditions, and decisionmaking processes. Key variables concerning institutions include staff size and skills, salaries and incentives, legal authority, bureaucratic culture, fiscal resources, centralization, coordination, and commitment to the task of rural development.

Some design issues in rural road projects call for the specialized skills of a trained social scientist (sociologist or anthropologist) who can assess the likely role of each of these variables in determining the outcome of a particular project. There is a small but growing community of social scientists who have the requisite skills and are familiar with the technical and economic issues raised by rural road projects. Because they have both project experience and sociological expertise, social scientists should be included whenever possible on project preparation teams and should also be involved in project evaluation.

It may be more effective to employ such scientists as consultants than to divert the limited time of generalist staff into social analysis outside of their own areas of competence. It is not always possible, however, for a professional social scientist to be a permanent member of the planning team that follows a project from identification to evaluation. For this reason, it is important to develop social analysis skills among project and program planners from other disciplines. These skills include the ability to assess the social and cultural factors in each situation which require further study by a specialist. They also include the ability to identify opportunities for enhancing a project's social impact and to design and implement an institutional framework that will promote and respond to local initiative. A social perspective in transport sector analysis should lead to the identification of projects that correspond more closely to people's mobility and communications needs, as well as expediting commodity movements.

The objectives of rural road projects may be to help increase agricultural production, to provide services and amenities to the rural population, to generate asset-creating employment, or to meet needs for personal mobility. Achievement of these objectives depends on people's behavioral response to the project. Will extension agents visit more farms if access is made easier? Will farmers adopt new technology and invest in inputs? Will teachers and doctors come to live in the community? Will the community be willing and able to maintain the improved road? Will people travel more to sell their products, to seek employment, or to participate in social and political activities? What other constraints will affect people's response to the road? These questions can be adequately answered only by a project planner with social analysis skills, and frequently only by a professional social scientist.

Rural road projects may also have unintended negative social consequences. For example, increases in land value caused by road improvements may be captured largely by wealthy persons, often outsiders, who buy up small farms in advance of construction. Such actions contribute to the impoverishment of already disadvantaged rural households. Several social scientists predicted the disastrous effect that Brazil's BO 360 road in the Amazon basin would have on the indigenous people, environment, and agriculture. Unfortunately, the financing for this road went ahead, and its actual negative impacts led subsequently to the formal recognition that the project had been a mistake. If such impacts can be anticipated, the project design can include mitigating measures such as land registration in the impact zone or controls over land transfers during the project period. Thus, possible negative outcomes of a project should always be assessed so that remedial actions can be built into its design.

Identification: How Planners Plan Roads

Rural transport is a derived demand, arising out of the basic needs of rural people for food, shelter, employment, health, education, security, and social contact.[14] The need for improvements in a country's rural transport and communications infrastructure should be identified through country economic and transport sector work. Country economic analysis describes the characteristics of the population and identifies the constraints which prevent the country from realizing its productive potential. It is frequently found that poverty is most prevalent in rural areas and that alleviating it requires overcoming a transport constraint (among others). In both agriculture and transport sector work, the need to invest in rural road improvements may also become apparent through the analysis of other projects and programs.

Rural road improvements become part of national investment programs in one of three ways. The first is when the major highway network of a country is completed and highway planners turn their attention to rural roads. This often results in a centrally planned program executed on a national scale, in which investments are spread among regions in response to political and social as well as economic priorities. Examples of such programs are Colombia's *Caminos Vecinales* and Kenya's Rural Access Roads Program. The cost of such programs is likely to be high in relation to available resources, since the objective is to provide at least a minimum level of service to the entire rural population.

A second approach is to include rural road improvements in rural or regional development investment packages, as has been done, for example, in Malawi and Côte d'Ivoire. In such cases, the selection and design of transport improvements is likely to be based on the transport demand associated with the production and marketing of a particular commodity or on the needs of service providers, rather than on priorities expressed by the beneficiary population. Construction is usually carried out by mechanized means, and local people have little to say about the location or design standards of the roads. As a result, local people may be reluctant to assume responsibility for road maintenance after the project is over.

Irrigation projects often include roads constructed along embankments as a by-product of canal construction. Such roads are intended to provide access to the canals and pumping stations for maintenance purposes, but they may also serve a wide spectrum of other transport needs. Forestry projects often construct temporary, low-standard logging roads, which then provide access to forest areas for shifting cultivators or even permanent settlers. In integrated agricultural development projects, especially where an agricultural commodity is to be produced in order to supply a processing plant, road improvements are mainly intended to ensure the timely transport of inputs and outputs. In other words, such improvements are planned primarily to transport goods rather than to meet the mobility needs of people in the project area. Any benefit to the people is an additional windfall from the project.

A third approach to rural development is for a government to make funds available to rural communities to undertake projects of their own choice. Examples of this include the INPRES program of rural improvements in Indonesia, and the PIDER programs for rural development in Mexico. Often the primary rationale of such a program is to provide employment, although asset creation is presumed to be an important consequence. Wherever such programs have been implemented, communities have placed rural road improvements high on the list of projects to be carried out. Lack of technical know-how, insufficient funds, and lack of social organization for maintenance at the village level, however, have meant that such investments do not always provide the anticipated level of service. They may deteriorate rapidly after construction and thus generate only limited long-term benefits to rural communities.

Each of these approaches raises questions that may need to be answered during project preparation by a professional social scientist. For example, how can a centrally planned program tap into local knowledge and resources? What should be the social criteria for prioritizing investments? In a rural or regional development package, how should the road construction component be coordinated with the activities of other agencies? Will there be competition for the available labor force? In a self-help program, can technical assistance be provided in a way that will not undermine community initiative? What communication strategies will be most effective in explaining the need for regular maintenance, and how can local skills and resources be developed for this purpose? What data does a project need to answer these questions and how might it be obtained most efficiently? Should such questions arise, the planner may want to consider including the services of a professional sociologist or anthropologist as part of the project design team.

Three basic questions should always be considered during project identification. The first is: what is the appropriate technology for carrying out rural road improvements, and how will it affect employment? This appears to be a technical question, but in fact the answer depends largely on demographic patterns and the socioeconomic level of development in the project area. The choice of an appropriate technology takes into account such factors as population density and settlement patterns, soil and terrain, present and future traffic levels and types, alternative uses of labor, local skills and materials, and local forms of work organization. The short-run employment benefits of labor-based construction may need to be weighed against the long-run benefits of constructing roads by machine-intensive methods while subsequently maintaining them by labor-based methods.

A second question that should be asked at the identification stage concerns the structure of rural transport services and its implications for the social costs and benefits of the project.[15] Who owns the vehicles that serve the project area and thus will benefit from the savings in transport costs? Are there barriers to the free entry of project beneficiaries into the transport service sector? Who is providing these services now (for example, headloading or animal transport) and are they likely to be displaced as a result of the road improvement? Will the project provide them an opportunity for more productive employment? The project planner may decide, on the basis of this information, to structure the project somewhat differently or to include additional components, such as credit for vehicle purchase or complementary investments in agriculture, to help ensure that benefits actually reach the intended beneficiaries or to compensate individuals who may be harmed by the project.

Third, planners should consider how the proposed rural road program will fit into the country's legal and administrative structure serving rural areas. Who will maintain the roads once they are constructed? Will they have the resources needed to carry out this responsibility? Will they be able to identify maintenance needs, organize its execution, and supervise the work? Should the project include technical assistance and training to develop the necessary skills within local institutions? This assessment requires close collaboration between members of the planning team, agency officials, and local authorities. The project's assumptions regarding maintenance must be made explicit and responsibility assigned to a specific institution or community group during project preparation.

A related question frequently raised at the identification stage concerns the potential impact of a rural road improvement on migration patterns. In general, planners want rural roads to deliver goods and services and thus to enhance the perceived quality of life in rural areas so that rural-urban migration becomes less attractive. Yet they often fear that, by facilitating personal travel, road improvements may tend to make migration more attractive. There is no simple answer to this question. Research has shown that people certainly do respond to road improvements with more personal travel.[16] However, most rural people are attached to the land and to their small, close-knit communities. Thus, they respond to road improvements by adopting migration strategies (whether temporary, seasonal, or permanent) that will enable them to return frequently to their home communities.

Social Analysis in Project Design

Most of the detailed work of project design is, or should be, done during the project preparation stage. When rural road projects are part of a national program of road improvements, this goal is generally fulfilled. In contrast, when they are part of agricultural or rural development projects, roads often receive inadequate attention during the preparation stage, and when funds are provided to communities for self-help projects, rural roads may be hardly planned at all. Lack of attention to social issues in project design means not only costly delays and technical errors but also that many opportunities for maximizing benefits and minimizing costs to rural residents may be missed.

Subproject Selection

Since resources are rarely sufficient to meet all identified needs, the project planner must often select from among a number of specific subproject alternatives those which promise to be socially and economically the most rewarding. A useful approach may be to map the location of population centers and service centers such as markets, schools, and clinics in relation to the existing network of main roads, and then to screen the proposed subprojects in terms of the population served or the services provided per kilometer of road or per unit cost of construction. Subprojects with a high social priority can then be evaluated according to a set of economic criteria. Rural people can understand this process and the reasoning behind it, and a reasonably representative group of beneficiaries or local decisionmakers should participate in the screening and selection process.

Several strategies for public participation in planning rural roads have been identified in Bank-assisted projects.[17] At the lowest level, local people are merely asked to provide the information that planners need to evaluate subprojects and make design decisions. Almost all Bank-funded road programs rely on some sort of local information. A second level is reached when communities are allowed to initiate subproject proposals. This approach is fairly common throughout Latin America and is found in parts of Africa and Asia as well. Next comes the situation in which beneficiaries are invited to participate in making detailed design decisions, such as the choice of a specific alignment, size and placement of structures, or use of local materials. This is particularly likely to occur in labor-intensive programs such as those in Mexico and Colombia. A more sophisticated approach allows for beneficiary participation in the process of subproject selection. This occurs in rural infrastructure programs such as those in Indonesia, Korea, and the Philippines. In a few cases, it is possible simply to make funds available and let rural communities take full responsibility for the preparation and execution of the project. This is done, for example, in the secondary roads program in Brazil.

Needs Assessment

Planners responsible for project preparation will need to learn about the mobility needs of people in the project areas and the constraints which they perceive as preventing those needs from being fulfilled. These data are rarely available for areas where rural road improvements are being planned. Interviews with local authorities, line agency officials, and other local notables may elicit some of the needed information. However, different social groups have differing—and at times conflicting—transport needs. Care must be taken, therefore, to reach at least some of the people who can speak for less powerful groups, such as women and children, students, landless laborers, and ethnic minorities.[18] Consequently, adequate analysis of local needs depends on having sufficiently detailed socioeconomic knowledge to determine which groups should be consulted.

When communities are expected to commit resources of their own, such as land, materials, or contributions for the payment of workers, the local system of decisionmaking should be evaluated, preferably by a social scientist, to determine whether the planned use of these resources is consonant with the priorities of the people who own and use them. For example, if land is collectively owned and distributed to households or clans for their use on an annual basis, a collective decision involving all potential users will be the best way of ensuring an undisputed right-of-way for a road. Traditional social structures can also be used to mobilize resources for new activities, if these activities are consistent with the customary functions of the group.[19] Working directly with local leaders during project preparation also creates a communication channel which can help moderate the impact of sociocultural changes during the course of project implementation.

Engineering Design

Sociologists can help project engineers understand how the design characteristics of the proposed improvements will affect people's lives in the project area. Land may be taken out of production by the road, for example, and land values in the rest of the project area will be dramatically restructured.[20] Which social groups will benefit from these changes, and which will bear the costs? Will production increases on adjacent lands translate into increased incomes or more regular employment for landless laborers? How will dust and drainage from the road affect the productivity of adjacent farmlands? Will space be provided for pedestrian and other slow-moving traffic? Roads often cut right through the middle of rural villages. Will adequate provision be made for pedestrian safety?

The planned technology of road construction should be examined in detail during project preparation to see how it fits with the employment needs and the availability of labor in the project area. Will the road require workers at the same time as the peak labor demand for planting or harvest? Will it interfere with normal patterns of seasonal migration of labor? Who will be employed in road work and who controls access to these jobs? Will women be offered an equitable opportunity to participate in such work? Through training and organization for road work, can local people acquire new skills that can be used to satisfy other needs on a self-help basis?

Resettlement

Project planners must ensure that adequate arrangements are made for the resettlement of households that are physically displaced by, or lose farming land to, the project.[21] Population displacement requirements

should be minimized as much as possible by locating new road alignments at a safe distance from existing structures and by building improved roads on existing alignments. Consultation with communities
early in the project's preparation can help identify potential displacement
problems that can be avoided through alternative design decisions.

However, at times the widening of existing roads or physical constraints governing the siting of new roads will require, for safety reasons,
the removal of structures in the road right-of-way. This imposes severe
costs on the affected households that cannot readily be remedied through
the payment of cash compensation. In rural road projects, a relatively
small number of families should be affected in any one community, and
it should be possible to replace the lost housing and land assets without
forcing these families to leave the community. Project planners should
identify the individuals affected by road-related displacement requirements, and should consult with local authorities and service providers to
ensure that their needs are met through a resettlement plan to be funded
as part of the project.[22]

Large-scale resettlement should not occur in connection with rural
road projects, although large-scale resettlement requirements can be
caused by major highway projects passing through rural or peri-urban
areas. Where a highway project will displace significant numbers of
households, it may be necessary to identify a resettlement site or sites
and to plan for assistance to the affected population in moving to the new
sites and re-establishing productive activities. In China, for example,
when a provincial road cuts through a densely populated and intensively
cultivated rural area, local procedures require the payment of compensation for cultivated land, as well as a settlement allowance, totalling up
to twenty times the estimated annual output value of the acquired land.
In addition, the road agency and the local authorities are required to find
new employment for the displaced farmers, either in other agricultural
production enterprises or in industry.

Institutional Issues

Project preparation teams should consider how the rural road project
or project component fits into the overall administrative structure for
rural development. How far down the line can technical responsibility
for roads be decentralized?[23] Can paraprofessionals be used to improve
communications between agency staff and local communities?[24] How is

the programming of road improvements to be coordinated with the detailed planning of other agencies that will be using the roads to provide services? Would it make sense for the project to provide credit for vehicle purchase, or to support rural industries engaged in transport-related activities such as blacksmithing, cart construction, or bicycle repair? What can be done to build up a road maintenance capacity in the appropriate agency or local authority?

The rural road program in Mexico provides a good example of how a rural infrastructure project can be used to catalyze community organization and develop local capacity for self-sustained growth.[25] The implementing institution, SAHOP (Secretariat for Human Settlements and Public Works), is well-organized and adequately staffed down to the district level. Its annual work program is determined as a result of priorities expressed by local communities and, at the provincial level, is coordinated with the programs of other agencies. When communities request a rural road improvement, they are visited by SAHOP "promoters," who explain the nature of the program and the need for subsequent road maintenance. These promoters encourage the community to form a committee which is legally empowered to enter into a contractual relationship with the government. A written agreement specifies and schedules the resources to be provided by the government and the community, taking into account seasonal variations in labor demand for agriculture.

Where possible, rural road projects in Mexico use labor-intensive methods. This provides employment and transfers skills to the communities to meet the needs for subsequent road maintenance. The community association recruits and pays workers (with funds provided by SAHOP on the basis of kilometers completed at an agreed rate), and takes responsibility for the security of tools and equipment. By the time a project is over, the community association is in a good position to provide routine road maintenance on a contractual basis. It may also undertake additional projects, either in collaboration with other government agencies or on a self-help basis.

Although the results of this program are satisfactory at the community level, there is no institutional mechanism for coordinating efforts between communities. Because the transport network is made up of many interdependent parts, this oversight may cause significant difficulties for some communities. The energy and commitment to change manifested in self-help efforts depend greatly on the quality of local leadership, which may vary considerably within a given area. Without a social mechanism through which one community can exert pressure on another, more remote areas may be poorly served despite their best efforts, if communities closer to the main roads fail to maintain their part of the network.

Social Issues in Project Appraisal

The appraisal team is responsible for ensuring that a project will produce a general increase in human welfare without unduly penalizing any particular groups, especially those already disadvantaged. This means that the high cost of road improvements to society as a whole should bring a substantial increase in the welfare of the project area population. A well-prepared project will have gathered all of the basic information needed for appraisal, defined project objectives, proposed a plan of action, assigned institutional responsibilities for implementation, and presented cost estimates for project activities. Project appraisal includes assessment of the technical and sociocultural feasibility of the project design, as well as of its economic costs and benefits and their likely distribution among different social groups.

Technical Feasibility

Insofar as the issue of technical feasibility involves assumptions about human behavior, it, too, should be subject to social analysis. Are enough adequately and appropriately trained people available to carry out the project? Will the planned incentives be sufficient to induce these people to participate in this project rather than in some alternative activity? What are the assumptions about expatriate technical assistance, and how will this affect the way local people and host country planners see the project? Are the outputs expected of workers reasonable in view of their health and nutritional status and their family responsibilities? Perhaps some additional interventions should be planned to make sure that people are able to perform as expected.

Sociocultural Feasibility

The issue of sociocultural feasibility has to do with social or cultural constraints that affect the way people react to project incentives or opportunities. For example, if farmers are to invest additional time in agriculture in response to a price incentive, they may have to decrease the time they spend on certain social or ritual activities which also have value for them. Expecting women to benefit from the marketing of cash crops implies a series of assumptions regarding the ability of women to travel, to interact with strangers, to handle money, and to participate in household decisionmaking. Increased utilization of education, health, extension, or credit services may depend not only on improved access but also on cultural norms governing the patterns of interaction among people in the project area, and between them and various types of outsiders.

Social feasibility is especially an issue when some form of local participation in project implementation is planned. Such activities must be appropriate to local perceptions of needs and resources. Community contributions must be carefully planned so as not to penalize the poorer sectors of society while the wealthier individuals reap the full benefits of the improvement. (This danger is particularly prevalent where there is a large landless labor force in rural areas.) Plans for mobilizing local resources such as land, labor, or materials must be examined to see how they fit with traditional social mechanisms for accomplishing similar tasks.[26] The locus of leadership, power, and decisionmaking within the community needs to be understood in order to determine how the community can commit the required resources.

Institutional Issues

Institutional aspects of a project also need special attention at the appraisal stage. What is the source of authority of the executing agency for the road component, and where does it get its political support? Is it a new institution that will have to develop a whole set of working relationships with the agencies and local authorities already involved in the rural development process? How will its activities affect the ability and willingness of these agencies or authorities to assume responsibility for maintaining the roads? Should the project include a component explicitly designed to transfer management and maintenance skills to rural communities?

A review of some fifty Bank-assisted projects with rural road components identified a number of institutional issues related to project success: the degree of decentralization, the use of new versus existing institutions, public versus private sector implementation, political commitment, beneficiary participation, interagency coordination, and human resource development.[27] Each of these issues has implications for project planning, construction, and maintenance. This review concluded that the ultimate objective of institution-building components in rural road projects should be to strengthen institutional capacities at the local level, and that the lead role of the road-building agency should be clearly confined to a transitional stage in the rural development process.

Local Participation

Given the limited amounts of available resources relative to growing transport needs, project planners increasingly rely on rural communities to mobilize part of the resources needed to implement projects. This reliance is particularly marked with respect to road maintenance, where communities are often expected to assume recurrent costs needed to assure project sustainability. In the 1980s, the World Bank undertook case studies in Colombia, Benin, and Burundi to investigate the relationship between local participation in rural road planning and construction and subsequent responsibility for road maintenance. Comparative analysis of these case studies and other material showed that strong local leadership, the use of appropriate technology, successful transfer of organizational and financial skills, and actual accrual of benefits to the target population were the key factors in project sustainability.[28]

However, "participation" is a term requiring careful definition. All too often, planners expect rural people to participate in the costs and benefits of a project without participating in decisionmaking. If participation is to mean more than simple cost sharing, there are several basic issues that require sociological assessment.

First, it is not always clear *who* should participate in road project decisionmaking. Roads often crosscut local administrative units, and few representative bodies span wide regions. In addition, a road that benefits one community may be disadvantageous for another located on an old communication route or specialized in transport services. Both communities should be involved in project decisions. Second, *how* people participate lends itself to sociological input. Traditional public works organizations such as the *mink' a* in Andean America offer considerable local authority and, moreover, are a recognized way to tap local opinions.[29] Some alternative steps which have proven helpful in determining local opinion include bringing village councils into project planning as early as possible; arranging informal meetings between project authorities and residents; and making legal contracts between project planners and local leadership groups. NGOs can sometimes offer useful institutional support that not only provides a voice for local concerns but also offers a ready-made channel for project authorities to contact beneficiaries.

How much communities can participate is also of vital importance. While many communities can and do carry out road construction and repairs, few can afford to repair damages caused by major landslides or other large-scale natural calamities. Participatory designs must distinguish between tasks beneficiaries can reasonably be expected to handle and tasks which will require public sector intervention.

In Liberia and Madagascar, sociologists participating in project appraisal evaluated the potential for local participation in rural road maintenance. Their assessment of the potential role of communities and small contractors was based on an analysis of local institutions, labor requirements, migration patterns, and cultural constraints. The sociologists recommended appropriate institutional arrangements for maintaining the roads, including recruitment, supervision, and payment of workers, and ways of transferring administrative skills to contractors and communities. They found, for example, that persons with the needed skills were locally available, but that communities were not organized and empowered to raise the needed funds or provide effective supervision for self-help efforts. The projects were, therefore, designed to strengthen community capabilities, both by allocating funds from the central government and by providing technical training.

Distribution of Costs and Benefits

The social aspects of project appraisal call for analyzing the distribution of costs and benefits among different groups within the project area and between project area residents and outsiders. Broadly speaking, the capital costs of rural road improvements are paid for by the country as a whole, unless the funds are derived from a specific source of revenue (such as a fuel tax), or part of the costs are recovered from users (such as by collecting tolls). The recurrent costs of road maintenance, however, tend to fall on local communities, which rarely have sufficient revenues to meet them. In addition, communities may make contributions to capital costs by donating land, labor, or local materials or by providing tools, housing, or support services for construction workers. Whether these activities result in costs or benefits to local communities depends primarily on whether they are paid for under the project.

The economic benefits of rural road projects derive from the employment generated during the construction period (and, to a much lesser extent, during the operating period) and from the savings in transport costs over the lifetime of the investment. The extent to which these two benefits will accrue to the intended beneficiaries should be carefully examined at appraisal. The magnitude and distribution of employment benefits will depend largely on the choice of construction technology and the method of implementation (force account or contractors). The incidence of transport cost savings depends to a large extent on the structure of rural transport services and the shifts expected as a result of the project. In a competitive transport market, cost savings will be passed on to the consumer, but where monopsonistic practices prevail, road improvements may simply result in a larger profit margin for the (often externally based) purveyors of transport services.

The distribution of these benefits among different groups within the beneficiary communities should be carefully considered. For example, will women be permitted to participate in road work? What about members of minority groups or migrant laborers coming into the community? Will access to employment be controlled by a few individuals who will have an opportunity to divert a portion of the benefits to their own pockets? Might this be, however, a more cost-effective way to provide for the organization of casual labor than by setting up a full-scale bureaucracy?

The highly competitive and atomized nature of rural transport services in most countries means that transport cost savings are in fact fairly widely distributed among the rural population. Nevertheless, the distribution of transport cost savings depends on patterns of vehicle ownership and on the social relationships in which transport services play a role. To the extent that savings in freight transport costs are passed on, they naturally accrue largely to the consumers (in the case of inputs) or to the producers (in the case of outputs) of bulk commodities: traders, cooperatives, government agencies, and larger farmers. Savings in passenger transport costs, passed on in the form of fare reductions or increments in the quality and quantity of service, tend to benefit heads of household and younger men, since they travel more frequently than other groups.[30]

In addition to the direct costs and benefits of rural road improvements, indirect costs and benefits may be differentially distributed within a project area. For example, the value of land adjacent to an improved road rises in relation to land elsewhere in the project area. Roads may encourage people to seek work over a wider area or even to move away in search of more permanent employment. This may have a profound effect on family structures and productive patterns in the project area.[31] Finally, road improvements will make a remote area more attractive for investment by outsiders and thus encourage the exploitation of local resources (timber, for example) in ways that may or may not benefit project area residents.

The impacts of rural road construction on new settlements are especially noticeable in the humid tropics. Roads planned as part of new settlements (see chapter 5) can produce local population explosions far in excess of anticipated growth. In Brazil, Peru, and Panama, anthropologists have been asked to assess at appraisal the potential impacts of rural road programs on indigenous people. In the Brazilian and Peruvian cases, the roads have opened avenues for spontaneous colonization over and above the level intended by the governments. In the Panamanian case, large cattle ranchers who are already interspersed in tribal territory will be the most immediate beneficiaries of the road program, and improved access to markets may inspire them to encroach even more on tribal land. In all three cases, measures related to land titles for the indigenous people living in the vicinity of the road have been made an integral part of the project. Unless these measures are successful, local people will face invasion or alienation of their lands because of the new roads.

In an appraisal of the Chiapas Rural Road Project in Mexico, sociologists assessed the ways in which road access might change production and labor migration patterns in indigenous communities. Special attention was also paid to the social organization of the trucking industry serving the area and its possible effect on the outcome of the project. Criteria for subproject selection were established which made explicit allowance for the social goals of the program by relating the minimum acceptable rate of return to the degree of deprivation in target communities compared to the project area as a whole.

Impact studies under way or recently completed in several countries shed some light on the longer-term social costs and benefits of rural road projects. In Kenya, for example, female-headed households experienced less income instability than male-headed households in sample road impact areas; this was attributed to the role of remittances in the rural economy from male wage-earners living away from home.[32] In the state of Bihar, India, local researchers found that travel by marginal farmers and landless laborers, presumably in search of additional income-earning opportunities, increased following rural road improvements, while similar travel by landowning farmers declined after the project.[33] This study also documented more rapid change in attitudes regarding modern medicine and family planning in areas served by improved rural roads than in control areas. Recently completed studies in Benin and Tunisia, and planned studies in Niger, should provide further insights into changes rural roads can bring about in rural welfare within the constraints imposed by specific social contexts.

Social Sensitivity in Project Supervision

The main concerns during supervision of rural road projects are that road construction meets technical standards, that costs are kept to a minimum consistent with the desired level of service, and that plans are carried out in accordance with the agreements reached between planners, agency officials, and local authorities. Supervisory staff can often provide a good deal of informal technical assistance and training to counterparts who are responsible for the day-to-day management of projects. Finally, project supervision often helps facilitate coordination between different agencies by introducing a neutral third party and by intensifying social contact between agency staff and others involved in the project process.

At the supervision stage, social issues tend to be identified only when they become obstacles to successful implementation. These issues are apt to be institutional in nature, although they may relate to project beneficiaries if local people have been insufficiently involved in the planning process. For example, in a project in Papua New Guinea, road costs increased greatly because of unresolved issues regarding land tenure and land acquisition. Local labor availability may also become an issue if it has not been adequately addressed during project preparation. Theft of tools and construction camp security may become a problem if local authorities have not been asked to assume some work site responsibility, and especially if local residents do not support the project.

A feeder road project in Benin is an example of how social analysis skills can be used in project supervision. This project was originally designed to be implemented using labor-intensive methods in the more densely populated parts of the country. As the project progressed, changes in the rural economy made agricultural employment more attractive than road work. As a result, there was a shortage of laborers for the project. Civil service regulations precluded a change in the daily wage for road workers, and at the same time they protected workers' rights to remain on the permanent payroll after completing a fixed period of service. After analyzing incentives and constraints affecting the employer-employee relationship, supervisory staff and consultants recommended changes, such as supplemental noncash payments through food for work, limited length of employment for casual workers, use of contracts for maintenance tasks, and partial mechanization of quarry operations. These new procedures responded both to the changing needs of beneficiaries and to the project's needs for increased productivity.

A common problem in project implementation is the lack of sufficient trained staff to carry out the various tasks. Possible causes for this can include: an absolute shortage of skilled manpower in the country; an inappropriate educational system which produces people who, though technically trained, cannot function competently in a field situation; low wages, which make rural road work less attractive than other employment opportunities for suitably trained personnel; or the failure of the government to support the program by assigning adequate numbers of staff and freeing them from other responsibilities. Trained manpower shortages can be overcome only through long-range training programs that allow for high levels of attrition. Incentive systems can be changed to encourage better performance or to attract better qualified staff; however, this requires an understanding of the full range of possible incentives and disincentives and the cultural context in which they operate. The motivation of many individuals, particularly in the civil service, will depend on their perceptions of political support for the program emanating from central government officials.

When adequate staffing is a problem for project implementation, the gap is often filled by expatriate technical assistance or international volunteers. Although it may help to improve performance in the short run, this solution can also have negative effects. It increases the social distance between technical staff and laborers, and encourages host country planners to believe that they no longer have final responsibility for the success of the project. It may discourage some local staff who might otherwise improve their skills in order to move up in the hierarchy. Finally, unless technical assistants are strongly encouraged to view training as one of their major responsibilities, there is an inevitable tendency to neglect training activities in favor of direct action to improve project performance.

When governments are unable to field adequate numbers of appropriately qualified staff, project supervisors may consider transferring some of the implementation responsibilities to the private sector. This could mean dealing with local labor contractors, truck and tractor owners, fuel and repair shops, and material and tool suppliers. For this reason, procurement regulations for rural road programs need to be kept as simple and flexible as possible, to take advantage of the opportunities offered by local supply systems. Even if these appear to be economically less efficient than centrally controlled procurement, the time saved and the stimulus provided to the rural economy would often justify such a course.

Supervision teams need to be sensitive to changes in the political environment of rural road programs at both the national and local levels. Building a short stretch of road which has no apparent economic justification may be part of the price paid for local political support. Employment opportunities in road work are likely to be politically controlled, and a local power shift may cause a substantial turnover in the work force. At the national level, political support may be essential from the regional development authorities and the line agencies, whose success in delivering services depends on good access to rural areas, as well as from representatives of beneficiary communities. This support will help secure continued allocations of counterpart funds from the central government, and will also help establish the basis for a future commitment to road maintenance.

If rural road projects are to meet their objectives, the road improvements must be coordinated with plans for the delivery of other inputs and services needed for rural development, as well as with plans for collecting, storing, and marketing the increased output from rural areas. Supervision teams should therefore be concerned with the quantity, quality, and frequency of information flows between the executing agency and the other institutions in the rural development process, including both the public and the private sector. Ideally, coordinated planning should take place at a decentralized level where it can be responsive to local needs and priorities and can take advantage of local initiatives.

Rural road projects have sometimes been used to introduce the concept of coordinated planning at the local level. It is appropriate for a road-building organization to take the lead initially, since adequate access roads may be a prerequisite for many other forms of assistance. Some road-building agencies have used this position to consolidate a power base and have succeeded in maintaining a leading role in the rural planning process. In the long run, however, development planning for rural areas should be guided by local people, with the planning of infrastructure improvements relegated to a supporting role.

Evaluating Project Performance

Project evaluation begins with the formulation of anticipated effects and the collection of baseline data during the preparation stage. Throughout project implementation, key indicators of potential impacts should be monitored and communicated to project managers so that negative impacts can be avoided or mitigated as they develop and positive impacts can be enhanced. The implementation process itself can be monitored, and social analysis skills applied to the identification and resolution of implementation problems. This process of formative feedback may lead to significant changes in project design—for example, the use of new subproject screening criteria, the provision of new types of technical assistance, or the addition of new components such as credit for vehicle purchase.

In-depth evaluation comes at the end of a project or even later, when long-run effects have had time to be felt. It addresses the full range of project processes and expected impacts, as well as any unanticipated changes during the project period. Such evaluation should, in principle, be done by host country nationals in order to maximize feedback to planning and implementing agencies for future project work. It is important that local social scientists as well as economists and engineers become involved in this evaluation process, so that distributional issues will be raised and unanticipated social changes resulting from the project will be recognized. If local social scientists cannot be found for this purpose, donors will find it useful to include a professional social scientist on the expatriate team for project evaluation. Of course, project beneficiaries should be regularly consulted throughout the monitoring and evaluation process.

Experience in social impact evaluation on rural roads suggests a number of social variables that should be considered. It is a good approach to define a "zone of influence" around each road and to use this for collecting data and assessing impacts. First, a clear distinction should be drawn between residents of the project area and outsiders. Traffic flows on the improved road may show that benefits are accruing largely to outsiders: traders, transporters, and government officials who use the road to reach their clientele. The extent to which these benefits are in fact "passed through" (or "trickle down") to project area residents merits close examination. Consumers in urban areas may also benefit from cost savings; if the cost of basic foodstuffs is reduced for poor urban consumers, the net social impact may not be negative even if few benefits accrue to rural areas. However, if prices to urban consumers are kept artificially low, there will be little incentive for farmers to increase production and the roads will have less impact on the rural economy.

A second key variable is vehicle ownership, which affects the ability of households in the project area to capture the benefits of rural transport improvements. A rapid increase in the number of vehicles owned, particularly in the number of bicycles and motorcycles, is often observed after roads have been improved. These private vehicles help to meet transport needs that cannot be met by public bus and truck services. Local people may also enter or expand rural transport services in response to reduced costs. New support services such as mechanical workshops and bicycle repair shops may spring up, and locally adapted vehicles may be developed.

Income and access to consumer credit are, of course, factors in determining who is able to capitalize on the road improvement by investing in a vehicle. Age, sex, and ethnicity are also closely related to vehicle use and ownership. Social or cultural constraints may in some contexts strongly affect the propensity of women to use new modes of transport. Some consideration should be given to the effects of the road improvement on people who continue to use traditional modes of transport.

Land tenure and farm size are also significant variables related to the effects of roads in rural areas. If project area residents are renting from absentee landholders, rents may be raised to recover the increase in land values adjacent to the new road. Sharecropping arrangements should be carefully examined to see who benefits from an increase in farmgate prices. Wealthier, better educated farmers or urban residents may try to buy up all available land, forcing poorer families to survive on less land or to leave the land entirely.

Road improvements help create opportunities for a range of innovative behavior: more personal travel, new farming technologies, new types of employment, new services, new leisure activities, new consumption patterns, and greater participation by local people in the process of rural development. Whether people decide to adopt these new activities depends on their psychological and physical characteristics, their place in the household and the community, and their culturally based perceptions of the costs and benefits associated with each new opportunity. Project evaluation looks at the amount and direction of long-term behavioral change in response to road improvement, and assesses whether the project has improved the general welfare of the country and the project area population, without undesirable side effects on any particular group.

Conclusion

This chapter argues that rural road projects would benefit greatly from improved collaboration between project planners, engineers, and social scientists. Rural roads are among the most powerful agents of social change in much of the developing world. Much more work needs to be done to understand the process of social change and to direct it toward the goals of true development. Qualified and experienced social scientists have important contributions to make in this process: they help to define key issues, obtain relevant data, analyze institutional and community structures and processes, and prepare workable solutions. Even more importantly, perhaps, social scientists help keep attention focused on the relationship of rural road project activities to the needs and concerns of rural people. Thus, "putting people first" serves to make rural development projects more efficient and also more cost-effective in reaching their goals.

Notes

This chapter is an expanded and updated version of material prepared for discussion in the World Bank's Sociology Group and for publication in Bank Staff Working Papers. It reflects insights gained from evaluations of rural road projects in Kenya, India, Benin, Niger, and Tunisia. Helpful comments on the original version from Michael Bamberger, Esra Bennathan, Leslie Brownrigg, Michael Cernea, Andrew Mercer, Brigitta Mitchell, Ossi Rahkonen, and Deborah Rubin, are here gratefully acknowledged. This revised version has also benefited from more recent collaboration with Henri Beenhakker, Frank Cancian, Steve Carapetis, Scott Guggenheim, Jeffrey Gutman, Clell Harral, Richard Hartwig, Sven Hertel, Sunita Kikeri, Manohar Lal, Uma Lele, Peter Cook, and Norman Uphoff among many others.

1. An early attempt to conceptualize the role of rural infrastructure in alleviating rural poverty is found in Judith Tendler, *New Directions for Rural Roads*, AID Program Evaluation

Discussion Paper no. 2 (Washington, D.C.: U.S. Agency for International Development, March 1979).

2. The major constraints on agricultural development as perceived by rural area residents are access to land, water, and markets, in that order. If access to land and water are assured, roads are generally the next priority, followed by rural electrification. Recently, storage and marketing facilities, as well as renewable energy investments, have also been included in rural development projects. Other components, such as health, education, extension, and credit, often contain a significant element of infrastructure investment. In addition, these components often provide vehicles and support for the transport costs associated with service delivery programs.

3. Southeast Asian Agency for Regional Transport and Communications (SEATAC), "Study of Transport Investment and Impact on Distribution of Income in Remote Areas," February 1979.

4. See Ayse Kudat, "Participation of Women in the Rural Access Road Program in Kenya," prepared for World Bank, Projects Policy Department (Washington, D.C., 1981, processed).

5. The role of rural transport in relation to the efficient functioning of rural labor markets is increasingly recognized by economists. See, for example, Ossi J. Rahkonen *et al.*, "Study of Rural Mobility and Communications in Mexico," Draft Final Report, World Bank Transportation Department (Washington, D.C., March 1983, processed).

6. Uma Lele, *The Design of Rural Development: Lessons of Experience* (Baltimore: Johns Hopkins University Press, 1975).

7. H. L. Beenhakker and A. M. Lago, *Economic Appraisal of Rural Roads: Simplified Operational Procedures for Screening and Appraisal*, World Bank Staff Working Paper no. 610 (Washington, D.C., 1983); Clell Harral, *The Study of Labor and Capital Substitution in Civil Engineering Construction* (World Bank, Washington, D.C., processed, 1978); Basil Coukis, ed., *Labor-Based Construction Programs: A Practical Guide for Planning and Management* (New Delhi, India: Oxford University Press, 1983).

8. The list of Bank-financed rural road projects for which formal ex post evaluations have been completed by 1989 includes Senegal Feeder Roads (1983), Upper Volta Rural Roads (1985), First and Second Benin Feeder Roads (1986), Kenya Rural Access Roads (1986), Cameroon Feeder Roads (1987), Liberia Feeder Roads (1987), Tunisia First Rural Roads (1987), and Niger Feeder Roads (1988). In addition, rural road programs have formed important components in highway lending, for example, in Honduras and the Dominican Republic. Of course, the number of agricultural and rural development projects involving roads for which evaluations have been completed is much larger. However, these reports typically pay little attention to the road component, and it is difficult to separate the effects of roads from those of other investments made in such projects.

9. For a detailed discussion of such policy issues, see Steve Carapetis, Henri L. Beenhakker, and J. D. G. F. Howe, *The Supply and Quality of Rural Transport Services in Developing Countries: A Comparative Review*, World Bank Staff Working Paper no. 654 (Washington, D.C., August 1984).

10. See, for example, I. A. Barwell, G. A. Edmonds, J. D. G. F. Howe, and J. de Veen, *Rural Transport in Developing Countries* (London: Intermediate Technology Publications, 1985); also, Gordon Hathway, *Low-cost Vehicles* (London: Intermediate Technology Publications, 1988).

11. Uma Lele, "Agriculture and Infrastructure," paper prepared for a World Bank Symposium on Transportation and Structural Adjustment, Baltimore, May 6–8, 1987. See also Peter D. Cook and Cynthia C. Cook, "Methodological Review of the Analysis of the Impacts of

Rural Transportation in Developing Countries," paper presented at the International Conference on Transportation and Economic Development, Williamsburg, Virginia, 1989.

12. See, for example, William E. Smith, Francis J. Lethem, and Ben A. Thoolen, *The Design of Organizations for Rural Development Projects*, World Bank Staff Working Paper no. 375 (Washington, D.C., March 1980).

13. The literature to 1979 is reviewed in Devres, Inc., *Socio-Economic and Environmental Impacts of Low Volume Rural Roads*, AID Program Evaluation Paper no. 7 (Washington, D.C.: USAID, February 1980). See also the eight case studies on rural roads by USAID program evaluation teams in Thailand, Philippines, Jamaica, Honduras, Colombia, Sierra Leone, Liberia, and Kenya, and the *Summary Report on Rural Roads Evaluation* (Washington, D.C.: USAID, March 1982).

14. John Howe and Peter Richards, eds., *Rural Roads and Poverty Alleviation* (London: Intermediate Technology Publications, 1984).

15. Some pertinent issues and possible mitigating measures are pointed out in Carapetis, Beenhakker, and Howe, *op. cit.*

16. Cynthia C. Cook, "Review of Research on Personal Mobility in Rural Areas of the Developing World," paper presented at the Twenty-fifth Anniversary Meeting of the Transportation Research Forum (Washington, D.C., November 1983).

17. Community participation in rural road planning, construction, and maintenance are further discussed in Cynthia C. Cook, "Demography of the Project Population," in K. Finsterbusch, J. Ingersoll, and L. Llewellyn, eds., *Fitting Projects: Methods for Social Analysis for Projects in Developing Countries* (Boulder, Colo.: Westview Press, 1990).

18. Robert Chambers, *Rural Development: Putting the Last First* (London: Longman, 1983). Further insights into the problems of data collection are given in chapter 14 of this volume.

19. For example, the Sukuma in Tanzania have traditionally seen road maintenance as the specific responsibility of the young adult male age set.

20. Some useful guidance for identifying land tenure and land use issues related to project design can be found in Raymond Noronha and Francis J. Lethem, *Traditional Land Tenure and Land Use Systems in the Design of Agricultural Projects*, World Bank Staff Working Paper no. 561 (Washington, D.C., 1983).

21. For a detailed treatment of forced population displacement and resettlement, see chapter 6 of this volume.

22. See Michael M. Cernea, *Involuntary Resettlement in Development Projects,* Policy Guidelines in World Bank Financed Projects. World Bank Technical Paper no. 80 (Washington, D.C., 1988). See also *From Unused Social Science Knowledge to Policy Creation: The Case of Population Resettlement,* DDP 342, Harvard Institute for International Development, Harvard University (Cambridge, May 1990).

23. See, for example, Dennis A. Rondinelli, John R. Nellis, and G. Shabbir Cheema, *Decentralization in Developing Countries: A Review of Recent Experience*, World Bank Staff Working Paper no. 581 (Washington, D.C., July 1983).

24. Milton J. Esman, *Paraprofessionals in Rural Development: Issues in Field-level Staffing for Agricultural Projects*, World Bank Staff Working Paper no. 573 (Washington, D.C., 1983).

25. See also the comments on Mexico by Norman Uphoff in chapter 13 of this volume.

26. This does not mean, of course, that traditional social mechanisms are always desirable for development. Where forced labor has been used in the past for rural public works, it may be necessary to dissociate the project from this experience in the minds of the people by adopting a totally different method of labor recruitment, such as individual contracts.

27. Institutional issues related to rural roads are discussed in Ossi J. Rahkonen, Cynthia C. Cook, and Steve Carapetis, "Institutional Aspects of Rural Road Projects," in *Highway Investment in Developing Countries*, prepared by the Institution of Civil Engineers (London: Thomas Telford Ltd., 1983).

28. See Cynthia C. Cook and Sunita Kikeri, "Local Participation in Rural Road Projects," paper presented at the annual meeting of the American Sociological Association, Chicago, August 1987.

29. See, among others, Stephen Brush, *Mountain Field and Family* (Philadelphia: University of Pennsylvania Press, 1977).

30. This does not mean that rural women fail to benefit from rural road improvements. See Mary Elmendorf and Deborah Merrill, "Social-economic Impact of Development in Chan Kom: Rural Women Participate in Change" (Washington, D.C.: World Bank Transportation Department, 1977, processed) for an interesting discussion of the direct and indirect effects of road access on the structure of opportunities for women in rural Mexico.

31. Such effects have been the subject of detailed study as part of the monitoring and evaluation program set up in association with the Kenya Rural Access Roads Programme. For a preliminary report, see Ayse Kudat, "Participation of Women in the Rural Access Road Program in Kenya," *op. cit.*

32. U.S. Agency for International Development, "Assessment of the Socio-economic Impacts of the Kenya Rural Access Road Programme" (prepared by Devres, Inc., April 1984).

33. Manohar Lal and M. P. Pandey, "Social-economic Conditions and Mobility Patterns in Some Road Influence Areas [in Bihar, India]," paper presented at the Fourth International Conference on Low-volume Roads, Ithaca, New York, August 1987.

PART VII

Evaluation

Editor's Note

Some development specialists still believe that taking social considerations into account entails substantially increased costs, with only the expectation of uncertain, nonquantifiable, and unprovable project benefits. The preceding chapters in this book have shown that in case after case this assumption is not correct. Not only does a failure to consider the social and cultural context of a project invite inappropriate design at best (and user hostility at worst), but also it usually leads to projects that are ultimately ineffective, wanted neither by their supposed beneficiaries nor by the investing public agencies. For this reason, a constant theme of all the chapters in this volume has been the need to bring sociological and anthropological concepts into project design from the beginning.

Kottak's reflective chapter presents more evidence to buttress this argument, evidence based on a thorough review of sixty-eight primary evaluations of completed projects. The review was undertaken to "harvest the benefits of hindsight for designing better and culturally more sensitive proposals." Kottak discusses projects which failed, as well as projects which succeeded. Through his secondary analysis of ex post findings on both kinds of projects, Kottak is able to show conclusively that sociocultural analysis makes a significant difference in the chances for projected success.

The payoff from some analysis is sometimes measurable in concrete economic terms: Kottak found that the average economic rate of return for rural development projects which have incorporated sociocultural analysis was more than double that for projects which had been poorly appraised from a sociological viewpoint.

Kottak notes that a "people orientation" involves considerably more than encouraging direct participation in project design and implementation. Many of the underlying principles of social structure, which are explicit in sociological models, are buried in cultural practice and are not necessarily articulated conceptually by members of a cultural group; yet these principles have to be understood and taken into account when development interventions are designed and implemented. Residence rules, division of labor, kinship, culturally informed resource distribution, management of collectively owned and used resources, and other basic features discussed by Kottak vary tremendously from one geographic area to another. His retrospective analysis of project results confirms how essential it is for the technical experts to recognize and address this cultural variability with the help of professional sociologists.

Kottak's dissection of past projects permits him to specify which social variables and approaches have proved crucial to a project's success or failure and should undoubtedly be built into future projects. Thus, his finding that sound, culturally informed social engineering was as important as technical or financial considerations in project preparation is not solely a diagnosis, but a strong recommendation.

12

When People Don't Come First: Some Sociological Lessons from Completed Projects

Conrad Phillip Kottak

This chapter draws on my initial (1985) analysis of selected ex post evaluation findings, as well as on two subsequent comparative studies of project reports by the World Bank and the U.S. Agency for International Development (USAID), to assess the function and value of sociological expertise in various stages of the project cycle. The social expert has the unique role of identifying social organization and harnessing it for the success of the project. The social organization of the project area, in its formal and informal aspects, constitutes a crucial variable of the development environment that may remain invisible if there is no social analyst to draw it out. Development teams that lack social expertise often perceive project participants as no more than a collection of people—potential beneficiaries, to be sure—rather than as structured groups of active individuals with their own strategies, organizational patterns, beliefs, perceptions of needs, motivations, and desires to help plan and implement changes that will affect their own lives and those of ensuing generations.

The broadest conclusion and recommendation of this study is the generalized need for informed social strategies for economic development. The problem of social underdesign for innovation must be corrected. To the extent possible, each project must have a socially informed and culturally appropriate design and implementation strategy. Social engineering is as important as technical or financial or economic considerations. Too many local needs call out for solutions to waste money funding projects that are inappropriate in one place, but needed in another or are unnecessary anywhere. The present chapter originated in a study examining the association between the sociocultural fit of projects that were economic successes and the adequacy of preproject social analysis. The results show that attention to issues of sociocultural compatibility pays off in economic terms—among others, in economic rates of return twice as high as those of the socially insensitive and inappropriate projects. Sociocultural planning for economic development is not simply socially desirable; it is demonstrably cost-effective.

My belief, shared with other contributors to this volume, is that people should come first at all stages of the development projects that affect them. Putting people first in development interventions means eliciting the needs for change that they perceive; identifying culturally compatible goals and strategies for change; developing socially appropriate, workable, and efficient designs for innovation; using, rather than opposing, existing groups and organizations; drawing on participants' informal monitoring and evaluation of projects during implementation; and gathering detailed information before and after implementation so that socioeconomic impact can be accurately assessed. These tasks are specific illustrations of the continuous need for social expertise from identification to impact evaluation.

The present synthesis demonstrates that proper social designs for implementation and sensitivity to social issues also have financial benefits as assessed, for example, by such measures as economic rate of return and long-term sustainability of benefit flows. Repeated confirmation of the importance of social design in comparative studies, whether based on statistical analysis or on case analysis, reaffirms the growing belief—held not just in the World Bank and other international development agencies, but also in consulting firms and developing countries generally—that proper social analysis and engineering leads to positive results—both social and economic.[1]

A caveat is necessary, however. Although social experts can offer valuable generalizations and recommendations with respect to specific subsectors, world areas, and sociopolitical systems, each project needs its own social analysis to reflect its individual features and goals.

Although greater use of social expertise by international development agencies is certainly in order, the heaviest burden of incorporating sociological knowledge throughout the project cycle will rest on borrowing agencies and governments, as they more carefully identify, prepare, design, implement, and socially evaluate development programs. The involvement of indigenous anthropologists and sociologists—as part of the specific information resources of each host country—will be particularly important here.

Secondary Analysis of Social Evaluation Findings

This chapter reviews my own and other more recent analyses of primary evaluations made of completed development projects, to harvest the benefits of hindsight for designing better and culturally more sensitive development proposals. Several kinds of evaluation studies are carried out by the World Bank. At the completion of each project, two documents are prepared. The first, the Project Completion Report (PCR), is written by the borrowing country, sometimes with assistance from the division of the Bank that was responsible for the project. (Previously they were written by Bank staff themselves.) These reports were not, for the most part, used in my 1985 study. The second Bank document, the project Performance Audit Report (PPAR), is prepared not by the project staff, but by an independent department of the Bank, the Operations Evaluation Department (OED), which reports directly to the Bank's Executive Directors. It compares the actual achievements of the project with its objectives at the time of appraisal. The PPAR is also sent to the borrowing government. USAID reports comparable to PCRs and PPARs were used by a 1987 study of 212 USAID-assisted projects.

A third type of Bank investigation is called an Impact Evaluation Report (IER). The IER differs from the other two evaluation exercises. It is carried out only for selected projects, and then only five or more years after project completion and after the PPAR has been written. In addition, the impact evaluations are more broadly focused on the general social and economic effects lasting in the project area after the project itself has been completed. Impact evaluations have often been carried out with the participation of sociologists and anthropologists, and provide useful examples of social analysis done in the Bank. Twenty-five such IERS formed the basis of Cernea's 1987 study of "Farmer Organizations and Institution Building for Sustainable Development."[2]

The present review encompassed a content analysis of sixty-eight ex post evaluation reports—fifty-seven PPARs and eleven IERS—to uncover the main lessons regarding the sociocultural variables of Bank-assisted rural development projects. In addition, I examined fourteen project appraisal reports so that I could more accurately assess the extent to which sociocultural analysis contributed to initial project design.

It must be emphasized that the sixty-eight project reports that I reviewed were chosen purposely to facilitate the identification and understanding of social and cultural issues in project design, implementation, and impact. Individual PPARs were selected for secondary analysis on the basis of the quality, detail, and depth of the material related to social issues, and not in order to build a random sample and determine frequencies. Although I attempted to obtain a broad geographic and sectoral spread among the projects, the findings of my study should be considered illustrative of particular problems rather than as representative in any statistical sense of the entire universe of Bank-assisted projects, or even Bank-assisted rural development projects. Furthermore, most of the projects evaluated here were designed during the 1960s and early-1970s, when the development community was less convinced than at present about the value of social expertise throughout the project cycle. More recent projects have paid greater attention to issues of sociocultural fit and socially appropriate strategies. Still, my main conclusions have been replicated by subsequent comparative studies involving more than 200 different projects of similar diversity and geographic spread.

The lessons offered here (some of which echo recommendations made in previous chapters) are drawn both from positive experiences in which proper social design or implementation strategies proved a key ingredient in project success, and from selected negative situations in which the project designers were less aware of the social organization of the beneficiaries. The lessons are drawn from *past* experience, although the study of USAID-assisted projects focused on the recent past—reports prepared mainly in 1985 and 1986. The reader should also bear in mind that some of the effects of these projects could not have been anticipated, probably even with social analysis.[3]

Many of the experiences documented here illustrate the tendency to address technical and financial factors and to neglect social issues. Perhaps the most significant finding of my 1985 study is that attention to social issues, which presumably enhances sociocultural fit and results in a better social strategy for economic development, pays off in concrete economic terms: the average economic rates of return for projects that were socioculturally compatible and were based on an adequate understanding and analysis of social conditions were more than twice as high as those for socially incompatible and poorly analyzed projects.

How did I assess sociocultural compatibility or incompatibility? Many PPARS and IERS often stated explicitly that certain features of project design or implementation were culturally inappropriate or unworkable. I coded each project as socioculturally compatible or not on the basis of either explicit statements in the primary documents or my own identification of a notable lack of fit between project goals or implementation strategy and local culture. Since no project designed for change can be completely compatible with tradition, projects were coded as incompatible only when the lack of social fit was substantial and obvious.

A few examples will clarify my coding procedure. Several African projects wrongly assumed that the participating units would be small European-type nuclear family farms rather than extended families and descent groups. An Ethiopian settlement project paid no attention to incentives or traditions in attempting the immediate conversion of pastoral nomads into sedentary cultivators. An Asian project promoted cultivation of nontraditional crops in areas where the labor demands of the new crops would directly compete with those of paddy, the dietary staple. A few projects ignored or made counterproductive assumptions about women's roles in the given mode of production and distribution.

Sociocultural compatibility and the other social, cultural, and socio-economic variables used in my study were constructed independently of the economic rate of return. Only after the social coding had been done did I process the information provided in the Bank documents I was analyzing on rates of return, which is usually given on a separate basic data sheet. This procedure helped eliminate the possible tendency to identify projects as socially incompatible once they were known to be economic failures. Indeed, the rates of return of the projects assessed as culturally incompatible ranged from negative to 59 percent, the highest rate in the study, whereas those of projects judged to be compatible ranged from negative to 47 percent.

The regional and sectoral distribution of the reports considered for my study is shown in table 12-1.

Since social sensitivity and cultural fit are key issues here it is necessary to identify at the outset the factors encompassed by these terms. The main sociocultural dimensions of economic development include the social organizations (both formal and informal) of the project area population; issues of stratification, ranking, and ethnicity; sex-based

Table 12-1.   *Distribution of Evaluation Reports by Region and Sector*

Region and sector	Number	Percent
Region		
Africa	33	48.5
Asia	16	23.5
Latin America and Caribbean	11	16.2
Other	8	11.8
Total	68	100.0
Sector		
Irrigation	18	26.5
Agricultural and multisectoral rural development	19	27.9
Settlement	12	17.6
Livestock	12	17.6
Fisheries	3	4.4
Other	4	5.9
Total	68	99.9

division of labor and gender roles; and systems of values and motivations—particularly as they relate to customs of production and exchange. Because the subfield known as economic anthropology is concerned with systems of production, distribution, consumption, and economic motivations in rural areas of developing countries, the work of the applied anthropologist covers some of the same territory as that of the agricultural economist, agronomist, or microeconomist. It is critical that this territory be understood for successful project design—whether the expert doing the study is a socially sensitive economist or an economic anthropologist.

Anthropological concerns are also linked with political analysis, in that national cultural traditions and procedures, including government policy, are relevant to the success of the project, but the primary data available for my study were not sufficiently detailed to allow examination of this linkage. (Some policy issues are discussed by Cernea 1987 and the USAID study.) It must also be pointed out than many of the reviewed projects in all the secondary studies were bad for a combination of reasons, including mistakes in planning and implementation, and not merely because their social engineering was poor. Conversely, there is no reason to expect that even the most careful social analysis can make a success of a project with poor technical or economic design.

In my 1985 study I attempted to quantify the sociocultural dimensions of projects described in ex post evaluation documents by constructing certain variables and coding each case. The discussions of the cases will make clear the criteria for judging such issues as sociocultural compatibility or fit. Among the specific cultural and socioeconomic variables considered were:

- Compatibility of the project with sociocultural conditions in the target area
- Problems resulting from inadequate sociocultural study or analysis
- Problems with incentives to participate in the project
- Poor estimation of labor availability
- Success of fee collection
- Problems related to the neglect of women's roles, stratification, and ethnicity
- Land tenure problems
- Use of existing cooperatives or participants' groups
- Quality and appropriateness of the sociocultural design
- Quality and appropriateness of implementation
- Notable flexibility during implementation
- Effect on equity (relative distribution of wealth).

Of course, assessing cultural compatibility as an ex post exercise, especially when there is insufficient information in the audit or other evaluation reports, is a judgmental endeavor. What is important is not counting spuriously precise percentages, but identifying the trends and issues of project processes, as well as the mechanisms through which a better social fit can be routinely incorporated into preparation, formulation, and appraisal of projects.

Social Design for Innovation

The social design strategies proposed here, on the basis of past successes and failures, are relevant to *all* project types. In my 1985 study the thirty projects (from the set of fifty-seven PPARs) in which project design was judged to be compatible with traditional cultural and local socioeconomic conditions in the targeted area had an average estimated rate of return at audit of 18.3 percent, compared with 8.6 percent for the twenty-seven projects in which sociocultural incompatibilities were identified. Again, it is necessary to caution that inasmuch as the reports examined were purposively selected, this finding has value not as a "hard," probability sample-based statistic, but as a trend indicator, significant for reflection. It *is* my belief that a random sample of worldwide development projects would also demonstrate a strong association between adequate social strategy and economic success.

The Fallacy of Overinnovation

Successful projects appear to avoid what might be called the fallacy of overinnovation. They might be seen as social science applications of the rule formulated by the paleontologist A. S. Romer to explain the origin of land-dwelling vertebrates.[4] Romer's rule points out that the ancestors of land dwellers lived in pools of water that disappeared during seasonal droughts. Legs gradually evolved out of fins not to enable these creatures to live full time on the land, but to carry them back to water as particular pools dried up. In other words, a feature that proved essential to land life originated to maintain an aquatic existence.

Systems theorists, paleobiologists, and social scientists alike have used Romer's rule to predict and explain change. The general lesson is that the goal of stability can be the main impetus for change. Evolution occurs incrementally as gradually changing systems keep on attempting to maintain themselves (as they gradually change). Because economic development is, after all, simply another term for (planned) socioeconomic evolution, Romer's rule is applicable.

To apply Romer's rule to economic development is certainly not to argue against change; the evolution of legs, which originally led Romer to his formulation, was undeniably a significant innovation that provided dramatic new opportunities for diversification and development. Applying Romer's rule, we can infer that smallholders usually wish to change in order to maintain what they have. Change thus appears as an adaptive strategy, necessary for self-maintenance within a constantly changing environment. Although most peasants in the contemporary world want certain changes in their life-styles, the motives that modify their behavior are usually provided by their traditional culture and the concerns of everyday existence. Their goals are not abstractions such as "learning a better way," "progressing," "increasing technical know-how," "improving efficiency," "adopting modern techniques," or "preserving biodiversity." Rather, their objectives are concrete, limited, and specific: increasing yields in a rice field, amassing enough food and cash to host a ceremony, getting a child through junior high school, or paying the tax collector. Furthermore, the goals and values of subsistence-oriented smallholders differ from those of people who are accustomed to producing for cash, and these different value systems must be taken into account during planning. Quite simply, to ignore these goals and values, for whatever reason, is to invite problems.

Following Romer's rule, realistic, workable, and sustainable projects promote change but not *over*innovation. Not one of the successful projects sampled in any of the comparative studies aimed at revolutionary changes in smallholders' lives. Implicit in all successful projects was the goal of changing so as to maintain. In other words, many minor changes are possible if the objective is to preserve a system while making it function more effectively.

The successful projects also had appropriate social designs for innovation—they tended to incorporate indigenous cultural practices and social structures for implementation. Cernea links grass roots mobilization to long-term success—to achieving project sustainability.

One irrigation project identified as both an economic and social success in my 1985 study was Sri Lanka's Mahaweli Ganga Development Project, which did not attempt fundamental changes in the existing cropping system, but tried to improve it with proven technical packages. The farmers were experienced irrigators who could easily adapt to increased water availability and the more rigorous time frame imposed by double cropping (the cultivation of two successive, rather than inter-cropped, annual cereals on the same piece of land). Given a free market for paddy, project farmers, who traditionally both ate and sold rice, stepped up production and consequently increased their incomes. Of the fourteen appraisal reports I examined, this was one of the most sensitive to social, cultural, and local economic conditions, which is unusual because of its early date.

I found that double cropping, which succeeded in this Sri Lanka project, was actually adopted in fewer than half (five out of eleven) of the projects that proposed it. The data examined suggest that double cropping is culturally incompatible and not normally a cost-effective option in areas of sparse population, such as throughout much of Sub-Saharan Africa. Either an intensive year-round labor supply or reliable machinery is necessary for such continuous use of land. As a general rule, double cropping is viable in sparsely populated areas only when inputs are readily available for mechanized farming and landholdings are large enough to make this kind of farming profitable. For example, in the only West African project in which double cropping was successfully implemented, a project authority provided inputs and mechanical plowing. In a Madagascar project, planners ignored the fact that the postcolonial shift in rice production from large colonial estates to smallholdings made careful social planning necessary, and they erroneously assumed that peasants could muster the labor (or afford the machinery) to double crop although population density was less than fifteen people per square kilometer (erroneously reported in the appraisal report as ninety per square kilometer!). The project's objectives were never attained. The problems in this case may have owed as much to faulty economic analysis as to lack of a proper preproject social feasibility study.

A double-cropping design should therefore be based on a detailed analysis of labor and input availability and farmer incentives. Anthropologists know that peasants have traditionally been motivated to intensify production in order to meet subsistence needs, pay taxes or rents, or meet social—particularly ceremonial—demands. For example, the peasants in this unsuccessful Madagascar project want cash primarily to purchase ceremonial goods. The uninformed planners who expected them to double crop ignored the fact that peak labor demands for the second crop would have come during the ceremonial season—which provided the main incentive to produce and sell more.

Sociocultural Fit

The role of cultural fit is illustrated by the Tanzania Tea Development Project, which worked best in areas where farmers already had a tradition of growing tea. Coffee projects in Ethiopia and Burundi appropriately concentrated on each country's leading export and cash crop, already widely cultivated by smallholders. In a successful project in Malawi, traditional local social structure was allowed to orient the formation of village committees.

Although, in general, smallholders are unlikely to cooperate with projects that require major changes in their daily lives—especially ones that interfere too much with customary subsistence pursuits—some drastic changes can be very successful. For example, land reform, by reallocating land rights in highly stratified areas, permits smallholders to go on cultivating traditional fields in return for a greater share of the product.

From a sociocultural perspective, settlement projects are perhaps the most interesting type of development scheme because they remove people from their homelands and native sociocultural contexts and establish them in new surroundings. The average estimated rate of return at audit for the twelve settlement projects examined (13.9 percent) is close to the average rate for the total set of reports (13.5 percent), but the settlement projects cluster more neatly than other types into two polar groups of economic successes (eight) and failures (four).

Design and implementation issues are closely connected in these cases, and several such issues are illustrated by a highly successful Senegal resettlement project with a rate of return of 59 percent. Its success is based on the fact that during implementation people put themselves first, even though planners had not. As the audit report notes, the social design was faulty mainly because of inaccurate socioeconomic information. In addition, there was an inappropriate social bias: the farm model of the appraisal report was again that of the European-type small family farm instead of the extended family, which is the basic unit of social organization in Senegal. The social forms and cultural values of the people certainly were not considered in the social design for innovation. Contradicting the designers' assumption that Western-style family farms would develop in the project area, however, the participants went right on using their ancestral social organization and transferred their extended kinship networks to project lands. Although this spontaneous use of extended family ties had not been anticipated, it proved so effective that the ex post evaluation called it "triggered settlement" and suggested it be replicated in other West African projects. The audit considers triggered settlement cost effective because in a kin-based society the extended family networks attract additional settlers and therefore foster spontaneous settlement. The report cites a village study showing that twice as many people as estimated benefit from the project because members of the extended families of the original settlers had joined them in the project area. "If the level of investment at the beginning of the project appears substantial in terms of the number of families, it becomes quite acceptable in relation to the total number of people actually involved."[5] Thus, the settlers turned out to be neither the European small-family farmers modeled at appraisal, nor the cultureless beings of a settlement "blueprint."[6] In their new setting they, simply and unsurprisingly, used the traditional principles of their old society to structure their new one.

Participants in a Papua New Guinea smallholder development project did not appear to attract their extended kin to the project area, but they *had* used their profits to maintain their family ties by revisiting their homelands and investing in its social life and ceremonials. Although the settlers came from different ethnic and tribal backgrounds, the high cash incomes that followed rapid growth and high productivity of oil palms were eminently compatible with widespread New Guinean "big man" systems involving competition for wealth and capital accumulation. Although farmers' organizations evolved slowly among the unrelated settlers, community social relations were good, and the government considered this a positive experiment in nation building. Again, such interethnic and interlinguistic mingling fit well with Papua New Guinea customs, where interlinguistic marriage is common, as is multitribal participation in common religious movements oriented toward material benefits (cargo cults).

The successful Malaysian Jengka Triangle Project I and Johore Land Settlement Project are parts of ongoing settlement programs managed by the experienced Federal Land Development Authority (FELDA). The Jengka project exemplifies the strategy that has earned FELDA the charge of paternalism from its critics for doing virtually everything for the settlers: clearing the forest, planting (rubber or oil palms), performing early maintenance, and establishing village block settlements with associated infrastructure. Settlers are awarded homes and established plantations. Costs are recovered through deductions from what producers deliver to the FELDA-oriented oil palm mills. The government strategy is to provide landless peasants with land and greater wealth: Jengka farmers enjoy incomes four times those of the rural poor from whose ranks they came.

Despite very high costs per acre and per beneficiary, FELDA, as the Johore project audit concludes, has been one of the most successful and experienced settlement agencies in the world. FELDA schemes have proved to be replicable and economically viable and to yield an adequate financial rate of return both for settlers and for FELDA itself. FELDA's policy on targeted income per beneficiary has been based on the need to create farming units large enough to withstand the world price fluctuations that are a constant risk for rubber and oil palm. This means that equity considerations have been balanced against the need for plots large enough (six to fourteen acres) to be economically viable. FELDA projects, in their design, appropriately anticipate world price variations.[7]

FELDA-type settlement schemes cannot be expected to work universally, but only under certain socioeconomic conditions: dense population, social stratification, land shortage, income disparities, and an economy based at least partly on cash. In such circumstances, landless peasants appear willing to leave their home communities and join with strangers in new socioeconomic systems. A nuclear family kinship system may also be necessary if such projects are to work. FELDA's strategy could work in the Philippines or Korea but would not in most parts of Sub-Saharan Africa, rural North Africa, or Oceania, where extended families and other kinds of kinship systems are encountered.

When People Don't Come First: Development Incompatibilities

Projects tended to be less successful when the planners on the project preparation teams ignored established socioeconomic and cultural patterns. More than half (59 percent) of the reports examined in my 1985 study drew attention to problems that arose because during project preparation or appraisal important socioeconomic information was either lacking, insufficiently analyzed, or ignored.

Some of the cases illustrate a project's inadequate regard for, and consequent lack of fit with, existing sociocultural conditions. A South Asian irrigation project to promote the cultivation of onions and chilies overoptimistically expected these crops to fit into a preexisting labor-intensive system of rice growing. "The average farmer . . . cultivates about three acres of paddy land in the valley bottoms, requiring about 220 days of labor input with peaks at transplanting and harvest times. These labor peaks are competing with time required for chili or onion production. Confronted with this situation, farmers gave priority to their subsistence crop: paddy." Because these cash crops were not only new to the local culture, but also in conflict with existing crop priorities and other interests of farmers, they were not successfully adopted.

Another Asian irrigation project ignored known social obstacles in the target area to forming water users' organizations and relied instead on the force of ministerial decrees, which farmers refused to follow. A West African project asked farmers to spray only immature cocoa trees, when efficiency, cost effectiveness, and custom dictated that the mature trees planted alongside them should also be sprayed; the project also pushed a fertilizer program that had not been field-tested and that proved unnecessary.

The most socioculturally naive and incompatible of the twelve settlement schemes I reviewed was an irrigation project in Ethiopia that was eventually canceled and redesigned after land reform. The main fallacy was the attempt to convert nomadic Afar pastoralists into sedentary cultivators. Project designers totally ignored the traditional land rights of the Afar tribe and proposed using their territory for commercial farms and converting the Afars into small farmers. Although noting that the conversion of "illiterate, nomadic pastoralists into cash crop farmers is a long and difficult process," the project preparation team and the appraisal nevertheless proposed that holdings be mechanically prepared for cropping, as the trainee settlers were taught to sow, weed, irrigate, and harvest. Would an experienced and culturally sensitive agency be doing this teaching? Not at all: "Settlement is . . . subject to other severe constraints, arising not only from the reluctance of Afar nomads to adopt a settled way of life, but also from AVA's [the implementation authority's] limited capacity to train them and provide supporting services."

As the audit points out, this project illustrates the tendency to address technical and financial factors in design and evaluation while glossing over cultural variables. In fact, the appraisal report is a seventy-five page document that devotes just one paragraph each to traditional production patterns, land use, and farming practices—and these in Ethiopia generally, not specifically, in the project area. A pilot study of sixty-seven families is mentioned, but there is no detailed information about it, and the appraisal report, while promoting conversion from nomadic to settled patterns, fails to say whether the prospective beneficiaries had been consulted about their projected fate. There was no social design for creating the new community and no role specified for social experts during implementation. The Afars were expected to give up a way of life they had known for generations in order to work three times as hard growing rice and picking cotton for commercial farmer bosses: "The project would create employment for the local Afars and for unemployed workers from the highlands. The AVA settlement would eventually settle 800 families, and the settlement farms would also hire labor seasonally for cotton picking."

The conclusion is obvious that particular attention should be given to social variables at an early stage in the project process. Detailed preliminary study might even have suggested that this project not be funded at all. Certainly the raiding that thwarted implementation could have been predicted by a sensible social expert.

The Tanzania Flue-cured Tobacco Project, which aimed at settling 15,000 farmers to grow tobacco, was also culturally insensitive and tried to overinnovate. The cooperative cultivation that the project promoted might have succeeded in already settled, communally oriented villages based on extended kinship, but cooperatives proved to work poorly in settlements made up of strangers who had no prior basis for mutual trust. Again, there was no careful social design for forging a community out of strangers so as to facilitate cooperative production. The ex post evaluation report notes that the project might have supported rehabilitation in areas that already cultivated tobacco, but chose not to. Although established growers were considered inefficient, their experience might have been harnessed for development through effective extension.

No effort was made to choose settlers who had a special interest in tobacco cultivation, and insufficient attention was paid to regional and national determinants of farmers' incentives. Most villagers chose to grow maize rather than tobacco; maize not only fed them, but also enjoyed a cash advantage (given increasing urban demand) over tobacco. Because of farmers' rational actions, concludes the audit, the tobacco project turned into a reasonably successful maize development project. Again, both faulty economic analysis and dubious sociocultural fit contributed to the problems.

The group of twelve livestock projects considered in my study provides some significant examples of design flaws related to socially unplanned innovation and to cultural incompatibility. Although not necessarily representative of all Bank-assisted livestock projects, this group had a particularly low level of success, with an average rate of return of only 2 percent. The failures reflect national planners' assumptions and preconceptions about livestock development strategies and the complex economic and cultural characteristics of pastoral societies.

Livestock development projects have incorporated different types of intervention. In general, the least successful have tried to replace the pastoral production system with ranching. The emphasis on ranches has often been at the insistence of borrower national agencies which give more weight to the project's increase in beef production than to its possible effects on pastoral populations. Other projects, however, do not aim at such comprehensive restructuring of the social organization of the production system and concentrate instead on improving specific com-

ponents: dairying or veterinary services, research on breeding and disease control, and marketing and slaughtering facilities. Some projects
include training and extension components, especially for agropastoral
populations which depend on agriculture and raise livestock as a secondary occupation.

Not only the overambitious objectives of many livestock projects, but
also the intrinsically complex characteristics of these populations make
success unlikely when major social restructuring is envisaged over short
intervals. Pastoralists often live in barely accessible, sparsely populated,
and poorly watered areas. They are highly mobile, constantly assessing
the available resources for both the human and animal populations. Their
patterns of social organization are subtly adapted to life in a very delicate
balance with their physical and animal environment, and the risks of
upsetting this adaptation with improper or overly rapid changes are high.
In addition, the remoteness of their lives inevitably limits data collection,
supervision, fee collection, law enforcement, and monitoring and evaluation. This complex of factors makes it all the more difficult, even for
experienced social scientists, to predict the shape of successful development interventions.

The observation that the social organization of ranching is often
culturally problematical and not yet acceptable in societies structured by
extended kinship and descent can be derived from the evaluation report
on the Papua New Guinea Smallholder Livestock Project, which failed:
"The profitability of livestock was expected to encourage additional
enclosure of common lands, permitting the evolution of private land
rights which would promote individual initiative. Eventually livestock
raising would give way to crop production. Thus, the cattle lending
program was seen as an instrument of both short- and long-term economic and social development." The anticipated outcome—enclosed,
private crop lands—reveals planners' biases against communal tenure
and even against livestock. In contrast, if it had been recognized that New
Guineans live in societies structured by kinship, descent, and marriage,
where land is communally rather than privately owned, the designers
could have built on the intrinsic development resources of the existing
social organization and designed a project that used, rather than opposed,
these native institutions.

This culturally incompatible Papua New Guinea livestock scheme also
illustrates the fallacy of overinnovation and of a socially insensitive
development strategy that fails to justify change in terms of locally

perceived needs. Such abstract goals as promoting "the evolution of private land rights," "individual initiative," or even "long-term economic development" may be familiar to national and international planners, but they are certainly not so conceptualized by tribal peoples.

This stress on abstract and general development "requirements" rather than local needs as local people perceive them has apparently been a frequent characteristic of livestock projects. The Madagascar Beef Cattle Project, for instance, was thought to be the initial step toward modernizing the livestock sector in Madagascar. In the Sudanese savanna, groups that had been herding for centuries were to be taught "better" range management. Criticism of such goals does not, of course, imply that pastoralists in developing countries cannot be taught better range management or improved animal husbandry techniques. The point is, rather, that livestock projects need concrete people-oriented objectives, culturally attuned technologies, and social implementation strategies that count on the people's ability to perceive the problems to be solved. The importance and cost-effectiveness of considering specific, rather than abstract goals, and of understanding key constraints in the local setting, are also emphasized in the report on USAID projects.

In Indonesia, the abstract goal of one livestock project was "adoption of advanced technology." The audit concluded that "the transfer of new or unfamiliar technology from a developed to a less developed country is particularly dangerous when there is little or no local expertise to monitor and evaluate the transfer." Another inappropriate innovation proved to be the use of slope grazing instead of the Japanese system of stall feeding in Korea's Dairy Beef Project. The choice might have been reversed if an economist, geographer, or anthropologist had insisted that the Japanese system would be culturally more appropriate for a densely populated country such as Korea with smallholdings and no dairying traditions than would a model borrowed from practices in New Zealand or Australia.

In an African beef cattle project, because the local agency was oblivious to social realities and because the Bank in the late 1960s and early 1970s paid limited attention to customary rights and questions of land tenure, there was overconfidence in the (abstract) rule of formal law. The borrowing agency said that project area lands were government owned; perhaps in the sense that the government held modern legal title to some project lands, this was true. Also included in the project area, however, were village lands on which traditional grazing rights were in force, although not legally registered. This fact was ignored in planning. When a few thousand local people, whose existence the appraisal mission had failed to notice, began to tear down fences, burn pasture, and rustle the Brahman cattle (as their ancestors had always done, living outside the national net of effective law and order), a government minister told the Bank he would ask the villagers to leave the project area. The local people, however, continued their guerrilla actions against the Australian-type ranches that had been established on their ancestral lands. The problems diminished only after expatriate management was replaced with nationals, who used traditional pacts (blood brotherhood) between villages to end the rustling.

The Bank livestock projects that have encountered serious problems because of deficiencies in their social design have had one or two features in common: they have superimposed parastatal corporations on traditional livestock production units, or in areas characterized by communal grazing they have tended to modify the grazing pattern without changing the social organization of the pastoralists to correspond. Failure rates of these kinds of projects have been high, not only in the Bank, but also in all other development agencies.

People-oriented Strategies for Implementation

Previous Bank studies call attention to the variety of (usually informal) organizational forms invented by peasant societies for production, savings, and credit. Those studies rightly contend (echoing Romer's rule) that instead of regarding traditional organizations as a constraint, they might better be used as a resource for development: "A sound modernization policy should make the best use of all available resources, including available social organizations, when they are amenable to developmental activities. On the other hand, the need to strengthen, change, and develop these organizations themselves should not be overlooked."[8]

Indeed, from a survey of 164 appraisal reports, Cernea's 1982 study found that 40 percent describe "intuitive" attempts to incorporate production-related peasant organizations as implementation units. Specifically, these reports indicated that the projects either considered traditional cooperative economic patterns or intended to encourage community self-help or to establish farmers' production or marketing groups during implementation.

The Cernea survey covered appraisal reports (the design at the beginning of the project). In contrast, subsequent reviews of actual achievements at project completion suggest that existing social organizations were being systematically involved in development programs to a lesser extent than initially intended.

If the development potential of group action and traditional social organization is intuitively recognized in design, why is it so rarely harnessed effectively? Analysis of the ex post evaluations indicates three main reasons: there was inadequate socioeconomic knowledge in project preparation; project management units lacked the social skills to carry out the social engineering goals of the project; and culturally biased and often incompatible social designs were used (often unconsciously). The social design for innovation in many of the projects examined appears to have been based either on Euro-American social groups and property concepts—individualistic production units, private property held by individuals or a couple and worked by a nuclear family (parents and children)—*or* on cooperative systems at least partially based on models used to implement development goals in Eastern Bloc socialist countries.

Since neither model has an unblemished record in developing countries, an alternative is needed: greater use of Third World social models for Third World development. Those models are to be found in such traditional social forms as the clans, lineages, and other extended kinship groups (with their communally held estates and resources) of Africa, Oceania, and several other Third World regions. The argument here is that the most productive strategy for change is to base the social design for innovation on traditional social forms in the project areas. Many Third World governments will find this recommendation compatible with their national development policies, and certain suggestions in this chapter concerning the use of indigenous social expertise in development planning and implementation may be particularly relevant.

In the projects reviewed here, existing target area cooperative patterns are rarely analyzed in depth. This is simply part of the general lack of detailed and accurate social and institutional knowledge at the design stage, which leads to a deficient or inappropriate social strategy for implementation. Appropriate groups with development potential are ignored. Inappropriate, unworkable, or unnecessary new organizations are formed, and assumptions about individual motivations conflict with traditional communal values.

Farmers' Associations

Farmers' organizations were assigned a role in project implementation in fewer than half (seven out of eighteen) of the irrigation projects reviewed in my 1985 study. Although newly formed cooperatives and associations tended to fare badly, the incorporation of traditional groups proved to be a sounder development strategy. For example, in Bank-assisted irrigation projects in Korea, the Philippines, and Peru, local water users' associations were found to manage tertiary canals effectively when the groups are small, to link with extension activities, to develop clear rules of operation, and to have a strong leadership.

A counter example is provided by a Thai irrigation project in which the operation and maintenance of tertiary canals were expected to be the responsibility of farmers organized into Water Users' Groups (WUGS). Water distribution was to be the paid responsibility of a farmer elected by members of each WUG. The audit concludes that the WUGS existed mainly on paper and the canals were poorly maintained, water distribution was inequitable, and downstream farmers faced water shortages. Similar WUG failures have been noted in Indonesia. In both Thailand and Indonesia, WUG problems reflected inadequate consideration of social, cultural, and local economic factors in design and implementation. In the one area of the Thai project where WUGS were successful, canals were short enough to ensure social homogeneity, and government agencies supported the WUGS through inputs and credits and facilitated the marketing of crops. Successful WUGS can be predicted in areas in which cooperative canal management has long been based on kinship, descent, and marriage ties or in which rules of water allocation are enforced by traditional leadership among non-kin owners of adjacent plots of land. Borrowers might heed these lessons in planning and implementation strategies.

In Senegal, the existing cooperative structure was not considered a suitable farmers' organization for Bank-assisted projects. Accordingly, the implementing authority introduced producers' groups on an experimental basis for the Senegal River Polders Project. Formed on the basis of traditional social groups and lines of authority, each group consisted of twelve to fifteen family heads and was represented by a "chief," who dealt directly with the implementing agency in regard to input supplies, credit recovery, and marketing. The ex post evaluation concludes that, despite other project problems, these groups did a better job than the government agency in maintaining agricultural equipment and suggests expanding their functions.

In the nineteen projects for area development examined in my 1985 study, as in some of the irrigation schemes, underdesign for social innovation showed up in infrequent or inappropriate use of traditional social organizations, associations, and cooperatives as implementation units. Existing cooperatives were only a bit more common in the area development schemes than in the irrigation projects. Existing cooperatives identified at appraisal were assigned an important implementing role in a very unsuccessful credit program in Niger. The PPAR for this project contrasts the seeming preproject strength of Niger's cooperatives with the usual situation in Africa: "Past experience with farmer groups in Africa, organized as cooperatives or credit societies, has been—with very few exceptions—rather negative. By uncritically transferring patterns tried out in different parts of the world, the founders or promoters of cooperatives seemed to have neglected socioeconomic factors dominating the African rural setting." The relatively large cooperatives that some Bank-assisted projects have established have failed to give farmers a feeling of trust and individual care. In other instances, cooperatives have been too small to support the cost of managers, accountants, and staff, and their members thus derive lower returns than those obtainable from private merchants, who are more flexible and efficient.

What about new cooperatives? In Ethiopia's Wolamo First Agricultural Development Project an "excellent" extension organization taught farmers agricultural and cooperative principles, but beneficiaries preferred to sell to private traders. The audit notes that without direct access to urban or foreign markets cooperatives were in a weak position from the outset. It recommends that in promoting cooperative marketing, the Bank consider the national chain of distribution, and that it avoid sponsoring small units in isolated areas. Commenting on the audit, the division responsible for the project suggested that it would increase administrative overhead to develop cooperative unions and that private traders might handle smallholders' marketing more efficiently than cooperatives.

Although cooperatives were assigned no role in the Burundi First Arabica Coffee Improvement Project, the villagers spontaneously organized communal self-help activities in implementing bridge building and other components, and the audit suggests that cooperative factory stores could have been established. These factory stores could have received coffee cherries in exchange for staples, so that the factories would have had a consistent coffee supply and the farmers would have had access to competitively priced staples. Such a cooperative could have provided a diffuse and flexible organizational structure able both to assess farmers' technical needs and to articulate their demands. In Tanzania, collective tea farming worked when organized spontaneously by villagers, but the communal tea farms initiated by regional authorities failed.

This study of ex post evaluations therefore concludes that cooperatives tend to be most successful when they are based on preexisting, local, and communal institutions. An extension of this generalization is that new cooperatives will tend to succeed in nuclear-family systems, whereas in descent-based societies the successful cooperatives will be those that use traditional descent and formal marriage structures to recruit and bond their membership.

Participant groups other than cooperatives contributed to five of the nineteen area development projects considered in my 1985 study. In the Senegal Casamance Rice Project, for example, the original over-centralized management and formal cooperative structure were replaced with a management unit that worked closely with village communities. Extension workers were generalists in charge of a small population and area. The monitoring and evaluation procedure compared affected and unaffected farmers. The evaluation documents conclude that flexibility in implementation was the main reason for the project's success. In a rural infrastructure project in Korea the combination of a strong and experienced implementing organization and grass roots participation of the beneficiaries helped ensure project success. Cernea's more recent (1987) study of twenty-five Bank-assisted projects broadens these findings by documenting the sustainable development potential of culturally appropriate grass roots organizational stabilization.

Flexibility, involvement of beneficiaries, drawing on preexisting social units, and monitoring of local conditions are part and parcel of socially sound implementation strategies. No standard implementation strategy will do for all projects. The fallacy of applying culturally alien development designs to varying countries and conditions has been examined previously. A related fallacy is that of seeing developing countries as an undifferentiated group. Livestock projects in Brazil and Paraguay had good rates of return (8 and 11 percent, respectively), because the provision of livestock credit responded to needs perceived by beneficiaries and the projects were compatible with the cultures. Both nations had long cattle-raising histories, and the lowland South American livestock patterns fit the development model used by the project better than would the animal care traditions of Africa, Asia, and Oceania.

Models for Success

Lessons from negative cases suggest the remedies, some of which have already been discussed, but some successful livestock development experiences can teach something, too. Although only partial successes, they suggest three models for further investigation.

LOW DENSITY MODEL. In Chad a project to dig new wells and rehabilitate others throughout pastoralists' traditional territory seemed more culturally appropriate than the usual ranch model of livestock development. As with irrigation projects, rehabilitation proved much more successful economically than the new construction. The project still failed, however, because of civil unrest (known at appraisal) and Bank delays as a result of rigid procedures. Better timing, greater Bank flexibility, and a primary focus on rehabilitation might be tried in another area of low population density.[9]

EUROPEAN RANCHER MODEL. In Brazil and Paraguay the provision of livestock credit through subloans to experienced, middle- and large-scale ranchers is one way to increase meat supplies and achieve satisfactory rates of return. The implementation strategy for such projects has no need for elaborate technical assistance, overseas training, or expatriate management. This model cannot, however, be expected to do much to reduce relative poverty.

HIGH DENSITY, MIXED ECONOMY MODEL. There are indications that if social bias can be eliminated, certain livestock-related projects may succeed in areas of relatively high population densities and mixed economies. Four tentative examples are India Drought Prone, Korea Dairy Beef, Uganda Beef Cattle, and Rwanda Mutara Agricultural Development Projects. The population densities of Uganda, Rwanda, India, and Korea, respectively, are 53, 200, 205, and 390 per square kilometer. One might generalize that people in these countries are packed

densely enough for effective implementation and are sufficiently motivated by family needs and pressure on resources to diversify and intensify
production.[10]

The Uganda Beef Cattle Project was judged by the ex post evaluation
to be one of the more successful livestock projects in Africa. It introduced
cattle herding to a region recently freed of tsetse fly infestation. The
project did not conflict with relevant local and regional socioeconomic
conditions, but rather made good use of them. Stock was introduced from
Kenya and was therefore adapted to regional ecology. Herding is a
culturally appropriate activity in Uganda, and once the tsetse fly was
eliminated people simply extended their traditional practice to fill a new
niche. The project used a mixture of ranch types: government, cooperative, and private. Project aims were compatible with traditional land
tenure, especially in Buganda, where fences and small farms were
customary and proved compatible with the private property and grazing
goals of the project. And Uganda's population is sufficiently concentrated (53 per square kilometer nationally, but higher in Buganda) for
effective supervision, extension, animal health care, marketing, input
delivery, and the like. This project's eventual problems were due to
political factors rather than to cultural incompatibility.

The group ranch subproject of the Rwanda Mutara Agricultural Development Project was initially considered to be the riskiest component
because there was no previous experience in Rwanda, and the people
affected were traditionally seminomadic. The appraisal mission (wisely,
it would seem) replaced a cooperative ranch concept proposed by the
government with group ranches based on communal grazing rights.
Pastoralist families were settled on delineated ranches, each of which
benefited from exclusive pasture rights, veterinary services, and plots
(1.5 hectares per family) for cultivation. About a thousand families were
installed on sixty-three ranches, the project was well accepted by the
beneficiaries, and veterinary fees were collected successfully.

The ex post evaluation attributes the success of the group ranch
subproject to three factors: the traditional grazing rights of the pastoral
communities were properly appreciated and well respected; the technical
package was adequately designed and proved appealing to pastoralists;
and the project turned out to be the main shield of pastoralists against
immigration and anarchic occupation of land by farmers.[11] One might
add the factor of population density (200 per square kilometer), which

has the same implications already mentioned for Uganda. Indeed, the audit notes that Rwandan pastoralists probably understand that the increasing population pressure on land leaves them little chance to survive unless they intensify their animal production methods and start cultivating part of their plots—both of which the project beneficiaries have done.

The most successful irrigation projects also tended to be located in densely populated areas (as were traditional irrigation systems). Extension and implementation are facilitated when people are more concentrated and easier to reach. However, the land tenure problems that frequently affect irrigation schemes are also found where dense population places pressure on scarce land and water. Socioeconomic stratification was usual in areas where irrigation projects were implemented, as was a history of nationwide, rather than tribal, organization. This is important because a usual correlate of nation-state organization is a developed legal code to arbitrate disputes over land ownership. Traditions of litigation and conflict combine with population pressure and stratification to create tenure problems in irrigation-based societies. Consequently, land tenure problems were reported much more often for the irrigation projects (44 percent in my 1985 study) than for the other agricultural or livestock projects (16 percent).

Equity

A fact of life is that irrigation projects are more likely than others to widen income disparities, even though they may simultaneously increase crop production and decrease absolute poverty. The reports on irrigation projects were much more likely than those for other subsectors to include statements about the project's impact on income distribution. However, virtually all the projects considered in the 1985 study were designed and implemented before the Bank's enunciation of its focus on poverty.[12] Because poverty alleviation was not a principal goal of most of the projects, the detailed pre- and postproject socioeconomic information necessary to evaluate the reduction of both absolute and relative poverty tends to be absent. If poverty alleviation is to be assessed in the future, social expertise will be essential. The main conclusion here (despite the paucity of detailed socioeconomic data for pre- and postproject comparisons) is that although irrigation projects increase production, there is a significant risk that they will widen the preexisting disparities in wealth.

For example, a polders project in Senegal in which only 14 percent of participants were classified as low-income reportedly increased income disparities and especially benefited absentee landlords and nonfarmers. A sound implementation procedure (reliance on traditional social structure) helped make the project an economic success, but apparently worked against income redistribution. Traditional leaders, drawn from the ranks of "noble" families, formed effective production groups and cooperatives to purchase and maintain equipment.

The goal of preventing wealth disparities from widening may not be clear-cut. How, for example, do we recognize inequality when we see it? Social anthropological knowledge may inform such assessments in ways that simple economic measurements cannot. Some evaluation reports seemed to confuse social *ranking* with stratification. In many Third World societies, the basic social organizations are clans, lineages, and other descent groups. Certain branches may be ranked higher than others and thus considered "noble," though actual differences in wealth and power between branches are slight. In descent groups, elders often control the labor and access to resources of their juniors; but since young people will eventually become elders, the situation is unlike socioeconomic stratification, in which differences in wealth and power are major and lifelong.

In Madagascar's Lake Alaotra Irrigation Project, for example, many large-scale and "noble" landlords were identified in the initial ex post evaluation as drawing disproportionate benefits. Later, however, sociological in-depth analysis (during impact evaluation) ascertained that they were clan leaders holding estates in trust for numerous dependents. Developers therefore need to know more than in whose name the land happens to be registered. Often *all* the members of a descent group work on and benefit from what turns out on in-depth analysis to be a joint or communal estate, although it is registered in the name of only one person. Allocation of benefits through ranked descent groups in traditional societies is very different from appropriation of surplus in a class-structured society.

It is therefore necessary to pay careful attention to the nature of ranking and resource allocation in the project area, in order to determine whether major class-based contrasts—or more innocuous forms of ranking—will be preserved or sharpened by the project?

Overview

The broadest conclusion and recommendation of this chapter is the general need for social engineering; the sociocultural characteristics of affected people must be systematically taken into account for sound development strategies. The consequences of underdesign for social innovation must be corrected. Each project must have a socially informed and culturally appropriate design and implementation strategy, and a social expert is best trained to provide this. Not only international donors, but also local agencies and consulting firms must recognize that social expertise is necessary at project identification to sort out the relevant sociocultural factors and fit the project to them. After identifying compatible projects centered around people's perceived needs, social expertise is again necessary to devise efficient and socially compatible implementation strategies. Identifying needs and planning projects that address them with socially informed implementation strategies are tasks that challenge governments to make greater use of national resources—their own social experts, indigenous anthropologists and sociologists—in development planning. Evaluation of project impact will also be facilitated by the routine use of social expertise to gather and analyze accurate socioeconomic information on the project area before, during, and after implementation. Sociocultural engineering for economic development is not simply socially desirable; it is demonstrably cost-effective.

Many of the projects reviewed here did not "put people first" because they were designed and initiated at a time when the need for a social strategy, and the results of its absence, were less apparent. Those that did succeed usually did so because of the sensitivity, skills, and intuition of experienced planners rather than careful social engineering. Flaws in social design, identified in thirty-six (53 percent) of sixty-eight projects sampled in 1985, caused many projects to fail or to achieve less than could have been achieved.

Several evaluation reports stress the relationship between design and implementation. Many designs were virtually impossible to implement because they lacked proper incentives for participation and acceptance of project goals. The evaluation of an African integrated rural development project states that most of the problems attributed to poor management were products of faulty design. Indeed, in all but fourteen projects, good (or poor) design accompanied good (or poor) implementation. In six cases project deficiencies were attributed to implementation rather than design flaws, and in eight good implementation—usually because of flexibility and the reformulation of the project—helped overcome design errors. The obvious recommendations, echoed in the 1987 USAID study, are to improve social design and to ensure that flexibility is built into implementation strategy.

The main findings of my 1985 study, pertaining to the cases and variables examined, and extending across the different sectors of rural development, will now be summarized. In the thirty-two cases (47 percent of the reviewed projects) in which the PPAR or IER specifically called attention to deficiencies in sociocultural *design*, the average rate of return was less than half that of the thirty-six projects in which no such problems were identified.[13]

Problems with participants' *incentives* were reported for 37 percent of the projects and extended evenly across all the sectors. Significant *flexibility* in implementation was noted in only 35 percent of the projects, most obviously in the area development projects, where it is particularly needed.

Human resources—specifically, the availability of manpower—was misestimated in 32 percent of the projects, usually when farming was a component. In all but two of the twenty-two reported cases, the local supply of labor was assumed to be more abundant than it really was.

Land tenure problems were reported in 34 percent of the projects, most frequently in irrigation, livestock, and settlement projects, but for different reasons related to the density of population and social stratification among irrigators, traditional migratory grazing rights over large areas and interethnic contacts among pastoralists, and tribal rights and historically discordant land-tilting procedures affecting new settlements.

Socioeconomic stratification was specifically mentioned as a project problem in just fifteen reports. This result is inconclusive, however, because stratification in fact affected a larger number of projects. When relative poverty alleviation is a goal, stratification needs greater attention during planning and implementation, especially in irrigation projects.

Ethnicity, specifically tensions between various ethnic groups, was signaled in twenty-two of the evaluation reports, most frequently for settlement projects (26 percent), livestock projects (42 percent), and area development (32 percent). For irrigation projects, stratification rather than ethnicity is the key issue of social differentiation.

Design and implementation problems related to the neglect of *women's roles* was mentioned in just six of the reports, too few for analysis. The

PPARS of a few West African projects, however, called attention specifically to socially incompatible assumptions about the roles and activities of women. Some recommendations in these audits can be reiterated: If women are to be prominent agricultural producers, female personnel should be drawn into the extension system; associations of female producers should be carefully investigated; and production and marketing units that exclude women will not function effectively in a cultural tradition or in a project that expects women to produce and sell. The USAID report provides a lengthy review of issues of women in development, based on statistical analysis and case discussion. In my 1985 Bank study, neglect of women's roles was simply a corollary of the generalized lack of a socially informed design and implementation strategy. Specific discussion of men's roles was almost as rare as the mention of women.

Participants' groups were encountered most frequently in projects with an agricultural component. These groups were most effective when based on traditional social organizations or the socioeconomic similarity of members. Examples include local and regional descent groups in Africa; small groups of traditionally connected, socioeconomically equal users of tertiary canals in a few areas of Asia; traditional ranked groups in West Africa; and groups of literate middle- and upper-income settlers in Peru and Malaysia. Although the use of traditional groups as implementation units furthered project production goals, it sometimes contributed negatively to income distribution.

In almost half the cases, however, it was impossible to assess the distributional impact of a project on the basis of the information available in the ex post evaluation papers. If poverty alleviation and more equitable income distribution are to be assessed for current and future projects, the quality of socioeconomic information collected before, during, and after project implementation must be improved. The need for such information leads to a brief discussion of some larger and more general sociocultural parameters of Bank-assisted development.

Information Gathering and the Culture of the Development Agency

This review has focused on the extent to which development projects have paid attention to and been compatible with the traditional culture, society, and economy of the target population. However, the fullest possible analysis of the sociocultural dimensions of agriculture and rural development projects would recognize that there are two larger domains in which sociocultural issues affect project success. One, obviously, is the national culture—the traditions, policies, resources, and characteristic procedures of each member country. Government pricing policies, for example, influence a project's success by increasing or decreasing participants' incentives to produce and sell certain crops. Governments sometimes make overly optimistic appraisals of their abilities to implement projects. Political forces and special interest groups oppose changes that might threaten their traditional advantages. These factors affect planning, implementation, and impact evaluation, but are not the focus of the present review.

A second more general domain is the culture of the international development agency—its properties as a multilevel sociocultural system with its own organizational goals, communication networks, information flows, authority lines, territorial imperatives, incentives, rewards and penalties, associations, conflicts, rituals, work habits, and decisionmaking procedures. A subdivision of this culture might be called the "culture of information gathering"—that is, the customary procedures for gathering and evaluating sociocultural data during design, implementation, and ex post evaluation. It appears that in many development organizations the task of collecting socioeconomic data has traditionally been assigned to the microeconomist when one is available. Among the projects reviewed here, some failures are attributable simply to faulty economic analysis, others to inadequate sociocultural understanding or insensitivity to the role of participants' traditions in making a project successful; still others, perhaps the majority of problem projects, are attributable to both. If microeconomists (rather than professional sociocultural analysts such as sociologists and anthropologists) are to continue their traditional role as principal project socioeconomic analysts (which may not be the most cost-effective option), they need more sociocultural training and sensitivity.

An in-depth ethnographic study of the culture of the development agency or agencies would be needed to determine the specifics of how problems arise and are perpetuated, and what might be done to correct them. But even a brief exposure to the culture of one such agency, as revealed through its documents and input from staff, can suggest some recommendations for change.

There is a need, for example, for better information flow between departments and divisions. Lessons drawn from project experience, audits, and impact evaluations have sometimes been ignored in planning follow-ups, as some of the ex post evaluation studies have signaled. One solution might be to have a fairly permanent member of the agency staff serve as a social analyst. Social specialists and generalists could help link these indigenous "country experts" into a larger information network. Anthropologists, rural sociologists, and other social experts have developed many cross-culturally valid generalizations about relationships between economy, society, and culture.

Better sociocultural background information not only is needed in identification, preparation, and appraisal of each project, but also must be woven obviously and systematically into project design. Too often, even when attention has been paid to cultural factors and local socioeconomy, this information is relegated to an annex of a preparation or appraisal document, where it is less likely to be read, heeded, or questioned than material in the main report. The provision of sociocultural information should not become an empty ritual. There is no value in having a section called "Social Aspects" in a preproject document if a social perspective has not been used to develop objectives and to design an implementation strategy. For example, if existing grass roots associations are to be used in implementation, much value will be added if their social characteristics, number, effectiveness, and location are thoroughly known and the manner of their use clearly charted.

The importance of a socially sensitive perspective in data collection and evaluation has been stressed in other chapters in the present volume and is underlined here.[14] Social expertise is important both in design and during identification, preparation, and appraisal, for if the socioeconomic impact (including the project's positive or negative contribution to production and equity) is to be assessed, there must be a reliable preproject data base. The role of social expertise in the ex post evaluation of impact is a corollary of this.

A social perspective is also needed during implementation and supervision, although some projects call for greater social sensitivity than others. For example, in fishery projects, credit procedures can increase stratification of the industry and thereby undermine the individual initiative on which offshore fishing productivity rests. In projects directed toward pastoral populations, effective extension seems to be especially important and implementation units deserve close attention. The common thread is the need for more accurate information on the sociocultural context and effects throughout the project cycle.

In an insightful article about development strategy, David Korten contrasts the blueprint model used by most developmental organizations with a "learning process" model that he considers more useful and cost-effective.[15] The learning process model attempts to involve prospective beneficiaries at all stages of the project cycle. People initiate and help plan the changes that will affect them, and the implementation strategy is based on flexibility and feedback from the project participants. A close working relationship throughout the project cycle between socially sensitive planners and the local population is also advocated by Norman Uphoff (see chapter 13). It is part and parcel of promoting a constructive participatory strategy for fitting development projects to people.

No matter who initiates the project, it is most likely to succeed when it is directed toward the proven expertise of the target population, when it addresses locally recognized needs, and when it makes proper use of existing social groups and structures for implementation. The culturally specific incentives necessary to obtain local participation will become apparent through socioeconomic and cultural study during preparation and appraisal. Social expertise can help in locating and formulating the people-initiated projects that respond to concrete problems local people perceive and that introduce changes participants themselves wish to make. Sociologists can also help locate the pockets of poverty that equity programs should address. Often anthropologists (indigenous or foreign) who have worked in a particular area can venture an immediate opinion about where needs are greatest or make an educated guess about a project's likely equity effects. Some social anthropologists are generalists, others are specialists who concentrate on a country or geographic area (such as the Near East and North Africa), sector (such as irrigation or fishing), theory, or topic. Experts should be matched with particular types of projects according to their specialties. Social analysts selected to work on development projects should have been previously concerned with socioeconomic change in their research.

The need for greater attention to cultural and socioeconomic factors in the project area will not invariably require international development agencies to assign a foreign anthropologist or sociologist throughout a project cycle. It will, however, necessitate greater reliance by governments on indigenous social expertise, and more training in sociocultural engineering for international agency staff. Ex post evaluation reports (particularly audits) make routine references to the field trips that under-lie the audits, but they rarely specify the amount of time actually spent in the project area or the nature and extent of social inquiry. The kind of data collection that is needed requires more than discussion in towns and cities with government figures and high-level implementation authori-ties. Rural development planning requires rural field work, and imple-mentation and evaluation (both by the country and by lenders and development agencies) must be based on visits to villages and interviews with the affected people. Good social engineering means that people come first—throughout the project cycle.

In the impact evaluation study for one African irrigation project, the full range of technical problems (improper canal construction and drain-age) was immediately revealed by villagers, during ex post evaluation, to an international team that included both a national and a foreign social expert. These issues might never have been revealed had only officials been consulted. Furthermore, peasants reported that they had been quick to perceive the project's technical flaws years earlier as it was being implemented. Had anyone sought out their input early on, they said, the project might have been changed for the better during the implementation period.

Putting people first therefore means recognizing that each project generates its own unpaid monitoring and evaluation team—the local participants who experience the project firsthand as it is implemented, and who must live with its results for years after the consultants have left. It should be a fairly simple matter for governments, consulting firms, and local development agencies to tap this information pool and put it to productive use.

Notes

Many Bank staff members have read and commented helpfully on this chapter and previous drafts, and their willingness to share their insights and knowledge is gratefully acknowledged. They include Michael Cernea, Clive Collins, Cynthia Cook, Jack Duloy, Fred Hotes, Jack Kordik, Francis Lethem, John Malone, Kathryn McPhail, Donald Pickering, Christian Polti, Owen Price, Deborah Rubin, and Montague Yudelman.

1. Michael A. Cernea, "Farmer Organizations and Institution Building for Sustainable Agricultural Development," *Regional Development Dialogue*, no. 2 (1988). The study referred to in this article involved the case analysis of twenty-five projects.

2. Most of the eleven IERS reviewed for this study have been done by sociologists or anthropologists. Among those who have been involved in the field research and writing of IERS

are James Anderson, Jean-Francois Barres, Marilyn Gelber, Neville Dyson-Hudson, Lina Fruzetti, Repeli Hau'ofa, and Conrad Kottak.

3. This analysis has been based mainly on information contained in documents prepared *after* project completion. There are other, potentially informative ways to test the relationship between adequate social analysis and the economic success of projects. One would involve using preproject materials—for example, for the same group of projects examined in the present study—as the basis for an evaluation of their social analysis. Thereafter and independently, the correlation between the use of preproject social expertise and economic success as measured by the economic rate of return could be calculated. Such a research design would provide an interesting test of the findings of the present study.

4. A. S. Romer, *Man and the Vertebrates*, vol. 1, 3d ed. (Hammondsworth, Eng.: Penguin Books, 1960).

5. All quotations in the text are from World Bank evaluation materials, unless otherwise specified.

6. David C. Korten, "Community Organization and Rural Development: A Learning Process Approach," *Public Administration Review* (September–October 1980), pp. 480–512.

7. This important lesson from FELDA partially contradicts the belief that project failures because of international price fluctuations are beyond the designers' control. See, for example, World Bank, *IDA in Retrospect: The First Two Decades of the International Development Association* (New York: Oxford University Press, 1982), p. 64.

8. Michael A. Cernea, "Modernization and Development Potential of Traditional Grassroots Peasant Organizations," in Mustafa O. Attir, Burkart Holzner, and Zdenek Suda, eds., *Directions of Change: Modernization Theory, Research, and Realities* (Boulder, Colo.: Westview, 1982), p. 133. Cernea also found that projects generally allowed traditional organizations only a secondary role in the overall project effort.

9. A Bank staff member suggested that "in the nomadic situation increased water availability along the migration route will permit herds to stay longer in a particular location. This can lead to overgrazing and land degradation, so well numbers and distribution need to be carefully balanced with carrying capacity of the grazing land under adverse rainfall assumptions."

10. If population density is to be used effectively in planning projects and evaluating their success, statistics must be gathered on a regional as well as a national basis.

11. Were the sixteen families (on the average) on each range recruited with reference to traditional kinship or descent groups? This seems a fourth probable reason for success, but the (otherwise extremely informative) evaluation materials do not say.

12. World Bank, *Focus on Poverty* (Washington, D.C., 1983).

13. It is important to repeat that the measures being correlated—the economic rate of return and sociocultural deficiencies—were calculated independently of one another.

14. See chapter 14 by Robert Chambers and chapter 2 by E. Walter Coward, Jr.

15. Korten, "Community Organization."

PART VIII

Participation

Editor's Note

If "people's participation" in financially induced development programs is to be more than a trendy slogan, planners and managers must face the task of *organizing* participation—they identify and mobilize the specific social actors whose participation is sought, and open the practical ways in which they could participate in project design, execution, and monitoring.

To chart such ways, Norman Uphoff uses a "problem map": he starts with a discussion of problems confronted in projects lacking adequate popular participation. He then analyzes several areas in project planning where planners will have to seriously rethink project design if they hope to bring more people into the decisionmaking process. Uphoff not only brings together many issues raised in the preceding chapters of this book, but also addresses theoretical and methodological questions concerning the integration of the project's social actors into project planning.

Uphoff begins by reviewing three rural development projects in Ghana, Mexico, and Nepal. Despite their relatively innovative designs, all three projects were hindered by an excessive dependence on centralized, nonparticipatory planning. Even where planners started to allow for consultation, as in the Mexican case, further analysis showed that lasting patterns of social organization for participation were not established.

The experience garnered from these three cases is used to define five ways of ensuring beneficiaries' participation in project design and implementation. First, the degree of participation desired must be made clear at the outset and in a way acceptable to all concerned parties. Second, there should be realistic objectives for participation and allowance must be made for the fact that some stages of planning, such as design consultation, will be relatively protracted, while other phases, such as the transfer of assets for utilization, will be shorter. Third, in most parts of the world specific provisions for introducing and supporting participation are needed. Although these will, of course, vary according to local patterns of social organization, in general it seems desirable to use existing local organizations. If existing organizations are insufficient or inadequate for the purpose, careful analysis should lead to the design of facilitating organizations congruent with local culture. Fourth, there must be an explicit, adequate financial commitment to popular participation. Goodwill is not enough. Fifth, there must be plans to share responsibilities in all stages of the project cycle. Beneficiaries involved in the planning and execution of projects are better informed and more committed to make the project work than are people suddenly handed an asset to which they have contributed nothing.

Uphoff discusses participation not merely in project decisionmaking, but also in gathering the knowledge used to design a project. He notes areas in which local expertise can make a substantive contribution to project design: obtaining socioeconomic data; monitoring and evaluating the project; checking the validity of sociocultural information gathered by outsiders; providing technical knowledge; and contributing spatial and historical information about similar earlier projects and the reasons for their success or failure.

In the chapter's final section, Uphoff addresses the issue of working with local organizations and notes that some institutions are more suitable than others for carrying out development programs. Chief among the potential pitfalls are the dangers that the elite of the community will co-opt the hierarchially induced development program for their own exclusive profit. Nearly as difficult a problem is how to prevent bureaucratization and organizational rigidity from setting in. Sustaining participatory projects may well turn out to be more difficult than initiating them.

Uphoff's chapter provides a not so gentle reminder of an unfortunate tendency to see the people as "the problem" and the technicians, bureaucrats, and planners as "the solution." Not only does this attitude reflect a jaundiced view of exactly who is supposed to benefit from the project, but it also effectively excludes the contributions that even people with limited resources can and should make.

13

Fitting Projects to People

Norman Uphoff

Putting people first in development projects comes down to tailoring the design and implementation of projects to the needs and capabilities of people who are supposed to benefit from them. No longer should people be identified as "target groups." Rather, if we must speak of them abstractly, we should consider them as "intended beneficiaries." They are to be benefited, rather than "impacted."[1] In design and implementation we have only intentions, since our knowledge of how to improve the productivity and well-being of the poor majority is limited. We can and should be clear about *whom* we expect to benefit, and *how*, but we cannot be certain our efforts will bear the desired fruits until the processes of economic and social change have been put in motion. Fortunately, some of the unanticipated outcomes can be favorable. The probabilities of gaining momentum, rather than losing it, in the course of carrying out projects should be greater to the extent that the mode of design and implementation reflects a "learning process" approach.[2] This should enlist the participation of intended beneficiaries as much as feasible in all aspects of project operations.

This chapter considers some actual project experiences and establishes how development expenditures are likely to be more worthwhile to the extent that projects are planned in ways that involve the intended beneficiaries in decisionmaking, implementation, evaluation, and of course benefits.[3] First I review experience with three rural development projects in rather different developing countries. These projects were planned with little input from the intended beneficiaries, and the ensuing problems and insufficient results derive from the top-down approach taken. In various ways the projects have been modified to become more open to people's participation, and progress has become more satisfactory.[4] This demonstrates that projects should be fitted to people.

Some general conclusions about *what* people can contribute to the planning and implementation of projects are then drawn from varied field experiences and recent developments in social science research and thinking on participation.[5] Also discussed is how, with the benefit of sociological theory and administrative practices, projects can be better conceived and carried out to put people first.

Problems with a Nonparticipatory Approach

To understand better what is likely to happen when people are not put first and when project design proceeds in more technocratic ways, with assumptions that technicians and administrators not only know best but know enough, consider three integrated rural development projects in Nepal, Ghana, and Mexico.[6] The countries themselves are drawn from Asia, Africa, and Latin America and represent quite different levels of economic and administrative development. They fall in the bottom, middle, and top third of developing countries according to per capita income—World Bank figures show them to be, respectively, seventh, forty-first, and seventy-first from the bottom out of ninety countries.

Three Rural Development Projects

All three projects were funded in part by loans from the World Bank, and its staff played a role in their design. It should be understood that these projects were for their time relatively innovative and thus deserve some credit even if they were less successful than desired. Knowledge concerning participatory modes of development—including the desirability of promoting them and the steps involved—has much advanced since the early or middle 1970s when these projects were initiated. It is easier to display hindsight than foresight when pointing out problems in the approach and results, and I take no satisfaction in making critical appraisals. The purpose is to highlight experience in a way that enables us to learn from it, so that foresight in design and implementation becomes clearer.

NEPAL. The first project to be considered is the Rasuwa-Nuwakot Development Project in Nepal. The project loan of $8 million was to improve an area covering 29,000 families in the two districts of Nuwakot and Rasuwa north of Kathmandu. The project included intensified agricultural extension work with improved crop varieties, farmer training, marketing, and research; livestock development; irrigation extension; improvements in the availability of agricultural inputs; control of soil erosion; health centers and village water supplies; trails and bridges; and cottage industries. It was assumed that participation, in implementation if not planning, would flow through the *panchayats* (the partyless local government system) following procedures for decentralized planning laid down in the District Administration Plan of 1975. These local institutions have now been abolished in part because they were unrepresentative of people's interests.

The area is noteworthy for its extreme poverty and the extremely poor transportation and communication infrastructure serving rugged mountain areas. An average family landholding is 0.6 hectare scattered in five pieces. Income is so low as to have little meaning in monetary terms. Food production covers only two-thirds to three-fourths of consumption, and one-third of adult males must migrate out of the area during part of each year to add to family income. The people are, in spite of or because of this, very hardworking and enterprising, extracting an existence from an environment distinguished for its beauty and its penury.

Even a critical reviewer of the project describes it as a "new and important landmark in the history of rural development in the country."[7] Other agencies have encountered similar or greater problems in rural development projects in the hills of Nepal, but many problems in the design and implementation of this one could be traced, in the words of a Nepalese government official, to the "lack of participatory process in plan formulation."

The existing planning procedures for the project are not based on the understanding of the critical ingredients of participation, namely participation in decisionmaking, participation in implementation, including resource mobilization, participation in benefit sharing, and participation in evaluation. Where the villagers undertook projects on their own, such as the forest regeneration project in Belkhot Panchayat discussed earlier, the participation of the local people in terms of all these dimensions was total. But when it came to the planning of activities under the [World Bank] project, their participation was only partial and limited to the need identification and subsequent implementation of a few rural works projects such as drinking water, suspension bridges, [and so on.] In most other sectoral activities, the participation of the people at the village level was simply nonexistent.[8]

The project staff, however, were satisfied if they could get the district-level panchayats somewhat involved in planning and implementation despite the limitations and social biases of these institutions. (The issue of village-level participation will be discussed below.) Some of the experience of this project has been encouraging, at least in communities where there was active participation.

GHANA. The Upper Region Agricultural Development Project in northern Ghana was planned for the same length of time and same period as the Nepal project. It was much larger, however, with a loan of $21 million to be applied to a region covering 10 percent of Ghana's population (125,000 families) and 40 percent of its cattle. Ninety Farm Service Centers were to provide extension and management services to farmers, and there would be loans and inputs to improve production on 118,000 hectares. In addition to projecting huge increases in the yields of traditional crops, the planners expected to increase livestock production with the establishment of ten 2,000-hectare ranches. Agricultural research was to be strengthened, seed production was to be increased, and a pilot adult literacy scheme was planned. Both health and nutrition components were designed, and small-scale irrigation and soil conservation activities were to be augmented.

This complex of activities was to be undertaken in the poorest and most remote part of Ghana. The Upper Region has much in common with the Sahel, and its inhabitants are afflicted by a long, harsh dry season each year. What needs to be done to improve the people's livelihood is fairly obvious, but *how* to accomplish this is not. The soils are poor, the level of literacy very low (10 percent), and parasitic and other diseases are endemic. The traditional sociopolitical structures persist, though they are changing in response to influences from the state, the market, and the world culture.

The project design effort was not very protracted or participatory, certainly less so than in retrospect the situation warranted.[9] Farmers were to be represented at the highest levels of project management, and farmer groups were to be involved in the credit and agricultural improvement activities. But neither provision was part of the initial design or implemented satisfactorily. Subsequent efforts moved in the direction of broader farmer participation, with some encouraging results. Certainly any project as large and ambitious as this one will encounter some problems and misunderstandings. The question is whether more involvement of farmers and other rural residents could have reduced mistakes in project planning and facilitated implementation once the project was under way.

MEXICO. Of the three projects, PIDER in Mexico is the largest and most ambitious project, planned to affect 22 percent of the rural population and half of the rural poor in identified "microregions." The first phase (PIDER I) began in 1973 and was expanded in a second phase (PIDER II) contemporary with the projects in Ghana and Nepal. This has been succeeded by PIDER III. For the 1977–82 period, planned investment was $700 million, of which 25 percent is covered by a World Bank loan. Inasmuch as PIDER was conceived as an investment program for rural development rather than as a conventional project, its approach has been more open-ended, with less advance specification of program content and technologies. This leaves more scope for working out details in some consultation with the affected population.

Initially PIDER adopted a fairly conventional style of operation, although its organization was innovative. A fairly small staff in the president's office coordinated the investment program, which was implemented by nearly two dozen government agencies with a staff of 3,000 professionals. One objective was to get regular line ministries and corporations working more effectively with the rural population. The initial approach to the people was, however, as paternalistic and technocratic as was customary with these agencies.

World Bank appraisal materials for PIDER II strongly emphasized the need for community participation:

There has been increasing recognition of the importance of participation, not only to give more decisionmaking influence to program beneficiaries, but also to ensure that the program infrastructure and services achieve their original intention. The real participation of village groups in investment programming and decisionmaking continues to be limited. PIDER, however, is now involved in various special programs to increase beneficiary participation in both the programming and execution of the program. PIDER staff have become increasingly concerned that unless there is real participation in all phases of the program, the potential for proper operation and maintenance of the program investments will be greatly reduced.

PIDER differs from most other projects in the amount of attention methodically devoted in recent years to making the process of investment planning and implementation more genuinely participatory.[10] This reorientation, as the statement just cited suggests, has grown out of the initial experience of PIDER.

With large sums of money at stake, it is understandable that in each of the three countries there was a great hurry to prepare and implement the project as quickly as possible. But each project had a number of problems, almost in proportion to the extent that it was introduced without substantial local participation. Because each project was complex, with many components, it is not surprising that various faults in formulation are noticeable. Contributing to the problems were inefficient technical approaches, missed opportunities, exaggerated expectations, insufficient preparation in the countries themselves, and the speed with which project formulation was undertaken, especially in the hills of Nepal and the savanna of Ghana where data are scarce and proven technical solutions even scarcer. Since the governments had limited expertise and capacity, solutions were often sought from the outside rather than by working closely with the rural population in an inductive manner. Nor were the ideas of field-level government staff mobilized as they might have been in a more participatory process although the experience and suggestions of staff could have helped make the investment more cost-effective over time.

Project Components

It is true that projects have to be formulated and designed within the framework of existing government structures and procedures. Still, the justification for most projects is that they introduce innovations. World Bank staff commonly say they cannot and should not impose new approaches on the government in Bank-funded projects, yet many local project staff feel that innovations are financed only if they are favorably assessed by Bank economic and technical experts. The situation is similar for other donor agencies as well.

In view of the experimentation with rural development initiatives in other parts of Nepal and the ineffectiveness of conventional approaches, it is striking how little institutional innovation was supported in the Nepal project. Health service delivery was through standard (and passive) health posts which have a spotty record. No apparent consideration was given to the use of paraprofessionals and community participation to get more active health programs as was done by another donor with the Ministry of Health.[11] The forest development strategy was to hire guards and erect fencing, even though cheaper and more effective community-based forestry programs were known.[12]

The water supply component, one of the better parts of the project, was built on the construction strategy begun by the Local Development Department. Contributions of labor and available materials from the community were augmented by cement, pipes, and the like from UNICEF (United Nations Children's Fund), with financial and material support from the central government. Agricultural credit was channeled through the government-directed village cooperatives (*sajha*). This appeared to incorporate a participatory dimension to the project, but in reality it did not, because of the social biases and poor performance of these groups.[13]

In Ghana some of the agricultural technologies chosen were rather inappropriate, though to its credit the project did not promote tractorization, which is not only economically inefficient if government subsidies are taken into account, but also agronomically dubious.[14] The project appraisal correctly labeled tractorization as a "modern and expensive form of shifting cultivation." The intermediate technology of bullock plows was not thought through economically, however. Since a plow cost twenty-four times the average per capita cash income in the area and two-thirds of the farm households did not have bullocks, the innovation was beyond their capacity.[15] The heavy emphasis on the use of chemical fertilizers was also questionable.

I do not have any data on similar shortcomings in the formulation of the PIDER project, though there might have been some. Because the project was more open-ended, it was apparently less prone to get locked into inappropriate technologies or misdirected service delivery mechanisms.

Agricultural Targets

The agricultural projections made by all three projects were less than realistic, and their accuracy could have been increased by consultation with farmers. The Nepal project's own data showed that yields of the four major crops had been declining over the previous five years in the two districts (except for wheat in Nuwakot). Nevertheless, the planners predicted that within just four years yields would increase 50 to 100 percent with the use of fertilizer and 19 to 38 percent without. (The lower figure was for rainfed areas, the higher figure for irrigated areas.)

In Ghana the plans assumed that in just five years, with only the improvement of small dams for minor irrigation, yields would go up by 113 percent for subsistence crops.[16] The area planted in improved or advanced varieties was expected to go from 25,000 hectares preproject to 133,000 hectares in five years, which implied an annual increase of 40 percent. PIDER had somewhat less exaggerated expectations of "full development" within six years, when yields of rainfed crops (corn and beans) would be up by 50 to 67 percent, while irrigation was expected to boost yields as much as 100 percent. Such increases were based on experiment station results, not on experience in farmers' fields, and were, predictably, not achieved.

I point to these figures and to the deficiencies in project formulation to suggest that more realistic and beneficial projects could have been formulated by engaging the experience and ideas of farmers and technicians working in the project area. To plead that this might take "too much time" is to assign no cost to the inefficient use of resources because unrealistic components of a project have been approved.

Technical Choices

It is not the function of the sociologist to point up faults in the technical design of a project, but some problems have come to light in the projects under consideration with respect to technology. One common failing of many project designers is to underestimate the technical knowledge of local people, which social scientists could bring out. This was pointed up in one of the villages in Nepal where a check dam was to be built.

Although this project was undertaken for the benefit of the local people they were little involved in its planning. When the time came for implementation, the local people wanted to have it built on a [stronger] foundation ... [which] was not included in its design and estimate, and so the request was not complied with. Even the gabion wire mesh was made by labor imported from India which local people could easily have made or been trained to make. As it turned out, in the last monsoon, the dam gave in at the base, thus confirming the apprehension of the villagers, who now want a new one built in its place.[17]

More serious problems of design can be identified in the Battar irrigation scheme, which was a costly part of the Nepal project.[18] This was a marvel of engineering design, involving lift pumps and piped water to supply each of the 120 individual 2-hectare units. It would give precise water control to farmers provided they had electricity. Farmers told a visiting USAID official in 1977 that they would have preferred to use a gravity flow system with technologies they knew and could manage themselves.[19] As the farmers had feared, the water supply was interrupted whenever hydroelectric power was diverted to Kathmandu. Moreover, farmers pointed out that the system of piping water to the field did not allow the cold river water to warm in the sun, as happens in a gravity-channel system, and the crops do not do as well because of the differences in water temperature.[20] Since farmers were given no voice in design decisions, their farm operations suffer.

One cannot assume that rural people have all the necessary technical knowledge to make sound design judgments in every case. But neither should it be assumed that those who live in the environment and know it intimately have nothing to contribute. The attitude of the project designers in Nepal toward farmers is indicated by this statement: "Following review within [the central government] and decision on the form of organization to be adopted, there would be a short public information campaign to advise the farmers of what is intended and ensure their willing [sic] participation."

In Ghana, the "contact groups" designed to transmit technical advice to farmers included no women, even though women do a large share of farm work.[21] Social factors were also ignored in the design of PIDER'S livestock development component. Conflicting interests between those who own cattle and those who do not would predictably affect the extent to which the two groups cooperated, but this was not considered. Consequently, fences were broken, pastures destroyed, and regulations could not be enforced. The factors overlooked in planning, one might say, took revenge. In this project, appropriate measures would have involved landless laborers in the cattle development planning process.[22]

The design of the irrigation component in PIDER, having paid little attention to land tenure, turned out to polarize incomes. Although some differentiation of incomes may have been unavoidable, the design could have focused on complementary income-generating activity elsewhere so that the irrigation component would not be so unbalancing.[23] In recent years, the World Bank has become more concerned with assessing the implications of land tenure for the distribution of project benefits, but such assessment is subject to the availability of reliable socioeconomic information.

Implementation

In implementation, all three projects encountered problems of coordination and delay, some of which could be attributed to the way people were left out of the design phase. In Nepal, two-thirds of the way through the project period, only 22 percent of planned funds had been expended, and most of this had been on the "easy" part: vehicles, equipment, buildings, and the like. At the end of the fourth year (80 percent of project period), project expenditure was 52 percent of the planned amount. One reason for this was the overcentralization of the implementation process, most of it directed from Kathmandu. There was too little opportunity to make appropriate changes, additions, or deletions to the plans in the field. Though district-level planning was written into the project, it was not effectively activated.[24]

The situation was worse in the Upper Region of Ghana, where the lack of consultation in the design process contributed to a lack of integration and to inordinate delays. The Departments of Rural Development and Cooperatives had been only marginally involved in planning. Even the core activities of irrigation, mechanization, and seed production were not integrated in the project. After two years, the Agricultural Development Bank had not made a single loan to small farmers.

With some effort, 108 contact groups of farmers were finally formed in 1979 to test new technology on trial plots and to get loans. But work was delayed by bureaucratic wrangling between the Project Management Unit and the Farmers' Services Company (FASCOM) over who should authorize loans. By the time the dispute was resolved, more than half the groups had broken up, judging that the bureaucracy was up to its "usual tricks."[25] Neither the Project Management Unit nor FASCOM was really accountable to farmers. A new effort in 1980 to set up Farmer Committees was reportedly more successful.

The PIDER project has made a detailed analysis of the reasons for its shortcomings. It found 40 percent of them were due to lack of coordination and complementary investments, 30 percent were due to lack of technical assistance, and 15 percent each were due to lack of beneficiary maintenance and poor initial technical design. These findings indicated that PIDER management needed to strengthen coordination: "emphasizing improved *local-level* programming and continued efforts to reorient the way participating agencies *interact with* beneficiaries at the grass root level."[26]

The following strong statement in the project appraisal for PIDER II is attributed to the research center (CIDER) which had been monitoring project implementation: "CIDER insists that the root cause of poor operation and maintenance is the lack of small farmer participation in the early stages of programming." This view reflects the fact that problems were observed in some project sectors and relatively greater success in others. In particular, road building stood out as an area of accomplishment of the PIDER program. Village road committees introduced much more community participation in road building and maintenance than in other PIDER activities. The length of roads in the microregions was increased from 25,000 to 100,000 kilometers in six years. Moreover, good maintenance through community participation was reported by CIDER after surveys in the microregions. In contrast, the water supply systems were less effectively installed and maintained because of having been introduced in a technocratic manner.[27]

PIDER, CIDER, and their World Bank collaborators have been attempting to develop and institutionalize methodologies for participation, although some of the bureaucratic line agencies in Mexico are reluctant to empower local organization.

Different Kinds of Participation

There are many possible kinds of participation, and *who* participates and *how* may be more crucial to project success than any purely quantitative expression of participation. Researchers can reasonably disagree about what is to be considered "participation," but it should be possible to assess the results of different approaches, assumptions, and mechanisms. Without setting up any absolute standard for judging participation, we can see that these projects tended toward what might be called "pseudoparticipation," although there is also evidence of a few genuine and productive approaches. Readers can use whatever definitions and criteria they like to assess the experience of these projects.

Nepal

Interestingly, the appraisals of both the Nepal and Ghana projects acknowledge the willingness of farmers to innovate. The Nepal appraisal documents emphasized:

Despite isolation and life at subsistence levels, villagers cannot be called "conservative." They generally understand the importance of innovations—improved seed types, use of fertilizers, and acceptance of new crops (wheat). Furthermore, there are no dietary or customary obstacles to innovation. There is recognition of the need for formal education of both sexes. Villagers are keenly aware of their needs and have their own priorities. In a brief and limited survey of villages the expressed needs, in order of priority, were: (i) drinking water supplies; (ii) better irrigation/more water; (iii) improved seed and better supply of seeds; (iv) improved trails and more bridges; (v) potatoes; and (vi) sheep. These priorities were further expressed in a memorandum "Requirements for Development of Nuwakot District," prepared by Village Panchayats and presented to the District Panchayat. In practice, however, the acceptance of innovations has been limited and temporary. The general peasant attitude to government and governmental programs is one of distrust and suspicion. The most important reasons are: (a) The discontinuity and failure of government programs. Seed supply programs have been irregular and different types of seeds have been supplied on each occasion; (b) Lack of trained personnel who are adequately remunerated; (c) Lack of awareness and non-communication of programs.

The reasons cited for "limited and temporary" acceptance of innovations by villagers have little to do with the villagers themselves and rather more to do with the government's performance. Yet in spite of this, the project was designed to depend entirely on government personnel. In the project design the planners claimed to be taking social factors into account by decentralizing government services to subcenters—several different training centers and seed and livestock exchanges. But saying that "more effective development of the Panchayat system [would be encouraged] to allow greater participation in project development" was no more than a bow toward the concept.[28]

To be sure, if the panchayat system were to take on more responsibilities it could possibly facilitate participation, but the very way government planners conceived of panchayat involvement made it unlikely that independent initiative and ideas would be fed into the process. Various infrastructure construction plans were to be placed before the District Assembly "for information," but only those to be financed out of local resources would require approval by the assembly.

This provision of a minimum level of necessary participation in decisionmaking—if local resources were to be forthcoming—appeared to be more a matter of ratification than of formulating and making decisions. Shrestha says of such exercises: "At the district level, too, the participation of the people represented by the district panchayat was only of dubious validity. In most cases targets were already approved and included in the national programmes and budget requests of the sectoral ministries even before they were presented to the district panchayat or its committees—a *fait accompli.*"[29]

A realistic rejoinder could be that the panchayats were not representative of the majority of interests in the rural areas in any case. The small farmers, the landless, the lower castes, and tribal populations, not to mention women, were greatly underrepresented.[30]

The main role of the World Bank was to provide financing, so it could not implement the project outside the government's framework. But greater sensitivity to existing biases in decisionmaking and benefits would have been in order for the team which prepared and designed the project before appraisal. Some efforts could have been made to support more participatory institutions complementing the panchayat system. At the same time as the World Bank project was being implemented, the FAO in cooperation with the Agricultural Development Bank of Nepal was introducing multipurpose development activities in the project area through the Small Farmer Development Program (SFDP).[31] These activities were clearly more effective than, and were subsequently incorporated into, the World Bank–assisted project.

The staff responsible for the project were not opposed to participation. Rather, they assumed that working with the district panchayat—on their own terms, to be sure—provided adequate participation. Village panchayats were asked to submit plans, but since they were given no control over resources, their plans amounted only to shopping lists. Village proposals were integrated into a district plan by the project coordinator's office in Kathmandu for approval by the district panchayat. The competence and commitment of panchayat leadership certainly varied from one place to the next (as did the caliber of government officials who would implement the project's activities if local bodies did not). The project staff found that in about half a dozen cases, where supportive local leaders headed village panchayats, participation was "fantastic" and implementation of activities went "like wildfire."[32] More of such participation would have been welcome, but the lack of responsible initiative was seen as the fault of lagging rural communities, and not as related to the attitudes and practices of the project staff.

Ghana

The initial approach to participation in Ghana was less substantial than in Nepal. To be sure, the appraisal materials indicated that the Upper Region's population would benefit from "increased farmer participation in local development and decisionmaking." Such language is encouraging, but the mechanisms for this participation were extremely limited. The appraisal materials acknowledged the willingness of farmers to be involved in agricultural improvement:

> Previous development work has shown that farmers are willing to adopt new practices which offer real benefits; there is already an established trade in purchased inputs in the Region. Immediate production improvements are expected simply from a wider distribution of goods and services in the Region; thereafter improvements would be sustained through demonstration, instruction, and deliberate concentration of technical and managerial research into problems confronting the smallholder.

Yet the role envisioned for the smallholder was passive rather than active: "Farmer contact and market penetration would be achieved through a series of retail ventures operated at strategically sited service centers, from which extension staff would also operate . . . It is expected that service centers would become focal points of agricultural and farmers' association activity; site selection and demarcation would be made on this premise."

Unfortunately, the farmers' associations referred to were not implemented from the outset. When contact groups were finally set up instead, they were treated so cavalierly that over half disbanded. Those which remained were essentially one-man contact groups, each a single "progressive farmer" or "opinion leader," as extensionists referred to them. When queried about the advisability of channeling all information and inputs through (and maybe to) only one person, a district officer responded: "This is the way we have always done the job."[33]

The project formulation was not hostile to participation, merely unrealistic about what would constitute this. It started from the premise that "expert and experienced direction and management would be imperative from the outset." To this it added that "some form of *active* farmer participation [was] also desirable in order to provide a constant spur to management and clientele. *Ideally* this should be attained through both equity [financial] participation and Board representation." However good this sounds, these two kinds of participation were set up in extremely truncated form.

"Equity participation" meant building up mandatory farmer shares in the Farmers' Services Company (FASCOM) through a *compulsory* 2.5 percent markup on the prices charged for all farm inputs. The shares would be held in trust for the farmers by the Bank of Ghana. It was assumed that since all recipients of inputs could be identified, dividends could *eventually* be made payable to individuals or groups of farmers. It was expected that in five years farmers' equity would have reached 12 percent of issued capital and that, as one appraisal assumption put it, control of the company would "one day" fall into the hands of the farmers. So much for "active" farmer participation.

The board representatives referred to were three farmers (out of thirteen members) on the FASCOM Board of Directors. These farmers were appointed by the project manager, though eventually they were to be elected by shareholding members of the farmers' association. The scope for popular input into decisionmaking in such bodies was slim. FASCOM was permitted to provide inputs only to those farmers approved by the project's technical staff. Such a restriction was understandable to prevent inputs from being resold or smuggled out of Ghana, but it cut out farmers' responsibility for managing resources since they had no say in something as basic as eligibility for services or loans. For the first years of the project farmers were represented on the FASCOM board but not in managing the

Farmer Service Centers, which were much closer to the farmers' situation. Farmer members of the FASCOM board expressed embarrassment over how little input they were able to make to project decisions.

The farmers' associations spoken of in the project documentation did not get set up until 1980 when forty-two Farmers' Committees were established to give users some voice in decisionmaking for the Farmer Service Centers. The pilot attempts were judged successful, with a tremendous turnout of farmers; service center facilities were even constructed by farmers rather than by contractors as previously planned. This recast the whole approach to farmer participation, which was earlier conceived as furthering project goals more than farmers' interests.

A strategy of farmer participation without an organizational base is dubious, as was eventually realized in the project. The original design combined grandiose agricultural plans with minimal organizational ones, which neglected the most elementary principles of sociological and psychological analysis.

Although more participation by farmers in project design is not guaranteed to produce a more implementable and beneficial balance, it would probably have made the project more realistic and increased the people's commitment to it. As the project was formulated, it was unlikely that any project manager or technical staff could have made it succeed along the lines laid out.

Mexico

The approach to participation taken in the PIDER project was not initially much better than that found with the other two, but the question of increasing local participation and making it more effective was taken seriously as ongoing evaluation studies by CIDER revealed problems with the initial approach. Although there have undoubtedly been some lapses and shortcomings, the participatory procedures have been tested, revised, and formalized to replace the imposition of programs from above with a system providing for an element of bottom-up planning.

Some of the approaches to fostering participation prescribed even in the formulation of PIDER II proved misdirected. Since most of the rural poor lived within *ejidos* (communal organizations established after the Mexican Revolution), the Department for Organization and Development of Ejidos (SOFE) sent out multidisciplinary brigades, so that ejidos could be involved in detailed planning of new investments; that way, they could participate in all new PIDER construction and share equally in all benefits. Unfortunately, SOFE staff did not involve campesinos fully in the process of planning PIDER investments. Staff members, coming fresh from the university, had difficulty working with campesinos and adjusting to the conditions of poverty and isolation they were encountering. Also, the staff did not get cooperation from other government departments, so this attempt to promote participatory development, despite the intention expressed by PIDER management and the fine language of the project documentation, was largely ineffective.

The Agrarian Reform Secretariat staff tried to involve campesinos in PIDER activity by working through local authorities such as municipal chiefs, teachers, and ejido presidents. It was assumed that local leaders would generate community participation as well as provide an independent link to the state-level technical secretariat. The interests served by this kind of "link" need to be examined, since consistent evidence suggests that many such leaders use their connections more for self-advancement than for community benefit.[34] The new methodologies developed by PIDER and CIDER were supposed to offset this by wider consultation within each community.

One approach used was to select activities on the basis of petitions, primarily from elected leaders and not through village assemblies:

> These petitions were assessed and investments then selected in light of their technical and economic feasibility, and in view of existing financial constraints.
>
> The initial "petitioning process" has not involved all the groups and strata in the villages (particularly the poorer ones). It has also suffered in particular from not following the procedure of integrating the final list of projects selected by the PIDER staff within the context of beneficiary priorities (stated explicitly) and within an explicit village-level and intra-microregional development strategy.[35]

Accordingly, the framework now outlined for planning from below stipulates more face-to-face contact with a full range of community members, not merely consideration of petitions received.

The emerging methodology requires technical staff to start the program design process by leaving their offices, rather than letting all community contact go through lower-status extension agents. The three stages are: *diagnosis* of local problems with the community participating; *preliminary programming* of investment projects, which involves discussion among many parties including government agencies; and *final programming,* at which stage agreements are reached among all concerned. Meetings are to be held with the whole community to identify problems, make suggestions, and set priorities for action. Staff are told to grasp and explore relationships among different groups within the community, and to recognize differences in interest and capability among them. They should talk with small groups to elicit ideas from the reticent members and check out problems and solutions with the evidently disadvantaged.

The guidelines and procedures eventually formulated state that there is to be *self*-definition of interests by community members and that officials are *not* to be regarded as the interpreters of farmers' interests. Moreover, the community assessment should actively seek out various sets of interests, not listen to only a few leaders or take the first investment ideas proposed. There needs to be a thorough diagnosis of each community in its own terms. Following this is an iterative planning process in which complementarity and integration of activities is sought.[36]

One limitation is that this process still "does not promote stable forms of peasant self-organization, which would themselves mobilize and support the active involvement of peasant groups in development activities." Cernea elaborates on this:

> The community meetings organized by PIDER programming teams with various segments of the village population are a useful, but only transitory, short-lived form of group action. Between the meetings that take place in the diagnosis stage and those in the final programming stage, there is no permanent structure of group action generated by PIDER in the target communities. The social structure that emerges in the process of interaction between the planners and the local community is not maintained and sustained after the field team departs.
>
> Participation must be self-perpetuating, not dependent on visits by outsiders. To sustain participation in the long run, PIDER should explore ways to help build more stable social-organization structures within the peasant communities. Such structures would be a powerful means both in fostering peasants' participation in government sponsored action and in supporting peasant groups' organization for more efficient production and marketing activities.[37]

Unfortunately, government agencies have shown little enthusiasm for establishing any broadly based or multifunctional local organizations.

Organizations such as village road committees or self-help groups organized through ejidos are acceptable, but any more ambitious and
mobilizing institutions are discouraged by most officials.[38] This represents a limitation, but as long as specialized functional organization is
possible, there seems good reason to proceed with it.

The emphasis in the emerging participatory methodology for PIDER on
reaching out to and listening to the poorer strata of the rural community
is a welcome advance. This is one reason PIDER holds out more promise
of contributing to broader-scale rural development that do the other two
projects. It offers more than resources or technology to the poor majority
and offers them some voice and some channels for improving their lives.
This is a stimulus to development too often neglected.

Project Design and Implementation

Conceptualizing these and other project experiences makes it possible
to delineate various methodologies to be used—and approaches to be
avoided—so that the intended beneficiaries of projects become more
productive ends as well as means of development. Here I draw particularly on the project experiences accumulated during field work under the
Rural Development Participation Project, especially the Gal Oya water
management and irrigation rehabilitation project in Sri Lanka, with
which I have been closely associated. Knowledge about how to support
and organize participation in projects, and what kinds of participation are
most important and appropriate, is still being accumulated and analyzed.
The suggestions here are intended to contribute to a growing understanding of such participation.

Clarity and Concurrence about Participation

To begin, it is important to recognize that "participation" can refer to
many different things, not all of which are relevant or desirable in any
specific project context. Overly enthusiastic and uncritical advocates of
participation have impeded its extension as much as have its adversaries.
Social research has arrived at a stage at which it is possible—in fact,
imperative—to be more precise about "participation."

Table 13-1 shows how certain kinds of participation may be identified
as more or less relevant to a specific project. To be sure, these distinctions

Table 13-1. *Possible Relevance of Different Kinds of Participation in Typical Projects*

Probably more relevant	Probably less relevant (or perhaps irrelevant)
Decisionmaking in agricultural credit project	
Proposed beneficiaries (PBs) deciding whether to have a group credit program in their community; the effectiveness of the project requires acceptance of responsibility for such credit.	PBs deciding that the project will extend credit on individual rather than group basis; administrative feasibility must be taken into account, though planners would want to know PBs' attitudes and experience on this.
PBs deciding on membership of local committees to administer loans to farmers; planners would want committees that command respect in the community.	PBs deciding whether project will be administered through Ministry of Agriculture or Development Bank; planners would want to know PBs' experience and attitudes toward each, however.
PBs deciding on location of offices to administer credit; planners would want offices to be accessible and want farmers to identify with program.	PBs deciding how many offices would be built with project funds; implications of having more or fewer offices might be discussed with PB representatives before finalizing number.
PBs deciding on individual eligibility for loans; planners would want local knowledge of character, credit-worthiness, and so on.	PBs deciding on interest rate to be charged; this relates to overall project financing.

have been suggested, as examples, in a nonparticipatory (deductive) way. In a real project situation, relevant kinds of participation can be determined in consultation with some of the intended beneficiaries. Proposals for various kinds of participation should be checked out with the intended beneficiaries to ascertain whether they are feasible and acceptable. We have already seen how failure to do this in the Ghana project led to substantial problems. Some modifications in the project design may be necessary if the consultations reveal shortcomings.

It is easy to put in very general provisions for participation in a project design, but it can also be misleading and detrimental. In the Gal Oya

Table 13-1   *(continued)*

Probably more relevant	Probably less relevant (or perhaps irrelevant)
Implementation of rural health project	
PBs constructing "health hut" with own labor and local materials (possibly with some government contribution).	PBs providing medicines to be stocked and distributed in health hut; PBs might advise on most effective or acceptable kinds.
PBs selecting villager to be trained as paraprofessional operating program of health hut.	PBs training the paraprofessional to operate program of health hut.
Benefits of vocational education project	
PBs gaining steady employment and income after training.	PBs becoming more marriageable as result of training.
Evaluation of rural industries project	
PBs assessing quality of products from new industries, since these have to satisfy consumers.	PBs assessing impact of project on balance of payments through import substitution or on economy through backward linkages (demand for raw materials).

project in Sri Lanka assisted by USAID, the project documents called for farmer participation in water management after physical rehabilitation of the irrigation system, but there was no agreement by the Irrigation Department (ID), which was the implementing agency, to expand farmer responsibility. The ID regarded farmers' participation as simply doing what they were told: following schedules set by engineers, rotating water on command, and so on. The only specific provision for farmer participation was that they would provide labor for rehabilitating (desilting and reshaping) all field channels in the scheme, but this was never discussed with or agreed to by farmers. Fortunately, through farmers' organizations and interaction with ID staff, once officials tried in good faith to involve farmers in the redesign of the system, farmers were willing to contribute their labor. Had existing negative attitudes between farmers and officials continued, it is unlikely such cooperation could have been attained. Not all needs and agreements can be laid out before a project begins, since projects are ongoing, problem-solving ventures.[39] But more precision and consultation than is usual at present would help achieve project goals.

Realistic Objectives

Unless there is adequate consultation with proposed beneficiaries, and sometimes even then, it is easy for planners to specify targets that foreordain failure. For instance, the Gal Oya project paper stated that all 19,000 farmers in the area would be organized within the four-year life of the project, but the means of introducing and supporting the new organizations had not been spelled out. Fortunately, the project paper also provided that the Agrarian Research and Training Institute (ARTI) in Sri Lanka would work with the Irrigation Department to develop an organizational model for water users' associations. During implementation this assignment evolved into the larger responsibility for recruiting, training, and fielding institutional organizers. Thus a *process* for farmer organization was developed which could carry beyond the project area once refined and validated.

Flexibility is part of the requirement of realism. Participatory capacity cannot be built like a road or a dam; it must be developed. (This is why, I believe, the term "institutional development" has replaced the earlier "institution building.") Rigid schedules are inappropriate and can lead to initiatives or pressures that impede long-term progress. It is recognized that providing for participation may sometimes slow the progress at certain stages such as planning or implementation, but neglecting participation can create similarly dogged delays, and capital-intensive approaches are prone to different kinds of breakdowns. It is not clear that, overall, participatory approaches are slower.[40] Moreover, a realistic approach can pay off materially in terms of maintenance and resource mobilization.[41] Exaggerated expectations, in contrast, may short-circuit the participatory processes and direct efforts back into the conventional bureaucratic channels.

Introducing Participation

Unless the intended beneficiaries are already organized and accustomed to involvement in formal development programs, some procedures for introducing participation should be explicitly worked out. Procedures will be needed to acquaint beneficiaries with the project from the beginning, to elicit their ideas and suggestions, to encourage and assist appropriate modes of organization for institutionalizing participation, and to monitor progress so that changes in the approach can be made whenever problems arise or better means can be identified. It is not easy for government agencies, or sometimes even private voluntary organizations (which sometimes have a tradition of paternalism), to shift into a more interactive mode of operation. Generally nongovernmental organizations are in a better position to initiate or support participatory processes, however.

For the Gal Oya project, one proposal was to create water users' associations and to entrust responsibility for forming them to the Irrigation Department. Given the department's palpable distrust and disrespect of farmers, however, a different approach seemed necessary, using persons in new catalytic roles (institutional organizers) who could be "honest brokers" between farmers and technical staff.[42] In contrast to deductive planning, which assumes that the ends and means are both clear enough to be specified in advance, the effort proceeded according to what could be called inductive planning. The ARTI set forth hypotheses about what was needed and what would work in that situation. Work was planned accordingly, but continually assessed and reassessed as evidence accumulated.

Efforts need not always start from scratch. Although one should not expect to transfer or import "models" of organization from one situation to the next, one can learn much from experience elsewhere. In the Gal Oya case, explicit consideration was given to the roles and strategies employed by the National Irrigation Administration in the Philippines[43] and the Small Farmer Development Programme in Nepal. These pioneer programs provided a basic model which ARTI modified according to its best estimate of what would work in the Gal Oya context.

Investing in Participation

One complaint sometimes heard from government or donor agency personnel is that participation does not "move money." This refers not only to possible delays in getting expenditures approved and made, but to the fact that "software" seldom costs as much as "hardware" in projects. In fact, a project's success commonly turns as much (if not more) on the software—the social organization, the communication channels, ongoing evaluation studies, training systems, and the like—which make a new technology utilized and productive. Yet governments and donor agencies are surprisingly reluctant to invest resources in the complex of activities associated with participation at the design and implementation stages. In the Gal Oya project, the planned investment in socioeconomic activities—baseline, monitoring, and evaluation studies, as well as farmer organization—was only about 5 percent of the total, even though the returns from physical rehabilitation of the irrigation system depended crucially on attuning it to the actual sociocultural situation and on bringing farmers into the management of the system.

Perhaps as significant as the reluctance to invest in software is the tendency to give it short shrift in the implementation process. The parts of the project that involve more money and represent more physical "progress" tend to displace support of the social and institutional components. A serious effort to bring beneficiaries into project planning and implementation requires a willingness not only to invest in training, supportive research, and evaluation, but also to provide a staff skilled in developing operable patterns of social organization and patient in working to organize beneficiaries.

The displacement of the social organizational components is well exemplified by the first Range and Livestock Management Project in Botswana, designed, financed, and staffed by USAID. Initially, this project was to develop socially acceptable and economically viable groups of small stockholders which would adopt improved systems of range and livestock management. Although the project was designed, sensibly, as a research program to foster and examine appropriate systems, its purpose became, instead, to establish more than a dozen group ranches within communal grazing areas, along classic three-paddock lines—"Texas ranches for groups." Unfortunately, USAID had no staff with the training or skills for the complex sociological task of organizing groups and sustaining their structure and activities. "After largely futile and misunderstood initial attempts to develop group ranches, the goal was reduced to establishing only three such ranches. In 1977, the project was phased out, having managed to get only one ranch, with fifteen members, off to a very shaky and problematic start."[44] An investment of staff and time in figuring out how to get such groups established (the original project purpose) would have produced much better results.[45]

Creating Appropriate Expectations

A commonly cited fear is that consulting with the intended beneficiaries about their problems and possible solutions will raise exaggerated
expectations of what will be done for them. Rather than arouse such
hopes, governments and technical agencies seem to prefer delivering
benefits at a time and place of their own choosing in order to keep control.
In the process, however, there is no assurance that they will be delivering
the most needed benefits, or even correct ones.

As long as governments wish to play paternalistic roles and to perpetuate dependency, they must expect people's demands and expectations
to be focused on what governments (and foreign donors) can do for them.
A participatory approach, in contrast, expects a significant degree of
self-reliance from the people.[46] When identifying and formulating a
project, government agencies should present development initiatives as
involving something given or received from the intended beneficiaries,
some commitment of local resources to the project's creation and particularly to its maintenance. This means that the exact dimensions, timing,
and purpose of the project must be agreeable to the community, or
resource commitments will not be forthcoming or sustained. This provides a test of the project's value, as long as the government's expectations of what can be mobilized from poor communities are realistic. A
participatory approach means bringing people into not only
decisionmaking but also resource mobilization and management. Agencies must give up some degree of control in this process, but the
advantages of a finely tuned program and a measure of local self-reliance
should more than compensate. If rural people know that creating a stream
of new benefits will require some inputs from them, expectations should
not become extreme. And the mobilization of local resources should
produce more, and more sustainable, benefits than if the government
sought to provide them all by itself.

Information Needs

To some extent, no amount of preproject research is going to reveal
all the information and knowledge needed for design and implementation. In the process of carrying out projects, new data and insights will
emerge, and project design and redesign should be flexible enough to

accommodate them. Yet there is value to be gained from investing in an initial and continuing knowledge base through sociological and economic research, paralleling whatever technical research is needed. A less cursory design process in the Gal Oya case, for example, would have revealed that the command area to be rehabilitated was 50 to 60 percent larger than the official figures (which did not count private lands or encroached areas under cultivation). If such information had been available at the outset, more realistic schedules and investment estimates would have been possible and planners would have foreseen the difficulties of establishing water users' associations when diverse forms of land tenure had to be incorporated.

From the outset, the Sri Lanka case project provided a role for a "knowledge-building institution," as David Korten recommends, in this case the Agrarian Research and Training Institute. This brought the same advantages which Cernea points out for the PIDER project in Mexico, where CIDER (the Research Center for Rural Development) helped with baseline studies, evaluation, and social methodologies. CIDER gave project managers both objective feedback and innovative ideas to redirect efforts more fruitfully as the project proceeded. A similar role was played in the Philippines by the Institute of Philippine Culture (Ateneo de Manila) and the Asian Institute of Management for an irrigation program.[47] Such social science action-research efforts account for a relatively small portion of the total project cost, but they make the rest of the expenditure much more productive. The independence of viewpoint and the theoretical foundations of knowledge-building institutions are important contributions as long as their staff are willing to collaborate with project designers and managers.

Participatory Approaches to Data Gathering

The way in which information is sought and assessed can itself be exceedingly "top-down" and nonparticipatory, and the value of the information is likely to be reduced accordingly. The sample survey is a well-known methodology often used for gathering data on communities and their problems, but as Gabriel Campbell and his associates have shown from surveys and resurveys in Nepal, this approach is liable to have many errors.[48] One way of making data gathering participatory is to involve rural people in keeping records of agricultural inputs and production, as done by the ARTI with farmers in Gal Oya to gain an understanding of the existing system of irrigation. More complex methods of acquiring knowledge about indigenous practices are possible, even among largely illiterate populations, as John Hatch has shown from his work with Bolivian peasants.[49] If the data gathering is done in a fairly conventional manner, it can and should be checked out with the communities being surveyed, as Louise Fortmann has described in Botswana.[50] This process can correct misinterpretations of the data and engage rural people in remedying the problems and attitudes suggested by the outside studies.

Technical Contributions

Officials may readily concede that socioeconomic information from rural people is useful in project planning and operation, but still be reluctant to engage farmers in discussions of a technical nature, assuming that poorly educated persons have little to contribute in this sphere. Yet, as seen above, villagers may offer insights of merit even on matters as technical as where to locate a dam or whether a method of construction would be adequate. The record of washed-out dams in Nepal, Philippines, and Mexico reported above should persuade technicians to query and listen to rural people on more than just socioeconomic matters. Rural people can be wrong—but then so can engineers and agronomists.

That indigenous technical solutions can sometimes be superior to what modern technology has to offer is shown by the construction of suspended bridges in the Baglung district of Nepal. There local committees used their own technology to construct bridgeheads of stone rather than cement and to fasten planks with homecast iron rods. With steel cable provided by the government, they put up bridges as much as 300 feet long, two to three times more quickly than the public works department and at as little as one-eighth the cost, by relying on community labor and technology.[51]

Spatial Information

Perhaps because most project planning and evaluation is done by economists, there is a tendency to think in terms of aggregate numbers and to look for averages and statistical distributions. In the real world in which people live and participate, places and spatial distributions count for much more. In all the projects I worked with—in Botswana, Costa

Rica, Jamaica, Sri Lanka, Tunisia, and Yemen—too little of the information available was organized spatially. If district or subdistrict data were at hand, they were still averages or aggregates. A lack of maps was most disconcerting for the Sri Lanka irrigation project. Population concentrations, distances, and the ubiquitous distinctions between head-end and tail-end areas had to be known before organizational efforts could be undertaken. In the Jamaican integrated rural development project assisted by USAID, ignorance of geographical factors clearly impeded participation. The project was planned to cover certain watersheds, but their boundaries did not coincide with the boundaries of administrative units (parishes) or existing social units (towns) which shaped patterns of interaction and cooperation. Both the participatory organizations and the criteria for project eligibility were conceived in hydrological terms that did not correspond to the sociological or administrative realities people knew and understood. So one of the lessons learned is that to support participatory initiatives, one needs to be aware of the social map, as well as the geographical map, of the area.

Historical Information

Developers tend to think that they are starting with a clean slate and that they can do whatever seems most promising. In fact, there is always some legacy. One reason for considering history is that it will greatly affect the willingness of the intended beneficiaries to take an active role in the proposed project.

Involving intended beneficiaries in project design and implementation is one way of bringing knowledge of past development experience to bear on the new effort. The local people will know what, if anything, has been tried before and what, if anything, worked. There seems almost a compulsion within development agencies to confirm the saying that "history repeats itself." Indeed, when projects "reinvent the wheel" they usually end up in square one with a plan which has already failed. Gene Ellis recounts a sad example of a design team that planned to introduce an ox-drawn plow in rural Ethiopia but made no effort to learn whether anything like that had been tried before (it had) and what the results were (failure because of soil conditions).[52] The designers of the integrated rural development project in Jamaica did not profit from the experience, positive or negative, of the Christiana Area Land Authority, which had begun work twenty years earlier and continued to operate in the very same area, though the purposes of the projects were almost identical.

Working with Local Organizations

Often local organizational structures that could facilitate participation in projects are either very weak or nonexistent. In Gal Oya, Sri Lanka, it was necessary to introduce water users' associations. But more often than outsiders realize, there are institutional structures that can be worked with or should at least be considered for some role. A Japanese donor agency planned a project in the northern part of the Philippines to reconstruct irrigation in 8,000 acres. It was oblivious to the existence of *zanjeras,* indigenous water user groups that have an effective system for operation and maintenance. The reconstruction would have destroyed the physical as well as the social infrastructure according to which these groups operated.[53]

The Jamaica project called for soil conservation measures and agricultural improvements to be channeled through some local organization but did not specify which. A Cornell team assessed the existing Jamaica Agricultural Society (JAS), which had branches in the project area, and concluded it would be a satisfactory vehicle since it was representative of farmers who were familiar with the area.[54] The project management nevertheless chose to establish altogether new organizations. Ironically, these new "Development Committees" had to be formed through meetings of the JAS chapters, and within two years the two organizations were practically indistinguishable. The project ended up describing its effort as one of "revitalizing" JAS branches.

Not all existing organizations, particularly the most informal ones, are suitable channels for formal development programs. But there are advantages to working with established institutions at the local level wherever they exist and are reasonably suited to project purposes. Cernea reviewed 164 World Bank rural development projects in thirty-seven countries and found that more than 40 percent provided for the creation or strengthening of some kind of farmer groups. "The main reason for the presence of such project provisions, in the absence of a formal policy, was the intuitive perception or the empirical conviction of the individual staff involved in the design or appraisal of projects that the development process needs to rely upon and promote the structured self-organization of the small producers for their own interests."[55]

There is a growing body of evidence that such organizations are productive. The World Bank study of twenty-five completed agricultural projects reported by Cernea and cited above (see note 5) found local grass root organizations to be a prime factor contributing to the long-term sustainability of project benefits, while their absence was identified as a key cause of nonsustainability.

What are the characteristics of local organizations most likely to function beneficially? This question has been addressed by analyzing a sample of 150 organizations from across the developing world.[56]

- *Informal modes of operation* were generally more successful than more formal ones. Highly formal procedures and roles usually reduced membership control because the members were unfamiliar with the proceedings and so elites could more easily become dominant.

- Performance was best when *decisionmaking* in organizations was shared between an executive committee (or set of committees) and a general assembly of all members. The purely executive mode of operation was generally unsuccessful, apparently because it limited membership participation.

- *Horizontal linkages* with similar organizations at the same level and *vertical linkages* with organizations above and below led to a system of organization that had more capacity and stability. "Unlinked" organizations operating in isolation performed generally poorly.

- *Size* was not a significant factor explaining organizational success. That larger organizations had slightly higher performance scores was probably a consequence rather than a cause of their success. On the other hand, small organizations that were vertically and horizontally linked had some of the highest average scores.

- *Linkage to government agencies* by itself did not contribute to greater success. The most "linked" organizations were under the control of officials rather than members or leaders, and this was a recipe for failure. Government linkage where local organizations were connected to other membership organizations at the same or different levels did have positive results.

- One of the strongest statistical explanations for local organizations' contribution to rural development goals was their impetus—who took the *initiative* to start them? Those established by community members or leaders had much higher performance scores than those created by outside agencies.
- When government or nongovernmental agencies worked to establish local organizations through *catalysts*—people specially recruited, trained, and deployed to work with communities in a nonbureaucratic manner—results were almost as good as when the organizations were initiated from the communities themselves.[57]

It is important that any agency be flexible when working with such institutions. Nongovernmental organizations are often more effective in undertaking this. The exact form of organization that is appropriate will vary from project to project, but some form is likely to be needed. It is best to begin by looking at what channels already exist whereby local people mobilize resources and solve problems.

Proceeding Realistically

There may be a temptation, when an existing organization is identified for involvement in a project or a new one is being formed, to load many responsibilities upon it. This must be avoided, and participatory activities must be consistent with the structures provided. In the Botswana project it was asked why groups set up by the government to manage small catchment dams were not working. Part of the answer was that the groups were expected to collect a set fee for all cattle watered at the dams, to pay for maintenance of the facilities. The fee, it turned out, was set much higher than needed, since the maintenance could be done by voluntary labor or ad hoc collections—practices much more acceptable in the semimonetized economy of rural Botswana. The dam groups did not meet regularly as was prescribed because the dams were important sources of water only during a few months of the year, and members were absent from the area during part of the year. The government had clearly misunderstood the context in which it was, with good intentions, delegating management responsibility to farmers.[58]

A state-of-the-art analysis of 150 cases from Africa, Asia, and Latin America found a consistent association between multiple functions and local organization performance, qualitatively as well as quantitatively.[59] But this does not mean that organizations should start with many functions. The weight of evidence seems to suggest that successful local organizations begin with only one or a few highly salient activities. As these are performed well, and as members gain both competence and confidence in their organization, the scope of its activity can and probably should expand. But the direction and pace of such expansion should be up to the members and leaders, not to outsiders.

Sometimes the project design is inconsistent with its participatory intentions. In the Jamaican project, soil conservation measures were all financed and undertaken on an individual basis, even though the benefits would have increased if all the farmers on a hillside had invested in such measures simultaneously. The group channels the project sought to work through were thus superfluous for its conservation (and agricultural) programs. Without an integrating concept, it is not surprising that new organizations did not take root.[60]

Avoiding Cooptation

By now, many persons have been made sensitive to the dangers that outsiders, with funding, may coopt community leaders, and even ideas, and bend them to outside priorities and perceptions. This is seen as a distortion of development efforts. In reverse cooptation, local leaders from advantaged groups may coopt the project efforts when a participatory approach is taken. This has been reported in the PIDER case, though special measures were introduced to get a more balanced view of people's needs. A similar methodology has been worked out for implementing the Resource Conservation and Utilization Project in Nepal. Representatives are invited from adjacent villages to attend a planning meeting, and it is specified that some of the representatives should be women and some should come from lower castes. After the whole assembly meets for some time, it divides into three discussion groups, one for male upper castes, one for male lower castes, and one for women. Field tests thus far have indicated that views and needs of less advantaged sectors can get fed into the planning process in this way.[61]

Although it is desirable to avoid having project plans and benefits coopted by the better-off elements of rural society, it should not be assumed that this stratum is always inimical to progress for lower strata or that it can be readily bypassed.[62] In a comparative study of forty-one cases in seven countries, Development Alternatives, Inc., found that in almost all, "the local power structure either actively participated in the new development initiative or formally approved of it."[63] As Robert B. Charlick also found in a similar number of cases where *animation rurale* techniques were used, involvement of the traditional leadership did not correlate in either direction with project effectiveness or distribution of benefits.[64] Although one should be sensitive to the potential hazards of the local elite's preempting benefits, it may make more sense to try to make existing leaders accountable to their constituency rather than to have outsiders screen leaders.

Avoiding Dependence

When government or donor agencies work with local organizations, their manner of giving or withholding funds is likely to create a psychology of dependency, which is the antithesis of development. The strategy of "assisted self-reliance" tries to foster self-sufficiency in local organizations. To achieve some autonomy, organizations must mobilize some of their own resources and not depend entirely on outside sources. In addition, government and donor agencies need to be willing to let the organizations make and learn from their own mistakes. This advice is difficult to accept, but it will be easier if one openly recognizes that officials and their agencies are also liable to make mistakes.

Some organizations will probably lag behind others. In such instances, it will be more effective (and efficient) to work with the groups that are proceeding well and to rely primarily on the demonstration effect to motivate the laggards. Good examples will persuade and instruct more than exhortations can. The very successful self-help water supply program in Malawi, which has brought good water to more than 500,000 persons at relatively low cost within ten years, conveys the following message to communities: "This is not the government's water scheme, it is yours. It will only work if you are willing to work. And it is you, rather than the government, that will make the decision on whether to proceed, on organizing yourselves into committees, and on deciding the order in which various villages would participate."[65]

If certain communities have difficulties or liabilities to overcome, they may need and deserve special attention or assistance. The Saemaul Undong movement in Korea differentiates the aid it gives communities by their level of advancement. But the purpose is to contribute to greater local initiative and capacity for improving production and the quality of life.

Reorienting Bureaucracies

Not many government agencies are both willing and able to work cooperatively and responsively with the intended beneficiaries. It is common for planners, administrators, and technicians to view the people somehow as "the problem" and to regard themselves as embodying "the solution." In practice, the situation may be reversed: the attitudes and performance of government staff often constitute barriers to developmental change. Noncooperation or so-called resistance to change by the people may reflect adverse experiences with previous government programs, condescending approaches, and ill-informed advice. People's behavior is likely to be an adaptation to an insecure or unpredictable environment, which includes the behavior of government personnel.

Whatever may be the genesis of estrangement between bureaucrats and the public, ending it requires incremental and reinforcing changes on both sides. To the extent that the people can be encouraged to take responsibility for self-reliant development, negative stereotypes about peasants or illiterates will be changed. The people will also gain some bargaining power as long as the government values resource-saving or resource-generating activity. I have observed that the behavior and attitudes of at least some officials can be changed by demonstrations of the seriousness and skill of the people in dealing with local problems.

Most agencies have a doctrine, more often implicit than explicit, which prescribes preferred ends and means, projects a particular self-image, and shapes relations with client groups, encouraging or discouraging participation. A classic doctrine implied in most forestry departments is that their task is to protect trees from people. For such departments to work with residents in and near forests in schemes of community management is almost unthinkable. (The so-called social forestry projects contrast with most government-sanctioned forestry, which emphasizes large-scale, block-stand, commercial operations.) However, the strong financial support provided in recent years to social forestry projects, the efforts to trigger corresponding institutional changes, and the move to take account of sociological factors affecting people's behavior with regard to trees have started to yield changes even in entrenched forestry department bureaucracies.[66]

It is sad but true that most government agencies around the world are not oriented toward working effectively with intended beneficiaries, but have a legacy of paternalistic or technocratic, if not authoritarian, relations with their publics. When seeking to promote more participatory methods of development, one should not expect the agencies involved to have the necessary skills and motivation already. To be sure, differences in their present attitudes and performance will indicate how much reorientation may be needed to effect collaborative development efforts with beneficiaries. Elsewhere I have discussed a strategy of bureaucratic reorientation, which is likely to be needed as part of a larger project initiative.[67] Donor agencies are also likely to need some reorientation of their own personnel practices, rules, incentives, and procedures if they are to be consistently supportive of participatory projects.[68]

Monitoring and Evaluation

If, as suggested already, a project design should be regarded as presenting hypotheses about the most significant barriers to improved production and well-being in a particular area or population and about how to eliminate them, monitoring and evaluation are essential elements of government support. Many technicians and administrators are loathe to admit that they may not have all the answers, and so they write up and implement projects with an exaggerated certainty. Yet experience shows this to be misplaced and even harmful. A participatory approach to development requires from the outset greater modesty on the part of the "experts" concerning what they know and can accomplish. This is not to suggest that more educated and experienced persons have no role in development efforts. On the contrary, their fund of knowledge should be put at the service of a joint problem-solving effort involving local leaders and residents as well as officials at all levels and any relevant outsiders who have knowledge of the environment and its problems or of similar situations and solutions.[69]

It is important that monitoring and evaluation be fully participatory, and that persons who represent many different roles and statuses be encouraged to interact. In particular, central government decisionmakers should get out into the field, as members of evaluation teams, so they can see and hear for themselves what is going on. In a participatory strategy the conventional model of specialization and division of labor works against sharing information and forging common understandings.

One of the paradoxes of getting participation is that promoting bottom-up development often requires top-down efforts. This was seen in the discussion of using catalysts or promoters—recruited, trained, and fielded from the center—to work with rural people at the periphery and to build up organizational capacities among them. Similarly, people at different levels of government, from field-level staff to top-level officials, also need to observe the outcome of project efforts, particularly by talking with the beneficiaries, who are rarely consulted purposefully and systematically about how well a project's objectives have been fulfilled. Unless government officers themselves participate in the evaluation that also involves beneficiaries, the persons who control outside resources affecting rural communities will not fully comprehend how those resources can be utilized more effectively. In other words, participation should not be confined to project clientele. It should be conceived in ways that mobilize the best ideas and energies of persons at all social levels. In this way it should be possible to get greater benefits from scarce material resources in a world in which nonmaterial resources hold the key to the greatest gains in productivity.[70]

Conclusions

The question is often asked whether the participatory approach advocated here can get and keep the support it needs. Donors' commitment to it may be only nominal, and deliberate or unthinking "shortcuts" around participation are common in project planning and implementation. Moreover, donors are constrained by the orientations and interests of recipient or borrowing governments which often do not want much input from the public.

One can construct a litany of reasons why a participatory approach may not be accepted or followed through seriously. Governments commonly favor the upper and middle classes because they are better endowed with political resources and their political loyalty is worth more. The poor are assumed to be passive and grateful receivers of benefits from government programs, becoming thereby also loyal followers. Those possessing power and wealth are usually determined to keep it, so a number of implicit assumptions are made about the poorer sectors: (a) they are preordained to remain poor, (b) they are entitled to paternalistic services but not to access to power and wealth, and (c) they are incapable of participating in planning and implementation.[71] This is a stereotyped view, but one finds it applied in many if not most developing countries.

What chance is there of having sufficient support to work as discussed here with local organizations? Certainly there are situations in some countries where a participatory approach is unlikely to gain acceptance or become effective. But the stereotyped view should not obscure all possibilities for working in this desirable mode. Some changes have been occurring that favor programs "bringing in the poor," not just as beneficiaries, but as partners.

- The expectation that strictly technocratic, nonparticipatory approaches can "deliver the goods" has lost credibility in recent years. Both poverty and populations continue to grow. Political elites are seldom monolithic, and some leading actors will perceive incentives to champion bottom-up approaches. These may not be conceived as reversing the status hierarchy, but they would open opportunities for more participation than now because of favorable ideological orientations, fear of present disorder, or apprehension over what an increasingly unjust future otherwise holds for the next generation.
- Governments are facing overwhelming fiscal problems, with a triple burden of budget deficits, foreign exchange shortages, and mounting external debts. There is more need than before to mobilize local resources both for capital and recurrent costs and to put all available resources to their best possible uses. Meeting both these needs requires greater local participation.
- The capabilities of the poor majority have been upgraded over the last thirty years by education, health, communication, and other investments. Self-management of development tasks is now more feasible. The poor are more confident as well as more competent to handle responsibilities of decisionmaking and implementation.

Thus, although the interests of the rich have not changed, the situation in which they find themselves has. History shows recurrent efforts at political mobilization by persons both from elite backgrounds and from within the poor majority. Where the idea of participation is accepted, to be sure, it may get directed into strengthening political organizations rather than functional organizations like water user associations. The former give politicians more of a hand in distributing political benefits and claiming support for electoral or other purposes. Also, the latter kind of organizations might be taken over by potential or actual dissidents. In fact, one finds rural people themselves usually anxious to avoid politicization of their organizations since it diminishes the internal solidarity and external acceptability they need to promote the interests of their members. The danger to governments from local organizations is less than often thought, so long as governments are willing to work with organizations of, by, and for the people. Under such circumstances, ground rules of nonpartisanship are mutually agreeable, and beneficial to the government and to the poor.

We have identified three objectives of participatory development—*efficiency, equity,* and *empowerment.*[72] There is general support for efficiency because resources are mobilized and utilized to best advantage. Elites gain from this and so do program beneficiaries. Equity can also be broadly accepted since central elites gain broad-based political appreciation from fairer distribution of opportunities. However, some influential opposition to equity is likely because local elites lose from greater equity. How much support the goal of equity can command in specific situations depends on the interplay of political forces from above and from below. But one should bear in mind that the issue involves more than stereotyped conflict between "the elites" and "the masses."

Most controversy comes over the third objective, as neither central nor local elites are likely to be enamored with the outcome of empowerment. Some of this is the price that must be paid for getting local assumption of financial and management responsibilities, which is ever more needed as resource constraints beset national governments. Purely technocratic approaches are increasingly discredited now and local capabilities are increasing, thanks to the successes of development programs in education, health, and other areas. Under current conditions, political balances are tilting toward a participatory approach. If not a perfect alternative, it becomes an ever more salient one.

Readers may have noted that the establishment of such an approach in the irrigation sector in the Philippines, described in chapter 3 by Bagadion and Korten, was approved and supported by the Marcos regime in the Philippines. Some of the most significant local organizations giving rural people a substantial degree of self-management in agricultural development are the farmers' associations in Taiwan, started by the Chiang Kai-shek government there.[73] The New Community movement (Saemaul Undong) established in the Republic of Korea is another case where a conservative government found it desirable to devolve a substantial amount of development responsibility to local levels.[74]

These examples are not intended to suggest that privileged sectors will always readily accept an expanded role for those "below" them economically, socially, and politically, or that conservative governments' version of participatory development is the most one should hope and work for. Rather, one should see that there is a range of political circumstances, just as there are a variety of political motives, which may become more hospitable for bottom-up development efforts than is apparent in advance.

Notes

1. The misuse of this word, making a noun into a transitive verb, reflects the casual "top-down" thinking that permeates the approach of many development professionals. Having some (any) impact is thought to signify a success without specifying what *kind* of impact was achieved.

2. David C. Korten, "Community Organization and Rural Development: A Learning Process Approach," *Public Administration Review* (September–October, 1980), pp. 480–511.

3. The discussion here will follow the analytical framework developed by the Rural Development Committee at Cornell University. This framework clarifies the three "dimensions" of participation: *who?* (who participates), *what?* (in what kinds of participation), and *how?* (what are the qualitative aspects—voluntary or coercive participation, continuous or ad hoc). These concepts and issues are elaborated in John Cohen and Norman Uphoff, *Rural Development Participation: Concepts and Measures for Project Design, Implementation and Evaluation* (Ithaca, N.Y.: Rural Development Committee, Cornell University, 1977); and Norman Uphoff and John Cohen, "Participation's Place in Rural Development: Seeking Clarity through Specificity," *World Development,* vol. 8, no. 3 (March 1980), pp. 213–36.

4. Indeed, thirteen of twenty-five World Bank projects reviewed by Michael Cernea had not achieved sustainability in large measure because they failed to institutionalize participation. See Michael Cernea, "Farmer Organizations and Institution Building for Sustainable Development," *Regional Development Dialogue,* vol. 8, no. 2 (Summer 1987), pp. 2–7.

5. The analysis here has been enriched by work in half a dozen countries and a number of state-of-the-art reviews and special studies under the Rural Development Participation Project. This project was carried out by the Cornell Rural Development Committee between 1977 and 1982, with financial assistance from the Office of Rural Development in the U.S. Agency for International Development (USAID).

6. The projects were not randomly selected, and I cannot say how typical they are, but there is no reason to believe that as a set they are unrepresentative. I had worked in Nepal and Ghana and knew people who had studied the integrated rural development projects there in some detail; in the case of Mexico the project was well documented and I could talk with persons acquainted with its operation.

7. Bihari K. Shrestha, "Nuwakot District (Nepal)," in *The Practice of Local-level Planning: Case Studies in Selected Rural Areas in India, Nepal and Malaysia* (Bangkok: U.N. Economic and Social Commission for Asia and Pacific, 1980), p. 99. This article by the joint secretary of the Nepal Ministry for Local Development drew on his field studies of local development planning and implementation in three village panchayat areas sampled within the project area.

8. Shrestha 1980. These conclusions are supported by former Secretary and later Minister of Finance Bharat B. Pradhan, "Strategy of the Development of Small Farmers through Group Approach: The Case of Nepal," paper read at the workshop on Small Farmers Development and Credit Policy, organized by the Agricultural Development Bank of Nepal and the Department of Agricultural Economics, Ohio State University, April 1980, Kathmandu.

9. A case study done during 1979–80 by Mohamed Ibn Chambas reported: "I was profoundly impressed with the degree of ignorance and misconception about URADEP [the project] in the Upper Region—even among urban government officials, not to mention the mass of rural people. The project manager once told me that one of his biggest tasks in the project was fighting erroneous ideas about the objectives of URADEP and presenting a correct perspective of what the project is about." ("The Politics of Agriculture and Rural Development in the Upper Region of Ghana: Implications of Technocratic Ideology and Non-Participatory Development," Ph.D dissertation, Cornell University, 1980, pp. 202–3; for a project history, see ibid., pp. 172–75.)

10. See Michael Cernea, *A Social Methodology for Community Participation in Local Investments: The Experience of Mexico's* PIDER *Project*, World Bank Staff Working Paper no. 598 (Washington, D.C., August 1983). Of special significance for promoting participation within PIDER was the evaluation and methodological work done by the Research Center for Rural Development (CIDER) associated with the project until 1981. This is the kind of knowledge-building institution which D. Korten ("Community Organization") advises be associated with rural development projects so that some systematic learning process can occur.

11. Don Chauls and Padma Raj Bhandari, "Nepal Community Health Leader Project," *Rural Development Participation Review,* vol. 2, no. 1 (Fall 1980), pp. 12–14.

12. J. G. Campbell, *Community Involvement in Conservation: Social and Organizational Aspects of the Proposed Resource Conservation and Utilization Project in Nepal* (Kathmandu: USAID, November 1979).

13. Most farmers could have told project planners of the weaknesses of the *sajha*, which are documented in K. N. Sharma, "Involvement of the Poor in Rural Development through People's Organizations in Nepal," paper written for the Rural Organizations Action Programme of the Food and Agriculture Organization (FAO) in 1977. The project appraisal documents did note that loan procedures were cumbersome and required changes to meet the needs of small farmers. It is doubtful, however, that these changes would have eliminated the domination of the cooperatives by richer farmers to their own advantage.

14. On the economic inefficiency of tractor cultivation in northern Ghana, see Fred W. Winch, "Costs and Returns of Alternative Rice Production Systems in Northern Ghana: Implications for Output, Employment, and Income Distribution," Ph.D. dissertation, Michigan State University, 1976.

15. See Chambas, "The Politics of Agriculture," pp. 211–12, and the appraisal materials.

16. The planning figures for yield increases were: millet 57 percent, sorghum 86 percent, dwarf sorghum 140 percent, maize 167 percent, rice 144 percent, groundnuts 100 percent, yams 125 percent, cowpeas 450 percent, and cotton 50 percent. If such exaggerated figures were used to arrive at an economic benefit-cost ratio to justify the project, it ultimately served neither the interest of the borrowing government nor the lending agency.

17. Shrestha, "Nuwakot District," p. 93. Coincidentally, this same thing happened at Laur in the Philippines, where the National Irrigation Administration took a more participatory approach to construction of irrigation systems. Laur was one of the first such efforts, and the engineers would not yet trust the local people's judgment when told that the dam they had designed was not strong enough to withstand the flood level. The dam was built with people's labor and money contributions, according to the engineer's design, and was washed out by

monsoon rains several months later as the people had predicted. See Frances F. Korten, *Building National Capacity to Develop Water Users' Associations: Experience from the Philippines*, World Bank Staff Working Paper no. 528 (Washington, D.C., 1982), p. 14. Michael Cernea reports a similar experience within the PIDER project in Mexico where a dam collapsed as the rural people had predicted. See Cernea, *A Social Methodology for Community Participation*.

18. Some Bank staff reported that this component was not desired by them but was included at the insistence of country agencies.

19. Personal communication from John Eriksson.

20. This scheme is described in detail in *Management Study on Battar Irrigation Project* (Kathmandu: Agricultural Projects Service Centre, 1977).

21. Chambas, "The Politics of Agriculture," p. 208.

22. Michael Cernea, *Measuring Project Impact: Monitoring and Evaluation in the PIDER Rural Development Project—Mexico*, World Bank Staff Working Paper no. 332 (Washington, D.C., June 1979), pp. 59–65.

23. Cernea 1979. pp. 54–59. In fact, complementary PIDER investments tended to be concentrated in the few localities that received water works, which further concentrated income.

24. Shrestha, "Nuwakot District," pp. 97–99. "It is often complained in the district as well as in the centre that the different sectoral agencies hold appraisal [document] provisions as sacrosanct as the teachings in the Gita, the Hindu equivalent of the Bible. But there are no institutional compulsions to do otherwise" (p. 98).

25. Implementation problems are discussed in some detail in Chambas, "The Politics of Agriculture," pp. 186–99.

26. Cernea, *Measuring Project Impact*, pp. 25–26, emphasis added. This is the first conceptualization of the "bureaucratic reorientation" idea elaborated in David C. Korten and Norman Uphoff, *Bureaucratic Reorientation for Participatory Rural Development*, NASPAA Working Paper no. 1 (Washington, D.C.: National Association of Schools of Public Affairs and Administration, 1981).

27. The agency handling water supply (SOP) was reorganized in 1977, and the appraisal materials say: "SOP will probably draw heavily on [PIDER] experiences in getting villager participation in maintenance of feeder roads to encourage the same villagers to take a much stronger interest in water system maintenance. Also, SOP is likely to obtain a significantly higher villager participation in actual construction activities along the piecework or contributed-labor systems worked out in feeder road programs." On the widely observed connection between beneficiary participation in design and construction of water supply systems, on the one hand, and system operation and maintenance, on the other, see *Village Water Supply*, A World Bank Paper (Washington, D.C., March 1976), pp. 17, 63–65, and 68. On the roads program, see the chapter by Edmonds in G. A. Edmonds and J. D. F. G. Howe, eds., *Roads and Resources: Appropriate Technology in Road Construction in Developing Countries* (London: Intermediate Technology Development Group for ILO), pp. 123–34.

28. When the king of Nepal toured the district, the complaints from panchayat spokesmen and villagers about being ignored by the project were so vociferous that he instructed the project to work more closely with the panchayats. Personal communication from P. S. J. B. Rana, the district's M. P. and now minister in cabinet.

29. Shrestha, "Nuwakot District," p. 99.

30. Shrestha wrote in an early draft of "Nuwakot District" that "Nepali society is stratified along social and economic lines which also largely determine the locus of political power in the local social structure. Thus, while the existence of elective process for the selection of

leaders might give the semblance of their accountability to them, the presence of this structural dimension in the interpersonal relationship between people is likely to vitiate the benefits of the democratic process and the interest of the low-income groups may not be adequately represented in the allocation of scarce resources. Therefore, in order to overcome the consequences of stratification for them, further institutional arrangements need to be studied to ensure the full-fledged participation of the low-income groups in the decisionmaking process for the allocation of resources" (November 1979, p. 4; this statement was deleted in the published version). On the panchayat system and how representation of the poor, however limited at the village level, is entirely missing at the district level, see Frederick Gaige, *Regionalism and National Unity in Nepal* (Berkeley: University of California Press, 1975), chap. 7.

31. An impact study found that SFDP groups had income more than 50 percent higher than control households in the area, with remarkable gains in social services and human resources as well, all through activities initiated by the farmer groups, assisted by SFDP group organizers. *Impact Study of Small Farmers Development Project: Nuwakot and Dhanusha Districts* (Kathmandu: Agricultural Projects Service Centre, February 1979). On the development contributions of these groups, see also Dharam Ghai and Anisur Rahman, "The Small Farmer Groups in Nepal," *Development: Seeds of Change* (Rome: Society for International Development, 1981), pp. 23–28; also their paper, *Rural Poverty and the Small Farmers' Development Programme in Nepal* (Geneva: Rural Employment Policies Branch, International Labour Office, 1979).

32. Personal communication from David Mitchnik.

33. Chambas, "The Politics of Agriculture," pp. 205–8.

34. The phenomenon of *caciquismo* is widely recognized by close observers of rural Mexico as impeding equitable and active local development efforts. See Rudolfo Stavenhagen and others, *Neo-Latifundismo y Exploitacion* (Mexico City: Nuestro Tiempo, 1975); and Rudolfo Barta and others, *Caciquismo y Poder Politico en el Mexico Rural* (Mexico City: Siglo Vientiuno, 1978).

35. Cernea, *Measuring Project Impact*, p. 69.

36. One suggestion was that the visiting team initially meet with the whole village but then, without advance notice, break up and meet spontaneously with smaller groups in different parts of the village. Persons who had refrained from talking in the larger meeting would thus have an opportunity to speak up without the surveillance of more powerful villagers, who could not cover all of the smaller, dispersed discussions.

37. Cernea, *A Social Methodology for Community Participation.*

38. See the discussion in Merilee Grindle, "Prospects for Integrated Rural Development: Evidence from Mexico and Colombia," *Studies in Comparative International Development,* vol. 17, nos. 3–4 (Fall–Winter 1982), pp. 124–49.

39. Albert O. Hirschman, *Development Projects Observed* (Washington, D.C.: Brookings Institution, 1967). On the Gal Oya Project experience, see the author's *Learning from Gal Oya: Possibilities for Participatory Development and Post-Newtonian Social Science* (Ithaca, N.Y.: Cornell University Press, 1990).

40. Uma Lele in her study, *The Design of Rural Development: Lessons from Africa* (Baltimore, Md.: Johns Hopkins University Press, 1975), has suggested that, in the initial stages, a project may have to expand slowly to allow the staff to develop an adequate understanding of what is possible and what is needed and to delegate genuine responsibility to local organizations. But there can be compensating accelerations later, and long-term prospects are better.

41. In a slum improvement project in Calcutta, once the government set up special committees to involve urban residents in redesigning their local communities, the rate of initial implementation was slower, but the pace subsequently accelerated and the maintenance of improvements was much better. It also became possible for the government to introduce taxation in the urban sector, which had been political anathema before. See Norman Uphoff, "Political Considerations in Human Development," in Peter T. Knight, ed., *Implementing Programs of Human Development*, World Bank Staff Working Paper no. 403 (Washington, D.C., 1980), p. 30.

42. This approach is analyzed in Norman Uphoff, "People's Participation in Water Management: Gal Oya, Sri Lanka," in Jean Claude Garcia-Zamor, ed., *Public Participation in Development Planning* (Boulder, Colo.: Westview Press, 1985), pp. 131–78; and in "Activating Community Capacity for Water Management: Experience from Gal Oya, Sri Lanka," in D. C. Korten, ed., *Community Management: Asian Experience and Perspectives* (West Hartford: Kumarian Press, 1987), pp. 201–19.

43. This experience is analyzed in chapter 3 by Benjamin U. Bagadion and Frances F. Korten.

44. Marcia Odell and Malcolm Odell, *The Evolution of a Strategy for Livestock Development in the Communal Areas of Botswana*, Pastoral Network Paper no. 10b (London: Overseas Development Institute, July 1980).

45. Examples of projects that "moved" large amounts of donor funding *because of* beneficiary participation are given in Norman Uphoff, *Local Institutional Development: An Analytical Sourcebook with Cases* (West Hartford: Kumarian Press, 1986), pp. 259–60.

46. A strategy of "assisted self-reliance" is proposed in Milton J. Esman and Norman Uphoff, *Local Organizations: Intermediaries in Rural Development* (Ithaca, N.Y.: Cornell University Press, 1984), pp. 262–65, and elaborated in "Assisted Self-Reliance: Working With, Rather Than For, the Poor," in J. L. Lewis, ed., *Strengthening the Poor: What Have We Learned?* (New Brunswick, N.J.: Transaction Books, 1988), pp. 47–59.

47. D. Korten, "Community Organization"; Bagadion and F. Korten, chapter 3 in this volume; and Cernea, *Measuring Project Impact*.

48. Standard survey questions were asked by trained Nepali enumerators in three villages, and the results were later compared with what several months of probing and observation revealed about the people's attitudes, knowledge, income, landholding patterns, and so on. Survey results were found to overstate or understate the true situation by large margins (100, 200, 300 percent or sometimes more). The major conclusion was that *nonsampling* error exceeds sampling error by far, and thus smaller-scale, more intensely conducted studies would produce more valid information than conventional surveys of large numbers of respondents. See Gabriel Campbell, Ramesh Shrestha, and Linda Stone, *The Use and Misuse of Social Science Research in Nepal* (Kathmandu: Research Centre for Nepal and Asian Studies, Tribhuvan University, 1979).

49. Hatch got peasants to help write a "textbook" on indigenous practices in agriculture, home economics, health, and the like, which could aid any outside agency wishing to work with and improve the situation of these highland communities. "Peasants Who Write a Textbook on Subsistence Farming: Report on the Bolivian Traditional Practices Project," *Rural Development Participation Review*, vol. 2, no. 2 (Winter 1981), pp. 17–20.

50. Louise Fortmann, "Taking the Data Back to the Village," *Rural Development Participation Review*, vol. 3, no. 2 (Winter 1982), pp. 13–16. Evaluation can itself be done in a more participatory manner as described by the author in "Participatory Evaluation of Farmer Organizational Capacity for Development Tasks," *Agricultural Administration and Extension*, vol. 30, no. 1 (September 1988), pp. 43–64.

51. Prachanda P. Pradhan, *Local Institutions and People's Participation in Rural Public Works in Nepal* (Ithaca, N.Y.: Rural Development Committee, Cornell University, 1980).

52. Gene Ellis, "Development Planning and Appropriate Technology: A Dilemma and a Proposal," *Rural Development,* vol. 9, no. 3 (1981).

53. E. Walter Coward, Jr., addresses this issue and discusses this particular case in chapter 2 above. See also Norman Uphoff, *Improving International Irrigation Management through Farmer Participation: Getting the Process Right* (Boulder, Colo.: Westview Press, 1986).

54. Arthur Goldsmith and Harvey Blustain, *Local Organization and Participation in Integrated Rural Development in Jamaica* (Ithaca, N.Y.: Rural Development Committee, Cornell University, 1980).

55. Michael Cernea, "Modernization and Development Potential of Traditional Grassroots Peasant Organizations," in Mustala O. Attir, Burkart Holzner, and Zdenek Suda, eds., *Directions of Change: Modernization Theory, Research, and Realities* (Boulder, Colo.: Westview Press, 1982), p. 132.

56. See Esman and Uphoff, *Local Organizations,* for the methodology and results of this analysis.

57. Ibid., pp. 163–69, 253–58. For an excellent analysis of the "catalyst" role, see S. Tilakaratna, *The Animator in Participatory Rural Development: Concept and Practice* (Geneva: ILO, 1987).

58. See Emery Roe and Louise Fortmann, *Season and Strategy: The Changing Organization of the Rural Water Sector in Botswana* (Ithaca, N.Y.: Rural Development Committee, Cornell University, 1982).

59. See Esman and Uphoff, *Local Organizations*, pp. 139–41.

60. See Harvey Blustain, *Agricultural Development and Resource Management in Jamaica: Lessons for Participatory Development* (Ithaca, N.Y.: Rural Development Committee, Cornell University, 1982).

61. Donald Messerschmidt, Bhimendra Katuwal, Udaya Gurung, and Bharat Devkota, "Gaun Sallah: Village Dialogue Method for Local Panchayat Planning, A Discussion Paper Based on Pilot Field Tests" (Kathmandu: Agricultural Projects Service Centre, March 1983; draft).

62. This is the conclusion of Lenore Ralston, James Anderson, and Elizabeth Colson, *Voluntary Efforts in Decentralized Management* (Berkeley: Institute of International Studies, University of California, 1981), pp. 18–21.

63. See David G. Gow and others, *Local Organizations and Rural Development: A Comparative Reappraisal,* vols. 1 and 2 (Washington, D.C.: Development Alternatives, Inc., 1979).

64. Robert B.Charlick, *Animation Rurale Revisited: Participatory Techniques for Improving Agricultural and Social Services in Five Francophone Nations* (Ithaca, N.Y.: Rural Development Committee, Cornell University, 1984).

65. See Gus Liebenow, "Malawi: Clean Water for the Rural Poor," *American Universities Field Staff Reports,* Africa, no. 40 (1981), p. 5. The organizational strategy for this program is laid out in Colin Glennie, *A Model for the Development of a Self-Help Water Supply Program,* Technology Advisory Group Working Paper no. 1 (Washington, D.C.: World Bank, 1982).

66. See chapter 9 by Scott Guggenheim and John S. Spears; and Uphoff and others, *Managing Irrigation: Analyzing and Improving the Performance of Bureaucracies* (New Dehli: Sage Publications, 1990).

67. D. Korten and Uphoff, *Bureaucratic Reorientation,* cited above.

68. Judith Tendler, *Inside Foreign Aid* (Baltimore, Md.: Johns Hopkins University Press, 1975); and Coralie Bryant, "Organizational Impediments to Making Participation a Reality: 'Swimming Upstream' in AID," *Rural Development Participation Review*, vol. 3, no. 1 (Spring 1980), pp. 8–10.

69. Participation applies not only to rural people but also to lower-level staff, who have much experience and many ideas to contribute but are usually overlooked in efforts to expand participation in planning from central government personnel to intended beneficiaries. See Robert Chambers, *Managing Rural Development: Ideas and Experience from East Africa* (Uppsala: Scandinavian Institute of African Studies, 1974).

70. See Harvey Leibenstein, "Allocation Efficiency versus 'X-Efficiency'," *American Economic Review* (June 1966), pp. 392–415.

71. This point was suggested by Richard Holloway, Asia Regional Field Director for CUSO, upon the first edition of this book.

72. Esman and Uphoff, *Local Organizations*, pp. 24–28. An additional characteristic, ecological sustainability, needs to be explored further.

73. See Benedict Stavis, "Rural Local Governance and Agricultural Development in Taiwan," in N. Uphoff, ed., *Rural Development and Local Organization in Asia*, vol. 2: *East Asia* (New Delhi: Macmillan, 1982), pp. 166–271.

74. Saemaul Undong is hardly a model of "democratic" local development but a good deal of decision-making power came to rest with rural community councils and leaders, partly as a political counterweight to urban interests. One of the most recent published assessments of Saemaul is by S. Y. Yoon, "Women and Collective Self-Reliance: South Korea's New Community Movement," in S. Muntemba, ed., *Rural Development and Women: Lessons from the Field*, vol. 2 (Geneva: ILO, 1985), pp. 147–72.

PART IX

Collection of Social Data

Editor's Note

In putting people first, social information plays a key part. But the methods of eliciting information about people are often too time-consuming or badly applied.

A common argument against using sociologists or anthropologists during project preparation is that they will require endless years to carry out detailed field studies, the results of which would by then have doubtful utility for projects by then far advanced or long finished. Social information is consequently dismissed because of the allegedly intractable time constraints of the project cycle. It is not an exaggeration to state that, over a long period, a crisis-sized shortage of social data and social knowledge has weakened many development interventions.

Robert Chambers discusses four interlocked defects that he identified in the process of generating, analyzing, and using social data in rural development. First, things have been put ahead of people. Second, poorer people have been neglected and they have come last of all. Third, conventional methods of social investigation have often not been cost-effective. Fourth, information has been acquired and analyzed mainly or only by outsiders, without the rural people's own involvement in the generation and use of knowledge.

Over the past decade, researchers involved in development work have significantly refined their approaches and techniques. Some traditional methods have been revised or adapted, and new time-efficient and cost-effective instruments for eliciting field data are being invented and tested. As a result of refreshing epistemological developments there are now simplified methods of investigation and more frequent use of participatory observation, experiments, pilot schemes, and the like.

Chambers proposes a set of shortcut and participatory procedures to elicit social information. He highlights the progress in molding rapid assessment procedures made during the late-1980s in several developing and developed countries. Advocating new procedures, Chambers indicts what he calls "rural development tourism," characterized by superficial trips to project areas and their easily reached environs. He also criticizes the "quick and dirty" or "long and dirty" survey approaches to data collection. The danger of rural development tourism is that an antipoverty bias directs the visitor toward the better-off people and places. In contrast, long-term anthropological field studies provide a more complete and less obviously biased picture, but they are overly time-consuming and often unrelated to implementation issues. The middle road is that of rapid rural appraisal or participatory rural appraisal, which attempt to construct in a short time a sensitive and practically relevant picture of the local population and their concerns.

The following chapter describes a wide menu of methods that can be used as alternatives or in combination, depending on local circumstances and on what needs to be known. Among them are various forms of direct observation, "do-it-yourself" methods, imaginative use of key informants, group interviews, and chain of interviews, mapping and aerial photographs, diagrams, ethnohistories, ranking procedures, stratifying procedures, stories and portraits, secondary data review, and others.

Underlying all these procedures is the idea that the rural people themselves are the most knowledgeable, but often the most overlooked resource for information on local problems and activities. Therefore, the professional use of these new investigation techniques promise a shortcut for obtaining accurate sociocultural information quickly. If accepted by the professional communities working on preparing development projects, such investigative approaches may make social analysis a much more practical and feasible endeavor in regular project work.

14

Shortcut and Participatory Methods for Gaining Social Information for Projects

Robert Chambers

The prior chapters have presented the case for putting people first. This case is based not just on ethical grounds, though many find the ethical obligations sufficient on their own. It is also highly practical. With repeated experience, evidence has built up to demonstrate that where people and their wishes and priorities are not put first, projects that affect and involve them encounter problems. Experience also shows conversely that where people are consulted, where they participate freely, where their needs and priorities are given primacy in project identification, design, implementation, and monitoring, then economic and social performance are better and development is more sustainable. There are, and always will be, other environmental and managerial factors that influence how well or how badly a project does. Irrespective of these influences, evidence shows that in rural development, putting people first is a necessary condition for good performance whenever local people are involved.

Information: What and Whose

In putting people first, social information plays a key part. For learning about and understanding people, their needs and priorities, and discovering the wider implications of social and cultural conditions, the approaches and methods of eliciting information are critical but often neglected or badly applied.

In the normal development project and professional practice, especially in the 1960s and 1970s, four interlocked defects stand out in the processes of generating, analyzing, and using social information in rural development.

First, things have come before people. Aid agencies and government organizations have tended to be staffed and influenced by engineers, economists, and statisticians—professionals concerned mainly with the physical and with the figures. In the sequence of the project cycle, survey and construction precede operation. In the early stages of many projects, then, physical and biological surveys and information dominate, as do professions and disciplines such as cartography, soil science, hydrology, engineering, agronomy, animal science, forestry, and economics—which are concerned primarily with physical, biological, and numerical aspects of a project rather than its social dimensions. Where people are taken into account, they are more often counted than listened to or learned from. Early project implementation is also often preoccupied with things—with the construction of roads, buildings, and other works. People, and the professions and disciplines concerned with people—such as sociology, social anthropology, and agricultural extension—are treated like poor relations. Social scientists tend to be called in later, if at all, to deal with "the people problem"—to persuade people to move to make way for the dam lake, to overcome the "constraint" of nonparticipation, to adapt the program to local cultural norms, or to transfer the technology generated on the research station. People have come last.

Second, poorer people have been easily neglected. They are the least accessible to outsiders, the least articulate, the least organized, the least likely to be able to complain or resist, and politically, the least important to persuade. Isolated, powerless, and silent, their priorities and needs have been low on the agenda. If people have come last, the poorer people have come last of all.

The third defect is that conventional methods of social investigation have often not been cost-effective. Decisionmakers need information that is relevant, timely, true, and usable. In rural development, a great deal of the information generated has been, in various combinations, irrelevant, late, wrong, or unusable. It has also been costly to obtain, process, analyze, and digest. Information gathering has been inefficient. Criteria of cost-effectiveness have not often been applied, and manifest inefficiency has sometimes been met by demanding not better information, or less of it, but more. All too often, the social information obtained has been useless or misleading, and late or out-of-date.

Fourth, information has been acquired, owned, and analyzed mainly or only by outsiders. In the first edition of *Putting People First*, reflecting the development ethos of the late-1970s and early-1980s, I wrote that "the challenge is to find more cost-effective ways for outsiders to learn about rural conditions." That remains a challenge. But significantly, it was "our" knowledge—and capacity to gain knowledge—that seemed to count, not "theirs." The sustainability of development and empowerment, which are associated with rural people's own generation and use of knowledge, were not on the agenda.

Concerning these four defects, the 1980s have witnessed shifts of emphasis, though sometimes only localized and on a small scale. As we enter the 1990s, there is wider awareness in development circles of the priority of people, and particularly of the poorer people, than there was in earlier decades. Some social investigations have become more cost-effective: new shortcut approaches and methods have been invented and developed, some of them adopting the rubric of rapid rural appraisal (RRA); and these methods have gradually spread. There is also increasing concern with practical questions about who gains and has knowledge and who has the ability to use it. With more attention paid to the issue of sustainability through the participation and empowerment of rural people, especially the poor, it is increasingly recognized that it matters who generates and "owns" knowledge, and whose capacity to learn and analyze is enhanced. Participatory research, participatory action research, participatory agricultural research, and participatory rural appraisal are all finding their places in the new vocabulary of development.

Against this background, the challenge is to develop and spread approaches and methods to gain social information for rural development projects, making them more cost-effective for outsiders to undertake and more participatory for rural people to sustain. With this in mind, the chapter reviews the rationale and range of some shortcut and participatory methods and assesses some of their potentials. The question is: how can the needed information be gained and used, by whom, and with what costs and effects. To seek answers, let us start by examining in more detail the defects of what is often still normal practice.

The Two Traps of Outsiders

In practice, most outsiders are still trapped by two sets of inappropriate methods for generating the social information they seek and need. These have been referred to as the "quick-and-dirty" and the "long-and-dirty" methods, where dirty means not cost-effective.

Quick and Dirty

The most common form of quick-and-dirty appraisal is rural development tourism—the brief rural visit by the urban-based professional.[1] This can be very cost-effective with the outstanding individual; one example is Wolf Ladejinsky, who in two remarkable, short field trips to India saw what was happening in the green revolution and reported it years before plodding social scientists came to the same conclusions carried out to two spurious decimal points.[2] But more commonly, rural development tourism introduces biases that mask the perception of rural poverty, reinforce underestimates of its prevalence, and prevent understanding of its nature. These antipoverty biases are:

- *Spatial (urban, tarmac, and roadside).* The poorer people are often out of sight of the road, having sold out and moved away. They tend to be concentrated in regions remote from urban centers and to live on the fringes of villages or in small inaccessible hamlets.[3]
- *Project.* Outsiders link up with networks that channel them from urban centers to rural places where there are projects, where something initiated by outsiders is happening or is meant to be happening, to the neglect of nonproject areas.
- *Personal contact.* Rural development tourists tend to meet the less poor and the more powerful, men rather than women, users of services rather than nonusers, adopters rather than nonadopters, the active rather than the nonactive, those who have not had to migrate, and (inevitably) those who have not died. In all cases the bias is against perceiving the extent of deprivation.

- *Dry season.* In many tropical environments the wet season is the worst time of year, especially for the poor, since it brings hard work, food shortages, high food prices, high incidence of disease, and high indebtedness.[4] Urban-based professionals, however, usually travel in the post-harvest dry season when things are better.
- *Politeness and protocol.* Courtesy and convention may deter rural development tourists from inquiring about and meeting the poor people. The visitor is also short of time, and the poorer people stand at the end of the line.

Moreover, these biases interlock. The prosperity after harvest of a male farmer on a project beside a main road close to a capital city may color the perceptions of a succession of influential officials and foreigners. The plight of a poor widow starving and sick during the wet season in a remote and inaccessible area may never in any way impinge on the consciousness of anyone outside her own community. The biases pull together to direct attention toward those who are better-off, and away from those who are poorer and more deprived.

Many other defects of quick-and-dirty investigators are well known, but a short list can serve as a warning:

- Quick-and-dirty investigators lack rapport with respondents, who give misleading replies that may be deferential, prudent, or designed to avoid penalties or gain benefits and who may evade sensitive topics, state social ideals not actual practice, and so on.
- Investigators—especially outsiders who are "old hands" and who "know it all"—fail to listen. They want to talk and teach rather than learn, and they reinforce misperception and prejudice by projecting their own ideas and selecting their own meanings.
- Investigators overlook the invisible—they observe physical things and activities, but not social and cultural relationships. They may not ask about or correctly understand crucial social facts such as patron-client relations, factions, informal organizations, norms, indebtedness, interest rates, wages, and control of assets and decision making within the family.
- Investigators see only a "snapshot"—a moment in time. Cyclical and periodic events such as seasonal activities and regular weekly markets may never be uncovered, and trends, often more important than a static view of current conditions, are easily missed.

This list could be lengthened, but the point is that quick appraisal can be seriously misleading, especially when it concerns the poor. Rapid is often wrong.

Long and Dirty

At the other extreme, traditions of academic research value long and costly investigations that often collect a massive volume of data. The real or imagined requirements of doctoral research induce students to seek safety and respectability by avoiding shortcuts and finding out more, not less. So social anthropologists immerse themselves for long periods in alien cultures, and sociologists and agricultural economists plan and perpetrate huge questionnaire surveys. Sometimes the outcome is academically excellent and makes a long-term contribution to understanding and action. All too often, however, the delays are excessive: the social anthropologist's field work is published (if at all) ten years later; the massive survey takes years to process, if it is processed at all.

In its still-not-uncommon pathological form, the multidisciplinary survey questionnaire has thirty or more pages, each discipline with its questions, which if asked are never coded, or if coded never processed, or if processed and printed out never examined, or if examined never analyzed and written up, or if analyzed and written up never read, or if read never understood and remembered, or if understood and remembered—never actually used to change action. Large-scale multidisciplinary rural surveys must be one of the most inefficient industries in the world. Benchmark surveys are often criticized and yet these huge operations persist, often in the name of the science of evaluation; they preempt scarce national research resources and generate mounds of data and papers, which are an embarrassment to all, until white ants or paper shredders clean things up.

Some social investigations are long and clean. Nothing in this chapter should undervalue them. Many of the insights of social anthropologists and sociologists later prove useful. Development anthropology has many practitioners now who have shown the capacity to make substantial contributions to projects. As for surveys, some of the best repeatedly monitor the same villages or people over a long period. Examples are the health and nutrition work of the Dunn Nutrition Unit, Cambridge, in Keneba village in the Gambia, the International Centre for Diarrheal Disease Research in Matlab Thana, Bangladesh, and the social and agricultural village survey of the International Crops Research Institute for the Semi-arid Tropics (ICRISAT) in India.[5] Another example is the study of processes and time-trends of access to and use of common property natural resources by the poor rural people, as carried out by N. S. Jodha in Madhya Pradesh and Rajasthan, India.[6] Such types of findings can be generated only through long, systematic research. Shortcut methods may not be an adequate tool to investigate such processes. Careful, patient, in-depth research is often needed in addition to rapid investigation procedures, as are revisits to areas and people earlier studied.

That said, it is still probably true in the early 1990s that most large-scale surveys, leaving aside those of a strict census type, are monumentally inefficient both in the quality of data obtained and the long delays entailed by the analysis and reporting of survey data. Ironically, the most useful information from large questionnaire surveys often comes not from the survey itself but from informal observations by those who conduct it.[7] Often, the survey's statistics are hardly used at all, even if the data are processed. With large surveys, long is often lost.

In Search of Cost-effectiveness: Rapid Rural Appraisal

The search for appraisal methods has sought to find a middle zone between quick-and-dirty and long-and-dirty, toward a zone of greater cost-effectiveness, one of approaches and methods that are fairly-quick-and-fairly-clean. People in many disciplines and professions have taken part in this search. In the 1980s, some of the inhibitions of earlier decades, which deterred writing and publication, have fallen away and a large literature has been published on what has come to be known as rapid rural appraisal (RRA). "Hard," refereed professional journals have accepted papers based on methods that have come to be recognized for their own rigor. Areas in which contributions have been made include appraisal and analysis concerning: agroecosystems; natural resources, forestry and the environment; irrigation; health and nutrition; farming systems and research; marketing; organizations; and social, cultural, and economic conditions.[8] Two major pioneering institutions have been the University of Khon Kaen in Northeast Thailand and the International Institute for Environment and Development in London.[9]

These developments must not distract from the major obstacles to new and shortcut methods that persist in most of the professional world, including colleges and universities. The words of one participant at an RRA conference in 1979 are still valid: "by the time people leave university the damage has been done"—inappropriate professional attitudes and rigidity in methods have been imparted and internalized. Another participant had been forced to abandon the employment of university graduates as enumerators because of their questionnaire mentality, and had instead used high school students who were more flexible and more open to learning from respondents.[10] One major blockage has been an over-reverence for formal statistical methods and a failure to treat them as servant and not as master.[11] More generally, professional value systems and rewards, and sheer inertia and conservative respectability have deterred improvisation in learning about rural conditions. Better, it has been thought, to be long and legitimate than to be short and suspect.

RRA has, though, developed its own rationale, principles, and rigor.[12] Different schools with different emphases have evolved. Special strengths have been the use of multidisciplinary teams and semi-structured interviewing by Khon Kaen; spatial, temporal, and social diagramming by IIED; and community participation by the Kenya National Environment Secretariat and Clark University. Many others have also evolved approaches and methods for special purposes. All, however, share five basic principles and practices:

- *Optimizing tradeoffs.* The concept of tradeoffs is basic. It relates the costs of collection and learning to tradeoffs between the quantity, relevance, timeliness, truth, and actual beneficial use of information. The paradoxical principle here is optimal ignorance. This means knowing what is not worth knowing, and not trying to find it out. It also includes knowing when enough is known and then abstaining from trying to find out more. A corollary of optimal ignorance is appropriate imprecision, or avoiding measurement or precision that is not needed.
- *Offsetting biases.* Deliberate efforts are made to offset biases, such as those of rural development tourism, by taking time instead of rushing, listening instead of lecturing, probing instead of passing on to a new topic, and being unimportant instead of important. The principle here is bias reversal, deliberate action to gain an unhurried, balanced, and representative view—to see and learn about what is usually out of sight or not mentioned.

- *Triangulating.* A menu of methods is available à la carte, to be used as need and opportunity arise. The range of methods recorded and available is growing. This permits the application of the principle of triangulation.[13] Triangulation means using more than one method or source (often three) for the same information. Examples include the use of research methods with different approaches or informants to obtain the same data; the sampling of units (initially one from near the middle, and one from toward either end of a distribution); and team composition, to represent different disciplines or even to add to a team in the course of investigation.
- *Learning directly from and with rural people.* Knowledge of rural people is fundamental to RRA for social information, and also for much physical information. The scope and validity of much indigenous technical knowledge is now widely recognized. The principle here is direct, face-to-face learning by outsiders with rural people.
- *Learning rapidly and progressively.* The process of RRA involves rapid and progressive learning, which is flexible—changing concerns, directions, priorities, and methods; interactive—with intensive exchanges of information and ideas between people; iterative—returning to questions, places, and informants; and, at its best, improvising and inventive—devising new methods and tailoring actions to needs. The principle here is conscious exploration; making judgments and decisions about what to do next on the basis of what has been discovered so far, not according to a blueprint, but as an adaptive learning process.

The Menu of Methods

In the late 1980s there was still no comprehensive manual of RRA methods, although several organizations produced their own guides.[14] A summary listing can illustrate some of the range and diversity of methods available.

- *Secondary data review.* A review of published and unpublished data, which can take many forms, including surveys, studies, annual reports, trip reports, travel books, ethnographic literature, articles, maps, aerial photographs, satellite imagery, and computer data files.

- *Direct observation.* Personal visits and observations with time to follow up on what is seen. An observational checklist is one aid to systematic observation.
- *Do-it-yourself.* Much briefer participant observation than in the normal social anthropological mode can take the form of undertaking a rural activity oneself. This allows insights and prompts the volunteering of information that would otherwise not be accessible.
- *Key indicators.* Key indicators can be shortcuts to insights about rural social conditions and change, especially when suggested by rural people themselves.[15]
- *Semi-structured interviews.* Informal interviews with checklists but without questionnaires, which permit probing and following up on the unexpected, without the requirement that all the checklist points must be covered in any one interview.[16]
- *Key informants.* Identifying those best able to inform on particular topics, or to give special points of view, whether individually or as groups.
- *Group interviews.* Interviews and discussions with groups, whether casually encountered (such as coffeeshop or teashop groups); specialized or focus groups of similar people; structured groups with an organized composition to represent different points of view, capabilities, or knowledge; and community groups.[17]
- *Chain of interviews.* Sequences of interviews, whether to cover knowledge of stages of a process (such as following a crop from land preparation through cultivation, harvest, marketing, processing, storage, sale, and cooking to consumption), or to follow through on similar topics from early to later contacts, as when group interviews lead to the identification of individuals who are key informants.[18] Repeat interviews in different contexts, including walks with observation, can be part of this.
- *Transects and group walks.* Systematic walks (or in large areas, rides or drives), for example from the highest to the lowest point, visiting and observing diverse conditions en route, including the poorer people and microenvironments.
- *Mapping and aerial photographs.* The use of formal maps, whether general or specialized, and the preparation of informal maps based on observation and on local knowledge.[19] The use of aerial photographs as aids to ecological, social, and political mapping and to identifying longitudinal change.[20]

- *Diagrams.* The use of diagrams to express, share, and check information. These include diagrams to represent information that is spatial, for example for transects; temporal, including trend lines for changes over the years, and seasonal calendars for changes within years for dimensions such as labor, diet, disease, cropping practices, prices, livestock fodder, rainfall, migration, and tree use; social, including links and overlaps between groups and institutions at the community level; and concerning processes. Types of diagrams include sketches, bar diagrams, histograms, flow diagrams, Venn diagrams, and decision-trees.[21] Venn diagrams (also known in South Asia as *chapati* diagrams) have been used to identify village institutions and their interrelationships.
- *Ranking, stratifying, and quantification.* Methods for eliciting knowledge and preferences from informants, which are both quick and enjoyable, have been used.[22] Aids to quantification and ranking include the Atte board, informal pie diagrams, and various systems of questioning.[23] Wealth ranking has proved a quick and accurate method for stratifying a rural population and has been tested and found to be effective in several different environments.[24]
- *Ethnohistories.* These are histories recalled and recounted by rural people. In one notable example, cultivator biographies were elicited with respect to a particular crop, cassava, in the Dominican Republic.[25] In another, information was obtained on changes in child-rearing practices in Ghana, with three generations of mothers as informants.[26]
- *Stories, portraits, and case studies.* These are anecdotes and descriptions of people and households, farming systems, social groups, villages, events, customs, practices, or other aspects of rural life, designed to portray conditions as one part or stage in understanding.[27]
- *Team interactions.* The deliberate organization of team interactions is part of many RRAS. The classic example is Hildebrand's *sondeo* technique, originating in Guatemala, in which social and biological scientists are paired, changing partners each day. This technique has also been adopted in Australia.[28]
- *Key probes.* Sometimes an exceptionally revealing key question can be identified, as in the fishermen's survey reported by Pollnac in chapter 8. Although "more sophisticated techniques of collection and analysis of data could have been used," he found that simply asking fishermen why they sold to one middleman rather than to

another was sufficient to produce information on which to base two operationally significant recommendations.

- *Questionnaires.* Late and light. If a questionnaire is needed, it is usually devised late in the investigation, tied in with dummy tables that are known to be needed, kept short and simple, and immediately analyzed.

The above methods are described to indicate some of the range of options available but do not cover them all. The cost-effectiveness of these methods depends on how appropriately and well they are used. However, where RRA methods have been compared with more conventional methods, they have proved reasonably accurate and almost always more cost-effective.

Adisak and Cernea have documented that four large sample surveys based on long questionnaires for evaluating extension impact in Thailand had an average cost of 1.3 million bhat each, while four rapid and in-depth sociological studies on small samples carried out much faster by the same evaluation unit each cost only 82,000 bhat, or fifteen times less.[29] Furthermore, four years later none of the large-scale surveys were fully processed and analyzed, while the four rapid cases had already long been analyzed and interpreted and their findings used by project management.[30] In a similar case, Collinson wrote that, in studying a local farming system, a lengthy and costly formal verification survey had always confirmed the findings of his shorter, cheaper, and informal exploratory survey.[31] Later, in Kenya, this finding was supported when a quick, informal agricultural investigation was carefully compared with a longer and more expensive formal one and showed insignificant differences between the two.[32]

In several cases where RRA methods have been compared with conventional surveys, they have proved not simply just as good but more accurate and informative. In Kenya, an investigation of the role of wild indigenous plants in land use systems was conducted both through a formal random sample of sixty-three households, and through group interviews and informal interviews with a chain of informants from "average" to expert. The formal survey took three times as long and resulted in the same information as the informal approach, but with less detail and coherence.[33] In a subhumid zone in Nigeria, a study of browse quality found a high correlation between rankings given by different pastoralists and that the pastoralists' information was more practical and timely than a laboratory chemical analysis.[34] In a pastoral community in Kenya, Barbara Grandin's wealth ranking not only showed a 0.97 correlation with a ranking of households based on a survey of livestock units, but also brought to light a number of census errors.[35] RRA methods, well used, are not only cost-effective; for insight and accuracy they are also quite often the best.

Participatory Rural Appraisal

Most of the methods mentioned involve outsiders learning from, and sometimes with, rural people. The mode of RRA presented, though, is primarily extractive. When outsiders are obtaining information for the identification, preparation, appraisal, monitoring, and evaluation of some sorts of projects, these extractive methods have obvious uses. But knowledge can also be generated by more participatory approaches, in which investigation and analysis are carried out more by rural people themselves, in which they "own" the information, and in which they articulate their priorities.

Participatory rural appraisal (PRA) belongs to, draws on, and overlaps with other members of a family of approaches that have been or are participatory in various ways. These include the community development of the 1950s and 1960s, the dialogics and "consciencization" of Paulo Freire, participatory action research, and the work of activist NGOs in many parts of the world, which have encouraged and enabled poor people to undertake their own analysis and action.[36]

PRA has adapted and further developed RRA methods in a participatory mode, increasingly enabling rural people to use them for their own analysis. Recent developments include participatory approaches to community natural resource assessment, management, and development evolved in Kenya by the National Environment Secretariat, in association with Clark University, and in India by the Aga Khan Rural Support Programme in Gujarat in association with the IIED.[37] These draw on the agroecosystems analysis developed by Gordon Conway and others, emphasizing transects, trend and seasonal analysis, social mapping, and problem and opportunity identification by and with rural people themselves, leading to community action.[38] Most recently, MYRADA, an NGO in South India, has taken this further, by developing powerful and popular new methods, such as participatory mapping and modeling, and by emphasizing changes in outsiders' behavior and new ways of establishing rapport.[39]

A parallel development has been farmer participation in agricultural research. Methods have been developed to enable farmers better to analyze their farming systems, assess their own needs, and improve the effectiveness of their own experiments.[40]

Visual observation is a common element in much PRA. This means that both rural people and outsiders can together see, discuss, point at, manipulate, and alter physical objects. This differs from the questionnaire interview mode in which information is transferred from the words of the interviewee onto the private paper of the interviewer, without the interviewee being able to check and correct what is written, the information being then taken away and analyzed elsewhere separately, and often by someone else. Visual observation takes two main forms.

The first is the simple and commonsense practice of show-and-tell: discussing a technology, plant, animal, farming, or social activity *in the field*, or where the practice or activity is taking place.

The second is shared diagramming. This can take many forms and new ones are being invented. Aerial photographs can provide templates for participatory mapping: they are often easily and enthusiastically interpreted by rural people in different countries and continents. They have been applied to mapping of land use and tenure for local-level planning by and with rural people and for identifying the boundaries between social groups, either by drawing on transparent overlays or directly on the photographs with chinagraph pencils. Maps and other diagrams and models can be drawn or made on the ground where many people can see, alter, and correct them. Stones, pellets, sticks of different sizes or lengths, and other local material can be used for shared quantification, ranking, and indication of trends. Analytical games of various sorts can be devised and used. Not only does visual sharing make information available to outsiders who would otherwise not have access; it also makes explicit to rural people the knowledge they already have in a diffuse way, helps them to develop and share it, allows crosschecking between individuals, and enhances analysis by rural people themselves.

Participatory rural appraisal changes and reverses roles. Outsiders are less extractors of information, and more catalysts and facilitators. Such investigation and analysis can be carried out more with rural and poor people themselves. New knowledge is generated and owned more by them. In the process they gain in confidence and thus are empowered. And development projects and initiatives that follow are likely to be more participatory and so, more sustainable.

Potentials and Dangers

Rapid rural appraisal (using the term here and below to include participatory rural appraisal) has many applications. Most obviously these include assessments of emergency situations, reconnaissance for time-bound government programs and policy requirements, and the investigation of particular topics. Besides these, two applications deserve special mention.

The Project Process

As stated or implied throughout this book, the use of RRA with a focus on social information can substantially improve the current project process used by development and government agencies.

RRA can be used to offset the tendency for the early stages of projects to be dominated by things rather than people, by technical experts (engineers, economists, biological and physical scientists) in the absence of social scientists, and by the interests of the better-off rather than by those of the poorer.[41] A clear example is the stage of project identification. If conceived in the narrow sense of having and establishing the idea of a project, then identification is easily influenced by those with special interests or local power. J. Price Gittinger's classic textbook, which devotes only one page out of 443 to "identification," recommends and perpetuates the narrow nonparticipatory manner of identifying projects. The textbook says:

> The first stage in the (project) cycle is to find potential projects. There are many, many sources from which suggestions may come. The most common will be well-informed technical specialists and local leaders. While performing their professional duties, technical specialists will have identified many areas where they feel new investment might be profitable. Local leaders will generally have a number of suggestions about where investment might be carried out.[42]

In this formulation, the process of identification is open to the normal biases of professionals and to the suggestions of the members of local elites. Such an approach will rarely give rise to projects that originate in the needs of the poorer rural people. In contrast, systematic RRA, when used for consulting them in an unhurried and sensitive manner, enabling them to analyze their conditions and formulate their priorities, should lead to different and more equitable projects and agendas.

RRA also has a big part to play later in the project cycle. The appraisal stage is the most obvious but at least as important are monitoring and evaluation, mid-term reviews, and adjustments in the learning process. All too often, monitoring and evaluation are superficial, measuring indicators that do not reflect changes in well-being, or failing to penetrate multiple causality. As Uphoff points out in chapter 13, monitoring and evaluation should be participatory, involving both rural people and government officers. Longitudinal applications of RRA methods at intervals and participatory trend analysis can monitor and reveal changes and the underlying causes, using indicators such as real wages for agricultural laborers, in- and out-migration, fuel availability by type and use, changes in diet, and the nutritional status of children.

RRA can also provide the rapid and accurate feedback necessary for a learning process style of project implementation, with "planning by successive approximation," and mid-course changes. Badly done, it can reinforce error. Well done, without rushing, it can considerably improve performance.

Training, Awareness, and Keeping Up-to-date

A second potential of RRA is for training and awareness. RRA has many applications in education and training institutions and for the professional formation of staff in government offices, NGOs, and technical agencies. On education, Michael Cernea points out in the first chapter how crucial it is for universities to avoid producing "new cohorts of socially incompetent technical experts or technically illiterate sociologists." Team RRAS are one potent means for avoiding or compensating for this danger. They induce rapid learning from colleagues and clients alike; personal, disciplinary, and departmental barriers break down. Some higher education institutions have already used RRA with their students and staff. The Institute of Rural Management at Anand in India, as part of a two-year course, has its staff and students spend a month in a village with an agenda of topics to investigate, such as the daily lives and problems of a group of poorer people. The University of Khon Kaen in Thailand had by early 1985 involved staff of at least sixteen university departments in field RRAS. The experiences of these and other institutions indicate that, as a standard part of university and institute training, a well-conducted RRA focused on the poorer rural people can sharpen professional skills, and generate new social commitment.

RRA methods can also be used for training, awareness, and updating the perceptions of field and headquarters staff of governments and NGOS. There is an unknown potential for training field staff in RRA methods to perceive and relate to the diversity of rural conditions, legitimating and helping much more decentralized and differentiated actions at the local level than what are currently found in large field bureaucracies. Staff can be taught interview methods such as those for ranking, which induce them to learn from and use the categories and criteria of their rural clients.

Older, senior staff, trapped in the higher levels of bureaucracies in urban centers are often decades out-of-date in their direct experience of rural conditions, apart from what they "learn" through biased rural development tourism and at second or third hand. For them, RRA methods can both liberate and update, through direct, informal contact with rural people.

Dangers of Unsuccessful Initiatives

RRA approaches and methods also have dangers. They could be over-sold, too rapidly adopted, badly done, and then discredited, to suffer an undeserved, premature burial as has occurred with other innovative research approaches. They could be used hurriedly, so that RRA becomes no more than a legitimating label for biased and superficial rural development tourism. They could be misinterpreted as a sufficient substitute for in-depth social investigation of rural life and conditions, and so undermine support for the good longitudinal studies that will always be needed. There will always be value in some large, repeated surveys like the national sample survey in India or the extended fieldwork of an individual anthropologist for in-depth comprehensive basic research. But these can now be complemented by the use of the new methods of RRA. Used well—optimizing tradeoffs, offsetting biases, triangulating and crosschecking, and learning rapidly and progressively from and with rural people—RRA methods provide an increasingly well-developed, cost-effective, and powerful means for gathering and analyzing social and other data.

Moreover, RRA methods resonate with aspects of the new development paradigm that puts people before things. The contrast between development paradigms is expressed in table 14-1.

These contrasts can be overdrawn. Most successful initiatives are a mixture of elements from each. Projects for physical infrastructure will always be needed. They require the application of universal rules, for instance as in building bridges. Precisely because these rules are universally valid, physical projects like bridges are relatively easy to implement. A much greater challenge is presented by projects that involve people, as well as things. As Bagadion and Korten have shown with irrigation in the Philippines in chapter 3, the participatory approach requires a basic shift in norms and attitudes from conceiving just the building of a physical system to developing the social organization capable of using and sustaining the system on a long-term basis. Many other similar cases and arguments for the paradigm that puts people first have been presented and analyzed in this volume.

Table 14-1. *Physical and Human Paradigms for Development*

Aspect	Physical	Human
Point of departure	Things	People
Mode	Blueprint	Learning process
Goals	Predetermined	Evolutionary
Analytical assumptions	Reductionist	Holistic
Keyword	Planning	Participatory planning
Locus of decisionmaking	Centralized	Decentralized
Relationship with clients	Controlling, inducing	Enabling, empowering
Methods	Standardized and universally applicable	Diverse and locally evolved and adapted
Technology for clients	A fixed package of options (table d'hôte)	A varied basket of options (à la carte)
Project output	Infrastructure	Competence and choice

Conclusion

To put people first, and to put poorer people first of all, requires action to support the organization and empowerment of poorer people to enable them to make effective demands. It requires institutions that are strong and sustainable and policies to support them. RRA, including participatory rural appraisal, is one point of entry among many others.

Even so, by making outsiders more self-critical about what they learn and mislearn, and making their learning more efficient and up-to-date; by making more time for the poorer to be heard and to take part; by encouraging the poorer to participate in analysis; and by bringing senior staff and poor people face-to-face—in ways such as these RRA methods promise an unmeasurable potential for changing behavior, awareness, and policy.

It is the beginning of wisdom to recognize that we, the professionals, are much of the problem and that they, the poorer, are much of the solution. In the late 1980s, these insights became more accepted than they were a decade earlier. In the 1990s, conceptual acceptance can be translated into more systematic action. An immense inertia of "normal" professional values, rewards, and behavior continues to impede change. This reinforces learning from above, not below, serving the richer, not the poorer, and standardizing not differentiating. Fortunately, we now have, in the growing family of RRA approaches and methods, one means to help reverse these tendencies.

More and more professionals—in government departments, in universities, in donor agencies, and in NGOs—are recognizing and practicing reversals—in putting people before things, in putting the poorer before the less poor, in learning from people and not just teaching them, in decentralizing instead of concentrating power, and in valuing and supporting diversity instead of standardization. The need for putting people first is more and more clearly seen and felt, not just by social scientists but across the whole range of disciplines and departments. RRA has its part to play in reinforcing and spreading this insight and conviction in the movement for sustainable social justice and development. However modestly, it has the potential to help make the 1990s increasingly a decade for reversals, for diversity, and for putting people first. The methods are better known than before. Lack of tools cannot be an excuse. It is less a question of what to do, than one of deciding to do it. Putting people first, and putting the poorer first of all, is now more than ever a matter of personal and professional choice and commitment.

Notes

Major sources include: *Agricultural Administration*, vol. 8, no. 6 (1981); Richard Longhurst, ed., "Rapid Rural Appraisal: Social Structure and Rural Economy," *IDS Bulletin*, Institute of Development Studies, University of Sussex, vol. 12, no. 4 (1981); Khon Kaen University, *Proceedings of the 1985 International Conference on Rapid Rural Appraisal, Rural Systems Research and Farming Systems Research Projects*, Khon Kaen, Thailand, 1987; Jennifer A. McCracken, Jules N. Pretty, and Gordon R. Conway, *An Introduction to Rapid Rural Appraisal for Agricultural Development* (IIED, 1988) and the series *RRA Notes* (1988), both issued from the International Institute for Environment and Development, London; National Environment Secretariat, Kenya, and others, *Participatory Rural Appraisal Handbook*, published by World Resources Institute, Washington, D.C.; and the PRA/PALM (participatory learning methods) series, 1990, issued by MYRADA, Bangalore, India.

1. For a more-detailed description of the pathology of rural development tourism, and its antipoverty biases, see Robert Chambers, *Rural Development: Putting the Last First* (Harlow, Eng.: Longman, 1983), pp. 10–26, and Mick Moore, "Beyond the Tarmac Road: A Guide for Rural Poverty Watchers," in Richard Longhurst, ed., "Rapid Rural Appraisal: Social Structure and Rural Economy," *IDS Bulletin*, vol. 12, no. 4 (1981), pp. 47–52.

2. Wolf Ladejinsky, "The Green Revolution in Punjab: A Field Trip," *Economic and Political Weekly*, vol. 4, no. 26 (1969); Ladejinsky, "The Green Revolution in Bihar—the Kosi Area: A Field Trip," *Economic and Political Weekly*, vol. 4, no. 39 (1969).

3. Joseph Ssennyonga, "The Cultural Dimensions of Demographic Trends," *Populi*, vol. 3, no. 2 (1976), pp. 2–11. Moore ("Beyond the Tarmac Road," p. 47) describes one part of rural Sri Lanka: "The proportion of houses with earth floors ranged from 14% in one locality to 41% in another. The remarkable fact is that one could drive along all the motorable roads in these localities and see scarcely a single mud floored house."

4. See Susan Schofield, "Seasonal Factors Affecting Nutrition in Different Age Groups and Especially Preschool Children," *Journal of Development Studies*, vol. 11, no. 1 (1974), pp. 22–40; Robert Chambers, Richard Longhurst, and Arnold Pacey, eds., *Seasonal Dimensions to Rural Poverty* (London: Frances Pinter, 1981); and Robert Chambers, "Health, Agriculture and Rural Poverty: Why Seasons Matter," *Journal of Development Studies*, vol. 18, no. 2 (1982), pp. 217–38.

5. T. S. Walker and J. G. Ryan, *Village and Household Economics in India's Semi-arid Tropics* (Baltimore, Md.: Johns Hopkins Press, 1990).

6. N. S. Jodha, "Market Forces and Erosion of Common Property Resources," in *Agricultural Markets in the Semi-arid Tropics* (Patancheru, India: ICRISAT, 1985), pp. 263–77.

7. See, for example, Steven Franzel and Eric Crawford, "Comparing Formal and Informal Survey Techniques for Farming Systems Research: A Case Study from Kenya," *Agricultural Administration*, vol. 27 (1987), pp. 13–33.

8. Sources are too numerous to cite, and there is a large associated literature. Two accessible bibliographies are Somluckrat W. Grandstaff and Apisit Buranakanonda, "Bibliography on Rapid Rural Appraisal," in Khon Kaen University, *Proceedings of the 1985 International Conference on Rapid Rural Appraisal*, Khon Kaen, Thailand (1987), pp. 327–42; and Jennifer

A. McCracken, Jules N. Pretty, and Gordon R. Conway, *An Introduction to Rapid Rural Appraisal for Agricultural Development* (London: International Institute for Environment and Development (IIED), 1988), with an annotated bibliography on pp. 81–94.

9. See Khon Kaen University 1987, and George W. Lovelace, Sukaesinee Subhadira, and Suchint Sumaraks, eds., *Rapid Rural Appraisal in Northeast Thailand: Case Studies* (Khon Kaen, Thailand: Khon Kaen University, 1988); the Sustainable Agriculture Programme of IIED had by 1990 published a substantial series of reports and monographs on rapid rural appraisal and agroecosystems analysis conducted in countries including Ethiopia, Fiji, India, Pakistan, Sudan, and Zimbabwe; written by Gordon Conway, Jennifer McCracken, Jules Pretty, and Ian Scoones. IIED produces *RRA Notes*, an informal bulletin available free of charge on request; the bulletin was so heavily supplied with material that six issues were published in the first year.

10. Rosalind Eyben, "Rapid Appraisal in Non-formal Education: An Account on an On-going Research Experience with a United Nations Project," paper to the Conference on Rapid Rural Appraisal, at IDS, University of Sussex, December 4–7, 1979.

11. See Mick Moore, "Denounce the Gang of Statisticians, Struggle against the Sample Line, Unite the Researching Masses against Professional Hegemony," paper to the Conference on Rapid Rural Appraisal at IDS, University of Sussex, December 4–7, 1979, and Anthony Ellman, "Rapid Appraisal for Rural Project Preparation," *Agricultural Administration*, vol. 8, no. 6 (1981), p. 465.

12. For the rationale, principle, and rigor of RRA see Deryke Belshaw, "A Theoretical Framework for Data-economizing Appraisal Procedures to Rural Development Planning," in Longhurst 1981; Ian Carruthers and Robert Chambers, "Rapid Appraisal for Rural Development," *Agricultural Administration*, vol. 8, no. 6 (1981), pp. 415–17; and Khon Kaen University 1987, pp. 3–102, especially Neil Jamieson "The Paradigmatic Significance of Rapid Rural Appraisal," pp. 89–102.

13. Khon Kaen University 1987, pp. 9–13.

14. For example, IIED, "Meals for the Millions in Kenya," Save the Children Fund (USA) in Sudan; the National Environment Secretariat, Kenya; and the Northeast Rainfed Agricultural Development Project in Thailand; see also Michael M. Cernea, *Re-Tooling in Applied Social Investigation for Development Planning: Some Methodological Issues,* opening address to the International Conference on Rapid Assessment Methodologies, November, 1990, Washington, D.C.

15. N. S. Jodha, "Poverty Debate in India: A Minority View," *Economic and Political Weekly*, special issue (November 1988), pp. 2421–27.

16. Semi-structured or informal interviewing is described in several sources, including Michael Collinson, "A Low Cost Approach to Understanding Small Farmers," *Agricultural Administration*, vol. 8, no. 6 (1981), pp. 433–50; Robert Rhoades, *The Art of the Informal Agricultural Survey*, (Lima, Peru: International Potato Center, 1982); Khon Kaen University 1987, pp. 129–43; and Krishna Kumar, "Conducting Key Informant Interviews in Developing Countries," USAID, Washington, D. C., (1989).

17. For group interviewing, see Dennis J. Casley and Krishna Kumar, *The Collection, Analysis, and Use of Monitoring and Evaluation Data* (Baltimore, Md.: Johns Hopkins Press, 1988), pp. 26–40; and Robert Chambers, Arnold Pacey, and Lori Ann Thrupp, eds., *Farmer First: Farmer Innovation and Agricultural Research*, (London: Intermediate Technology Publications, 1989), pp. 127–46.

18. Dianne Rocheleau and others, "Local Knowledge for Agroforestry and Native Plants," in Chambers, Pacey, and Thrupp 1989, pp. 20–22.

19. Anil Gupta and IDS Workshop, "Maps Drawn by Farmers and Extensionists" in Chambers, Pacey, and Thrupp 1989, pp. 86–92.

20. Brian Carson, "Appraisal of Rural Resources Using Aerial Photography: An Example from a Remote Hill Area in Nepal," in Khon Kaen University 1987, pp. 174–90; Dick Sandford, "A Note on the Use of Aerial Photographs for Land Use Planning on a Settlement Site in Ethiopia," *RRA Notes* no. 6, pp. 18–19; Peter Dewees, "Aerial Photography and Household Studies in Kenya," *RRA Notes* no. 7 (1989), pp. 9–12; and Robin Mearns, "Aerial Photographs in Rapid Land Resource Appraisal, Papua New Guinea," *RRA Notes* no. 7 (1989), pp. 12–15.

21. McCracken, Pretty, and Conway 1988 and Gordon Conway, "Diagrams for Farmers," in Chambers, Pacey, and Thrupp 1989, pp. 77–86.

22. See *RRA Notes*, no. 1, and Robin Mearns, "Direct Matrix Ranking in Papua New Guinea," *RRA Notes*, no. 3, pp. 11–15.

23. For the Atte board see David Barker, "Appropriate Methodology: An Example Using a Traditional African Board Game to Measure Farmers' Attitudes and Environmental Images," *IDS Bulletin*, vol. 10, no. 2 (1979), pp. 37–40; for pie diagrams see Simon Maxwell, "Rapid Food Security Assessment: A Pilot Exercise in Sudan," *RRA Notes*, no. 5, pp. 15–21.

24. Barbara Grandin, *Wealth Ranking in Smallholder Communities: A Field Manual* (London: Intermediate Technology Publications, 1988).

25. Louk Box, "Virgilio's Theorem: A Method for Adaptive Agricultural Research," in Chambers, Pacey, and Thrupp 1989, pp. 61–67.

26. Gill Gordon, "Finding Out About Child (0–5 years) Feeding Practices," paper to the Conference on Rapid Rural Appraisal, at IDS, University of Sussex, December 4–7, 1979.

27. McCracken, Pretty, and Conway 1988, pp. 31–32.

28. Peter Hildebrand, "Combining Disciplines in Rapid Appraisal: The Sondeo Approach," *Agricultural Administration*, vol. 8, no. 6, pp. 423–32, and Peter Ampt and Ray Ison, "Riparola Rapids Rural Appraisal to Identify Problems and Opportunities for Agroeconomic Research and Development in the Forbes Shire, NSW," School of Crop Sciences, University of Sydney, December 1988.

29. Adisak Sreensunpagit, "Monitoring and Evaluation of Extension: Experience in Thailand," in Michael Cernea, J. Coulter, and J. F. A. Russell, eds., *Agricultural Extension by Training and Visits: The Asian Experience* (Washington, D. C.: World Bank, 1983).

30. Michael Cernea, "Evaluation of Farmers' Reactions to Extension Advice," M. Cernea, J. Coulter, and J. F. A. Russel, eds., *Agricultural Extension by Training and Visits: The Asian Experience* (Washington, D.C.: World Bank, 1983).

31. Collinson 1981, p. 444.

32. Franzel and Crawford 1987.

33. Rocheleau and others in Chambers, Pacey, and Thrupp 1989, p. 21.

34. Wolfgang Bayer, *Browse Quality and Availability in a Farming Area and a Grazing Reserve in the Nigerian Subhumid Zone*, report to the ILCA Subhumid Zone Program, Kaduna, Nigeria (May 1986) and "Ranking Browse Species by Cattle Keepers," *RRA Notes*, no. 3, pp. 4–10.

35. Grandin 1988, p. 31.

36. See Paulo Freire, *Pedagogy of the Oppressed* (New York: Seabury Press, 1970); Ponna Wignaraja, "Ten Years of Experience with Participatory Action Research in South Asia— Lessons for NGOs and Peoples' Organizations," in Richard Holloway, ed., *Doing Development: Government, NGOs and the Rural Poor in Asia*, (London: Earthscan Publications in association with CUSO, 1989), pp. 30–40; David Watson and Richard Holloway, eds., *Changing Focus: Involving the Rural Poor in Development Planning* (Oxford and New Delhi: IBH, 1989); and David C. Korten, ed., *Community Management: Asian Experience and Perspectives* (West Hartford, Conn.: Kumarian Press, 1987).

37. *Participatory Rural Appraisal Handbook*, National Environment Secretariat, Nairobi, and Clark University, Second Draft, June 21, 1989, and Charity Kabutha and Richard Ford, "Using RRA to Formulate a Village Resource Management Plan, Mbusangi, Kenya," *RRA Notes*, no. 2, pp. 4–11. Jennifer A. McCracken, *Participatory Rapid Rural Appraisal in Gujarat: A Trial Model for the Aga Khan Rural Support Program (India)* (London: IIED, 1988).

38. Gordon R. Conway, Jennifer A. McCracken, and Jules N. Pretty, *Training Modes for Agroecosystem Analysis and Rapid Rural Appraisal*, (London: IIED, November 1987).

39. See *Experimental Agriculture*, vol. 24, no. 3 (six papers on farmer participatory research, edited by John Farrington, 1988); John Farrington and Adrienne Martin, *Farmer Participation in Agricultural Research: A Review of Concepts and Practices*, AAU Occasional Paper no. 9 (London: Overseas Development Institute, 1988); *Participatory Technology Development in Sustainable Agriculture* (Leiden, Netherlands: ILEIA, April 1989); Stephen D. Biggs, *Resource-poor Farmer Participation in Research: A Synthesis of Experiences from Nine National Agricultural Research Systems* (The Hague, Netherlands: ISNAR, June 1989); and Chambers, Pacey, and Thrupp 1989. An ODI annotated bibliography on farmer participation in research is forthcoming.

40. Roland Bunch, *Two Ears of Corn: A Guide to People-Centered Agricultural Improvement* (Oklahoma City, Okla.: World Neighbors).

41. Robert Chambers, "Normal Professionalism and the Early Project Process," Discussion Paper no. 247, IDS, University of Sussex (July 1988).

42. J. Price Gittinger, *Economic Analysis of Agricultural Projects*, 2d ed. (Washington, D.C.: World Bank, 1982), p. 21.

Notes on the Contributors

Benjamin U. Bagadion was the assistant administrator for operations of the National Irrigation Administration (NIA) in the Philippines until his retirement from the government in 1985. Since then he has been a consultant to several irrigation projects in Bangladesh, Indonesia, Nepal, Sri Lanka and, Thailand, and the NIA–Ford Foundation program in the Philippines. His publications include *Developing Viable Irrigators' Associations: Lessons from Small Scale Irrigation Development in the Philippines,* written with Frances Korten, *Water User Organizational Needs and Alternatives,* and *Farmers Involvement and Training in Irrigation Water Management.*

Michael M. Cernea is senior adviser, social policy and sociology, at the World Bank, Washington, D.C. He obtained his Ph.D. at the University of Bucharest and has held research and teaching positions in Romania. In 1970–71 he was a fellow at the Center for Advanced Studies in the Behavioral Sciences at Stanford University, and in 1979–80 he was a fellow at the Netherlands Institute for Advanced Studies in Social Sciences. He has published and edited several books on the sociology of agricultural cooperatives, sociology of mass culture, diffusion of innovations, agricultural extension, and evaluation research. He joined the World Bank as a sociologist in 1974 and has conducted sociological fieldwork on development projects in Algeria, China, India, Mexico, Senegal, Tanzania, Thailand, and other countries.

Robert Chambers is a fellow of the Institute of Development Studies at the University of Sussex in England. He holds an M.A. in history from Cambridge University and a Ph.D. in public administration from Manchester University. His long-term involvement with development issues has included managing rural development schemes in Kenya, carrying out rural research in India, Kenya, and Sri Lanka, training for development administration in East Africa, and other consultancies for operational work. From 1975 to 1976 he was evaluation officer with the Office of the High Commission for Refugees, and in 1981–83 he worked in India with the Ford Foundation. His many publications include *Managing Rural Development; Rural Development:Putting the Last First*, and the jointly edited *Seasonal Dimensions of Rural Poverty.*

Cynthia C. Cook is a sociologist with the World Bank's Africa Region Environment Division. Prior to the creation of that division, she worked in the Bank's Transportation Department and Transportation Division for Africa. Before joining the Bank, she worked for consulting firms and research organizations on policy analysis, program design and evaluation, social analysis, and socioeconomic impact assessment for development projects in the United States and abroad.

E. Walter Coward, Jr. was a professor of rural sociology and Asian studies at Cornell University until recently, when he joined the Ford Foundation as director of the foundation's Rural Poverty and Resource Program. His research interests have focused on the sociological aspects of irrigation development in Asia, with particular attention to the community irrigation sector.

Neville Dyson-Hudson is professor of anthropology at the State University of New York, Binghamton. Educated at Cambridge and Oxford, he has been studying East African pastoral groups for thirty years and has done extended field research among the Karimojong (Uganda), Bisharin (Sudan), and Turkana and Maasai (Kenya). He worked two years at the

International Livestock Centre for Africa in Kenya and more briefly in Ethiopia, Botswana, and Mali. He has been a consultant to the World Bank on livestock and rural development projects in Botswana and Kenya and an agricultural research project in Sudan. He has also been involved in a multidisciplinary long-term study of pastoral populations in northwest Kenya (the South Turkana Ecology Project) sponsored by the U.S. National Science Foundation.

David M. Freeman is professor and chairman of the Sociology Department, Colorado State University. He holds an M.A. from the University of Pittsburgh, and a Ph.D. in international studies from the University of Denver. Dr. Freeman served for two years as a program planning officer in the Near East–South Asia Division of the Peace Corps, 1962–64. He has worked with the Colorado State University water management teams on problems of irrigation in the Indus Valley of Pakistan and in India. He has done sociological work in natural resources and river basin planning for the U.S. Department of Agriculture's Forest Service. Dr. Freeman has recently published *Local Organizations for Social Development: Concepts and Cases of Irrigation Organization in South Asia.*

Scott Guggenheim is an anthropologist working with the World Bank. Following several years of research with the National Institute of Anthropology and History in Mexico City, he obtained his Ph.D. from the Johns Hopkins University, with a thesis on rural differentiation in the Philippines. He has done ethnographic fieldwork in Colombia, Mexico, and the Philippines. His publications include "Power and Protest in the Countryside" (with Robert Weller); "Cock or Bull: Cockfighting and Social Change in the Philippines;" and "Compadrazgo, Baptism, and the Symbolism of Natural Birth" (with Maurice Bloch).

Frances F. Korten received a Ph.D. in social psychology from Stanford University and did research, management work, and teaching in connection with family planning programs in Central America and irrigation and social forestry programs in Southeast Asia. She is currently assistant representative to the Philippines for the Ford Foundation. Her publications include *Transforming a Bureaucracy: The Experience of the Philippine National Irrigation Administration* (with Robert Siy) and *Casebook for Family Planning Management: Motivating Effective Clinic Performance* (with David C. Korten).

Conrad Phillip Kottak received his Ph.D. in anthropology from Columbia University in 1966 and is professor of anthropology at the University of Michigan and a faculty associate of the Institute for Social Research. In 1988 Dr. Kottak was elected chair of the General Anthropology Division of the American Anthropological Association (AAA) and is serving on the AAA Presidential Panel on Sociocultural Transformation and Its Difficulties in Preindustrial and Industrializing Societies. His books include *The Past in the Present: History, Ecology and Cultural Variation in Highland Madagascar; Assault on Paradise: Social Change in a Brazilian Village; Prime-Time Society: An Anthropological Analysis of Television and Culture;* and fifth editions, now being prepared, of *Cultural Anthropology* and *Anthropology: The Exploration of Human Diversity*. Dr. Kottak's most recent research project, now in progress, is a study of risk perception and ecological consciousness in contemporary Brazil.

Max K. Lowdermilk received his Ph.D. in extension education and master's degree in rural sociology from Cornell University. He was a water management extension specialist in India with the U.S. Agency for International Development and an agricultural development agent in Pakistan. In 1974 he joined the Colorado State University interdisciplinary water management team to work in Pakistan on problems of on-farm water management. He later became director of international education, Colorado State University, and published extensively on problems of diffusion of improved agricultural technology and water management. He has been a consultant to the World Bank and USAID on irrigation and extension. Currently on the sociology faculty at Colorado State University, Dr. Lowdermilk is also serving now as farmer organization unit leader on a USAID-funded project in Egypt.

Richard B. Pollnac is professor of anthropology at the University of Rhode Island. For the past fifteen years he has been involved in fisheries development as a research associate with the International Center for Marine Resources Development. He has carried out field research on several development-related subjects in Africa, Latin America, the Middle East, and Southeast Asia and has also conducted field research on fishermen's cooperatives in Ecuador, Indonesia, and Panama and on the social impact of extension services in the Azores. His most recent publications include *Evaluating the Success of Fishermen's Organizations in Developing Countries* and *Monitoring and Evaluating the Impacts of Small-Scale Fishery Projects.*

Thayer Scudder is professor of anthropology at the California Institute of Technology, Pasadena, and director of the Institute for Development Anthropology, Binghamton, New York. Educated at Harvard University, he has since 1956 pursued research interests related to new land settlement, river basin development, and long-term community studies. His publications deal particularly with the Kariba Dam Project in Central Africa and with dam relocation and new land settlement worldwide. He has worked as a consultant for the World Bank, USAID, and other organizations on projects in Africa, Asia, and the Middle East. Currently he is revising for publication a book-length report prepared for USAID on the experience with river basin development in Africa.

John S. Spears received his degrees in forestry and agriculture from the Universities of Wales and Oxford (United Kingdom) and British Columbia (Canada). He was a conservator of forests in Kenya for fifteen years and worked for ten years with the Food and Agriculture Organization–World Bank Cooperative Program in Rome, primarily on the preparation of forestry conservation projects. In 1976 he joined the World Bank as its forestry adviser and was one of the principal authors of the Bank's Forestry Sector Policy Paper published in 1978. In 1986 he was appointed chief of the Bank's Environmental Policy Research Division and has played a role in reorienting the Bank's activities to give greater emphasis to sustainable natural resource management and containment of environmental pollution. He is currently a senior adviser with the Consultative Group on International Agricultural Research.

Norman Uphoff is professor of government at Cornell University and newly appointed director of the Cornell International Institute for Food, Agriculture, and Development. Previously he served as chair of the Rural Development Committee and director of the South Asia Program at Cornell. From 1977 to 1982 he directed the Rural Development Participation Project at Cornell, funded by USAID. He has been a consultant to the World Bank, USAID, the Asian Development Bank, the Food and Agriculture Organization, the Ford Foundation, the African Development Foundation, and several other agencies. His most recent book, based on experience helping to introduce farmer organizations for improving irrigation management in Sri Lanka, is *Learning from Gal Oya: Possibilities for Participatory Development and Post-Newtonian Social Science.* His other books on particupatory development include *Local Organizations: Intermediaries in Rural Development* (with Milton Esman); *Local Institutional Development: An Analytical Sourcebook with Cases;* and *Improving International Irrigation Management with Farmer Participation: Getting the Process Right.*

Index

Abel, M. E., 128

Ablasser, Gottfried, 149

Accelerated Mahaweli Project (Sri Lanka), 148, 149, 150, 154, 159, 164, 166, 172, 173, 175, 176, 178, 182, 439

Aerial photographs, 526, 530

Afforestation. *See* Forestry projects

Africa: age groups in, 382; deforestation and, 301, 307; double cropping in, 440; ethnic issues and, 231, 232, 236, 241, 242; evaluation and, 435, 441, 443, 447, 459, 462, 463; farmer groups and, 451; fishery projects in, 263, 270, 279; forestry and, 317, 325, 333, 343, 364, 374, 375; livestock projects and, 453, 454; participation and, 470, 500; roads and, 401, 409; settlement and, 152, 155, 156, 178, 443; tribal people and, 231, 232, 236, 241, 242. *See also* Livestock production (African pastoral societies); Livestock projects (East Africa); *names of specific African countries*

Agencies. *See* Development agencies

Agricultural development projects. *See* Rural development projects

Agricultural extension services. *See* Extension services

Agricultural Land Settlement (World Bank issues paper), 151

Agricultural settlement. *See* Settlement projects

Agriculture: deforestation and, 305, 307; development planning and social sciences and, 4; evaluation analysis and, 451, 460; forestry and, 301, 374; industry and, 177; irrigation participatory projects and, 76, 100; irrigation projects and, 114, 120; land-based resettlement strategy and, 205–6; participation and, 471, 472, 476, 479; road projects and, 400, 404, 406, 414; settlement projects and, 148, 150, 159, 164, 175–76, 183; tribal, 313

Agroforestry, 305, 310, 314–18; family, 370–72, 373, 374, 375; social organization of, 314–18. *See also* Forestry participatory programs; Forestry projects

irrigators' associations and, 76–77; nonparticipatory programs compared with, 91–104; norms and attitudes and, 89–90; organization and, 93–97; participation and, 491, 506; participatory approach development, 75–76; personnel and, 81–82; pilot programs and, 54, 78, 79, 81, 82, 84, 101, 104–7; policy and procedures and, 75, 82–89; post-construction assistance and, 88–89; project appraisal and 75–76; project cycle and, 104–7; social science and, 73–74, 75, 81; sociologist and, 57, 75, 78, 79, 91; sociotechnical profiles and, 83; staff and, 81–82, 83, 84, 85, 86–87, 88–90, 91, 100; water distribution and, 95–96, 101; World Bank and, 75–76, 80

Irrigation projects: action research and water user association example and, 26–27; agency planning and, 47–50; agriculture and, 114, 120; anthropologists and, 128, 137; design and, 47, 50, 54, 56, 71, 74, 78; development agencies and, 50; displacement and, 190, 191, 210; evaluation and, 50, 443–44, 450–51, 453, 455, 458, 459; feasibility studies and, 53–54, 55, 56, 71; Ghana and, 476; infrastructure and, 50, 54; institutions and, 46, 48, 49, 50–53, 53–57, 59–63, 69, 70, 85–86; local institution building and, 53–57, 85–86; local irrigation systems and, 54, 57, 58; organization and, 117, 126, 128, 139; planning and, 47, 50, 54, 57, 78, 85, 106, 131, 139; project appraisal of Sri Lanka, 55; project implementation as social process and, 47; project preparation and beneficiaries of, 18; regional field studies and, 44–45, 53; regional field study (India) and, 63–68; regional

field study (northern Sumatra) and, 58–63; regional field study (project planning) and, 68–70; resettlement and, 206, 211; resource mobilization and, 49, 50; rural roads and, 405; settlement, 152, 166, 176, 181; social interaction and, 47; social organization and, 44, 46, 47, 48, 49, 50, 53–57, 69–70, 71, 74, 77, 78, 84, 102, 103, 119, 137; socioeconomic surveys and, 50–53; sociologists and project identification and, 17; sociology of (conceptualizing), 48–50; Sri Lanka and, 489, 490

Irrigation system construction, 117, 136; costs and, 77, 91, 97–98; costs and associations and, 102–3; hiring and contracting and, 86–87; irrigators' associations and, 77, 103; lead-time before, 84–85; Palampur irrigation system, 64–65; participatory and nonparticipatory programs compared, 92, 93; Pidie irrigation system and, 62; pilot programs, 78; post-construction assistance and, 88–89, 90; social objectives and, 74

Irrigation system maintenance, 49, 50, 117, 136; NIA and, 76, 96, 101; operation and sociology and, 43, 69, 114–18; Palampur system and, 64, 65–66, 67; Pidie system and, 60, 62, responsibility for, 138; staffing and, 129–30, 131; in Thailand 126, 128, 134, 136, 450

Irrigation system rehabilitation, 46, 117; assumptions concerning, 47, 50; field studies and, 70–71; government and, 46; organization building and, 122, 124; Philippine project and, 53–54, 56–57, 80; risk of failure and, 47; sociologist and, 50; Sri Lanka and, 55–56; state-financed contemporary, 46; Sumatra and, 69